JINDŘICH FÜGNER

Vltava wa

Tisk z hloubky.
Copyright 1926.

# PRAHA
# PRAG
# PRAGUE

JAN KAPLAN
&
KRYSTYNA NOSARZEWSKA

# PRAHA
# PRAG
# PRAGUE

## THE TURBULENT CENTURY
## DAS TURBULENTE JAHRHUNDERT
## LE SIÈCLE TURBULENT

KÖNEMANN

# CONTENTS IN

# INTRODUCTION

## 1900–1918: Under the Double Eagle

The beginning of the twentieth century saw Prague as a cultural metropolis within the Austro-Hungarian Empire: a golden city of steeples and spires where three cultures, Czech, German and Jewish, met and mingled on the banks of the Vltava (Moldau). In 1900 Prague had 514,345 inhabitants. The German bourgeoisie and Austrian nobility made up 5 per cent of the population; they possessed two theaters, a huge concert hall, two universities, five high schools and two newspapers. Because of their wealth, they formed the city's upper class. Jews constituted 4 per cent of the population. More than half of them regarded themselves as Germans; they spoke German, attended German universities and in general were strongly attracted to German culture. They lived mainly in the Old Town. Among the Jewish middle classes were many writers, scientists and artists; they represented the strongest liberal faction, although Zionist ideas later became quite fashionable among the younger generation. The rest of the city's inhabitants were Czechs, who, although they formed the middle and lower classes, "nevertheless owned everything, the country, the land, the original traditions," as the journalist Willy Haas (1891–1973) wrote. At the turn of the century the Czechs stood on the threshold of national and cultural emancipation and tensions between them and the wealthy Germans were always close to exploding.

In this complicated ethnic and political landscape, artists from all over Europe relentlessly created magnificent works, as if inspired by Prague's imaginative architecture, with its fusion of Slav, German and Italian aesthetic elements. However, the spirit of National Awakening, which had begun in the nineteenth century mainly in the Czech language, had by the late 1890s become the dominant force in architecture, sculpture and music too. With the emergence of the Czech middle class, landmarks of the new consciousness were built to propagate Czech arts, Czech language, Czech history and Czech legends. These included the gold-crested National Theater which opened in 1883, built with funds raised by Czechs after the Austrian state refused money, and the National Museum erected in 1890. Prague was being re-Slavicized: the

The German Opera House (today Prague State Opera).
Das Deutsche Opernhaus (heute Prager Staatsoper).
L'Opéra allemand (aujourd'hui Opéra national de Prague).

# EINLEITUNG

## 1900–1918: Unter dem Doppeladler

Zu Beginn des 20. Jahrhunderts war Prag eines der kulturellen Zentren der österreichisch-ungarischen Monarchie: In der Stadt mit den goldenen Kirchturmspitzen an den Ufern der Moldau (Vltava) lebten über 500.000 Einwohner aus drei Kulturen – der tschechischen, der deutschen und der jüdischen. Das deutsche Bürgertum und der österreichische Adel, die nur etwa fünf Prozent der Bevölkerung ausmachten, stellten aufgrund ihres Reichtums die städtische Oberschicht. Ihnen gehörten zwei Theater, eine große Konzerthalle, zwei Universitäten, fünf Höhere Schulen und zwei Zeitungen. Auch die meisten der mehr als 20.000 Juden bezeichneten sich als Deutsche; sie sprachen Deutsch, besuchten deutsche Universitäten und zeigten ein großes Interesse an deutscher Kultur. Sie lebten größtenteils in der Altstadt. In der jüdischen Mittelschicht gab es viele Schriftsteller, Wissenschaftler und Künstler, die zu den Liberalen zählten. Gerade in der jüngeren Generation aber fand zionistisches Gedankengut zunehmend Anklang. Die übrigen Einwohner waren Tschechen, die die Mittel- und Unterschicht bildeten; ihnen gehörte jedoch alles: »Der Staat, das Land, die eigentlichen Traditionen«, wie der Journalist Willy Haas (1891–1973) schrieb. Als um die Jahrhundertwende die Tschechen an der Schwelle zu nationaler und kultureller Emanzipation standen, wurden die Spannungen zwischen ihnen und den reichen Deutschen immer größer.

In dieser komplizierten ethnischen und politischen Landschaft schufen Künstler aus ganz Europa eine Fülle großartiger Werke, die von der phantasievollen Architektur Prags und deren Mischung aus slawischen, deutschen und italienischen Elementen inspiriert zu sein scheinen. In den späten 90er Jahren des 19. Jahrhunderts wurde dann das tschechische Nationalgefühl, das zunächst nur die tschechische Sprache erfaßt hatte, zur treibenden Kraft von Architektur, Bildhauerei und Musik. Mit dem Aufstieg der tschechischen Mittelklasse kam ein neues Bewußtsein auf, das die tschechische Kunst, die tschechische Sprache, die tschechische Geschichte und ihre Mythen in den Vordergrund drängte. Beispiele dafür sind das von Josef Schulz entworfene und 1890 fertiggestellte Nationalmuseum und das mit einem goldenen Dach versehene Nationaltheater, das 1883 mit tschechischen Geldern erbaut wurde, nachdem der österreichische Staat die finanzielle Unterstützung verweigert hatte. Prag wurde re-slawisiert: Die Arbeiten der Künstler nahmen die politischen Veränderungen vorweg, die sich nun vollziehen sollten.

Vor allem die tiefe Abneigung des österreichischen Kaisers Franz-Josef (1830–1916) den Tschechen gegenüber – so ist er trotz seines Titels »König von Böhmen« nie offiziell im Veitsdom gekrönt worden und war auch nur selten in Prag zu Besuch – führte diese immer mehr zu der Überzeugung, ihr Schicksal selbst in die Hand nehmen zu müssen, um nicht länger Bürger zweiter Klasse im eigenen Land zu sein. Eine der zahlreichen politischen Gruppierungen, die dafür eintrat, war die kleine, aber einflußreiche »Realistische Partei«, die der Univer-

# INTRODUCTION

## 1900–1918: Prague sous l'aigle bicéphale

Au début du XXe siècle, Prague est une grande métropole culturelle, au cœur même de l'empire austro-hongrois. Dans cette magnifique cité hérissée detours et des flèches de ses nombreuses églises, trois cultures se rencontrent et s'entremêlent: la tchèque, l'allemande et la juive. En 1900, la ville compte 514 345 habitants. La bourgeoisie allemande et la noblesse autrichienne représentent 5 pour cent de cette population. Ensemble, elles possèdent deux théâtres, une vaste salle de concerts, deux universités, cinq lycées et deux journaux. Leur richesse en fait la classe dominante de la capitale. Les Juifs – 4 pour cent de la population – se considèrent allemands pour plus de la moitié d'entre eux. Ils parlent allemand, étudient dans les universités allemandes, et sont généralement fortement attachés à la culture allemande. Ils vivent essentiellement dans la vieille ville. Les classes moyennes juives comptent de nombreux écrivains, scientifiques et artistes, et représentent la faction la plus fortement libérale, bien que les idées sionistes commencent à devenir à la mode parmi les membres des jeunes générations. Le reste des habitants est composé de Tchèques qui, bien qu'ils forment la classe moyenne et les classes inférieures, «possèdent néanmoins tout, le pays, la terre, les traditions originales», comme l'écrit le journaliste Willy Haas (1891–1973). Au tournant du siècle, les Tchèques sont au seuil de leur émancipation culturelle et nationale, et, à tout instant, des tensions menacent d'éclater entre eux et les riches Allemands.

Dans ce paysage ethnique et politique complexe, des artistes venus de toute l'Europe ont sans discontinuité créé des œuvres magnifiques, comme s'ils étaient inspirés par l'architecture si fertile de la cité qui fusionne des éléments slaves, allemands et italiens. L'esprit du Réveil National qui a débuté au XIXe siècle, essentiellement à travers la langue tchèque, devient à la fin des années 1890 la source principale d'inspiration en architecture, en sculpture et en musique. Parallèlement à l'émergence d'une classe moyenne tchèque, cette prise de conscience nouvelle se manifeste dans l'édification de monuments chargés de propager les arts tchèques, la langue tchèque, l'histoire et les légendes tchèques. Parmi eux, le

The National Theater.
Das Nationaltheater.
Le Théâtre national.

work of the city's artists anticipated the political changes that were about to take place.

Franz Josef I (1830–1916), Emperor of Austria-Hungary and King of Bohemia (although he was never formally crowned in St Vitus Cathedral), came rarely to Prague to see his subjects. As 1908, the sixtieth anniversary of his reign approached, Czechs were becoming increasingly certain that one day they would control their own destiny and would cease to be second-class citizens in their own land. Among the many political parties reflecting this new confidence was the Realistic Party, a small but influential group founded in 1900 by university professor Tomáš Garrigue Masaryk (1850–1937).

To the Prague Germans it was becoming apparent that they were a community on the defensive, gradually losing their dominant position in the politics and culture of the city. Prague, for them, was becoming a quicksand. In reaction to the rise of Czech nationalism, they turned to the anti-Semitic and anti-Slav doctrines of Pan-Germanism, which at the same time were influencing the young Adolf Hitler (1889–1945) in Vienna. Fights between students from the rival Czech and German universities were not uncommon. The Austrian police kept a close watch on these political conflicts and, just before the Emperor's visit to Prague in 1907, made a series of preventive arrests of known Czech radicals.

The fatal shots fired at the Archduke Franz Ferdinand d'Este, heir to the Austro-Hungarian throne, by a young Serbian nationalist, Gavrilo Princip, in Sarajevo on 28 June 1914 started a chain of events leading to the First World War and put an end to the old Europe. As part of the Habsburg Empire, the Czechs were drawn into the war on the side of the Central Powers (Germany, Austria-Hungary, Turkey and Bulgaria), but they were reluctant belligerents. From the beginning of the war, most Czechs sympathized with the Allied Powers, particularly the Slav Serbs and Russians, and many were not prepared to fight for the Habsburgs. Deserters created legions which fought alongside the Allies in France, Italy and Russia.

By the middle of the war, Czech ambitions had gone beyond autonomy in favor of total independence, a demand articulated abroad by exiled leaders such as Tomáš Masaryk and Edvard Beneš (1884–1948). They were joined by a Slovak, Milan Rastislav Štefánik (1880–1919) and the idea of Czechs and Slovaks creating a common state became more real. At home a nationalist underground movement was formed. The authorities responded with a series of arrests in which thousands were rounded up and some sentenced to death in show trials. But, as the tide of war turned against the Central Powers and US President Woodrow Wilson proclaimed self-determination for the Czech and Slovak peoples, it was already too late for the Habsburgs and their Emperor Karl I (1887–1922), who had succeeded his grandfather Franz Josef in 1916. He proclaimed an amnesty and relaxed police repression in an attempt to save his throne, but he was never to visit his Bohemian kingdom. In Prague he was nicknamed Karl the Last. On 28 October 1918 the underground Czechoslovak National Council staged a bloodless coup in the name of the

sitätsprofessor Tomáš Masaryk (1850–1937) im Jahre 1900 gegründet hatte.

Die Deutschen in Prag sahen ihre beherrschende Position in der politischen und kulturellen Szene der Stadt allmählich schwinden. Als Reaktion auf den tschechischen Nationalismus wandten sich viele der antisemitischen und antislawischen Ideologie des Pan-Germanismus zu, der zur gleichen Zeit großen Einfluß auf Adolf Hitler (1889–1945) in Wien ausübte. Kämpfe zwischen den Studenten der rivalisierenden tschechischen und deutschen Universitäten waren an der Tagesordnung. Als der Kaiser 1907 einen Besuch in der Stadt plante, stellte die österreichische Polizei denn auch vorsorglich eine Reihe von bekannten tschechischen Radikalen unter Arrest.

Mit den tödlichen Schüssen des jungen serbischen Nationalisten Gavrilo Princip auf Erzherzog Franz-Ferdinand d'Este, den österreichisch-ungarischen Thronfolger, am 28. Juni 1914 in Sarajevo begann der Erste Weltkrieg. Als Teil des Habsburgerreiches wurden die Tschechen auf Seiten der Achsenmächte (Deutschland, Österreich-Ungarn, Türkei und Bulgarien) in den Krieg hineingezogen, obwohl ihre Sympathien zumeist den alliierten Mächten, besonders den slawischen Serben und den Russen, galten. Viele Tschechen desertierten aus den Habsburger Armeen und kämpften auf der Seite der Alliierten in Frankreich, Italien und Rußland.

Auf dem Höhepunkt des Krieges hatte sich der Wunsch der Tschechen nach Autonomie in die Forderung nach völliger Unabhängigkeit gewandelt, die vor allem von den im Exil lebenden Führern wie Tomáš Masaryk und Eduard Beneš (1884–1948) erhoben wurde. Ihnen schloß sich der Slowake Milan Rastislav Štefánik (1880–1919) an, wodurch die Idee eines gemeinsamen tschechischen und slowakischen Staates Gestalt anzunehmen begann. In der Heimat bildete sich eine nationalistische Untergrundbewegung, auf die die Behörden mit einer Serie von Verhaftungen reagierten, der Tausende zum Opfer fielen. In groß angelegten Schauprozessen wurden sogar einige Todesstrafen verhängt. Als die Achsenmächte immer größere Verluste hinnehmen mußten und der amerikanische Präsident Wilson das Selbstbestimmungsrecht für das tschechische und slowakische Volk verlangte, konnten die Habsburger und ihr Kaiser Karl I. (1887–1922), der 1916 auf seinen Großvater Franz-Josef gefolgt war, den Thron nicht mehr retten. Zwar gewährte der Kaiser noch eine Amnestie und lockerte den Druck der Polizei, aber er sollte sein böhmisches Königreich niemals mehr besuchen. In Prag erhielt er den Spitznamen Karl der Letzte. Am 28. Oktober 1918 unternahm der im Untergrund operierende tschechoslowakische Nationalrat im Namen der neuen Tschechoslowakischen Republik einen unblutigen Staatsstreich, der dreihundert Jahre tschechischer Geschichte im Zeichen der Habsburger beendete und Prag wieder zur nationalen Hauptstadt werden ließ.

Der berühmteste deutschsprachige Dichter, der in Prag geboren wurde und dort seine Kindheit verbracht hatte, war der Österreicher Rainer Maria Rilke (1875–1926). Seine Beziehung zu den Tsche-

Musée national, de Josef Schulz achevé en 1890, et le Théâtre national de Josef Zitek, construit en 1881, grâce à des fonds levés par les Tchèques après que l'État autrichien ait refusé de financer ce projet. Prague est donc en cours de re-slavisation: l'œuvre de ses artistes anticipe les changements politiques qui sont sur le point de se produire.

François-Joseph (1830–1916), empereur d'Autriche-Hongrie et roi de Bohême (bien qu'il n'ait jamais été couronné dans la cathédrale saint-Guy), ne rend que rarement visite à ses sujets à Prague. À l'approche de 1908, soixantième anniversaire de son règne, les Tchèques sont de plus en plus certains qu'ils vont bientôt prendre en main leur destinée et cesseront d'être des citoyens de seconde classe dans leur propre pays. Parmi les nombreux partis politiques qui reflètent ce nouvel espoir figure le Parti Réaliste, groupe réduit mais influent, fondé en 1900 par le professeur d'université Tomáš Garrigue Masaryk (1850–1937).

Pour les Allemands de Prague il devient alors clair qu'ils sont une communauté sur la défensive, perdant peu à peu sa position dominante dans la politique et la culture de la cité. Pour eux, Prague est un banc de sable mouvant. En réaction à la montée du nationalisme tchèque, il se tournent vers les doctrines antisémites et antislaves du pangermanisme, qui, au même moment, influencent le jeune Adolf Hitler alors à Vienne. Les bagarres entre étudiants des universités tchèques et allemandes rivales ne sont pas rares. La police autrichienne surveille de près ces conflits politiques et, juste avant la visite de l'empereur à Prague en 1907, se livre à une série d'arrestations de Tchèques connus pour leurs idées radicales.

Les coups de feu tirés sur l'héritier du trône austro-hongrois, l'archiduc François-Ferdinand d'Este, par le jeune nationaliste serbe Gavrilo Princip à Sarajevo le 28 juin 1914 déclanche une succession d'événements qui aboutira à la Première Guerre mondiale et la fin de la vieille Europe. Appartenant à l'empire des Habsbourg, les Tchèques sont entraînés dans la guerre aux côtés des puissances centrales (Allemagne, Autriche-Hongrie, Turquie et Bulgarie), mais se battent sans enthousiasme. Dès le début du conflit, la plupart des Tchèques sympathisent avec les puissances alliées, en particulier les Slaves de Serbie et de Russie, et beaucoup d'entre eux ne se sentent pas prêts à se battre pour les Habsbourg. Des déserteurs forment des légions qui se battent aux côtés des Alliés en France, en Italie, et en Russie.

Au milieu de la guerre, les ambitions tchèques vont maintenant au-delà de l'autonomie et portent sur une indépendance totale, demande exprimée à l'étranger par des leaders exilés comme Tomáš Masaryk et Edvard Beneš (1884–1948). Ils sont rejoints par un Slovaque, Milan Rastislav Štefánik (1880–1919) et l'idée d'un État commun aux Tchèques et aux Slovaques commence à prendre corps. Sur place, un mouvement nationaliste clandestin se forme. Les autorités répondent par une série d'arrestations qui voient des milliers de personnes arrêtées au cours de rafles et certaines condamnées à mort dans des procès de circonstances. Lorsque le sort de la guerre se retourne contre les puissances centrales et que le

new Czechoslovak Republic. Three hundred years of Czech history under the Habsburgs' thumb had come to an end and Prague emerged once more as the national capital.

The most famous German-speaking poet, who was born in Prague and spent his early years there, was the Austrian Rainer Maria Rilke (1875–1926). His relationship with the Czechs was always complicated. He called the Czech poets "a childish people, full of unfulfilled wishes, having ripened overnight." He was also critical of Prague German, which, cut off from "proper" German, was to him as dead and dry as medieval Latin, and of its offspring, *Kuchelböhmisch*, a German–Czech pidgin spoken by the two nationalities. In Jewish families there was the additional influence of *Mauscheldeutsch*, a sort of germanized Yiddish, though its influence was not pervasive.

However, the limitations of Prague German did not stop good writers from using it creatively. Franz Kafka (1883–1924), born in Prague and writing in German – and, like all the germanized Jews, living in a kind of vacuum – wrote in a remarkably unadorned style, concise, neutral and sometimes almost pedantic. His linguistic purity was a stand against the inflated style adopted by his contemporaries in order to compensate for the limited resources of Prague German. Kafka's work (most of it published posthumously) was deeply infused with the atmosphere of the city. He called Prague "a little mother that has claws." Watching the gradual disappearance of the old Jewish ghetto, he told Gustav Janouch: "In us all it still lives – the dark corners, the secret alleys, shattered windows, squalid courtyards, noisy bars, and sinister inns. We walk through the broad streets of the newly built town. But our steps and our glances are uncertain. Inside we tremble just as before in the ancient streets of our misery. Our heart knows nothing of the *asanace*, the slum clearance which has been achieved. The unhealthy old Jewish town within us is far more real than the new hygienic town around us. With our eyes open we walk through a dream: ourselves only a ghost of a vanished age."

While Kafka and other members of the German–Jewish literary circle frequented the city's cafés, institutions integral to Habsburg culture, Czech writers, such as Jaroslav Hašek (1883–1923), the subversive *bon vivant* (who established the Party of Moderate Progress Within the Bounds of the Law) and author of *The Good Soldier Švejk*, were to be found in Prague's beerhouses, churning out satires against their Habsburg masters and the absurdity of the First World War. Taverns and coffeehouses were the birthplaces of manifestos and polemical texts, while artists and writers debated on art for art's sake and whether literature should contain a political message.

With the clearing of the Ghetto in the 1890s and early 1900s and the construction of a gracious boulevard giving access to the river (now called Pařížská), the city begun to assume the familiar shape we know today. Two stadiums and three bridges were built in the first decade of the century in order to serve the proud new owners of

A quaint courtyard of old Prague.
Malerischer Innenhof in der Altstadt von Prag.
Cour pittoresque dans le vieux Prague.

chen war immer kompliziert. So bezeichnete er die tschechischen Dichter als »ein kindisches Volk, voll von unerfüllten Wünschen, die über Nacht reif geworden waren«. Darüber hinaus übte er Kritik an der deutschen Sprache in Prag, die er in ihrer Isolation vom »richtigen« Deutsch für so tot und vertrocknet hielt wie mittelalterliches Latein, und am lokalen Dialekt, dem *Kuchelböhmisch*, einer von Deutschen und Tschechen verwandten Mischsprache. In jüdischen Kreisen wurde zudem noch *Mauscheldeutsch* – eine Art eingedeutsches Jiddisch – gesprochen, das sich aber nicht allgemein durchsetzte.

Ungeachtet dieser Vorurteile gelangten einige Prager Autoren zu Weltruhm. Franz Kafka (1883–1924), ein in Prag geborener deutscher Jude, der in der slawischen Welt wie in einem Vakuum lebte, hatte einen bemerkenswert klaren Stil – präzise, neutral und manchmal fast pedantisch. Seine sprachliche Brillanz bildete das Gegengewicht zum schwülstigen Stil seiner Zeitgenossen, die damit die begrenzten Möglichkeiten des Prager Deutsch zu über- spielen versuchten. Kafkas Werke (von denen die meisten posthum veröffentlicht wurden) sind eng mit der Atmosphäre der Stadt verwoben. Er bezeich-nete Prag als »Mütterchen mit Krallen«. Ange-sichts der langsamen Auflösung des alten jüdischen Ghettos schrieb er 1902 an seinen Freund Gustav Janouch: »Das alles lebt noch in uns – die dunklen Ecken, die geheimen Gäßchen, zerbrochenen Fen-ster, die heruntergekommenen Hinterhöfe, die lauten Bars und die düsteren Kneipen. Wir gehen durch die breiten Straßen einer neugebauten Stadt. Aber unse-re Schritte und unsere Blicke sind unsicher. Innerlich zittern wir genauso wie in den alten Straßen unseres Unglücks. Unsere Herzen wissen nichts von der Assanierung, von der Beseitigung der Elendviertel, die stattgefunden hat. Die ungesunde alte jüdische Stadt in uns ist viel lebendiger als die neue hygieni-

président américain Woodrow Wilson proclame le droit à l'autodétermination des peuples tchèques et slovaques, il est déjà trop tard pour les Habsbourg et le nouvel empereur, Charles Ier (1887–1922) qui succède à son grand-père François-Joseph en 1916. Il proclame une amnistie et calme la répression policière pour sauver son trône, mais ne se rend jamais dans son royaume de Bohême. À Prague, il est surnommé Charles dernier. Le 28 octobre 1918, le Conseil national tchécoslovaque clandestin organise un coup d'État sans effusion de sang au nom de la république tchécoslovaque. Trois siècles d'histoire tchèque sous la férule des Habsbourg touchent à leur fin, et Prague redevient la capitale d'une nation.

L'Autrichien Rainer Maria Rilke (1875–1926), célèbre poète germanophone est né à Prague et y a passé son enfance. Ses relations avec les Tchèques ont toujours été assez complexes. Il parle des poètes tchèques comme «d'un peuple enfantin, empli de désirs inassouvis mûris en une nuit». Il critique également l'allemand parlé à Prague, qui, coupé de la «vraie» langue allemande est à sons sens aussi mort et desséché que le latin du Moyen Âge. Il n'est pas plus tendre avec le *Kuchelböhmisch*, un sabir germano-tchèque parlé par les deux nationalités. Dans les familles juives, joue de plus l'influence du *Mauscheldeutsch*, sorte de yiddish germanisé, même s'il n'est pas très répandu.

Les limites de l'allemand pragois n'empêchent cependant pas de bons écrivains de l'utiliser de manière créative. Franz Kafka (1883–1924), né à Prague et écrivant en allemand – qui comme tous les Juifs germanisés vit dans une sorte de bulle – écrit dans un style remarquablement épuré, concis, neutre, presque pédant parfois. Sa pureté linguistique relève aussi d'une attitude face au style enflé adopté par ses contemporains pour compenser les faiblesses de l'allemand de Prague. L'œuvre de Kafka (publiée pour sa plus grande partie après sa mort) est profondément marquée par l'atmosphère de la ville. Il appelle Prague «la petite mère qui a des griffes». Observant la disparition graduelle du vieux ghetto juif, il dit en 1902 à son ami Gustav Janouch: «Tout vit encore en nous – les sombres recoins, les allées secrètes, les fenêtres brisées, les cours sordides, les bars bruyants et les auberges sinistres. Nous marchons dans les larges rues de la ville nouvellement construite. Mais nos pas et nos regards sont incertains. À l'intérieur de nous-mêmes, nous tremblons comme naguère dans les anciennes ruelles de notre misère. Notre cœur ne sait rien de l'asanace, de la destruction des taudis qui a été accomplie. La vieille ville juive malsaine qui est en nous est beaucoup plus réelle que la nouvelle ville hygiénique autour de nous. Les yeux ouverts, nous marchons dans un rêve: nous ne sommes que les fantômes d'un âge révolu.»

Pendant que Kafka et les autres membres des cercles littéraires judéo-allemands fréquentent les cafés de la ville, institutions éminentes de la culture habsbourgeoise, les écrivains tchèques, tel Jaroslav Hašek (1883–1923), bon vivant subversif qui a fondé le «Parti du Progrès modéré dans les limites de la loi» et auteur du *Brave soldat Švejk*, se

Albert Einstein, photographed in Prague.
Albert Einstein, fotografiert in Prag.
Albert Einstein, photographié à Prague.

automobiles. The citizens of Prague worshipped their machines. In 1911 Jan Kašpar, an engineer, flew from Pardubice to Prague – and survived.

A number of famous people passed through the city in the century's first two decades. Albert Einstein taught physics at the Prague German University in 1911–12 and was paid handsomely for his efforts (8672 crowns). In January 1912, from the back room of a building on Hybernská, Vladimir Ilyich Lenin and the Bolsheviks seized control of the Russian Social Democratic Party, expelling the Mensheviks (and converting some Czechs in the process).

In 1902 an exhibition by the French sculptor Auguste Rodin (1840–1917), the last genius of straightforward representation, made a great impact on local artists. Sculptors like Josef Myslbek (1848–1922) seemed more traditional than the French avant-garde, but his statue of St Wenceslas, unveiled in Wenceslas Square in 1912, was nevertheless recognized as a magnificent work. In the Old Town Square a monument to Jan Hus, best-known Czech religious reformer, was erected. Hus (born c.1371) represented proud Czech nationalism. He was burnt at the stake in 1415 for preaching against the Church's practices and in favor of the right to serve Mass in Czech.

Some sculptors tried their hand at architecture, including František Bílek (1872–1941), whose highly original villa was completed in 1911. Taking a wheatfield as his theme, his design symbolized the harvest and the mystical ripening of the nation's desires. Painter Antonín Slavíček (1870–1910) adapted the principles of Impressionism to the muddy-golden colors of Prague and the Czech landscape.

The greatest impact in the arts in this period, however, was made by the new style called the *secese* in Czech (from the Austrian Sezession) and

sche Stadt um uns herum. Mit offenen Augen gehen wir durch einen Traum: Wir selbst sind nur die Geister eines vergangenen Zeitalters.«

Besuchten Kafka und andere Mitglieder des deutsch-jüdischen Literatenzirkels die Kaffeehäuser der Stadt – jene Markenzeichen der Habsburger Kultur –, kamen die tschechischen Autoren wie der subversive Lebemann Jaroslav Hašek (1883–1923), Gründer der »Partei des gemäßigten Fortschritts in den Grenzen des Gesetzes« und Autor des *Braven Soldaten Schwejk*, in den Prager Kneipen zusammen. Hier entstanden ihre Satiren gegen die Habsburger Obrigkeit und die Absurditäten des Krieges. Kneipen und Kaffeehäuser waren die Geburtsorte von Manifesten und polemischen Texten. Künstler und Schriftsteller debattierten an diesen Orten über die Kunst um der Kunst willen und stritten darüber, ob Literatur eine politische Botschaft enthalten dürfe.

Mit der Sanierung der Altstadt um die Jahrhundertwende, der das Judenviertel zum Opfer fiel, und dem Bau des eleganten Boulevard zur Moldau hin (der heutigen Pařížská-Straße) nahm die Stadt allmählich die Gestalt an, in der wir sie heute kennen. Nach 1900 wurden zwei Stadien und für die stolzen neuen Besitzer von Automobilen drei Brücken errichtet. Die Prager liebten den technischen Fortschritt. So flog 1911 der Ingenieur Jan Kašpar von Pardubice nach Prag – und überlebte.

Berühmte Leute hielten sich in diesen Jahren in der Stadt auf: Albert Einstein unterrichtete von 1911–12 Physik an der Deutschen Universität, wofür er mit 8672 Kronen entlohnt wurde. Im Januar 1912 übernahmen Lenin und seine Bolschewiken im Hinterzimmer eines Gebäudes auf der Hybernská-Straße die Russische Sozialdemokratische Arbeiterpartei und schlossen die Menschewiki aus (wobei auch einige Tschechen zu ihnen überliefen).

1902 wurde in Prag eine Ausstellung des französischen Bildhauers Auguste Rodin (1840–1917), des letzten Genies der gegenständlichen Darstellung,

Work in progress on the St Wenceslas statue.
Arbeiten an der Wenzelsstatue.
La statue de saint Venceslas en travaux.

Lenin taking a stroll on the Charles Bridge.
Lenin beim Spaziergang auf der Karlsbrücke.
Lénine se promenant sur le pont Charles.

retrouvent dans les brasseries de Prague, multipliant les satires contre leurs maîtres autrichiens et l'absurdité de la Première Guerre mondiale. C'est dans les tavernes et les cafés que naissent manifestes et textes polémiques, qu'artistes et écrivains débattent de l'art pour l'art et de la nécessité pour la littérature de proposer un message politique.

Avec la destruction du ghetto dans les années 1890 et au début des années 1900, et l'ouverture d'un élégant boulevard débouchant sur la rivière (rue Pařížská), la ville commence à prendre le visage familier que nous lui connaissons aujourd'hui. Deux stades et deux ponts sont construits au cours de la première décennie du siècle pour répondre aux attentes des fiers propriétaires d'un nouveau moyen de locomotion : l'automobile. Les Pragois adorent les machines. En 1911, Jan Kašpar, un ingénieur, vole de Pardubice à Prague et en réchappe.

Un certain nombre de personnages célèbres séjournent dans la ville pendant les vingt premières années du XXe siècle. En 1911–12, Albert Einstein enseigne la physique à l'Université allemande qui le paye généreusement (8 672 couronnes). En janvier 1912, d'une pièce sur cour d'un immeuble de la rue Hybernská, Vladimir Illitch – Lénine – et les Bolcheviques prennent le contrôle du parti social-démocrate russe et en expulsent les Mencheviks (convertissant quelques Tchèques à leurs idées dans le même élan).

En 1902, une exposition du sculpteur français Auguste Rodin (1840–1917), dernier génie de la représentation figurative, exerce une forte influence sur les artistes locaux. Un sculpteur comme Josef Myslbek (1848–1922) peut sembler plus traditionnel que l'avant-garde française, mais il est certain que sa statue de saint Venceslas, dévoilée place Venceslas en 1912, est une œuvre splendide. Sur la place de la Vieille ville, un monument à Jean

generally known as Art Nouveau. A sensuous flowing line, often taking the form of a highly stylized, floral design, became almost compulsory in architecture, painting, graphic art, sculpture, and the applied arts. The delicate, soft, undulating line combined sensitivity with eroticism, two favorite elements of Prague's artists; it provided an excuse for endless depictions of beautiful women. Alfons Mucha (1809–1939) made a very good living out of this credo. He had become world famous for his Sarah Bernhardt posters when he lived in Paris and continued his highly decorative technique after his return to Prague in 1910, designing jewelry, biscuit tins, banknotes and calendars. In the end he decided "to jump off the train going nowhere," as he put it, and devoted the final thirty years of his life to his *Slav Epic*, a series of massive paintings executed on canvas sails.

The first architect to try out the new style successfully was the talented Jan Kotěra (1871–1923) with his house at 775 Wenceslas Square (1900). Among the greatest Art Nouveau buildings in Prague is the Evropa Hotel (1903–4), covered with lacy golden and green floral motifs. However, perhaps the city's outstanding example of the style is the *Obecní dům* (Municipial House), completed in 1911, which on the outside appears to be neo-Baroque, while inside it is pure Art Nouveau. A list of those who contributed to it reads like a "Who's Who?" in the Czech arts. Top architects (Antonín Balšánek, Osvald Polívka), sculptors (Josef Mařatka, František Úprka, Bohumil Kafka, Ladislav Šaloun) and painters (Max Švabinský, Mikoláš Aleš, Karel Špillar, Jan Preisler) created this most remarkable landmark. The brilliant Alfons Mucha was also involved. Not only did he paint the allegory of Prague in the

Koruna (Crown) Palace.
Das Koruna (Krone) Palais.
Le Palais de la Couronne.

eröffnet, die einen tiefen Eindruck bei den örtlichen Künstler hinterließ. Diesen Einfluß spiegelt das Denkmal des Bildhauers Ladislav Šaloun für Jan Hus, den um 1371 geborenen tschechischen Reformator und Sinnbild des tschechischen Nationalismus, auf dem Altstädter Ring. Hus war 1415 wegen seiner antiklerikalen Ideen und seiner Forderung, die Bibel auf tschechisch lesen zu dürfen, auf dem Scheiterhaufen verbrannt worden. Andere Prager Bildhauer blieben ihrem traditionellen Stil verhaftet. So schuf Josef Myslbek (1848–1922) für den Wenzelsplatz die Statue des Heiligen Wenzel, ein heroisches Reiterstandbild, das 1912 enthüllt und von den Zeitgenossen auch als großartiges Kunstwerk angesehen wurde.

Einige Bildhauer arbeiteten zudem als Architekten. 1911 ließ František Bílek (1872–1941) sein Wohn- und Atelierhaus nach eigenen Entwürfen erbauen: Es gleicht eher einer symbolischen Plastik, für die Bílek das Thema des Weizenfeldes als Sinnbild für die Ernte und das mystische Reifen nationaler Wünsche gewählt hatte. Auch der Impressionismus hat seine Spuren in Prag hinterlassen. So hat der Maler Antonín Slavíček (1870–1910) diese Malweise mit den staubig-goldenen Farben der Prager und der tschechischen Landschaft verbunden.

Den größten Einfluß auf die Kunst dieser Epoche übte jedoch der neue Stil aus, den die Tschechen *secese* (nach dem österreichischen Sezession) nannten und der allgemein als Art Nouveau oder Jugendstil bekannt ist. Sinnlich fließende Linien, oft in Form stark stilisierter Pflanzen oder Blüten, wurden zum vorherrschenden Prinzip in Architektur, Malerei, Bildhauerei, Graphik und im Kunsthandwerk. Feine, weiche, wellenförmige Linien verbanden Sensibilität und Erotik – zwei beliebte Themen der Prager Künstler, die eine Vielzahl von Darstellungen schöner Frauen schufen. Dieses Bekenntnis zu Sinnlichkeit und Schönheit machte Alfons Mucha (1869–1939) weltberühmt. In seiner Pariser Zeit hatte er mit Plakaten für Sarah Bernhardt große Erfolge errungen. Als er 1910 nach Prag zurückkehrte, übertrug er seine höchst dekorative Technik auf die Entwürfe von Schmuck, Keksdosen, Geldscheinen und Kalendern. Am Ende entschloß sich Mucha, »von dem Zug, der nirgendwo hin führte, abzuspringen«, und widmete die letzten 30 Jahre seines Lebens seinem *Slawischen Epos*, einer Serie von monumentalen Bildern auf Segeltuch.

Als Begründer der modernen tschechischen Architektur gilt der Architekt Jan Kotěra (1871–1923), der sein Haus am Wenzelsplatz 775 (1900) erfolgreich im neuen Stil erbaute. Eines der größten Jugendstil-Gebäude in Prag ist das Hotel Europa (1903–04), dessen Fassade mit spitzenartigen goldenen und grünen Pflanzenmotiven überzogen ist. Der berühmteste Bau dieser Epoche ist jedoch das Repräsentationshaus (*Obecní dům*), das 1911 fertiggestellt wurde. Weist die Fassade noch Elemente des Neobarock auf, so ist der Innenraum im reinsten Jugendstil gestaltet. Die Architekten Antonín Balšánek und Osvald Polívka hatten zur Ausschmückung die besten tschechischen Künstler ihrer Zeit verpflichtet: Bildhauer wie Josef Mařatka, František Úprka, Bohumil Kafka, Ladislav Šaloun und Maler wie Max Švabinský, Mikoláš Aleš; Karel Špillar und Jan Preisler. Unter ihnen befand sich der

Hus, célèbre réformateur religieux, est érigée. Hus (né vers 1371) symbolise en fierté du nationalisme tchèque fier. Il est brûlé vif en 1415 contre les pratiques de l'Église et en faveur du droit de dire la messe en tchèque.

Certains sculpteurs s'essayent à l'architecture. František Bílek (1872–1941) édifie une villa très originale en 1911. Sur le thème du champ de blé, sa conception symbolise le temps de la moisson et le mûrissement mystique des désirs de la nation. Le peintre Antonín Slavíček (1870–1910) adapte les principes de l'Impressionnisme aux tonalité dorées de Prague et du paysage tchèque.

Mais la grande nouveauté esthétique de cette période, celle qui exerce l'impact artistique le plus fort est un style appelé *secese* (dérivé de la *Sécession* autrichienne) et connu ailleurs sous le nom d'Art Nouveau. La fluidité sensuelle des formes, souvent inspirée de motifs floraux très stylisés, devient presque la norme en architecture, peinture, sculpture arts graphiques, sculpture et arts appliqués. Les lignes délicates, ondulantes et douces marient la sensibilité à l'érotisme, deux éléments favoris des artistes pragois. C'est aussi une excuse pour des représentations sans fin de la beauté féminine. Alfons Mucha (1860–1939) tire un excellent parti financier de ce mouvement à la mode. Il deviendra célèbre dans le monde entier pour ses affiches sur Sarah Bernhardt lors de son séjour à Paris, et poursuivra sur cette voie très décorative après son retour à Prague en 1910, concevant des bijoux, des boîtes à biscuits, des billets de banque et des calendriers. Finalement, il se décide « à sauter d'un train qui ne mène nulle part », comme il l'écrit, et consacre les trente dernières années de sa vie à *L'Épopée slave*, une série d'immenses peintures exécutées sur de la toile de voile.

Le premier architecte à s'essayer avec succès au nouveau style est le talentueux Jan Kotěra (1871–1923). Il l'applique à un immeuble 775 place Venceslas (1900). Parmi les plus intéressants immeubles Art Nouveau de Prague figure l'Evropa Hotel (1903–04), orné d'une dentelle de motifs décoratifs floraux or et vert. L'exemple pragois le plus remarquable de ce style est cependant peut-être l'*Obecní dům* (maison municipale) achevée en 1911, qui semble néo-baroque vue de l'extérieur, mais est pur Art Nouveau à l'intérieur. La liste de ceux qui contribuent à sa décoration est un peu le Who's Who des artistes tchèques du début du siècle. De grands architectes (Antonín Balšánek, Osvald Polívka), des sculpteurs (Josef Mařatka, František Úprka, Bohumil Kafka, Ladislav Šaloun) et des peintres (Max Švabinský, Mikoláš Aleš, Karel Špillar, Jan Preisler) participent à la création de ce remarquable monument. Le brillant Alfons Mucha ne pouvait en rester à l'écart. Non seulement il peint une allégorie de Prague dans le bureau du maire, mais en dessine également le mobilier et les rideaux, brodés et décorés de perles de verre couleur rubis. Les salles officielles (Art Nouveau slovaque et oriental) sont de petits bijoux de décoration intérieure. L'hôtel de ville possède également des salons d'exposition, la salle de concert Smetana, un café, un restaurant et une élégante marquise de fer embellie de verre opalescent et coloré qui donnent au bâtiment son caractère si novateur.

Mayor's Room but he also designed the furniture and curtains, embroidered and studded with ruby-colored beads. The ceremonial rooms (Slovak and Oriental Art Nouveau) are little gems of interior design. The Municipal House also has exhibition halls, the Smetana concert hall, a café, a restaurant and the elegant iron awning embellished with stained glass and milky opal, all of them demonstrating the exuberant inventiveness that gave the building its new character.

The Art Nouveau buildings, often tinted with verdigris – which translates poetically as "the green of Greece," dusty bluish-green pigment which forms on copper, bronze and brass, always enhanced with pale gold decorative motifs – blend elegantly with medieval cupolas and turrets of the same colors.

Beneath the Vyšehrad Hill several Cubist houses, designed by Josef Chochol (1880–1956), sprang up in 1913, inspired by Picasso's and Braque's geometric depictions of objects and figures as if seen simultaneously from many different angles. Nowhere was Cubism seized upon more eagerly than in Prague. It influenced not only architecture but also painting, the applied arts, and stage design. But architecture is its most extraordinary manifestation: Prague is the only city in the world with Cubist buildings. They were possibly inspired not only by Picasso's and Braque's paintings but also by the city's own Renaissance houses with their "sgraffiti" (a decorative technique based on drawing and scratching): when viewed from a distance, an optical illusion makes the surface of the buildings seem three-dimensional.

Among the best ambassadors of Czech culture were the composers Antonín Dvořák (1841–1904), Leoš Janáček (1854–1928) and Bedřich Smetana (1824–84). On the recommendation of the Emperor, Dvořák, whose opera *Rusalka* (The Water Nymph) was premièred at the National Theater in 1901, was made a Member of Parliament for his services to music. Three years later he died, leaving behind not only the nine symphonies and the operas that made him a world-acclaimed artist, but also a considerable body of dance music, including the famous Prague Waltzes. Dvořák was buried with pomp and ceremony in the most elegant resting place Prague could offer her illustrious artists: the small Vyšehrad cemetery, high on the top of the legendary hill. The cemetery is both a burial place and, in effect, an open-air gallery. Sculptures by Josef Myslbek, Jan Štursa, Ladislav Šaloun, František Bílek and others vie for attention, making the cemetery a surprisingly lively place: Prague's answer to Père-Lachaise.

Prague's first permanent "house of moving pictures" was opened in 1907 in Karlova, showing short comic films to the delight of an appreciative audience. Its owner, Viktor Ponrepo, was a magician. He charged not only for seats but standing places as well, and acted as cashier, usher, projectionist, commentator and host, all in one.

Prague was not only a cultural center but a sports' capital as well. There were two football clubs, SK Slavia, founded in 1892, and AC Sparta, established two years later. The Czechs played their first international ice-hockey match, against France, in

berühmte Alfons Mucha: Er malte nicht nur die Allegorie auf Prag im Salon des Primators, sondern entwarf auch die Möbel und Vorhänge, die mit Stickereien und rubinroten Perlen verziert waren. Die großen Festsäle (im slowakisch und orientalischen Jugendstil) sind wahre Kleinodien der Innenarchitektur. Das Repräsentationshaus beherbergt darüber hinaus auch Ausstellungsräume, den Smetana-Saal, ein Café und ein Restaurant. Seine auffälligsten Merkmale sind die große Glaskuppel und der prächtige gußeiserne Portikus mit einer kunstvollen Bleiverglasung. All diese Elemente bezeugen den überreichen Erfindungsreichtum, der dem Gebäude seinen persönlichen Charakter verleiht.

Die Jugendstil-Gebäude, die häufig mit Grünspan überzogen waren, fügten sich mit ihren blaß-goldenen dekorativen Elementen elegant in die Fülle der gleichfarbigen mittelalterlichen Kuppeln und Kirchturmspitzen ein.

Unterhalb des Vyšehrad entstanden in den Jahren 1911–13 eine Reihe kubistischer Gebäude nach Entwürfen von Josef Chochol (1880–1956), die von den Objekten und Figuren Picassos und Braques inspiriert waren. Diese hatten die kubischen Werte zum Gestaltungsprinzip erhoben und versuchten, die Körperhaftigkeit eines Objektes durch ein Neben- und Übereinanderordnen seiner Vorder- und Seitenflächen in die Fläche umzusetzen. Nirgendwo anders wurde der Kubismus so begeistert aufgenommen wie in Prag. Er beeinflußte nicht nur die Malerei, das Kunsthandwerk und die Bühnenbildnerei, sondern vor allem auch die Architektur, die eine außergewöhnliche, eigenständige Fassadengestaltung entwickelte: Prag ist die einzige Stadt auf der Welt mit kubistischen Gebäuden. Einen zusätzlichen Einfluß übten möglicherweise die Renaissancehäuser der Stadt mit ihren »Sgraffiti« aus – einer auf Zeichnungen und Reliefarbeiten beruhenden dekorativen Technik, die die Gebäudeflächen dreidimensional erscheinen läßt.

Zu den besten Botschaftern der tschechischen Kultur gehörten die Komponisten Antonín Dvořák (1841–1904), Leoš Janáček (1854–1928) und Bedřich Smetana (1824–84). Auf Empfehlung des Kaisers wurde Dvořák, dessen Oper *Rusalka* (Die Wassernixe) 1901 im Nationaltheater uraufgeführt wurde, für seine Verdienste um die Musik zum Mitglied des tschechischen Parlaments ernannt. Als er drei Jahre später starb, hinterließ er nicht nur zehn Opern und neun Symphonien, die ihn weltberühmt machten, sondern auch zahlreiche Werke der Tanzmusik, einschließlich der bekannten Prager Walzer. Dvořák wurde mit großem Zeremoniell in der elegantesten Grabstätte, die Prag ihren berühmten Künstlern zu bieten hatte, auf dem Friedhof des Vyšehrad bestattet. Dieser Ehrenfriedhof ist zugleich eine Freiluft-Galerie: Skulpturen von Josef Myslbek, Jan Štursa, Ladislav Šaloun, František Bílek und anderen machen ihn zu einem überraschend lebendigen.

Prags erstes ständiges »Lichtspielhaus« wurde 1907 in der Karlsgasse eröffnet und zeigte dem begeisterten Publikum ein Programm witziger Kurzfilme. Sein Besitzer, Victor Ponrepo, von Beruf Zauberer, verlangte für Sitz- und Stehplätze Eintritt. Bis zu seinem Tod 1926 arbeitete er gleichzeitig als

Cubist door of Diamant (Diamond) House.
Kubistische Tür am Diamant-Haus.
Porte cubiste de la maison du Diamant.

Les immeubles Art Nouveau, souvent teintés de vert-de-gris – qui se traduit poétiquement en tchèque par « vert de Grèce » – le bleu vert poussiéreux des oliviers, s'unit élégamment au bleu-vert et aux ors pâles du Musée national et des autres coupoles et flèches de la ville.

Au pied de la colline de Vyšehrad, deux maisons cubistes conçues par Josef Chochol (1880–1956), sont édifiées en 1913. Elles s'inspirent de la représentation d'objets et de figures vues simultanément sous plusieurs angles différents qu'ont exploré Picasso et Braque. Nulle part, le cubisme n'est adopté avec plus d'allant qu'à Prague. Il influence non seulement l'architecture, mais aussi la peinture, les arts appliqués et les décors de théâtre. Mais l'architecture est sa manifestation la plus extraordinaire : Prague est la seule ville au monde à posséder des immeubles cubistes. Ils ont pu être inspirés par les peintures de Picasso et de Braque, mais également par les maisons Renaissance de la ville à *sgraffiti* (technique décorative reposant sur le dessin et le grattage) qui, vus à une certaine distance, créent un effet d'optique en trois dimensions.

Parmi les meilleurs ambassadeurs de la culture tchèque figurent également les compositeurs Antoín Dvořák (1841–1904), Leoš Janáček (1854–1928), et Bedřich Smetana (1824–1884). À l'initiative de l'Empereur, Dvořák dont l'opéra *Rusalka* (La Nymphe des eaux) a été donné pour la première fois au Théâtre national en 1901, est fait membre du parlement pour services rendus à la musique. Trois ans plus tard, le compositeur disparaît, laissant derrière lui non seulement les neuf symphonies et les opéras qui l'ont fait acclamer dans le monde entier, mais également une œuvre considérable de musique de danse dont les fameuses *Valses de Prague*. Dvořák est enterré avec pompe dans le plus élégant lieu de repos éternel que la ville pouvait offrir à l'un de ses fils illustres, le petit cimetière de Salvin, au sommet de l'antique colline de Vysehrad. Cet

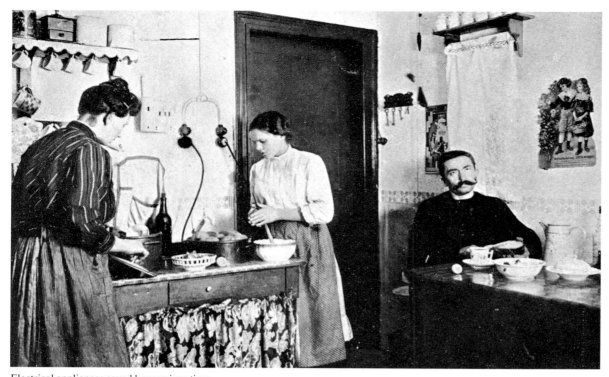

Electrical appliances saved housewives time.
Zeitersparnis für Hausfrauen durch Elektrogeräte.
Les appareils électriques font gagner du temps à la ménagère.

1909 and two years later became European Champions. The Austrian Speed-Skating Championship took place in 1907 on the frozen Vltava; in those days the river was still the best skating rink in the city. The first horse races at Chuchle were held in 1906, not only reviving gambling but also serving as ideal fashion catwalks. The Austrian uniforms had won first prize for their elegance at the Military Design Show in Paris in 1900, so the men walked with pride, trying to impress the ladies.

However, the generation of young women who had suddenly discovered hiking, skiing, cycling and driving seemed to be distracted from the traditional interest of love. Czech women, like their counterparts all over Europe, were resolved to escape the confines of the housewife's narrow world. Milena Jesenská (1896–1944), a journalist and friend of Kafka, wrote, "I want to use all my strength not to remain little." At the turn of the century the women of Prague stood on the brink of the social revolution that would free them once and for all from the medieval world of their mothers. But that revolution started innocently, when they demanded to do what the boys always did: swimming on Žofín Island, racing down the river, playing tennis and skating on the frozen Vltava. Once they were allowed to participate in philosophical discussions in Café Arco or Slavia, and to analyze Dr Freud, there would be no turning back.

One notable champion of women's equality was Tomáš Masaryk himself, who adopted his American wife's name Garrigue in recognition of their partnership. Charlotte Garrigue Masaryk was politically active, as was her daughter Alice, who, after being imprisoned by the Austrians on charges of treason, wrote, "Every experience helps

Kassierer, Platzanweiser, Vorführer, Kommentator und Moderator (Gastgeber).

Aber Prag war nicht nur eine Kulturmetropole, sondern auch ein Zentrum des Sports. Es gab zwei Fußballvereine: SK Slavia, gegründet 1892, und der zwei Jahre später ins Leben gerufene AC Sparta. 1909 bestritten die Tschechen ihr erstes internationales Eishockeyspiel gegen Frankreich; zwei Jahre später wurden sie schon Europameister. 1907 fanden die österreichischen Meisterschaften im Eisschnellaufen auf der zugefrorenen Moldau statt, die damals noch die beste Eisbahn der Stadt war. Das erste Pferderennen wurde 1906 in Chuchle durchgeführt. Es belebte nicht nur das Wettgeschäft, sondern war zugleich ein idealer Ort für die Modewelt. Die Männer flanierten stolz in den österreichischen Uniformen, die 1900 auf der Pariser Ausstellung für Militär-Design wegen ihrer Eleganz den ersten Preis gewonnen hatten.

Die neue Generation junger tschechischer Frauen, die gerade das Wandern, Ski-, Rad-, und Autofahren für sich entdeckt hatte, hatte andere Interessen. Wie ihre Geschlechtsgenossinnen in ganz Europa waren sie entschlossen, den Grenzen der Hausfrauenwelt zu entfliehen. Milena Jesenská (1896–1944), eine Journalistin und Freundin Kafkas schrieb: »Ich will alle meine Kraft einsetzen, um nicht klein zu bleiben.« Um die Jahrhundertwende standen die Frauen von Prag an der Schwelle zur sozialen Revolution, die sie endgültig von der mittelalterlichen Welt ihrer Mütter befreien sollte. Anfangs waren es harmlose Forderungen nach dem, was die Jungen schon immer durften: Schwimmen an der Sophieninsel, Rudern auf dem Fluß, Tennis spielen und Eislaufen auf der zugefrorenen Moldau. Als ihnen die Teilnahme an den philosophischen

endroit, outre sa fonction pratique, est également un musée en plein air. Les sculptures de Josef Myslbek, Jan Štursa, Ladislav Šaloun, František Bílek et d'autres se font concurrence pour attirer le regard du visiteur, transformant ce cimetière en un lieu étonnement vivant.

La première « Maison du cinématographe » de Prague ouvre ses portes en 1907, rue Karlova, et projette des courts métrages comiques à la plus grande satisfaction de l'assistance. Son propriétaire, Victor Ponrepo, est à l'origine un magicien. Il fait payer non seulement les fauteuils mais aussi les places debout, et joue le rôle de caissier, d'ouvreur, de garde, de commentateur et d'accueil, et ce jusqu'à sa mort en 1926.

Prague n'est pas seulement un centre culturel, mais également une capitale du sport. Deux clubs de football se partagent les faveurs des amateurs, le SK Slavia, fondé en 1892, et l'AC Sparta, créé deux ans plus tard. En 1909, les Tchèques jouent leur premier match international de hockey sur glace contre la France et deviennent champions d'Europe deux ans plus tard. Le championnat autrichien de patinage de vitesse sur glace se tient en 1907 sur la Moldau gelée, la rivière étant alors la meilleure des patinoires. Les premières courses de chevaux sont organisées à Chuchle en 1906, lançant à la fois la pratique des paris et un nouveau haut lieu de l'élégance féminine. Les uniformes autrichiens ont remporté le premier prix d'élégance à l'Exposition militaire de Paris en 1900, et les officiers se pavanent volontiers dans leurs superbes tenues.

Cependant, la génération de jeunes femmes qui vient de découvrir coup sur coup les joies de la marche à pied, du ski, du vélocipède et de la conduite automobile ne semble plus aussi intéressée par les relations amoureuses traditionnelles. Les femmes tchèques, comme leurs sœurs de toute l'Europe, ont bien l'intention de s'échapper des confins étroits de leur univers domestique. Milena Jesenská (1896–1944), journaliste et amie de Kafka, écrit : « Je veux utiliser tout ma force pour ne pas rester une enfant. » Au tournant du siècle, les Pragoises sont à l'avant-garde de la révolution sociale qui va les libérer une fois pour toutes du carcan médiéval qu'ont connu leurs mères. Cette révolution commence presque innocemment lorsqu'elles demandent le droit de faire ce que les hommes ont toujours fait : nager sur l'île de Sophie, courir le long de la rivière, jouer au tennis, patiner sur la Moldau gelée. Lorsqu'elles sont autorisées à participer aux discussions philosophiques du Café Arco ou du Café Slavia, et à se pencher sur les théories du Docteur Freud, le point de non-retour est atteint.

L'un des champions les plus notables de l'égalité des femmes est Tomáš Masaryk lui-même, qui a adopté le nom de famille de son épouse américaine, Garrigue, pour marquer leur union. Charlotte Garrigue Masaryk participe à la vie politique, ainsi que sa fille Alice, qui, après avoir été emprisonnée par les Autrichiens pour trahison, écrit : « Dans la vie, toute expérience nous apporte quelque chose, et celle-ci est certainement plus intéressante que la

us in life, and this is truly better than the Ladies' Home Journal experience which many women have."

In contrast to the optimism emanating from the American Club of Czech Ladies (established in 1865), Prague's educated Jewish women felt dark despair. They were shocked to discover that among the homeless refugees from Galicia who flooded the city in 1914, the women and girls were working, while the men and boys studied the Talmud. Journalist Grete Fischer wrote: "War, 1914, meant helplessness for us, because there was no role for us."

## 1918–1939: The Reign of the Czech Lion

On 18 October 1918, in Washington, Tomáš Masaryk proclaimed the birth of free Czechoslovakia and on 28 October the jubilant Republic celebrated its first day of independence. It was a thoroughly democratic creation, because, as Masaryk said, it had no native dynasty, no native aristocracy and no native professional army; and the President himself was the son of a Slovak coachman and a Moravian housemaid. The population was 13.6 million (almost 7 million Czechs, just under 2 million Slovaks and 3.1 million Germans, with the remainder comprising Hungarians, eastern and northern Slavs and Jews). In 1921 Prague had 676,657 inhabitants. The importance of the city's new position was underlined by the incorporation of thirty-seven neighboring communities and towns, including Karlín, Kralovské Vinohrady and Žižkov. By 1939, the population had risen to 962,200.

Some of the more objectionable symbols of Habsburg domination were swept away, such as the Marshal Radetzky monument, or the statue of the Virgin Mary in the Old Town Square. To some, this statue represented the triumph of the Counter-Reformation and the forced re-Catholicization of the Czechs. Some said that the destruction of the Virgin Mary column was revenge for the defeat of the Czechs on the White Mountain, where in 1621 they lost their independence to the Catholic Habsburg armies. Most of the double-headed eagles on public buildings were replaced by the Lion of Bohemia, though some of them survive today.

Almost overnight, the new President became head of one of the wealthiest countries in Europe. Czechoslovakia inherited almost 70 per cent of the Empire's industry, which included textile and glass production, automobile and aircraft manufacture, electrical engineering, coalmining and others. However, very soon an industrial crisis developed. With the collapse of the Empire, the old markets disappeared. Unemployment rose to 200,000 and the country took four years to recover.
In 1920 a general strike, which had begun as a quarrel over property, polarized the social democratic parties and in mid-May 1921 the Communist Party of Czechoslovakia (KSČ) emerged. It quickly became the second strongest party in the new country. Because its members often met in the Karlín district of Prague, they became

Diskussionen im Café Arco oder dem Slavia und die Analyse von Dr. Freud schließlich gestattet wurde, war die Revolution nicht mehr aufzuhalten.

Ein wichtiger Vorkämpfer für die Gleichberechtigung der Frau war Tomáš Masaryk, der den Mädchennamen Garrigue seiner amerikanischen Frau als Ausdruck ihres partnerschaftlichen Verhältnisses angenommen hatte. Charlotte Garrigue Masaryk war wie ihre Tochter Alice politisch aktiv. Nachdem letztere wegen Verrats von den Österreichern inhaftiert worden war, schrieb sie: »Jede Erfahrung hilft uns im Leben, und das ist sicherlich besser als die Frauenzeitschrifts-Erfahrungen, die viele Frauen machen.«

## 1918–1938: Unter der Regentschaft des tschechischen Löwen

Am 18. Oktober 1918 wurde in Paris die Unabhängigkeitserklärung des tschechischen Volkes veröffentlicht, die Thomás Masaryk in Washington konzipiert hatte, und am 28. Oktober die erste freie Tschechoslowakische Republik ausgerufen. Sie war eine durch und durch demokratische Einrichtung – weil es, wie Masaryk feststellte, keine einheimische Dynastie, keinen einheimischen Adel und keine eigene Berufsarmee gab. Ihr Präsident war der Sohn eines slowakischen Kutschers und eines mährisches Hausmädchens. Das Land zählte 13,6 Millionen Einwohner, davon fast 7 Millionen Tschechen, knapp 2 Millionen Slowaken und 3,1 Millionen Deutsche; die übrige Bevölkerung setzte sich aus Ungarn, Ruthenen, Polen und Juden zusammen. 1921 hatte Prag 676.657 Einwohner. Die neue Rolle der Metropole wurde durch die Eingemeindung von 37 benachbarten Gemeinden und Städten wie Karlín, Kralovské Vinohrady und Žižkov unterstrichen. 1939 war die Bevölkerung auf 962.200 angestiegen. Als Symbole der verhaßten Habsburgerherrschaft riß man Denkmäler wie das des Marschalls Radetzky oder die Statue der Jungfrau Maria

lecture du *Ladies' Home Journal*, seule expérience du monde extérieur que connaissent de nombreuses femmes.»

Comparées aux dames du Club américain, fondé en 1865, qui respiraient l'optimisme, les femmes juives cultivées de Prague étaient plongées dans une détresse profonde. Elles furent choquées de découvrir que les femmes et jeunes filles réfugiées de Galicie, qui affluèrent dans la ville en 1914, travaillaient pendant que les hommes et les garçons se consacraient à l'étude du Talmud. La journaliste Grete Fischer écrit: «La guerre de 1914 a été synonyme d'impuissance pour nous, car aucun rôle n'était prévu pour les femmes.»

## 1918–1938: Le règne du lion tchèque

Le 18 octobre 1918, à Washington, Tomáš Masaryk proclame la naissance de la Tchécoslovaquie libre, et le 28 octobre la jeune république célèbre le premier jour de son indépendance. C'est la création d'une authentique démocratie, puisque, comme le fait remarquer Masaryk, le pays ne possède ni dynastie royale, ni aristocratie, ni armée professionnelle et que le président lui-même est né d'un cocher slovaque et d'une femme de ménage morave. La population s'élève à 13,6 millions d'habitants (dont 7 millions de Tchèques, un peu moins de 2 millions de Slovaques et 3,1 millions d'Allemands, le reste étant composé de Hongrois, de Slaves du Nord et de l'Est et de Juifs). En 1921, Prague compte 676 657 habitants. L'importance du nouveau statut de la ville est souligné par l'incorporation dans ses limites de trente-sept communes voisines dont Carlin, Kralovské Vinohrady et Žižkov. En 1939, le chiffre de la population s'élève à 962 200 personnes.

Certains des symboles les plus controversés de la domination des Habsbourg sont effacés, comme le monument au maréchal Radetzky ou la statue de la

Tearing down the Austro-Hungarian eagle.
Das Ende des österreichisch-ungarischen Adlers.
La fin de l'aigle austro-hongrois.

Unemployed people searching for jobs.
Arbeitslose auf der Suche nach Arbeit.
Chômeurs à la recherche de travail.

known as the "Karlín Boys". The most zealous amongst them was the illegitimate son of a poor country girl, Klement Gottwald (1896–1953). His devotion was spotted in Moscow, where he was to spend a considerable time in the late 1930s.

Under President Masaryk's democratic regime, the new nation prospered and an advanced social-security system was introduced. In 1929, however, Czechoslovakia, like many other countries, was hit by the Great Depression. For a time work prospects were bleak. The Republic's highest unemployment figure was recorded in 1933, when 738,000 people were out of work. Many men left their homes to wander the countryside, living in caves or sleeping under an open sky. They sang sentimental songs and read cheap novels about the Wild West, and gazed dreamily into sparkling fires. They gave rivers American-Indian names (Rio Grande was the most popular) and dressed in cowboy hats adorned with rabbit tails. The phenomenon was called *tramping* in Czech. Some *tramps* built log cabins and settlements, where they lived until the economic situation improved.

Between the wars, Prague was a major center of modern European art – the second favorite city, after Paris, of the avant-garde artists of the period. Experiments inspired by Le Corbusier (1887–1965) took place in modern architecture, including the Mánes building (1928; housing a restaurant, club room and gallery for the artistic group Mánes), the Perla (1927–31; the former ARA department store), the Baťa building in Wenceslas Square (1927–29) and the exclusive Terraces restaurant in Barrandov (1929).

Residential districts such as Dejvice reflected the new Functionalist ideas as well as the fashionable social and political concepts of the democratic Republic. They demonstrated a more economical approach to architecture: Functionalism freed itself from ornamental detail; its simple, straight lines looked elegant and timeless. But Functionalism did not penetrate the old city center, as if it was not good enough for those used to the lavish richness of Baroque.

auf dem Altstädter Ring nieder. Letztere repräsentierte für manche den Triumph der Gegenreformation und die gewaltsame Re-Katholisierung der Tschechen. Nach anderer Auffassung war ihre Zerstörung eine Rache für die Niederlage am Weißen Berg, durch die die Tschechen 1621 ihre Unabhängigkeit an die katholischen Habsburger verloren hatten. Auch wurden die meisten Doppeladler auf öffentlichen Gebäuden durch den böhmischen Löwen ersetzt, nur wenige haben bis heute überlebt.

Fast über Nacht war der Präsident zum Staatsoberhaupt eines der reichsten Länder Europas geworden. Die Tschechoslowakei hatte fast 70 Prozent der Industrie des ehemaligen Kaiserreiches geerbt, darunter die Textil- und Glasproduktion, die Automobil- und Flugzeugindustrie, die Elektrotechnik und die Kohlenförderung. Doch mit dem Zusammenbruch des Kaiserreiches verschwanden auch die alten Märkte, so daß das Land schon bald von einer schweren Wirtschaftskrise erfaßt wurde. Die Zahl der Arbeitslosen stieg auf 200.000 an. Erst nach vier Jahre war die Rezession beendet.

1920 führten Streitigkeiten um Eigentumsfragen zu einem Generalstreik, der die sozialdemokratischen Parteien spaltete. Mitte 1921 wurde die Kommunistische Partei der Tschechoslowakei (KSČ) gegründet, die sich schnell zur zweitstärksten Partei im Land entwickelte. Weil ihre Mitglieder oft in Karlín zusammentrafen, wurden sie als »Karlín-Jungs« bezeichnet. Einer ihrer Anführer war Klement Gottwald (1896–1953), der illegitime Sohn eines armen Landmädchens, dessen Engagement auch in Moskau nicht verborgen blieb. Ende der dreißiger Jahre verbrachte er einige Zeit in dieser Stadt.

Unter Präsident Masaryks demokratischem Regiment erlebte die neue Nation eine wirtschaftliche Blütezeit, die eine Reihe fortschrittlicher Sozialgesetze mit sich brachte. Nach 1929 erfaßte die Weltwirtschaftskrise auch die Tschechoslowakei. Die Zahl der Arbeitslosen stieg beständig und erreichte 1933 mit 738.000 ihren Höhepunkt seit Bestehen der Republik. Viele Männer verließen ihre Häuser, um auf dem Lande zu vagabundieren, lebten in Höhlen oder schliefen unter freiem Himmel. Ihr Vorbild war der Wilde Westen, den sie aus Groschenromanen kannten: Sie sangen sentimentale Lieder, starrten verträumt in die knisternden Lagerfeuer, gaben den Flüssen Indianernamen (am beliebtesten war der Rio Grande) und trugen mit Kaninchenschwänzen verzierte Cowboyhüte. Die Bezeichnung im Tschechischen für diese Lebensweise ist – gleich dem englischen Wort – *tramping*. Einige *tramps* bauten sogar Blockhütten und Siedlungen, in denen sie lebten, bis sich die wirtschaftliche Situation gebessert hatte.

In der Zeit zwischen den Weltkriegen entwickelte sich Prag zu einer Metropole für moderne europäische Kunst, die nach Paris zum Treffpunkt der Avantgardekünstler wurde. Im Bereich der modernen Architektur übten die Entwürfe Le Corbusiers (1887–1965) großen Einfluß aus, wovon das Mánes-Haus (Sitz des Vereins Bildender Künstler, 1928 mit einem Restaurant, einem Clubraum und einer Galerie), das Perla-Gebäude (1927–31); das frühere

Sainte Vierge sur la place de la vieille ville. Pour certains, elle représentait le triomphe de la contre-réforme et la re-catholicisation forcée des Tchèques. Pour d'autres c'était une revanche sur la défaite de ceux-ci à la bataille de la Montagne blanche (1621) où ils avaient perdu leur indépendance face aux armées autrichiennes. La plupart des aigles à deux têtes des bâtiments publics furent remplacés par le lion de Bohême, bien que quelques emblèmes impériaux aient survécu jusqu'à nos jours.

Presque du jour au lendemain, le nouveau président devient le dirigeant de l'un des plus riches pays d'Europe. La Tchécoslovaquie a hérité de près de 70 pour cent de la puissance industrielle de l'empire qui comprend, entre autres, des usines de textile et de verrerie, d'automobiles, d'avions et d'appareils électriques, des mines de charbon. Une crise industrielle se développe rapidement. Avec l'effondrement de l'empire, les marchés traditionnels disparaissent. Le chômage touche 200 000 personnes et il faudra quatre longues années au pays pour recouvrer sa prospérité.

En 1920, une grève lancée à l'occasion d'une querelle sur des problèmes de propriété mobilise les partis sociaux-démocrates, et, au milieu du mois de mai 1921, est fondé le Parti communiste de Tchécoslovaquie (KSČ). Il va rapidement devenir le second parti du pays. Parce que ses membres se réunissent souvent dans le quartier de Prague appelé Karlín, ils reçoivent le surnom de «ceux de Karlín». Le plus actif d'entre eux est le fils illégitime d'une pauvre fille de la campagne, Klement Gottwald (1896–1953). Son dévouement est remarqué à Moscou, où il passe de très longs séjours à la fin des années 30.

La nouvelle nation prospère sous le régime démocratique du président Masaryk tandis qu'un système moderne de sécurité sociale est mis en place. En 1929, cependant, la Tchécoslovaquie, comme de nombreux autres pays, est touchée par la Grande dépression. Pendant un temps, le marché du travail n'a plus rien à offrir. En 1933, la République enregistre un taux record de chômage avec 738 000 sans travail. Beaucoup d'entre eux quittent leurs maisons, errent dans les campagnes, dormant dans des cavernes ou à la belle étoile. Ils chantent des chansons sentimentales et lisent des romans bon marché sur l'Ouest américain, et se réunissent pour rêver autour de feux de bois. Ils donnent aux rivières des noms américains (le rio Grande est le plus populaire) et mettent des chapeaux de cow-boys ornés de queues de lapin. Le phénomène est appelé en tchèque *tramping*. Des *tramps* construisent des cabanes et des campements de rondins où ils vivent jusqu'à ce que la situation s'améliore.

Entre les deux guerres, Prague devient l'un des grands centres de l'art européen contemporain, second après Paris, pour les artistes d'avant-garde. En architecture se développent des tentatives inspirées par Le Corbusier (1887–1965), dont le bâtiment Mánes (1928; abritant un restaurant, une salle de réunion et une galerie pour le groupe d'artistes Mánes), le Perla (1927–31); ancien magasin ARA), l'immeuble Baťa de la place Venceslas (1927–29) et l'élégant restaurant des Terrasses à Prague–Barrandov (1929).

Banks, insurance companies and ministries favored Neoclassicism, which was imposing and monumental. Masaryk called on Jože Plečnik (1872–1957), a Slovenian architect, to give the complex of presidential buildings on the Hradčany Hill a new look, fit better for the new Republic. The majority of the buildings, gardens and terraces had been neglected; after their renovation, Plečnik added vases, huge bowls, an obelisk, staircases, columns and new terraces, which were inspired by the Classical period but looked timelessly modern. The result was solemn, decent and matter of fact, as though approved by a committee. Plečnik used the sturdiest granite found in the Czechoslovak mountains – diorite. However, the obelisk broke during transportation, as if foretelling the fragility of the new Republic.

Plečnik's other, and maybe more famous, work in Prague is the startlingly unconventional square Church of the Sacred Heart in Jiří z Poděbrad Square. Its large circular window displays a huge clock and the church is dun-colored, like the bare bricks from which it was built, both outside and inside.

When they first appeared, Plečnik's gloomy shapes seemed out of keeping with Prague's light-hearted spirit. As the years passed, however, the city assumed more and more of his sobriety. Life was not a series of Hašek's jokes, people realized, but resembled more the endless bricks in Plečnik's church, repetitious and boring, only rarely, when highlighted by the setting sun, seeming luminous, textured and magnificent.

Similar in its spirit of unornamented grandeur is Jan Zázvorka's National Liberation Monument (1932) on the top of Vítkov Hill. In the tall, granite-faced cube of the main hall lie the remains of an Unknown Soldier. This monumental building dominates the hill. The site was chosen to commemorate the battle of 1420, when the Hussite leader Jan Žižka (c. 1370–1424) defeated the Crusaders. His statue in front of the monument complements the style of the building. From the valley below, the one-eyed medieval warrior on his powerful steed forms a perfect silhouette against the sky. The biggest equestrian statue in Europe, it was designed by Bohumil Kafka (1878–1942) in the 1930s, though not finished and unveiled until 1950.

The sobriety of Neoclassicism and Functionalism meant these styles were suited to crematoria and tombstones. One of Plečnik's pupils, Alois Mezera, designed the Prague–Strašnice crematorium in 1930. Cremation became fashionable at the turn of the century. The first to be cremated was Vojtěch Náprstek in 1894. (He had spent his life promoting inventions and various progressive ideas, including the equality of women, and as well as his ashes he left behind the Náprstek Museum.)

Prague's first airport, at Kbely, came into operation in 1923, but something more modern was soon needed and in 1936 Ruzyně Airport was opened to cope with the growing international traffic.

A thriving literary culture continued in the pubs and cafés of the city, finding new metaphors of the absurd in the work of Charlie Chaplin, who, like Hašek's Švejk, was a little man caught up in the complicated machinery of modern times. Czech

Kaufhaus Ara), das Baťa-Gebäude auf dem Wenzels-platz (1927–29) und das exklusive Terrassen-Restaurant im Stadtteil Barrandov (1929) noch heute Zeugnis ablegen.

Die modernen sozialen und politischen Konzepte der demokratischen Republik und die neuen Ideen des Funktionalismus spiegelten sich in Wohngebie-ten wie Dejvice wieder. Diese Stilrichtung der modernen Architektur versuchte, die Erscheinungs-form ganz aus der Funktion eines Bauwerks abzulei-ten oder diese besonders zu betonen. Anstelle von ornamentalen Details wurden einfache, klare Linien bevorzugt, die elegant und zeitlos wirken.

Banken, Versicherungsgesellschaften und Mini-sterien zogen den imposanten und monumentalen Neoklassizismus vor. Masaryk beauftragte den slo-wenischen Architekten Jože Plečnik (1872–1957) mit der Modernisierung des Präsidentensitzes auf dem Hradschin, durch die die Anlage auf die Ver-hältnisse der jungen Republik abgestimmt werden sollte. Nach der Renovierung der Gebäude, Gärten und Terrassen erweiterte Plečnik den Komplex um Vasen, eine große Kugel, einen Obelisken, Treppen, Säulen und neue Terrassen, die vom Klassizismus dieser Zeit beeinflußt waren, aber gleichzeitig zeit-los modern erschienen. Das Ergebnis wirkte feier-lich, unauffällig und sachlich, als sei es von einem Ausschuß überprüft worden. Plečnik verwendete den härtesten Granit aus den tschechoslowakischen Bergen, den Diorit. Dennoch fiel der Obelisk beim Transport auseinander – ein Vorzeichen für die Zer-brechlichkeit der jungen Republik.

Eine weitere und vielleicht die bekanntere Arbeit Plečniks in Prag ist die aufregend unkonventionelle Herz-Jesu-Kirche auf dem Jiří z Poděbrad-Platz (1928–32). Fassade und Innenraum des Kubus sind aus einfachen Ziegelsteinen erbaut, deren Brauntöne auch für die gesamte Ausstattung übernommen wur-den. An der Ostseite erhebt sich ein ebenfalls als Kubus gestalteter Turm mit einer großen Uhr in dem ausladenden runden Fenster.

Anfänglich schienen Plečniks düstere Formen unvereinbar mit Prags leichtherzigem Geist. Im Laufe der Jahre aber nahm die Stadt mehr und mehr von seiner Nüchternheit an. Das Leben bestand nicht, wie die Menschen feststellten, aus einer Reihe von Hašeks Scherzen, sondern ähnelte vielmehr den endlosen Steinen in Plečniks Kirche: Sie waren gleichförmig und langweilig und schienen nur gele-gentlich, wenn sie von der untergehenden Sonne angestrahlt wurden, leuchtend, strukturiert und prächtig.

Eine ähnlich schlichte Ausstrahlung besitzt das Nationaldenkmal Jan Žižkas (1370–1424) auf dem Ziskov-Hügel. Der Monumentalbau, der von Jan Zázvorka erbaut wurde (1929–32), entstand an der Stelle, an der der Hussiten-Führer 1420 die Kreuzrit-ter besiegt hatte. In dem großen, mit Granit verklei-deten Würfel ruhen die Überreste eines unbekannten Soldaten. Bohumil Kafka (1878–1942) hat das Rei-terstandbild vor der Gedenkstätte auf die Architektur abgestimmt: Von dem darunterliegenden Tal aus gesehen, bilden der einäugige mittelalterliche Krie-ger und sein mächtiges Roß eine perfekte Silhouette gegen den Himmel. Dieses größte Reiterdenkmal Europas wurde bereits in den 30er Jahren entworfen, aber erst 1950 vollendet und enthüllt.

Plečnik's vase in the Hradčany gardens.
Plečniks Vase im Garten des Hradschin.
Le vase de Plečnik dans les jardins du Hradčany.

Des quartiers résidentiels comme Dejvice reflètent alors les nouvelles idées fonctionnalistes et les concepts sociaux et politiques à la mode dans la nouvelle démocratie. Ils témoignent d'une approche plus économique de l'architecture : le fonctionnalisme se libère du détail ornemental, ses lignes simples et droites paraissent élégantes et intemporelles.

Les banques, les compagnies d'assurance et les ministères adoptent un néoclassicisme monumental et imposant. Masaryk fait appel à Jože Plečnik (1872–1957), un architecte slovène, pour moderniser le complexe présidentiel du château de la colline de Hradčany, qui doit être adapté aux besoins de la nouvelle république. La plus grande partie des bâtiments, des jardins et des terrasses avait été longtemps négligée. Après leur rénovation, Plečnik installe des vases, d'énormes coupes, des obélisques, des escaliers, des colonnes et de nouvelles terrasses inspirées de la période classique mais d'aspect néanmoins moderne et intemporel. Le résultat est solennel, sans grande fantaisie, et a dû passer par l'approbation d'une commission. Plečnik utilise un granit très dur des montagnes tchécoslovaques, la diorite. Mais l'obélisque se brise pendant son transport, augurant mal de la solidité du nouveau régime.

La seconde intervention de Plečnik à Prague – peut-être plus célèbre encore – est sa surprenante et peu conventionnelle église carrée du Sacré-Cœur, place Jiří z Poděbrad. Sa grande rosace reçoit une énorme horloge, et l'église est fortement colorée comme les briques nues dont elle est construite, aussi bien à l'extérieur qu'à l'intérieur.

À leur apparition, les formes austères de Plečnik semblent bien éloignées de l'esprit de légèreté de la ville. Avec le temps, cependant, la capitale a de mieux en mieux assumé cette sobriété. Les Pragois ont compris que la vie n'est pas une suite de plaisanteries de Hašek, mais ressemble davantage aux alignements sans fin de briques de l'église de l'architecte, répétitifs et ennuyeux, mais lumineux, riches de toute une texture et splendides lorsqu'à de rares occasions le soleil vient les illuminer.

Jaroslav Seifert in later life.
Jaroslav Seifert in späteren Jahren.
Jaroslav Seifert à la fin de sa vie.

literature started gaining recognition abroad, thanks to Jaroslav Hašek and Karel Čapek. Čapek (1890–1938), novelist, essayist and playwright, defended humanist and democratic values. Hašek watched the nation's intoxication with democracy with a certain amusement. Only a few years earlier he had come face to face with a totalitarian regime: the Soviet Union at its birth. After deserting from the Austro-Hungarian army in 1915, he wandered through Russia. These were the days when anyone thought to be a capitalist or intellectual was seen as an enemy of the workers; famine raged and cannibalism was not uncommon. In order to survive, Hašek pretended to be a deaf-mute village idiot. Later he joined the Bolsheviks and revealed his journalistic talents. In 1917 he became the Red commissar of a region in Asia bigger than Czechoslovakia. It was the only time in his life that he stayed sober. After his return to Prague he took special pleasure in spreading the news of wild atrocities committed by the Bolsheviks, but no one took much notice of him – not even when he died in 1923. On two previous occasions he had falsely notified the authorities of his death and had obituaries published, and so the appearance of his real obituary was naturally assumed to be a joke.

In 1920–22 the Devětsil group was founded. It was an association of avant-garde poets, painters, architects, theater artists and journalists who declared themselves proponents of romantic Marxism. Artists gathered around the theoretician Karel Teige (1900–51), who advocated total simplicity in art, which was to be about the worker and for the worker. The best examples of this Proletarian art were the circus, burlesque film, football and books about the Wild West. (Teige himself, none the less, was a refined, erudite man, the walking antithesis of the naivete he preached.) Proletarian Art soon evolved into Poetism, which sought inspiration in fantasy and free associations, and Constructivism, which in architecture emerged as Functionalism.

Im Stil des Neoklassizismus und des Funktionalismus wurden viele Grabsteine und Krematorien gestaltet. Aufgrund des immer knapper werdenden Raums für Friedhöfe erfreuten sich letztere zunehmender Beliebtheit. Alois Mezera, ein Schüler Plečniks, entwarf in den 30er Jahren das Krematorium in Strašnice. Der erste, der dort eingeäschert wurde, war 1894 Vojtěch Náprstek. (Náprstek hatte zeit seines Leben Erfindungen unterstützt und verschiedene progressive Ideen – einschließlich der Gleichberechtigung der Frau – gefördert. Er hinterließ neben seiner Asche auch das Náprstek-Museum.)

Prags erster Flughafen in Kbely, der 1923 für den Flugverkehr geöffnet worden war, erfüllte schon bald nicht mehr die wachsenden Anforderungen der internationalen Luftfahrt. So entstand 1936 mit dem Bau des Ruzyně-Flughafens eine modernere Anlage.

Die blühende Literaturszene Prags spielte sich weiterhin in den Kneipen und Kaffeehäusern ab. Hier wurden neue Metaphern des Absurden in den Werken Charlie Chaplins gefunden, der, wie Hašeks Schwejk, als kleiner Mann in der komplizierten Maschinerie der »Modernen Zeiten« gefangen war. Dank Jaroslav Hašek und Karel Čapek fand die tschechische Literatur im Ausland allmählich Anerkennung. Čapek (1890–1938), Schriftsteller, Essayist und Dramatiker, setzte sich für die Wahrung humanistischer und demokratischer Werte ein. Hašek hingegen betrachtete die Begeisterung des Volkes für die Demokratie mit einer gewissen Belustigung. Er war nur wenige Jahre zuvor mit einem totalitären Regime – der Sowjetunion – in Berührung gekommen. Nachdem er 1915 aus der österreichisch-ungarischen Armee desertiert war, war er durch Rußland gereist. In diesen Jahren wurde jeder, von dem man annahm, er sei ein Kapitalist oder ein Intellektueller, als Feind der Arbeiterklasse angesehen. Hungersnöte wüteten, und Kannibalismus war keine Seltenheit. Um zu überleben, spielte Hašek einen taubstummen Dorftrottel. Später schloß er sich den Bolschewiken an und gab seine journalistischen Talente zu erkennen. 1917 wurde er zum Kommissar einer Region in Asien ernannt, die größer als die gesamte Tschechoslowakei war. Dies war die einzige Zeit in seinem Leben, in der er nüchtern blieb. Als er nach Prag zurückkehrte, machte er sich eine besondere Freude daraus, Nachrichten über die wilden Grausamkeiten der Bolschewiken zu verbreiten, aber keiner nahm Notiz von ihm – noch nicht einmal, als er 1923 starb. Da er bei zwei vorherigen Anlässen den Behörden fälschlicherweise seinen Tod gemeldet und einen Nachruf veröffentlicht hatte, hielt man den echten Nachruf ebenfalls für einen Scherz.

Anfang der 20er Jahre wurde die avantgardistische Gruppe Devětsil gegründet, der sich Dichter, Maler, Architekten, Theaterschauspieler und Journalisten anschlossen. Die Künstler, die sich als Vertreter des romantischen Marxismus bezeichneten, scharten sich um den Theoretiker Karel Teige (1900–1951). Dieser forderte eine vollkommen einfache Kunst, die den Arbeiter in den Mittelpunkt stellen und für den Arbeiter geschaffen werden sollte. Anschauliche Beispiele dieser Proletarischen Kunst fanden sich im Zirkus, in Filmpossen, beim Fußball und in Büchern über den Wilden Westen.

Le monument national de la Libération (1932) au sommet de la colline de Vítkov fait preuve du même esprit de grandeur dépouillée de tout ornement. Dans le grand cube plaqué de granit du hall principal ont été déposés les restes d'un soldat inconnu. Ce bâtiment monumental domine la colline. Le site a été choisi pour commémorer la bataille de 1420, lorsque le chef hussite, Jan Žižka (vers 1370–1424), battit les croisés. Face au monument, sa statue complète l'effet d'ensemble. Vu de la vallée, le guerrier médiéval borgne, monté sur son puissant destrier se découpe, impeccable silhouette sur le fond du ciel. Plus grande statue équestre d'Europe, dessinée par Bohumil Kafka (1878–1942) dans les années 30, elle ne fut terminée et inaugurée qu'en 1950.

Avec leur sobriété, le néoclassicisme et le fonctionnalisme conviennent idéalement aux crématoriums et aux monuments funéraires. L'un des élèves de Plečnik, Alois Mezera, conçoit ainsi le crématorium de Strašnice en 1930, où il est à la mode de se faire incinérer, d'autant plus que l'espace se fait rare dans les cimetières. Le premier Pragois à se faire incinérer avait été Vojtěch Náprstek, ardent défenseur des inventions et des idées progressistes – dont l'égalité pour les femmes. En 1894, il fait disperser ses cendres derrière le musée Náprstek.

Le premier aéroport de Prague, à Kbely, entre en service en 1923, mais est vite dépassé. En 1936, de nouvelles installations sont inaugurées à Ruzyně pour répondre aux besoins grandissants des vols internationaux.

La culture vivante se poursuit dans les pubs et les cafés de la ville, découvrant de nouvelles métaphores de l'absurde dans l'œuvre de Charlie Chaplin qui, comme le Švejk de Hašek, montre un individu perdu face à la machinerie complexe des temps modernes. La littérature tchèque commence à être reconnue à l'étranger, grâce à Jaroslav Hašek et Karel Čapek. Čapek (1890–1938), romancier, essayiste et auteur dramatique, défend les valeurs humanistes et démocratiques. Hašek observe l'engouement de son pays pour la démocratie avec un certain amusement. Peu de Tchèques s'étaient jusque-là retrouvés face à face avec un régime totalitaire : l'Union soviétique dans ses balbutiements. Après avoir déserté de l'armée austro-hongroise en 1915, l'écrivain avait erré à travers la Russie. À cette époque, tous ceux qui passaient pour des capitalistes ou des intellectuels étaient considérés comme des ennemis de la classe ouvrière. La famine faisait rage et les cas de cannibalisme fréquents. Pour survivre, il joua à l'imbécile sourd-muet. Ce fut la seule fois de sa vie où il cessa de boire. Plus tard, il révéla ses origines et, en 1917, devint commissaire des armées tchèques libres en Russie. De retour à Prague, il prend un plaisir particulier à faire connaître les atrocités commises par les bolcheviques, mais personne ne fait vraiment attention à lui, même lorsqu'il meurt en 1923. À deux occasions précédentes, il avait faussement averti les autorités de sa mort et avait fait publier des nécrologies, et l'on crut que cette nouvelle notice était une plaisanterie.

En 1920–22, le groupe Devětsil se forme pour protester contre une culture qui fait de la machine et du progrès une nouvelle religion. Des artistes se rassemblent autour du théoricien Karel Teige

The MGM cinema in Prague.
Das MGM-Kino in Prag.
Le cinéma MGM à Prague.

A well-known poet attracted to Proletarian art was Vítězslav Nezval (1900–58), who later became an advocate of Poetism and Surrealism. After the war he engaged his talents in glorifying Communism. Jaroslav Seifert (1901–85) was among the movement's other poets who were later to become famous; in 1984 he was awarded the Nobel Prize for Literature.

From Poetism sprang Surrealism, of which Teige went on to become a leading spokesman. The Surrealists, established in Prague in 1934, were the most left wing among the artists; initially they had very close ties with the Communist Party, but in 1938 they left their political mentors. In 1935 the French Surrealist poets Paul Éluard (1895–1952) and André Breton (1896–1966) visited Prague, lecturing on the new "ism". "Art never listens to an order," Breton told his Czech disciples. They took him for long walks through old streets where every house has some beautiful detail. "Prague," he wrote, "wrapped in its legendary magic, is truly one of those cities that has been able to fix and retain the poetic idea that is always more or less drifting aimlessly through space."

In 1924 Franz Kafka died, leaving instructions to his friend, Max Brod, to burn his manuscripts. But Brod ignored his request and devoted his life to promoting Kafka's slim volumes.

An indefinable guilt permeated Prague's Jewish literature in German. Oddly enough, the distress of isolation, the inability to adapt, the uprootedness also tormented some Jews writing in Czech. Bilingual Jews, such as Brod who wrote for German newspapers, opened many doors to Czech artists.

A new kind of entertainment had been brought from Paris at the turn of the century by architect Jan Kříženecký (1868–1921), who introduced the Lumière camera to Prague and began producing humorous short films. Soon these developed into lavish, almost Hollywood-style productions. In the 1920s about twenty films a year were made in Czechoslovakia; after the completion of the Barrandov Studios in 1934, the number increased to

(Teige selbst hingegen war ein kultivierter, belesener Mensch und der wandelnde Gegenbeweis für die von ihm geforderte Naivität.) Die Proletarische Kunst wandelte sich schnell in den Poetismus, der seine Inspirationen aus der Phantasie und der freien Assoziation bezog, und in den Konstruktivismus, der sich in der Architektur aus dem Funktionalismus entwickelte.

Ein bekannter Anhänger der Proletarischen Kunst war der Schriftsteller Vítězslav Nezval (1900–58), der später zum Verfechter des Poetismus und des Surrealismus avancierte. Nach dem Krieg nutzte er seine Talente zur Glorifizierung des Kommunismus. Der Lyriker Jaroslav Seifert (1901–85) ist ebenfalls diesem Kreis zuzurechnen, der später Berühmtheit erlangen sollte: 1984 wurde ihm der Literatur-Nobelpreis verliehen.

Aus dem Poetismus entwickelte sich der Surrealismus, als dessen Sprachrohr Teige bekannt wurde. Die Surrealisten, die sich 1934 in Prag konstituierten, galten in der Kunstszene als extrem links orientiert. Ihr politischer Mentor war die Kommunistische Partei, von der sie sich aber 1934 lösten. 1935, während eines Besuchs in Prag, propagierten die französischen surrealistischen Dichter Paul Éluard (1895–1952) und André Breton (1896–1966) die neue Richtung der modernen Literatur. »Die Kunst gehorcht niemals einem Befehl« erklärte Breton seinen tschechischen Schülern. Diese führten ihn auf langen Spaziergängen durch die alten Straßen, wo jedes Haus reizvolle Details aufwies. »Prag«, schrieb Breton, »eingehüllt in seine legendäre Magie, gehört wahrhaft zu den Städten, die in der Lage sind, die poetischen Ideen, die immer mehr oder weniger ziellos im Raum schweben, auf sich zu ziehen und zu halten.«

Als Franz Kafka 1924 starb, hinterließ er seinem Freund Max Brod (1884–1968) den Auftrag, seine Manuskripte zu verbrennen. Aber Brod ignorierte diese Bitte und widmete sich zeit seines Lebens der Verbreitung von Kafkas Werk.

Die jüdische Literatur Prags in deutscher Sprache ist von einer undefinierbaren Schuld durchdrungen. Merkwürdi- gerweise quälten die Schwierigkeiten der Isolation, die Unfähigkeit, sich anzupassen, und die Entwurzelung auch einige Juden, die in tschechischer Sprache schrieben. Juden, die Werke in beiden Sprachen verfaßten – wie Brod, der für deutsche Zeitungen arbeitete – öffneten tschechischen Künstlern viele Türen.

Eine neue Art von Unterhaltung wurde um die Jahrhundertwende aus Paris durch den Architekten Jan Kříženecký (1868–1921) eingeführt. Der Lumière-Schüler hatte die ersten beweglichen Bilder festgehalten und mit der Produktion humorvoller Kurzfilme begonnen. Aus diesen entstanden bald ausladende, fast Hollywood-ähnliche Leinwandstreifen. In den zwanziger Jahren wurden pro Jahr etwa 20 Filme in der Tschechoslowakei gedreht, nach der Fertigstellung der Barrandov-Filmstudios 1933 stieg die Zahl auf 30 bis etwa 50 an. Prag hatte 1933 mehr Kinos pro Einwohner als jede andere europäische Stadt. In den Barrandov-Studios, die sich im Besitz von Miloš Havel (ein Onkel des Präsidenten Václav Havel) und Max Urban befanden, entwickelte sich schließlich eine moderne Filmindustrie. Auf den sanften Hügeln in der Nähe der Studios

(1900–1951), qui défend l'idée d'une simplicité totale en art, un art concernant les travailleurs et créé pour eux. Les meilleurs exemples de cet art prolétarien sont le cirque, le film burlesque, le football et les livres de western (Teige lui-même n'en est pas moins un homme raffiné, érudit, antithèse vivante de la naïveté qu'il prêche). L'art prolétarien évolue bientôt en poétisme, qui recherche l'inspiration dans l'imaginaire et les associations libres, et le constructivisme, qui, en architecture, naît du fonctionnalisme.

Vítězslav Nezval (1900–1958) est un poète très célèbre sensible à cet art prolétarien; il se fera plus tard l'avocat du poétisme et du surréalisme. Après la guerre, il mettra ses talents au service de la glorification du communisme. Jaroslav Seifert (1901–1985) fait partie d'un autre groupe de poètes du même mouvement, qui accédera à la célébrité. En 1984, il recevra même le prix Nobel de littérature.

Du poétisme allait sortir le surréalisme, dont Teige sera l'un des plus importants porte-parole. Les surréalistes, qui apparaissent à Prague en 1934, font partie des artistes les plus à gauche. Initialement, ils entretiennent des liens très étroits avec le parti communiste, mais en 1938, abandonnent leurs mentors politiques. En 1935, les poètes surréalistes français Paul Éluard (1895–1952) et André Breton (1896–1966) séjournent à Prague et donnent une conférence sur ce nouveau mouvement. «L'art n'obéit jamais aux ordres», dit Breton à ses disciples tchèques qui l'entraînent dans de grandes promenades à travers la vieille ville, où chaque maison offre au regard un détail intéressant. «Prague», écrit-il, «noyé dans sa magie légendaire, est vraiment l'une de ces villes qui a su fixer et retenir l'idée poétique qui se déplace toujours plus ou moins sans but à travers l'espace.»

En 1924, Franz Kafka meurt en demandant à son ami Max Brod de brûler ses manuscrits. Brod ne respecte pas cette dernière volonté et consacre au contraire sa vie à faire connaître l'œuvre de l'écrivain.

Un sentiment indéfinissable de culpabilité est présent dans toute la littérature juive pragoise écrite en allemand. Curieusement, la détresse de l'isolement, l'incapacité à s'adapter, le problème des racines tourmentent également certains Juifs qui écrivent en tchèque. Les Juifs bilingues, comme Brod qui écrit pour des journaux allemands, apportent énormément aux artistes tchèques.

Une nouvelle forme de loisirs est importée de Paris au tournant du siècle par l'architecte Jan Kříženecký (1868–1921) qui rapporte à Prague une caméra Lumière et commence à produire des films humoristiques. Bientôt il passe à des productions plus ambitieuses, presque hollywoodiennes. Dans les années 20, vingt films environ sont réalisés chaque année en Tchécoslovaquie. Après la construction des studios Barrandov en 1934, ce nombre s'élèvera selon les années entre trente et quarante-neuf. En 1934, Prague possède plus de cinémas par habitant que n'importe quelle autre ville européenne, et une industrie cinématographique moderne se met finalement en place dans les studios Barrandov, propriété de Miloš Havel (oncle du président Václav Havel) et de Max Urban. Sur les collines voisines, de nombreuses villas élégantes et

between thirty and forty-nine. In 1934 Prague had more cinemas per capita than any other European city and at Barrandov, owned by Miloš Havel (uncle of President Václav Havel) and Max Urban, a modern film industry finally emerged. On the sloping hill next to the studios many elegant and luxurious villas were built for the stars – a Czech Beverly Hills.

While mainstream Czech cinema tried to imitate Hollywood films, the left-wing avant-garde filmmakers sought for inspiration in the Soviet art of the 1920s, which was revolutionary, experimental and daring. One film which became famous when it ran into censorship problems in the straitlaced USA was Gustav Machatý's *Ekstase* (Ecstasy, 1933). It was not actress Hedwig Kiesler's nudity that caused the trouble so much as close-ups of her face during sexual intercourse.

The *Osvobozené divadlo* (Liberated Theater) of the actor–playwrights Jan Werich (1905–80), Jiří Voskovec (1905–81) and the composer Jaroslav Ježek (1906–42) represented the spirit of Prague and the First Republic. With its brilliant satire, allusions to French and American culture, focus on democracy, its jazz and Surrealism and Dada, the theater became a vital part of the life of the capital. Voskovec and Werich's intellectual cabaret, ridiculed twentieth-century dictators and personified a witty and courageous stand against the advance of Nazism. In 1934 Voskovec and Werich had to evacuate the premises because of Fascist provocation.

Sport, and tennis in particular, became increasingly popular in Prague in the 1920s and 1930s. Ladislav Žemla and Jan Koželuh, winners of the Davis Cup in 1924, made it to the world top ten. Koželuh was world professional tennis champion from 1925 to 1930, and again in 1932. Jaroslav Skobla won the heavyweight weightlifting gold medal at the Los Angeles Olympics in 1932. In 1928 Eliška Junková won the Targa Florio in Sicily in her Bugatti, the only woman to have won the race to date. Czechs liked sport and the President, who, quite late in life, took up riding through the streets of Prague, was often surrounded by members of the famous sports organization *Sokol* (Falcon). *Sokol* was founded in 1862 by Miroslav Tyrš, a teacher of philosophy, who was convinced that the Olympic ideal of "healthy body, healthy spirit" would help the Czech nation rediscover its own identity. *Sokol* gymnasts often won Olympic medals, but the organization was persecuted for its patriotism. It was dissolved three times in its short history: first by the Habsburgs in 1915; then in 1941 by the Nazis, who imprisoned 20,000 members (nearly 5000 of them died in concentration camps); finally, in 1948, it was disbanded by the Communists, who replaced the famous *Sokol* festivals with *spartakiáda* – similarly monolithic events, but stripped of Czech patriotism and filled instead with slogans glorifying the new regime.

In Masaryk's Republic, the workers had their own group, the DTJ (*Dělnické tělocvičné jednoty*: Workers' Physical Training Units) and their own Workers Olympics. Catholics exercised in "a Christian discipline and spirit" in the *Československý Orel* (Czechoslovak Eagle Sports

wurden für die Stars viele elegante und luxuriöse Villen gebaut – ein tschechisches Beverly Hills.

Während das kommerzielle tschechische Kino sich auf die Imitation von Hollywood-Filmen beschränkte, suchten die linken Filmemacher der Avantgarde nach Insprirationen in der sowjetischen Kunst der zwanziger Jahre, die revolutionär, experimentell und gewagt war. Ein Film, der auf Grund seiner Zensurprobleme in den sittenstrengen USA berühmt wurde, war Gustav Machatýs *Ekstase* (Ekstase, 1933). Nicht die Nacktszene mit Hedwig Kiesler, sondern die Nahaufnahmen ihres Gesichts während eines Liebesakts, waren der Anlaß für die Schwierigkeiten.

Das *Osvobozené divadlo* (Befreites Theater) des Schauspielers und Dramatikers Jan Werich (1905–80), von Jiří Voskovec (1905–81) und des Komponisten Jaroslav Ježek (1906–42) repräsentierte den Geist von Prag und der Ersten Republik. Mit seinen brillanten Satiren, den Anspielungen auf die französische und die amerikanische Kultur, der Betonung der Demokratie und seinem Faible für Jazz, Surrealismus und Dada entwickelte sich das Theater zu einem wesentlichen Bestandteil des Lebens in der Hauptstadt. Voskovecs und Werichs intellektuelles Kabarett nahm die Diktatoren des 20. Jahrhunderts aufs Korn und vertrat einen gewitzten und mutigen Standpunkt gegenüber dem aufkommenden Nationalsozialismus. Wegen faschistischer Provokationen mußten Voskovec und Werich 1934 das Theater räumen lassen.

Sport und ganz besonders Tennis wurden in den 20er und 30er Jahren in Prag immer populärer. Die Gewinner des Davis-Cups von 1924, Ladislav Žemla und Jan Koželuh, kamen unter die ersten Zehn der Weltrangliste. Koželuh war von 1925 bis 1930 und dann wieder 1932 Tennisweltmeister. Jaroslav Skobla errang bei den Olympischen Spielen in Los Angeles 1932 im Gewichtheben die Goldmedaille. 1928 wurde Eliška Junková in ihrem Bugatti Siegerin der Targa Florio auf Sizilien; sie ist bis heute die einzige Frau, die das Rennen je gewonnen hat. Die Tschechen liebten den Sport, und der Präsident, der erst recht spät in seinem Leben anfing, durch die Straßen von Prag zu reiten, wurde oft von Mitgliedern der berühmten Turnvereinigung *Sokol* (Falke) begleitet. Die *Sokol* war 1862 von Miroslav Tyrš, einem Philosophielehrer, in der Überzeugung gegründet worden, daß das olympische Ideal »eines gesunden Geistes in einem gesunden Körper« der tschechischen Nation helfen würde, ihre eigene Identität wiederzufinden. *Sokols* Turner gewannen viele olympische Medaillen. Wegen ihres Patriotismus aber wurde die Organisation verfolgt und im Lauf ihrer kurzen Geschichte dreimal aufgelöst: 1915 von den Habsburgern, 1941 von den Nazis, die 20.000 Mitglieder festnahmen (von denen fast 5000 in Konzentrationslagern starben) und schließlich von den Kommunisten, die die berühmten *Sokol*-Feste durch die Spartakiaden ersetzten – ähnlich monolithische Veranstaltungen, die des tschechischen Patriotismus beraubt waren, dafür aber viele Slogans zur Verherrlichung des neuen Regimes beinhalteten.

In Masaryks Republik hatten die Arbeiter einen eigenen Verein, das DTJ (*Dělnické tělocvičné jednoty*: Sportgruppe der Arbeiter) und eigene

luxueuses s'élèvent pour les stars locales, sorte de Beverly Hills tchèque.

Si le cinéma populaire tchèque essaie d'imiter les films d'Hollywood, les réalisateurs d'avant-garde recherchent leur inspiration dans l'art soviétique des années 20, à la fois révolutionnaire, expérimental et audacieux. Un film devint très célèbre lorsqu'il rencontre des problèmes de censure aux États-Unis toujours aussi prudes : *Ekstase* (Extase, 1933), réalisé par Gustav Machatý. Ce n'est pas tant la nudité d'Hedwig Kiesler et son corps recouvert de mousse de savon qui provoquent des troubles, que les gros plans sur son visage pendant les scènes érotiques.

L'*Osvobozené divadlo* (Théâtre libéré) de l'acteur et auteur dramatique Jan Werich (1905–1980), Jiří Voskovec (1905–1981) et du compositeur Jaroslav Ježek(1906–1942), incarne l'esprit pragois de la première république. Avec sa satire brillante, ses allusions aux cultures française et américaine, sa programmation sur des sujets touchant à la démocratie, au jazz, au surréalisme et à dada, ce théâtre joue un rôle éminent dans la vie de la capitale. Les sketches de Voskovec et Werich, férus d'esprit Švejk, dans lesquels ils jouent, chantent et se querellent comme deux clowns inséparables ridiculisent les dictateurs de l'époque et mettent en scène des positions courageuses et pleines d'esprit contre l'avancée du nazisme. En 1934, Voskovec et Werich doivent quitter le théâtre à la suite de provocations fascistes.

Le sport, et le tennis en particulier, deviennent de plus en plus populaires au cours des années 20 et 30. Ladislav Žemla et Jan Koželuh, vainqueurs de la coupe Davis, font partie des dix meilleurs joueurs mondiaux. Koželuh est champion du monde professionnel de 1925 à 1930, puis en 1932. En 1932, Jaroslav Skobla remporte la médaille d'or d'haltérophilie aux Jeux olympique de Los Angeles. En 1928, Eliška Junková remporte la Targa Florio, en Sicile, dans sa Bugatti, seule femme à avoir jamais gagné cette course. Les Tchèques aiment le sport et le Président qui prend tardivement l'habitude de circuler à cheval dans les rues de la capitale, est souvent entouré par les membres de la célèbre association sportive *Sokol* (Le faucon). *Sokol* avait été fondé en 1862 par Miroslav Tyrš, professeur de philosophie et de biologie, convaincu que l'idéal olympique « d'un esprit sain dans un corps sain » aiderait la nation tchèque à retrouver son identité. Les gymnases de *Sokol* remportèrent souvent des médailles olympiques, mais l'association fut persécutée pour son patriotisme et dissoute trois fois pendant sa courte histoire : par les Habsbourg en 1915, par les nazis en 1941 – qui emprisonnèrent 20 000 de ses membres dont 5 000 périrent dans des camps de concentration – et finalement en 1948, lorsqu'elle fut démantelée par les communistes qui remplacèrent les célèbres fêtes des *Sokol* par des Spartakiades, manifestations également de masse, mais épurées de tout patriotisme tchèque remplacé par des slogans à la gloire du nouveau régime.

Dans la république de Masaryk, les travailleurs possèdent leurs propres associations sportives, le DTJ (*Dělnické těločvicné jednoty*: unités de formation physique des travailleurs) et leurs propres

Workers' Olympics in Prague.
Arbeiterolympiade in Prag.
Les Jeux Olympiques des Travailleurs, à Prague.

Club). Many children belonged to the Scouts, whose varieties included Wolf Cubs, Girl Scouts, Water Scouts, Camping Scouts, Catholic Scouts, Jewish Scouts and the Hungarian variety. Their mottoes "Be Prepared" and "Protect the Weak" were taught early on. Children's books with patriotic themes were published and the top graphic designers contributed to their imaginative outlook.

A sophisticated urban culture, which was greatly admired by foreign visitors, flourished in Prague during the inter-war years. In 1938 the city had seven universities, forty-one secondary schools, 115 vocational schools and 423 elementary schools. Illiteracy was virtually nonexistent (approximately 0.5 per cent). Prague boasted twenty theaters (with 27,303 seats), 103 cinemas (with 55,997 seats), thirty-seven puppet theaters, twelve archives, nineteen museums, 637 libraries with 5 million books in them, 2129 magazines (in 1935), 46,000 exhibited paintings and an estimated 149,600 radios.

In 1935 Tomáš Masaryk resigned his office and Edvard Beneš was elected as the new President. Masaryk died in 1937, a year before the Czechoslovak Republic was dismembered and her young democracy cut down in its prime.

Arbeiter-Olympiaden. Katholiken betrieben »in christlicher Disziplin und christlichem Geist« Sport im *Československý Orel* (Sportclub Tschechoslowakischer Adler). Viele Kinder waren bei den Pfadfindern, zu deren Untergruppen die »Wölflinge«, die Mädchenpfadfinder, die »Wasser-Pfadfinder«, die »Zelt-Pfadfinder«, die Katholischen Pfadfinder, die Jüdischen Pfadfinder und ungarische Varianten zählten. Schon früh lernten sie die Devisen »Allzeit bereit« und »Schützt die Schwachen«. Verlage veröffentlichten Kinderbücher mit patriotischen Themen und die besten Graphiker trugen zu deren phantasievollen Gestaltung bei.

In der Zeit zwischen den beiden Weltkriegen blühte in Prag eine hochentwickelte städtische Kultur, die bei ausländischen Besuchern große Bewunderung hervorrief. 1938 besaß die Stadt sieben Universitäten, 41 weiterführende Schulen, 115 Berufs- und 423 Grundschulen. Analphabetismus existierte praktisch überhaupt nicht (etwa 0,5 Prozent). Prag rühmte sich seiner 20 Theater (mit 27.303 Plätzen), 103 Kinos (mit 55.997 Plätzen), 37 Marionettentheater, 12 Archive, 19 Museen, 637 Bibliotheken mit 5 Millionen Büchern, 2129 Zeitschriften (1935), 46.000 ausgestellten Gemälden und schätzungsweise 149.600 Radios.

Als Tomáš Masaryk 1935 von seinem Amt zurücktrat, wurde Eduard Beneš zu seinem Nachfolger gewählt. Masaryk starb 1937 – ein Jahr bevor die tschechoslowakische Republik aufgelöst wurde und ihre junge Demokratie ein jähes Ende fand.

Jeux olympiques des Travailleurs. Les catholiques pratiquent le sport dans un esprit de discipline au sein de leur *Československý Orel* (Club sportif tchèque de l'aigle). De nombreux enfants appartiennent aux scouts, sous de multiples formes: louveteaux, jeannettes, scouts marins, scouts catholiques, scouts juifs et hongrois. Leurs devises « Sois prêt » et « Protège le faible » sont enseignées dès l'initiation. Des livres d'enfants à thèmes patriotiques sont publiés et les meilleurs illustrateurs y contribuent.

Une culture urbaine sophistiquée, très admirée par les visiteurs étrangers, s'épanouit ainsi à Prague entre les deux guerres. En 1938, la ville compte 7 universités, 41 lycées et collèges, 115 écoles professionnelles et 423 écoles préparatoires. L'analphabétisme est quasi inexistant (environ 0,5 pour cent). Prague se flatte de posséder 20 théâtres (27 303 places), 103 cinémas (55 997 places), 37 théâtres de marionnettes, 12 centres d'archives, 19 musées, 637 bibliothèques proposant 5 millions d'ouvrages, 2 129 magazines (en 1935), 46 000 peintures exposées et environ 149 600 postes de radio.

En 1935, Tomáš Masaryk démissionne de ses fonctions et Edvard Beneš lui succède. Masaryk meurt en 1937, un an avant le démembrement de la république tchécoslovaque et que la jeune démocratie ne soit piétinée.

## 1938–1945: Under the Swastika

On 1 October 1938, Hitler's army moved into the Sudetenland, where the large German population enthusiastically welcomed the annexation of the Czechoslovak territory to the Third Reich. Earlier that year 90 per cent of the Sudeten Germans had voted for the pro-Nazi Sudetendeutsche Partei led by Konrad Henlein (1898–1945) and Karl Hermann Frank (1898–1946). Promising to protect the Sudeten Germans "with the German shield and the German sword," Hitler was already threatening to carve up the rest of Czechoslovakia. The country had been offered as a sacrificial lamb by France and the United Kingdom in a vain attempt to buy peace for Europe: in September 1938 they had signed the Munich Agreement with Germany and Italy, recognizing Hitler's territorial claim to the Sudetenland. Neville Chamberlain, the British Prime Minister, told his government, "I have nothing to be ashamed of." Nevertheless, ashamed he was, because he promised the Czechs a loan of £10 million.

On 1 October 1938 Poland, encouraged by the Germans, annexed a slice of north-eastern Czechoslovakia, Těšínsko (in Silesia). In November, Hungary followed the example and seized the southern parts of Slovakia and Ruthenia, dismembering Czechoslovakia from below.

Edvard Beneš was forced to resign the presidency on 5 October and left for England. Emil Hácha (1872–1945) was sworn in as the new President. Since August 1938 the Czech army, well equipped with the latest technology, had been on stand-by. However, orders to fight and defend never came. Helpless, the soldiers watched their homeland shrinking; but the men on the streets of Prague often voiced their anger and humiliation.

German refugees who were against Hitler's rise to power had been arriving in Prague since he became Chancellor in 1933. German and Austrian Jews joined the exodus, attempting to flee the terror to which they had been subjected for the last few months. They had been stripped of their property and passports; moreover, with the introduction of the Nazi's "racial laws," they had been robbed of their dignity.

German cavalry riding along the embankment.
Deutsche Kavallerie auf der Uferstraße.
La cavalerie allemande le long d'un quai.

## 1938–1945: Unter dem Hakenkreuz

Am 1. Oktober 1938 marschierten Hitlers Truppen im Sudetenland ein, wo die große deutsche Bevölkerung die Annexion des tschechoslowakischen Gebietes begeistert begrüßte. Bei den Wahlen wenige Monate zuvor hatten 90 Prozent der Sudetendeutschen für die den Nazis nahestehende Sudeten- deutsche Partei unter der Führung von Konrad Henlein (1898–1945) und Karl Hermann Frank (1898–1946) gestimmt. Mit dem Versprechen, die Sudetendeutschen »mit dem deutschen Schild und dem deutschen Schwert« zu beschützen, drohte Hitler bereits, auch den Rest der Tschechoslowakei zu zerschlagen. Vergeblich hatten Frankreich und Großbritannien das Land als Opferlamm angeboten, das den Frieden in Europa erkaufen sollte: Im September 1938 hatten sie mit Deutschland und Italien das Münchener Abkommen unterzeichnet, in dem Hitlers Gebietsansprüche auf das Sudetenland anerkannt wurden. Der britische Premierminister Neville Chamberlain erklärte seiner Regierung: »Es gibt nichts, wofür ich mich schämen müßte.« Dem war anscheinend nicht so, denn er bot den Tschechen eine Anleihe von 10 Millionen Pfund an.

Am 1. Oktober 1938 annektierte Polen, durch die Deutschen ermutigt, einen Teil der nordöstlichen Tschechoslowakei, die Region Těšínsko (in Schlesien). Im November folgte Ungarn diesem Beispiel und übernahm die südlichen Teile der Slowakei und Rutheniens, womit die südliche Hälfte der Tschechoslowakei aufgeteilt war.

Eduard Beneš wurde auf Grund des außenpolitischen Drucks gezwungen, am 5. Oktober seine Präsidentschaft niederzulegen, und ging nach England. Emil Hácha (1872–1945) wurde als neuer Präsident vereidigt. Seit August 1938 hatte die mit neuesten Technologien bestens ausgestattete tschechische Armee in Bereitschaft gestanden. Aber der Befehl, zu kämpfen und das Land zu verteidigen, kam nicht: Hilflos mußten die Soldaten zusehen, wie ihr Heimatland zusammenschrumpfte. Die Menschen in den Straßen von Prag aber brachten häufig ihre Wut und ihr Gefühl der Erniedrigung zum Ausdruck.

Seit Hitler 1933 Reichskanzler geworden war, kamen deutsche Flüchtlinge, die gegen seine Machtergreifung gewesen waren, nach Prag. Deutsche und österreichische Juden schlossen sich diesem Exodus an, um dem Terror zu entgehen, dem sie in den letzten paar Monaten ausgesetzt gewesen waren. Man hatte ihnen ihr Eigentum und ihre Pässe abgenommen und – was noch schlimmer war – durch die neuen nationalsozialistischen »Rassengesetze« waren sie auch ihrer Würde beraubt worden.

Am 25. Dezember 1938 starb der Schriftsteller Karel Čapek. Gerade noch rechtzeitig, am Vorabend der »Großen Dunkelheit«, entwischte der Schöpfer des Wortes »Roboter« den deutschen Erfindern der Massenvernichtungsmethoden. Sein Bruder Josef Čapek (1887–1945), ebenfalls ein bekannter Schriftsteller und Maler, hatte dieses Glück nicht. Er starb ein paar Jahre später in Bergen-Belsen.

Am 14. März 1939 riefen die slowakischen Faschisten die Unabhängigkeit ihres Landes aus. Noch am gleichen Tag wurde Emil Hácha nach

## 1938–1945: Prague dans l'ombre de la croix gammée

Le 1er octobre, les armées hitlériennes font leur entrée dans les Sudètes, dont l'importante population allemande accueille avec enthousiasme l'annexion de ce territoire tchécoslovaque. Peu avant, la même année, 90 pour cent des Allemands des Sudètes avaient voté pour le Sudetendeutsche Partei pro-nazi de Konrad Henlein (1898–1945) et de Karl Hermann Frank (1898–1946). Promettant de protéger les Allemands des Sudètes «avec le bouclier allemand et le glaive allemand», Hitler menace déjà de dépecer le reste de la Tchécoslovaquie. Le pays est sacrifié par la France et le Royaume-Uni dans une vaine tentative d'acheter la paix européenne : en septembre 1938, les deux démocraties signent les accords de Munich avec l'Allemagne et l'Italie, reconnaissant les revendications territoriales de Hitler sur les Sudètes. Neville Chamberlain, le Premier ministre britannique, commente à son retour à son gouvernement : «Il n'y a rien là dont je doive avoir honte.» C'est sans doute néanmoins une certaine honte qui l'amena à promettre aux Tchèques un prêt de 10 millions de £.

Le 1er octobre 1938, la Pologne, encouragée par les Allemands, annexe une partie de la Tchécoslovaquie du Nord, en Silésie. En novembre, la Hongrie suit cet exemple et s'empare des régions méridionales de la Slovaquie et de la Ruthénie, participant à son tour au démembrement de la Tchécoslovaquie.

Edvard Beneš est forcé de démissionner de la présidence le 5 octobre et se réfugie en Angleterre. Emil Hácha (1872–1945) prête serment comme nouveau président. Depuis le mois d'août 1938, l'armée tchèque, bien équipée en armement des plus modernes, est mobilisée. Les ordres de défense et d'attaque ne viendront jamais. Les soldats impuissants verront leur pays sombrer, mais des manifestations dans les rues de Prague témoigneront de la colère et de l'humiliation des habitants.

Des adversaires allemands de Hitler dès son arrivée au pouvoir s'étaient réfugiés en grand nombre à Prague à partir de 1933. Les Juifs allemands et autrichiens les suivirent dans cet exode, tentant de fuir la terreur brune. Ils avaient été dépouillés de leurs biens et de leur passeport, et les lois raciales nazies voulaient leur ravir leur dignité.

Le 25 décembre 1938, meurt l'écrivain Karel Čapek, juste à temps. À la veille de la «grande obscurité», le créateur du mot «robot» échappait ainsi aux Allemands qui allaient inventer des méthodes d'extermination à la chaîne. Son frère Josef Čapek (1887–1945), auteur dramatique et peintre connu, eut moins de chance : il mourut quelques années plus tard à Bergen-Belsen.

Les fascistes de Slovaquie déclarent leur indépendance le 14 mars 1939. Le même jour, Emil Hácha est convoqué à Berlin où, après de sévères pressions, il cède et signe un document demandant à Hitler de prendre le peuple tchèque sous la protection du Reich. Le lendemain, 15 mars, les troupes allemandes font leur entrée dans Prague et le Führer rend une brève visite à l'ancien fief des rois de Bohême. Les Pragois sont dans les rues,

On 25 December 1938 the writer Karel Čapek died. Just in time. On the eve of "the Great Darkness," the creator of the word "robot" gave the slip to the German innovators of assembly-line extermination methods. His brother, Josef Čapek (1887–1945), also a well-known author and painter, was not so lucky. He died a few years later in Bergen-Belsen.

Slovakia's Fascists declared an independent state on 14 March 1939. That same day, Emil Hácha was called to Berlin, where, after severe intimidation and bullying, he gave in and signed a paper requesting Hitler to take the Czech people under the protection of the Reich. The next day, 15 March, German troops marched into Prague and Adolf Hitler paid a brief visit to this ancient seat of Bohemian kings. People lined the streets, helpless and stricken with sorrow. As the German columns moved into Wenceslas Square, the weeping crowds bared their heads and sang the National Anthem. Masaryk's Czechoslovakia, the one indisputably Western-style democracy in Central Europe during the 1930s, had ceased to exist.

The Protectorate of Bohemia and Moravia was established as part of the Greater German Reich. When Emil Hácha arrived at Hradčany (Prague Castle) on the night of 15 March, his new masters were already in and he had to use the servant's entrance – a symbol of the new relationship between Czechs and Germans.

Hitler appointed as first Reichsprotektor Baron Konstantin von Neurath (1873–1956), a conservative aristocrat; his deputy, however, was the Sudeten German Karl Hermann Frank, a rabid Nazi and a Czech-hater. Soon the Gestapo and SS made their presence felt. The first to be sent to concentration camps were students. At a national demonstration on 28 October 1939 a young medical student, Jan Opletal, was wounded by a German bullet; he died on 11 November. A large number of students attended his funeral four days later. Fights between the students and the city's Germans broke out, serving as a pretext for SS reprisals against the intelligentsia. Twelve hundred students were arrested, nine of their leaders were executed and the Prague universities were closed down. Five thousand Jewish refugees, including anti-Nazi journalists, were rounded up and sent to concentration camps. A number of despairing people trapped in the Protectorate committed suicide.

Initially, the most visible change in Prague was the switch to driving on the right, implemented within eleven days of the occupation. Most of the population displayed passive resistance to the Nazis' New Order. They ignored Hitler's birthday, and laid bunches of flowers on the Jan Hus statue and on the monument to former US President Woodrow Wilson outside the main railway station. The reburial of the nineteenth-century poet Karel Hynek Mácha produced another demonstration of national empathy.

After the German blitzkrieg on Poland in September 1939, the presence in Prague of the SS and the Gestapo became more menacing. The only consolation to the Czechs was that England and France had declared war on Germany. Stalin, however, signed the Nazi–Soviet pact with Hitler

Berlin gerufen, wo er nach heftigen Einschüchterungsaktionen eine Erklärung unterzeichnete, daß er das Schicksal des tschechischen Volkes und Landes vertrauensvoll in die Hände des Führers lege. Einen Tag später, am 15. März, marschierten deutsche Truppen in Prag ein, und Hitler stattete dem alten Sitz der böhmischen Könige einen kurzen Besuch ab. Hilflos und sorgenvoll säumte die Bevölkerung die Straßen. Als die deutschen Kolonnen den Wenzelsplatz erreichten, nahm die Menge ihren Hut ab und sang die Nationalhymne. Masaryks Tschechoslowakei, die einzige unzweifelhaft westliche Demokratie der 30er Jahre in Mitteleuropa, gab es nicht mehr.

Das Protektorat Böhmen und Mähren wurde Teil des Großdeutschen Reiches. Als Emil Hácha in der Nacht des 15. März auf dem Hradschin ankam, waren die neuen Herren bereits da, und er mußte den Dienstboteneingang benutzen – ein Zeichen für die neuen Beziehungen zwischen Tschechen und Deutschen.

Adolf Hitler ernannte den konservativen Aristokraten Baron Konstantin von Neurath zum ersten Reichsprotektor. Dessen Staatssekretär wurde allerdings der Sudetendeutsche Karl Hermann Frank, ein fanatischer Nazi und Tschechen-Hasser. Bereits kurze Zeit später wurden Gestapo und SS aktiv. Die ersten, die der Verfolgung ausgesetzt wurden, waren die Studenten. Als es auf der Beerdigung des jungen Medizinstudenten Jan Opletal, der während einer nationalen Demonstration am 28. Oktober 1939 von einer deutschen Kugel verwundet worden und am 11. November gestorben war, zu Auseinandersetzungen zwischen Studenten und deutschen Bewohnern der Stadt kam, nahm die SS dies zum Vorwand, gegen die Intellektuellen vorzugehen. 1.200 Studenten wurden verhaftet, neun ihrer Anführer hingerichtet und die Prager Universitäten geschlossen. Auch wurden 5.000 jüdische Flüchtlinge, einschließlich anti-nationalsozialistischer Journalisten, festgenommen und in Konzentrationslager geschickt. Einige Verzweifelte, die keinen Ausweg aus dem Protektorat mehr sahen, nahmen sich das Leben.

Anfänglich war die auffälligste Veränderung in Prag die Umstellung vom Links- auf das Rechtsfahren, die innerhalb von elf Tagen nach der Besetzung eingeführt wurde. Ein Großteil der Bevölkerung leistete passiven Widerstand gegen die Neue Ordnung der Nationalsozialisten: Sie ignorierten den Geburtstag des Führers Geburtstag, legten aber Blumensträuße an die Jan-Hus-Statue und an das Monument des früheren amerikanischen Präsidenten Woodrow Wilson vor dem Hauptbahnhof. Die erneute Beisetzung des im 19. Jahrhundert verstorbenen Dichters Karel Hynek Mácha führte zu einer weiteren Welle nationaler Sympathien.

Nach dem deutschen Blitzkrieg in Polen im September 1939 wurden die Aktionen der SS und der Gestapo in Prag immer bedrohlicher. Der einzige Trost für die Tschechen war die Tatsache, daß England und Frankreich Deutschland den Krieg erklärt hatten. Andererseits aber hatte Stalin den sowjetisch-deutschen Pakt mit Hitler unterzeichnet und sich damit der Zerstörung des polnischen Staates angeschlossen. Im Protektorat hob die Nazi-Propaganda wiederholt hervor, daß den Tschechen dieses Schicksal nur durch die Unterordnung unter

désespérés. Lorsque les colonnes allemandes arrivent sur la place Venceslas, la foule se décoiffe et chante l'hymne national. La Tchécoslovaquie de Masaryk, la seule indiscutable démocratie occidentale d'Europe centrale au cours des années 30, cesse d'exister.

Un protectorat de Bohême et de Moravie est ainsi créé dans le cadre du Reich allemand. Lorsqu'Emil Hácha arrive au Hradčany (château de Prague), pendant la nuit du 15 mars, ses nouveaux maîtres sont déjà là, et il doit emprunter l'entrée de service, symbole des nouvelles relations entre les Tchèques et les Allemands.

Hitler nomme premier Reichsprotektor le baron Konstantin von Neurath (1873–1956), un aristocrate conservateur, mais son vrai représentant reste cependant l'Allemand des Sudètes Karl Hermann Frank, nazi féroce qui hait les Tchèques. Bientôt la Gestapo et les S.S. font sentir leur présence. Les premiers à être envoyés en camps de concentration sont les étudiants. Lors d'une manifestation nationale le 28 octobre 1939, un jeune étudiant en médecine, Jan Opletal est blessé par une balle allemande et meurt le 11 novembre. Un grand nombre de ses condisciples assiste à ses funérailles quatre jours plus tard. Des bagarres éclatent entre eux et les Allemands de la ville, prétexte pour les S.S. de déclencher des représailles contre l'intelligentsia. Mille deux cents étudiants sont arrêtés, neuf de leurs responsables exécutés et les universités de Prague fermées. Cinq mille réfugiés juifs, y compris des journalistes antinazis partent pour les camps de concentration. Un certain nombre de réfugiés, piégés dans ce Protectorat, se suicident.

Au début, le changement le plus visible dans les rues de Prague est le passage à la conduite à droite décidé dans les onze jours qui suivent l'occupation. La plus grande partie de la population résiste passivement au nouvel ordre nazi. Elle ignore l'anniversaire de Hitler et dépose des bouquets devant la statue de Jan Hus et le monument à l'ancien président américain Woodrow Wilson, près de la gare principale. Le changement de sépulture du poète du XIXe siècle Karel Hynek Mácha déclenche une autre manifestation de solidarité nationale.

Après la Blitzkrieg allemande de septembre 1939 en Pologne, la présence à Prague des S.S. et de la Gestapo se fait plus menaçante. La seule consolation pour les Tchèques est que la Grande-Bretagne et la France déclarent la guerre à l'Allemagne. Staline,

Academics taking part in Jan Opletal's funeral.

Akademiker nehmen an der Beerdigung von Jan Opletal teil.

Des professeurs assistent aux funérailles de Jan Opletal.

A Nazi parade in the Old Town Square.
Eine Naziparade auf dem Altstädter Ring.
Défilé nazi place de la Vieille ville.

and joined in the destruction of the Polish state. In the Protectorate, Nazi propaganda emphasized that the Czechs had avoided a similar fate only by accepting subordination to the Reich. According to Frank, the Czechs had Hitler to thank for the fact that their towns were not in ruins and the blood of thousands of young Czechs had not been spilled.

There were two places of terror in Prague: Petschek Palace, which housed the Gestapo, and Pankrác prison (later equipped with a guillotine). The Gestapo gradually penetrated the home resistance and eliminated them by imprisonment or by forcing them to collaborate. The last to receive this treatment were the Communists. Their most famous martyr, according to post-war Communist legend, was the journalist Julius Fučík (1903–43). Not only did he refuse to betray his comrades but he also managed to write a book, *The Report from the Gallows*. According to a high-ranking Czech police official who saw Gestapo interrogation methods, "unless they were absolute heroes, everybody talked within twenty-four hours." Tragically, the most trusted members of the Communist resistance received instructions to betray non-Communist networks to the Gestapo, and did so. Even at this stage, the Communists took care to eliminate potential opposition.

One of the greatest Czech resistance heroes was Josef Mašín (1896–1942). He belonged to a group called *Tři králové* (Three Kings), which passed on intelligence to Edvard Beneš, who had set up a government-in-exile in London, and also organized acts of sabotage. Betrayed by an informer, Mašín was arrested by the Gestapo but fought bravely. For three months he withstood torture, never disclosing a single name. He was executed at Kobylisy, with seventy others, on 30 June 1942. The German who interrogated him said that Mašín was the most courageous adversary he had ever encountered.

das Reich erspart geblieben sei. Laut Frank sollten sie Hitler dankbar dafür sein, daß ihre Städte nicht in Trümmern lagen und nicht das Blut von Tausenden junger Tschechen vergossen worden war.

Es gab zwei Schauplätze des Terrors in Prag: den Petschek-Palast, der Sitz der Gestapo, und das Pankratius-Gefängnis (das später mit einer Guillotine ausgestattet wurde). Die Gestapo ging schrittweise gegen den Widerstand vor und konnte ihn allmählich ausschalten, indem sie seine Mitglieder entweder ins Gefängnis steckte oder zur Kollaboration zwang. Die letzten, die diese Behandlung erfuhren, waren die Kommunisten. Ihr berühmtester Märtyrer war der Journalist Julius Fučík (1903–43), der nicht nur den Verrat seiner Kameraden verweigerte, sondern dem es auch noch gelang, ein Buch zu schreiben: *Der Bericht vom Galgen*. Dies war ungewöhnlich, denn nach Aussagen eines hochrangigen tschechischen Polizeibeamten, dem die Befragungsmethoden der Gestapo vertraut waren, »sprach jeder, selbst wenn er noch so heldenhaft war, innerhalb von 24 Stunden«. Tragischerweise erhielten die vertrauensvollsten Mitglieder des kommunistischen Widerstandes die Anweisung, nichtkommunistische Netzwerke an die Gestapo zu verraten, und taten dies auch. Selbst zu diesem Zeitpunkt waren die Kommunisten darauf aus, eine mögliche Opposition auszuschalten.

Einer der größten Helden der tschechischen Widerstandsbewegung war Josef Mašín (1896–1942). Er gehörte einer Gruppe mit dem Namen *Tři králové* (Drei Könige) an, die Informationen an Eduard Beneš und dessen Exilregierung in London weitergab und Sabotageakte organisierte. Mašín wurde von einem Denunzianten verraten und von der Gestapo verhaftet. Drei Monate widerstand er der Folter, ohne einen einzigen Namen preiszugeben. Mit 70 anderen wurde er am 30. Juni 1942 in Kobylisy hingerichtet. Die Deutschen, die ihn verhörten, bezeichneten Mašín als den mutigsten Gegner, den sie jemals getroffen hatten.

Nach Provokationen der SS ernannte Hitler im September 1941 Reinhard Heydrich (1902–1942), den Stellvertreter Himmlers, zum stellvertretenden Reichsprotektor. Heydrich, Liebhaber von Wagner-Musik, Sportler, Soldat, das Gehirn vieler bösartiger Pläne, war zugleich ein Massenmörder. Er rief sofort das Kriegsrecht aus, richtete das Ghetto Theresienstadt als Übergangslager für tschechische Juden auf ihrem Weg zu den Todeslagern weiter im Osten ein und veranlaßte die unmittelbare Exekution derjenigen, die unter dem Verdacht standen, mit Beneš' Exilregierung Kontakt zu halten. Im Januar 1942 war er Vorsitzender der Wannsee-Konferenz in Berlin, auf der die »Endlösung der Judenfrage« unter dem Codenamen »Reinhard« beschlossen wurde. Heydrichs Aufgabe bestand darin, die Verteilung und Überführung der 10 Millionen europäischen Juden in die Todeslager zu organisieren. Er galt als sehr ehrgeizig und hatte sogar in der Abwehr und in der Wehrmacht einen schlechten Ruf wegen des Terrors, den er im Osten mit seinen speziellen Mordkommandos ausübte. Seine Einsatzgruppen erschossen Juden, Zigeuner, Polen und Russen.

Als die Nazis im März 1939 Böhmen und Mähren besetzten, lebten 56.000 Juden in Prag, darunter 15.000 deutsche Flüchtlinge. Schon bald

cependant, signe un pacte avec Hitler et participe à l'anéantissement de l'État polonais. Dans le Protectorat, la propagande nazie fait comprendre aux Tchèques qu'ils n'ont échappé à un sort similaire qu'en acceptant leur subordination au Reich. Selon Frank, les Tchèques doivent être reconnaissants à Hitler de ce que leurs villes ne sont pas en ruines et que le sang de milliers de jeunes n'a pas été répandu.

Deux lieux symbolisent la terreur qui règne à Prague : le palais Peček, siège de la Gestapo, et la prison Pankrác (plus tard équipée d'une guillotine). La Gestapo infiltre peu à peu la Résistance et l'élimine en emprisonnant ses membres ou en les forçant à collaborer. Selon un responsable de haut rang de la police tchèque, témoin des méthodes d'interrogatoire de la Gestapo, « à moins d'être un héros absolu, tout le monde parlait en moins de vingt-quatre heures ». Les derniers à recevoir ce traitement sont les communistes. Leur plus illustre martyr, selon la légende communiste d'après-guerre, est le journaliste Julius Fučík (1903–1943). Non seulement il refuse de trahir ses camarades, mais réussit à écrire un livre, *Rapport d'une geôle*. Tragiquement, les membres de la résistance communiste reçurent instruction de trahir les réseaux et le firent. Dès cette époque, les communistes prennent soin d'éliminer toute opposition potentielle.

L'un des plus grands héros de la résistance tchèque est Josef Mašín (1896–1942). Il appartient à un groupe appelé *Tři králové* (les trois rois), qui travaille en sous-main pour Edvard Beneš chef du gouvernement en exil à Londres et organise des actions de sabotage. Trahi par un informateur, Mašín est arrêté par la Gestapo mais se comporte avec un rare courage. Pendant trois mois, il supporte la torture sans livrer un seul nom. Il sera exécuté à Kobylisy, avec soixante-dix autres résistants, le 30 juin 1942. Les Allemands qui l'avaient interrogé déclarèrent qu'il avait été l'adversaire le plus courageux jamais rencontré.

En septembre 1941, après une provocation S.S. et une manœuvre de Frank, Hitler remplace von Neurath par un gouverneur plus dangereux. Le bras droit de Heinrich Himmler, Reinhard Heydrich (1902–1942), s'installe au château de Hradčany, comme nouveau protecteur du Reich. Amateur de Wagner, sportif, soldat, instigateur de nombreux projets pervers, Heydrich est un tueur à grande échelle. Il ordonne immédiatement la loi martiale, fait du ghetto de Terezín un camp de transit pour les Juifs tchèques en route vers les camps de la mort installés à l'Est, et l'exécution de partisans suspectés d'être en contact avec le gouvernement en exil de Beneš. En juin 1942, il préside la conférence du Wannsee à Berlin où est décidée la solution finale à laquelle est donnée le nom de code de « Reinhard ». La tâche de Heydrich était d'organiser le transit et l'acheminement de 10 millions de Juifs européens vers les camps de la mort. Homme d'une ambition féroce, il s'était fait une mauvaise réputation même auprès de l'armée allemande pour la terreur déchaînée à l'Est par ses escadrons de la mort (*Einsatzgruppen*) qui assassinaient Juifs, Gitans, Polonais et Russes.

Lorsque les nazis occupent la Bohême-Moravie en mars 1939, 56 000 Juifs se trouvent à Prague,

In September 1941, following SS provocation and intrigue by Frank, Hitler replaced von Neurath with a more lethal ruler. Himmler's deputy, Reinhard Heydrich (1902– 42) was installed at Hradčany as the new Acting Reichsprotektor. A Wagnerian music lover, sportsman, soldier and the brain behind many devious plans, Heydrich was a mass killer. He immediately ordered martial law, the establishment of the Terezín ghetto as a transit camp for Czech Jews on their journey to death camps further east, and the execution of people suspected of staying in touch with Beneš's government-in-exile. In January 1942 he chaired the Wannsee Conference in Berlin where the Final Solution was decided on and codenamed "Reinhard." Heydrich's task was to organize the transit and delivery of 10 million European Jews to the death camps. A fiercely ambitious man, he had a bad reputation even among the *Abwehr* and the *Wehrmacht* for the terror he unleashed in the East with the special killing squads (*Einsatzgruppen*) which murdered Jews, Gypsies, Poles and Russians.

When the Nazis occupied Bohemia–Moravia in March 1939 there were 56,000 Jews in Prague, of whom 15,000 were German refugees. Various anti-Jewish laws were soon issued, along the lines of the Nazi Nuremberg Laws. In June 1939 Neurath issued a decree excluding Jews from the economic life of the Protectorate and forcing them to register their assets. Their businesses were taken over by German "trustees" who would supervise their sale or "aryanization." Adolf Eichmann, who headed the SS's Central Office for Jewish Emigration, arrived in Prague in June 1939 demanding the expulsion of 70,000 Jews within a year. After September 1939, Nazi policy became increasingly radical. Segregation was introduced in public places. Gradually, Prague Jews were excluded from public service and from all social, cultural and economic organizations. Forced out of apartments, denied access to a wide range of goods, not allowed to travel in front carriages, having to wear the yellow star, they were being prepared for deportation. Transports to Terezín started in November 1941; from there prisoners were usually sent to Auschwitz-Birkenau, the death camp near Cracow in occupied Poland.

Of 39,395 Jews taken to Terezín from Prague during the war, 31,709 perished, either in the ghetto or in the camps. The Jews' apartments were reassigned to SS men and their property redistributed among corrupt officials; anything left was sent to Germany. A large collection of religious objects and archives relating to Jewish life was gathered by the SS for preservation, intended to form the basis of a museum of the extinct Jewish race after the Final Solution had been carried through. Prague synagogues and burial places were left intact: they provided a picturesque backdrop for the gruesome project. As early as 1942, exhibitions were held for SS officers, who showed a morbid interest in the people they were murdering.

On Beneš's orders, Jan Kubiš (1913–42) and Jozef Gabčík (1912–42), two soldiers of the Free Czechoslovak Armies based in Britain, were sent to assassinate Heydrich. They were trained for their mission by the English SOE (Special Operations

wurde eine Reihe anti-jüdischer Bestimmungen entsprechend den Nürnberger Gesetzen erlassen. Im Juni 1939 verabschiedete Neurath einen Erlaß, der die Juden aus dem wirtschaftlichen Leben im Protektorat ausschloß und sie zur Registrierung ihres Vermögens zwang. Ihre Geschäfte wurden von deutschen »Treuhändern« übernommen, die deren Verkauf oder »Arisierung« beaufsichtigten. Adolf Eichmann, der der »Zentralstelle für jüdische Auswanderung« der SS vorstand, kam im Juni 1939 nach Prag und forderte die Abschiebung von 70.000 Juden innerhalb eines Jahres. Ab September 1939 wurde die Politik der Nationalsozialisten zunehmend radikaler. An öffentlichen Orten wurde eine Trennung eingeführt und die Juden Schritt für Schritt von den sozialen Leistungen und aus allen gesellschaftlichen, kulturellen und wirtschaftlichen Organisationen ausgeschlossen. Man vertrieb sie aus ihren Wohnungen, verbot ihnen den Erwerb vieler Güter, die Benutzung der vorderen Waggons im öffentlichen Verkehr, ordnete das Tragen des gelben Sterns an und bereitete damit alles für die Deportation vor. Die Transporte nach Theresienstadt begannen im November 1941; von dort schickte man die Gefangenen im allgemeinen nach Auschwitz-Birkenau, dem Todeslager nahe Krakau im besetzten Polen.

Von den 39.395 Juden, die während des Krieges nach Theresienstadt verschleppt wurden, verschwanden 31.709 Menschen. Die Wohnungen der Juden wurden an SS-Männer übergeben und ihre Besitztümer unter den korrupten Beamten verteilt; sofern etwas übrig blieb, wurde es nach Deutschland geschickt. Die SS legte eine umfangreiche Sammlung von Kultgegenständen und anderen Materialien zum jüdischen Leben an, die den Grundstock für ein Museum über die ausgerottete jüdische Rasse nach der Durchführung der »Endlösung« bilden sollte. Prags Synagogen und Friedhöfe blieben intakt; sie boten einen malerischen Hintergrund für das grausame Vorhaben. Schon 1942 gab es Ausstellungen für SS-Offiziere, die ein morbides Interesse an den Menschen zeigten, die sie ermordeten.

In Beneš' Auftrag wurden Jan Kubiš und Jozef Gabčík, zwei Soldaten der in Großbritannien stationierten Freien Tschechoslowakischen Armee, entsandt, um Heydrich zu ermorden. Die englische SOE (Special Operations Executive) hatte sie eigens für diese Mission ausgebildet. Am 27. Mai 1942 verwundeten sie Heydrich mit einer Bombe an einer Straßenecke im Prager Vorort Libeň; er starb ein paar Tage später an einer Wundinfektion. Heydrich war der hochrangigste Offizier, der während des Zweiten Weltkriegs von Widerstandskämpfern ermordet worden ist.

Der Terror, den die SS nach Heydrichs Ermordung in Prag ausübte, war gnadenlos. Die Gestapo nahm irrtümlich an, daß Lidice, ein Dorf in der Nähe von Prag, in irgendeiner Form mit den Soldaten aus England in Verbindung gestanden hatte. Auf Hitlers Befehl wurde das Dorf von der Landkarte des Protektorats ausradiert. Alle Männer wurden erschossen, alle Frauen in Konzentrationslager deportiert und die rassisch geeigneten Kinder zur »Arisierung« nach Deutschland verschleppt. Jeden Tag hallten in den Straßen Prags über Lautsprecher die Namen der Menschen wider, die hingerichtet worden waren.

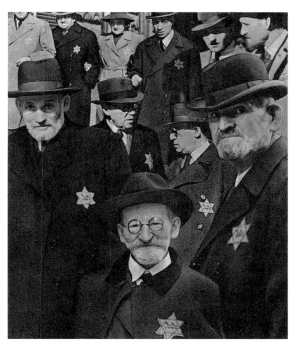

Antisemitic photograph "Typical Prague Jews," 1941.
Antisemitische Fotografie »Typische Prager Juden«, 1941.
Photographie antisémite «Juifs typiques de Prague», 1941.

dont 15 000 sont des réfugiés allemands. Diverses mesures antisémites sont immédiatement promulguées dans l'esprit des lois racistes de Nuremberg. En juin 1939, Neurath publie un décret excluant les Juifs de la vie économique du Protectorat et les forçant à déclarer leurs biens. Leurs activités sont reprises par des «administrateurs» allemands chargés de superviser leur vente ou leur «aryanisation». Adolf Eichmann, qui dirige le Bureau central S.S. pour l'émigration juive, arrive à Prague en juin 1939 et demande l'expulsion de 70 000 Juifs dans l'année. À partir de septembre 1939, la politique nazie se radicalise encore davantage. La ségrégation est introduite dans les lieux publics. Peu à peu, les Juifs de Prague sont exclus de tous les services publics et de toutes les associations sociales, culturelles et économiques. Chassés de leur appartement, interdits d'achat de nombreux produits, empêchés de voyager dans les voitures de tête des trains, obligés de porter l'étoile jaune, ils sont préparés à la déportation. Les transports vers Terezín commencent en novembre 1941. De là les hommes et les femmes sont habituellement envoyés à Auschwitz-Birkenau, le camp de la mort voisin de Cracovie, en Pologne occupée.

Des 39 395 Juifs déportés de Prague à Terezín pendant la guerre, 31 709 périront, dans le ghetto ou dans les camps. Les appartements des Juifs sont donnés aux S.S. et leurs biens distribués aux officiels du régime. Tout ce qui subsiste est expédié en Allemagne. Une importante collection d'objets religieux et d'archives de la vie juive est rassemblée par les S.S. pour former la base d'un musée sur l'extinction de la race juive, une fois la solution finale appliquée. Les synagogues et les cimetières de Prague sont laissés intacts et fournissent un décor pittoresque au projet sanguinaire. Dès 1942, des expositions sont organisées pour les officiers S.S., qui montrent un intérêt morbide pour le peuple qu'ils sont en train d'assassiner.

Executive). On 27 May 1942, on a sharp corner in Libeň in the Prague suburbs, they wounded him with an impact bomb; a few days later he died of blood poisoning. He was the highest-ranking officer to be killed by resistance forces during the Second World War.

The SS terror unleashed upon Prague after Heydrich's assassination was merciless. The Gestapo mistakenly thought that Lidice near Prague was somehow connected with the soldiers sent from England and on Hitler's orders Frank erased the village from the map of the Protectorate. All the men were shot and all the women sent to a concentration camp; the children were taken to the Reich to be germanized. Every day, the streets of Prague resounded with the names of people who had been executed read through loudspeakers. On 18 June, betrayed by one of their fellow parachutists, Gabčík and Kubiš along with five other Czechoslovak soldiers were surrounded in the St Cyril and St Methodius Church in Resslova. After a gun battle with the Waffen SS guard battalion, those fighting in the choir were killed and those in the crypt committed suicide rather than surrender. The Czech Orthodox priests were immediately arrested for aiding the parachutists. About 5000 men and women died in the subsequent wave of terror, among them many brave members of the *Sokol* organization.

On 3 July 1942, 250,000 people took part in a rally in Wenceslas Square, swearing an oath of allegiance to the Third Reich. A small group of Hácha's government officials, led by Emmanuel Moravec (1893–1945), the most prominent collaborator in the puppet government, appeared in front of the cameras singing the Czech National Anthem with their hands raised in a Nazi salute.

Despite Karl Hermann Frank's impressive record in subjugating the Czechs, he did not get the desired post of Reichsprotektor. Perhaps Hitler did not want the Sudeten Germans to feel that they were masters of the Protectorate. Almost immediately after Heydrich's assassination, Hitler sent another SS General, Kurt Daluege (1897–1946), who was not known for his intelligence but who was a pure German. In 1943 he was replaced by Wilhelm Frick (1877–1946).

Heydrich's assassination and the highly publicized destruction of Lidice, which was filmed by two film crews, one German and one Czech, helped Beneš achieve two goals: there could be no doubt that Czechoslovakia was on the Allies' side and Beneš became established as the country's president-in-exile. The events justified the Czechoslovak government's expulsion of the country's 2.5 million Sudeten Germans in 1945.

From the early days of the occupation, Prague was decorated with the symbols of her enslavement. Swastikas fluttered from every flagpole, huge portraits of Hitler were displayed on his birthday and pictures and plaques of a predatory German eagle grasping the world in its talons appeared in the city squares and on government buildings. When the SS regiments were taking their oath of allegiance, their symbol, two silver runes against a black background, looked like huge bolts of lightning

Hácha and his government on 3 July 1942, Wenceslas Square.
Hácha und seine Regierung am 3. Juli 1942, Wenzelsplatz.
Hácha et son gouvernement le 3 juillet 1942, place Venceslas.

Durch den Verrat eines Kameraden konnten Gabčík und Kubiš zusammen mit fünf anderen Widerstands-kämpfern in der Kirche St. Kyrill und Method in der Resslova-Straße gestellt werden. In einem Feuerge-fecht mit der Waffen-SS wurden alle, die sich im Chor der Kirche aufhielten, getötet; die anderen, die sich in der Krypta verbargen, zogen den Selbstmord einer Übergabe vor. Unmittelbar darauf wurden die orthodoxen Priester wegen Unterstützung der Widerstandskämpfer verhaftet. Insgesamt mußten etwa 5.000 Männer und Frauen als Folge des Atten-tats ihr Leben lassen, unter ihnen viele tapfere Mit-glieder der *Sokol*.

Am 3. Juli 1942 nahmen 250.000 Menschen an einer Demonstration auf dem Wenzelsplatz teil und schworen einen Treueeid auf das Dritte Reich. Eine kleine Gruppe von Angehörigen der Regierung Hácha erschien unter Führung von Emmanuel Moravec (1893–1945), dem bekanntesten Kollabo-rateur der Marionettenregierung, vor der Kamera und sang mit zum Nazi-Gruß erhobener Hand die tschechische Nationalhymne.

Trotz seiner beeindruckenden Erfolge bei der Unterjochung der Tschechen erhielt Karl Hermann Frank nicht den vakanten Posten. Vielleicht wollte Hitler nicht, daß die Sudetendeutschen sich als die Herren des Protektorats betrachteten. Kurz nach der Ermordung Heydrichs sandte er einen anderen SS-General, Kurt Daluege (1897–1946), der nicht gera-de für seine Intelligenz, dafür aber als überzeugter Deutscher bekannt war. 1943 wurde er von Wilhelm Frick (1877–1946) abgelöst.

Heydrichs Ermordung und die propagandistisch vielfach genutzte Vernichtung von Lidice, die von zwei Filmteams – einem deutschen und einem tschechischen – aufgenommen worden war, halfen Beneš in zweifacher Hinsicht: Es gab keinen Zweifel mehr daran, daß die Tschechoslowakei auf der Seite der Alliierten stand, und Beneš wurde als Führer der Exilregierung anerkannt. Diese Ereignisse rechtfer-tigten auch die Anordnung der tschechoslowaki-schen Regierung, 2,5 Millionen der im Lande lebenden Sudetendeutschen 1945 auszuweisen.

Schon seit den ersten Tagen der Besatzung wurde Prag mit Symbolen der Unterwerfung überhäuft. Hakenkreuzfahnen flatterten an jeder Fahnenstange, große Hitler-Porträts wurden zu seinem Geburtstag ausgestellt, Bilder und Plaketten mit einem räuberi-

Sur ordre de Beneš, Jan Kubiš (1913–1942) et Jozef Gabčik (1912–1942), deux soldats des armées de la Tchécoslovaquie libre basées en Grande-Bretagne, sont envoyés pour assassiner Heydrich. Ils sont préparés à leur mission par le SOE britannique. Le 27 mai 1942, à un carrefour de Liben, dans la banlieue de Prague, ils le blessent. Quelques jours plus tard, il meurt d'un empoisonnement du sang. Il est le S.S. du plus haut rang tué par la Résistance au cours de la Seconde Guerre mondiale.

La terreur S.S. se déchaîne alors sur Prague. La Gestapo pensant à tort que Kubiš et Gabčik se cachent à Lidice près de Prague, Frank fait raser le village sur les ordres de Hitler. Tous les hommes sont tués, les femmes déportées en camp de concentration, les enfants envoyés en Allemagne pour y être germanisés. Chaque jour, les rues de Prague résonnent des noms de ceux qui ont été exécutés, lus par hauts-parleurs. Le 18 juin, trahis par un de leurs compagnons parachutistes, Gabčik, Kubiš et cinq autres soldats tchèques sont encerclés dans l'église Saint-Cyrille et Saint-Méthode de la rue Resslova. Après une bataille au fusil contre un bataillon de gardes S.S., les résistants sont tués, et ceux qui se trouvent dans la crypte se suicident plutôt que de se rendre. Les prêtres orthodoxes tchèques sont immédiatement arrêtés pour avoir aidé les parachutistes. Environ 5 000 hommes et femmes meurent dans la vague de terreur qui s'ensuit, dont de nombreux membres de l'association *Sokol*.

Le 3 juillet 1942, 250 000 personnes prennent part à une manifestation place Venceslas et jurent fidélité et allégeance au Troisième Reich. Un petit groupe d'officiels du gouvernement Hácha, conduit par Emmanuel Moravec (1893–1946), le collaborateur le plus en vue de ce gouvernement fantoche, paraît devant les caméras et chante l'hymne national tchèque, la main tendue formant le salut nazi.

Malgré les impressionnants efforts déployés par Karl Hermann Frank pour imposer le joug allemand aux Tchèques, il ne sera jamais récompensé du titre de Reichsprotektor. Hitler ne voulait peut-être pas que les Allemands des Sudètes se sentent maîtres du protectorat. Presque immédiatement après l'assassinat de Heydrich, le Führer envoie un autre général S.S., Kurt Daluege (1897–1946), pur allemand mais peu réputé pour son intelligence. En 1943, il est remplacé par Wilhelm Frick (1877–1946).

L'assassinat de Heydrich et la destruction de Lidice, qui connaît un vaste écho, (elle est filmée par deux équipes de cinéma, une allemande et une tchèque), aident Beneš à atteindre deux de ses objectifs : il est maintenant certain que la Tchécoslovaquie se trouve aux côtés des Alliés et il devient le représentant officiel en exil de son pays. Ces événements serviront à justifier l'expulsion de Tchécoslovaquie de 2,5 millions d'Allemands des Sudètes en 1945.

Dès les premiers jours de son occupation, Prague est décorée des symboles de son esclavage. Les svastikas flottent à chaque mât, d'énormes portraits de Hitler sont déployés lors de son anniversaire et l'aigle germain prédateur emportant le monde dans

jabbing the cobblestones of the Old Town Square. From the summer of 1941 the letter "V", proclaiming faith in German victory, was painted on trams and buildings. It was an offence to deface, alter or ridicule this "V"; whenever this happened, the whole neighborhood was punished by a collective fine and the confiscation of radios. Hitler's architect Albert Speer visited the city and fantasized about transforming its architecture into something more monumental and Germanic.

A blackout was imposed almost from the start of the war. The darkened streets, dimmed car and tram lights and shuttered windows made the city look almost unreal. Along with the blackout came rationing, but the citizens of Prague had close ties with neighboring villages and seemed to get by. Workers in arms factories received extra tobacco and shoes. The Germans cultivated the working class, whose contribution was vital for the efficient operation of the war industry. One third of Nazi armaments came from Protectorate factories. By February 1943 all men aged between sixteen and sixty-five and all women between seventeen and forty-five were eligible for industrial conscription. As the war went on, conditions worsened for everyone. Benefits were eroded and wages frozen. Rations were restricted and black-market prices soared. People were urged to save electricity and gas. Petrol and tyres were not available to private citizens. Buses and trucks were powered by coal gas, carried in a sausage-shaped balloon on the roof. The Czech comedian Vlasta Burian (1891–1962) resolved this problem by driving around the city in a coach pulled by five matched horses. Bikes and trams carried the rest of the population.

As part of their war against intellectuals, the Nazis encouraged writing that celebrated the working class (thus providing an eerie taste of things to come). In March 1942 they sponsored a competition for novels, poetry and short stories on the life of the workers. The winners included pieces entitled *The Boys in Blue Overalls*, *Men under Prague* and *Women from Smoke*. However, a Surrealist entry entitled *An Imaginary Interview with Employees of a Condom Factory*, would have been regarded as an example of "degenerate art", that is, had it been submitted. Soon after the invasion, the Prague Surrealists went underground and continued painting and writing, basically for each other. They also helped each other. Toyen (Marie Čermínová; 1902–80) hid her fellow Surrealist Jindřich Heisler (1914–53), a Jew, from the Nazis. The Surrealists' opposition to a dictatorial regime became their trademark, and their anti-logic, anti-boring-art stand became apparent in these years – a "cultural resistance" to the Nazis' Socialist Realism. The Nazis (and later the Communists) regarded their art as decadent, subversive and dangerous.

Cinemas during the war showed innocuous comedies, wildlife films and compulsory propaganda newsreels. The bulletins were often used to intimidate the population and to hunt people down. At the end of May 1942, for example, when a bicycle, briefcase, Sten gun and coat belonging to Gabčík and Kubiš were found after their attack on Heydrich, they were shown in newsreels *ad nauseam*, urging informers to come forward.

Prague's streets were festooned with swastika flags.
Die Straßen von Prag, geschmückt mit Hakenkreuzfahnen.
Les rues de Prague decorées de drapeaux à la swastika.

schen deutschen Adler, der die Welt in seinen Krallen hält, erschienen auf den Plätzen und an den Regierungsgebäuden der Stadt. Als die SS-Regimente ihren Treueeid schworen, schien sich ihr Markenzeichen – zwei silberne Runen auf schwarzem Untergrund – wie große Blitzstrahlen in das Kopfsteinpflaster des Altstädter Platzes zu bohren. Seit Sommer 1941 malte man den Buchstaben »V« als Zeichen für den Glauben an den deutschen Sieg auf Straßenbahnen und Gebäude. Es galt als Verbrechen, dieses »V« zu verunstalten, zu verändern oder zu karikieren; wo immer dies geschah, wurde die gesamte Nachbarschaft kollektiv bestraft und die Radios konfisziert. Albert Speer, der Architekt Hitlers, träumte bei einem Besuch der Stadt davon, ihre Architektur monumentaler und »germanischer« zu gestalten.

Bald nach Beginn des Krieges wurden Verdunkelungen angeordnet. Die dunklen Straßen, die abgeblendeten Auto- und Straßenbahnlampen und die geschlossenen Fensterläden ließen die Stadt beinahe unwirklich erscheinen. Mit der Verdunkelung kam die Rationierung, aber die Einwohner Prags unterhielten enge Verbindungen zu den benachbarten Dörfern und arrangierten sich mit den Bedingungen. Arbeiter in Munitionsfabriken erhielten Extrarationen Tabak und Schuhe. Die Deutschen unterstützten die Arbeiterschaft, deren Kooperation für eine erfolgreiche Rüstungsindustrie notwendig war. Ein Drittel der Nazi-Waffen stammte aus den Fabriken des Protektorats. Seit Februar 1943 konnten alle Männer im Alter zwischen 16 und 65 und alle Frauen zwischen 17 und 45 zur Rüstungsindustrie herangezogen werden. Im Verlauf des Krieges verschlechterten sich die Bedingungen für alle. Vergütungen wurden gestrichen, die Löhne eingefroren, die Rationen verkleinert, und die Schwarzmarktpreise schossen in die Höhe. Die Einwohner mußten sparsam mit Strom und Gas umgehen; Benzin und Reifen waren für Privatpersonen nicht erhältlich. Busse und Lastwagen wurden mit Kohlengas angetrieben, das sie in wurstförmigen Ballons auf den Wagendächern mitführten. Der tschechische Komödiant Vlasta Burian (1891–1962) löste das Problem dadurch, daß er mit einer fünfspännigen Kutsche durch die Stadt fuhr. Fahrräder und Straßenbahnen beförderten den Rest der Bevölkerung.

Als Teil ihres Kampfes gegen die Intellektuellen förderten die Nazis eine Literatur, die die Arbeiterklasse feierte (und lieferten damit einen unheimli-

ses serres apparaît sur les places publiques et les bâtiments officiels. Lorsque les régiments S.S. prêtent serment d'allégeance, leur symbole – deux runes argentées sur un fond sombre – semblent deux éclairs géants plantés dans les pavés de la place de la vieille ville. À partir de l'été 1941, la lettre « V » proclamant la foi dans la victoire allemande, est peinte sur les trams et les bâtiments. L'effacer, la modifier ou la ridiculiser est un délit. Lorsque cela se produit, tout le quartier est puni par une amende collective et les radios sont confisquées. L'architecte de Hitler, Albert Speer visite la ville et fantasme sur sa transformation en quelque chose de plus monumental et germanique.

Un *black-out* est imposé quasiment depuis le début de la guerre. Les rues sombres, les phares des trams et des voitures maquillés, et les volets fermés donnent une apparence presque irréelle à la cité. Le rationnement suit bientôt, mais les Pragois ont conservé des liens étroits avec les villages avoisinants et s'organisent assez bien. Les ouvriers des fabriques d'armement reçoivent des dotations supplémentaires de tabac et de chaussures. Les Allemands prennent soin de la classe ouvrière, dont la contribution est essentielle à l'effort de guerre. Un tiers des armements allemands viennent des usines du Protectorat. En février 1943, tous les hommes de seize à soixante-cinq ans et toutes les femmes de dix-sept à quarante-cinq ans peuvent être réquisitionnés pour la conscription industrielle. La guerre se poursuivant, les conditions de vie de la population se détériorent. Les bénéfices diminuent et les salaires sont gelés. Les rations sont réduites et les prix du marché noir explosent. Il est fermement conseillé d'économiser le gaz et l'électricité. Les particuliers ne peuvent plus acheter d'essence ou de pneus, et les bus et les camions fonctionnent au gaz de charbon, emmagasiné dans un réservoir oblong fixé sur leur toit. Le comédien tchèque Vlasta Burian (1891–1962) résout le problème en se déplaçant dans une voiture tirée par cinq chevaux de la même couleur, tandis que les bicyclettes et les trams transportent le reste de la population.

Dans leur lutte contre les intellectuels, les nazis encouragent les écrits qui célèbrent la classe ouvrière (avant-goût étrange de ce qui allait survenir). En mars 1942, ils organisent un concours de roman, de poésie et de nouvelles sur la vie des travailleurs. Parmi les vainqueurs figurent des contributions intitulées *Les garçons en bleu de travail*, *Les hommes sous Prague*, *Femmes de fumée*. Une participation surréaliste intitulée *Entretien imaginaire avec les employés d'une fabrique de préservatifs*, fut cependant considérée comme une provocation. Peu après l'invasion, les surréalistes pragois passent dans la clandestinité et continuent à peindre et à écrire essentiellement entre eux et à s'entraider. Toyen (Marie Čermínová, 1902–1980) cache son compagnon surréaliste Jindřich Heisler (1914–1953), Juif. Les surréalistes s'engagent ouvertement dans leur opposition au régime dictatorial, tandis que s'affirment leurs positions contre l'art logique, contre l'art ennuyeux, « résistance culturelle » au réalisme socialiste nazi. Les nazis, et plus tard les communistes, considèrent leur mouvement comme une forme d'art décadente, subversive et dangereuse.

Joseph Goebbels visiting Prague.
Joseph Goebbels bei einem Besuch in Prag.
Visite de Joseph Goebbels à Prague.

Three German theaters catered for the 40–50,000 Germans in Prague in 1940. German music-lovers attended classical concerts at Rudolfinum or in the Philharmonic Opera. Heydrich paid tribute to his father, the composer Bruno Heydrich (1863–1938), by having his works performed in Wallenstein Palace. On the eve of his assassination Heydrich sat with his wife Lina listening to his father's music and before he died he quoted to Himmler lines from Bruno's opera *Amen*: "The world is just a barrel-organ which the Lord God turns Himself. We all have to dance to the tune which is already on the drum".

Various dignitaries visited the city during the war, among them Joseph Goebbels (1897–1945), who came to assess the Barrandov Film Studios. "I have fallen totally in love with this city," he enthused in his diary. "It exudes the German spirit and must become German again." As Propaganda Minister, he knew very well the importance of controlling the media and the Nazis acquired two thirds of Barrandov, to which they added two other studios (one in Radlice and the other one in Hostivař). Goebbels expanded the studio complex, building the largest sound stage in Europe. If the film medium was regarded by Goebbels as an important propaganda tool, theaters were expendable. In November 1944 the Czech theaters were closed as part of total mobilization and actors were assigned to the war industry.

Hitler's favorite director, Leni Riefenstahl (b. 1902), made her film *Tiefland* in Prague. She was impressed by the Czech film technicians' hard work. Many technicians, directors and actors worked on German films and the spelling of their names was changed to look more Germanic. The architect Jan Zázvorka was turned into Johan Sasworka, Bedřich Veverka to Friedrich Walldorf, Martin Frič to Fritsch, Adina Mandlová to Lil Adina (her stage name was created by Goebbels himself) and so on. A number of German propaganda films (including the

chen Vorgeschmack dessen, was kommen sollte). Im März 1942 finanzierten sie einen Wettbewerb für Romane, Gedichte und Kurzgeschichten über das Leben der Arbeiter. Die Gewinner waren Beiträge mit Titeln wie *Die Jungs in den blauen Overalls*, *Männer in Prag* und *Frauen aus Rauch*. Ein surrealistischer Beitrag mit dem Titel *Ein imaginäres Interview mit Arbeitern einer Kondom-Fabrik* wäre wahrscheinlich, wenn er vorgelegt worden wäre, als Beispiel »entarteter Kunst« betrachtet worden. Kurz nach der Invasion waren Prags Surrealisten in den Untergrund gegangen, wo sie für sich selbst weitermalten und schrieben. Sie unterstützten einander, wie beispielsweise Toyen (Marie Čermínová; 1902–1980), die ihren Surrealistenkollegen, den Juden Jindřich Heisler, vor den Nazis versteckte. Die Opposition gegen ein diktatorisches Regime wurde zum Markenzeichen der Surrealisten, und ihre unlogische Kunst gegen die Langeweile formierte sich als »kultureller Widerstand« gegen den Sozialen Realismus der Nazis, die diese Kunst (wie später die Kommunisten) für dekadent, subversiv und gefährlich hielten.

Während des Krieges zeigten die Kinos harmlose Komödien, Naturfilme und die obligatorischen Propagandaberichte. Die Nachrichten wurden oft dazu benutzt, die Bevölkerung einzuschüchtern und Leute aufzuspüren. Als beispielsweise Ende Mai 1942 ein Fahrrad, ein Aktenkoffer, ein leichtes Maschinengewehr und ein Mantel aus dem Besitz von Gabčík und Kubiš nach dem Attentat auf Heydrich gefunden wurden, zeigten die Nachrichten immer wieder diese Gegenstände und forderten Informanten auf, sich zu melden.

Drei deutsche Theater standen den 40–50.000 Deutschen in Prag 1940 zur Verfügung. Deutsche Musikliebhaber besuchten klassische Konzerte im Rudolfinum oder in der Philharmonie. Heydrich ehrte seinen Vater, den Komponisten Bruno Heydrich (1863–1938), indem er seine Arbeiten im Palais Wallenstein aufführen ließ. Am Vorabend seiner Ermordung lauschte Heydrich zusammen mit seiner Frau Lina Kompositionen seines Vaters, und vor seinem Tod zitierte er vor Himmler Zeilen aus der Oper seines Vaters *Amen*: »Die Welt ist nur ein Leierkasten, auf dem der Herrgott selbst spielt. Wir müssen alle nach der Musik tanzen, die schon auf der Trommel ist.«

Verschiedene Würdenträger besuchten die Stadt während des Krieges. Unter ihnen war auch Joseph Goebbels (1897–1945), der die Barrandov-Studios besichtigen wollte. »Ich habe mich total verliebt in diese Stadt«, schrieb er begeistert in sein Tagebuch. »Sie strömt über vor deutschem Geist und muß wieder deutsch werden.« Als Propagandaminister wußte er sehr genau, wie wichtig die Kontrolle der Medien war. So erwarben die Nazis zwei Drittel von Barrandov, denen sie zwei weitere Studios (eines in Radlice und ein anderes in Hostivař) hinzufügten. Goebbels erweiterte den Studiokomplex und baute die größte Tonfilmbühne Europas. Während er die Filmindustrie als wichtiges Propagandainstrument ansah, hielt er die Theater für überflüssig. Im November 1944 wurden sie als Teil der totalen Mobilmachung geschlossen und die Schaupieler der Rüstungsindustrie unterstellt.

Pendant la guerre, les cinémas projettent des comédies anodines, des films sur la vie sauvage et des actualités de propagande. Les bulletins servent souvent à intimider la population et à pourchasser des gens. Fin mai 1942, par exemple, lorsqu'une bicyclette, une serviette, une mitrailleuse Sten et un manteau appartenant à Gabčik et Kubiš sont trouvés après leur attentat contre Heydrich, des bandes d'actualité projetées *ad nauseam* incitent les spectateurs à la délation.

Trois théâtres allemands répondent aux besoins de distraction des 40 à 50 000 Allemands qui résident à Prague en 1940 (armée comprise). Les mélomanes allemands assistent à des concerts au Rudolfinum ou à l'Opéra philharmonique. Heydrich rend hommage à son père, le compositeur Bruno Heydrich (1863–1938), en faisant jouer ses œuvres au palais Wallenstein. La veille de son assassinat, il écoute encore la musique de son père en compagnie de sa femme Lina, et avant sa mort, il citera à Himmler quelques phrases de son opéra, *Amen*: «Le monde n'est qu'un orgue de Barbarie dont le Seigneur joue Lui-même. Nous devons tous danser sur les airs qui sont sur le cylindre.»

Divers dignitaires allemands visitent la ville pendant la guerre, dont Joseph Goebbels (1897–1945), qui vient prendre possession des studios cinématographiques Barrandov. «Je suis tombé totalement amoureux de cette ville», écrit-il avec enthousiasme dans son journal. «Elle exsude l'esprit allemand, et doit redevenir allemande.» Ministre de la propagande, il est parfaitement conscient de l'importance du contrôle des médias, etles nazis acquièrent les deux tiers de Barrandov, auxquels ils ajoutent deux studios supplémentaires (l'un à Radice, l'autre à Hostivař). Goebbels agrandit ce complexe cinématographique, et construit le plus grand studio pour film sonore d'Europe. S'il considère le cinéma comme un instrument important pour la propagande, le théâtre n'est pas indispensable à ses yeux. En novembre 1944, les théâtres seront fermés dans le cadre d'une mobilisation générale, et les comédiens affectés à l'industrie de guerre.

La réalisatrice préférée de Hitler, Leni Riefenstahl (née en 1902), réalise son film *Tiefland* à Prague. Elle est impressionnée par le travail des techniciens tchèques. Beaucoup de techniciens, de réalisateurs et d'acteurs travaillent sur des films allemands et leurs noms sont modifiés pour avoir l'air plus allemand. L'architecte Jan Zásvorka devient Johan Sasworka; Bedřich Veverka, Friedrich Walldorf; Martin Frič, Martin Fritsch; Adina Mandlová, Lil Adina (son nom de scène fut trouvé par Goebbels lui-même)… Un certain nombre de films de propagande allemande (dont le très antisémite *Juif Süss*) furent produits à Barrandov, ainsi qu'un petit nombre de films d'évasion tchèques. Barrandov reste au-delà de la portée des bombardiers alliés jusqu'en 1944, et les installations tournent à plein rendement. Pendant les six années d'occupation, quatre-vingt films allemands sont réalisés à Prague. En 1944, neuf films tchèques sont produits, contre quarante-neuf en 1937.

Aucune œuvre artistique n'est réalisée pendant ces années de guerre. La médiocrité et la loyauté sont seules récompensées. Un certain

anti-Semitic *Jud Süss*) were produced at Barrandov, as well as a small number of Czech escapist movies. Barrandov was beyond the range of the Allied bombers until 1944, so the technical facilities could be used to their full potential. During the six years of occupation, eighty German films were made in Prague. In 1944 there were nine Czech films, compared with forty-nine in 1937.

Nothing of significant artistic importance was produced in the war years. Mediocrity and loyalty were rewarded. A number of Jewish artists and producers either fled the country or perished in concentration camps. Hugo Haas (1901–68), the actor and director, managed to escape just before the outbreak of the war. The two beloved Prague clowns Voskovec and Werich (and their composer Ježek) knew that their anti-Fascist plays would earn them a trip to a concentration camp and left for the United States in January 1939.

By the summer of 1944, Germany and her partners were gradually being expelled by the Allies from the conquered European, North African and Asian territories. In Fascist Slovakia the Communists organized an uprising (29 August 1944). For two months they fought against the much better-armed enemy and Germany was forced to invade her former ally, eventually defeating the Slovaks.

Partisans became active in the mountains in early 1945 as a wave of parachute groups dropped by the Russians to encourage disruption behind Nazi lines. On 23 April the Czech government-in-exile, which Beneš had re-formed under Soviet supervision and which was now established in Russian-held territory at Košice in Slovakia, broadcast an appeal to the Czech nation calling for an uprising. Nazi radio replied with a threat to destroy Prague, but still the uprising began on 5 May. The Czechs knew of Hitler's suicide of 30 April 1945 and were hoping that the Americans, who were already in Plzeň, 90 kilometers away, would reach the capital within a day or two. But US General George S. Patton (1885–1945) was not allowed to go to Prague: in the bargaining between the Western Allies and the USSR, the city had been pledged to the Soviet army.

Everything would have gone according to Stalin's plan but for the 1st division of the Russian National Liberation Army under General K. Bunyachenko. Known as *vlasovci* after their leader General Andrei Vlasov (1900–46), they were Russian soldiers captured by the Germans who had expressed a willingness to fight Communism. In 1944 the Nazis pledged support for the formation of a Russian National Liberation Committee (KNOR) in order to buy their loyalty. When the Prague uprising began, however, the *vlasovci*, hoping to save their skins, switched sides and turned on their SS allies.

The uprising was announced in a radio broadcast at 6 a.m. and soon both Communists and non-Communists were fighting street battles against the Germans. The spring breeze was filled with the scent of lilacs and of freedom. Just behind the National Museum, the radio station became the focus of the resistance. Over 1500 barricades were built. The western suburbs of Prague and Ruzyně airport soon

Hitlers Lieblingsregisseurin, Leni Riefenstahl (geboren 1902) drehte ihren Film *Tiefland* in Prag. Sie war beeindruckt vom Fleiß der tschechischen Filmtechniker. An der Produktion deutscher Filme waren viele Techniker, Regisseure und Schauspieler beteiligt, deren Namensschreibweisen verändert wurden, damit sie deutscher aussahen. Der Architekt Jan Zázvorka wurde zu Johan Sasworka, Bedřich Veverka zu Friedrich Walldorf, Martin Frič zu Fritsch, Adina Mandlová zu Lil Adina (ihren Künstlernamen hatte Goebbels selbst entworfen) und so weiter. In Barrandov wurde eine Reihe deutscher Propagandafilme (einschließlich des antisemitischen *Jud Süß*) produziert; außerdem entstanden hier einige tschechische Filme, die vom Alltag ablenken sollten. Da Barrandov bis 1944 außerhalb der Reichweite der alliierten Bomber lag, konnte man die technischen Möglichkeiten voll ausschöpfen. Während der sechsjährigen Besatzung wurden 80 deutsche Filme in Prag gedreht. 1944 produzierte man neun tschechische Filme, 1937 waren es noch 49 gewesen.

In den Kriegsjahren entstanden keine bedeutenden Kunstwerke; statt dessen wurden Mittelmäßigkeit und Loyalität belohnt. Viele jüdische Künstler und Produzenten verließen entweder das Land oder verschwanden in den Konzentrationslagern. Dem Schauspieler und Regisseur Hugo Haas (1901–68) gelang noch kurz vor Kriegsausbruch die Auswanderung. Die beiden beliebten Prager Clowns Voskovec und Werich (und ihr Drehbuchautor Ježek) sahen voraus, daß sie wegen ihrer antifaschistischen Stücke verfolgt werden würden, und reisten im Januar 1939 in die USA aus.

Ab Sommer 1944 wurden Deutschland und die Achsenmächte von den Alliierten Schritt für Schritt aus den eroberten Gebieten in Europa, Nordafrika und Asien vertrieben. In der faschistischen Slowakei organisierten die Kommunisten am 29. August 1944 einen Aufstand. Zwei Monate lang kämpften sie gegen einen weitaus besser gerüsteten Feind, schließlich sah sich Deutschland zum Einmarsch in die Gebiete seines früheren Alliierten gezwungen, um den Aufstand niederzuschlagen.

Anfang 1945 wurden Partisanen in den Bergen aktiv, nachdem einige Fallschirmspringereinheiten von den Russen abgesetzt worden waren, um hinter der Nazi-Front Unruhe zu stiften. Am 23. April rief die tschechische Exilregierung, die Beneš unter sowjetischer Aufsicht neu formiert hatte und die jetzt im von der Sowjetunion besetzten Gebiet Košice in der Slowakei saß, die tschechische Nation über Radio zum Aufstand auf. Der Sender der Nazis antwortete mit der Drohung, Prag zu zerstören, aber am 5. Mai begann der Aufstand. Die Tschechen hatten bereits von Hitlers Selbstmord am 30. April 1945 erfahren und hofften nun, daß die Amerikaner, die bereits im 90 Kilometer entfernten Pilsen standen, in 1-2 Tagen die Hauptstadt erreichen würden: Aber General Patton (1885–1945) hatte keine Erlaubnis, in Prag einzumarschieren: In den Verhandlungen zwischen den westlichen Alliierten und der UdSSR war die Stadt der sowjetischen Armee zugesprochen worden.

Vlasov soldier during the Prague uprising.
Wlassow-Soldat während des Prager Aufstandes.
Soldat de Vlasov pendant le soulèvement de Prague.

nombre d'artistes et de producteurs juifs fuient le pays ou meurent dans les camps de concentration. Hugo Haas (1901–1968), acteur et réalisateur réussit à s'échapper juste avant que la guerre n'éclate. Les deux clowns pragois si populaires, Voskovec et Werich (et leur compositeur Ježek) savaient que leurs sketchs musicaux antifascistes leur vaudraient les camps de concentration et fuient vers les États-Unis en janvier 1939.

À l'été 1944, l'Allemagne et les puissances de l'Axe sont peu à peu repoussées par les Alliés des territoires conquis en Europe, en Afrique du Nord et Asie. Dans la Slovaquie fasciste, les communistes organisent un soulèvement (29 août 1944). Pendant deux mois, ils se battent contre un ennemi bien mieux armé et l'Allemagne est obligée d'envahir son ancien allié, pour finir par battre les Slovaques.

Les Résistants entrent en action dans les montagnes début 1945 lorsque les Russes commencent des lâchers de parachutistes pour encourager les soulèvements derrière les lignes allemandes. Le 23 avril, le gouvernement tchèque en exil, reformé par Beneš sous contrôle soviétique et installé à Košice en Slovaquie occupée par les Russes, lance à la radio un appel au soulèvement de la population tchèque. La radio nazie réplique par la menace de détruire Prague, mais le soulèvement débute néanmoins le 5 mai. Les Américains se trouvent déjà à Pilsen, à 90 km, mais le général Patton (1885–1945) n'est pas autorisé à entrer dans Prague. Dans le marchandage entre les Alliés occidentaux et l'URSS, la ville a été cédée à l'armée soviétique.

Tout se serait déroulé selon le plan de Staline sans la première division de son armée nationale russe de libération dirigée par le général Bunyachenko. Connue sous le nom de *Vlasovci* d'après le général Andrei Vlasov, cette armée était composée de soldats russes capturés par les

Soviet marshals Koniev and Rybalko, 1945.
Die sowjetischen Marschälle Koniev und Rybalko, 1945.
Deux maréchaux soviétiques, Koniev et Rybalko, 1945.

came under the control of Vlasov's well-armed divisions. Without their intervention, Prague might have shared the fate of Warsaw. The only thing the Vlasov soldiers wanted from the Czechs in return was asylum. But the Czech Communists were not prepared to pay the political price attached to that demand. Granting asylum to the *vlasovci* would have been a political faux pas, for, even though Vlasov's men had helped to save Prague, they had previously been traitors to the Soviet Union and in Stalin's eyes that could never be forgiven.

On 7 May 1945 a German delegation signed an act of unconditional surrender at Rheims. Fighting was to end on all fronts at 23:01 hours on 8 May. By the early hours of 8 May the *vlasovci* were leaving the battleground, fearing the approaching Red Army. They hoped to reach the safety of American lines. Just before their departure, one of them said to Stanislav Ausky, a Czech member of the reconnaissance, "You got rid of one dog, but the second is about to jump at your throat." Deprived of the *vlasovci* support, there was little the poorly armed and untrained civilians in Prague could do against the determined German troops, but while the SS were still slaughtering women and children in the suburb of Krč, the German General Rudolf Toussaint asked to be allowed to pull out of Prague unhindered. The Czechs, prepared to make concessions to end the fighting, opened the barricades and after 4 p.m. on 8 May the Germans started leaving the city. However, the ceasefire collapsed when the Red Army, arriving from Berlin, entered the suburbs the next day. Shortly after midday Marshal Ivan S. Koniev's troops took control of the city. They were greeted by the citizens of Prague with relief and joy. The Reds hunted down the *vlasovci* and shot many of them without trial. Those who reached American lines were handed over to Stalin; labor camp or execution was their usual fate. Their vital role in saving Prague from the SS terror was erased from both Czech and Soviet history.

Alles wäre nach Stalins Plan verlaufen, wäre da nicht die Erste Division von Wlassows Russischer Nationaler Befreiungsarmee unter General Bunyachenko gewesen. Die sogenannten *Vlasovci*, wie sie nach ihrem Führer General Andrei Vlasow (1900–46) genannt wurden, waren russische Soldaten in deutscher Gefangenschaft, die den Wunsch geäußert hatten, gegen den Kommunismus zu kämpfen. 1944 hatten die Nazis die Bildung eines Russischen Nationalen Befreiungskommitees (KNOR) unterstützt, um damit die Treue von Wlassows Soldaten zu erkaufen. Als der Prager Aufstand begann, wechselten die *Vlasovci* in der Hoffnung, ihre Haut retten zu können, die Fronten und wendeten sich gegen ihre SS-Kameraden.

Nachdem der Aufstand in einer Radiosendung um 6 Uhr morgens bekanntgegeben worden war, lieferten sich Kommunisten und Nicht-Kommunisten blutige Straßenschlachten mit den Deutschen. Die Frühlingsluft war erfüllt vom Duft des Flieder und der Freiheit. Die Radiostation unmittelbar hinter dem Nationalmuseum entwickelte sich zum Zentrum des Widerstandes. Mehr als 1.500 Barrikaden wurden errichtet. Die westlichen Prager Vororte und der Flughafen Ruzyně gerieten schnell unter die Kontrolle von Wlassows gutausgerüsteten Divisionen. Ohne ihre Intervention hätte Prag möglicherweise das Schicksal Warschaus ereilt. Das einzige, was sie von den Tschechen als Gegenleistung verlangten, war die Gewährung von Asyl. Aber die tschechischen Kommunisten zeigten sich nicht bereit, den politischen Preis zu bezahlen, der mit dieser Forderung verbunden war. Asyl für die *Vlasovci* wäre ein politischer Fehler gewesen, denn, obwohl sie den Kommunisten zum Sieg verholfen hatten, hatten sie vorher die Sowjetunion verraten, und das war in Stalins Augen unverzeihlich.

Am 7. Mai unterzeichnete eine deutsche Delegation in Reims die bedingungslose Kapitulation. An allen Fronten sollten die Kämpfe am 8. Mai um 23:01 Uhr aufhören. In den frühen Morgenstunden des 8. Mai verließen die *Vlasovci* aus Angst vor der heranrückenden Roten Armee das Schlachtfeld. Sie hofften, sich hinter die amerikanische Frontlinie in Sicherheit bringen zu können. Unmittelbar vor ihrem Abzug sagte einer von ihnen zu Stanislav Ausky, einem tschechischen Mitglied der Aufklärungstruppe: »Ihr seid einen Hund losgeworden, aber der nächste setzt schon zum Sprung auf eure Kehle an.« Ohne die Unterstützung der *Vlasovci* konnten die schlecht bewaffneten und ungeübten Zivilisten in Prag wenig gegen die entschlossenen deutschen Truppen ausrichten. Während aber die SS noch immer Frauen und Kinder in der Prager Vorstadt Krč ermordete, bat der deutsche General Rudolf Toussaint um die Erlaubnis, ungehindert aus Prag abzuziehen. Die Tschechen waren zu Konzessionen bereit, um die Kämpfe zu beenden, und öffneten die Barrikaden. Am 8. Mai nach 4 Uhr nachmittags begannen die Deutschen mit dem Abzug aus Prag. Der Waffenstillstand brach jedoch zusammen, als die Rote Armee, die aus Berlin vorstieß, am nächsten Tag die Vororte der Stadt erreichte. Kurz nach Mittag übernahmen die Truppen von Marschall Iwan S. Koniew die Kontrolle über die Stadt. Sie wurden von den Prager Bürgern mit Erleichterung und Freude begrüßt. Die Rote Armee

Allemands et ayant exprimé leur volonté de combattre le communisme . À l'automne 1944, les nazis aidèrent à la formation d'un Comité national russe de libération (KNOR) pour acheter la loyauté des soldats de Vlasov. Lorsqu'éclate le soulèvement de Prague, les *Vlasovci*, pour sauver leur peau, se retournèrent contre leurs alliés SS.

Le soulèvement est annoncé à la radio à 6 heures, et bientôt communistes et non-communistes se battent dans les rues contre les Allemands. La brise du printemps était pleine de l'odeur des lilas et du parfum de la liberté. Située juste derrière le Musée national, la station de radio devint le Q.G. de la Résistance. Plus de 1 500 barricades sont élevées. Les banlieues ouest et l'aéroport de Ruzyně tombent rapidement sous le contrôle des divisions bien armées de Vlasov. Sans leur intervention, Prague aurait pu partager le sort de Varsovie. La seule chose que demandaient aux Tchèques les soldats de Vlasov était un asile. Mais les communistes tchèques n'étaient pas prêts à payer le prix politique d'une telle demande. Accorder cet asile aux *Vlasovci* aurait été provoquer la colère de Staline pour lequel, si ces hommes avaient participé à la victoire communiste, ils avaient d'abord trahi l'Union soviétique ce qui était impardonnable à ses yeux.

Le 7 mai 1945, une délégation allemande signe l'acte de reddition inconditionnelle à Reims. Les combats doivent cesser sur tous les fronts à 23 heures 01 le 8 mai. Au petit matin du 8 mai, les soldats de Vlasov quittent le champ de bataille, devant l'avancée de l'Armée rouge. Ils espèrent atteindre les lignes américaines. Juste avant leur départ, un *Vlasovci* dit à Stanislav Ausky : « Vous vous êtes débarrassés d'un chien, mais le second va vous sauter à la gorge. » Sans le soutien militaire des *Vlasovci*, les Pragois mal équipés et mal formés ne pouvaient grand-chose face aux troupes allemandes déterminées, mais pendant que les S.S. assassinaient encore des femmes et des enfants dans le faubourg de Krč, le général allemand Toussaint demanda à pouvoir quitter Prague en laissant la ville intacte. Les Tchèques prêts à faire des concessions pour accélérer la fin des combats, ouvrent les barricades, et à 16 heures le 8 mai, les troupes allemandes commencent à quitter la ville. Le cessez-le-feu est rompu le lendemain lorsque l'Armée rouge qui arrive de Berlin pénètre dans les faubourgs. Peu après midi, les troupes du maréchal Ivan S. Koniev prennent le contrôle de la cité. Les Rouges pourchassent les *Vlasovci* et en fusillent un grand nombre sans procès. Ceux qui réussissent à atteindre les lignes américaines seront remis à Staline et envoyés dans des camps de travail ou devant des pelotons d'exécution. Leur rôle essentiel dans le sauvetage de Prague de la terreur S.S. sera gommé de l'histoire tchèque et de l'histoire russe.

Le peuple de Prague prend alors sa revanche sur les Allemands abandonnés. Les ex-collaborateurs de la Gestapo sont les plus féroces. Les pendaisons et les lynchages se multiplient et des svastikas sont peintes sur le front des Allemands de Prague internés dans diverses prisons et dans le stade de Strahov. Ils sont forcés à démonter les barricades et à enterrer les morts. Les soldats russes se livrent à de nombreux viols sur les jeunes femmes. Le NKVD (la sécurité d'État soviétique) se saisit des dossiers de la Gestapo

The people of Prague took revenge on the Germans left behind. One-time Gestapo collaborators were the most ferocious. There were hangings and lynchings, and swastikas were painted on the foreheads of Prague Germans interned in various prisons and in the Strahov sports stadium. They were forced to clear barricades and bury the dead; young women were often raped by the Soviet soldiers. The NKVD (Soviet state security) agents seized the Gestapo's files and took them to Moscow, where lists of collaborators were studied carefully. A number of these people were later recruited to join the Communist Party.

Frank was captured in Plzeň by the Americans and handed over to the Czechs to stand trial. In 1946 he was sentenced to hang and tickets to his execution at Pankrác prison were given to various groups, including the Lidice women who had survived their concentration-camp internment. Kurt Daluege and two commandants of Terezín, Seidl and Rahm, met the same fate. Konrad Henlein, the Gauleiter of the Sudetenland, who had played a leading role in the destruction of the pre-war Czechoslovak state, slashed his wrists when it became obvious that he would be handed over to the Czechs.

The Czechoslovak government established in Košice – known as the National Front – included a number of Communists imposed on Beneš by Stalin. They were the first to be returned to Prague, in a Soviet plane. Beneš was kept captive under the pretext of security and illness; he had no freedom of movement or communication. He was allowed back to Prague a week later: after all, he still had one important trump card – his considerable popularity at home. He was greeted with tremendous enthusiasm: the packed streets were decorated with his portrait and Stalin's, and with Czechoslovak and Soviet flags. The people never suspected that they had just been conquered by the Red Army.

verfolgte die *Vlasovci* und erschoß viele ohne Verhandlung. Diejenigen, die die amerikanischen Linien erreichten, wurden Stalin übergeben; Arbeitslager oder Hinrichtung war ihr Schicksal. Die wichtige Rolle, die sie bei der Rettung Prags vor dem SS-Terror gespielt hatten, wurde sowohl aus der tschechischen als auch aus der sowjetischen Geschichtsschreibung getilgt.

Die Bürger von Prag übten Rache an den zurückgebliebenen Deutschen, wobei sich einstige Gestapo-Kollaborteure besonders hervortaten. Es kam zu Hinrichtungen und Ermordungen; Prager Deutschen, die in verschiedenen Gefängnissen und im Strahov-Stadion interniert waren, wurden Hakenkreuze auf die Stirn gemalt. Sie mußten Barrikaden abbauen und die Toten begraben; junge Frauen wurden häufig von sowjetischen Soldaten vergewaltigt. Die Agenten des NKWD (der sowjetischen Staatssicherheit) beschlagnahmten die Gestapo-Unterlagen und brachten sie nach Moskau, wo die Listen mit Kollaborateuren sorgfältig gelesen wurden. Eine Reihe dieser Leute rekrutierte man später als Mitglieder der Kommunistischen Partei.

Frank wurde in Pilsen von den Amerikanern verhaftet und den Tschechen zum Gerichtsprozeß übergeben. 1946 verurteilte man ihn zum Tode durch den Strang und verteilte Eintrittskarten an verschiedene Gruppen anläßlich seiner Exekution im Pankratius-Gefängnis. Unter ihnen waren auch Frauen aus Lidice, die die Internierung im Konzentrationslager überlebt hatten. Kurt Daluege und zwei Kommandanten von Theresienstadt, Seidl und Rahm, ereilte dasselbe Schicksal. Konrad Henlein, der Gauleiter des Sudetenlandes, der eine führende Rolle bei der Zerschlagung des tschechischen Staates gespielt hatte, schnitt sich die Pulsadern auf, als klar war, daß er den Tschechen übergeben werden sollte.

In der tschechoslowakischen Regierung in Košice – bekannt als Nationale Front – waren auch eine Reihe von Kommunisten, die Beneš von Stalin aufgezwungen worden waren. Sie kehrten als erste in einem sowjetischen Flugzeug nach Prag zurück. Beneš aber wurde unter dem Vorwand der Sicherheit und einer Erkrankung gefangengehalten; er durfte sich weder frei bewegen noch mit der Außenwelt Kontakt aufnehmen. Erst eine Woche später wurde ihm die Rückkehr nach Prag gestattet; schließlich besaß er noch einen wichtigen Trumpf – seine außerordentliche Popularität. Beneš wurde bei seiner Ankunft ein begeisterter Empfang bereitet: die vollgestopften Straßen waren mit seinen und Stalins Porträts dekoriert, überall hingen tschechoslowakische und sowjetische Fahnen. Die ahnungslose Menge wußte nicht, daß sie gerade von der Roten Armee erobert worden waren.

Frank facing the death penalty.
Frank zum Tode verurteilt.
Frank condamné à la mort.

et les expédie à Moscou où les listes de collaborateurs sont étudiées. Un certain nombre de ces gens seront ultérieurement recrutés par le parti communiste.

Frank est capturé à Pilsen par les Américains et remis aux Tchèques pour y subir son procès. En 1946, il est condamné à être pendu, et des billets pour assister à son exécution à la prison de Pankrác sont distribués à divers groupes, dont les femmes de Lidice qui ont survécu à leur séjour en camp de concentration. Kurt Daluege et deux commandants de Terezín, Seidl et Rahm, connaissent le même sort. Konrad Henlein, le Gauleiter des Sudètes, qui avait joué un rôle moteur dans la destruction de l'État républicain d'avant-guerre, s'entaille les poignets lorsqu'il est certain d'être livré aux Tchèques.

Le gouvernement tchécoslovaque de Košice – appelé Front national – comprend un certain nombre de communistes imposés à Beneš par Staline. Ils sont les premiers à revenir à Prague, dans un avion soviétique. Beneš est retenu sous des prétextes de sécurité et de maladie et se voit privé de toute liberté de mouvement ou de communication. Il est autorisé à se rendre à Prague une semaine plus tard et pourrait encore avoir une carte à jouer, celle de son immense popularité. Une foule immense envahit les rues décorées de portraits de Benes et de Staline et de drapeaux tchécoslovaques et soviétiques. L'accueil du président est enthousiaste. Il est acclamé par une population qui n'as pas encore compris que le pays vient d'être conquis par l'Armée rouge.

### 1945–1989: In the Shadow of the Red Star

Prague survived the war relatively unscathed. The most visible destruction was caused by American bombers, whose pilots claimed that they mistook the city for Dresden. The neo-Gothic wing of the Town Hall in the Old Town Square was destroyed by the Germans during the uprising. The ruin was photographed often and used as a subtle propaganda symbol to show Prague's scars. By 1947 its shell had been cleared, although other ruins stayed untouched until the 1990s. Rationing continued – coupons were in circulation for another eight years. Although the Czechs inherited a huge armaments industry, everything else was in short supply, including culture. However, that situation was soon remedied.

In 1946 Beneš's government decided to pay tribute to the Czech Philharmonic, which was about to celebrate its 50th anniversary, with a music festival. The victorious Allies each sent a participant (usually a well-known composer or conductor). The festival was named the "Prague Spring," and it opened on 12 May with Bedřich Smetana's symphonic poem *Má vlast*. It was so successful that it became an annual event.

The first post-war international Surrealist exhibition was held in Prague in 1947 and was attended by President Beneš and his wife. Paintings and collages by Toyen, Jindřich Štyrský (1899–1942), Karel Teige as well as works from France, the USA, Spain, the Soviet Union and other countries were featured. It seemed that freedom, democracy and the desire to build a new and just world had prevailed, together with the basic needs to play and to create.

At the same time, the smoothest of Communist takeovers had already begun. Under an agreement signed by Beneš in Moscow in March 1945, the Communists – led since 1929 by Klement Gottwald – became one of the chief parties in the National Front, with eight seats in the Cabinet, including the Ministry of the Interior. In the elections of May 1946 – the country's last free elections for more than four decades – the Communist Party of Czechoslovakia (KSČ) polled 38 per cent of the vote. However, the democratic parties in the National Front were

Portraits of Beneš, Gottwald, Stalin and Nejedlý.
Porträts von Beneš, Gottwald, Stalin und Nejedlý.
Portraits de Beneš, Gottwald, Staline et Nejedlý.

### 1945–1989: Im Schatten des Roten Sterns

Prag hatte den Krieg relativ unbeschädigt überlebt. Die größten Zerstörungen waren durch amerikanische Bomber verursacht worden, deren Piloten nach eigener Aussage die Stadt mit Dresden verwechselt hatten. Während des Aufstandes war der neugotische Flügel des Rathauses auf dem Altstädter Marktplatz von den Deutschen zerstört worden. Diese häufig fotografierte Ruine wurde als geschicktes Propagandamittel genutzt, um Prags Narben zu zeigen. Aber bereits 1947 war das Gebäude restauriert, andere Ruinen hingegen sind bis in die 90er Jahre liegen geblieben. Rationierungen wurden nach dem Kriege beibehalten, Coupons blieben noch für die nächsten acht Jahre im Umlauf. Die Tschechen hatten zwar eine große Rüstungsindustrie geerbt, aber alles andere – so auch die Kultur – war knapp. Diese Situation sollte sich allerdings bald ändern.

Aus Anlaß ihres 50. Geburtstags ehrte die Beneš-Regierung 1946 die Tschechische Philharmonie mit einem Musikfestival, zu dem jeder der siegreichen Alliierten einen Teilnehmer – in der Regel einen bekannten Komponisten oder Dirigenten – entsandte. Das Festival erhielt den Namen »Prager Frühling« und wurde am 12. Mai mit Bedřich Smetanas symphonischem Gedicht *Má vlast* eröffnet. Es wurde ein so großer Erfolg, daß man es von nun an jährlich wiederholte.

Die erste internationale Nachkriegsausstellung in Prag fand 1947 zum Thema »Surrealistische Kunst« statt, der auch Präsident Beneš und seine Gemahlin einen Besuch abstatteten. Es wurden Bilder und Collagen von Toyen, Jindřich Štyrský (1899–1942), Karel Teige sowie Werke aus Frankreich, den USA, Spanien, der Sowjetunion und anderen Ländern gezeigt. Freiheit, Demokratie und der Wunsch nach einer neuen Welt schienen sich, verbunden mit dem einfachen Verlangen nach Spiel und Kreativität, durchsetzen.

Gleichzeitig aber hatte die sanfteste aller kommunistischen Machtübernahmen bereits begonnen. Nach einem Abkommen, das Beneš im März 1945 in Moskau unterzeichnet hatte, wurde die kommunistische Partei, deren Vorsitzender seit 1929 Klement Gottwald war, eine der führenden Parteien innerhalb der Nationalen Front mit acht Sitzen im Kabinett, einschließlich dem des Innenministers. Bei den Wahlen vom März 1946 – den letzten des Landes für mehr als 40 Jahre – erhielt die Kommunistische Partei der Tschechoslowakei (KSČ) fast 38 Prozent der Stimmen. Dennoch sahen die demokratischen Parteien der Nationalen Front keinen Anlaß, ihren größten Gegner zu fürchten, sondern blickten vielmehr zuversichtlich auf die nächsten Wahlen, die 1948 stattfinden sollten. Es hatte den Anschein, als würde die anfängliche Unterstützung des Kommunismus nachlassen; während die KSČ zu diesem Zeitpunkt aber bereits fast die Kontrolle übernommen hatte.

Nachdem die tschechoslowakische Regierung 1947 die Teilnahme am Marshall-Plan – das amerikanische Hilfsprogramm für das vom Krieg zerstörte Europa – beschlossen hatte, wurden drei ihrer Minister nach Moskau berufen. Stalin behandelte die Tschechen schon jetzt wie ungehorsame Kinder. Ihnen wurde ausdrücklich nahegelegt, ihre Entschei-

### 1945–1989: Prague sous l'étoile rouge

Prague avait traversé la guerre relativement intacte. Les destructions les plus visibles venaient des bombardements américains, dont les pilotes avouèrent avoir cru qu'il s'agissait de Dresde. L'aile néogothique de l'hôtel de ville sur la place de la vieille ville fut détruite par les Allemands pendant le soulèvement. Cette ruine souvent photographiée fut utilisée comme subtil symbole de propagande pour montrer les blessures subies par la ville. En 1947, elle fut démolie, mais d'autres ruines restèrent en l'état jusqu'aux années 1990. Le rationnement continua et fonctionna sous forme de coupons pendant huit années supplémentaires. Si les Tchèques avaient hérité d'une énorme industrie de l'armement, tout manquait, y compris les activités culturelles, mais la situation allait vite s'améliorer.

En 1946, le gouvernement Beneš décide de rendre hommage à la Philharmonie tchèque qui doit célébrer son cinquantième anniversaire par un festival de musique. Les Alliés envoient chacun un participant (généralement un compositeur ou un chef d'orchestre célèbre). Le Festival reçoit le nom de Printemps de Prague, et ouvre sur le poème symphonique de Bedřich Smetana, *Má vlast* (ma patrie) le 12 mai. Il remporte un tel succès que l'on décide alors de l'organiser chaque année.

La première exposition internationale surréaliste d'après-guerre se tient à Prague en 1947 et reçoit la visite du président Beneš et son épouse. Des peintures et des collages de Toyen, Jindřich Štyrský (1899–1942) et Karel Teige sont présentés aussi bien que des œuvres originaires de France, des États-Unis, d'Espagne, d'Union soviétique et d'autres pays. Il semble qu'avec le besoin fondamental de jouer et de créer, la liberté, la démocratie et le désir de reconstruire un monde nouveau et juste vont l'emporter.

Au même moment, le coup d'État communiste le plus subtil commence à se mettre en place. Selon un accord signé par Beneš à Moscou en mars 1945, les communistes – dirigés depuis 1929 par Klement Gottwald – sont devenus l'un des principaux partis du Front national, détenant huit portefeuilles dans le cabinet, dont celui du ministère de l'Intérieur. Aux élections de mai 1946, les dernières élections libres pour plus de quarante ans, le Parti communiste de Tchécoslovaquie (KSČ) remporte 38 pour cent des suffrages. Les partis démocratiques du Front national ne veulent pas voir les manœuvres de leur principal rival et attendent les élections suivantes, prévues pour 1948. Il semble alors que l'aura du communisme décline dans la population, mais le KSČ a déjà pratiquement pris le contrôle de la situation.

Lorsqu'en 1947, la Tchécoslovaquie a déclaré qu'elle allait d'accepter le plan Marshall (l'aide américaine à la reconstruction de l'Europe), les ministres sont appelés à Moscou. Staline traite les Tchèques comme des enfants dissipés et les convainc de revenir sur leur décision. Le ministre des Affaires Étrangères Jan Masaryk (1886–1948, fils de Tomáš Masaryk) déclare : « Je suis allé à Moscou en ministre tchécoslovaque et en suis revenu en laquais soviétique. » En novembre 1947,

dismissive of their main rival's future and were looking forward to the next elections, scheduled for 1948. It seemed that initial support for Communism was declining, but by this time the KSČ was almost in control.

When in 1947 Czechoslovakia decided to join the Marshall Plan (US aid to war-devastated Europe), ministers were called to Moscow. Stalin was already treating the Czechs as naughty children. They were told to reverse their decision, and they did. Foreign Minister Jan Masaryk (1886–1948; Tomáš Masaryk's son) said, "I went to Moscow as a Czechoslovak Minister and came back a Soviet lackey." In November 1947 an attempt was made to assassinate him and two other non-Communist ministers. He was powerless when so-called Action Committees, usually consisting of a cleaner, a doorman and another menial worker, were set up in his ministry and valuable employees were dismissed. The Communists infiltrated the police, the security services and the army. Leaving nothing to chance, they armed the proletariat with new Soviet rifles, gave them red armbands and set them to patrol streets and stations. These were the so-called People's Militia. When students tried to march to the Castle in a gesture of support for President Beneš, the police and People's Militia blocked their way and scattered them with clubs. The Action Committees took over local administration, newspapers, banks, utilities and the buildings of the opposition parties. These committees, like the armed militias, were illegal.

On 12 February 1948 twelve non-Communist ministers resigned in protest against the Communists' takeover of the police. On the afternoon of 25 February, Klement Gottwald confronted President Beneš in Hradčany. Under the explicit threat of the armed militias – and deserted by the armed forces, whose commander, General Ludvík Svoboda (1895–1979), a secret KSČ member, ordered them not to intervene – Beneš yielded to Gottwald's demands, giving him a free hand to form a government. The empty places were filled by members of the KSČ and, when Beneš resigned on 2 June, Gottwald became President. The Communist takeover was complete. On 3 September, feeling utterly betrayed, Beneš died.

The most tragic postscript to those three turbulent post-war years came on 10 March 1948 when the body of Jan Masaryk was found outside the Černín Palace in Loretánské náměstí. For many years the official story was that he had thrown himself from a window, but, according to František August, a senior officer in the Czechoslovak State Security Organization (StB) who later escaped to the West, Masaryk was murdered on the orders of the NKVD because he planned to leave Czechoslovakia. The man who organized his death was Major Augustin Schramm, who in turn was shot soon after. The man officially accused of shooting Schramm was promptly executed. The man who knew the identity of Schramm's real killer was murdered as well, his body stuffed in a sack and burnt in a blast furnace in Ostrava. All documents relating to the case were destroyed in the early 1960s.

dung zurückzuziehen, und das taten sie auch. Außenminister Jan Masaryk (1886–1948, Sohn von Tomáš Masaryk) sagte: »Ich ging nach Moskau als tschechischer Minister und kehrte als Lakai Moskaus zurück«. Im November des Jahres entkamen er und zwei andere nicht-kommunistische Minister nur knapp einem Attentat. Masaryk war machtlos, als sogenannte »Aktionskomitees«, die in der Regel aus einem Mitglied des Reinigungspersonals, einem Wachmann und einem Handwerker bestanden, in seinem Ministerium eingerichtet und dafür andere wichtige Mitglieder entlassen wurden. Systematisch durchsetzten die Kommunisten Polizei, Geheimdienste und Armee mit ihren Mitgliedern. Um nichts dem Zufall zu überlassen, wurden die Arbeiter mit russischen Waffen versorgt, bekamen rote Armbinden und patrouillierten als sogenannte Volksmiliz durch die Straßen und Bahnhöfe. Als Studenten sich zu einem Marsch auf die Burg zusammenschlossen, um ihre Unterstützung für Präsident Beneš zum Ausdruck zu bringen, blockierten Polizei und Volksmiliz den Weg und trieben die Menge mit Schlagstöcken auseinander. Die Aktionskomitees übernahmen die Lokalverwaltung, Zeitungen, Banken, öffentliche Einrichtungen sowie die Gebäude der oppositionellen Parteien. Dabei waren sie genauso illegal wie die bewaffneten Milizen.

Am 20. Februar 1948 gaben zwölf nicht-kommunistische Minister aus Protest gegen die kommunistische Übernahme der Polizei ihren Rücktritt bekannt. Am Nachmittag des 25. Februar trafen Klement Gottwald und Präsident Beneš auf dem Hradschin zusammen. Unter dem spürbaren Druck der bewaffneten Milizen – und vom Militär im Stich gelassen, dessen Kommandant General Ludvík Svoboda (1895–1979), ein geheimes KSČ-Mitglied, ein Eingreifen untersagt hatte – mußte sich Beneš Gottwalds Forderungen beugen und die neue Ministerliste unterzeichnen. Die vakanten Sitze wurden von der KSČ besetzt. Als Beneš am 2. Juni von seinem Amt als Staatspräsident zurücktrat, wurde Gottwald sein Nachfolger. Die kommunistische Macht- übernahme war vollzogen. Beneš starb am 3. September mit dem Gefühl, von allen Seiten betrogen worden zu sein.

Das tragischste Ereignis am Ende dieser drei turbulenten Nachkriegsjahren geschah am 10. März 1948, als man den Leichnam Jan Masaryks unter dem Fenster seiner Dienstwohnung im Czernin-Palast auf dem Loretánské-Platz fand. Über viele Jahre wurde die offizielle Version aufrechterhalten, Masaryk habe sich aus dem Fenster gestürzt. Aber nach den Aussagen von František August, einem höheren Offizier des tschechoslowakischen Staatssicherheitsdienstes (StB), der später in den Westen floh, war Masaryk auf Anordnung des NKWD ermordet worden, weil er die Tschechoslowakei habe verlassen wollen. Major Augustin Schramm, der die Ermordung organisiert hatte, wurde selbst kurze Zeit später erschossen. Derjenige, den man offiziell für Schramms Ermordung anklagte, wurde prompt hingerichtet. Der Mann aber, der um die Identität von Schramms wahrem Mörder wußte, fiel einem Attentat zum Opfer; man stopfte seinen Leichnam in einen Sack und verbrannte ihn in einem Hochofen in Ostrava. Alle Unterlagen zu dem Fall wurden in den frühen 60er Jahren vernichtet.

une tentative d'assassinat est fomentée contre lui et deux autres ministres non-communistes. Il se retrouve sans pouvoir face aux soi-disant Comités d'Action qui se constituent dans son ministère – généralement une femme de ménage, un portier et un autre employé subalterne – pendant que ses collaborateurs de valeur perdent leur poste. Ne laissant rien au hasard, les communistes arment le prolétariat de nouveaux fusils soviétiques, leur attribuent des bandeaux rouges et les envoient patrouiller dans les rues et les gares, sous le nom de Milice du Peuple. Lorsque des étudiants marchent sur le Château pour soutenir le président Beneš, la police et la milice bloquent leur route et les rouent de coups. Les Comités d'Action prennent en main l'administration locale, les journaux, les banques, les services publics et les immeubles des partis d'opposition. Comme les milices, ces comités sont illégaux.

Le 12 février 1948, douze ministres non-communistes démissionnent pour protester contre la prise en main de la police par les communistes. L'après-midi du 25 février, Klement Gottwald a une confrontation avec le président Beneš au Hradčany. Sous la menace explicite des milices armées – et abandonné par les forces armées dont le chef, le général Ludvík Svoboda (1895–1979), appartient secrètement au KSČ – Beneš doit céder aux exigences de Gottwald, et lui demande de former un gouvernement. Les postes vacants sont occupés par des membres du KSČ et à la démission de Beneš, le 2 juin, Gottwald devient président. La prise du pouvoir par les communistes est totale. Le 3 septembre, se sentant complètement trahi, Beneš meurt.

Le post-scriptum le plus tragique de ces années d'après-guerre mouvementées se produit le 10 mars 1948, lorsque le corps de Jan Masaryk est découvert devant le palais Czernin, place Loretánské. Pendant de nombreuses années, la version officielle restera qu'il s'était jeté lui-même du haut des fenêtres, mais selon František August, haut responsable de la Sécurité d'État tchécoslovaque (StB) qui passera plus tard à l'Ouest, Masaryk a été assassiné sur les ordres du NKVD, parce qu'il projetait de quitter la Tchécoslovaquie. L'homme qui organisa ce meurtre fut le major Augustin Schramm, lui-même tué peu après. L'homme officiellement accusé d'avoir tiré

People's Militia in the Old Town Square.

Volksmiliz am Altstädter Ring.

La Milice populaire, place de la Vieille ville.

Klement Gottwald (center) and Rudolf Slánský (right).
Klement Gottwald (Mitte) und Rudolf Slánský (rechts).
Klement Gottwald (au centre) et Rudolf Slánský (à droite).

Jan Masaryk's death marked the end of the democratic era. Many other lives were extinguished in the wake of the February coup. Among them was Milada Horáková, a hero of the underground and a Nazi concentration-camp survivor, then a democratic Member of Parliament in 1945–48, who was tried on trumped-up charges of treason and executed in 1950. In that year alone, fourteen executions and fifty-two life sentences were handed out. Many shopkeepers and tradesmen were dragged off to prison, where they awaited trial by the so-called People's Tribunals, whose decisions were based not on law but on "sound class feeling." In all, 50,000 people were arrested. The prison near Ruzyně airport became notorious. Many Catholic priests (including two bishops) and 2500 monks were jailed and the monasteries and churches closed. The citizens of Prague dreaded Thursdays and Fridays, when the Central Committee met: new arrests were made on those two days.

Photographs of Stalin, in which his pockmarked complexion was retouched to a velvety-peach smoothness, were snapped up by the faithful and displayed in offices and private flats. At mass rallies Prague Young Communists chanted: "We are the new generation, we are Gottwald's generation." They took an oath of allegiance to the Soviet Union. Young parents gave Russian names to their newborn children: "Ivan" was the most popular. Various slogans became part of the new faith, including Maxim Gorky's "Man – that has a proud ring to it."

The Party idealists worked to implement free medical care, old-age pensions and vacations for the workers. Housing, jobs and culture were to be redistributed equally to everybody. Industry was nationalized, farms collectivized and history rewritten for the new generation. Children were encouraged to denounce their parents as reactionaries. The Minister of Education, Moscow-trained Zdeněk Nejedlý, wasted no time in purging teachers with pro-Western or democratic sympathies.

Socialist B-movies were shown in the cinemas. A great hit was *Cossacks from the Kuban*, which portrayed happy life on a collective farm. Films

Der Tod Jan Masaryks markierte das Ende der demokratischen Ära. Viele Menschen verloren im Zusammenhang mit den Vorfällen im Februar ihr Leben. Unter ihnen war Milada Horáková, eine Heldin der Widerstandsbewegung und Überlebende des Konzentrationslagers, die von 1945 bis 1948 als Mitglied der demokratischen Parteien im Parlament saß. Sie wurde wegen angeblichen Hochverrats angeklagt und 1950 hingerichtet. Allein in diesem Jahr verhängte man 14 Hinrichtungen und 52 lebenslängliche Haftstrafen. Viele Ladenbesitzer und Kaufleute kamen ins Gefängnis, wo sie ihren Prozeß vor dem sogenannten Volkstribunal erwarteten, dessen Urteile nicht auf dem Gesetz, sondern auf dem »gesunden Klassenbewußtsein« beruhten. Insgesamt wurden 50.000 Menschen verhaftet, berüchtigt war das Gefängnis am Ruzyně-Flughafen. Viele katholische Priester (einschließlich zweier Bischöfe) und 2.500 Mönche wurden inhaftiert und die Klöster und Kirchen geschlossen. Die Bürger von Prag fürchteten die Donnerstage und Freitage, an denen das Zentralkomitee tagte, denn an diesen beiden Tagen fanden neue Verhaftungen statt.

Fotos von Stalin, auf denen sein pockennarbiges Gesicht mit einer samtenen Pfirsichhaut retouchiert war, stellten seine Anhänger in Büros und Privatwohnungen auf. Auf Großveranstaltungen rief die kommunistische Jugend: »Wir sind die neue Generation, wir sind Gottwalds Generation«. Sie schwor einen Treueeid auf die Sowjetunion, junge Eltern gaben ihren Kindern russische Namen, von denen »Iwan« der beliebteste war. Verschiedene Schlagworte wurden Teil des neuen Glaubensbekenntnisses, beispielsweise Maxim Gorkis: »Der Mensch – das hat einen stolzen Beiklang.«

Die Idealisten in der Partei setzten sich für eine freie medizinische Versorgung, freie Renten und Urlaub für die Arbeiter ein. Wohnraum, Arbeit und Kultur sollten gleichmäßig an alle verteilt werden. Die Industrie wurde verstaatlicht, die Landwirtschaft kollektiviert und die Geschichte für die neue Generation umgeschrieben. Man ermutigte Kinder, ihre Eltern als Reaktionäre zu denunzieren. Der in Moskau ausgebildete Erziehungsminister Zdeněk Nejedlý machte kurzen Prozeß mit Lehrern, die ihre pro-westlichen oder demokratischen Sympathien nicht verbargen.

Die Kinos zeigten sozialistische Filme zweiter Klasse. Ein großer Kassenschlager war *Kuban-Kosaken*, der das glückliche Leben auf einem kollektivierten Bauernhof beschrieb. Zumeist handelten solche Filme von Saboteuren und Spionen, die versuchten, die Einheit der Arbeiterklasse zu zerstören. Die Buchläden waren vollgestopft mit Büchern über die große Verschwörung gegen die Partei und den Genossen Stalin. 1951 hing der Verfolgungswahn wie eine dicke Wolke über Prag, selbst die Anhänger der Kommunisten blieben nicht vom Terror verschont. Zwischen 1948 und 1954 war jeder 20. Hingerichtete ein Kommunist und selbst die Getreuesten waren nicht sicher. Eines der prominenten Opfer der Säuberungswelle war der Generalsekretär der KSČ, Rudolf Slánský (1901–52) – ein pathologischer Dogmatiker mit großem Anerkennungsbedürfnis und Machthunger und selbst Initiator politischer Säuberungen: Im November 1952 fand im Pankratius-Gerichtshof der spektakulärste Schauprozeß der

sur Schramm fut promptement exécuté. Celui qui connaissait l'identité réelle du tueur de Schramm fut également assassiné, son corps jeté dans un sac brûlé dans une chaudière à Ostrava. Tous les documents concernant cette affaire ont été détruits au début des années 60.

La mort de Jan Masaryk marque la fin de la période démocratique. De nombreuses autres vies seront sacrifiées au coup d'État de février. Ainsi Milada Horáková, héros de la clandestinité, survivant des camps de concentration et député démocrate en 1945–48, sera jugé sur des charges montées de toutes pièces pour trahison et exécuté en 1950. Au cours de cette seule année, quatorze exécutions ont lieu et cinquante-deux condamnations à mort sont prononcées. De nombreux commerçants sont traînés en prison, où ils attendent leur procès devant les «tribunaux du peuple», dont les décisions ne s'appuient pas sur la loi, mais sur «un juste sentiment de classe». En tout, 50 000 personnes sont arrêtées, et la prison proche de l'aéroport de Ruzyně devient célèbre. De nombreux prêtres catholiques (y compris deux évêques) et 2 500 moines sont incarcérés et des monastères et des églises fermés. Les Pragois en viennent à redouter les jeudis et les vendredis, jours de réunion du Comité central, où les arrestations se font plus nombreuses.

Des photographies de Staline, dont la peau tavelée est retouchée pour lui donner une douceur de pêche, sont placardées par les fidèles dans les bureaux et les appartements. Lors de manifestations de masse, les jeunesses communistes scandent pendant des heures jusqu'à ce que leurs cordes vocales n'en puissent plus: «Nous sommes la nouvelle génération, nous sommes la génération Gottwald.» Ils jurent allégeance à l'Union soviétique «J'aimerai toujours l'Union soviétique» et débordent d'énergie et d'enthousiasme, même si ces débordements ne donnent rien de très concret. De jeunes parents donnent des noms russes à leurs enfants, «Ivan» étant le plus populaire. De nombreux slogans confortent cette nouvelle foi, dont celui de Maxim Gorky: «Homme et fier de l'être».

Les idéalistes du Parti travaillent à l'amélioration du système de santé, des retraites et des congés pour les travailleurs. Le logement, le travail et la culture doivent être redistribués à égalité. Les industries sont nationalisées, les fermes collectivisées et l'histoire réécrite pour la nouvelle génération. Les enfants sont encouragés à dénoncer leurs parents réactionnaires. Zdeněk Nejedlý, ministre de l'Éducation formé à Moscou, ne perd pas de temps à purger le système de l'enseignement des professeurs à sympathies pro-occidentales ou démocratiques.

Des films de catégorie B mais socialistes sont projetés dans les cinémas. Un des plus grands succès est *Cosaques du Kuban*, qui fait le portrait du bonheur de vivre dans une ferme collective. Les films montrent souvent des saboteurs et des espions essayant de nuire à l'unité de la classe des travailleurs. Les librairies sont remplies d'une vaste littérature sur la grande conspiration contre le Parti et le Camarade Staline. En 1951, la paranoïa se répand sur Prague, telle un nuage chargé. Les convaincus eux-mêmes ne sont pas exclus de la terreur. Au cours des années 1948–54, un exécuté

typically featured saboteurs and spies striving to disrupt the unity of the working class. The bookstores were stocked with extensive literature about the great conspiracy against the Party and Comrade Stalin. By 1951 paranoia hung over Prague like a thick cloud. The believers themselves were not excluded from the terror. In the years 1948–54, one in twenty of those executed was a Communist. Not even the most ardent were safe. Rudolf Slánský (1901–52), First Secretary of the KSČ – a dogmatist pathologically eager for recognition and power and instigator of political purges – was tried and executed. In November 1952 the most spectacular show trial of the Stalin era took place in Prague's Pankrác court. All fourteen accused were former Party officials, eleven of them Jewish. They were charged with being "traitors, Trotskyists, Titoists, Zionists, bourgeois nationalists and enemies of the Czech people." Most of them, under coercion, confessed to everything "for the good of the Party." Eleven were hanged and cremated, and their ashes turned over to the StB for disposal. The driver of the official limousine displayed typical Czech humor, saying to the StB men, "This is the first time I've carried fourteen people in this car – the three of us and those eleven in the sack." They scattered the ashes on an icy road outside Prague.

According to some members of Klement Gottwald's personal guard, from then on he took to drink. Following Stalin's orders was not the easiest job for the Moscow-trained President. The Soviet leader died on 5 March 1953. Soon after returning from his funeral, Gottwald himself died of syphilis (on 14 March). The Vítkov National Memorial was turned into his mausoleum and his mummified body was kept on display by an army of doctors, engineers and make-up artists from the Barrandov film studios, until in 1963 he was finally cremated. Antonín Zápotocký (1884–1957) succeeded to the presidency and Party leadership. On his death in November 1957 he was succeeded by Antonín Novotný (1904–75).

Between 1945 and 1948 the economy had looked promising. But after the coup Moscow demanded a complete realignment of Czechoslovakia's trade with the Soviet Union. The emphasis was to be on heavy industry. A centralized economic planning system was set up in Prague to decide total production, manpower, investment and even prices. Inflation became a major problem and in 1953 the currency was drastically reformed. Strikes broke out in factories; they were swiftly and brutally put down by Communist Border Guard units.

In November 1956 these same units were drafted to help the pro-Soviet elements quash the Hungarian uprising. Aid from Czechoslovakia to Hungary consisted not of food, as some thought, but of truckloads of truncheons. The bloody suppression of the Hungarian insurgents by the Soviet army caused panic in Prague.

The legendary days when for every ordinary citizen in Prague there were three journalists, four painters and five authors were long gone. Instead, for every citizen there was an informer willing to turn him in on the strength of gossip. People withdrew into themselves and became secretive. Wearily, they watched the black Tatra limousines,

Stalin-Ära statt. Alle 14 Angeklagten, darunter Slánský, waren ehemalige Parteibonzen, elf von ihnen Juden. Sie wurden als »Verräter, Trotzkisten, Titoisten, Zionisten, bürgerliche Nationale und Feinde des tschechischen Volkes« angeklagt. Die meisten von ihnen gestanden nach der Anwendung von Druckmitteln alles »zum Wohle der Partei«. Man hängte und verbrannte elf der Angeklagten und übergab ihre Asche der StB. Der Fahrer der Staatslimousine bewies den typisch tschechischen Sinn für Humor, als er zu den StB-Männern sagte: » Das ist das erste Mal, daß ich 14 Leute in meinem Auto befördere: uns drei und die elf in dem Sack.« Die Asche wurde auf einer vereisten Straße außerhalb Prags verstreut.

Nach Angaben einiger Mitglieder seiner persönlicher Wache verfiel Gottwald von diesem Zeitpunkt an dem Alkoholismus. Für den in Moskau ausgebildeten Präsidenten war es nicht immer einfach, Stalins Anordnungen zu folgen. Der sowjetische Führer starb am 5. März 1953. Kurz nach seiner Rückkehr von Stalins Begräbnis (am 14. März) verstarb Gottwald an Syphilis. Die nationale Gedenkstätte Vítkov wurde zu einem Mausoleum umgewandelt und eine Armee von Ärzten, Ingenieuren und Maskenbildnern aus den Barrandov-Studios konservierten Gottwalds mumifizierten Leichnam, bis er schließlich 1963 verbrannt wurde. Antonín Zápotocký (1884–1957) folgte ihm als Präsident und Parteiführer. Nach dessen Tod im November 1957 übernahm Antonín Novotný (1904–1975) diese Ämter.

Zwischen 1945 und 1948 hatte sich die tschechische Wirtschaft positiv entwickelt. Nach der Machtübernahme aber forderte Moskau eine völlige Neuorganisation des tschechischen Handels mit der Sowjetunion. Den Hauptteil der tschechischen Exporte in die UdSSR machte die Schwerindustrie aus. In Prag wurde ein zentralisiertes System zur Wirtschaftsplanung geschaffen, das alle Entscheidungen über Produktion, Arbeitskraft, Investitionen und sogar über die Preise fällte. Die Inflation stieg so stark an, daß 1953 eine tiefgreifende Währungsreform durchgeführt wurde. Daraufhin brachen in den Fabriken Unruhen aus, die kommunistische Grenzschutzeinheiten schnell und brutal beendeten.

Im November 1956 wurden dieselben Einheiten zur Unterstützung der pro-sowjetischen Elemente gegen das ungarische Aufbegehren rekrutiert. Die tschechische Hilfe für Ungarn bestand nicht aus Lebensmitteln, wie einige glaubten, sondern aus Schlagstöcken. Die blutige Unterdrückung des ungarischen Aufstandes durch die Rote Armee löste in Prag Panik aus.

Die legendären Zeiten, in denen auf jeden Prager Bürger drei Journalisten, vier Maler und fünf Schriftsteller kamen, waren lange vorbei. Statt dessen fiel auf jeden Bürger ein Informant, der bereit war, ihn auf Grund von Gerüchten zu denunzieren. Die Menschen zogen sich zurück und wurden immer verschlossener. Müde beobachteten sie die schwarzen Tatra-Limousinen mit ihren Haifischflossen-Kotflügeln und verhängten Fenstern, die die Rote Bourgeoisie von und zum Hradschin fuhren. Die verarmte Bevölkerung bezahlte für deren Villen, Jagdhütten und Luxusgüter. Oft standen die Men-

A black Tatra car crossing the Charles Bridge.
Schwarze Tatra-Limousine beim Überqueren der Karlsbrücke.
Tatra noire traversant le pont Charles.

sur vingt est communiste. Même les plus ardents ne sont pas en sécurité. Rudolf Slánský (1901–1952), secrétaire général du KSČ, dogmatiste pathologiquement avide de reconnaissance et de pouvoir et instigateur des purges politiques, est littéralement écrasé par la machine du Parti. En novembre 1952, le plus spectaculaire des procès à grand spectacle de l'ère stalinienne se déroule au tribunal pragois de Pankrác. Les quatorze accusés sont d'anciens responsables du parti, onze Juifs. On les accuse d'être des « traîtres, trotskistes, titistes, sionistes, nationalistes bourgeois et ennemis du peuple tchèque ». La plupart d'entre eux avouent tout et n'importe quoi « pour le bien du parti ». Onze sont pendus et incinérés, et leurs cendres données à la Sécurité d'État pour être dispersées. Le chauffeur d'une limousine officielle, faisant preuve d'un humour tchèque typique, dira aux policiers : « C'est la première fois que je transporte quatorze personnes dans cette voiture, nous trois et les onze dans le sac. » Les cendres sont disséminées sur une route glacée de la banlieue de Prague.

Selon quelques membres de la garde personnelle de Klement Gottwald, c'est à ce moment que celui-ci se met à boire. Suivre les ordres de Staline n'est pas un travail facile, même pour le président formé à Moscou. Le dictateur soviétique meurt le 5 mars 1953. Rentrant des funérailles de Staline, Gottwald disparaît à son tour le 14 mars. Le Mémorial national de Vítkov est transformé en mausolée où son corps momifié est exposé, gardé par une armée de médecins, de techniciens et de maquilleurs des studios de cinéma de Barrandov, jusqu'en 1963, date où l'on se décida à l'incinérer. Antonín Zápotocký (1884–1957) lui succède à la présidence et à la tête du Parti. À sa mort, en novembre 1957, il est remplacé par Antonin Novotný (1904–1975).

De 1945 à 1948, l'économie avait semblé pleine de promesses, mais après le coup d'État, Moscou exige brutalement une réorientation complète du commerce tchèque vers l'Union soviétique. L'accent doit être mis sur l'industrie lourde. Un système de planification économique centralisé est créé pour décider de la production, de la main d'œuvre des investissements et même des prix. L'inflation

Wenceslas Square in the 1960s.
Wenzelsplatz in den sechziger Jahren.
La place Venceslas dans les années 60.

with their shark-like fins and curtained windows carrying the Red bourgeoisie to and from Hradčany. The impoverished population paid for their villas, hunting lodges and luxuries. People queued for food, often during their working hours. Bureaucracy reigned and very little was done. "We pretend to work and they pretend to pay us," it was often said.

Slowly, however, change crept in. A gradual coalescence of change-seeking groups – in particular economists, social scientists, writers, filmmakers and students, as well as Slovaks (who felt that their interests were disregarded) and some progressive Party officials – helped the country move away from hardline Communism towards the fusion of Socialism, democracy and nationalism it had once enjoyed. From the early 1960s, it was public knowledge that the Communist system was bankrupt.

In January 1963, at a symposium on contemporary prose, attacks were made on the restrictions of Socialist Realism. In May Kafka was rehabilitated. Tourists were allowed to visit Prague in order to boost the flow of hard currency. Gradually, a fresh breeze was being felt in Czechoslovak culture. Simultaneously, people began to dare to criticize the Soviet Union. In the spring of 1965 the Czechs refused to add to the slogan "20th Anniversary of the Liberation of Czechoslovakia" the important words: "by the Soviet Army." To add insult to injury, during the May Day celebrations students carried a banner inscribed "Long Live the Soviet Union but at its own expense." During a performance of *Hamlet* the leading actor Radovan Lukavský received wild applause when, with great feeling, he declaimed that "Something is rotten in the state of Denmark." By now even the policemen in the cultural section of the StB knew that Lukavský did not mean Denmark.

By 1967 a relatively free decentralized market economy had gradually been introduced. Disenchantment with the Soviet model was by now

schen während ihrer Arbeitszeit für Lebensmittel an. Die Bürokratie regierte, und nur wenig wurde getan. »Wir tun so, als ob wir arbeiten, und sie tun so, als ob sie uns bezahlen« hieß es häufig.

Aber langsam stellten sich Veränderungen ein. Eine allmähliche Verbindung von reformfreudigen Gruppen – darunter besonders Wirtschafts- und Sozialwissenschaftler, Schriftsteller, Filmemacher, Studenten, Slowaken (die ihre Interessen vernachlässigt sahen) und einige progressive Parteigenossen – unterstützten das Land auf seinem Weg vom strengen Kommunismus hin zu der Mischung von Sozialismus, Demokratie und Nationalismus, die das Land schon einmal regiert hatte. Seit den frühen 60er Jahren war es allgemein bekannt, daß das kommunistische System bankrott war.

Im Januar 1963 wurde auf einem Symposion für zeitgenössische Prosa Kritik an den Einschränkungen des Sozialistischen Realismus laut. Im Mai desselben Jahres rehabilitierte man Kafka. Touristen war der Besuch in der Stadt erlaubt, um den Zufluß harter Währungen zu fördern. Allmählich konnte die tschechische Kultur eine frische Brise verspüren. Gleichzeitig wagten die Menschen allmählich, Kritik an der Sowjetunion zu üben. Im Frühjahr 1965 weigerten sich die Tschechen, den Parolen zum »20. Jahrestag der Befreiung der Tschechoslowakei« die wichtigen Worte »durch die sowjetische Armee« hinzuzufügen. Diese Ablehnung erfuhr noch eine Steigerung, als Studenten während der Demonstrationen zum 1. Mai ein Transparent mit den Worten »Lang lebe die Sowjetunion, aber auf ihre eigenen Kosten« trugen. Während einer Aufführung von *Hamlet* erhielt der Hauptdarsteller Radovan Lukavský tosenden Beifall, als er mit tiefer Empfindung deklamierte: »Es ist etwas faul im Staate Dänemark«. Zu diesem Zeitpunkt wußten sogar die Polizisten in der Kulturabteilung des StB, daß Lukavský nicht Dänemark meinte.

Bis 1967 war schrittweise eine relativ freie, dezentralisierte Marktwirtschaft eingeführt worden. Die tschechische kommunistische Partei fühlte sich vom sowjetischen Modell enttäuscht, unter den Intellektuellen nahm die Opposition zu. Auf dem vierten Parteitag der tschechischen Schriftstellergewerkschaft im Juni 1967 wurde die »führende Rolle der Partei« kritisiert. Der Autor Ludvík Vaculík (geboren 1926) wies darauf hin, daß die Menschen keine garantierten Bürgerrechte besäßen, es keine objektiven Kontrollorgane gebe und daß sogar die Gerichte in der Hand der Partei lägen.

Im Oktober desselben Jahres protestierten 1.500 Studenten der Prager Technischen Universität gegen ihre Lebensbedingungen in der Studentenstadt Strahov. Die Polizei trieb sie mit Tränengas und Schlagstöcken auseinander. Alexander Dubček (1921–92) und andere Reformer innerhalb der Partei, die mit den Studenten in Kontakt standen, kritisierten die harte Linie der Polizei und forderten Veränderungen, die insbesondere die Vorreiterrolle der Partei betrafen. Novotnýs Regime sah sich mit einer ernsthaften Führungskrise konfrontiert. Zwar kam im Dezember der sowjetische Staatschef Leonid Breschnew (1906–1982) noch zu einem kurzen Besuch, aber im Januar 1968 trat Novotný von

s'étend et, en 1953, la monnaie est radicalement réformée. Des grèves éclatent dans les usines, vites étouffées par des interventions brutales des unités de gardes-frontières communistes.

En novembre 1956, ces mêmes unités aideront les éléments pro-soviétiques à étouffer le soulèvement hongrois. L'aide de la Tchécoslovaquie à la Hongrie consistait non en nourriture, comme certains le pensaient, mais en camions de matraques. La sanglante répression des insurgés hongrois par l'armée soviétique provoque une panique à Prague.

La période légendaire ou pour chaque Pragois ordinaire on comptait trois journalistes, quatre peintres et cinq auteurs dramatiques était révolue depuis longtemps. Pour chaque habitant, on peut maintenant compter un informateur prêt à colporter n'importe quel ragot. Les gens se referment sur eux-mêmes et deviennent secrets. Le front soucieux, ils regardent passer les grandes limousines Tatra aux ailes effilées comme des nageoires de requin et aux fenêtres tendues de rideaux qui transportent la *nomenklatura* communiste vers le château. La population appauvrie paie pour leurs villas, leurs relais de chasse et leur vie luxueuse. Les gens font la queue pour la nourriture, souvent pendant leurs heures de travail. La bureaucratie règne et presque rien n'aboutit. « Nous prétendons travailler, et ils prétendent nous payer », disait-on alors.

Lentement, cependant, les choses changent. L'union informelle de groupes avides de changement – en particulier d'économistes, de sociologues, d'écrivains, de réalisateurs de films et d'étudiants et de Slovaques qui pensent que leurs intérêts sont négligés – aide le pays à s'éloigner de la ligne communiste dure et à aller vers cette fusion de socialisme, de démocratie et de nationalisme que le pays avait un moment connue. À partir des années 60, il devint évident que le système communiste va tout droit vers la banqueroute.

En janvier 1963, lors d'un symposium sur la prose contemporaine, des attaques sont lancées contre les contraintes du réalisme socialiste. En mai, Kafka est réhabilité. Les touristes peuvent de nouveau visiter Prague, ne serait-ce que pour faire rentrer des devises. Peu à peu, un souffle plus léger se fait sentir dans la culture tchécoslovaque. Dans le même temps, les gens commencent à oser critiquer l'Union soviétique. Au printemps 1965, les Tchèques refusent d'ajouter au slogan « XXème anniversaire de la libération de la Tchécoslovaquie », les trois mot si importants : « par l'Armée rouge ». Pour ajouter l'insulte à la blessure, des étudiants portent lors du défilé du 1er mai une bannière proclamant « Vive l'Union soviétique, mais à ses frais ». Au cours d'une représentation de *Hamlet*, le grand acteur Radovan Lukavský est frénétiquement applaudi lorsqu'il déclame : « Il y a quelques chose de pourri au royaume de Danemark. » Même les policiers de la section culturelle de la StB comprennent alors qu'il ne pense pas au Danemark.

En 1967, une économie de marché relativement libre est introduite. Le désenchantement par rapport au modèle soviétique est maintenant fortement ressenti dans le parti communiste tchèque, et une opposition grandissante se développe au sein de

strongly felt throughout the Czech Communist Party, and among the intelligentsia opposition continued to grow. At the Fourth Congress of the Czechoslovak Writers' Union in June 1967 "the leading role of the Party" was criticized, with the writer Ludvík Vaculík (b. 1926) pointing out that the citizen had no guaranteed civil rights, no objective control and even the courts were in the Party's grip.

On 31 October of that year 1500 students of the Prague Technical College's Strahov hostel protested about their living conditions. The police dispersed them with teargas and clubs. Alexander Dubček (1921–92) and other Party reformers who were in touch with the students attacked the hardline policies, urging changes, especially in the concept of the Party's leading role. Novotný's regime faced a serious leadership crisis. The Soviet leader Leonid Brezhnev (1906–82) paid a brief visit in December, but in January 1968 Novotný resigned.

The pent-up demand for reforms gathered momentum. Censorship was relaxed, the truth about trials in the 1950s began to be told and the enthusiastic masses indicated their support for "the democratic model of a Socialist society which would fully correspond to Czechoslovak conditions." On 27 June 1968 a manifesto entitled *Dva tisíce slov* (2000 Words), written by Ludvík Vaculík, appeared in the magazine *Literarní listy* (Literary Leaves), pressing for faster liberalization.

The 1960s were exciting times for Prague. A more relaxed censorship and an explosion of talent in the arts affected everyone's life profoundly. The theaters staged Eugène Ionesco (1909–94) and Samuel Beckett (1906–89), Edward Albee (b. 1928) and Friedrich Dürrenmatt (1921–90). High artistic quality and irreverent productions made theaters such as the *Semafor* (Semaphore), *Divadlo Na zábradlí* (Theater on the Balustrade), *Divadlo za branou* (Theater beyond the Gate) and *Činoherní klub* (Drama Club) immensely popular. The Theater on the Balustrade became well known for staging brilliant mime – an art form that flourishes in Prague. Ladislav Fialka (1931–91), the famous pantomime artist, performed there, as he had in the 1950s; in the late 1960s Jan Grossman (1925–93) directed plays there; and the playwright (and future President) Václav Havel (b. 1936) began his career there as a stagehand. His first play, *The Garden Party*, was performed at the theater in 1963.

Bohumil Hrabal (1914–97) emerged as the leading novelist of the 1960s. His book *Closely Observed Trains* (1967) was made into a film by Jiří Menzel (b. 1928) and won an Oscar in 1967. It is a gently poetical film, showing everyone as human, war as absurd and heroism as accidental; it contains quirky erotic scenes and genuinely funny moments. Miloš Forman (b. 1932) made *The Firemen's Ball*, released in 1968 and nominated for an Oscar. It was a vicious satire on inefficient Socialist bureaucracy and mocked human failings such as greed, pomposity, smugness and self-importance. It was one of the cruellest as well as one of the funniest among the Czechoslovak New Wave productions. The Communists hated it because it ridiculed the working class – "which of course was not good for their business," as Forman commented drily in his autobiography. Vojtěch Jasný (b. 1925) won the

seinem Posten als Erster Sekretär des Zentralkomitees zurück. Sein Nachfolger wurde Dubček.

Endlich wurde der aufgestauten Forderung nach Reformen entsprochen: Die Pressezensur wurde aufgehoben, die Bevölkerung erfuhr die Wahrheit über die Prozesse der 50er Jahre. Die begeisterten Massen zeigten ihre Unterstützung für »das demokratische Modell einer sozialistischen Gesellschaft, das mit den tschechischen Bedingungen völlig übereinstimmte«. Am 27. Juni 1968 erschien in der Zeitschrift *Literarní listy* (Literarische Blätter) das »Manifest der 2000 Worte« (*Dva tisíce slov*) von Ludvík Vaculík, in dem er eine schnellere Liberalisierung verlangte.

Die 60er Jahre waren eine aufregende Zeit für Prag. Dank der gelockerten Zensur setzte das Geistesleben zu einem Höhenflug an und erlebten Literatur, Theater und Film eine neue Blüte. Die Theater führten Stücke von Eugène Ionesco (1909–94) und Samuel Beckett (1906–89), Edward Albee (geboren 1928) und Friedrich Dürrenmatt (1921–90) auf. Die *Semafor*-Kleinbühne, das *Divadlo Na zábradlí* (Theater am Geländer), das *Divdlo za branou* (Theater hinter dem Tor) und der *Činoherni Club* (Schauspiel-Club) waren wegen ihrer hohen künstlerischen Qualität und ihrer respektlosen Produktionen äußerst beliebt. Das »Theater am Geländer« wurde durch seine großartigen Pantomimen berühmt – eine Kunstgattung, die sich in Prag zur vollen Blüte entfaltete. Hier trat in den 50er Jahren der Pantomine Ladislav Fialka (1931–91) auf, arbeitete Jan Grossman (geboren 1936) in den späten 60er Jahren als Regisseur und hier begann der Dramatiker (und spätere Präsident) Václav Havel seine Karriere als Kulissenschieber. In diesem Theater gab Havel 1963 sein Debüt mit dem Schauspiel *Das Gartenfest*.

Bohumil Hrabal (1914–97) avancierte zum führenden Romanschriftsteller der 60er Jahre. Sein Buch *Reise nach Sondervorschrift, Zuglauf überwacht* wurde von Jiří Menzel (geboren 1928) verfilmt und gewann 1967 einen Oskar. Dieser sanft poetische Film zeichnet alle Beteiligten von ihrer menschlichen Seite, erklärt den Krieg für absurd und Heldentum für ein Zufallsprodukt; er enthält eigenwillige erotische Szenen und ausgesprochen komische Momente. *Der Feuerwehrball* von Miloš Forman (geboren 1932) wurde 1968 vorgestellt und für einen Oskar nominiert. Der Film ist eine bösartige Satire auf die völlig uneffiziente sozialistische Bürokratie und karikiert menschliche Schwächen wie Gier, Prahlerei, Blasiertheit und Wichtigtuerei. Er zählt zu den grausamsten, aber gleichzeitig auch zu den witzigsten Produktionen der tschechoslowakischen »Neuen Welle«. Die Kommunisten lehnten den Film ab, weil er die Arbeiterklasse lächerlich mache, »was natürlich nicht gut für ihr Geschäft war«, wie Forman in seiner Autobiographie trocken anmerkte. 1968 gewann Vojtěch Jasný (geboren 1925) für *Alle meine guten Landsleute* den Sonderpreis der Jury in Cannes. Věra Chytilová (geboren 1929) hatte die Freiheit, mit ihren absonderlichen Phantasien zu spielen, wie beispielsweise in *Gänseblümchen*, 1960. Ihre Filme galten als »experimentell«, weil sie den traditionellen Handlungsfaden ablehnte. Der wahrscheinlich spektakulärste Film der 60er Jahre aber war Františeks Vláčils (geboren 1924) *Markéta Lazarová*, ein episches

A still from the film *Markéta Lazarová*.
Standphoto aus dem Film *Markéta Lazarová*.
Image du film *Markéta Lazarová*.

l'intelligentsia. Au quatrième congrès de l'Union des Écrivains tchécoslovaques, en juin 1967 « le rôle moteur du Parti », l'écrivain Ludvík Vaculík (né en 1926) montre que les droits civiques ne sont pas garantis, que les contrôles objectifs n'existent pas, et que même les tribunaux sont aux mains du Parti.

Le 31 octobre de la même année, 1500 étudiants de la cité du Collège technique Strahov protestent contre leurs conditions de logement. La police les disperse avec des matraques et du gaz lacrymogène. Alexander Dubček (1921–1992) et d'autres réformateurs du Parti en contact avec les étudiants lancent des attaques contre la ligne dure, réclamant des changements, en particulier dans le concept de rôle moteur du Parti. Le régime de Novotný se trouve face à une sérieuse crise de pouvoir. Le leader soviétique Léonid Brejnev (1906–1982) se rend à Prague en décembre pour une brève visite, mais en janvier 1968, Novotný démissionne.

La demande de réformes, jusqu'alors refoulée, se libère d'un coup. La censure se relâche, la vérité sur les procès des années 50 commence à se faire jour, et des masses enthousiastes apportent leur soutien au « modèle démocratique d'une société qui réponde pleinement aux conditions tchécoslovaques ». Le 27 juin 1968, un manifeste intitulé « 2000 mots », rédigé par Luvík Vaculík, est publié dans le magazine *Literarní listy* (Feuilles de littérature). Il demande l'accélération de la libéralisation.

Pour Prague, les années 60 sont passionnantes. Une censure moins présente et une explosion de talents artistiques donnent à chacun le goût de revivre. Les théâtres montent des pièces de Eugène Ionesco (1909–1994) et de Samuel Beckett (1906–1989), d'Edward Albee (né en 1928) et de Friedrich Dürrenmatt (1921–1990). Des spectacles irrévérencieux et de haute qualité artistiques sont donnés dans des théâtres comme le *Semafor*, le *Divadlo Na zábradlí* (Théâtre sur la balustrade), le *Divadlo za branou* (Théâtre derrière les Portes) et l'immensément populaire *Činoherní klub* (Club dramatique). Le Théâtre sur la balustrade devient célèbre par ses brillantes pantomimes, forme d'art

Soviet tanks on the streets of Prague in 1968.
Sowjetische Panzer 1968 in den Straßen von Prag.
Tanks soviétiques dans les rues de Prague, en 1968.

Special Jury Prize at Cannes for *All My Good Countrymen* in 1968. Věra Chytilová (b. 1929) was allowed to experiment with her whimsical fantasies, such as *The Daisies*, 1960. Her films were described as "experimental" because she refused to spoil them with a traditional plot. But perhaps the most spectacular film made in the 1960s was František Vláčil's (b. 1924) *Markéta Lazarová*, an epic canvas set in the barbaric Middle Ages. This personal ode to paganism has the quality of a painting and is visually the most stimulating film ever made in Czechoslovakia, as well as being the most expensive in the history of Communist cinema. (Money was lavished on the production, because Vláčil's script was based on a novel by Vladislav Vančura (1891–1942), the Communist writer who died in the wave of Gestapo terror after Heydrich's assassination.)

In the months leading up to the Prague Spring, as the period came to be known (its name borrowed from the annual music festival), ordinary Czechs were allowed to travel to the West. For many it was their first encounter with those described in Communist vernacular as "decadent imperialists, workers' bloodsuckers, American barbarians, architects of germ warfare" – and what they found they loved. The Beatles, hippies, day-glo colors, geometric patterns, and ads fired the imagination of the Czech visitors. They had always suspected that the West was ahead, contrary to Communist propaganda, but they had not been prepared for the abundance of images created by inventive minds. They returned home with many new ideas and the feeling that they had finally become part of a civilized Europe.

At home, the media were reporting on politically sensitive stories and, gently at first, probing both the past and the present. But many people did not see the dark clouds gathering above the Castle and Dubček's reformers: they were too preoccupied with the "lightness of being." Also, as ever, they were

Gemälde aus dem barbarischen Mittelalter. Diese persönliche Ode an den Paganismus ist von den Bildern her der schönste, aber auch der teuerste Filme, der jemals in der kommunistischen Tschechoslowakei gedreht worden ist. (Die Produktion wurde großzügig mit finanziellen Mitteln ausgestattet, weil Vláčils Drehbuch auf einem Roman des kommunistischen Schriftstellers Vladislav Vančura (1891–1942) beruhte, der während der Terrorwelle der Gestapo nach der Ermordung Heydrichs gestorben war.)

In den Monaten des Prager Frühling, wie diese Periode nach dem alljährlichen Musikfestival später genannt wurde, durften alle Tschechen ins westliche Ausland reisen. Für viele von ihnen war es die erste Begegnung mit denjenigen, die in der kommunistischen Propaganda als »dekadente Imperialisten, Blutsauger der Arbeiterklasse, amerikanische Barbaren und Begründer der biologischen Kriegsführung« beschrieben wurden – und sie mochten das, was sie vorfanden. Die Beatles, die Hippies, Leuchtfarben und geometrische Muster beflügelten die Phantasie der tschechischen Besucher. Trotz der kommunistischen Propaganda hatten sie immer vermutet, daß der Westen ihnen voraus war, aber auf die Überfülle der Bilder, die phantasievolle Geister geschaffen hatten, waren sie nicht vorbereitet. Sie kehrten mit vielen neuen Ideen und dem Gefühl zurück, endlich ein Teil des zivilisierten Europas geworden zu sein.

Daheim berichteten die Medien über politisch umstrittene Themen und untersuchten zunächst behutsam Vergangenheit und Gegenwart. Aber die Menschen sahen nicht die dunklen Wolken, die sich über dem Hradschin und Dubčeks Reformern zusammenbrauten. Sie waren zu sehr mit der »Leichtigkeit des Seins« beschäftigt. Außerdem wurden sie – wie immer – im Unklaren gelassen: Das Säbel-Rasseln ließ sich außerhalb der Korridore des Hradschin nicht vernehmen.

spécifiquement pragoise. Ladislav Fialka (1931–1991) le célèbre mime y joue, comme dans les années 50. À la fin des années 60, Jan Grossman (1925–1993) y dirige des pièces et l'auteur dramatique – et futur président – Václav Havel (né en 1936) y commence sa carrière comme machiniste. Sa première pièce *La Fête en plein air* y est jouée en 1963.

Bohumil Hrabal (1914–1997) est le plus célèbre romancier des années 60. Son livre *Trains étroitement surveillés* (1967) est porté à l'écran par Jiří Menzel (né en 1928) et remporte un oscar la même année. C'est une œuvre gentiment poétique, montrant l'humanité cachée en chaque être, que la guerre est absurde et l'héroïsme un accident de l'histoire. Il contient de petites scènes érotiques maladroites et des moments très drôles. Miloš Forman (né en 1932) réalise *Le Bal des pompiers* en 1968 qui lui vaut une nomination aux Oscars. Il s'agit d'une satire habile sur l'inefficacité de la bureaucratie socialiste, qui se moque de travers humains comme la rapacité, le goût des honneurs, la suffisance, la vanité. C'est l'une de productions les plus cruelles et les plus drôles de la nouvelle vague tchécoslovaque. Les communistes la haïssent parce qu'elle ridiculise la classe ouvrière, «ce qui bien sûr n'était pas bon pour leurs affaires », comme le commentera sèchement Forman dans son autobiographie. Vojtěch Jasný (né en 1925) remporte le prix spécial du jury au Festival de Cannes pour *Mes chers concitoyens* en 1968. Věra Chytilová (née en 1929), peut se lancer dans la mise en scène de son imaginaire personnel, comme avec *Les Petites Marguerites* (1960). Ses films sont qualifiés d'expérimentaux car elle se refuse à les gâcher par une construction traditionnelle. Mais la réalisation la plus spectaculaire des années 60 est sans doute *Markéta Lazarová* de František Vláčil (né en 1924), saga se déroulant au Moyen-Âge. Cette ode très personnelle au paganisme possède la qualité d'une fresque. C'est le film le plus stimulant visuellement jamais tourné en Tchécoslovaquie et le plus coûteux de l'histoire du cinéma communiste. L'argent n'avait pas posé de problème car le script de Vláčil adaptait un roman de Vladislav Vančura (1891–1942), écrivain communiste mort lors de la vague de terreur nazie qui avait suivi l'assassinat de Heydrich.

Dans les mois qui mènent au «Printemps de Prague», selon le nom que prendra cette période, les Tchèques reçoivent l'autorisation de voyager à l'Ouest. Pour nombre d'entre eux, c'est la première rencontre avec des gens décrits dans la vulgate communiste comme «des impérialistes décadents, des suceurs du sang des travailleurs, des barbares américains, architectes de la guerre bactériologique » et ils apprécient ce qu'ils découvrent. Les Beatles, les hippies, les pantalons à pattes d'éléphant, Twiggy, les couleurs fluo et les motifs géométriques font rage. Les couleurs, les publicités, l'argent et un nouveau rythme tournent les têtes des Tchèques. Ils ont toujours suspecté l'Occident d'être en avance, mais ne sont pas préparés à une telle abondance d'images, à tant d'imagination. Ils reviennent dans leur pays pleins d'idées nouvelles, et avec le sentiment qu'ils sont enfin redevenus des Européens civilisés.

kept in the dark: the sabre-rattling was not heard outside the corridors of the Castle.

On 20 August 1968, shortly after 11 p.m., Soviet commandos landed at Ruzyně airport. Tanks disembarked from the heavy Antonov planes. By dawn the massive airlift had deposited an entire airborne division. At the same time, Soviet, Polish, Hungarian and Bulgarian troops crossed Czechoslovakia's borders. These were the first units of the half million Warsaw Pact troops and 5000 tanks that were to occupy Czechoslovakia in the next few days. On 21 August Dubček and his colleagues were abducted by KGB men, led by a loyal StB officer (Lieutenant Colonel Bohumil Molnar) and flown to Moscow, where they were bullied and intimidated. The "negotiations" with the kidnapped men had one object: to legitimize the invasion. "Sasha" Dubček, a pre-war Communist brought up in the Soviet Union and a participant in the Slovak uprising of 1945, wrote in his memoirs (published posthumously in 1993): "It took the drastic personal experience of the coming days and months for me to understand that I was in fact dealing with gangsters." When they returned to Prague on 28 August they were beaten men. Their attempt at "Socialism with a human face" had been extinguished. They signed the Moscow Agreement, which effectively rolled back the reforms of the Prague Spring. The document legalized the invasion and brought back censorship. It also foreshadowed a treaty regularizing the temporary presence of Soviet troops (authorized by the Czechoslovak Parliament in October 1968).

The Soviet tanks that drove through the streets of Prague were often led by StB collaborators. However, it seemed that the Soviet agents, legal (like Soviet Embassy or Aeroflot employees) and "illegal" (those who had taken Czech citizenship and pretended to be loyal Czechoslovaks), were already

Gustáv Husák, architect of the "normalization."
Gustáv Husák, Architekt der »Normalisierung«.
Gustáv Husák, architecte de la « normalisation ».

Am 20. August 1968, kurz nach 23 Uhr, landeten sowjetische Kommandos auf dem Ruzyně-Flughafen. Aus den schweren Antonow-Maschinen wurden Panzer entladen. Bis zum Morgengrauen hatte die gewaltige Luftbrücke eine gesamte Luftlandedivision abgesetzt. Gleichzeitig überquerten sowjetische, polnische, ungarische und bulgarische Truppen die tschechoslowakischen Grenzen. Es waren die ersten Einheiten von einer halben Million Soldaten und 5.000 Panzern des Warschauer Paktes, die in den nächsten paar Tagen die Tschechoslowakei besetzten. Am 21. August wurden Dubček und seine Kollegen durch KGB-Offiziere unter der Führung eines kommunistentreuen StB-Offiziers (Oberst Bohumil Molnar) verhaftet und nach Moskau geflogen. Schikanen und Einschüchterungen folgten. Die »Verhandlungen« mit den entführten Männern hatten nur ein Ziel: die Legitimation der Invasion. »Sascha« Dubček, ein Kommunist aus der Vorkriegzeit, der in der Sowjetunion aufgewachsen war und an der nationalen Erhebung der Slowakei 1945 teilgenommen hatte, schrieb in seinen Memoiren (die 1993 posthum erschienen): »Es brauchte die dramatische persönliche Erfahrung der folgenden Tage und Monate, damit ich begriff, daß ich es hier tatsächlich mit Gangstern zu tun hatte.« Dubček und seine Gesinnungsgenossen kehrten am 28. August als geschlagene Männer zurück. Ihr Versuch eines »Sozialismus mit menschlichem Antlitz« war gescheitert. Sie unterzeichneten das Moskauer Abkommen, durch das die Reformen des Prager Frühlings rückgängig gemacht wurden. Das Kommuniqué legalisierte die Invasion und führte die Zensur wieder ein. Darüber hinaus erlaubte es die begrenzte Anwesenheit sowjetischer Truppen in der Tschechoslowakei (Es wurde durch das tschechische Parlament im Oktober 1968 ratifiziert.).

Die sowjetischen Panzer, die durch die Straßen Prags fuhren, wurden oft von StB-Kollaborateuren geleitet. Anscheinend befanden sich sowjetische Agenten sowohl legal (wie die Mitarbeiter der sowjetischen Botschaft oder der staatlichen Fluggesellschaft Aeroflot) als auch »illegal« (wie diejenigen, die die tschechische Staatsbürgerschaft angenommen hatten und sich als treue tschechoslowakische Bürger ausgaben) bereits in Schlüsselpositionen, als die Invasion stattfand. Sie brauchten kaum Unterstützung und konnten schnell nach den aus Moskau eintreffenden Anordnungen handeln. Täglich gab es Auseinandersetzungen zwischen Zivilisten und sowjetischen Soldaten. Tschechische Mädchen wurden vergewaltigt, Geschäfte von sowjetischen Truppen geplündert. (Der Duty-Free Shop in Ruzyně war sofort nach der Landung ausgeräubert worden.) In Prag starben 25 Menschen bei Straßenkämpfen. Wütende Bürger schmierten überallhin Parolen, auch auf russische Panzer: »Der Russische Zirkus ist in der Stadt. Tiere bitte nicht füttern.« »Die Deutschen wollten uns bloß für tausend Jahre. Die Russen wollen uns für immer.« »Mit Brüdern wie euch bitten wir Mütterchen Rußland um Geburtenkontolle.« »Hilfe gesucht: ein Marionetten-Premierminister, ein Sprecher der Nationalver- sammlung, ein erster Sekretär, ein Vorsitzender der Nationalen Front. Nur Anfragen von Verrätern erwünscht. Bitte melden sie sich bei der sowjetischen Botschaft.« Ein Patriot kritzelte einfach zwei

À Prague, les médias commencent à traiter de sujets politiques sensibles et, prudemment dans un premier temps, explorent le présent et le passé. Mais beaucoup ne veulent pas voir les sombres nuages qui s'amoncellent au-dessus du Château et des réformateurs de Dubček. Chacun est trop préoccupé par la « légèreté de l'être ». Comme toujours, l'information circule mal. Le bruit des traîneurs de sabre ne sort pas des couloirs du Château.

Le 20 août 1968, peu après 11 heures, des commandos soviétiques débarquent à l'aéroport de Ruzyně, avec leurs tanks transportés par les lourds Antonov. Dans le même temps, des troupes soviétiques, polonaises, hongroises et bulgares pénètrent en Tchécoslovaquie, avant-garde des 500 000 soldats du Pacte de Varsovie et des 5 000 tanks qui vont occuper le pays en quelques jours. Le 21 août, Dubček et ses collègues sont arrêtés par des hommes du KGB conduits par un officier du StB (le lieutenant-colonel Bohumil Molnar) et envoyés par avion à Moscou où ils sont soumis à toutes sortes de pressions et d'intimidations. Les « négociations » avec ces hommes enlevés n'ont qu'un seul objet : légitimer l'invasion. « Sasha » Dubček un communiste d'avant-guerre élevé en Union soviétique et qui a participé au soulèvement slovaque de 1945 écrira dans ses mémoires publiées après sa mort en 1993 : « Il me fallut la terrible expérience personnelle des jours et des mois qui suivirent pour comprendre que je traitais en fait avec des gangsters. » Ce sont des hommes blessés qui rentrent à Prague, le 28 août. Leur tentative de « socialisme à visage humain » est terminée. Ils ont signé l'Accord de Moscou qui annule concrètement les réformes du Printemps de Prague. Le document légalise l'invasion et rétablit la censure. Il annonce également un traité de régularisation de la présence temporaire des troupes soviétiques, légalisée par le parlement tchécoslovaque en octobre 1968.

Les tanks soviétiques qui sillonnent les rues de la ville sont souvent pilotés par des collaborateurs du StB. Il est probable que les agents soviétiques légaux (comme le personnel de l'ambassade ou de l'Aéroflot) et « illégaux » (qui ont pris la nationalité tchèque et prétendent être de loyaux citoyens tchécoslovaques) occupaient déjà des positions clés au moment de l'invasion. Ils agissent sur les ordres de Moscou. Des incidents quotidiens éclatent entre civils et soldats soviétiques. De jeunes Tchécoslovaques sont violées, et des magasins pillés par les troupes soviétiques. La boutique hors-taxe de Ruzyně l'a été dès leur atterrissage. À Prague, 25 personnes moururent lors d'échauffourées. Des citoyens en colère inscrivent partout des graffitis vengeurs, y compris sur les tanks russes : « Le cirque russe arrive! Ne pas donner de nourriture aux animaux », « Les Allemands nous voulaient pour mille ans, les Russes pour toujours », « Avec des frères comme vous, on voudrait que la mère Russie pratique la contraception », « On demande un Premier ministre fantoche, un président de l'Assemblée nationale, un premier secrétaire, un président du Front national. Réservé aux traîtres. Contacter l'Ambassade soviétique. » Un patriote

The John Lennon memorial wall.
Die John-Lennon-Gedenkwand.
Le mur-mémorial de John Lennon.

in key positions when the invasion took place and did not need much help. They could act swiftly on orders from Moscow. There were daily clashes between civilians and Soviet soldiers. Czechoslovak girls were raped, and shops were looted by Soviet troops. (The duty-free shop at Ruzyně was raided immediately after the landing.) In Prague, 25 people died in skirmishes. Angry citizens scribbled slogans everywhere, including on Soviet tanks: "Russian circus in town! Do not feed the animals;" "The Germans wanted us for only a thousand years, the Russians for ever;" "With brothers like you, we beg mother Russia to practice contraception;" "Help wanted: one puppet Prime Minister, one National Assembly Speaker, one First Secretary, one National Front Chairman. Only traitors need apply. Contact Soviet Embassy." And one patriot simply scrawled two letters which more than anything else expressed the feelings of the people: "M = M" – Moscow equals Munich.

That August week in 1968 was not all defeat. The unprecedented unity of the Czechoslovak people achieved two objectives: it prevented the establishment of a quisling government and forced Leonid Brezhnev to return the Czech leaders unharmed. This defiant spirit ruled Prague until the following spring.

In November, 60,000 students went on strike to protest against the erosion of the Dubček's Action Program. On 1 January 1969, after ringing in the New Year, thousands of people poured on to the streets chanting: "Go home!" Then on 16 January in Wenceslas Square a twenty-year-old student of philosophy, Jan Palach, set himself on fire in protest at the Soviet invasion. His funeral was attended by 800,000 people. Jan Zajíc, aged eighteen, became the second human torch, and other youngsters were ready to commit suicide for the same reason. One man said to the American journalist Alan Levy, who witnessed the events of 1968 and 1969, "What a country we live in, where the only light for the future is the burning body of a young man."

In March 1969 the Czechoslovak ice-hockey team defeated the Soviet Union 3–2 in Stockholm. The people of Prague rushed into the streets, told jokes against the Russians and drank to the

Worte, die mehr als alle anderen die Stimmung der Menschen zum Ausdruck brachte: »M = M. Moskau gleich München.«

Aber diese Augustwochen des Jahres 1968 brachten nicht nur Niederlagen. Die beispiellose Einigkeit des tschechischen Volkes zwang Moskau zum Kurswechsel: Zum einen wurde von der Einrichtung einer Kollaborationsregierung abgesehen, zum anderen mußte Breschnew die tschechischen Führer unbeschadet zurückschicken. Dieser trotzige Geist beherrschte Prag bis zum folgenden Frühjahr.

Am 17. November begannen 60.000 Studenten einen Streik, um gegen den Zusammenbruch von Dubčeks Aktionsprogramms zu protestieren. Am 1. Januar, nachdem das neue Jahr eingeläutet worden war, strömten Tausende von Menschen auf die Straßen und sangen: »Geht nach Hause, geht nach Hause!« Am 16. Januar 1969 verbrannte sich der 21jährige Philosophiestudent Jan Palach auf dem Wenzelsplatz aus Protest gegen die sowjetische Invasion. An seiner Beerdigung nahmen 800.000 Menschen teil. Der 18jährige Jan Zajíc war die nächste lebende Fackel, und auch andere junge Menschen waren zum Selbstmord für diese Sache bereit. Ein Mann sagte dem amerikanischen Journalisten Alan Levy, der die Ereignisse der Jahre 1968 und 1969 als Augenzeuge miterlebte: »In was für einem Land leben wir! Hier ist das einzige Licht der Zukunft der brennende Körper eines jungen Mannes.«

Als im März 1969 das tschechoslowakische Eishockeyteam die Sowjets in Stockholm mit 3:2 besiegte, strömten die Bewohner Prags auf die Straßen, erzählten sich Witze über die Russen und tranken auf das siegreiche Team. Parolen erschienen auf dem Wenzelsplatz, auf dem sich die größte Menschen-menge zusammengefunden hatte. Der KGB und der StB nutzten die Gelegenheit, um eine Provokation zu inszenieren. Geheimagenten warfen Steine auf die Büros der sowjetischen Luftfahrtgesellschaft Aeroflot und zertrümmerten Scheiben. Für schuldig wurden sofort die Prager und Dubček befunden, der angeblich nicht in der Lage war, Ordnung zu bewahren.

Am 17. April 1969 wurde Dubček von Moskau zum Rücktritt gezwungen und durch Gustáv Husák ersetzt. Der Generalsekretär der KPČ wurde 1975 schließlich auch Staatspräsident. Von nun an hatten die Stalinisten alles unter fester Kontrolle. Husák fragte Breschnew um Rat, was mit den Menschen zu geschehen habe, die sich hartnäckig weigerten, die Rückkehr zum Status Quo zu akzeptieren. Der sowjetische Führer gab nur ein Wort zur Antwort: »Progolodat« (»Hungere sie aus«). Nach dieser Anordnung legte Husák dem tschechoslowakischen Volk ein neue soziale Vereinbarung vor: Vergeßt die Vergangenheit und eure Rechte, dafür erhaltet ihr Lebensmittel und ein ruhiges Dasein. Während dieser Zeit der »Normalisierung« wurden 500.000 Menschen wegen ihrer Unterstützung der Reformen aus der Partei ausgeschlossen; eine Million verloren ihren Arbeitsplatz oder wurden degradiert. Hunderten von Kindern »gefährlicher« Eltern wurde die höhere Bildung verweigert. Universitätsprofessoren mußten Fenster putzen, Künstler arbeiteten an Dampfkesseln, Dichter maßen die Wasserhöhe der Stauseen und lebten in Eisenbahnwaggons. Politische Gefangene fertigten Lüster – ein Fortschritt

inscrit deux lettres qui plus que toute autre phrase traduisent les sentiments du peuple : « M = M », Moscou = Munich.

Cette terrible semaine d'août 1968 n'est pas seulement symbolique de défaite. L'unité sans précédent manifestée par le peuple tchécoslovaque aura atteint deux objectifs : elle empêche l'établissement d'un gouvernement type Quisling et force Brejnev à épargner les leaders tchèques. Cet esprit de défi allait régner à Prague jusqu'au printemps suivant.

En novembre, 60 000 étudiants se mettent en grève pour protester contre l'abandon du programme réformateur de Dubček. Le 1er janvier 1969, après avoir salué la nouvelle année, des milliers de personnes envahissent les rues de la capitale en criant : « Rentrez-chez vous ! » Puis, le 16 janvier, sur la place Venceslas, un étudiant en philosophie âgé de vingt ans, Jan Palach, se suicide par le feu en signe de protestation contre l'invasion soviétique. Ses funérailles sont suivies par 800 000 personnes. Jan Zajíc, dix-huit ans, est la seconde torche humaine et d'autres jeunes gens se préparent au suicide pour les mêmes raisons. Un homme confie au journaliste américain Alan Levy, témoin des événements de 1968 et 1969 : « Quel est ce pays, où la seule lumière qui nous montre le futur est le corps embrasé d'un jeune homme. »

En mars 1969, l'équipe de hockey sur glace tchécoslovaque bat l'équipe de l'Union soviétique à Stockholm par 3 à 2. Le peuple de Prague, y compris des étudiants de pays socialistes voisins, se précipite dans les rues, fait des plaisanteries contre les Russes et boit à l'équipe victorieuse. Des slogans apparaissent autour de la place Venceslas envahie par une immense foule euphorique. Des agents des services spéciaux jettent des pierres sur la façade de la compagnie aérienne soviétique Aéroflot et en brisent les vitres. L'incident est reproché aux Pragois et à Dubček qui n'est pas capable de maintenir l'ordre. Selon František August, si la Tchécoslovaquie avait perdu le match, les bureaux de l'Aéroflot auraient subi le même sort, qui aurait été imputé au ressentiment des Pragois pour leur défaite.

Le 17 avril 1969, Dubček est forcé de démissionner par Moscou et Gustáv Husák (1913–1991) est élu premier secrétaire du KSČ (il devint président en 1975). Les Staliniens sont de nouveau fermement aux commandes. Husák se tourne vers Brejnev pour lui demander conseil sur ce qu'il doit faire d'un peuple qui refuse avec obstination de retourner à son état précédent. Le leader soviétique lui répond d'un mot : « Progolodat » (Coupez-leur les vivres). Husák impose alors un nouveau contrat à son peuple : oubliez le passé et vous aurez en échange de la nourriture et l'apaisement. Pendant cette période appelée « normalisation », 500 000 membres sont expulsés du Parti pour avoir soutenu les réformes ; 1 million de personnes sont licenciées ou rétrogradées ; des centaines d'enfants de parents « dangereux » se voient interdits d'éducation supérieure. Des professeurs d'université deviennent laveurs de carreaux. Des artistes alimentent des chaudières. Des poètes sont chargés de mesurer le niveau de réservoirs et vivent dans des wagons. Des

victorious team; slogans appeared around Wenceslas Square, where the largest crowds gathered. The KGB and StB, however, used the occasion to stage a provocation. Intelligence agents stoned the offices of the Soviet airline Aeroflot, shattering the windows. The blame was laid squarely on the citizens of Prague and on Dubček, who supposedly was unable to maintain order.

On 17 April 1969 Dubček was forced by Moscow to resign and Gustáv Husák (1913–91) was elected First Secretary of the KSČ; he became President in 1975. Now the Stalinists were firmly in control. Husák turned to Brezhnev for advice on what to do with people who stubbornly refused to accept the return to the status quo. The Soviet leader said just one word, "Progolodat" ("Starve them out"). Accordingly, Husak imposed a new social contract on the Czechoslovak people: forget the past and your rights in return for food and a quiet life. During this period of "normalization," 500,000 were expelled from the Party for supporting the reforms; 1 million people were fired or demoted; hundreds of children of "dangerous" parents were banned from entering higher education. University professors were made to clean windows. Artists worked in boiler rooms. Poets measured the water-levels of reservoirs and lived in wagons. Political prisoners made crystal chandeliers (an improvement on the past, when labor in uranium mines was their usual fate).

Half a million people emigrated. New Wave film directors Miloš Forman and Ivan Passer (b. 1933) left, as did novelist Milan Kundera (b.1929), who became famous when his book *The Unbearable Lightness of Being* was published in France in 1984; it was later made into a film that wove in documentary shots of the invasion. Musicians, painters, animators, engineers, teachers and students decided to leave; 70 per cent were young, many of them graduates or highly skilled. One of the most famous émigrés, in 1975, was Martina Navrátilová, for whom the Socialist tennis scene became too small and too oppressive. The brain drain was ignored by the leadership. They thought they could afford it.

Spying became an art. Embassies and foreign diplomats were closely watched. Any clerk, janitor, porter, maid or chimneysweep might be a high-ranking StB agent. Prague had no fewer than eighty restaurants with permanently bugged tables, to which foreign diplomats would be led by StB agents posing as waiters. The StB also used prostitutes – often beautiful intelligence agents – to lure diplomats and visiting sportsmen.

Political trials started in the early 1970s. Many people were imprisoned. Harassment became the StB's main activity. They interrogated detainees for many hours without a break, subjecting them to coercion and 24-hour surveillance; they slashed car tires, cut brake cables and threw sugar into petroltanks. They always tried to extract something, looking for a vulnerable spot. "Don't tell them anything," said Olga Havlová (Havel's first wife, who died in 1996), "not even the name of your dog."

In 1977 a group of civil rights campaigners – among them Jan Patočka, Jiří Hájek and Václav Havel – formed the Charter 77 group to demand

gegenüber der Vergangenheit, als die Arbeit in den Uranminen ihr Schicksal war.

Eine halbe Million Menschen wanderte aus. Die tschechoslowakischen Regisseure der »Neuen Welle«, Miloš Forman und Ivan Passer (geboren 1933) verließen das Land ebenso wie der Schriftsteller Milan Kundera (geboren 1929), der 1984 in Frankreich mit seinem Buch *Die Unerträgliche Leichtigkeit des Seins* berühmt wurde. In der späteren Verfilmung wurden Dokumentaraufnahmen von der Invasion verarbeitet. Musiker, Maler, Zeichner, Ingenieure, Lehrer und Studenten entschlossen sich zur Emigration; 70 Prozent waren junge Leute, darunter viele Universitätsabsolventen und hochqualifizierte Kräfte. Eine der bekanntesten Emigranten war Martina Navrátilová, für die 1975 die sozialistische Tennisszene zu klein und repressiv wurde. Die Führungsriege nahmen diesen Brain-drain nicht ernst; sie glaubte, sich die Abwanderung leisten zu können.

Spionage wurde immer weiter perfektioniert. Man überwachte Botschaften und ausländische Diplomaten. Jeder Angestellte, Pförtner, Schornsteinfeger, Klempner und jedes Zimmermädchen konnte ein hochrangiger StB-Agent sein. Es gab nicht weniger als 80 Restaurants in Prag, deren Tische mit Wanzen versehen waren; als Kellner getarnte StB-Agenten führten ausländische Diplomaten dorthin. Der StB setzte auch Prostituierte – oft sehr attraktive Geheimagentinnen – ein, um Politiker und Sportler auf Besuchsreise auszuhorchen.

In den frühen 70er Jahren begannen politische Prozesse, viele Menschen wurden ins Gefängnis gesteckt. Quälereien gehörten zu den Hauptaktivitäten des StB. Er befragte Inhaftierte über mehrere Stunden ohne Unterbrechung und stellte sie für 24 Stunden unter polizeiliche Überwachung. Es wurden Autoreifen zerschnitten, Bremskabel durchtrennt und Zucker ins Benzin gekippt. Auf der Suche nach Schwachstellen versuchten die Agenten immer, irgendetwas herauszubekommen. »Sag' ihnen nicht das geringste«, sagte Olga Havlová (Havels erste Frau, die 1996 starb), »nicht einmal den Namen deines Hundes.«

1977 gründete eine Gruppe von Bürgerrechtlern – unter ihnen Jan Patočka, Jiří Hájek und Václav Havel – die Charta 77. In ihrer Grundsatzerklärung forderten sie die Einhaltung der Menschenrechte. Die Machthaber reagierten mit der Verhaftung der Unterzeichner, von denen Jan Patočka nach einem intensiven Polizeiverhör starb. Seine Beerdigung in Břevnov wurde zu einer Demonstration des StB-Sadismus. Man setzte Helikopter und Motorräder ein, um die Reden und Gebete zu übertönen und filmte die Trauernden, von denen viele hinterher ihren Arbeitsplatz verloren, in der Presse denunziert wurden und ins Gefängnis wanderten. Trotzdem trug die Charta 77 1980 über 1000 Unterschriften, darunter die von etwa 100 Dissidenten. Sie trugen sogenannte »Dissi-Taschen« mit sich herum, die vollgestopft waren mit verbotener Literatur, und riskierten damit ihre sofortige Verhaftung.

Die Prager Jugend kommunizierte mit der Regierung über ihre Graffities. Die mit psychedelischen Bildern geschmückte »John-Lennon-Mauer«, die die Gärten des Malteserordens begrenzt, war ursprünglich eine Erinnerungsstätte für den berühm-

Building housing estates in the suburbs.
Bau von Wohnhäusern in den Vororten.
Construction de logements en banlieue.

prisonniers politiques fabriquent des lustres de cristal, progrès par rapport au passé où ils étaient condamnés à travailler dans les mines d'uranium.

500 000 personnes choisissent d'émigrer. Les réalisateurs de films de la nouvelle vague comme Miloš Forman et Ivan Passer (né en 1933) partent, comme le romancier Milan Kundera (né en 1929), célèbre pour son livre *L'Insoutenable légèreté de l'être*, publié en France en 1984, et adapté pour le cinéma avec des extraits de documentaires sur l'invasion. Des musiciens, des peintres, des animateurs, des ingénieurs, des professeurs et des étudiants décident de quitter le pays. 70 pour cent d'entre eux sont jeunes, un grand nombre diplômés ou très qualifiés. L'un des plus célèbres émigrés d'asile, en 1975, est Martina Navrátilová, pour laquelle même l'atmosphère du tennis socialiste est devenue oppressante.

Espionner devient un art. Les ambassades et les diplomates étrangers sont placés sous haute surveillance. Tout employé, portier, huissier, femme de chambre on ramoneur peut être un agent du StB de haut niveau. Prague ne compte pas moins de quatre-vingt restaurants aux tables équipées de micros, et où les diplomates étrangers sont servis par des agents du StB. Celui-ci utilise également des prostituées – souvent très belles – pour égarer les diplomates ou les sportifs de passage.

Les procès politiques commencent au début des années 70. De nombreuses personnes sont emprisonnées. Le harcèlement devient la principale activité du StB. Ses agents interrogent les détenus pendant des heures d'affilée, les soumettant à une coercition et une surveillance de 24 heures sur 24. Ils crèvent les pneus des voitures, coupent les câbles de frein, jettent du sucre dans les réservoirs d'essence, essayant toujours de trouver le point faible. « Ne leur dites rien », disait Olga Havlová (première femme de Havel, morte en 1996), « même pas le nom de votre chien.»

En 1977, un groupe de défenseurs des droits civils – dont Jan Patočka, Jiří Hájek et Václav Havel – fondent le groupe de la Charte 77 pour réclamer l'application des droits humains fondamentaux. Les autorités répliquent en arrêtant les signataires, et Jan Patočka meurt à l'issue d'un interrogatoire musclé

basic human rights. The authorities retaliated by arresting the signatories, and Jan Patočka died after intensive police interrogation. His funeral in Břevnov was a display of refined StB sadism. They used a helicopter and motorbikes to drown the speeches and prayers, and they filmed the mourners, many of whom were subsequently fired from their jobs, denounced in the press and imprisoned. By 1980, however, Charter 77 had over 1000 signatures. Among them was a core of about 100 dissidents. They carried "dissi" bags full of forbidden literature, risking an instant jail sentence.

The youth of Prague communicated with the government through their graffiti. The psychedelic John Lennon Wall which shrouds the Knights of Malta Gardens began as a shrine to the famous pop star and pacifist, but developed into a forum for pouring out grievances against the state. Its artists were arrested by the police and the wall was assaulted with whitewash.

A number of major construction projects were carried out in Prague during the Husák régime. One of the most famous was the 216-meter television tower in Žižkov, seen from every part of Prague and known as "Husák's Finger." It was designed as a massive jamming station to knock out all foreign transmissions, but by the time it was operational in 1989, it became just an ordinary television transmitter. Also during the "normalization" period, Prague's efficient underground was built. Some of its stations were designed as protective shelters, equipped with steel doors sunk into the floor or hidden in the walls. The city's housing shortage was tackled by erecting huge, uniform estates in the suburbs. The most famous, called the Southern City, was planned for 138,000 people. Its prefabricated high-rise blocks were so alike that each one had to be painted with a different symbol to prevent the tenants getting lost. The north–south six-lane highway which cuts through Prague's picturesque center was one of the follies of the Communist planners, and faceless, domineering buildings – such as the Federal Parliament next to the National Museum, or the New Stage, an alien glass structure next to the National Theater – brought an invasion of ugliness. The shapes, walls and textures exude gloom and doom, and a lack of talent. To make matters worse, some of the buildings from that period were built using radioactive material.

Prague citizens waiting for a train to take them to their *chatas*.
Prager Bürger warten auf den Zug zu ihren *chatas*.
Pragois attendant un train qui les emportera vers leurs *chatas*.

ten Popstar und Pazifisten, entwickelte sich aber zu einem Forum für Klagen gegen den Staat. Die Künstler wurden von der Polizei verhaftet und die Mauer übertüncht.

Während der Regierung Husáks wurde in Prag eine Reihe bedeutender Bauten realisiert. Der berühmteste ist der 216 Meter hohe Fernsehturm in Žižkov, der überall in Prag zu sehen ist und den Spitznamen »Husáks Finger« trägt. Ursprünglich war er als riesiger Störsender gedacht, der alle ausländischen Übertragungen fernhalten sollte, aber als er 1989 in Betrieb genommen wurde, arbeitete er nur als Sendeturm. In der Zeit der »Normalisierung« wurde auch Prags moderne U-Bahn angelegt. Einige ihrer Stationen sollten als Bunker dienen und waren mit in den Boden eingelassenen oder hinter Mauern versteckten Stahltüren ausgestattet. Der Wohnungsnot in der Stadt begegnete man mit der Errichtung großer, einheitlicher Wohnblocks in den Vorstädten. Die bekannteste von ihnen, die sogenannte Südstadt sollte 138.000 Menschen aufnehmen. Ihre Hochhäuserblocks aus Fertigteilen sahen so gleich aus, daß sie mit verschiedenen Symbolen bemalt werden mußten, damit sich die Bewohner nicht verliefen. Die Nord-Süd-Autobahn, die Prags malerisches Zentrum zerschneidet, gehört zu den Fehlgriffen kommunistischer Stadtplaner und die gesichtslosen, die Szenerie beherrschenden Gebäude – wie das Parlament nördlich des Nationalmuseums und die Neue Szene, ein fremdartiger Glas-Beton-Bau neben dem Nationaltheater – zeugen von einer Invasion der Scheußlichkeit. Die Formen, Mauern und Materialien strahlen nicht nur Düsternis aus, sondern zeugen auch von mangelndem Talent. Was die Sache noch verschlimmert: Einige der Gebäude dieser Zeit wurden unter Verwendung radioaktiven Materials errichtet.

de la police. Ses funérailles à Břevnov sont l'occasion d'un étalage du sadisme raffiné du StB qui se sert d'un hélicoptère et de motos pour couvrir les discours et les prières, puis filme les assistants dont beaucoup seront par la suite licenciés de leur travail, dénoncés dans la presse et emprisonnés. En 1980, cependant, la Charte 77 avait recueilli plus de 1 000 signatures, dont celles d'un noyau de 100 dissidents. Ils portaient des sacs « dissi » pleins de littérature interdite, risquant une mise en prison immédiate.

La jeunesse de Prague communique avec le gouvernement par l'intermédiaire de graffitis. Le psychédélique « Mur de John Lennon » qui entoure les jardins des chevaliers de Malte commence comme en hommage à la pop star pacifiste, puis se transforme en forum d'affichage des doléances contre l'état totalitaire. Ses artistes seront arrêtés par la police et le mur passé à la chaux.

Un certain nombre d'importants projets de construction sont menés à bien à Prague sous le régime Husák. L'un des plus célèbres est la tour de télévision de 216 m de haut de Žižkov, qui se voit de toute la ville. Elle a été conçue comme une énorme installation de brouillage pour interdire toutes les émissions de l'étranger, mais, à son inauguration en 1989, sera transformée en relais de télévision ordinaire. C'est également sous la période de « normalisation » qu'est construit l'efficace métro pragois. Certaines de ses stations sont conçues comme des abris, on peut les obturer à l'aide de portes d'acier dissimulées dans le sol ou les murs. Le manque de logements est traité en partie par la construction d'énormes immeubles en banlieue. Le grand ensemble le plus fameux, appelé « Cité du Sud », est prévu pour 138 000 habitants. Ses tours et ses blocs se ressemblent tellement que chacun a dû être peint d'un symbole explicite pour éviter que les locataires ne se perdent. L'autoroute nord-sud qui passe à travers le pittoresque centre de la capitale est une autre folie des urbanistes communistes ainsi que les énormes immeubles anonymes du Parlement fédéral, à côté du Musée national, ou de la Nouvelle Scène, tout en verre, près du Théâtre national, qui donnent le sentiment que la ville se laisse envahir par la laideur. Les formes, les murs et les textures exsudent l'ennui, et le manque de talent. Pour rendre les choses pires encore, certains des immeubles de cette période sont construits en matériaux radioactifs…

## 1989–2000: The Pendulum Years

On 17 November 1989 about 15,000 students gathered in a peaceful rally to commemorate the death of student Jan Opletal, murdered by the Nazis in 1939. The so called "Velvet Revolution" began when the police brutally tried to disperse the demonstrators in Národní třída. Over 100 were arrested and 145 injured. The students demanded fundamental social changes and a dialogue with the Party, calling for democracy, liberty and human rights. The spontaneous protest continued, with actors, writers, artists and musicians joining in. On 20 November students began sit-ins, in and outside Prague. About 150,000 people gathered in the city center, threatening massive strikes. On 21 November First Secretary Miloš Jakeš (b 1922) called for calm, while simultaneously he tried to find a way of crushing the disenchanted intelligentsia. From a balcony of the Melantrich House in Wenceslas Square Václav Havel spoke for the first time, receiving an ovation.

Havel came to embody the spirit of the gentle, civilized revolution that was to force the Communists from power. The Soviet Union could no longer support its satellites. Its resources were gone and it could not afford the price of its own stagnation. The collapse of Communism began with the Soviet leader Mikhail Gorbachev's reforms, which in 1989 led to the break-up of the Soviet Empire and the reunification of Germany.

In Prague the Civic Forum was established to represent the interests of the people. On 26–27 November it and the striking workers brought down the Communist government. On 10 December President Gustáv Husák resigned and Alexander Dubček was elected Chairman of the Federal Assembly. On 29 December Václav Havel became President of Czechoslovakia.

For many months the citizens of Prague were intoxicated with freedom and happiness. Religion came into the open. Catholics rejoiced, thanking St Agnes and the Infant Jesus of Prague (a little statue of colored wax in the church of Virgin Mary the Victorious) for the miracle of the Velvet Revolution. Pope John Paul II visited the city in 1990 and the mass he celebrated in Letná Plain was televised. White-clad monks appeared on the streets, underground priests revealed themselves. In fear of persecution, they had led a double life. Of 200 priests ordained in the 1970s and 1980s, eighty turned out to be married men and had to be laicized. A full-time rabbi, sporting a black hat, arrived after a crash-course in rabbinical studies to take care of the 1000-strong Jewish community.

Restaurants, cafés, fast-food chains, guest-houses, family hotels, boutiques and souvenir shops mushroomed overnight. Exotic objects appeared on the shelves. Colorful advertisements were plastered on trams and buildings. To begin with, Prague became a dumping ground for out-of-date Western goods, although expensive boutiques were soon established.

## 1989–2000 : Die Jahre des Umschwungs

Am 17. November 1989 versammelten sich etwa 15.000 Studenten zu einer friedlichen Demonstration, um an den Tod ihres 1939 von den Nazis ermordeten Kommilitonen Jan Opletal zu erinnern. Die sogenannte »Samtene Revolution« nahm ihren Anfang, als Sicherheitskommandos die Demonstranten in der Národní třída gewaltsam auseinanderzutreiben versuchten. Mehr als 100 Menschen wurden verhaftet und 145 verletzt. Die Studenten forderten grundlegende Veränderungen und den Dialog mit der Partei, sie riefen nach Demokratie, Freiheit und Menschenrechten. Der spontane Protest, dem sich Schauspieler, Schriftsteller, Künstler und Musiker anschlossen, weitete sich aus. Am 20. November begannen die Studenten mit Sit-ins innerhalb und außerhalb Prags. Etwa 15.000 Menschen versammelten sich im Stadtzentrum und drohten mit massiven Streiks. Am 21. November forderte Generalsekretär Miloš Jakeš (geboren 1922) die Menschen zum Stillhalten auf, während er gleichzeitig nach Wegen suchte, die desillusionierten Intellektuellen auszuschalten. Von einem Balkon des Melantrich-Hauses auf dem Wenzelsplatz hielt Václav Havel seine erste, von Akklamationen begleitete Ansprache.

Havel war die Symbolfigur dieser sanften, zivilisierten Revolution, die das kommunistische Regime zur Abdankung zwang. Die Sowjetunion konnte ihre Satelliten nicht länger unterstützen, denn ihre Ressourcen waren am Ende und sie war unfähig, die eigene Stagnation zu finanzieren. Der Zusammenbruch des Kommunismus begann mit den Reformen des kommunistischen Führers Michail Gorbatschow, die 1989 zur Auflösung des sowjetischen Imperiums und zur Wiedervereinigung Deutschlands führten.

Zur Vertretung der Interessen des Volkes wurde in Prag das Bürgerforum gegründet. Seine Forderungen, denen die Arbeiter durch einen Generalstreik Nachdruck verliehen, führten am 26. und 27. November zum Sturz der kommunistische Regierung. Am 10. Dezember trat Präsident Gustáv Husák zurück. Alexander Dubček wurde zum Vorsitzenden der Bundesversammlung ernannt und am 29. Dezember fand die Wahl Václav Havels zum Präsidenten der Tschechoslowakei statt.

Viele Monate hindurch waren die Bürger Prags von Freiheit und Glück erfüllt. Die Glaubensgemeinschaften wurden wieder Teil des öffentlichen Lebens. Die begeisterten Katholiken dankten St. Agnes und dem Prager Jesulein (eine kleine Statue aus gefärbtem Wachs in der Kirche St. Maria de Victoria) für das Wunder der Samtenen Revolution. Während des Besuchs von Papst Johannes Paul II. 1990 wurde die Messe, die er auf dem Letná-Plateau feierte, vom Fernsehen übertragen. Mönche erschienen in den Straßen, Priester aus dem Untergrund gaben sich zu erkennen. Aus Angst vor Verfolgungen hatten sie ein Doppelleben geführt. Von 200 Priestern, die in den 70er und 80er Jahren geweiht worden waren, hatten 80 geheiratet und waren aus den kirchlichen Ämtern ausgeschieden. Ein Vollzeit-Rabbiner mit schwarzem Hut kam nach

## 1989–2000: Les années de velours

Le 17 novembre 1989, 15 000 étudiants environ se rassemblent pacifiquement pour commémorer la mort de l'étudiant Jan Opletal, assassiné par les nazis en 1939. La « Révolution de velours » débute lorsque la police essaie de disperser brutalement les manifestants sur la Národní třída. Plus de 100 personnes sont arrêtées et 145 blessées. Les étudiants réclament des changements fondamentaux dans la société, un dialogue avec le Parti et exigent l'instauration de la démocratie et des droits de l'homme. La protestation spontanée s'amplifie, rejointe par les acteurs, les écrivains, les artistes et les musiciens. Le 20 novembre, les étudiants commencent des sit-in dans et en dehors de Prague. Environ 150 000 personnes se rassemblent au centre de la ville, menaçant de déclencher une grève massive. Le 21 novembre, le Premier secrétaire, Miloš Jakeš (né en 1922) adjure la foule de rester calme, tout en tentant parallèlement de trouver un moyen de discréditer l'intelligentsia désenchantée. D'un balcon de la maison Melantrich, sur la place Venceslas, Václav Havel prend la parole pour la première fois ; il reçoit un accueil enthousiaste.

Havel en vient à incarner l'esprit de cette révolution douce et civilisée qui va bouter les Communistes hors du pouvoir. L'Union soviétique n'a plus alors les moyens de soutenir ses satellites. En pleine crise économique, elle ne peut même plus supporter le coût de sa propre stagnation. L'effondrement du communisme commence avec les réformes de Mikhaïl Gorbatchev qui, en 1989, mènent à l'éclatement de l'empire soviétique et à la réunification de l'Allemagne.

À Prague, se crée un Forum civique qui représente les intérêts du peuple. Le 10 décembre, le président Gustav Husák démissionne et Alexander Dubček est élu président de l'Assemblée fédérale. Le 29 décembre Václav Havel devient président de la Tchécoslovaquie.

Pendant de nombreux mois, les Pragois seront enivrés de bonheur et du sentiment de la liberté recouvrée. La religion fait sa réapparition. Les catholiques se réjouissent, remerciant sainte Agnès et l'Enfant Jésus de Prague (petite statue de cire dans l'église de la Vierge Marie Victorieuse) pour le miracle de cette révolution de velours. Le Pape Jean-Paul II se rend à Prague en 1990, et la messe de Saint-Guy est télévisée. Des moines vêtus de blancs se promènent dans les rues, ainsi que des prêtres, contraints jusqu'alors à la clandestinité. Par crainte de la persécution, ils avaient dû mener une double vie. Sur les 200 prêtres ordonnés dans les années 70 et 80, quatre-vingt s'étaient mariés et sont bannis de rangs de l'Église. Un rabbin à plein temps, portant un chapeau noir, arriva après avoir suivi un cours accéléré en études rabbiniques pour s'occuper de la communauté juive qui ne comptait plus que 1 000 membres.

Des restaurants, des cafés, des chaînes de restauration rapide, des pensions, et des boutiques de souvenirs ouvrent du jour au lendemain. Des objets exotiques venus de pays lointains surgissent dans les

The museums to Lenin and Klement Gottwald were closed. Its murals overpainted, its façade cleaned, the Gottwald Museum on Rytiřská became a bank almost overnight. Socialist Realist statues from all over the city were taken to Raná, outside Prague, where they were put into storage. The Soviet army moved out, leaving behind devastated apartment blocks and quantities of undetonated bombs, bullets, mortar rounds, grenades, mines and artillery shells. Roads were renamed: all the Red Army squares and Soviet marshal boulevards disappeared, to be replaced by names of Czech heroes and martyrs, such as Tomáš Masaryk or Jan Palach. The main railway station officially reclaimed its old name, Woodrow Wilson Station, and a modest plaque was unveiled bearing words from Wilson's 1917 declaration of war: "The World Must Be Made Safe for Democracy."

A market economy was launched by Václav Klaus, the pragmatic Prime Minister and leader of the right-wing Civic Democratic Party (ODS). Privatization and the restitution of private property were the government's two main policies. Under the privatization program, assets were sometimes sold off for remarkably low prices and the new Republic also, perhaps inevitably, became a haven for money-laundering. Openness to foreign investment attracted much capital, but less than had been hoped. Klaus, who was regarded as the great pupil of British Prime Minister Margaret Thatcher, introduced a number of taxes of which the Czechs had not even dreamed, including value-added tax (DPH), set at the high level of 22 per cent. Klaus made the Czech crown convertible, managed to keep inflation down to 10 per cent and made Prague the fourteenth best city for business in Europe. (In 1994 Warsaw was seventeenth and Moscow twenty-ninth.)

Between 1990 and 1993, Czech GDP fell by 26 per cent. In a Western economy that would mean a deep depression, lay-offs and strikes. Here, however, there are almost no strikes, and the creation of new businesses and jobs has meant that unemployment is almost non-existent (0.5 per cent in Prague and 3 per cent in the rest of the country). Various loopholes in the law have also encouraged a flourishing black economy, a hidden productivity which helps the country thrive.

It was Václav Klaus who engineered the split between the Czechs and the Slovaks, after the elections in June 1992, in which the ODS was elected in the Czech regions and the left-wing HZDS in Slovakia. On 1 January 1993 the two republics went their separate ways.

*Lustrace* (screening), a process to weed out top Communists from positions of political power was introduced soon after the Velvet Revolution. Communists were banned from top jobs until the year 2000 – although almost overnight (through their trade contacts, know-how and money) they exchanged their political muscle for economic dominance. *Rudé krávo*, a staunchly anti-Communist publication, printed a list of more than 140,000 names of alleged StB collaborators. Many were innocent, however, while the names of some well-known agents were missing. For a nation whose motto is "Truth Will Prevail," it was the greatest disappointment. Ironically, the truth became

einer kurzen Ausbildung in die Stadt, um sich um die 1000 Mitglieder der jüdischen Gemeinde zu kümmern.

Über Nacht schossen Restaurants, Cafés, Imbißketten, Gasthäuser, Familienhotels, Boutiquen und Souvenirläden wie Pilze aus dem Boden. Exotische Objekte erschienen in den Regalen. Farbenprächtige Werbetafeln wurden an Straßenbahnen und Gebäuden angebracht. Zunächst war Prag ein Markt für aus der Mode gekommene westliche Güter, aber schon bald wurden teure Boutiquen eröffnet.

Die Museen für Lenin, Fučík und Klement Gottwald wurden geschlossen. Fast über Nacht verwandelte sich das Gottwald-Museum auf der Rytiřská-Straße, nachdem die Wandgemälde übertüncht und die Fassade gereinigt worden war, in eine Bank. Aus der ganzen Stadt brachte man die Statuen des Sozialistischen Realismus in ein Lager nach Raná, außerhalb Prags. Die Rote Armee zog ab und hinterließ heruntergekommene Wohnblocks und große Mengen Munition. Straßen wurden umbenannt: Alle Plätze der Roten Armee und Boulevards mit den Namen sowjetischer Marschalls verschwanden und wurden durch die Namen der tschechischen Helden und Märtyrer wie Tomáš Masaryk und Jan Palach ersetzt. Am Hauptbahnhof, der offiziell seinen alten Namen, Woodrow-Wilson-Bahnhof, zurückerhielt, wurde eine bescheidene Plakette enthüllt, auf der die Worte der Kriegserklärung Wilsons von 1917 eingraviert waren: »Die Welt muß sicher gemacht werden für die Demokratie.«

Der pragmatische Premierminister und Führer der rechtsgerichteten Demokratischen Bürgerpartei (ODS) Václav Klaus führte die Marktwirtschaft ein. Privatisierung und Rückgabe des Privateigentums waren die beiden Hauptaufgaben der Regierung. Im Rahmen des Privatisierungsprogramms wurden staatliche Unternehmen manchmal zu ausgesprochen niedrigen Preisen verkauft, so daß die neue Republik sich – vielleicht unvermeidlich – zu einem Sammelbecken der Geldwäscher entwickelte. Die Offenheit für ausländische Investoren ließ große Kapitalmengen ins Land fließen, allerdings weniger, als man erwartet hatte. Klaus, der als Musterschüler der britischen Premierministerin Margaret Thatcher galt, führte eine Reihe von Steuern ein, von deren Existenz die Tschechen noch nicht einmal geträumt hatten, darunter die Mehrwertsteuer (DPH), die bei 22 Prozent lag. Klaus machte darüber hinaus die tschechische Krone konvertibel und konnte die Inflation unter 10 Prozent halten. Auch brachte er Prag in der Liste der attraktivsten Handelsstädte Europas auf Platz 14 (1994 stand Warschau auf Platz 17 und Moskau auf Platz 29).

Zwischen 1990 und 1993 sank das tschechische Bruttoinlandsprodukt um 26 Prozent. In einer westlichen Wirtschaft hätte eine solche Entwicklung zu tiefer Depression, Arbeitsniederlegungen und Streiks geführt. Nicht so in der Tschechoslowakei, hier konnte vielmehr durch die Schaffung neuer Unternehmen und Arbeitsplätze die Arbeitslosigkeit auf ein Minimum reduziert werden (0,5 Prozent). Zahlreiche Lücken im Gesetz ermöglichten eine blühende Schattenwirtschaft und eine versteckte Produktivität, die dem Wohlstand des Landes zugute kam.

rayons des magasins. Des affiches publicitaires bariolées apparaissent sur les trams et les immeubles. Au début, Prague devient le déversoir de produits occidentaux démodés, mais des boutiques de luxe ouvrent bientôt.

Les musées de Lénine, de Fučik et Klement Gottwald sont fermés. Fresques recouvertes, façade nettoyée, le Musée Gottwald, rue Rytiřská, est transformé en banque presque en une nuit. Les statues de style réaliste socialiste de toute la ville sont transférées dans des entrepôts à Raná, en banlieue. L'armée soviétique quitte le pays, laissant derrière elle des immeubles d'appartements dévastés et de grandes quantités de bombes, de balles, de grenades, de mines. Les rues changent de nom. Les places de l'Armée rouge et les boulevards au nom de maréchaux soviétiques disparaissent, pour être remplacés par les noms de héros et de martyrs tchèques comme Tomáš Masaryk ou Jan Palach. La gare principale reprend son nom ancien de gare Woodrow Wilson, et une modeste plaque est apposée portant le texte de la déclaration de guerre de Wilson en 1917 : « Le monde doit devenir un lieu sûr pour la démocratie. »

L'économie de marché est lancée par Václav Klaus, Premier ministre pragmatique et dirigeant du Parti Démocrate des Citoyens (ODS) de droite. La privatisation et la restitution des biens privés saisis est l'une des premières préoccupations du gouvernement. Les entreprises nationales sont parfois cédées pour des prix étonnamment bas, et la nouvelle république devient – c'était peut-être inévitable – un centre de blanchiment de l'argent. L'ouverture aux capitaux étrangers attire des investisseurs, bien que pas autant que l'on avait espéré. Klaus, considéré comme un élève de Margaret Thatcher, introduit un certain nombre d'impôts que les Tchèques n'avaient pas imaginés, comme une taxe à la valeur ajoutée de 23 pour cent. Il rend la couronne convertible, réussit à maintenir l'inflation à 10 pour cent et fait de Prague la quatorzième ville européenne la plus recherchée pour les affaires en 1994 (Varsovie étant dix-septième, et Moscou, vingt-neuvième.)

De 1990 à 1993, le PNB tchèque diminue de 26 pour cent. Dans une économie de type occidental, cela aurait signifié une profonde dépression, des licenciements et des grèves. Ici, cependant, le chômage reste presque inexistant (0,5 pour cent). De nombreuses insuffisances dans la loi encouragent une économie parallèle, dont la productivité alimente l'expansion que connaît le pays.

Václav Klaus organise la séparation entre les Tchèques et les Slovaques, après les élections de juin 1992, qui voient l'ODS élu dans les provinces tchèques et l'HZDS, de gauche, chez les Slovaques. Le 1er janvier 1993, les deux républiques décident de mener chacune leur vie en toute indépendance.

La *Lustrace* (filtration), le processus mis au point pour éliminer les communistes des positions politiques, est introduite, peu après la Révolution de velours. Les communistes se voient chassés des postes de responsabilités jusqu'en l'an 2000, mais très vite à travers leurs contacts commerciaux, leur savoir-faire et leur argent, ils passent de la domination politique à une position économique dominante. *Rudé krávo*, une publication fermement

even more elusive under the new democratic system. According to Czech writer Benjamin Kuras, a KGB-inspired operation named "Wedge" was instrumental in overthrowing the sclerotic Communist regime and its agents were planted in the new democratic organizations, as well as in various economic ventures. Since the Communists clawed their way back to power in Poland, the story has gained credibility.

The StB was formally dismantled, and the Czech Security and Information Service (BIS) established as a new body for the protection of constitutional democracy. Even in the mid-1990s, however, some politicians were claiming that eavesdropping and information-gathering occurred frequently. In such ways, little seemed to have changed. As one cynic commented, "It's everybody against everybody. Whoever has information has power."

After the collapse of Communism, historians were kept busy trying to rewrite the textbooks. Some had problems with certain political topics: to re-indoctrinate oneself is difficult and many never succeeded. People's souls remained in Communism, said one native of Prague.

The old aristocracy returned to their castles. Some of them even started using their titles again. In 1918 President Masaryk's administration had abolished titles, even forbidding aristocratic prepositions in legal documents. Instead, academic titles became the fashion. Members of *Sokol* always used the egalitarian "Brother" or "Sister." In the Communist era "Comrade" replaced everything else, although the High School of Marxism and Leninism (known, ironically, as *Dejvická Sorbonna*: the Dejvice Sorbonne) distributed academic titles indiscriminately to the most devout Communists. After the Velvet Revolution thousands of business cards with academic titles were printed. Most parliamentary deputies signed their names with some sort of title – not all genuine.

The introduction of a market economy allowed the enterprising to prosper and soon the city had a group of super-rich businessmen, and one woman. They established their own exclusive club, "Golem." Prime Minister Václav Klaus was one of its poorest members. Job opportunities opened up for women, creating a new class of female entrepreneurs. The "double burden" of job and housework became more bearable as shopping grew easier. Czech women ridiculed Western feminists who arrived in Prague with their banners, but there were not many women in the Czech Parliament (nineteen out of 200 in 1996) or in other traditionally male professions, and only five women painters (out of fifty-six) were featured at the permanent exhibition of modern Czech art (1900–60) which opened in 1995 in the Trade Fair Palace; the number of female artists has, however, grown considerably in the last two decades.
Expensive cars started to multiply as prosperity grew; within four years the number of cars in Prague tripled. Thrilled by their new-won freedom and badly out of practice, people drove too fast; 1994 saw over 150,000 accidents in the Czech Republic. Car fumes contributed to a dramatic increase in pollution. The smog in Prague soon became suffocating, especially in winter, when, in the mid-

Es war Václav Klaus, der die Abspaltung der Slowaken von den Tschechen nach den Wahlen im Juni 1992 auslöste, bei denen die ODS in den tschechischen Gebieten und die linksgerichtete HZDS in der Slowakei gewannen. Seit dem 1. Januar 1993 gehen die beiden Republiken getrennte Wege.

Kurz nach der Samtenen Revolution setzte der Prozeß der *Lustrace* (Überprüfung) ein, durch den führende Kommunisten aus politischen Machtpositionen entfernt wurden. Bis zum Jahre 2000 sollen Kommunisten keine hochrangigen Ämter bekleiden – aber sie haben dank ihrer wirtschaftlichen Kontakte, ihres Know-how und ihres Geldes fast über Nacht ihre politische Macht in eine wirtschaftliche Vormachtstellung verwandeln können. *Rudé krávo*, ein extrem anti-kommunistisches Organ, veröffentlichte eine Liste von über 140.000 Namen angeblicher StB-Kollaborateure, von denen viele unschuldig waren, während die Namen bekannter Spitzel fehlten. Dies war für die Nation, deren Motto »Die Wahrheit wird sich durchsetzen« lautete, eine besonders herbe Enttäuschung. Ironischerweise war die Wahrheit unter dem neuen demokratischen System noch weniger zu fassen. Nach den Worten des tschechischen Schriftstellers Benjamin Kuras stand hinter dem Sturz der abgewirtschafteten kommunistischen Regierung eine vom KGB angestiftete Operation namens »Keil«, deren Agenten in die neuen demokratischen Organisationen und in verschiedene Wirtschaftsprojekte eingeschleust wurden. Seitdem die Kommunisten in Polen wieder die Macht an sich gerissen haben, hat diese Version an Glaubwürdigkeit gewonnen.

Der StB wurde formell aufgelöst und der Tschechische Sicherheits- und Informationsdienst (BIS) als neues Organ zum Schutz der demokratischen Ordnung eingerichtet. Noch in der Mitte der 90er Jahre behaupteten Politiker, es gäbe zahlreiche Fälle von Bespitzelung. In dieser Hinsicht schien sich wenig geändert zu haben, wie ein Zyniker kommentierte: »Hier ist jeder gegen jeden. Wer die Informationen hat, hat auch die Macht.«

Nach dem Zusammenbruch des Kommunismus waren Historiker mit der Neuschreibung der Geschichte beschäftigt. Für einige waren bestimmte politische Themen problematisch: Die eigene Ideologie zu ändern ist schwierig, und manche schaffen es nie. Denn die Seele des Volkes verblieb im Kommunismus, wie ein Prager Bürger sagte.

Die alten Aristokraten kehrten auf ihre Schlösser zurück; manche trugen sogar wieder ihre Titel. 1918 hatte die Regierung des Präsidenten Masaryk diese abgeschafft, selbst aristokratische Präpositionen in Rechtsdokumenten waren verboten. An ihrer Stelle kamen akademische Titel in Mode. Mitglieder der *Sokol* redeten sich immer mit dem demokratischen »Bruder« oder »Schwester« an. In der kommunistischen Ära ersetzte »Genosse« alles andere, obwohl die Marxistische und Leninistische Hochschule (ironischerweise als *Dejvická Sorbona*, die Dejvice-Sorbonne, bekannt) wahllos besonders verdienten Kommunisten akademische Grade zuerkannte. Nach der Samtrevolution wurden Tausende von Visitenkarten mit akademischen Titeln gedruckt. Viele Parlamentsmitglieder unterzeichneten mit einem Titel – der nicht unbedingt echt war.

anticommuniste, imprime une liste de plus de 14 000 noms, tous de prétendus collaborateurs du StB. Beaucoup de ceux ainsi désignés à la vindicte publique sont innocents, alors que le nom de quelques agents connus manquent. Pour une nation dont la devise est «La Vérité prévaudra», c'est une grande déception. Ironiquement, la vérité devient encore plus évanescente sous le nouveau système démocratique. Selon l'écrivain tchèque Benjamin Kuras, une opération inspirée par le KGB et appelée «Wedge» joua un rôle fondamental dans le renversement d'un régime communiste sclérosé et ses agents furent implantés dans les nouvelles organisations démocratiques et dans de nombreuses opérations économiques. Depuis que les communistes ont réussi à reprendre le pouvoir en Pologne, cette histoire a gagné en crédibilité.

Le StB est réformé en Service tchèque de sécurité et d'information (BIS). Au milieu des années 90, il apparut que des agents espionnaient et réunissaient des dossiers sur des hommes politiques. Il semble donc que peu de choses aient changé. Commentaire d'un cynique : «C'est chacun contre chacun. Celui qui a l'information a le pouvoir.»

Après l'effondrement du communisme, des historiens sont chargés de réécrire les livres d'histoire. Certains rencontrent quelques difficultés avec certains sujets politiques, tant il est difficile de se réendoctriner soi-même. L'âme du peuple en est restée au communisme, a pu dire un habitant de Prague.

L'ancienne aristocratie est revenue dans ses châteaux. Certains Tchèques ont même recommencé à se prévaloir de leurs titres. En 1918, l'administration du président Masaryk avait aboli ces titres, interdisant même l'usage de prépositions aristocratiques dans les documents légaux. Les titres académiques devinrent alors à la mode. Des membres de l'association *Sokol* se servaient d'un «frère» ou «sœur» égalitaire. Sous les communistes «camarade» remplaça tout, même si la haute école du marxisme et du léninisme (ironiquement rebaptisée *Dejvická Sorbona* ; la Sorbonne de Dejvice) distribuait des titres académiques sans aucune discrimination aux communistes les plus dévots. Après la Révolution de velours, des milliers de cartes de visite comportant des titres académiques furent imprimées. La plupart des députés font accompagner leur nom d'un titre, parfois emprunté. Les nouveaux riches pragois succombent eux aussi à cette tentation.

L'introduction d'une économie de marché a permis à l'esprit d'entreprise de prospérer, et la ville a vu apparaître une classe d'hommes d'affaires extrêmement riches, dont une femme. Ils ont fondé leur propre club, très exclusif, le «Golem», dont le Premier ministre, Václav Klaus est l'un des membres les plus pauvres. Les possibilités d'emploi s'ouvrent pour les femmes, donnant naissance à une nouvelle classe de femmes chefs d'entreprise. Le «double fardeau» du travail et de l'entretien d'un foyer s'allège avec une plus grande facilité pour faire ses achats. Les femmes tchèques se sont moquées des féministes occidentales arrivées à Prague, drapeaux au vent, mais il n'y a toujours pas beaucoup de femmes au parlement (19 députés sur 200 en 1996) ou dans les professions

Jim Morrison's portrait admired by tourists.
Jim Morrisons Porträt, von Touristen bewundert.
Un portrait de Jim Morrison admiré par des touristes.

1990s, 200,000 households were burning low-quality lignite. On a few occasions the city was on smog alert and children were not allowed outdoors. In Prague children became twice as likely to contract respiratory illnesses as in Western Europe. Acid rain damaged statues of vulnerable limestone, and also affected old books.

Tourists came in millions. In 1989 over 23 million visited Prague; the number climbed to 90.5 million in 1994. The royal, the rich and the famous came to see the city's transformation and her architectural beauty. Many foreigners descended on the city because it was cheap (in the first two years); others came out of curiosity; some were looking for business opportunities. In 1917 Miloš Marten wrote, "For centuries [Prague] was a cove for pitiless adventurers. They came in droves from the four corners of the earth to plunder, make merry and lord it over the natives." His statement held true in the 1990s. The McDonaldization of the city was ruthless in its efficiency. It was no longer important to have identical Communist views – but to eat the same type of hamburger, that was chic. The foreign tobacco giants and food chains worked hard to create a "brand loyalty," but the people of Prague proved difficult to brainwash. Advertisements selling "image" failed, although information-oriented campaigns were more successful.

Freedom brought a deluge of commercialism and cheap culture. New tabloids, fashion magazines and foreign newspapers appeared. More television channels were launched, often showing soap operas, pornography, game shows and bingo. Jan Švankmajer, the Surrealist filmmaker, commented, "Communism was an ulcer on the body of civilization. When it was removed it didn't mean society was saved. In fact, it has gone to hell."

Liberation also brought an influx of Western-style crime. Casinos, brothels and pimping taxidrivers began doing good business. Wenceslas Square was divided between drug-dealers and pickpockets, who now and then raided trams and robbed passengers. Corruption was widespread in the police: in 1993, 288 policemen were charged with 376 crimes. Some security guards, often former StB members, were arrested for public-order offences. Gun-shops mushroomed. Arms, Semtex and radioactive material were all traded in Prague.

Durch die Einführung der Marktwirtschaft florierten die Unternehmen, in kurzer Zeit besaß die Stadt eine Reihe äußerst reicher Geschäftsleute, darunter eine Frau. Sie gründeten ihren eigenen, exclusiven Club, den »Golem«, zu dessen ärmsten Mitgliedern Premierminister Václav Klaus zählte. Frauen eröffneten sich neue Berufsmöglichkeiten, sie avancierten sogar zu Unternehmerinnen. Die Doppelbelastung von Arbeit und Haushalt wurde durch bessere Einkaufsmöglichkeiten erleichtert. Tschechische Frauen machten sich über Feministinnen aus dem Westen lustig, die mit ihren Schlagworten nach Prag kamen. Im tschechischen Parlament aber waren nur wenige weibliche Mitglieder vertreten (1996 waren es 19 von 200), ebenso in anderen traditionell von Männern dominierten Berufen. Und nur fünf Malerinnen (von 56) stellten auf der Dauerausstellung moderner tschechischer Kunst aus, die 1995 im Handelspalast eröffnet wurde. In den letzten beiden Jahren hat die Zahl der weiblichen Künstler allerdings beträchtlich zugenommen.

Mit wachsendem Wohlstand kamen auch immer mehr teure Autos in die Stadt; in vier Jahren hat sich die Zahl der Fahrzeuge verdreifacht. Beflügelt durch die neu gewonnene Freiheit lieben die Bewohner trotz mangelnder Fahrpraxis die Geschwindigkeit: 1994 ereigneten sich über 150.000 Unfälle in der tschechischen Republik. Autoabgase trugen zu einem dramatischen Anstieg der Umweltverschmutzung bei. Vor allem im Winter, in dem bis zur Mitte der 90er Jahre immer noch 200.000 Haushalte minderwertige Braunkohle verheizten, wurde der Smog in Prag unerträglich. Einige Male wurde in der Stadt Smogalarm ausgelöst und Kindern verboten, sich im Freien aufzuhalten. Die Gefahr einer Erkrankungen der Atemwege ist in Prag zweimal so hoch wie in Westeuropa. Saurer Regen begann die anfälligen Sandsteinstatuen zu zersetzen und richtete auch bei alten Büchern Schaden an.

Millionen von Touristen kamen nach Prag. 1989 waren es 23 Millionen, 1994 stieg die Zahl auf 90,5 Millionen. Adelige, Reiche und andere Berühmtheiten wollten die Verwandlung der Stadt und ihre Architektur bewundern. Viele Ausländer stiegen in der Stadt ab, weil sie (in den ersten zwei Jahren) preiswert war; andere statteten ihr aus Neugier einen Besuch ab, und wieder andere suchten Geschäftsmöglichkeiten. 1917 schrieb Miloš Marten: »Über Jahrhunderte war die Stadt eine Höhle für gnadenlose Abenteurer. In Trauben kamen sie aus allen Ecken der Welt, um zu plündern, sich zu vergnügen und sich gegenüber den Einheimischen als Herren aufzuspielen.« Diese Feststellung trifft auch auf das Prag der 90er Jahre zu. Der Triumphzug der Schnellimbisse war gnadenlos und effizient. Es war nicht länger von Bedeutung, die gleichen, kommunistischen Ansichten zu vertreten; statt dessen galt es als chic, den gleichen Hamburger zu essen. Die großen ausländischen Tabakfirmen und Lebensmittelketten bemühten sich eindringlich, »Markentreue« herzustellen, aber die Prager Bürger erwiesen sich als schwer manipulierbar: Anzeigen, die ein Image verkauften, schlugen fehl, während informationsorientierte Kampagnen Erfolg hatten.

traditionnellement masculines. Trois femmes peintres seulement étaient présentes à l'exposition permanente d'art moderne tchèque (1900–60) du Palais de la foire en 1995. Toutefois le nombre des femmes artistes a beaucoup augmenté ces dernières vingt années.

Les automobiles coûteuses se multiplient avec la prospérité. En quatre ans, le nombre de voitures à Prague a triplé. Fiers de leur liberté récemment acquise mais manquant de pratique, leurs conducteurs conduisent trop vite et il y a eu 150 000 accidents en 1994. Les fumées des moteurs contribuent dramatiquement à l'élévation de la pollution. Le brouillard de Prague est devenu suffocant, en particulier l'hiver, lorsque que 200 000 foyers brûlent encore un lignite de mauvaise qualité. À quelques occasions la ville a connu des alertes sérieuses, les enfants n'ayant pas le droit de quitter leur maison. Les petits Pragois ont deux fois plus de risques de contracter une maladie respiratoire qu'en Europe occidentale. Les pluies acides endommagent les statues en pierre calcaire fragile et s'attaquent aux vieux livres.

Les touristes affluent par millions. En 1989, Prague a reçu plus de 23 millions de visiteurs, et 90,5 millions en 1994. Des personnalités du monde entier viennent assister aux transformations de la ville. Beaucoup d'étrangers apprécient également le coût de la vie encore bon marché lors des deux premières années; d'autres sont poussés par la curiosité, certains attirés par les opportunités d'affaires. En 1917, Miloš Marten avait écrit «Depuis des siècles, c'était un havre pour des aventuriers sans pitié. Ils vinrent en foule des quatre coins de la terre pour piller, et profiter des indigènes» et ceci fut encore plus vrai dans les années 90. La «macdonalisation» de la ville s'est révélée d'une brutale efficacité. Il n'est plus important de partager les mêmes idées communistes, mais de manger la même nourriture. Le hamburger est chic. Les grandes sociétés de cigarettes et les chaînes d'épicerie travaillent dur pour créer une «fidélité de marque», mais les Pragois se montrent assez résistants au lavage de cerveau. Les annonces publicitaires vantant «l'image» ont échoué à l'inverse des campagnes plus orientées sur l'information.

La liberté a apporté un déluge de tentations commerciales et de culture bon marché. De nouveaux quotidiens, des magazines de mode et des journaux étrangers ont fait leur apparition. De nouvelles chaînes de télévision diffusent souvent des feuilletons, de la pornographie, des jeux de toutes sortes. Un certain nombre de cinémas ont fermé leurs portes, et ceux qui ont résisté projettent surtout des films américains de seconde zone, les vraies œuvres cinématographiques ayant du mal à se frayer un chemin parmi ces tombereaux de déchets. En 1996, s'est ouvert le premier café Internet. Jan Švankmajer, réalisateur de films surréalistes, a fait remarquer que «si le communisme avait été un ulcère sur le corps de la civilisation, son ablation ne signifiait pas que la société était sauvée. En fait, elle était partie pour l'enfer.»

La libération a également favorisé l'apparition d'activités criminelles de type occidental. Casinos,

One man kept uranium in a bank safe, another in a private flat. Gangsters – often Afghan war veterans – thrived; the Ukrainian mafia emerged as the most ruthless.

Theft was rife. The Communist legacy, summed up in the famous Czech saying "Who does not steal from the state, steals from his own family," did not die out. Car-theft was widespread; not even a car-clamp was safe in Prague. Sales staff stole from the shops they worked in. Employees stole from their firms. Art treasures disappeared from churches and museums.

Skinheads, reinforced by neo-Nazis from the former East Germany, organized marches. "Gypsies to the gas chambers," "Foreigners out," they shouted in Wenceslas Square in 1991. Ninety per cent of Czech Gypsies (6000) were murdered in German concentration camps, though Slovak Gypsies survived. Today's Bohemian Gypsies came from Romania (soon after the Second World War) or from Slovakia (Husák resettled them in the 1980s). With illiteracy, unemployment, the high crime rate, the introduction of new Czech citizenship laws and local racism, the community found itself in difficulties, but still Romany artists and musicians have managed to establish themselves in the Bohemian community, and singers such as Věra Bílá, whose voice combines raw coarseness with emotional warmth, and the experimental Iva Bittová have won widespread admiration.

In the heady days of the early 1990s, Prague saw all kinds of artistic activity. An East German Trabant car with four big human legs instead of wheels was displayed in the Old Town Square. Entitled *Quo Vadis?*, it was the work of David Černý, who also caused controversy by painting a tank commemorating the arrival of the Red Army in 1945 shocking pink. This caused heated discussions among the older citizens of Prague who regarded the Vlasov soldiers and not the Soviets as their liberators. Arguments intensified until the "liberation" issue was literally fought out by the Communists and their adversaries in front of the

Foreign newspapers flooded the capital.
Ausländische Zeitungen überfluteten die Hauptstadt.
Les journaux étrangers envahirent la capitale.

Die Freiheit brachte Kommerzialisierung und eine Flut billiger Kultur mit sich. Es erschienen neue Boulevardzeitschriften, Modemagazine und ausländische Zeitungen. Weitere Fernsehkanäle wurden eingerichtet, die Seifenopern, Pornofilme, Spielshows und Bingowettbewerbe zeigten. Der surrealistische Filmemacher Jan Švankmajer kommentierte: »Der Kommunismus war ein Geschwür auf dem Leib der Zivilisation. Seine Entfernung führte aber nicht zur Rettung der Gesellschaft. Tatsächlich fuhr sie zur Hölle.«

Die neue Freiheit führte zu einer Reihe typisch westlicher Verbrechen. Kasinos, Bordelle und Taxifahrer, die sich als Zuhälter verdingten, machten gute Geschäfte. Den Wenzelsplatz teilten sich Drogenhändler und als Taschendiebe arbeitende Sinti und Roma, die gelegentlich auch in den Straßenbahnen einfielen und die Passagiere ausraubten. Korruption war ein weitverbreitetes Übel in der Polizei: 1993 wurden 288 Polizisten wegen 376 Verbrechen angeklagt. Auf Grund von Verstößen gegen die öffentliche Ordnung verhaftete man einige Sicherheitsbeauftragte, darunter viele frühere StB-Mitglieder. Waffengeschäfte schossen wie Pilze aus dem Boden und Waffen, Semtex-Gas und radioaktives Material wurden gehandelt. Ein Mann hatte Uran in einem Banksafe aufbewahrt, ein anderer in einer Privatwohnung. Kriminelle – viele von ihnen ehemalige Afghanistan-Kämpfer – gingen in der Stadt ein und aus, wobei die ukrainische Mafia als besonders skrupellos galt.

Diebstähle waren weit verbreitet. Das kommunistische Vermächtnis, das sich in dem bekannten tschechischen Sprichwort »Wer nicht vom Staat stiehlt, beraubt seine eigene Familie« zusammenfassen läßt, blieb weiterhin lebendig. Bevorzugt wurden Autos gestohlen, nicht einmal Autokrallen waren in Prag sicher. Das Personal beraubte die eigenen Geschäfte und Angestellte stahlen in ihren Firmen. Kunstschätze verschwanden aus Kirchen und Museen.

Skinheads, die von Neonazis in der ehemaligen DDR unterstützt wurden, organisierten Demonstrationen. »Zigeuner in die Gaskammern« und »Ausländer raus« brüllten sie bei einer ihrer Versammlungen auf dem Wenzelsplatz im Jahre 1991. 90 Prozent der tschechischen Sinti und Roma (6.000) waren in den deutschen Konzentrationslagern ermordet worden, nur die slowakischen Sinti und Roma hatten überlebt. Die heutigen böhmischen Sinti und Roma waren kurz nach dem Zweiten Weltkrieg aus Rumänien gekommen oder von Husák in den 80er Jahren aus der Slowakei umgesiedelt worden. Sie hatten mit vielen Schwierigkeiten wie Analphabetismus, Arbeitslosigkeit, einer hohen Kriminalitätsrate, der Einführung des neuen tschechischen Bürgerrechts und örtlichem Rassismus zu kämpfen. Künstlern und Musikern aus der Gruppe der Roma gelang es jedoch, sich in der böhmischen Gesellschaft zu etablieren. Sängerinnen wie Věra Bílá, die in ihrer Stimme wilde Kraft mit emotionaler Wärme vereinte, und die experimentierfreudige Iva Bittová wurden weithin bewundert.

In den ungestümen Tagen der frühen 90er Jahre gab es in Prag alle Arten künstlerischen Engagements.

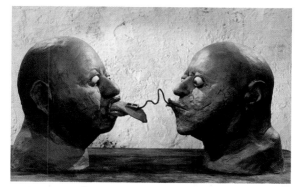

A still from Jan Švankmajer's film *Talking Heads*.
Standbild aus Jan Švankmajers Film *Talking Heads*.
Image du film de Jan Švankmajer, *Talking Heads*.

bordels, et chauffeurs de taxi rabatteurs se livrent à leur fructueux commerce. La place Venceslas est partagée entre revendeurs de drogues et voleurs à la tire, qui de temps en temps font une razzia sur un tram et pillent les voyageurs. La corruption se répand dans la police : en 1993, 288 policiers ont été poursuivis pour 376 délits. Des gardiens, souvent d'anciens membres du StB, ont été arrêtés. Les armureries se multiplient. Armes, Semtex, matériaux radioactifs, tout se trouve et se vend à Prague. On cache de l'uranium dans un coffre de banque, ou dans un appartement. Les gangsters – souvent des vétérans de la guerre en Afghanistan – sont omniprésents. La mafia ukrainienne est le groupe le plus brutal.

Le vol se porte bien. Le legs communiste résumé dans le fameux dicton tchèque «Celui qui ne vole pas l'État, vole sa propre famille» est toujours valable. Le vol de voiture est répandu. On vole même les sabots de Denver. Les vendeurs volent dans les magasins pour lesquels ils travaillent. Les employés volent leur entreprise. Des trésors artistiques disparaissent des musées et des églises.

Les skinheads, renforcés par les néonazis de l'ancienne Allemagne de l'Est, organisent des manifestations. «Les tziganes aux chambres à gaz», «Dehors les étrangers», ont-ils crié place Venceslas en 1991. 90 pour cent des tziganes tchèques (6 000) ont disparu dans les camps de concentration allemands, mais les slovaques ont été épargnés. Aujourd'hui les tziganes bohémiens sont d'origine slovaque (où Husák les avait relégués dans les années 80) et roumaine. Avec un taux élevé d'analphabétisme, de chômage, de crime, l'introduction des nouvelles lois de citoyenneté tchèques et du racisme local, cette communauté se trouve soumise à de multiples difficultés, mais les artistes et musiciens romanis ont réussi à s'établir en Bohême et des chanteurs comme Věra Bílá et Iva Bittová ont séduit par l'étrange et brutale beauté de leur musique.

Au cours des turbulentes journées du début des années 90, Prague a vu s'épanouir toutes sortes d'activités artistiques. Une vieille Trabant est-allemande, dont les roues étaient remplacées par quatre pieds humains a été exposée sur la place de la vieille ville. Intitulée *Quo Vadis?*, c'était l'œuvre de David Černý, lequel provoqua également une

The pink tank.
Der pinkfarbene Panzer.
Le tank rose.

"desecrated monument." The Soviet Embassy complained; Dubček apologized, but the disputes continued until the tank was removed to a military museum in Kbely.

The last film of the Czechoslovak New Wave, *The Ear*, by Karel Kachyňa (b. 1924), won a special award at the Cannes Film Festival, and was finally released in 1990. When it was first made the film, which brilliantly captures the paranoia of the Communist era and the omnipresent StB, was locked away by the censor for twenty years and Jiřina Bohdalová, who plays one of the two main parts, was banned from acting for ten years.

In 1992 Prague was recognized by UNESCO as a city of outstanding beauty and placed on its World Heritage list. Since then there has been a big drive to restore buildings and repair crumbling sidewalks. The marble and granite cobblestones were replaced in the elegant old patterns. New architecture sprang up on sites left vacant since the Second World War, trying to blend in with the historic Prague. The Dancing House, on the corner of the Embankment and Resslova, was designed by Frank O'Gehry and Vladimir Milunić and, as in the days of the First Republic when each artistic endeavor was greeted with lively discussion, it inspired tremendous bickering. The building's two towers seem to be bursting with movement – one is shaped like an hourglass, the other is crowned with a zany ball made out of stainless-steel mesh. One malicious architect commented, "Imagine having to live with an old joke for years and years." A new shopping mall called "Myslbek," in Na Příkopě, was opened in 1996 and also proved controversial, not as much for its heavy-handed design as for the consumerist philosophy it embodies.

But none of these endeavors caused as much commotion as the football finals in the European Championship of 1996, when the Czech team lost to Germany. An enormous crowd watched the match on a huge video screen in the Old Town Square, the Sparta followers celebrating midfielder Karel

Auf dem Altstädter Marktplatz wurde ein ostdeutschen Trabant gezeigt, der anstelle der vier Räder vier menschliche Beine hatte und den Titel *Quo Vadis* trug. Es war ein Werk von David Černý, der bereits eine kontroverse Debatte hervorgerufen hatte, als er zur Erinnerung an den Einmarsch der Roten Armee 1945 einen Panzer in grellem Rosa anmalte. Dieses Kunstwerk führte zu hitzigen Debatten mit den älteren Bewohnern Prags, die Wlassows Soldaten und nicht die Sowjets als ihre Befreier angesehen hatten. Die Auseinandersetzungen spitzten sich zu, bis die Kommunisten und ihre Gegner die Sache vor dem »entweihten Monument« im wahrsten Sinne des Wortes ausfochten. Die sowjetische Botschaft protestierte und Dubček entschuldigte sich, aber die Kontroverse dauerte an, so daß der Panzer schließlich in ein Militärmuseum in Kbely gebracht wurde.

Der letzte Film der tschechoslowakischen Neuen Welle, *Das Ohr* von Karel Kachyňa (geboren 1924), der einen Sonderpreis bei den Filmfestspielen in Cannes gewonnen hatte, konnte 1990 endlich der Öffentlichkeit vorgestellt werden. Bei seiner Erstaufführung war der Film, der auf brillante Weise den Verfolgungswahn der kommunistischen Ära und die Allgegenwart des StB zum Ausdruck brachte, von der Zensur einbehalten und für 20 Jahre weggeschlossen worden; eine der beiden Hauptdarsteller, Jiřina Bohdalová, erhielt für die nächsten 10 Jahre Schauspielverbot.

1992 erkannte die UNESCO Prag als eine Stadt von besonderer Schönheit an und nahm sie in die Liste des Weltkulturerbes auf. Seit dieser Auszeichnung werden die alten Gebäude restauriert und die zerfallenden Bürgersteige repariert. Pflastersteine aus Marmor und Granit wurden durch elegante alte Materialien ersetzt. Neue Gebäude entstanden auf den seit dem Zweiten Weltkrieg leerstehenden Grundstücken. Der Tanzpalast auf der Höhe der Resslova-Straße an der Uferpromenade, ein Werk des Amerikaners Frank O'Gehry und Vladimir Milunić löste wie in den Tagen der Ersten Republik,

controverse en peignant en rose un tank commémorant l'arrivée de l'Armée rouge en 1945. Pour les vieux Pragois, c'étaient les soldats de Vlasov et non les Soviétiques qui les avaient libérés. Les discussions s'intensifièrent jusqu'à ce que l'argument de la « libération » soit littéralement jeté sur la place publique par les communistes et leurs adversaires devant ce «monument déconsacré». L'ambassade soviétique éleva une protestation contre cette farce. Dubček s'excusa, mais la dispute se poursuivit jusqu'à ce que le tank soit déplacé dans le musée militaire de Kbely.

Le dernier film de la nouvelle vague tchécoslovaque, *L'Oreille* de Karel Kachyňa (né en 1924) a remporté un prix spécial au festival de Cannes, et a été finalement diffusé en 1990. Ce film, qui retrace brillamment la paranoïa de l'ère communiste et l'omniprésence du StB, avait été bloqué par la censure pendant vingt ans, et Jiřina Bohdalová, qui joue l'un des deux rôles principaux, interdite de scène pendant dix ans.

En 1992, Prague a été reconnue par l'Unesco comme une ville d'une beauté exceptionnelle et placée sur la liste du patrimoine de l'humanité. Depuis, l'on s'efforce de restaurer les bâtiments et de réparer la voirie. Les pavés de marbre et de granit ont été remis en place selon d'anciens et élégants motifs. De nouveaux immeubles s'élèvent sur des terrains abandonnés depuis la Seconde Guerre mondiale, s'efforçant de se fondre dans la Prague historique. Cet étrange immeuble, au coin de la rue Resslova, a été conçu par l'architecte américain Frank O'Gehry et Vladimir Milunić. Comme aux beaux jours de la première république, lorsque chaque nouvelle entreprise artistique s'accompagnait de discussions, il a suscité d'intenses querelles. Avec ses deux éléments cylindriques pressés l'un contre l'autre – l'un en forme de sablier, l'autre couronné d'une énorme boule de métal – idée de Václav Havel – il ressemble à un couple de danseurs. Un architecte malicieux a pu commenter : « Imaginez devoir vivre avec la même vieille plaisanterie année après année... » Un nouveau centre commercial appelé « Myslbek », dans Na Příkopě s'est ouvert en 1996 et a également déclenché une querelle. Ce n'est pas le cube de verre traversé par des rails d'acier en diagonale qui a provoqué la colère des gens, mais le nœud rouge, suggérant un cadeau bien emballé, la consommation et la philosophie de la consommation.

Mais aucune de ces réalisations ne provoqua un choc comparable à celui du championnat d'Europe de football de 1996 qui a vu l'équipe tchèque battue par les Allemands. Une foule immense a assisté au match devant un écran vidéo géant sur la place Venceslas, les partisans du club Sparta célébrant l'avant Karel Poborský, tandis que les fans du Slavia applaudissaient leur gardien de but, Petr Kouba. Les Tchèques se passionnent de même pour le tennis, et chaque année les enthousiastes se retrouvent (y compris souvent le Premier ministre) autour des courts de Štvanice ou se déroule l'Open Škoda.

Václav Klaus apprécie le sport, et voudrait que la culture soit régie par les forces du marché libre. Son attitude lui a valu des critiques multiples dont celles de Milan Knížák, directeur de l'Académie tchèque des beaux-arts qui a déclaré: «Nous avons besoin

Poborský, while the Slavia fans cheered on their goalkeeper Petr Kouba. The Czechs are also keen followers of tennis; each summer enthusiasts (often including Prime Minister Václav Klaus) flock to the Štvanice courts where the Škoda Open Championship is held.

Klaus enjoys sport, but would prefer culture to be governed by the forces of the free market. His attitude has won him criticism from many, including Milan Knížák, director of the Czech Academy of Fine Arts, who says, "We need culture that makes no money. Without such a culture there is no culture. We can't have an American system here because we have a different tradition... In Europe [culture is] more integrated: it lives more with the people." Art historian Jakub Outrata asks, "Do you think Klaus would have invented a rainbow? Never, because it would have cost too much money... pretty, but utterly useless."

The market economy has already strangled many cafés, the favorite sanctuaries of the city's artists, where ideas were traditionally tried out to the delight of friends and to the benefit of the public. "Is there an alternative?" some have wondered. One native of Prague said, "Have you ever heard of a great novel written in McDonalds? Greed will kill everything, because creating is about giving and if nobody is prepared to give any more ..."

In the last ninety years, Prague has witnessed a series of dramatic events providing a metaphor for the European experience of the twentieth century. The city lived through two world wars, three revolutions, two invasions and two occupations. It was the capital of five different Republics, of varying extent and political complexion. It also fell under three empires, the Austro-Hungarian, the Nazi and the Soviet, and outlasted them all.

The architects of the two totalitarian systems that have shaped our century visited Prague at key moments in their careers: Lenin took his first steps to power from here in 1912 and, twenty-seven years later, Hitler proudly surveyed his new conquest as

The presidential flag.
Die Präsidentenfahne.
Le drapeau présidentiel.

in denen fast jedes Kunstwerk mit lebhaften Diskussionen begrüßt wurde, eine heftige Kontroverse aus. Seine beiden Türme scheinen sich einander zuzuneigen – der eine ist wie ein Stundenglas geformt, den anderen krönt ein großer Metallbau aus einem nichtrostenden Sathlnetz. Ein übelmeinender Architekt kommentierte das Werk mit den Worten: »Stell dir vor, du müßtest mit dem selben alten Witz über Jahre hinweg leben.« Die neue Einkaufszone, die 1996 mit dem Namen »Myslbek« im Stadtteil Na Příkopě eröffnet wurde, löste ebenfalls Kontroversen aus. Der Grund war weniger das umstrittene Design als vielmehr die dahinterstehende Konsumphilosophie.

Aber keines dieser Projekte erregte die Gemüter so sehr wie das Endspiel der Fußball-Europameisterschaft 1996, als die Tschechen den Deutschen unterlagen. Eine riesengroße Menschenmenge verfolgte das Spiel auf einer großen Videoleinwand auf dem Wenzelsplatz. Die Fans von Sparta feierten ihren Mittelfeldspieler Karel Poborský, die Anhänger von Slavia bejubelten ihren Torhüter Petr Kouba. Die Tschechen sind auch begeisterte Tennisfans: Jeden Sommer treffen sich die Enthusiasten (häufig auch Premierminister Václav Klaus) im Tennisstadion in Štvanice, in dem die Offenen Škoda-Meisterschaften stattfinden.

Klaus ist ein großer Sportsfreund, würde es aber vorziehen, wenn die Kultur vom freien Markt gelenkt würde. Diese Haltung hat ihm von vielen Seiten Kritik eingebracht, so auch vom Direktor der tschechischen Akademie der Schönen Künste, Milan Knížák, der bemerkte: »Wie brauchen eine Kultur, die kein Geld einbringt. Wir können hier nicht nach dem amerikanischen System leben, denn wir haben eine andere Tradition. In Europa [ist die Kultur] stärker eingebunden: sie lebt näher an den Menschen.« Der Kunsthistoriker Jakub Outrata stellt die Frage: »Glauben Sie, Klaus hätte den Regenbogen erfunden? Niemals, denn das hätte zuviel Geld gekostet ... schön, aber vollkommen nutzlos.«

Die Marktwirtschaft hat bereits viele Cafés, die beliebtesten Treffpunkte der Prager Künstler, zugrunde gerichtet. Hier wurde traditionell zum Vergnügen der Freunde und zugunsten des Publikums mit Ideen experimentiert. »Gibt es eine Alternative?«, fragte man sich. Ein gebürtiger Prager antwortete: »Haben Sie schon einmal ewas von einem großen Roman gehört, der bei McDonalds geschrieben worden ist? Habsucht wird alles schlucken, weil Kreativität etwas mit Geben zu tun hat. Und wenn niemand mehr bereit ist zu geben...«

In den letzten 90 Jahren war Prag Zeugin einer Reihe dramatischer Ereignisse, die zur Metapher für die Erfahrungen im Europa des 20. Jahrhunderts wurden. Die Stadt erlebte zwei Weltkriege, drei Revolutionen, zwei Invasionen und zwei Besetzungen. Sie war die Hauptstadt fünf verschiedener Republiken unterschiedlichster Ausdehnung und politischer Gestalt. Sie mußte sich drei Weltreichen unterwerfen – dem österreichisch-ungarischen, dem nationalsozialistischen und dem sowjetischen – und sie hat alle überlebt.

Die Architekten zweier totalitärer Systeme, die unser Jahrhundert geprägt haben, kamen in entscheidenden Momenten ihrer Karrieren nach Prag: 1912

"The Dancing House."
»Das Tanzhaus«.
«Le dancing».

d'une culture qui ne s'intéresse pas à l'argent. Sans une telle culture, il n'y a pas de culture. Nous ne pouvons avoir le système américain parce que nous vivons sur une tradition différente. En Europe, la culture est plus intégrée : elle vit davantage avec les gens.» L'historien de l'art Jakub Outrata pose de son côté la question suivante : « Pensez-vous que Klaus aurait inventé un arc-en-ciel? Jamais, parce que cela lui aurait coûté trop d'argent... il l'aurait trouvé charmant, mais inutile.»

L'économie de marché a déjà étranglé de nombreux cafés, ces sanctuaires favoris des artistes de la ville où les idées s'échangent entre amis pour le plus grand bénéfice de tous. « Y a-t-il une alternative?» se demandent certains. Un vrai Pragois pense « Avez-vous jamais entendu parler d'un grand roman écrit dans un McDonald? L'attrait du gain tue tout, parce que créer c'est donner et que personne n'est plus préparé à donner... »

Au cours des quatre-vingt-dix dernières années, Prague a été le témoin d'une succession d'événements dramatiques, métaphore du destin de l'Europe au XXe siècle. Pendant cette période, la ville a vécu deux guerres mondiales, trois révolutions, deux invasions et deux occupations. Elle a été la capitale de cinq républiques différentes, d'une complexité politique variée. Elle a également subsisté sous le joug de trois régimes, l'austro-hongrois, le nazi et le soviétique, et leur a survécu.

Les architectes des deux grands systèmes totalitaires qui ont marqué l'histoire de notre siècle ont visité Prague à des moments clés de leur carrière : Lénine y fit ses premiers pas vers le pouvoir en 1912, et vingt-sept ans plus tard, Hitler y vint fièrement passer ses troupes en revue, ce qui allait directement mener à la Seconde Guerre mondiale.

Après 1945, Prague est devenue l'un des symboles de la guerre froide. Le coup de Prague de février 1948 a marqué la partition de l'Europe.

President Václav Havel arriving at an official function.
Präsident Václav Havel bei einem offiziellen Auftritt.
Le président Václav Havel dans ses fonctions officielles.

German troops marched in – an event that led directly to the Second World War.

After 1945 Prague became a symbol of the Cold War. The Communist seizure of power in February 1948 touched off containment and the partition of Europe. Behind the Iron Curtain, Prague was ruled by the most Stalinist regime in the Soviet bloc, and the city saw some of the biggest show trials and political purges in Eastern Europe. A brief interval of destalinization, the Prague Spring, was crushed by the Russian invasion in August 1968, which ended "Socialism with a human face" and closed the possibility of reform within the Soviet Empire. Prague was plunged into a political deep freeze, so called normalization, until the Velvet Revolution of November 1989 symbolized the end of the Cold War and the beginnings of a new Europe.

Unlike the other major cities of the region, Prague has survived these dramatic events with little physical damage. A citizen of 1914 would find much that was familiar in the late 1990s. But the century has left its mark in other ways. The Germans and the Jews – for long, important elements in Prague's urban mosaic – have gone. They have been replaced by thousands of Americans and other Western and Eastern Europeans, who have contributed enormously to the city's appearance, not only in terms of money, but also of expertise and their diverse talents. This Euro-American melting pot has had only an imperceptible effect on the natives of Prague with their Slavic souls, German pragmatism and streak of black Jewish humor. But one thing is purely Czech: the surreal, poetical fantasy which the people create with such ease.

unternahm Lenin von hier aus die ersten Schritte zur Macht, 27 Jahre später inspizierte ein stolzer Hitler nach dem Einmarsch deutscher Truppen seine neue Eroberung – ein Ereignis, das unmittelbar in den Zweiten Weltkrieg führte.

Nach 1945 wurde Prag zum Symbol des Kalten Krieges. Die kommunistische Machtübernahme im Februar 1948 löste die Eindämmung und die Teilung Europas aus. Hinter dem Eisernen Vorhang wurde Prag von dem am stärksten stalinistisch geprägten Regime im ganzen Ostblock regiert, die Stadt erlebte einige der größten Schauprozesse und politischen Säuberungen in Osteuropa. Die kurze Periode der Entstalinisierung, der Prager Frühling, wurde durch die russische Invasion im August 1968 zerschlagen, sie beendete den »Sozialismus mit menschlichem Antlitz« und machte eine Reform innerhalb des sowjetischen Imperiums unmöglich. Unter dem Schlagwort »Normalisierung« verfiel Prag in eine politische Eiszeit, bis die Samtene Revolution im November 1989 das Ende des Kalten Krieges und den Beginn eines neuen Europas einläutete.

Im Gegensatz zu den meisten großen Städten dieser Region überlebte Prag diese dramatischen Ereignisse mit wenigen äußerlichen Schäden. Ein Bürger des Jahres 1914 würde in den späten 90er Jahren auf viel Bekanntes stoßen. Aber das Jahrhundert hat auf andere Weise seine Spuren hinterlassen. Die Deutschen und die Juden – für lange Zeit wichtige Elemente in Prags städtischem Mosaik – sind verschwunden. An ihrer Stelle kamen Tausende von Amerikanern und anderen West- und Osteuropäern, die nicht nur mit ihrem Geld, sondern auch mit ihrer Erfahrung und ihren verschiedenen Talenten ent-

Derrière le rideau de fer, la ville était soumise au plus staliniste des régimes du bloc soviétique, et la cité fut témoin de quelques-uns des plus spectaculaires procès et purges politiques de l'Europe de l'Est. Après un bref intervalle de déstalinisation, le Printemps de Prague a été écrasé par l'invasion russe d'août 1968 qui a mis fin au «Socialisme à visage humain,» et empêché toute possibilité de réforme au sein de l'empire soviétique. Prague s'est vue plongée dans une période de glaciation politique, appelée «normalisation», jusqu'à ce que la Révolution de velours de novembre 1989 symbolise la fin de la guerre froide et le début d'une nouvelle Europe.

À la différence d'autres grandes villes de la région, Prague a survécu à tous ces événements sans grand dommage matériel. Un habitant de 1914 ne se sentirait pas dépaysé à la fin des années 90. Mais le cours du siècle a laissé des traces d'une nature différente. Les Allemands et les Juifs – longtemps importants éléments de la mosaïque humaine pragoise – ont disparu. Ils ont été remplacés par des milliers d'Américains, d'autres Occidentaux et Européens de l'Est, qui ont énormément contribué à la nouvelle apparence de la cité, non seulement en terme d'argent, mais également de compétence et de talent. Ce melting-pot euro-américain n'a eu qu'un effet imperceptible sur les natifs de Prague et leur âme slave, leur pragmatisme allemand et leur humour noir juif. Mais une chose reste purement tchèque : l'imagination surréaliste et poétique dont chacun semble doué.

Avec l'accélération de l'internationalisation, et la montée en force d'une culture unique qui éradique

As the globalization of life accelerates, and monoculture gradually eradicates national identities, Prague is still defending herself vigorously and surviving, thanks to her lack of English. Once the language barrier falls, Prague will fall as well. Her only unique feature then will be the architecture which has witnessed and absorbed her painful past, which has soaked in so much visual and intellectual talent, such an abundance of human energy that it holds the visitor captive and will not let him go.

At the end of the millennium the people of Prague have discovered one more asset: the least orthodox President there has ever been within the walls of Hradčany, Václav Havel. This is a man who sensed the absurdity of his fate when he found himself catapulted to his grand post. "Being in power means I am permanently suspicious of myself," he said. Soon after, he was seen zipping through the long castle halls on a scooter. He knew he was not a professional politician but that he had something else to offer. In the great tradition of another preacher, Jan Hus, Havel told people that they should persist in doing things if they firmly believe them to be good, regardless of when or whether they will pay off. In a sense, he was replying to all those people throughout history who looked for excuses, people to whom life is a "barrel-organ." He concentrated on moral issues, specifically on lies, cheating and betrayal. In a famous remark about not being able to prevent murderers and dictators from publicly stroking the heads of children, he showed his awareness of the subtle complexities of life. The people know that someone who sees life at such close range will not let them down. Life is a huge number of minutiae, and Prague itself is an accumulation of beautifully crafted detail.

Prague is a city which combines the rational with the absurd, pragmatism with a sense of humor, hard work with playfulness and flexibility. Since the Czechs are masters at inventing mitigating circumstances, they do not see world globalization as a threat to their city. Deep down they are flattered and pleased that Prague has been rediscovered as one of the world's great cities of culture, which, with the ending of the Cold War, has resumed its rightful place at the crossroads of Europe.

Krystyna Nosarzewska

scheidend auf das Stadtbild eingewirkt haben. Dieser euro-amerikanische Schmelztiegel hat auf die Prager mit ihrer slawischen Mentalität, ihrem deutschen Pragmatismus und ihrem jüdischen Sinn für schwarzen Humor kaum Einfluß genommen. Eine Sache ist allerdings rein tschechisch: die surreale, poetische Phantasie, die die Menschen mit einer solchen Leichtigkeit ins Leben rufen können.

In einer Zeit, in der die Globalisierung des Lebens zunimmt und eine Einheitskultur allmählich alle nationalen Eigenheiten verwischt, verteidigt die Stadt ihre Identität noch massiv und erfolgreich. Ein Grund hierfür ist das Fehlen englischer Sprachkenntnisse. Wenn diese Sprachgrenze erst gefallen ist, fällt auch Prag. Ihre einzige Besonderheit wird dann ihre Architektur sein – Zeugin ihrer schmerzlichen Vergangenheit, die sie mit so viel visueller und intellektueller Energie in sich aufgenommen hat, daß der Besucher von dem Überfluß an menschlicher Schaffenskraft ergriffen und gefesselt wird.

Am Ende des Jahrtausends haben die Menschen von Prag einen weiteren Schatz entdeckt, den unkonventionellsten Präsidenten, der jemals in den Mauern des Hradschin regiert hat: Václav Havel. Dieser Mann begriff die Absurdität seines Schicksals, als er sich plötzlich auf seinen großen Posten katapultiert sah. »Am Hebel der Macht mißtraue ich mir selbst die ganze Zeit«, sagte er. Kurze Zeit später sah man ihn auf einem Roller durch die großen Burghallen flitzen. Er wußte, daß er kein professioneller Politiker war, dafür aber etwas anderes zu bieten hatte. In der Tradition eines anderen Predigers, Jan Hus, ermahnte Havel das Volk, daß es hartnäckig die Dinge tun sollte, von denen es überzeugt sei, daß sie richtig seien – egal, ob und wann sich das Engagement auszahlen würde. In gewissem Sinne antwortete er damit auf all diejenigen Menschen in der Geschichte, die nach Entschuldigungen gesucht hatten, Menschen, für die das Leben ein »Leierkasten« ist. Er konzentrierte sich auf moralische Fragen, besonders auf Lügen, Betrug und Verrat. Mit der bekannten Äußerung, er könne es nicht verhindern, daß Mörder und Diktatoren in der Öffentlichkeit Kindern übers Haar streichen, brachte er seine tiefe Sensibilität für die Vielschichtigkeiten des Lebens zum Ausdruck. Das Volk weiß, daß es von jemandem, der das Leben in all seiner Komplexität sieht, nicht im Stich gelassen wird. Das Dasein setzt sich aus einer Vielzahl von Einzelheiten zusammen, so wie Prag selbst eine Ansammlung von wunderschön gestalteten Miniaturen ist.

Prag ist eine Stadt, die Vernunft mit dem Absurden, Pragmatismus mit einem Sinn für Humor und harte Arbeit mit Verspieltheit und Flexibilität verbindet. Weil die Tschechen Meister im Schaffen mildernder Umstände sind, sehen sie in der Globalisierung auch keine Gefahr für ihre Stadt. Tief in ihrem Inneren fühlen sie sich geschmeichelt und freuen sich über die Tatsache, daß Prag als eine der größten Kulturstädte der Welt wiederentdeckt worden ist und nach dem Ende des Kalten Krieges erneut ihren rechtmäßigen Platz an den Wegkreuzungen Europas eingenommen hat.

Krystyna Nosarzewska

peu à peu les identités nationales, Prague se défend encore vigoureusement et survit, grâce à son absence de la connaissance de l'anglais. Une fois que le barrage de la langue aura été franchi, la ville risque de tomber. Sa seule personnalité tiendra alors à son architecture qui témoigne de son douloureux passé, riche de tant de génie visuel et intellectuel, et de tant d'énergie qu'elle fascine à chaque fois le visiteur.

À la fin de ce millénaire, le peuple de Prague s'est découvert un capital supplémentaire : le moins orthodoxe de tous les présidents jamais installés au Hradčany, Václav Havel. Cet homme a senti l'absurdité de son destin lorsqu'il s'est trouvé catapulté au poste suprême. «Étant au pouvoir, signifie que je doute en permanence de moi-même», dit-il. Peu après, on l'aperçut en scooter dans les immense halls du palais. Il sait qu'il n'est pas un politicien professionnel mais qu'il a quelque chose d'autre à offrir. Dans la grande tradition d'un autre prédicateur, Jan Hus, Havel dit aux Tchèques qu'ils doivent persister à faire les choses s'ils pensent qu'elles sont bonnes, quoi qu'ils puissent en attendre en retour et quelle qu'en soit la date. En un sens, il réplique à tous ceux qui au cours de l'histoire ont cherché des excuses, à tous ceux pour lesquels la vie est un «orgue de Barbarie». Il concentre son action sur les enjeux moraux, en particulier sur les mensonges, les trahisons et les traîtrises. Dans une remarque célèbre disant que l'on ne pouvait empêcher les meurtriers et les dictateurs de caresser en public la tête des enfants, il a montré sa conscience des subtiles complexités de l'existence. Le peuple sait que quelqu'un qui sait observer la vie d'aussi près ne l'abandonnera pas. La vie est faite d'une immense quantité de détails, et Prague elle-même est une accumulation de merveilleux détails.

Prague est une cité qui marie le rationnel à l'absurde, le pragmatisme au sens de l'humour, le travail et la bonne humeur. Depuis que les Tchèques sont passés maîtres dans l'acceptation des circonstances du destin, ils ne voient pas la globalisation comme une menace contre leur ville. Au plus profond d'eux-mêmes, ils sont flattés et apprécient que Prague soit redécouverte comme une grande ville de culture, et que leur capitale ait enfin retrouvé, avec la fin de la guerre froide, sa juste place au carrefour de l'Europe.

Krystyna Nosarzewska

# Under the Double Eagle
# Unter dem Doppeladler
# Prague sous l'aigle bicéphale

The ubiquitous double-headed eagle, emblem of the Austro-Hungarian monarchy, was displayed on government buildings, like this one on the house U hybernů, the former Prague customs office, facing the square in front of the Powder Gate. When the Empire collapsed, most of the eagles were torn down, although a few can still be found.

Der allgegenwärtige doppelköpfige Adler, das Emblem der österreichisch-ungarischen Monarchie, schmückte Regierungsgebäude wie das Haus U hybernů, das ehemalige Prager Zollamt, das am Platz gegenüber des Pulverturms liegt. Nach dem Untergang des Kaiserreiches wurden viele der Bildnisse entfernt; einige sind allerdings immer noch zu sehen.

L'omniprésent aigle à deux têtes, symbole de la monarchie austro-hongroise, était apposé sur les bâtiments officiels, comme ici, sur U hybernů, l'ancien siège des douanes pragoises, face à la place devant la porte des Pondres. Lors de l'effondrement de l'Empire, la plupart de ces emblèmes furent détruits, mais quelques-uns se remarquent encore.

Wappen der österreich-ungarischen Kronländer.

Böhmen | Bosnien | Bukowina | Croatien | Dalmatien | Galizien | Kärnten | Krain

Küstenland

Mähren

ÖSTERR.REICHSWAPPEN | UNGAR.REICHSWAPPEN

Ob.Österr.

Nied.Österr.

Salzburg | Schlesien | Siebenbürgen | Slavonien | Steiermark | Tirol | Ungarn | Vorarlberg

Kartogr. Anst. v. G. Freitag & Berndt, Wien.

## The Imperial Habsburg Family

(1) The Emperor Franz Josef I (1830–1916) with his family. In his long life he endured many tragedies: the suicide of his son, Crown Prince Rudolf (1858–89), whose portrait hangs on the wall; the assassination of his wife Elisabeth, generally known as Sissi (1837–98), who is sitting behind the little girl, Archduchess Elisabeth (1883–1963). Franz Josef also outlived the man who stands behind him, the young Archduke Franz Ferdinand d'Este (1863–1914), who became heir to the Habsburg throne after the deaths of Crown Prince Rudolf and of his own father, Karl Ludwig (the Emperor's brother)and who was assassinated. The others in the group are (left to right): standing behind Sissi, Archduchess Valerie (1868–1924); Archduke Franz Salvator (1866–1939); Prince Leopold of Bavaria (1821–1912); Franz Josef's daughter, Archduchess Gisela (1856–1932); and Crown Princess Stefanie (1864–1945), widow of Crown Prince Rudolf. (2) The Habsburg's double-headed eagle (left) with the Hungarian coat of arms (right). Bohemia's coat of arms – a lion with two tails – is in the top left corner.

## Die kaiserliche Familie

(1) Kaiser Franz Josef I. (1830–1916) mit seiner Familie. In seinem langen Leben mußte er viele Schicksalsschläge hinnehmen: den Selbstmord seines Sohnes, Kronprinz Rudolf (1858–89), dessen Porträt an der Wand hängt, die Ermordung seiner Frau Elisabeth, besser bekannt als Sissi (1837–98), die hinter dem kleinen Mädchen, Erzherzogin Elisabeth (1883–1963), sitzt und die Ermordung des jungen Erzherzogs Franz Ferdinand d'Este (1863–1914), der hinter ihm steht. Dieser war nach dem Tod des Kronprinzen Rudolf und seines eigenen Vaters Karl Ludwig, einem Bruder des Kaisers, Erbe des Habsburgerthrons geworden. Die anderen Personen in der Gruppe sind (von links nach rechts): Erzherzogin Valerie (1868–1924) hinter Sissi, Erzherzog Franz Salvator (1866–1939), Prinz Leopold von Bayern (1821–1912), Erzherzogin Gisela (1856–1932), Tochter des Kaisers, und Kronprinzessin Stefanie (1864–1945), die Witwe des Kronprinzen Rudolf. (2) Der Habsburger Doppeladler (links) mit dem ungarischen Wappen (rechts). Das böhmische Wappen, ein Löwe mit zwei Schwänzen ist in der Ecke links oben.

## La famille impériale

(1) L'empereur François-Joseph Ier (1830–1916) et sa famille. Sa longue existence fut marquée de nombreuses tragédies : le suicide de son fils, le prince héritier Rodolphe (1858–1889) dont le portrait est accroché au mur, l'assassinat de son épouse Élisabeth, « Sissi » (1837–1898), assise derrière la petite fille, l'archiduchesse Élisabeth (1883–1963). François-Joseph vécut plus longtemps que le jeune archiduc François-Ferdinand d'Este qui fut assassiné (1863–1914) qui se tient derrière lui, et fut l'héritier du trône après la mort du prince héritier Rodolphe et de son propre père, Charles-Louis, frère de l'Empereur. Les autres membres du groupe sont, de gauche à droite : debout derrière Sissi, l'archiduchesse Valérie (1868–1924), l'archiduc François-Salvator (1866–1939), le prince Léopold de Bavière (1821–1912), la fille de François-Joseph, l'archiduchesse Gisèle (1856–1932) et la princesse héritière Stéphanie (1864–1945), veuve du prince héritier Rodolphe. (2) L'aigle impérial bicéphale des Habsbourg ( à gauche) et les armes de la Hongrie (à droite). Les armes de la Bohème – un lion à deux queues – se trouvent dans le coin gauche en haut.

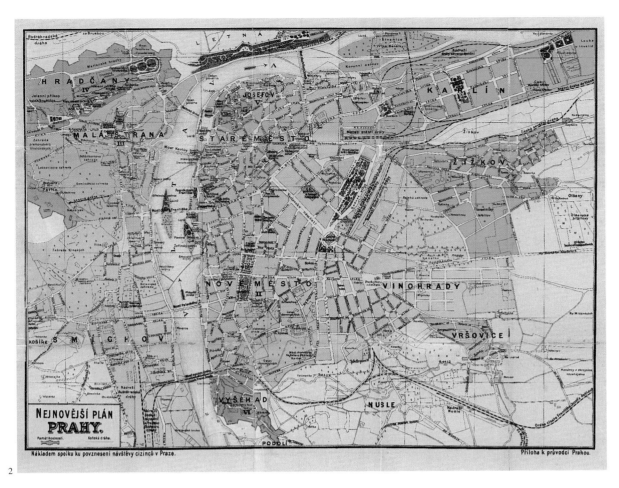

## Map of Austria-Hungary

(1) The Empire's 51 million subjects sang the Imperial anthem on the Emperor's birthday in 12 different languages. Besides 12 million Austrians and Germans, the Empire was composed of: 10 million Hungarians, 6.6 million Czechs, 2 million Slovaks, 5 million Poles, 4 million Ruthenes, 3.2 million Croats, 2 million Serbs, 2.9 million Romanians, 1.4 million Slovenes, 0.8 million Italians, 0.6 million Islamic Slavs and 0.5 million others.

(1, top right) The Austro-Hungarian Eagle. (2) According to a census of 31 December 1890, the population of Prague numbered 368,837 inhabitants, living in 9222 houses. At the turn of the century the city consisted of the following districts: Old Town I, New Town II, Little Quarter III, Hradčany IV, Josefov V, Vyšehrad VI, Holešovice VII, and Libeň VIII.

## Karte von Österreich-Ungarn

(1) Die 51 Mio. Untertanen des Kaiserreiches sangen zum Geburtstag des Kaisers die Nationalhymne in zwölf verschiedenen Sprachen. Neben den 12 Mio. Österreichern und Deutschen lebten im Kaiserreich 10 Mio. Ungarn, 6,6 Mio. Tschechen, 2 Mio. Slowaken, 5 Mio. Polen, 4 Mio. Ruthenen, 3,2 Mio. Kroaten, 2 Mio. Serben, 2,9 Mio. Rumänen, 1,4 Mio. Slowenen, 0,8 Mio. Italiener, 0,6 Mio. moslemische Slawen und 0,5 Mio. Menschen anderer Nationalitäten.

(1, oben rechts) Der österreichisch-ungarische Doppeladler. (2) Nach der Volkszählung vom 31. Dezember 1890 belief sich die Bevölkerung von Prag auf 368.837 Einwohner in 9.222 Haushalten. Um die Jahrhundertwende war die Stadt in folgende Distrikte unterteilt: Altstadt I, Neustadt II, Kleinseite III, Hradschin IV, Josefov V, Vyšehrad VI, Holešovice VII, Libeň VIII.

## Carte d'Autriche-Hongrie

(1) Les 51 millions de sujets de l'Empire chantaient l'hymne impérial en 12 langues différentes pour l'anniversaire de l'Empereur. En dehors de 12 millions d'Autrichiens et d'Allemands, l'Empire se composait de 10 millions de Hongrois, 6,6 de Tchèques, 2 de Slovaques, 5 de Polonais, 4 de Ruthènes, 3,2 de Croates, 2 de Serbes, 2,9 de Roumains, 1,4 de Slovènes, 0,8 d'Italiens, 0,6 de Slaves islamisés et 500 000 représentants d'autres nationalités.

(1, en haut à droite) L'aigle austro-hongroise. (2) Selon le recensement du 31 décembre 1890, la population de la capitale comptait 368 837 habitants, vivant dans 9 222 immeubles. Au tournant du siècle, la ville se composait des quartiers suivants: Vieille ville I, Nouvelle ville II, Le petit quartier III, Hradčany IV, Josefov V, Vyšehrad VI, Holešovice VII et Libeň VIII

4

## Monuments to the Empire

(1) The equestrian statue of Emperor Franz I (1768–1835) was the central part of this monument designed by Josef Max in 1845 after drawings by Josef Kranner from 1844, and unveiled in 1850. In 1893 it suffered the indignity of having a rope placed around its neck by some anti-Habsburg Czech youths. The statue was removed in 1919 (today it can be found in the lapidary of the Exhibition Grounds), while the empty neo-Gothic shell on Smetana Embankment remains a forgotten relic from the Habsburg past. (3) Field Marshal Johann Joseph Wenzel, Count Radetzky von Radetz (1766–1858) was a famous commander (he was a Czech, named Václav Rádetzký) who successfully managed to keep the Habsburg Empire united. A monument was erected to him for his 98th birthday, but he died before the unveiling in 1858. The monument, 2.84m high, was cast in Nuremberg from Italian guns captured in Custozza and given by the Emperor for this fitting tribute, and was the work of Kristian Ruben, Emanuel Max and Josef Max. Johann Strauss further enhanced the Marshal's myth in his famous *Radetzky March*. However, the Czechs were much less sentimental about the man and his statue. After the declaration of Czechoslovak independence, the monument was immediately covered with canvas and soon after the winter of 1919 it was dismantled (2). Today it is also displayed in the lapidary at the Exhibition Grounds. (4) The Franz Josef I suspension bridge, built by English architects in 1865–68, was 250m long and 9.5m wide. The chains were brought from England. It was pulled down in 1941 and Šverma Bridge stands in its place today.

## Monumente des Kaiserreiches

(1) Die Reiterstatue von Kaiser Franz I. (1768–1835) bekrönte ursprünglich das Monument, das nach Entwürfen von Josef Kranner 1844 errichtet wurde. Das Standbild stammt von Josef Max und wurde 1850 enthüllt. 1893 entweihten es junge Tschechen, Gegner der Habsburgermonarchie, indem sie eine Schlinge um dem Hals des Kaisers legten. 1919 wurde die Statue entfernt. Sie befindet sich heute im Lapidarium auf dem Ausstellungsgelände, während die leere neugotische Muschel am Smetana-Ufer als Überbleibsel des Habsburgerreiches vergessen wurde. (3) Feldmarschall Johann Joseph Wenzel, Graf Radetzky von Radetz (1766–1858) war ein berühmter Befehlshaber (er war Tscheche und hieß ursprünglich Václav Rádetzký), der die Einheit des Kaiserreiches bewahrte. Anläßlich seines 98. Geburtstages wurde er mit einem Denkmal geehrt, vor dessen Enthüllung er aber verstarb. Das 2,84 Meter hohe Monument – ein Werk von Kristian Ruben, Emanuel und Josef Max – wurde in Nürnberg aus italienischen Kanonen gegossen, die in Custozza erbeutet und dem Kaiser als angemessenen Tribut übergeben worden waren. Johann Strauß trug zum Mythos dieses Marschalls durch seinen berühmten *Radetzky-Marsch* bei. Die Tschechen allerdings waren dem Mann und seinem Denkmal gegenüber weniger sentimental eingestellt. Nach der Unabhängigkeitserklärung der Tschechoslowakei bedeckten sie das Monument sofort mit einem Segeltuch und entfernten es bald darauf im Winter 1919 (2). Heute steht es ebenfalls im Lapidarium auf dem Ausstellungsgelände. (4) Die Franz-Josefs-Brücke, eine Kettenbrücke, 1865–68 von englischen Architekten erbaut, war 250 m lang und 9,5 m breit. Die Ketten waren aus England mitgebracht worden. Sie wurde 1941 demontiert und später durch die Šverma-Brücke ersetzt.

## Les monuments impériaux

(1) La statue équestre de l'empereur François Ier (1768–1835) figurait au centre d'un monument dessiné par Josef Max en 1845 (après l'esquisse de Josef Kranner de 1844) et inauguré en 1850. En 1893, de jeunes opposants tchèques lui passèrent une corde au cou. La statue fut déplacée en 1919 et se trouve au lapidarium du champ de foire, son abri néogothique du quai Smetana se dressant telle une relique d'un passé habsbourgeois oublié. (3) Václav Rádetzký (1766–1858 ), un célèbre haut officier tchèque réussit à préserver l'unité de l'empire des Habsbourg. Un monument lui fut érigé à l'occasion de son 98e anniversaire, mais il mourut avant son inauguration en 1858. Le monument de 2,84 m de haut fut fondu à Nuremberg à partir de canons italiens pris à Custozza et offerts en hommage à l'Empereur. Il était l'œuvre de Kristian Ruben, Emanuel Max et Josef Max. Johann Strauss contribua au mythe du maréchal par sa *Marche de Radetzky*. Les Tchèques étaient néanmoins peu attachés à l'homme et à sa statue. Après la déclaration de l'indépendance tchécoslovaque, le monument fut immédiatement masqué derrière des toiles et démantelé au cour de l'hiver 1919 (2). Aujourd'hui, il se trouve également au lapidarium du champ de foire. (4) Le pont François-Joseph Ier, construit par des architectes anglais de 1865 à 1868, mesurait 250 m de long sur 9,5 m de large. Les chaînes provenaient d'Angleterre. Démoli en 1941, il fut remplacé par le pont Šverma.

## River Traffic

The river Vltava (Moldau), with a length of some 425km, flows from the springs of Šumava (Bohemian Forest) to its conflation with the Labe (Elbe) in Mělník. There were 47 ferries operating at the beginning of the 20th century. In 1860 a steamboat, called *Praha*, boasting enough space for 600 people, made her maiden voyage; in the first year 19,005 passengers were ferried on it. Most of those who used the steamers were peasants transporting their agricultural products to the capital. The number of steamboats increased from 11 in 1889 to 21 in 1913. The inhabitants of Prague often called the steamers "drunken little fishes" because of their many accidents. In 1898 the steamboat *Franz Josef I*, mooring near Palacký Bridge, exploded, breaking in half and sinking immediately with the loss of three lives. (5) Karel Tuček, one of Prague's eccentric inventors, in his propeller-powered boat, the *hydrobus*, 1912.

## Flußverkehr

Von ihrer Quelle in Šumava (Böhmerwald) fließt die Moldau (Vltava) auf einer Länge von etwa 425 km bis zur Elbe bei Mělník. Zu Beginn des 20. Jahrhunderts waren 47 Fähren in Betrieb. 1860 nahm ein Dampfschiff mit dem Namen *Praha*, das 600 Fahrgäste fassen konnte, den Verkehr auf und beförderte in seinem ersten Jahr 19.005 Passagiere. Die meisten von ihnen waren Bauern, die ihre landwirtschaftlichen Erzeugnisse in die Hauptstadt brachten. Von 1889 bis 1913 stieg die Zahl der Dampfschiffe von 11 auf 21. Wegen der zahlreichen Unfälle nannten die Prager sie »betrunkene kleine Fische«. 1898 explodierte der in der Nähe der Palacký-Brücke vertäute Dampfer *Franz Josef I*, brach in zwei Teile und sank auf der Stelle, drei Menschen starben bei diesem Unglück. (5) Karel Tuček, einer der exzentrischen Erfinder Prags, mit seinem propellergetriebenen Boot, dem *Hydrobus*, im Jahr 1912.

## Le trafic fluvial

Longue de 425 km, la Moldau prend sa source à Šumava (Forêt de Bohême) et se jette dans l'Elbe près de Mělník. 47 bacs étaient encore en service à Prague au début du XXe siècle. En 1860, le vapeur *Praha* capable de transporter 600 passagers fit son premier voyage. 19 005 voyageurs l'emprunteront dès sa première année d'exploitation. La plupart d'entre eux étaient des paysans qui apportaient leurs produits à la capitale. Le nombre de vapeurs passa de 11 en 1889 à 21 en 1913. Les Pragois surnommaient ces bateaux « les petits poissons saouls » car ils connurent de nombreux accidents. En 1898, le vapeur *Franz Josef I*, à l'ancre près du pont Palacký, explosa, se brisa en deux et sombra immédiatement, faisant trois victimes. (5) Karel Tuček, inventeur excentrique, aux commandes de son engin à hélice, l'*Hydrobus* en 1912.

1

2

3

4

5

## Flood Destroys the Charles Bridge

(Overleaf) On 4 September 1890 the Vltava swept away parts of the Charles Bridge and two Baroque statues, flooding all the Prague islands, 52 streets, many squares and numerous buildings. The flood was the result of extreme rainfall in Southern Bohemia and the water level reached 3.65m. The swollen river set loose boats, timber and wooden rafts, which caused most of the damage. At the time the event was described as a catastrophe comparable in magnitude only to the burning down of the National Theater in1881.

## Eine Flut zerstört die Karlsbrücke

(Folgende Seiten) Am 4. September 1890 spülte die Moldau Teile der Karlsbrücke und zwei Barockfiguren davon und setzte alle Prager Inseln, 52 Straßen, viele Plätze und zahlreiche Häuser unter Wasser. Infolge heftiger Regenfälle in Südböhmen war der Wasserstand auf 3,65 Meter angestiegen. Der angeschwollene Fluß riß Boote, Bäume und Holzflöße mit sich, die noch weitere Schäden anrichteten. Die Ereignisse wurden als eine Katastrophe angesehen, die in ihren Ausmaßen nur mit dem Brand des Nationaltheaters von 1881 verglichen werden konnte.

## Le pont Charles détruit par les inondations

(Pages-suivantes) Le 4 septembre 1890, la Moldau renversa plusieurs arches du Pont Charles, engloutit deux de ses statues baroques, recouvrit toutes les îles de Prague, 52 rues, de nombreuses places et bâtiments. L'inondation avait été provoquée par d'importantes chutes de pluie en Bohême du Sud et le niveau des eaux atteignit 3,65 m. La rivière en fureur charriait des bateaux, des poutres, des arbres qui provoquèrent la plupart des dommages. À l'époque, l'événement fut décrit comme une catastrophe comparable en importance à l'incendie du Théâtre national en 1881.

### The Vltava in Winter

(1, 2) Icemen cutting blocks of ice from the river to be sold to Prague beerhouses and butchers. (3, 5) Ice skating was regarded as a good place for befriending young women, who would be invited to skate with the same gesture (a man would take his hat off and ask a chaperone for permission) as when being invited to dance at a ball. Skates, which were hired at special stands, had to be strapped to the boots. Halifaxes, a Canadian model with heel and sole clamps, were introduced in 1884, but only the rich could afford them. (4) The frozen river was ideal for ice hockey, which was played from 1889 with a ball and a flat walking stick. The Czech players learned Canadian hockey (with hockey sticks and a puck) in 1909 when their team went to play in France and two years later they became European champions.

### Die Moldau im Winter

(1, 2) Arbeiter schlagen Eisblöcke aus dem Fluß, um sie in Prags Bierkellern und Metzgereien zu verkaufen. (3, 5) Schlittschuhlaufen galt als gute Gelegenheit, um junge Damen kennenzulernen. Sie wurden mit derselben Geste, mit der man sie bei einem Ball zum Tanz aufforderte, zum Eislaufen eingeladen: der Mann nahm den Hut ab und bat die Anstandsdame um Erlaubnis. Die Schlittschuhe, die an speziellen Ständen geliehen werden konnten, wurden unter die Schuhe geschnallt. Halifax-Schlittschuhe aus Kanada, die man mit Klammern an Sohlen und Fersen befestigte, kamen 1884 in Mode, aber nur die Reichen konnten sich diese leisten. (4) Der zugefrorene Fluß eignete sich ideal zum Eishockeyspielen. Das Spiel wurde seit 1889 mit einem Ball und flachen Spazierstöcken gespielt; 1909 lernten die tschechischen Spieler kanadisches Eishockey (mit Hockeyschlägern und einem Puck) bei einem Match in Frankreich, zwei Jahre später wurden sie Europameister.

### La Moldau en hiver

(1, 2) Des ouvriers découpent des blocs de glace sur les berges de la Moldau, qui seront vendus en ville aux brasseurs et aux bouchers. (3, 5) Le patin à glace est une occasion idéale pour rencontrer des jeunes femmes que l'on invite à patiner de la même façon qu'à danser: l'homme lève son chapeau et demande au chaperon la permission. Les patins loués dans des boutiques spéciales sont attachés aux chaussures par des sangles. Les « Halifax », modèle canadien à crochets, apparurent en 1884, mais seuls les plus riches pouvaient se les offrir. (4) La rivière gelée est un lieu parfait pour la pratique du hockey sur glace, que l'on joue depuis 1889 avec une balle et une canne. Les joueurs tchèques apprendront bientôt le hockey canadien (avec une canne différente et un palet). En 1909, leur équipe joua en France et devint championne d'Europe deux ans plus tard.

1

2

3

4

5

## Horse Power

Prague was one of the noisiest European cities because of the sound of hooves hitting the cobblestones and the rattle of wheels. Asphalt did not replace the cobblestones because the paviours stubbornly spread rumors that it was too slippery for horses. The drivers were incessantly yelling "Ó, ó, ó," which derived from the word *pozor* (watch out). Horse-drawn public transport came into operation on 23 September 1875 with the opening of the first horse-traction line. At the time of its greatest development in the 1890s, the Prague horse-traction transport system was nearly 19km long, with 117 cars and 528 horses. (1) Horse-drawn carriage in K mostu (now Mostecká). (2) Horse-driven carriages on the Charles Bridge. The last horse-drawn tram made its journey across Charles Bridge on 12 May 1905. (3) Traffic on Palacký Bridge (decorated with statues by Josef Myslbek, which nowadays can be found on the top of the Vyšehrad Hill). (4) Beer-cart driver. (5) Undertakers. (6) Grooming. (7) Carriage-cleaning. (8) Municipal-services inspector. (9) Cabby.

## Pferdestärken

Prag war wegen des Geklappers der Pferdehufe auf den Pflastersteinen und des Ratterns der Räder eine der lautesten Städte Europas. Die Pflastersteine wurden nicht durch Asphalt ersetzt, weil die Pflasterer hartnäckig das Gerücht verbreiteten, er sei zu glatt für Pferdehufe. Die Fahrer brüllten ununterbrochen »Ó, ó, ó«, was eigentlich für *pozor* (Achtung) stand. Mit der Eröffnung der ersten Pferdebahn-Linie am 23. September 1875 begann der pferdebetriebene öffentliche Nahverkehr. Während ihrer größten Ausdehnung in den 90er Jahren des 19. Jahrhunderts war die Prager Pferdebahn fast 19 km lang und besaß 117 Waggons und 528 Pferde. (1) In K mostu (heute Mostecká). (2) Kutschen der Pferdebahn auf der Karlsbrücke. Die letzte Pferdebahn überquerte am 12. Mai 1905 die Brücke. (3) Verkehr auf der Palacký-Brücke (mit Statuengruppen von Josef Myslbek, die heute auf dem Vyšehrad stehen). (4) Ein Bierkutscher. (5) Ein Leichenbestatter. (6) Das Striegeln. (7) Die Reinigung der Bahnen. (8) Städtische Aufseher. (9) Droschkenkutscher.

## À cheval

Avec le choc des fers claquant sur les pavés et le grincement des roues, Prague était l'une des villes les plus bruyantes d'Europe. L'asphalte ne remplaça pas les pavés car les paveurs sur la défensive répandirent la rumeur que les chevaux y glissaient. Les cochers criaient d'incessants «Ó, ó, ó» pour *pozor* (attention). La première ligne de transport public à cheval fut ouverte le 23 septembre 1875. Le réseau de près de 19 km de long était parcouru par 117 voitures et 528 chevaux. (1) Voiture à cheval rue Mostecká. (2) Les voitures à cheval empruntèrent le pont Charles entre 1883 et 1905. Le dernier tram hippomobile le franchit le 12 mai 1905. (3) La circulation sur le pont Palacký (orné de statues de Josef Myslbek, qui se trouvent maintenant sur la colline de Vyšehrad). (4) Cocher de char à bière. (5) Employés des pompes funèbres. (6) Bichonnage. (7) Nettoyage d'une calèche. (8) Employé municipal. (9) Cocher.

4

5

6

7

8

9

## Tramways

Prague's first electric tram appeared on 18 July 1891 as an advertising stunt to open the Bohemian Jubilee Exhibition. Trams were used not only for carrying passengers but also to transport food, coal to the city gasworks and rubbish to the communal dumping ground in Vysočany. The first trams were distinguished only by color combination, headlights and direction plates. In 1908 tramlines came to be denoted by numbers. By 1910 the combined length of 14 separate tramlines was 83km. There were 1828 employees, 357 electric cars and 195 trailers which carried over 49 million passengers annually. The Czech inventor František Křižík was the owner of the first tram licence (from Letná to Park Royal). In 1896 he started operating another tramline to the outskirts of Libeň and Vysočany. In 1897 *Elektrické podniky královského hlavního města Prahy* (Electrical Enterprises of the Royal Capital of Prague) was established, gradually taking over the tramlines and expanding the network.

## Straßenbahnen

Prags erste elektrische Straßenbahn kam am 18. Juli 1891 anläßlich der Eröffnung der böhmischen Jubiläumsausstellung auf die Straße. In den Straßenbahnen wurden nicht nur Fahrgäste, sondern auch Lebensmittel, Kohlen für die städtischen Gaswerke und Abfall für die örtliche Müllkippe in Vysočany befördert. Die Straßenbahnen unterschieden sich anfänglich nur durch ihre Farbkombinationen, Scheinwerfer und Streckenanzeigen voneinander, nach 1908 erhielten sie unterschiedliche Nummern. 1910 war das Streckennetz der 14 einzelnen Straßenbahnlinien 83 km lang, es gab 1.828 Angestellte, 357 elektrische Wagen und 195 Anhänger, die jährlich mehr als 49 Millionen Fahrgäste beförderten. Der tschechische Erfinder František Křižík war im Besitz der ersten Straßenbahnlizenz (von Letná zum königlichen Park). 1896 eröffnete er eine weitere Straßenbahnlinie in die Vororte Libeň und Vysočany. 1897 wurden die *Elektrické podniky královského hlavního města Prahy* (Elektrowerke der Königlichen Hauptstadt Prag) gegründet, die Schritt für Schritt die Straßenbahnlinien übernahmen und das Streckennetz erweiterten.

## Tramways

Le premier tramway électrique fit son apparition à Prague le 18 juillet 1891, à l'occasion de l'ouverture de l'exposition du Jubilé en Bohême. Les trams servaient non seulement à transporter des voyageurs mais également les produit alimentaires, le charbon vers les usines à gaz et les ordures vers la décharge communale de Vysočany. Les premiers trams se distinguaient par leur combinaison de couleurs, leurs phares et les plaques indiquant leur direction. En 1908, les lignes furent numérotées. Vers 1910, la longueur totale des 14 lignes représentait 83 km, et la compagnie employait 1 828 personnes, 357 voitures électriques et 195 motrices transportant chaque année plus de 49 millions de passagers. L'inventeur tchèque František Křižík fut le premier détenteur d'une licence d'exploitation de tram (de Letná au Parc Royal). En 1896, il lança une nouvelle ligne vers les banlieues de Libeň et de Vysočany. En 1897, *Elektrické podniky královského hlavního města Prahy* (Entreprise électrique de Prague capitale royale) fut fondée et reprit peu à peu toutes les lignes avant d'étendre son réseau.

UNDER THE DOUBLE EAGLE

2

## The Ghosts of the Ghetto

The former Prague Jewish ghetto was renamed "Josefov" in memory of the Habsburg Emperor Josef II (1741–90), who granted the Bohemian Jews a number of basic liberties. They were granted the right to learn crafts and pursue higher studies, to own land and to serve in the army. They were also allowed to practice their religion freely and to leave the ghetto. In 1860 Jews attained full equality with other races and nationalities in the eyes of the law. The Prague ghetto was incorporated into the rest of the city and virtually ceased to exist. At that time there were 8500 Jews in Prague, against a Christian population of 115,000. After 1860, when the more prosperous Jews had long since left the ghetto, it became a refuge for impoverished Christians as well as Jews. (1) The Old New Synagogue, with its fortress-like 13th-century walls, survived not only a few pogroms and fires but the "forces of progress" known in Czech as *asanace* (slum clearance, redevelopment). The Jewish Town Hall, with its famous Hebrew clock whose hands turn anti-clockwise, was another survivor of this sanitation program. (2) The cover illustration of a book on the Prague ghetto by Zikmund Winter, published in 1901.

## Die Geister des Ghettos

Zur Erinnerung an den Habsburger Kaiser Josef II. (1741–90), der den böhmischen Juden eine Reihe von Grundrechten zugestanden hatte, erhielt das frühere jüdische Ghetto Prags den Namen Josefov. Die Juden durften ein Handwerk lernen und höhere Schulen besuchen, Land besitzen und in die Armee eintreten. Auch war es ihnen erlaubt, ihre Religion frei auszuüben und das Ghetto zu verlassen. 1860 wurden die Juden den anderen Rassen und Nationalitäten gleichgestellt. Das Prager Ghetto wurde aufgelöst und in die Stadt integriert. Zu diesem Zeitpunkt gab es 8.500 Juden und 115.000 Christen in Prag. Nach 1860, als die reicheren Juden das Ghetto verließen, wurde es zum Wohnviertel für verarmte Christen und Juden gleichermaßen. (1) Die Altneusynagoge mit ihren burgähnlichen Mauern aus dem 13. Jahrhundert widerstand nicht nur einer Reihe von Progromen und Feuersbrünsten, sondern auch den »Kräften des Fortschritts«, wie man das tschechische Wort *asanace* (Assanierung oder Altstadtsanierung) auch übersetzen kann. Das jüdische Rathaus, dessen berühmte Uhr ein Zifferblatt mit linksläufigen Zeiger trägt, überlebte ebenfalls das Sanierungsprogramm. (2) Umschlagsillustration eines 1901 erschienenen Buches von Zikmund Winter über das Prager Ghetto.

## Les Fantômes du ghetto

L'ancien ghetto de Prague était appelé «Josefov» en souvenir de l'empereur Joseph II (1741–1790) qui avait accordé aux Juifs de Bohême un certain nombre de libertés fondamentales. Ils pouvaient pratiquer les métiers de leur choix, poursuivre des études supérieures, posséder des terres et servir dans l'armée. Ils étaient également libres de pratiquer leur religion et de quitter le ghetto. En 1860, les Juifs obtinrent l'égalité juridique complète avec les autres races et nationalités. Le ghetto de Prague fut incorporé au reste de la ville et cessa virtuellement d'exister. À cette époque, 8 500 Juifs vivaient dans la capitale pour une population chrétienne de 115 000 personnes. Après 1860, alors que les Juifs les plus prospères avaient depuis longtemps quitté le ghetto, celui-ci devint un refuge aussi bien pour les Juifs que les Chrétiens. (1) L'ancienne nouvelle synagogue aux murs fortifiés datant du XIIIe siècle survécut non seulement à quelques pogroms et incendies mais également aux «forces de progrès» de l'*asanace* (curetage des taudis, rénovation). L'hôtel de ville juif à la fameuse horloge hébraïque dont les aiguilles tournent à l'envers est un autre survivant de ce programme hygiéniste. (2) Couverture d'un livre sur le ghetto de Prague par Zikmund Winter, publié en 1901.

1

2

3

## Ghetto Life

Ignát Herrmann (1854–1935), the well-known Czech writer, gave a vivid description of life in the ghetto: "The whole place gave the impression that the rules of the outside world were in abeyance, and a solitary traveller was exposed to the mercy of other powers – invisible, mysterious and hostile. The streets were covered with filth and refuse; children ran about half-naked, and in front of the houses women performed intimate household tasks or sat about gossiping at the end of the day, having finished work and perhaps gone for an evening stroll. In many streets, house after house was a brothel.... Cheek by jowl with the haunts of vice and debauchery were the austere houses of believing Jews who locked their doors at nightfall, kept the Sabbath, and observed the high festivals in traditional style. While the taverns and coffee-houses rang with the crazy mirth of Saturday-night revellers, the synagogues and other houses of prayer, of which there were some forty in the Jewish quarter of Prague, would be filled with the monotonous chant of their congregation."

## Leben im Ghetto

Der bekannte tschechische Schriftsteller Ignát Herrmann (1854–1935) gab eine lebendige Beschreibung des Lebens im Ghetto: »Der ganze Ort vermittelt den Eindruck, als seien die Gesetze der äußeren Welt außer Kraft gesetzt. Der einsame Wanderer steht in der Gnade anderer Mächte – unsichtbar, mysteriös und feindlich. Die Straßen sind voller Schmutz und Abfall; halbnackte Kinder laufen herum und vor dem Haus sitzen Frauen und verrichten die intimsten Haushaltspflichten oder schwatzen am Ende des Tages, nachdem sie ihre Arbeit erledigt haben und einen Abendspaziergang machen. In vielen Straßen ist in jedem Haus ein Bordell ... Dicht an dicht stehen die Höhlen von Laster und Ausschweifung neben den kargen Häusern der gläubigen Juden, die zur Nacht die Tür verschließen, den Sabbath halten und die hohen Feste auf traditionelle Weise begehen. Während die Kneipen und Kaffeehäuser von den verrückten Freuden der samstäglichen Nachtschwärmer widerhallen, sind die Synagogen und anderen Gebetshäuser, von denen es im jüdischen Viertel von Prag etwa 40 gibt, erfüllt von dem monotonen Gesang der Gemeinde.«

## La vie du ghetto

Ignát Herrmann (1854–1935), le célèbre écrivain tchèque, a fourni une description très vivante du ghetto: « Tout donnait l'impression que les règles du monde extérieur étaient ici suspendues, et que le voyageur solitaire était à la merci de puissances autres – invisibles, mystérieuses, hostiles… Côte à côte avec les antres du vice et de la débauche, se dressaient les austères demeures des Juifs pratiquants qui fermaient leur porte à la tombée de la nuit, respectaient le sabbat et participaient aux grandes fêtes traditionnelles. Alors que les tavernes et les cafés résonnaient des réjouissances débridées du samedi soir, les synagogues et autres lieux de prière – on en comptait environ quarante dans le quartier juif de Prague – s'emplissaient du chant monotone des assemblées de fidèles. »

4

5

## The *Asanace* of the Ghetto

(1) In the 1890s the city authorities decided to raze the ghetto slums, the official reason being that the area's complete lack of sanitation made it a serious health hazard. In 1893–1915 far-reaching alterations took place over a 365,476 square meter area of the city, of which 272,984 square meters were in what is now Prague I district and 92,984 in the ghetto. The demolition was opposed by intellectuals and artists, to no avail. The labyrinth of medieval dwellings was replaced with large, elegant apartment buildings along wide boulevards. (2) The newly opened Mikulášska (now called Pařížská) provided access to the river.

## Die Assanierung des Ghettos

(1) Um 1890 beschloß die Stadtverwaltung den kompletten Abriß des Ghettos mit der offiziellen Begründung, es stelle ein Gesundheitsrisiko dar. Zwischen 1893 und 1915 fanden groß angelegte Umbauarbeiten auf einem Gebiet von 365.476 m² statt, von denen 272.984 m² zum heutigen Distrikt I und 92.984 m² zum Ghetto gehörten. Intellektuelle und Künstler kritisierten die Sanierungsarbeiten. Das Labyrinth aus mittelalterlichen Wohnungen wurde durch große elegante Wohnhäuser an breiten Boulevards ersetzt. (2) Die neu angelegte Mikulášska (die heutige Pařížská-Straße) öffnete sich zum Fluß hin.

## Le curetage du ghetto

(1) Dans les années 1890, les autorités municipales décidèrent de raser les taudis du ghetto, la raison officielle étant que l'absence totale d'hygiène de ce quartier menaçait la santé des citadins. De 1893 à 1915, d'importants travaux se déroulèrent sur un secteur de 365 476 m², dont 272 984 dans ce qui est aujourd'hui le quartier de Prague I et 92 984 dans le ghetto. Des intellectuels et des artistes s'opposèrent en vain à cette démolition. Le labyrinthe des vieilles demeures médiévales fut remplacé par de grands immeubles bordant de larges boulevards. (2) La nouvelle rue Mikulášska (aujourd'hui Pařížská, rue de Paris) donna un nouvel accès à la rivière.

## Art Nouveau

The "new style" *secese* was brought from Vienna (Sezession) and Paris (Art Nouveau) at the turn of the century. Born of a rebellion against Classicism (which was seen as stifling and dead) and permeated with *fin de siècle* mysticism, Art Nouveau searched for inspiration in living plants, animals and insects. In Prague the highly stylized floral designs and undulating, sensuous lines can be seen in beautiful grilles and shutters, stained-glass windows and doors, wrought-iron balconies and iron awnings, chandeliers and gates. The Czech artists who introduced the decorative curve not only combined it with floral shapes but often added human masks and naturalistic nudes of legendary Slav warriors (which were inspired by ancient Egyptians and Babylonians) as well as historical figures.

## Der Jugendstil

Aus Wien (Sezession) und aus Paris (Art Nouveau) kam um die Jahrhundertwende der »neue Stil«, die *Secese*. Aus der Rebellion gegen den Klassizismus (den man für steif und tot hielt) und durchdrungen vom Mystizismus des *Fin de Siècle*, suchte der Jugendstil seine Motive aus dem Bereich der Pflanzen, Tieren und Insekten. Überall in Prag finden sich kunstvoll stilisierte Blumendesigns und wellenförmige, sinnliche Linien auf wunderschönen Gittern und Fensterläden, auf bunten Glasfenstern und Türen, auf schmiedeeisernen Balkons, Kerzenleuchtern und Toren. Die tschechischen Künstler, die den dekorativen Bogen einführten, kombinierten diesen nicht nur mit verschiedenen Blumenformen. Oftmals fügten sie auch menschliche Masken und die naturalistisch dargestellten, nackten Körper legendärer, slawischer Krieger hinzu (die von den alten Ägyptern und Babyloniern inspiriert waren), sowie historische Figuren.

## L'Art Nouveau

Le *Secese*, le «nouveau style», fut importé de Vienne (Wiener Sezession) et de Paris (Art Nouveau) au tournant du siècle. Né d'une rébellion contre l'historicisme éclectique, jugé stérile, mort et imprégné de mysticisme fin-de-siècle, l'Art Nouveau recherchait son inspiration dans les végétaux, les animaux et les insectes. À Prague, des motifs floraux stylisés tout en courbes et en lignes sensuelles s'observent encore dans de superbes grilles, sur des volets, des vitraux, des portes, des balcons et des marquises de fer forgé, des lampadaires et des portails. Les artistes tchèques qui introduisirent ce sens de la courbe en décoration l'appliquèrent non seulement à des formes florales, mais également à des masques humains, des représentations nues (inspirées de l'Égypte et de Babylone) de guerriers slaves légendaires et de personnages historiques.

## Alfons Mucha

Alfons Mucha (1860–1939) was the most famous *secese* artist. He often drew or painted robust Slav beauties decorated with plaits and wreaths of elegant poppies, thistles, ivy, daisies, sunflowers and many other plants unknown to a town-dweller. His feeling for elegance was so apparent that he was asked to design jewelry, calendars, furniture, postage stamps, menus, banknotes, theater programs, posters (he became famous for his Sarah Bernhardt posters) and book illustrations. The Moravian country boy who was refused a place at the Prague Art Academy studied in Vienna and Paris, then traveled to the United States before returning to Prague, where he worked most notably on the Municipal House, the showcase of Prague Art Nouveau. His dream was to paint a monumental series of pictures called *The Slav Epic* (1910–28), which tells the legends and history of the Slavs. (1) Mucha with his wife, Marie. (2, 3) Mucha in his studio. (4) A detail of Mucha's stained-glass window in St Vitus Cathedral.

## Alfons Mucha

Alfons Mucha (1860–1939) war der bekannteste Künstler der *Secese*. Oft zeichnete oder malte er robuste slawische Schönheiten, die ihr Haar zu Zöpfen geflochten hatten und Blumengirlanden aus schön gewachsenem Klatschmohn, Disteln, Efeu, Gänseblümchen, Sonnenblumen und vielen anderen, dem Städter unbekannten Pflanzen trugen. Sein Gespür für Eleganz war so augenfällig, daß er mit Entwürfen für Schmuck, Kalendern, Möbeln, Briefmarken, Speisekarten, Geldscheinen, Theaterprogrammen, Plakaten (mit seinen Sarah-Bernhardt-Plakaten wurde er weltberühmt) und Buchillustrationen beauftragt wurde. Der Mann aus dem ländlichen Böhmen, der von der Prager Kunstakademie abgelehnt worden war, studierte in Wien und Paris, reiste dann in die USA und kehrte schließlich nach Prag zurück, wo er an der Ausstattung des Repräsentationshauses beteiligt war, das zum Vorzeigeobjekt des Jugendstil wurde. Er träumte von einem monumentalen Bilderzyklus mit dem Titel *Slawisches Epos* (1910–28), in dem er Szenen aus tschechischen Legenden und der Geschichte des Landes darstellte. (1) Mucha mit seiner Frau Marie. (2, 3) Mucha in seinem Studio. (4) Ein Ausschnitt aus Muchas Buntglasfenster im Veitsdom.

## Alfons Mucha

Alfons Mucha (1860–1939) est le plus fameux des artistes *secese*. Il dessinait et peignait souvent de robustes beautés slaves aux cheveux nattés parsemés de pavots, chardons, lierre, marguerites, tournesols et de multiples plantes inconnues des citadins. Son goût élégant était si apprécié qu'on lui commanda des bijoux, des calendriers, des meubles, des timbres-poste, des menus, des billets de banque, des programmes de théâtre, des affiches (dont celles si célèbres de Sarah Bernhardt) et des illustrations de livres. Morave né à la campagne, il fut refusé à l'Académie des Arts de Prague et fit ses études à Vienne et à Paris, puis voyagea aux États-Unis avant de revenir à Prague, où il travailla pour la Maison municipale, la grande vitrine de l'Art Nouveau tchèque. Son rêve était de peindre une série de fresques monumentales appelée L'*Épopée slave* (1910–1928), qui raconte les légendes et l'histoire des Tchèques. (1) Mucha et son épouse Marie. (2, 3) Mucha dans son atelier. (4) Détail d'un vitrail de Mucha dans la cathédrale Saint-Guy.

BOHU
VLASTI
UMĚNÍ KE
BANKA

KU CHVÁLE
K SLÁVĚ
CTI VĚNUJE
SLÁVIE

## The Municipal House

(1) The Municipal House (*Obecní dům*) was built on the site of the *Králův dvůr* (King's Court, on the right of the Gothic Powder Gate), which was demolished at the turn of the century. (2, 3) The Municipal House was built in 1905–11. It was a symbol of the Czech middle class's newly acquired wealth and power. The neo-Baroque building was designed by Antonín Balšánek and Osvald Polívka and the most famous Czech artists decorated the interiors in Art Nouveau style. It is a cultural center with exhibition halls and large auditoria as well as restaurants, cafés, conference rooms and offices. (4) Smetana Concert Hall. (5) The Mayor's Room, decorated by Alfons Mucha with murals symbolizing episodes from Czech history. (6, 7) The restaurant on the ground floor decorated with a painting, *Prague Welcoming Her Guests.* Milky opal and hand-carved crystal glass were used for the lights and the opulent clock.

## Repräsentationshaus

(1) *Obecní dům*, das Repräsentationshaus, wurde an der Stelle des um die Jahrhundertwende abgerissenen *Králův dvůr* (Königshof, unmittelbar neben dem gotischen Pulverturm) erbaut. (2, 3) Der neobarocke Bau entstand in den Jahren 1905 bis 1911 nach einem Entwurf von Antonín Balšánek und Osvald Polívka und symbolisierte den neuen Reichtum und die Macht der tschechischen Mittelschicht. Seine Innenräume wurden von den berühmtesten tschechischen Künstlern im Jugendstil ausgeschmückt. Als Kulturzentrum beherbergt er große Ausstellungsräume und Hörsäle sowie Restaurants, Cafés, Konferenzräume und Büros. (4) Der Smetana-Saal. (5) Alfons Mucha dekorierte den Primatorensaal mit Wandgemälden, die Episoden aus der tschechischen Geschichte darstellen. (6, 7) Das Restaurant im Erdgeschoß schmückt ein Bild mit dem Titel *Prag heißt seine Gäste willkommen.* Milchglas und handgeschliffenes Kristallglas wurden für die Lampen und die große Uhr verwendet.

## La maison municipale

(1) La Maison municipale, *Obecní dům*, s'élève sur le site du *Králův dvůr* (Palais royal) démoli au début du siècle, à droite de la Tour des Poudres de style gothique. (2, 3) Édifiée en 1905–1911, elle est le symbole de la montée en puissance de la nouvelle bourgeoisie tchèque. De style extérieur néobaroque, le bâtiment fut conçu par Antonín Balšánek et Osvald Polívka et les plus célèbres artistes tchèques en décorèrent l'intérieur en style Art Nouveau. Cette Maison est un centre culturel qui possède des salles d'exposition, de vastes auditoriums, des cafés, des restaurants, des salles de conférence et des bureaux. (4) Salle de concerts Smetana. (5) Salle du Bourgmestre, décorée par Alfons Mucha de fresques représentant des épisodes de l'histoire tchèque. (6, 7) Le restaurant du rez-de-chaussée, décoré d'un tableau sur le thème de *Prague honorant ses hôtes.* Les luminaires et la somptueuse horloge sont en opaline laiteuse et en cristal taillé à la main.

4

5

6

7

## J. Novák Department Store and Advertising

(2) The famous department store, where according to an advertisement one could buy "everything from a needle to a locomotive," was built in 1902–3 in Vodičková. The Art Nouveau building was designed by Osvald Polívka and its façade was decorated by Jan Preisler's allegorical mosaic depicting Commerce and Industry. (1) The stained-glass door by Osvald Polívka glows like butterfly wings when seen from inside, reminding one of Tiffanys lamps. (3, 4) J. Novák advertising stickers, which were glued to the covers of magazines, proved to be a popular selling gimmick. (5) Prague ham and sausages often featured in advertisements. (6) A sandwich-man advertising the sale of musical instruments. (7) A market in Vinohrady which sold various smoked meats, game, pheasant and rabbit as well as different kinds of fish. (8) Advertisement for fruit cordial. (9) Václav Sommer advertises his shoemaking establishment. Shoes were sewn and a shoemaker often visited his client at home. Later, when factory shoes appeared on the market, people called them "glued shoes."

## Das Kaufhaus J. Novák und die Reklame

(2) Das berühmte Kaufhaus, dessen Anzeigen damit warben, daß man hier »alles von einer Nadel bis zu einer Lokomotive« kaufen könne, wurde zwischen 1902 und 1903 nach einem Entwurf von Osvald Polívka an der Vodičková-Straße erbaut. Die Fassade des Jugendstil-Gebäudes ist mit allegorischen Mosaiken zu den Themen Handel und Industrie nach Vorlagen Jan Preislers geschmückt. (1) Osvald Polívkas Buntglastür leuchtet, von innen betrachtet, wie ein Schmetterling und erinnert an Tiffanylampen. (3, 4) Reklameaufkleber von J. Novák, die man an die Titelseiten von Zeitschriften klebte, erwiesen sich als beliebte Verkaufsschlager. (5) Prager Schinken und Würstchen waren häufig in Anzeigen zu sehen. (6) Ein Plakatträger wirbt Musikinstrumente. (7) Auf einem Markt in Vinohrady verschiedene Sorten von geräuchertem Fleisch, Wild, Fasanen, Kaninchen sowie einige Fischarten angeboten. (8) Anzeige für Fruchtlikör. (9) Václav Sommer wirbt für seine Schuhmacherwerkstatt. Die Schuhe wurden handgenäht und häufig kam der Schuhmacher seinen Kunden nach Hause. Als später fabrikgefertigte Schuhe im Handel erhältlich waren, bezeichnete man sie als Schuhe«.

## Le grand magasin Novák et sa publicité

(2) On pouvait tout acheter dans le célèbre grand magasin Novák construit en 1902–1903 rue Vodičková: «d'une aiguille à une locomotive». Le bâtiment Art Nouveau fut dessiné par Osvald Polívka et sa façade décorée de mosaïques allégoriques de Jan Preisler représente le Commerce et l'Industrie. (1) Vue de l'intérieur, la porte à vitraux d'Osvald Polívka flamboie comme des ailes de papillon exotique, un peu à la manière d'une lampe de Tiffany. (3, 4) Les autocollants publicitaires de Novák, collés sur la couverture des magazines, se révélèrent très efficaces. (5) Les saucisses et jambons de Prague faisaient souvent l'objet de publicités. (6) Un homme-sandwich engagé par un marchand d'instruments de musique. (7) Au marché de Vinohrady, l'on vendait des viandes fumées, du gibier et toutes sortes de poissons. (8) Publicité pour une liqueur aux fruits. (9) Publicité estivale pour les chaussures Václav Sommer. Les chausseurs venaient souvent à domicile. Les chaussures étaient alors cousues, et lorsque les modèles fabriqués en usine firent leur apparition, ils furent surnommés «chaussures collées.»

5

6

7

8

9

## Painting with Light

(1, 4) Prague's famous photographic studio belonged to Jan Langhans (1851–1919) at 37 Vodičková. He called himself "a court photographer to the English king, Persian shah, Parisian countess and Duchess Helena." Later he replaced his titles with his clients' coats of arms. His studio won top award at an exhibition in Paris in 1900. In 1922 the firm advertised that it owned over 500,000 negatives with portraits of famous personalities. (2) Reverse of a photograph featuring a studio's name. (3) A cover of the *Czech Amateur Photographer*. The Club of Amateur Photographers and its magazine were established in 1889. (5–8, 10) A selection of the so-called *kabinetky*. Prague studio photographers followed a trend called Pictorialism, competing successfully with portrait painters. The amount of silver used in the emulsion gave the photographs a painting-like quality and lent the shapes a certain sculpted softness, which cannot be found in modern photographs. New reproduction techniques, to which Czech photographers (such as Jakub Husník and Karel Klíč) made notable contributions, had a considerable effect on the growth of photography's social prestige. The first portable camera to be produced by a Prague firm appeared in the shops in 1885. (9) A portrait photographer at work.

## Licht im Bild

(1, 4) Jan Langhans (1851–1919) führte auf der Vodičková-Straße 37 das bekannteste Fotostudio in Prag. Er bezeichnete sich selbst als »Hoffotografen des englischen Königs, des Schah von Persien und der Pariser Gräfin und Fürstin Helena«. Später ersetzte er die Titel durch die Wappen seiner Kunden. Auf der Pariser Ausstellung von 1900 gewann sein Studio die höchsten Preise. 1922 warb das Unternehmen damit, daß es mehr als 500.000 Negative mit Porträts berühmter Persönlichkeiten besaß. (2) Rückseite einer Fotografie, auf der der Name eines Studios verzeichnet ist. (3) Ein Titelbild des *Tschechischen Amateurfotografen*. Der »Klub der Amateurfotografen« und seine Zeitschrift wurden 1889 gegründet. (5–8, 10) Eine Auswahl sogenannter *kabinetky*. Prager Studiofotografen nahmen den Trend des sogenannten Pictorialismus auf, der sich erfolgreich gegen die Porträtmaler behauptete. Der Silberanteil in der Fotoemulsion verlieh den Fotografien ein gemaltes Aussehen und gab den Konturen eine gewisse gemeißelte Weichheit, die man auf heutigen Fotografien nicht findet. Neue Reproduktionstechniken, an denen tschechische Fotografen (wie beispielsweise Jakub Husník und Karel Klíč) maßgeblichen Anteil hatten, trugen wesentlich dazu bei, das soziale Prestige der Fotografie zu erhöhen. 1885 erschien in den Geschäften die erste tragbare Kamera, die von einer Prager Firma hergestellt worden war. (9) Ein Porträtfotograf bei der Arbeit.

## Peindre avec la lumière

(1, 4) Le studio du photographe Jan Langhans (1851–1919), 37 rue Vodičková, était l'un des plus fameux de la capitale. Langhans s'intitulait «photographe de la cour du roi d'Angleterre, du chah de Perse, de comtesses parisiennes et de la duchesse Helena.» Plus tard, il remplacera ces titres par les blasons de ses clients. Son studio remporta un prix à l'exposition universelle de Paris, en 1900. En 1922, il déclara posséder plus de 500 000 négatifs de portraits de personnalités. (2) Verso d'une photo avec le nom de l'atelier. (3) Couverture du magazine *Le Photographe Amateur tchèque*. Le club des photographes amateurs et son magazine furent créés en 1889. (5–8, 10) Sélection de *kabinetky*. Les photographes de Prague suivaient la tendance pictorialiste et concurrençaient ainsi avec succès les peintres portraitistes. La quantité de sels d'argent utilisée dans l'émulsion donnait à leurs tirages une qualité picturale et une douceur qui ont disparu des photographies modernes. De nouvelles techniques de reproduction, auxquelles les photographes tchèques (comme Jakub Husník et Karel Klíč) fournirent des contributions remarquées, accrurent le prestige social de la photographie. Le premier appareil photo portatif fabriqué à Prague fut commercialisé dès 1885. (9) Un photographe de portraits au travail.

5

6

7

8

9

10

## The Poor and the Rich

(1) A typical second-hand shop advertising "old iron and skates bought and sold, best prices" in Pinkasova. The shop was demolished in 1908 during the slum clearance. (2) A yard with drying clothes, vats and tubs. Most families used outside toilets and corridor sinks. Often there was no running water and staircases were without gaslight, let alone electricity. The water from the river, which was drunk by all the inhabitants, made Prague at the turn of the century the European capital of typhoid. In 1906 the first water-filtering plant was established. By 1910 there were 134km of basic sewer pipes. Rubbish was taken out in open carts until 1909, when covered carts were introduced. (3) The poor eating soup outside the Franciscan monastery in U Milosrdných. (4) High-society ladies on an outing on Petřín Hill. (5, 6) The nobility attending horse races in Chuchle, near Prague. A sign of "good breeding" was a small head and a long lean body dressed in an impeccably cut uniform, instantly recognizable as "the Austrian gentleman." The Czech Countess Žofie Chotková (right, bottom picture), wife of Archduke Franz Ferdinand d'Este, the heir to the Habsburg throne.

## Arme und Reiche

(1) Ein typischer Gebrauchtwarenladen auf der Pinkasova-Straße, der mit dem Slogan wirbt: »Günstiger An- und Verkauf von altem Eisen und Kufen«. 1908 wurde der Laden im Zuge der Altstadtsanierung abgerissen. (2) Ein Innenhof mit Wäscheleinen, Fässern und Wasserkränen. Die meisten Familien benutzten Toiletten außerhalb des Hauses und Waschbecken auf dem Flur. Oft gab es kein fließendes Wasser und die Treppenhäuser waren ohne Beleuchtung. Durch das Flußwasser, das die Einwohner tranken, gab es in Prag um die Jahrhundertwende eine Vielzahl von Typhusfällen. 1906 wurde eine Wasserfiltrieranlage eingerichtet. 1910 gab es 134 km einfache Abwasserrohre. Bis 1909 fuhr man den Abfall auf offenen Karren aus der Stadt; erst danach wurden geschlossen Wagen verwendet. (3) Die Armen bei einer Suppenküche am Franziskanerkloster an der Straße U Milosrdných. (4) Damen der feinen Gesellschaft bei einem Ausflug auf dem Petřín-Hügel. (5, 6) Der Adel besucht Pferderennen in Chuchle bei Prag. Als Zeichen vornehmer Herkunft galten ein kleiner Kopf auf einem langen, schmalen Körper in einer gut sitzenden Uniform: daran war der »österreichische Gentleman« zu erkennen. Die tschechische Gräfin Žofie Chotková (rechts auf dem unteren Foto) war die Frau von Erzherzog Franz Ferdinand d'Este, dem Habsburger Thronerben.

## Les pauvres et les riches

(1) Typique boutique d'occasion de Pinkasova annonçant « On achète et vend à bon prix vieux fers et patins ». Elle fut démolie en 1908 lors du curetage des taudis. (2) Une cour avec linge qui sèche, barriques et tubs. La plupart des familles ne disposait que de toilettes extérieures et d'un évier dans le couloir. Souvent il n'y avait pas d'eau courante et les escaliers n'étaient éclairés ni au gaz ni – encore moins – à l'électricité. L'eau de la rivière bue par tous les citadins faisait de Prague la capitale européenne de la typhoïde. En 1906, est inaugurée la première installation de filtrage de l'eau. En 1910, la ville compte 134 km d'égouts collecteurs. Les ordures sont ramassées dans des chariots à découvert jusqu'en 1909, date à laquelle ils seront couverts. (3) Des pauvres mangeant une soupe devant le monastère franciscain de la rue Milosrdných. (4) Des dames de la haute société lors d'une garden-party sur la colline de Petřín. (5, 6) La noblesse assiste aux courses de chevaux à Chucle, près de Prague. Les « gentlemen autrichiens » se reconnaissaient à une tête fine sur un corps élancé vêtu d'un uniforme impeccablement coupé. La comtesse tchèque Žofie Chotková (à droite sur la photo du bas), épouse de l'archiduc François-Ferdinand d'Este, héritier du trône des Habsbourg.

4

5

6

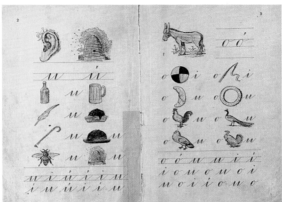

Rozvrh hodin.

## Children

(1, 2) Girls' class and boys' class, c. 1911. From 1848 children were taught the Czech language. In 1869, according to the new Austrian law, it became compulsory for children to attend an extended elementary school, starting at six years of age and finishing at 14. (3) School timetable belonging to a 4th-grade child, who attended school for six days a week and learned Czech, mathematics, German, religion, art and sports, with an additional three hours of violin and two hours of *Sokol* gymnastics. (4) Spelling book from 1902 issued by the Imperial Schoolbook Commission. (5) A studio photograph of a child at the turn of the century, wearing the customary sailor-suit. (6) Children parading through the streets of Prague in rococo costumes during holiday celebrations. (7) A group of boys at play.

## Kinder

(1, 2) Mädchen- und Jungenklassen um 1911. Seit 1848 unterrichtete man die Kinder in tschechischer Sprache. 1869 machte ein neues österreichisches Gesetz den Besuch einer verlängerten Grundschule für alle Kinder zwischen 6 und 14 Jahren zur Pflicht. (3) Stundenplan eines Kindes in der vierten Klasse. An sechs Tagen in der Woche lernte es Tschechisch, Mathematik, Deutsch, Religion, Kunst und Sport und erhielt drei Zusatzstunden in Violinunterricht und zwei Stunden *Sokol*-Gymnastik. (4) Eine Fibel von 1902, ausgegeben von der Kaiserlichen Schulbuchkommission. (5) Ein Studioporträt eines Kindes um die Jahrhundertwende im damals üblichen Matrosenanzug. (6) Während einer Festtagsfeier marschieren Kinder in Rokokokostümen durch die Prager Straßen. (7) Eine Gruppe von Jungen beim Spielen.

## Les enfants

(1, 2) Classe des filles et classe des garçons, vers 1911. À partir de 1848, l'enseignement fut dispensé en langue tchèque. En 1869, selon la nouvelle loi autrichienne, les enfants devaient obligatoirement aller à l'école de 6 à 14 ans. (3) Emploi du temps d'un élève du 4e degré, qui va à l'école six jours par semaine et apprend le tchèque, les mathématiques, l'allemand, la religion, l'art, les sports, sans compter trois heures de violon et deux heures de gymnastique *Sokol*. (4) Alphabet publié en 1902 par les éditions impériales. (5) Photographie de studio d'un enfant au tournant du siècle : il porte le classique costume marin. (6) Des enfants défilent dans les rues de Prague en costume style XVIIIe siècle, lors d'une fête des vacances. (7) Groupe de garçons jouant.

6

7

### Festivities and Tourism

By the turn of the century Prague had already become Europe's favorite city to visit, as the countless brochures and postcards show. (1) A beauty pageant called the Flower Queen competition, in Prague, 1910. (2) A Venetian night on the Vltava. (3) A dance was a rigidly formal affair, and each young woman carried with her a dance-engagement book with a tiny pencil tied to it. Men would book a dance and sign their name in an empty space. From the early 19th century the "Slavic balls" were instituted in Prague. At these balls the dance hall was decorated in the Bohemian national colors (red and white) and conversation in Czech only was allowed. (4, 8–11) Postcards and guide books with the most photographed views of Hradčany and the Charles Bridge. (5, 6) Greeting cards: the postman's bag and the girl's folder contain folding-picturebooks. (7) Membership card of the Czech Tourist Club, which was established in 1888. The *Sokol* sport organization was known for so-called "national pilgrimages" to places of historical importance to the Czechs. *Sokol* tried to combine sport with the newly discovered and carefully nurtured patriotism.

### Festlichkeiten und Tourismus

Prag war bereits um die Jahrhundertwende eines der beliebtesten Reiseziele Europas, wie man an den zahllosen Broschüren und Postkarten erkennen kann. (1) Ein Schönheitswettbewerb mit dem Namen Blumenkönigin-Wahl 1910 in Prag. (2) Eine venezianische Nacht auf der Moldau. (3) Ein Ball war eine ausgesprochen formelle Angelegenheit, und jedes junge Mädchen trug ihr Buch mit den Tanzverabredungen und einem kleinen, daran befestigten Bleistift mit sich herum. Männer buchten einen Tanz und trugen sich an den freien Stellen ein. Seit dem frühen 19. Jahrhundert wurden in Prag »Slawische Bälle« organisiert. Bei diesen Tanzveranstaltungen waren die Ballsäle in den böhmischen Nationalfarben (rot und weiß) dekoriert, und die Teilnehmer durften nur tschechisch sprechen. (4, 8–11) Postkarten und Reiseführer mit den beliebten Fotomotiven des Hradschin und der Karlsbrücke. (5, 6) Grußkarten: Die Tasche des Postboten und die Mappe des Mädchens enthalten Klappbilderbücher. (7) Mitgliedskarte des 1888 gegründeten Tschechischen Touristenklubs. Die Sportvereinigung *Sokol* war für ihre sogenannten »Nationalen Pilgerreisen« zu den für die Tschechen historisch bedeutenden Stätten bekannt. *Sokol* versuchte den Sport mit dem neu entdeckten und sorgsam gepflegten Nationalismus zu verbinden.

### Tourisme et festivités

Au tournant du siècle, Prague est déjà l'une des destinations touristiques préférées de l'Europe, et le sujet d'innombrables brochures et cartes postales. (1) Le défilé du «Concours de la Reine des fleurs», à Prague en 1910. (2) Nuit vénitienne sur la Moldau. (3) Danser était une activité très codifiée. Chaque jeune femme possédait un carnet de bal auquel était attaché un petit crayon. Les cavaliers réservaient leur tour en signant de leur nom dans l'espace qui leur était réservé. Au début du XIXe siècle sont créés des «bals slaves» : la salle de danse était décorée aux couleurs nationales de la Bohême (rouge et blanc) et seules les conversations en tchèque étaient permises. (4, 8–11) Cartes postales et guides touristiques avec les vues sans cesse reproduites du Hradčany et du Pont Charles. (5, 6) Cartes de vœux : le sac du facteur et le classeur de la fillette contiennent des dépliants. (7) Carte de membre du Club tchèque du Tourisme, fondé en 1888. L'association sportive *Sokol* organisait de célèbres «pèlerinages nationaux» vers des lieux marquants de l'histoire tchèque. *Sokol* essayait de mêler le sport à un patriotisme renaissant et soigneusement entretenu.

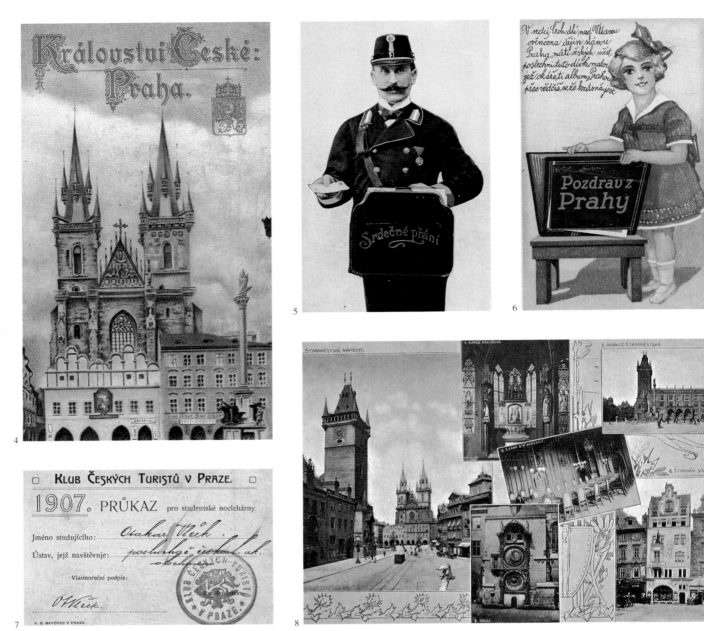

Královstuí České: Praha.

5

Srdečné přání

6

Pozdrav z Prahy

7

8

KNAPPŮV PRŮVODCE
PO
PRAZE
A OKOLÍ

S ČETNÝMI
ILLUSTRACEMI
A PLÁNEM
PRAHY

CENA
KOR. 1.—

NAKLADATEL M. KNAPP KNIHKUPEC
V KARLÍNĚ

9

PRAG

10

Illustrovaný
Průvodce
Prahou
a okolím.

Vydáno
Spolkem ku povznesení
návštěvy
cizinců
v
PRAZE.

Illustroval
Pavel Körber

Historická část
od prof. Jana V. Krecara

11

## "Roll out the Barrel"

(1–3) Inns, taverns and restaurants. In 1910 there were 1500 pubs and bars in Prague. Their names often referred to Czech history and its Slavonic roots – for example, At the Czech Crown, At the Czech Knight, At Slavonic Linden Tree, At Žižka Oak and others. Pubs were famous for their excellent Czech beer. Each pub had a regular clientele and the steady customer, *štamgast,* for whom a table was always reserved, was treated with reverence. The Czechs are the number-one consumers of beer in the world. We know that beer and wine were being made in Břevnov monastery in 993 when Bishop Vojtěch was consecrating the place, although the first written evidence of beer brewing comes from 1088. When assessing a beer one should judge its scent, fullness of taste, bitterness, pungency, clarity and the stability of its frothy head. (4) Brewery advertisement. (5) A postcard depicting one of the most famous Prague pubs, U Fleků, which has been brewing its own dark beer since 1499. Their renowned beer is called Bavarian and is a rare leaven 13° beer. Its taste is influenced by four types of malt: Pilsen, Bavarian, Caramel and Roasted Malt. Guests often played cards in pubs and restaurants. (7–10) Prague motifs on playing cards. (6, 11) A busy Prague restaurant.

## »Hoch die Gläser«

(1–3) Gasthäuser, Kneipen und Restaurants: 1910 gab es in Prag 1.500 Kneipen und Bars. Ihre Namen erinnerten oft an die tschechische Geschichte und ihre slawische Wurzeln, wie beispielsweise Zur tschechischen Krone, Zum tschechischen Ritter, Zur slawischen Linde, Zur Žižka-Eiche und andere. Die Kneipen waren wegen ihres ausgezeichneten tschechischen Bieres berühmt. Jede Kneipe hatte ihre Stammkunden, und der *štamgast,* für den immer ein Tisch frei war, wurde mit besonderer Aufmerksamkeit bedient. Die Tschechen sind die größten Bierkonsumenten der Welt. Es ist bekannt, daß bereits 993 zur Einweihung des Klosters Břevnov durch Bischof Vojtěch Bier und Wein hergestellt wurden. Das erste schriftliche Zeugnis über das Bierbrauen stammt jedoch aus dem Jahr 1088. Bier sollte man nach seinem Geruch, seinem Geschmack, seinem Grad an Bitterkeit, seiner Schärfe, Reinheit und der Festigkeit seiner Krone beurteilen. (4) Brauerei-Reklame. (5) Eine Postkarte mit dem Bild einer der berühmtesten Kneipen Prags, U Fleků: Hier wurde seit 1499 hauseigenes dunkles Bier unter dem Namen »Bayerisches« gebraut, das eine ungewöhnliche Gärung von 13° aufweist. Sein Geschmack entsteht durch vier verschiedene Malzsorten: Pilsener, Bayerisches, Karamel- und geröstetes Malz. Oft spielten die Gäste Karten in den Kneipen und Restaurants. (7–10) Prager Motive auf Spielkarten. (6, 11) Ein gut besuchtes Prager Restaurant.

## La culture des brasseries

(1–3) Auberges, tavernes et restaurants. 1 500 brasseries et bars existaient à Prague en 1910. Leur nom se référait souvent à l'histoire tchèque et aux racines slaves comme, par exemple : La Couronne tchèque, Le Chevalier tchèque, Le Tilleul slave, Au Chêne de Žižka, etc. Les brasseries étaient célèbres pour leur excellente bière. Chacune d'entre elles possédait sa clientèle d'habitués et de clients fidèles traités avec respect – le *štamgast* – pour lesquels une table était réservée en permanence. Les Tchèques sont les premiers consommateurs de bière du monde. On produisait déjà du vin et de la bière au monastère de Břevnov en 993 lorsque l'évêque Vojtěch le consacra, et la première mention écrite d'une activité de brasserie remonte à 1088. Une bière doit être jugée à son nez, à la plénitude de son goût, à son amertume, sa saveur, sa clarté et à la stabilité de sa mousse. (4) Publicité de brasserie. (5) Carte postale de l'une des plus célèbres brasseries pragoises, U Fleků, qui produisait sa propre bière brune depuis 1499. Cette bière renommée, appelée « bavaroise », titre 13°. Son goût vient de la présence de quatre malts différents : le Pilsen, le Bavarois, le Caramel et le Malt rôti. Les clients jouaient souvent aux cartes dans les brasseries et les restaurants. (7–10) Décor pragois de dos de cartes à jouer. (6, 11) Restaurants animés.

4

5

6

7

8

9

10

11

## Sporting Life

(1, 2) The most famous soccer teams in Prague were Slavia (established in 1892) and Sparta (1894). It was a man's sport, although one journalist wrote after seeing a match, "Soccer and rugby can be played by women; it is safe." (3) One of the world's oldest sports is wrestling. The Czech Gustav Frištenský became European champion in 1903, and from 1908 an Englishman, Eddy Pierce, started to teach boxing in Prague. (4) Pole-vaulting at the Slavia Club. (5) A match at Štvanice tennis courts. At the end of the 19th century tennis was played mainly by the upper classes, who had private tennis courts in their gardens. The first Championship of the Lands of the Czech Crown took place in 1895. The oldest club in the country is the ČLTK (Czech Lawn Tennis Club), founded in 1893. (6) Velodrome: cycling became popular after 1878 when the first permission to cycle was issued. The Cyclists Club was established in 1883. (7) The 25th International Athletic Games, organized by the Sparta Club. (8) Austrian army officers were the best at fencing.

## Sport

(1, 2) Die berühmtesten Prager Fußballklubs waren Slavia (gegründet 1892) und Sparta (gegründet 1894). Obwohl ein Journalist nach einem Spiel schrieb: »Fußball und Rugby können auch Frauen spielen, es ist ungefährlich«, blieb der Sport Männersache. (3) Ringen ist eine der ältesten Sportarten. 1903 wurde der Tscheche Gustav Frištenský Europameister, und ab 1908 gab der Engländer Eddy Pierce in Prag Boxunterricht. (4) Stabhochsprung im Klub Slavia. (5) Ein Spiel auf den Tennisanlagen von Štvanice. Am Ende des 19. Jahrhunderts war Tennis vor allem ein Sport der Oberschicht, die in ihren Gärten private Tennisplätze anlegen ließ. 1895 fand die erste Meisterschaft der Länder der Tschechischen Krone statt. Der älteste Klub des Landes ist der 1893 gegründete ČLTK (Tschechischer Rasentennisclub). (6) Nachdem 1878 die erste Fahrradlizenz erteilt worden war, erfreute sich der Radsport rasch großer Beliebtheit. 1883 entstand der Fahrradklub. (7) Der Klub Sparta organisierte die 25. Internationalen Athletischen Spiele. (8) Die österreichischen Offiziere waren ausgezeichnete Fechter.

## Le sport

(1, 2) Les plus célèbres équipes de football de Prague étaient la Slavia (fondée en 1892) et la Sparta (1894). Le football était réservé aux hommes, même si un journaliste écrivait alors : « Le football et le rugby peuvent être joués par les femmes ; ce sont des jeux sans danger. » (3) La lutte est l'un des plus anciens sports du monde. Le Tchèque Gustav Frištenský en devint champion d'Europe en 1903 et, à partir de 1908, l'Anglais Eddy Pierce vint enseigner la boxe dans la capitale. (4) Saut à la perche au club Slavia. (5) Match de tennis à Štvanice. À la fin du XIXe siècle, le tennis est le sport des élites, qui possèdent des courts dans leurs jardins. Le premier Championnat des États de la Couronne tchèque se déroula en 1895. Le club le plus ancien du pays était le ČLTK (Club tchèque de tennis sur gazon), fondé en 1893. (6) Vélodrome : le cyclisme devint populaire après 1878, lorsque le premier permis de circuler à vélo fut attribué. Le Club des cyclistes fut créé en 1883. (7) 25e Jeux Athlétiques Internationaux, organisés par le Club Sparta. (8) Les officiers de l'armée autrichienne étaient les meilleurs escrimeurs.

3

4

5

6

7

8

## Going to the Movies

(1) The man who brought the Lumière camera from France was the architect Jan Kříženecký (1868–1921), who is regarded as the father of Czech cinema. His work includes film of firemen in action, swimming baths in Žofín and impressions from *Sokol* rallies. Soon the Czech cinema had its own stars: Josef Šváb Malostranský (2) and Anna Sedlačková (3), who starred in countless silent one-reelers shot in the streets and courtyards of the city (4). Famous magician Viktor Ponrepo established the first permanent Prague cinema in 1907 in the house At the Blue Pike in Karlova. He was cashier, usher, commentator and host, all in one. Later he filmed his farewell on celluloid and projected it after the film, so from then on he did not have to shake hands with his cinemagoers. (5) A poster advertising Ponrepo's *Biograf* (cinema) and (6) the main door of the cinema. (7, 8) Interior of Prague cinemas. By 1910 there were 15 permanent cinemas.

## Kinobesuch

(1) Der Architekt Jan Kříženecký (1868–1921), der die Lumière-Kamera aus Frankreich mitbrachte, gilt als Vater des tschechischen Kinos. Zu seinen Werken gehört ein Film über Feuerwehrleute im Einsatz, Schwimmbäder auf der Sofieninsel und Eindrücke von den *Sokol*-Veranstaltungen. Das tschechische Kino hatte bald seine eigenen Stars: Josef Šváb Malostranský (2) und Anna Sedlačková (3) spielten in zahllosen kurzen Stummfilmen mit, die auf den Straßen und in den Innenhöfen der Stadt aufgenommen wurden. (4) 1907 richtete der bekannte Zauberkünstler Viktor Ponrepo das erste ständige Prager Lichtspielhaus im Haus Zur Blauen Pike in der Karlova-Straße ein. Er war Kassierer, Platzanweiser, Kommentator und Besitzer zugleich. Später bannte er seine Abschiedsworte auf Zelluloid und zeigte sie nach dem Film, so daß er sich nicht mehr von jedem Kinobesucher persönlich zu verabschieden brauchte. (5) Ein Plakat wirbt für Ponrepos *Biograf* (Kino). (6) Der Haupteingang des Kinos. (7, 8) Innenräume von Prager Kinos. 1910 gab es 15 ständige Lichtspielhäuser in der Stadt.

## Au cinéma

(1) L'architecte Jan Kříženecký (1868–1921), considéré comme le père du cinéma tchèque, fut le premier à rapporter de France une caméra Lumière. Il réalisa des films sur les pompiers en action, les piscines de Žofín et les rassemblements de *Sokol*. Le cinéma tchèque eut bientôt ses propres stars, comme Josef Šváb Malostranský (2) et Anna Sedlačková (3) qui jouèrent dans d'innombrables courts métrages muets tournés dans les rues et les cours de la capitale. (4) Le célèbre magicien Viktor Ponrepo fonda le premier cinéma pragois en 1907 dans la maison de «La Pique bleue», rue Karlova. Il était à la fois caissier, ouvreur, commentateur et hôte. Plus tard, il se filma lui-même disant au revoir à ses spectateurs, ce qui lui évitait de leur serrer la main en fin de séance. (5) Affiche publicitaire du *Biograf* (cinéma) de Ponrepo et (6) son entrée principale. (7, 8) Salles de cinéma de Prague. Vers 1910, existaient déjà 15 salles permanentes.

5

6

7

8

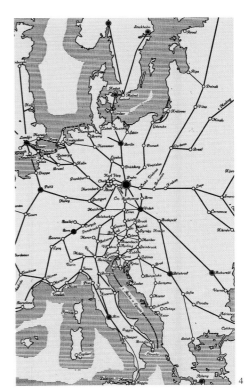

## Trains

The Austro-Hungarian Empire was linked by an extensive railway network. The Prague locomotive factory in Vysočany (known as "Českomoravská") produced the biggest and most powerful steam engines in Austria-Hungary while the Ringhoffer factory in Smíchov built the most luxurious carriages. The firm made the first ever locomotive in 1900. One of the newly produced engines set a new European speed record at 148km/h. An automobile factory was added to the plant in 1909 and the Praga car appeared on the streets of the capital. (1) By 1903 the number of engines produced had risen to 87, of which five were express locomotives. (2) An Austro-Hungarian passport. (3) Constructing a locomotive in the railway-engine department, which was added to the engineering works in 1899. (4) A map of the railway network, showing how closely Prague was interconnected with the rest of Central Europe. (5) One such luxury carriage was made for Franz Josef. After the collapse of Austria-Hungary it was used by Tomáš Masaryk. (6) Franz Josef station (designed by Josef Fanta, built in 1901–09) in Art Nouveau style, now known as the Main Station or Wilson Station.

## Eisenbahn

Das Kaiserreich Österreich-Ungarn war durch ein weites Eisenbahnnetz verbunden. Die Prager Lokomotivenfabrik in Vysočany (bekannt als »Českomoravská«)stellte die größten und schwersten Dampfmaschinen in ganz Österreich-Ungarn her, während in der Ringhoffer-Fabrik in Smíchov die elegantesten Waggons gebaut wurden. Im Jahre 1900 stellte die Firma die allererste Lokomotive her. Eine der moderneren Lokomotiven erreichte einen neuen Geschwindigkeitsrekord von 148 km/h. 1909 erweiterte man das Werk um eine Autofabrik, und Autos der Marke Praga erschienen auf den Straßen der Hauptstadt. (1) Bis 1903 hatte man 87 Lokomotiven gebaut, davon fünf Expressloks. (2) Ein österreichisch-ungarischer Paß. (3) Der Bau einer Lokomotive in der Eisenbahnabteilung des Motorenwerkes, die 1899 eingerichtet wurde. (4) Eine Karte des Eisenbahnnetzes, die zeigt, wie eng Prag mit dem übrigen Mitteleuropa verbunden war. (5) Ein luxuriöser Waggon, der für Franz Josef hergestellt worden war und den sein Sohn benutzte. Nach dem Zusammenbruch des Kaiserreichs diente er Tomáš Masaryk. (6) Der von Josef Fanta im Jugendstil entworfene Franz-Josef-Bahnhof (1901–09), der heute als Hauptbahnhof oder Wilson-Bahnhof bekannt ist.

## Les trains

L'empire austro-hongrois était parcouru par un important réseau de voies ferrées. La fabrique pragoise de locomotives de Vysočany (connu comme «Českomoravská») produisait les plus grosses et les plus puissantes machines à vapeur de l'Empire, tandis que l'usine Ringhoffer de Smíchov fabriquait les wagons les plus luxueux. L'entreprise fabriqua sa première locomotive en 1900 et l'un de ses modèles battit le record d'Europe de vitesse : 148 km/h. Elle s'intéressa à l'automobile en 1909, et l'on vit bientôt une voiture de marque Praga dans les rues de la capitale. (1) En 1903, le nombre de machines produites s'élevait à 87, dont cinq locomotives express. (2) Passeport austro-hongrois. (3) Construction d'une locomotive dans les ateliers ferroviaires qui complétèrent les ateliers de mécanique en 1899. (4) Carte du réseau ferré, montrant les nombreuses liaisons entre Prague et le reste de l'Europe centrale. (5) Wagon de luxe fabriqué pour François-Joseph, et utilisé par François-Ferdinand. Après l'effondrement de l'Autriche-Hongrie il servit, à Tomáš Masaryk. (6) Gare François-Joseph (conçue par Josef Fanta en style Art Nouveau, construite en 1901–09), aujourd'hui gare principale ou gare Wilson.

5

6

## The Wheels of Progress

The use of automobiles was steadily growing. Horse-drawn carriages were gradually replaced by taxis while annual motor shows held at the Holešovice Exhibition Grounds (2) presented the public with the latest models. Amongst the most popular cars of its day was the Praga automobile (1, 2), built in Jinonice. "Praga automobiles last for hundreds of thousands of kilometers" claimed the advertising slogan. From 1911 the company started building cars to its own original designs from parts made in Bohemia. The Praga became the number-one car in Austria-Hungary and by 1930 the Praga factory was producing more cars than all other Czechoslovak car manufacturers combined. It also made lorries, buses, armored vehicles, tractors, motorcycles and racing cars. (5, 6) By 1928 half of the capital's taxis were Pragas. (7) A car-race outside Prague. The car-race from Zbraslav to Jíloviště was the motoring event of the year.

## Die Räder des Fortschritts

Der Gebrauch von Automobilen nahm beständig zu. Schritt für Schritt wurden die Pferdewagen durch Taxen ersetzt, und eine jährliche Motorschau auf dem Ausstellungsgelände in Holešovice informierte die Bevölkerung über die neuesten Modelle. (2) Der in Jinonice gefertigte Praga (1, 2) gehörte zu den populärsten Wagen. »Praga-Autos halten Hunderttausende von Kilometern« behauptete der Werbeslogan. Seit 1911 baute die Firma Wagen in ihrem eigenen Design, mit Autoteilen, die in Böhmen hergestellt wurden. Der Praga war das beliebteste Auto in Österreich-Ungarn, 1930 produzierte die Praga-Fabrik mehr Fahrzeuge als alle anderen tschechischen Autohersteller zusammen. Man baute auch Last- und Panzerwagen, Traktoren, Motorräder und Rennwagen. (5, 6) 1928 waren die Hälfte aller Taxis Pragas. (7) Ein Autorennen außerhalb Prags. Das Rennen Zbraslav-Jíloviště war das wichtigste Motorsportereignis des Jahres.

## On n'arrête pas le progrès

L'automobile se répandit rapidement. Les voitures à chevaux furent peu à peu remplacées par des taxis et des salons furent organisés à Holešovice pour présenter au public les derniers modèles. (2) L'une des automobiles les plus populaires de son époque était la Praga (1, 2), construite à Jinonice. « Les automobiles Praga durent des centaines de milliers de kilomètres » proclamait son slogan publicitaire. À partir de 1911, l'entreprise monta des voitures d'après ses propres plans avec des pièces fabriquées en Bohême. La Praga était la voiture la plus vendue en Autriche-Hongrie et en 1930, l'usine Praga produisait davantage que tous les autres fabricants tchécoslovaques réunis. Elle fabriquait également des camions, des bus, des véhicules blindés, des tracteurs, des motocyclettes et des voitures de course. (5, 6) En 1928, la moitié des taxis de la capitale étaient des Praga. (7) Course de voitures dans les environs de Prague. La course de Zbraslav à Jíloviště était l'événement automobile de l'année.

## The Emperor Visits Prague

From the 15th to the 19th century the Habsburgs were Holy
Roman Emperors. Franz Josef I ruled the Empire from 1848 until
his death in 1916. His visits to Prague were infrequent. He ruled
from a distance, seeming more and more to be the weathered
centerpiece of a patinaed court. His most memorable visit to
Prague took place in 1907. As was customary, he took part in the
opening of public buildings, visited schools and museums, and
inspected many army installations. (1, 3) The Emperor arrives
to open the Čech Bridge. (2) Title page from The *Czech World*
showing Franz Josef I leaving the German Technical College in
Prague. (4) A card promoting the unity of the monarchy. (5) City
officials welcome the Emperor. (6, 7) Garlanded streets and
festive crowds welcome the Emperor.

## Der Kaiser besucht Prag

Vom 15. bis zum 19. Jahrhundert waren die Habsburger Kaiser
des Heiligen Römischen Reiches. Franz Josef I. regierte das
Kaiserreich von 1848 bis zu seinem Tod 1916. Er besuchte Prag
nur gelegentlich, regierte aus der Ferne und schien mehr und
mehr zum verwitterten Zentrum eines mit Patina überzogenen
Hofes zu werden. Sein denkwürdigster Besuch in Prag fand 1907
statt. Wie üblich nahm er an der Eröffnung öffentlicher Gebäude
teil, besuchte Schulen und Museen und inspizierte viele
Armeeinrichtungen. (1, 3) Der Kaiser eröffnet die Čech-Brücke.
(2) Das Titelbild der *Tschechischen Welt* zeigt Kaiser Franz
Josef I. beim Verlassen der Deutschen Technischen Hochschule
in Prag. (4) Eine Karte wirbt für die Einheit der Monarchie.
(5) Stadthonoratioren begrüßen den Kaiser auf dem Wenzelsplatz. (6, 7) Geschmückte Straßen und eine festlich gestimmte
Menge heißen den Kaiser willkommen.

## La visite de l'Empereur à Prague

Du XVe au XIXe siècle, les Habsbourg portèrent le titre
d'empereurs du saint empire germanique. François-Joseph Ier,
qui régna de 1848 à sa mort en 1916, ne séjourna que rarement
à Prague. Il régnait de loin, de plus en plus âgé et isolé au milieu
d'un rituel de cour figé. Sa visite la plus mémorable eut lieu en
1907. Selon la coutume, il inaugura des bâtiments publics, visita
des écoles et des musées et inspecta des installations militaires.
(1, 3) Arrivée de l'Empereur qui vient inaugurer le pont Čech.
(2) Couverture du *Monde tchèque*, montrant le souverain quittant
le lycée technique de Prague. (4) Carte à la gloire de l'unité
représentée par la monarchie. (5) Les officiels de la ville saluent
l'Empereur. (6, 7) Les vues décorées de guirlandes et la foule en
liesse accueillent l'Empereur.

5

6

7

### The Jubilee Exhibition

In 1908, the Czechs staged a large-scale display in the Holešovice Exhibition Grounds. This was to mark the 60th anniversary of the Emperor's accession to the throne. The exhibitors vied with each other to present their products in the most spectacular manner. Many pavilions were built for the occasion, including a model of an Ethiopian village. (1) A Jubilee postcard with the Emperor Franz Josef I. (2) Franz Ferdinand d'Este opening the Exhibition. (3–8) Postcards from the Exhibition.

### Die Jubiläumsausstellung

1908 veranstalteten die Tschechen aus Anlaß des 60. kaiserlichen Thronjubiläums eine große Schau auf dem Ausstellungsgelände in Holešovice. Aussteller wetteiferten miteinander, um ihre Exponate am spektakulärsten auszustellen. Viele Pavillons wurden eigens für diesen Anlaß errichtet. Zu den aufsehenerregendsten Ausstellungsstücken gehörte das Modell eines äthiopischen Dorfes. (1) Eine Jubiläumspostkarte mit dem Bild von Kaiser Franz Josef I. (2) Franz Ferdinand d'Este eröffnet die Ausstellung. (3–8) Postkarten der Ausstellung.

### L'exposition du Jubilé

En 1908, les Tchèques organisèrent une énorme exposition à Holešovice, pour marquer le soixantième anniversaire de l'accession de l'Empereur au trône. Une compétition s'instaura entre les exposants pour présenter leur production de la manière la plus spectaculaire. De nombreux pavillons furent construits à cette occasion, dont une reconstitution de village éthiopien, clou de l'exposition. (1) Une carte commémorative avec le portrait de François-Joseph. (2) François-Ferdinand d'Este déclare ouverte l'exposition. (3–8) Cartes postales de l'exposition

Pozdrav z Jubilejní výstavy v Praze 1908.

3

4

Jubilejní výstava v Praze 1908.

5

Pozdrav z Jubilejní výstavy w Praze 1908.

6

POZDRAV Z JUBILEJNÍ VÝSTAVY V PRAZE.

Habešské kouzlo.

7

JUBILEJNÍ VÝSTAVA V PRAZE 1908

8

UNDER THE DOUBLE EAGLE 103

### Sokol Rallies

The *Sokol* (Falcon) organization was established in 1862 by Miroslav Tyrš (1832–84), a teacher of philosophy and a great fan of ancient Greek history and culture. With the help of Jindřich Fügner (1822–64), the *Sokol* uniform (a red *Garibaldi* shirt, Czech patriot's coat with buttons and eyes, trousers made of Russian linen and a Slovak hat with a ribbon and falcon feather) was designed and the first gym built in Prague. *Sokol* combined sport activities with Slav nationalistic ideals. Large *Sokolské slety* (literally: flockings, gatherings) were held in the capital and other towns in Bohemia. Women had their own section, established in 1869, and in 1911 the equality of women was formally announced at one of the *Sokol* meetings. The masses saw in *Sokol* a national army. Members participated in important events, such as the transportation of the Bohemian crown jewels from Vienna to Prague. The last *Sokol* rally before the First World War took place in Brno in 1914 and was interrupted when the news of the assassination of Archduke Franz Ferdinand d'Este reached Bohemia. For their anti-Habsburg stand *Sokol* groups were dissolved by the authorities in 1915. Many members were imprisoned and executed. (1–5) Posters, postcards, poems and music compositions were the by-product of the rallies, which took place every four and later every six years. (6) *Sokol* emblem. (7) A gymnastic show on Letná Plain with thousands of members exercising. Many members became Olympic medallists.

### Sokol-Veranstaltungen

Die Organisation *Sokol* (Falke) wurde 1862 von Miroslav Tyrš (1832–84), einem Philosophielehrer und großem Verehrer der Geschichte und Kultur der alten Griechen, gegründet. Mit Hilfe von Jindřich Fügner (1822–64) wurde die *Sokol*-Uniform entworfen (ein rotes *Garibaldi*-Hemd, ein tschechischer Patriotenmantel mit Knöpfen und Ösen, Hosen aus russischem Leinen und ein slowakischer Hut mit Band und Falkenfeder) und die erste Sporthalle in Prag erbaut. *Sokol* verband sportliche Aktivitäten mit nationalistischen slawischen Idealen. Die großen *Sokolské slety* (wörtlich: Versammlungen) fanden in der Hauptstadt und an anderen Orten im Königreich Böhmen statt. 1869 wurde eine eigene Sektion für Frauen eingerichtet, 1911 deren Gleichberechtigung auf einem *Sokol*-Treffen offiziell erklärt. Die Mehrheit sah in der *Sokol* eine nationale Armee. Ihre Mitglieder nahmen an wichtigen Ereignissen teil, so am Transport der böhmischen Kronjuwelen von Wien nach Prag. Die letzte *Sokol*-Veranstaltung vor dem Ersten Weltkrieg fand 1914 in Brno statt und wurde unterbrochen, als die Nachricht von der Ermordung von Erzherzog Franz Ferdinand d'Este in Böhmen eintraf. Wegen ihrer antihabsburgischen Haltung wurde die *Sokol* 1915 von den Behörden verboten. Viele Mitglieder landeten im Gefängnis oder wurden hingerichtet. (1–5) Plakate, Postkarten, Gedichte und Musikkompositionen entstanden als Nebenprodukte der Veranstaltungen, die zunächst alle vier, später alle sechs Jahre abgehalten wurden. (6) *Sokol*-Emblem. (7) Eine Turnveranstaltung auf dem Letná-Plateau, an der Tausende von Mitgliedern teilnahmen. Viele von ihnen errangen olympische Medaillen.

### Les rassemblements de Sokol

L'association *Sokol* (le faucon) avait été créée en 1862 par Miroslav Tyrš (1832–1884), professeur de philosophie et adepte de l'histoire et de la culture de la Grèce ancienne. Avec l'aide de Jindřich Fügner (1822–1864), il dessina l'uniforme *Sokol* (une chemise rouge à la *Garibaldi*, le manteau des patriotes tchèques avec ses boutons et ses œilletons, des pantalons en lin russe et un chapeau slovaque orné d'un ruban et d'une plume de faucon) et fit construire un premier gymnase à Prague. *Sokol* associait des activités sportives aux idéaux nationalistes slaves. Les grands *Sokolské slety* (rassemblements) se tinrent dans la capitale et d'autres villes du royaume de Bohême. Les femmes disposaient de leur propre section, fondée en 1869 et, en 1911, leur égalité fut formellement proclamée au cours d'une grande réunion *Sokol*. Les masses voyaient dans *Sokol* une armée nationale. Les membres participèrent aux événements importants comme le transfert des joyaux de la couronne de Bohême de Vienne à Prague. Le dernier rassemblement de *Sokol* avant la Première Guerre mondiale se déroula à Brno en 1914 et fut interrompu par l'annonce de l'assassinat de l'archiduc François-Ferdinand. Les groupes *Sokol* furent dissous en 1915 par les autorités pour leur position anti-monarchique. De nombreux membres furent arrêtés et exécutés. (1–5) Affiches, cartes postales, poèmes et œuvres musicales accompagnaient les rassemblements qui se tenaient tous les quatre, puis tous les six ans. (6) Emblème *Sokol*. (7) Une démonstration de gymnastique donnée dans la plaine de Letná par des milliers de participants. De nombreux membres seront titulaires de médailles olympiques.

7

### The František Palacký Monument

František Palacký (1798 –1876), historian and statesman, was regarded as the man who resurrected the Czech national conscience. At the Slavonic Congress in 1848 he demanded equal rights for all nationalities: "Either we achieve a situation where we can say with pride: 'I am a Slav,' or we shall stop being Slavs." On 1 July 1912 the monument (2), designed by Stanislav Sucharda and full of historical symbols, was unveiled on the embankment. (1) Casting of bronze parts for the monument in a foundry in Brandýs nad Labem.

### Das František Palacký-Monument

Der Historiker und Politiker František Palacký (1798 –1876) galt als der Mann, der das tschechische Nationalbewußtsein wiedererweckte. Auf dem Slawistenkongreß von 1848 forderte er gleiche Rechte für alle Nationalitäten: »Entweder wir schaffen eine Situation, in der wir mit Stolz sagen können: ›Ich bin ein Slawe‹ oder wir sollten aufhören, Slawen zu sein.« Zu seinen Ehren entwarf Stanislav Sucharda ein Monument mit historischen Symbolen (2), das am 1. Juli 1912 am Kai enthüllt wurde. (1) In einer Schmiede in Brandýs nad Labem werden Bronzeteile des Denkmals gegossen.

### Le monument à František Palacký

František Palacký (1798 –1876), homme d'État et historien, est considéré comme l'un des initiateurs du réveil de la conscience nationale. Au Congrès slave de 1848, il réclama l'égalité des droits pour toutes les nationalités : « Soit nous arrivons à une situation ou nous pourrons être fiers de dire ‹ je suis un Slave ›, soit nous cesserons d'être des Slaves. » Le 1er juillet 1912, le monument (2) surchargé de symboles historique, dessiné par Stanislav Sucharda fut dévoilé sur le quai. (1) Fonte de différentes parties du monument en bronze dans une fonderie de Brandýs nad Labem.

## The Golden Shrine on the Vltava

(1) The illuminated National Theater at night. The theater was built in the late 19th century with money collected from the whole Czech nation. The sign above the entrance says "The Nation to Itself." The theater meant being equal with the Austrians and Germans, who had thriving cultural institutions. The neo-Renaissance building was designed by Josef Zítek and opened with Smetana's *Libuše* in 1881, but two months later the theater burned down. Under Josef Schulz's direction it was rebuilt and re-opened in 1883. The interiors and façades were lavishly decorated by leading artists. The theater was lovingly called *zlatá kaplička* (the golden little chapel). (2) Antonín Dvořák (1841–1904), composer of nine symphonies, 10 operas and much chamber and solo music. (3) Leoš Janáček (1854–1928), a composer deeply committed to the promotion of Moravian folk music. (4) Eduard Vojan (1853–1920) was considered the greatest actor on the Czech stage.(5) On 25 September 1913 Ema Destinnová (Emilie Pavlína Kitlová; 1878–1930) performed in the title role of Bedřich Smetana's *Libuše*. This gala performance was staged to mark the 30th anniversary of the opening of the National Theater. Richard Strauss described Destinnová as "One of the greatest singers of the 20th century with the most beautiful soprano voice."

## Der Goldene Schrein an der Moldau

(1) Das beleuchtete Nationaltheater bei Nacht. Das Theater war im späten 19. Jahrhundert mit finanzieller Unterstützung der gesamten tschechischen Bevölkerung erbaut worden, was die Inschrift über dem Eingang widerspiegelt: »Der Nation für sich selbst.« Der Bau war immer auch ein Symbol des tschechischen Nationalbewußtseins, denn die Österreicher und Deutschen unterhielten viele erfolgreiche kulturelle Institutionen. Das Gebäude im Stil der Neorenaissance von Josef Zítek wurde 1881 mit der Aufführung von Smetanas *Libuše* eröffnet, brannte aber bereits zwei Monate später ab. Unter der Leitung von Josef Schulz wurde es wiederaufgebaut, und 1883 fand die zweite Eröffnung statt. Innenräume und Fassade wurden von führenden Künstlern gestaltet. Das Theater wurde als *zlatá kaplička* (kleine Goldkapelle) bezeichnet. (2) Antonín Dvořák (1841–1904) komponierte neun Symphonien, zehn Opern sowie zahlreiche Kammermusikstücke und Werke für Solisten. (3) Leoš Janáček (1854–1928) war ein Komponist, der sich der Verbreitung der mährischen Volksmusik stark verpflichtet fühlte. (4) Eduard Vojan (1853–1920) galt als der bedeutendste tschechische Schauspieler. (5) Am 25. September 1913 sang Ema Destinnová (Emilie Pavlína Kitlová, 1878–1930) die Titelrolle in Bedřich Smetanas *Libuše* anläßlich einer Galaveranstaltung zum 30. Jahrestag der Gründung des Nationaltheaters. Richard Strauss nannte Destinnová »eine der größten Sängerinnen des 20. Jahrhunderts mit der schönsten Sopranstimme.«

## Un temple d'or sur la Moldau

(1) Le Théâtre national illuminé la nuit. Il fut construit à la fin du XIXe siècle grâce à des fonds collectés dans l'ensemble du pays. L'inscription de l'entrée proclame : « La nation à elle-même. » Le théâtre se voulait l'égal des prestigieux établissements allemands et autrichiens. Le bâtiment néo-Renaissance fut dessiné par Josef Zítek et ouvrit sur une représentation de *Libuše* de Smetana en 1881. Deux mois plus tard, il était victime d'un grave incendie. Reconstruit sous la direction de Josef Schulz, il fut reconstruit et rouvrit en 1883. Les intérieurs et les façades sont merveilleusement décorés par les plus grands artistes. Les visiteurs appelaient affecteusement ce monument: *zlatá kaplička* (la petite chapelle d'or). (2) Antonín Dvořák (1841–1904), compositeur de neuf symphonies, dix opéras et d'une importante œuvre de musique de chambre. (3) Leoš Janáček (1854–1928), compositeur très engagé. (4) Eduard Vojan (1853–1920), le plus grand acteur de la scène tchèque. (5) Le 25 septembre 1913, Ema Destinnová (Emilie Pavlína Kitlová; 1878–1930) interpréta le rôle titre de *Libuše* de Bedřich Smetana lors du gala du trentième anniversaire de la fondation du Théâtre national, sanctuaire de la vie culturelle tchèque. Richard Strauss décrivit Destinnová comme : « Une des grandes chanteuses du XXe siècle avec la plus belle voix de soprano qui soit. »

5

### Franz Kafka and German Culture

(1) A graduation photograph of Franz Kafka (1883–1924), one of the most important Prague writers of the 20th century. His works *The Trial, The Castle* and *Metamorphosis* became a part of the world's literary heritage in the second half of the 20th century. He died at 41 and was buried in the New Jewish Cemetery in Olšany. (2) Max Brod (1884–1968), Kafka's friend, writer, journalist, critic, and translator. In 1939 he was forced to flee Prague and settled in Tel Aviv. (3) Egon Erwin Kisch (1885–1948), the father of modern journalism, known in his day as the "Furious Reporter." He worked for the *Prager Tagblatt* (5), the most popular newspaper among the German-speaking population. (4) Gustav Meyrink (1868–1932), author of a mystical novel, *The Golem* – a haunting vision of the Prague ghetto interwoven with the legend of a man-like monster of clay created by a rabbi who gives the creature life. (6) Rainer Maria Rilke (1875–1926), poet born in Prague's New Town. He felt oppressed by Prague's provincialism and its linguistic ghetto. (7) Franz Werfel (1890–1945) was one of the most important German Expressionist poets and a playwright. His most famous books include *Forty Days* and *Verdi*.

### Franz Kafka und die deutsche Kultur

(1) Ein Foto von Franz Kafka (1883–1924), dem bedeutendsten Prager Schriftsteller des 20. Jahrhunderts, das anläßlich seines Universitätsexamens entstand. Seine Werke »Der Prozeß«, »Das Schloß« und »Die Verwandlung« gehören seit der zweiten Hälfte des 20. Jahrhunderts zum Kanon der Weltliteratur. Kafka starb mit nur 41 Jahren und wurde auf dem Neuen Jüdischen Friedhof in Olšany beerdigt. (2) Der Schriftsteller, Journalist, Kritiker, Übersetzer und Herausgeber Max Brod (1884–1968), ein Freund Kafkas, mußte 1939 Prag verlassen und emigrierte nach Tel Aviv. (3) Egon Erwin Kisch (1885–1948), der Begründer des modernen Journalismus, wurde von seinen Zeitgenossen »der Rasende Reporter« genannt. Er arbeitete für das *Prager Tagblatt* (5), die beliebteste Zeitung der deutschsprachigen Bevölkerung. (4) Gustav Meyrink (1868–1932) schrieb den mystischen Roman *Der Golem* – eine unheimliche Vision des Prager Ghettos mit der Legende des von einem Rabbi aus Ton geschaffenen menschenähnlichen Monsters. (6) Rainer Maria Rilke (1875–1926), der in der Prager Neustadt geborene Dichter, fühlte sich vom Provinzialismus Prags und der sprachlichen Isolierung erdrückt. (7) Franz Werfel (1890–1945) war einer der bedeutendsten deutschen Dichter und Dramatiker des Expressionismus. Seine bekanntesten Werke sind *Vierzig Tage* und *Verdi*.

### Franz Kafka et la culture allemande

(1) Portrait de Franz Kafka (1883–1924) en étudiant, il est l'un des plus importants écrivains pragois du XXe siècle. Ses écrits comme *Le Procès, Le Château* et *La Métamorphose* appartiennent aujourd'hui au patrimoine littéraire mondial. Il mourut à l'âge de 41 ans et fut enterré dans le nouveau cimetière juif d'Olšany. (2) Max Brod (1884–1968), l'ami de Kafka, écrivain, journaliste, critique et traducteur. En 1939, il fut obligé de fuir Prague et s'installa à Tel Aviv. (3) Egon Erwin Kisch (1885–1948), père du journalisme moderne, connu de son temps comme « le reporter alerte ». Il travaillait pour le *Prager Tagblatt* (5), le quotidien le plus populaire auprès de la population germanophone. (4) Gustav Meyrink (1868–1932), auteur du roman mystique *Le Golem*, vision onirique du ghetto de Prague mêlée à la légende d'un monstre d'apparence humaine créé par un rabbin. (6) Rainer Maria Rilke (1875–1926), poète né dans la Nouvelle ville de Prague. Il se sentait oppressé par le provincialisme pragois et son ghetto linguistique. (7) Franz Werfel (1890–1945) fut l'un des plus importants poètes expressionnistes et auteurs dramatiques allemands. Parmi ses œuvres les plus connues : *Quarante jours* et *Verdi*.

2

3

4

5

6

7

## Cubism

Czech painters, sculptors, designers and architects, inspired by Cubist ideas and by Pablo Picasso's and Georges Braque's paintings, created many excellent works of art. Prague is the only city in the world which boasts Cubist architecture. The geometrically three-dimensional façades rank among the most distinctive features of the city's appearance. (1) A house at 30 Neklanova (1913–14), designed by Josef Chochol (1880–1956). (2) The House at the Black Madonna (1911–12), designed by Josef Gočár (1880–1945), near completion. (3) Building Cubist houses under the Vyšehrad Hill (1911–13). Josef Chochol was the most radical Czech Cubist architect. (4) A Cubist "triple" house on Rašín Embankment (under the Vyšehrad Hill) designed by Josef Chochol and built in 1912–13. (5) The House at the Black Madonna in Celetná is home to a permanent exhibition of Czech Cubist art on its upper floors.

## Kubismus

Tschechische Maler, Bildhauer, Designer und Architekten schufen, inspiriert von kubistischen Ideen und den Bildern Pablo Picassos und George Braques, viele großartige Kunstwerke. Prag ist die einzige Stadt auf der Welt mit kubistischer Architektur. Die geometrisch dreidimensionalen Fassaden sind einzigartige Elemente im städtischen Erscheinungsbild. (1) Ein Haus an der Neklanova-Straße 30 (1913–14), das nach den Entwürfen von Josef Chochol (1880–1956) entstand. (2) Das Haus Zur Schwarzen Muttergottes (1911–12), nach den Plänen von Josef Gočár (1880–1945), kurz vor seiner Fertigstellung. (3) Der Bau kubistischer Häuser unterhalb des Vyšehrad (1911–13). Josef Chochol war der radikalste Verteter des tschechischen Kubismus. (4) Ein kubistisches Dreifamilienhaus am Rašín-Kai (unterhalb des Vyšehrad) nach den Entwürfen von Josef Chochol, erbaut 1912–13. (5) Das Haus Zur Schwarzen Muttergottes in Celetná beherbergt im Obergeschoß eine Dauerausstellung tschechischer Werke des Kubismus.

## Le cubisme

Les peintres, sculpteurs, designers et architectes tchèques inspirés par la théorie cubiste et les peintures de Pablo Picasso et de Georges Braque sont à l'origine de nombreuses remarquables réalisations. Prague est la seule cité au monde qui puisse se vanter de posséder des exemples d'architecture de ce style. Certaines façades géométriques en trois dimensions ajoutent un charme unique au paysage urbain pragois. (1) Maison, 30 rue Neklanova (1913–14) dessinée par Josef Chochol (1880–1956). (2) Maison de « la Madone noire » (1911–12), conçue par Josef Gočár (1880–1945), lors de son achèvement. (3) Maisons cubistes en construction près de la colline de Vyšehrad (1911–1913). Josef Chochol était le plus radical des architectes tchèques cubistes. (4) Villa pour trois familles 6–10 quai Rašínovo conçue par Josef Chochol et construit en 1912–1913. (5) Maison de « la Madone noire », rue Celetna (abrite aujourd'hui une exposition permanente des cubistes tchèques aux étages supérieurs).

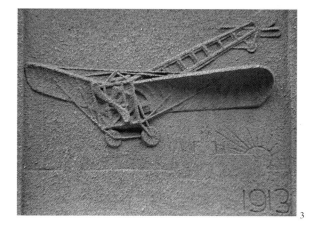

1913

I. veřejný vzlet aeroplanu

v Pardubicích

Ve prospěch Ústřední Matice Školské a Mor. Jednoty Severočeské.

Ve prospěch Ústřední Matice Školské a Mor. Jednoty Severočeské.

uspořádá český aviatik
inž. Jan Kašpar z Pardubic

v neděli 19. června 1910 mezi půl 6. a 8. hodinou odpol. za klidného počasí na vojenském cvičišti.

## Flying over Prague

(1) The spirit of the new age was best reflected in the flying feats of pioneer aviators such as the Czech Jan Kašpar (1883–1927), who flew from Pardubice to Prague in a French-built Blériot plane in 1911. (2) The French pilot Adolphe Pégoud (1889–1915), who performed many medal-winning, hair-raising flying stunts. He became a pilot in the First World War and was killed in action in 1915. (3) This house sign from 1913 shows the fragility of early aeroplanes. (4) Kašpar made his first tests in April 1910 in his Blériot, model XI, making flights of up to 2km. (5) Poster advertising Kašpar's "take-off from Pardubice on Sunday 19 June 1910 between 6 and 8 p.m., weather permitting." (6) Kašpar in a field in Prosek outside Prague. (7) Photomontage of Pégoud performing one of his aerobatic stunts above Hradčany.

## Der Flug über Prag

(1) Der Geist des neuen Zeitalters äußerte sich am deutlichsten in den Flugleistungen der Luftfahrpioniere wie des Tschechen Jan Kašpar (1883–1927), der 1911 in einem in Frankreich gebauten Blériot-Flugzeug von Pardubice nach Prag flog. (2) Der französische Pilot Adolphe Pégoud (1889–1915) vollführte viele haarsträubende Kapriolen in der Luft und gewann damit zahlreiche Medaillen. Im Ersten Weltkrieg wurde er Flieger und starb während eines Einsatzes 1915. (3) Dieses Hausschild von 1913 zeigt die Fragilität der frühen Flugzeuge. (4) Kašpar unternahm im April 1910 in seiner Blériot, Modell XI, seine ersten Versuche, indem er Strecken von bis zu 2 km flog. (5) Ein Plakat kündigt Kašpars »Flug von Pardubice am Sonntag, dem 19. Juni 1910, zwischen 18.00 und 20.00 Uhr, falls das Wetter es erlaubt« an. (6) Kašpar auf einem Feld in Prosek bei Prag. (7) Fotomontage: Pégoud führt einen seiner akrobatischen Kunstflüge über dem Hradschin vor.

## Prague, vue d'avion

(1) L'esprit des temps modernes se traduit particulièrement dans les exploits de pionniers de l'aviation comme le Tchèque Jan Kašpar (1883–1927) qui, en 1911, vola de Pardubice à Prague dans un aéroplane Blériot. (2) Le pilote français Adolphe Pégoud (1889–1915), auteur de terrifiantes acrobaties aériennes qui lui rapportèrent de nombreuses médailles. Pilote pendant la Première Guerre mondiale, il fut tué lors de l'opération en 1915. (3) Ce panneau de 1913 montre la fragilité des anciens avions. (4) Kašpar fit ses premiers essais en avril 1910 dans son modèle Blériot XI, volant sur près de 2 km. (5) Affiche annonçant le vol de Kašpar : « Décollage de Pardubice le dimanche 19 juin 1910 entre 18 et 20 heures, si le temps le permet. » (6) Kašpar dans un champ à Prosek à l'extérieur de Prague. (7) Photomontage de Pégoud exécutant un de ses numéros acrobatiques au-dessus de Hradčany. En 1914, les habitants de Prague furent subjugués par les démonstrations acrobatiques de ce risque-tout français.

6

7

KREMATORIUM

SPOLEK PRO SPALOVÁNÍ MRTVÝCH V PRAZE

zpopelní své členy úplně zdarma. Příspěvky od 1 kor. měsíčně. Šiřte tuto vysoce pokrokovou ideu! Pište ihned o prospekty. Adresa: KREMATORIUM, Praha

| LEDEN | ÚNOR | BŘEZEN | DUBEN |
|---|---|---|---|
| 1 Sob. 16 Ned. | 1 Uterý 16 Střed. | 1 Uterý 16 Střed. | 1 Pátek 16 Sob. |
| 2 Ned. 17 Pond. | 2 Stř. 17 Čtvrt. | 2 Střed. 17 Čtvrt. | 2 Sob. 17 Ned. |
| 3 Pond. 18 Uterý | 3 Čtvrt. 18 Pátek | 3 Čtvrt. 18 Pátek | 3 Ned. 18 Pond. |
| 4 Uterý 19 Střed. | 4 Pátek 19 Sob. | 4 Pátek 19 Sob. | 4 Pond. 19 Uterý |
| 5 Střed. 20 Čtvrt. | 5 Sob. 20 Ned. | 5 Sob. 20 Ned. | 5 Uterý 20 Střed. |
| 6 Čtvrt. 21 Pátek | 6 Ned. 21 Pond. | 6 Ned. 21 Pond. | 6 Střed. 21 Čtvrt. |
| 7 Pátek 22 Sob. | 7 Pond. 22 Uterý | 7 Pond. 22 Uterý | 7 Čtvrt. 22 Pátek |
| 8 Sob. 23 Ned. | 8 Uterý 23 Střed. | 8 Uterý 23 Střed. | 8 Pátek 23 Sob. |
| 9 Ned. 24 Pond. | 9 Střed. 24 Čtvrt. | 9 Střed. 24 Čtvrt. | 9 Sob. 24 Ned. |
| 10 Pond. 25 Uterý | 10 Čtvrt. 25 Pátek | 10 Čtvrt. 25 Pátek | 10 Ned. 25 Pond. |
| 11 Uterý 26 Střed. | 11 Pátek 26 Sob. | 11 Pátek 26 Sob. | 11 Pond. 26 Uterý |
| 12 Střed. 27 Čtvrt. | 12 Sob. 27 Ned. | 12 Sob. 27 Ned. | 12 Uterý 27 Střed. |
| 13 Čtvrt. 28 Pátek | 13 Ned. 28 Pond. | 13 Ned. 28 Pond. | 13 Střed. 28 Čtvrt. |
| 14 Pátek 29 Sob. | 14 Pond. | 14 Pond. 29 Uterý | 14 Čtvrt. 29 Pátek |
| 15 Sob. 30 Ned. | 15 Uterý | 15 Uterý 30 Střed. | 15 Pátek 30 Sob. |
| 31 Pond. | | 31 Čtvrt. | |

| KVĚTEN | ČERVEN | ČERVENEC | SRPEN |
|---|---|---|---|
| 1 Ned. 16 Pond. | 1 Střed. 16 Čtvrt. | 1 Pátek 16 Sob. | 1 Pond. 16 Uterý |
| 2 Pond. 17 Uterý | 2 Čtvrt. 17 Pátek | 2 Sob. 17 Ned. | 2 Uterý 17 Střed. |
| 3 Uterý 18 Střed. | 3 Pátek 18 Sob. | 3 Ned. 18 Pond. | 3 Střed. 18 Čtvrt. |
| 4 Střed. 19 Čtvrt. | 4 Sob. 19 Ned. | 4 Pond. 19 Uterý | 4 Čtvrt. 19 Pátek |
| 5 Čtvrt. 20 Pátek | 5 Ned. 20 Pond. | 5 Uterý 20 Střed. | 5 Pátek 20 Sob. |
| 6 Pátek 21 Sob. | 6 Pond. 21 Uterý | 6 Střed. 21 Čtvrt. | 6 Sob. 21 Ned. |
| 7 Sob. 22 Ned. | 7 Uterý 22 Střed. | 7 Čtvrt. 22 Pátek | 7 Ned. 22 Pond. |
| 8 Ned. 23 Pond. | 8 Střed. 23 Čtvrt. | 8 Pátek 23 Sob. | 8 Pond. 23 Uterý |
| 9 Pond. 24 Uterý | 9 Čtvrt. 24 Pátek | 9 Sob. 24 Ned. | 9 Uterý 24 Střed. |
| 10 Uterý 25 Střed. | 10 Pátek 25 Sob. | 10 Ned. 25 Pond. | 10 Střed. 25 Čtvrt. |
| 11 Střed. 26 Čtvrt. | 11 Sob. 26 Ned. | 11 Pond. 26 Uterý | 11 Čtvrt. 26 Pátek |
| 12 Čtvrt. 27 Pátek | 12 Ned. 27 Pond. | 12 Uterý 27 Střed. | 12 Pátek 27 Sob. |
| 13 Pátek 28 Sob. | 13 Pond. 28 Uterý | 13 Střed. 28 Čtvrt. | 13 Sob. 28 Ned. |
| 14 Sob. 29 Ned. | 14 Uterý 29 Stř. | 14 Čtvrt. 29 Pátek | 14 Ned. 29 Pond. |
| 15 Ned. 30 Pond. | 15 Střed. 30 Čtvrt. | 15 Pátek 30 Sob. | 15 Pond. 30 Uterý |
| | | 31 Ned. | 31 Střed. |

| ZÁŘÍ | ŘÍJEN | LISTOPAD | PROSINEC |
|---|---|---|---|
| 1 Čtvrt. 16 Pátek | 1 Sob. 16 Ned. | 1 Uterý 16 Střed. | 1 Čtvrt. 16 Pátek |
| 2 Pátek 17 Sob. | 2 Ned. 17 Pond. | 2 Střed. 17 Čtvrt. | 2 Pátek 17 Sob. |
| 3 Sob. 18 Ned. | 3 Pond. 18 Uterý | 3 Čtvrt. 18 Pátek | 3 Sob. 18 Ned. |
| 4 Ned. 19 Pond. | 4 Uterý 19 Střed. | 4 Pátek 19 Sob. | 4 Ned. 19 Pond. |
| 5 Pond. 20 Uterý | 5 Střed. 20 Čtvrt. | 5 Sob. 20 Ned. | 5 Pond. 20 Uterý |
| 6 Uterý 21 Střed. | 6 Čtvrt. 21 Pátek | 6 Ned. 21 Pond. | 6 Uterý 21 Střed. |
| 7 Střed. 22 Čtvrt. | 7 Pátek 22 Sob. | 7 Pond. 22 Uterý | 7 Střed. 22 Čtvrt. |
| 8 Čtvrt. 23 Pátek | 8 Sob. 23 Ned. | 8 Uterý 23 Střed. | 8 Čtvrt. 23 Pátek |
| 9 Pátek 24 Sob. | 9 Ned. 24 Pond. | 9 Střed. 24 Čtvrt. | 9 Pátek 24 Sob. |
| 10 Sob. 25 Ned. | 10 Pond. 25 Uterý | 10 Čtvrt. 25 Pátek | 10 Sob. 25 Ned. |
| 11 Ned. 26 Pond. | 11 Uterý 26 Střed. | 11 Pátek 26 Sob. | 11 Ned. 26 Pond. |
| 12 Pond. 27 Uterý | 12 Střed. 27 Čtvrt. | 12 Sob. 27 Ned. | 12 Pond. 27 Uterý |
| 13 Uterý 28 Stř. | 13 Čtvrt. 28 Pátek | 13 Ned. 28 Pond. | 13 Uterý 28 Střed. |
| 14 Střed. 29 Čtvrt. | 14 Pátek 29 Sob. | 14 Pond. 29 Uterý | 14 Střed. 29 Čtvrt. |
| 15 Čtvrt. 30 Pátek | 15 Sob. 30 Ned. | 15 Uterý 30 Střed. | 15 Čtvrt. 30 Pátek |
| | 31 Pond. | | 31 Sob. |

Úřadovny: Král. Vinohrady, Dolní Blanická číslo 1.

1910    1910

## Going Out in Style

(1) At the turn of the century a new trend came to Prague. A calendar (in Art Nouveau style) from 1910 advertises the *Crematorium – Society for the Burning of the Dead*, "which will incinerate its members almost for free. The fees start from 1 crown monthly. Do spread the very progressive idea! Write to us immediately for brochures. The address: Prague Crematorium." (2–5) Opulent Art Nouveau tombs at the Vyšehrad Cemetery, the city's most exclusive burial-place, where many famous Czech artists are interred.

## Abgang mit Stil

(1) Um die Jahrhundertwende setzten sich neue Trends in Prag durch. Ein Kalender (im Jugendstil) von 1910 wirbt für die *Krematorium – Gesellschaft zur Verbrennung der Toten*, »die ihre Mitglieder fast umsonst verbrennt. Die Mindestgebühr beläuft sich auf eine Krone pro Monat. Verbreiten Sie diese sehr fortschrittliche Idee! Fordern Sie sofort Broschüren an. Adresse: Prager Krematorium.« (2–5) Reich geschmückte Jugendstil-Grabsteine auf dem Vyšehrader Friedhof, Prags elegantester Ruhestätte, auf der viele berühmte tschechische Künstler bestattet sind.

## Partir avec élégance

(1) Au tournant du siècle, Prague connut une nouvelle mode. Un calendrier de style Art Nouveau datant de 1910 annonce la création du *Crematorium – la Société de crémation des morts* «qui incinère ses adhérents pratiquement gratuitement. À partir de 1 couronne par mois. Faites connaître cette idée si nouvelle! Demandez notre brochure. Adresse : le Crématorium de Prague.» (2–5) Opulents tombeaux Art Nouveau au cimetière de Vyšehrad, le plus élégant de Prague, où sont enterrés de nombreux grands artistes tchèques.

2

3

**RODINA MILDOVA**

PHDR PETR PUJMAN

ANNA MILDOVA
ROZ. BARTHOVA
*1.10.1848. +4.10.1900.
JUDr JOS. MILDE
ADVOKÁT.
*26.11.1839. +1.12.1900.
ANNA NATALIE
BARTOSOVA∞
ROZ. HENNEROVA
*14.5.1899. +12.9.1921.
JAROMIR MILDE
∞ ZAKLADATEL FIRMY
MILDE - ROESSLER ∞
VELKOZÁVOD LUCEBNINAMI
13.VIII.1871 +16.VI.1930.
JARMILA
HENNEROVA
ROZ.
ROESSLEROVA
*10.8.1899 +24.9.1978.
RNDr VOJTĚCH
PUJMAN CSc ∞
*9.I.1921 +24.2.1986.

| UNIV. PROF. | JUDr KAMIL HENNER | |
| REKTOR U K | 2.7.1861 | 19.5.1928 |
| MARIE HENNEROVÁ | ROZ. MILDOVA | |
| 12.3.1870 | | 19.10.1931 |
| AKADEMIK | UNIV. PROFESOR | |
| MUDr KAMIL HENNER | NEUROLOG | |
| 30.3.1895 | | 26.8.1967 |

4

**RODINA MAŠKOVA**
VÁCLAV MAŠEK
TOVÁRNÍK
MARIE MAŠKOVA

5

# ČESKÝ SVĚT

ROČNÍK X.    V PRAZE, DNE 3 ČERVENCE 1914    ČÍSLO 42.

Oběť sarajevské tragedie, rakouský následník trůnu František Ferdinand d' Este.

Do nádherně rozkvetlých zahrad konopišťského zámku, ještě oddechujících vonnými vzpomínkami, zalehly černé stíny smutku. Náhlou ranou zachvěla se celá veliká říše a tři mladičká osiřelá srdce dětská letěl se první ukrutnou bolestí života. Historie se dávno převalí přes událost, ale ta srdce si nikdy nebudou moci vzpomenouti na jarní konopišťské růže, aby se nezachvěla v hloubi. Vždyť se mezi nimi naposled loučila s otcem a matkou . . .
Foto Louis Vácha, Konopiště.

1

2

3

## The Heir to the Throne

The Archduke Franz Ferdinand d'Este (1863–1914), nephew of the Emperor Franz Josef, was heir to the Habsburg throne but his dislike for Vienna, which became even more intense following his morganatic marriage to the Czech Žofie Chotková (1868–1914), made him a virtual recluse at the Konopiště Castle (45km south-east of Prague). His passion for collecting and, above all, hunting became an overriding obsession. He killed over 300,000 animals during his life, which itself came to an abrupt end when he and his wife were shot in Sarajevo on 28 June 1914. His death led to a series of events which started the First World War, the complete disintegration of the Austro-Hungarian Empire and the creation of many Central European states. (1) The official portrait of Archduke Franz Ferdinand on the cover of *The Czech World* following his assassination. (2) Franz Ferdinand's coat of arms. (3) Franz Ferdinand, his wife Žofie Chotková and their three children: (from left) Ernst (1904–54), Maximilian (1902–62) and Sophie (1901–91). (4) Konopiště Castle. (5) The Archduke attending the races at Chuchle, near Prague. (6) A hunting weekend at Konopiště with Kaiser Wilhelm of Germany. (7) In Prague several places were named after the Archduke, including the bridge (today called Mánes) next to the Rudolfinum.

## Der Thronerbe

Erzherzog Franz Ferdinand d'Este (1863–1914), der Neffe von Kaiser Franz Josef, war Erbe des Habsburger-Throns. Aufgrund seiner Abneigung gegen Wien, die sich durch seine morganatische Ehe mit der Tschechin Žofie Chotková (1868–1914) noch verstärkte, lebte er wie ein Einsiedler auf Schloß Konopiště (45 km südöstlich von Prag). Seine Sammelleidenschaft und vor allem sein Interesse an der Jagd entwickelten sich zu einer Sucht. Er tötete mehr als 300.000 Tiere in seinem Leben, das selbst ein plötzliches Ende nahm, als er am 28. Juni 1914 in Sarajewo zusammen mit seiner Frau erschossen wurde. Sein Tod löste eine Serie von Ereignissen aus, die zum Ausbruch des Ersten Weltkriegs, zum völligen Zerfall des Kaiserreiches Österreich-Ungarn und zur Entstehung vieler mitteleuropäischer Staaten führte. (1) Das offizielle Porträt des Erzherzogs Franz Ferdinand auf dem Titelblatt der *Tschechischen Welt* nach seiner Ermordung. (2) Franz Ferdinands Wappen. (3) Franz Ferdinand mit seiner Frau Žofie Chotková und ihren drei Kindern: (von links) Ernst (1904–54), Maximilian (1902–62) und Sophie (1901–91). (4) Schloß Konopiště. (5) Der Erzherzog besucht ein Rennen in Chuchle in der Nähe von Prag. (6) Ein Jagdwochenende in Konopiště mit Kaiser Wilhelm II. von Deutschland. (7) In Prag benannte man mehrere Plätze einschließlich der Brücke in der Nähe des Rudolfinums (heute Mánes-Brücke) nach dem Erzherzog.

## L'héritier du trône

L'archiduc François-Ferdinand d'Este (1863–1914), neveu de l'empereur François-Joseph, était l'héritier du trône des Habsbourg. Son mépris pour Vienne, qui s'intensifia après son mariage morganatique avec la Tchèque Žofie Chotková (1868–1914), l'amena pratiquement à se retirer au château de Konopiště (à 45 km au sud-est de Prague). Sa passion des collections et surtout de la chasse devint presque une obsession. Il tua plus de 300 000 animaux au cours de sa vie avant d'être assassiné le 28 juin 1914 à Sarajevo. La mort de François-Ferdinand entraîna une série d'événements d'où allait éclater la Première Guerre mondiale, la désintégration de l'Empire austro-hongrois et la création de nombreux États nouveaux en Europe centrale. (1) Portrait officiel de l'archiduc François-Ferdinand sur la couverture du *Monde tchèque* après son assassinat. (2) Les armes de François-Ferdinand. (3) François-Ferdinand, son épouse Žofie Chotková et leurs trois enfants (à partir de la gauche) : Ernest (1904–1954), Maximilien (1902–1962) et Sophie (1901–1991). (5) L'archiduc assistant aux courses de Chuchle, près de Prague. (4) Château de Konopiště. (6) Week-end de chasse à Konopiště en compagnie de l'empereur Guillaume d'Allemagne. (7) Plusieurs lieux de Prague prirent le nom de l'Archiduc, dont le pont proche du Rudolfinum (aujourd'hui Pont Mánes).

4

5

6

7

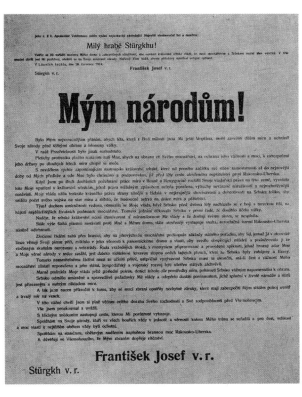

### "Off to the War!"

(1, 2) Young soldiers leaving Prague in 1914. Often they were transported in cattle trucks bearing the sign: "40 Men or 6 Horses." They were leaving behind a prosperous city which two years later started to experience hunger. Ration coupons were useless and peasants started exchanging food for pianos, jewelry and binoculars. Material for clothes was made from nettles, coffee from barley and beer was not available. The people smoked potato leaves, though some managed to grow tobacco. (3) Franz Josef's proclamation, "To My Nations," which was posted across the Empire on the declaration of war. (4) Newspaper headline: "War declared on Serbia." (5) The cover of a period song depicts a Prague soldier waving his goodbye to the city with the words "I'd like to see my beloved Prague one more time..." (6) Departing cavalry. (7) Troops on the Letná Plain ready to leave Prague. Czech soldiers were reluctant to fight for the Austro-Hungarian Empire. Many deserted and formed Czech legions in Russia, France and Italy, which later became the embryo of the Czechoslovak Republic's army.

### »Auf in den Krieg«

(1, 2) Junge Soldaten verlassen 1914 Prag. Sie reisten oft in Viehwaggons mit der Aufschrift: »40 Mann oder 6 Pferde«. Sie ließen eine wohlhabende Stadt zurück, die zwei Jahre später den Hunger kennenlernen sollte. Rationskarten waren nutzlos, und Bauern begannen, ihre Lebensmittel gegen Klaviere, Juwelen und Ferngläser einzutauschen. Bekleidungsmaterial war Nessel, Kaffee wurde aus Gerste hergestellt und Bier gab es nicht mehr. Die Leute rauchten Kartoffelblätter, obwohl es einigen gelang, Tabak anzubauen. (3) Franz Josefs Erklärung »An mein Volk«, die nach der Kriegserklärung im ganzen Reich verschickt wurde. (4) Schlagzeile in einer Zeitung: »Kriegserklärung gegen Serbien.« (5) Das Titelblatt eines Liederbuches zeigt einen Prager Soldaten, der seiner Stadt zum Abschied mit den Worten »Ich möchte noch einmal mein geliebtes Prag wiedersehen« zuwinkt. (6) Abfahrende Kavallerie. (7) Truppen auf dem Letná-Plateau warten auf den Abmarsch aus Prag. Tschechische Soldaten waren nur widerwillig bereit, auf der Seite des Kaiserreichs Österreich-Ungarn zu kämpfen. Sie desertierten und gründeten tschechische Legionen in Rußland, Frankreich und Italien, die später den Grundstock der Armee der tschechoslowakischen Republik bilden sollten.

### «C'est la guerre!»

(1, 2) Jeunes soldats quittant Prague en 1914. Ils étaient souvent transportés en chariots à bestiaux portant la pancarte « 40 hommes ou 6 chevaux.» Ils laissaient une cité prospère qui allait connaître la famine deux ans plus tard. Les coupons de rationnement devinrent inutiles et les paysans commencèrent à échanger de la nourriture contre des pianos, des bijoux, des jumelles. Les vêtements étaient fabriqués à partir d'orties, le café avec de l'orge et la bière était devenue introuvable. Les gens du peuple fumaient des feuilles de pomme de terre, mais certains arrivaient encore à cultiver du tabac. (3) Proclamation de François-Joseph « À mes nations », affichée dans tout l'Empire et annonçant la guerre. (4) Titre de journal : « La guerre contre la Serbie est déclarée.» (5) Couverture d'une chanson de l'époque montrant un soldat pragois disant adieu à sa ville : « Je voudrais revoir encore une fois ma chère Prague...» (6) La cavalerie prête pour le départ. (7) Plaine de Letná, les troupes sur le point de quitter la capitale. Les soldats tchèques n'avaient guère envie de se battre pour l'empire austro-hongrois. Beaucoup désertèrent et formèrent des légions tchèques en Russie, en France et en Italie, qui allaient devenir l'embryon de l'armée tchécoslovaque.

6

7

Psal sem list tento wám w žaláři w oko=
wách čakaje na zajtřie na smrt otsúzenie
maje.plnú nádeji ku pánu Bohu abych
prawdy bozie neustupowal a bludów·
kteréz sú na mě křiwi swědkowě swěd=
čili abych sě neodzřisáhl · · · · · · · · · ·
Také prosim · abyste sě milowali we=
spolek dobrých násilim tlačiti nedali
a prawdy kazdému přáli·

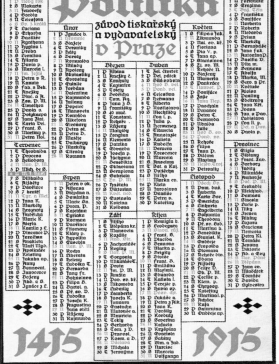

## The Jan Hus Monument

Lively debates among the city's artists and businessmen preceded the building of the Jan Hus monument. Hus is the most famous Czech religious reformer, who preached against practices of the church. He celebrated mass in Czech in Betlémská Chapel and wrote hymns in Czech. Besides revising Czech grammar, he created the motto "The truth shall prevail," which is embroidered on the Czech presidential standard. (1) He was burnt at the stake in Constance for refusing to recant, and his ashes were scattered in the Rhine. The unveiling of the almost finished monument, designed by (2) Ladislav Šaloun (1870–1946), planned for the 500th anniversary of Hus's death, took place in 1915 but in a very restricted manner under the watchful eye of the authorities, who feared an outbreak of nationalistic demonstrations. (3) A calendar commemorating the 500th anniversary of Jan Hus's death. (4–6) Construction of the monument, cast in bronze, in Staroměstké náměstí (Old Town Square).

## Das Jan-Hus-Denkmal

Dem Bau des Jan-Hus-Denkmals gingen lebhafte Debatten zwischen den Künstlern der Stadt und den Geschäftsleuten voraus. Hus ist der berühmteste tschechische Reformator, der die Kirche insbesondere wegen ihrer Ablaßpraktiken anprangerte. Er hatte viele Anhänger unter den Tschechen, die in der Bethlehemskapelle zusammenkamen, und schrieb seine Hymnen in Tschechisch. Außerdem überarbeitete er die tschechische Grammatik und prägte das Motto: »Die Wahrheit wird sich durchsetzen«, das auf der Präsidentenstandarte eingestickt ist. (1) Er wurde in Konstanz auf dem Scheiterhaufen verbrannt, weil er den Widerruf seiner Lehre verweigerte. Seine Asche streute man in den Rhein. Die Enthüllung des fast fertigen Denkmals, das nach den Plänen von (2) Ladislav Šaloun (1870–1946) zum 500. Todestag von Hus geplant war, fand 1915 in eingeschränkter Form unter den wachsamen Augen der Behörden statt, die eine Welle nationaler Demonstrationen befürchteten. (3) Ein Kalender erinnert an den 500. Todestag von Jan Hus. (4–6) Errichtung des Denkmals, das in Bronze gegossen ist, auf dem Staroměstké náměstí (Altstädter Ring).

## Le monument à la gloire de Jean Hus

Des débats animés entre artistes et bourgeois de la ville précédèrent la construction de ce monument à Jean Hus, le plus célèbre réformateur religieux tchèque, qui critiquait les pratiques cléricales. Il lisait la messe en tchèque à la Chapelle Betlémská et écrivait des hymnes en tchèque. Avant de réviser la grammaire tchèque, il créa la devise « La vérité prévaudra » brodée sur le fanion présidentiel. (1) Ayant refusé d'abjurer, il fut brûlé vif en 1415 à Constance, et ses cendres furent dispersées dans le Rhin. L'inauguration du monument presque achevé, dessiné par (2) Ladislav Šaloun (1870–1946), et prévue pour le 500e anniversaire de la mort du grand homme. Elle eut lieu en 1915, mais d'une manière très discrète, sous le contrôle des autorités qui craignaient que n'éclatent des démonstrations de nationalisme. (3) Calendrier commémorant le 500e anniversaire de la mort de Jan Hus. (4–6) Construction du monument en bronze à Staroměstké náměstí (ancienne place municipale).

4

5

6

Nach einer Aufnahme von E. Bieber

Kunstverlagsanstalt Gerhard Stalling, Oldenburg i. Gr.

*Die treuen Verbündeten 1915*

1

2

3

### Death of the Emperor

(1) Idealised portraits of Emperor Wilhelm II (1888–1918) and Emperor Franz Josef I (1848–1916). (2, 3) Post-war caricatures of the two rulers by Dr Desiderius. (4) Postcard of the Emperor at prayer. (5) In November 1916 the aged Franz Josef smoked his last cigar and soon died of bronchial pneumonia. He lay in state at the Hofburg in Vienna with violets decorating his chest. The flowers were stolen and later sold as a souvenir. (6) Portrait of Franz Josef I on the cover of *Besedy lidu* following his death. His successor, the Archduke Karl, was deposed when Austria-Hungary collapsed. Crowned as Karl the First (7), he became known as Karl the Last.

### Der Tod des Kaisers

(1) Idealisiertes Porträt der Kaiser Wilhelm II. (1888–1918) und Franz Josef I. (1848–1916). (2, 3) Karikaturen der beiden Herrscher von Dr. Desiderius aus der Zeit nach dem Weltkrieg. (4) Postkarte mit dem betenden Kaiser. (5) Im November 1916 rauchte der gealterte Franz Josef seine letzte Zigarre und starb kurz darauf an bronchialer Lungenentzündung. Er wurde in der Hofburg in Wien mit Veilchen auf der Brust aufgebahrt. Die Blumen wurden gestohlen und später als Souvenirs verkauft. (6) Porträt Kaiser Franz Josef I. auf dem Titelbild der *Besedy lidu* nach seinem Tode. Sein Nachfolger Erzherzog Karl mußte zwei Jahre später das Ende von Österreich-Ungarn mit ansehen. (7) Karl I., der Nachfolger Franz Josefs. Zu dieser Zeit erhielt er den Spitznamen Karl der Letzte.

### La mort de l'Empereur

(1) Portraits idéalisés de l'Empereur Guillaume II (1888–1918) et l'empereur François-Joseph Ier (1848–1916). (2, 3) Caricatures d'après-guerre des deux souverains par Dr. Desiderius. (4) Carte postale de l'Empereur en prière. (5) En novembre 1916, le vieil empereur fuma son dernier cigare et mourut d'une pneumonie. Son corps exposé à la Hofburg de Vienne, entouré de violettes. (6) Portrait de François-Joseph Ier en couverture de *Besedy lidu*, après sa mort. Les fleurs furent dérobées, puis vendues en souvenir. Son successeur, l'archiduc Charles, allait assister à l'effondrement de l'Autriche-Hongrie deux années plus tard. (7) Charles Ier, successeur de François-Joseph. Il fut bientôt appelé Charles dernier.

**An meine Völker!**

Der König von Italien hat **Mir** den Krieg erklärt.

Ein Treubruch, dessengleichen die Geschichte nicht kennt, ist von dem Königreiche Italien an seinen beiden Verbündeten begangen worden.

Nach einem Bündnis von mehr als dreißigjähriger Dauer, während-dessen es seinen Territorialbesitz mehren und sich zu ungeahnter Blüte ent-falten konnte, hat uns Italien in der Stunde der Gefahr verlassen und ist mit fliegenden Fahnen in das Lager Unserer Feinde übergegangen.

4

5

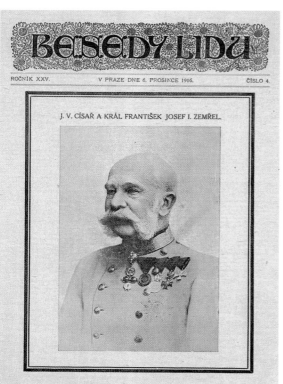

**BESEDY LIDU**

ROČNÍK XXV.     V PRAZE DNE 6. PROSINCE 1916.     ČÍSLO 4.

J. V. CÍSAŘ A KRÁL FRANTIŠEK JOSEF I. ZEMŘEL.

6

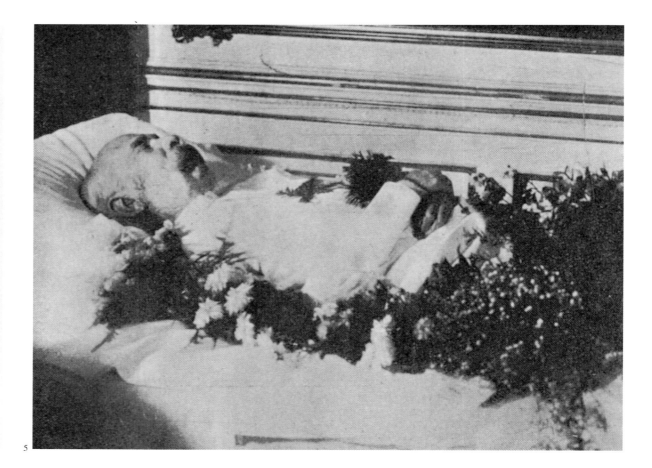

7

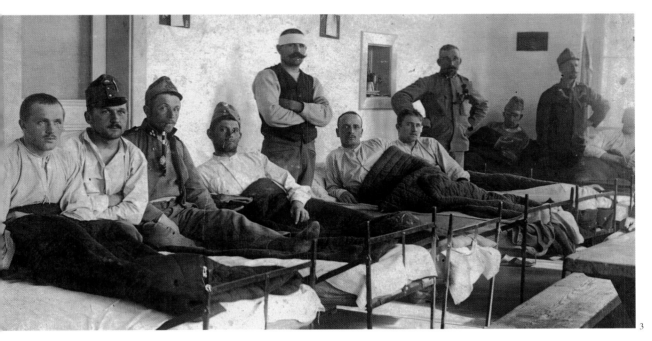

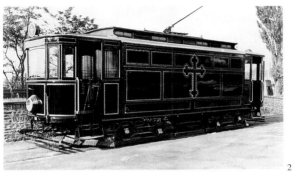

## Wartime in Prague

Although not directly affected by the war, conditions in Prague progressively worsened. (1) There were severe food shortages and general hardship. (3) Soon Prague had virtually turned into a giant hospital caring for thousands of wounded soldiers. During the First World War ambulance-trams carried 700,000 injured soldiers to hospitals, while a specially built funeral tram (2) was used to carry dead soldiers. The lower part of the carriage had enough space for two to four coffins and, in 1917–19, 1042 dead soldiers were transported from hospitals in Vinohrady to cemeteries in Olšany. (4) Food rationing coupons. (5) The International Red Cross building. (6) An advertisement for Prague coal merchants. (7) The song "My Comrade," written by Karel Hašler (1879–1941), one of the most famous composers of popular songs at the time, shows a Czech soldier dreaming of Prague. (8) A 1916 Christmas card sent from the front. (9) A small booklet containing a selection of letters by soldiers sent during the war to their families and friends.

## Prag in Kriegszeiten

Obwohl die Stadt nicht direkt vom Krieg betroffen war, wurden die Lebensbedingungen in Prag allmählich immer schwieriger. (1) Lebensmittel waren knapp und die Zeiten hart. (3) Bald verwandelte sich Prag in ein gigantisches Hospital für Tausende von Soldaten. Während des Ersten Weltkrieges beförderten Ambulanzbahnen 700.000 verwundete Soldaten in die Krankenhäuser. Für den Transport der Toten setzte man speziell für diesen Zweck gebaute Beerdigungsbahnen (2) ein, bei denen der untere Teil des Waggons genug Platz für zwei bis vier Särge bot. Zwischen 1917 und 1919 beförderte man 1042 tote Soldaten von den Krankenhäusern in Vinohrady auf den Friedhof von Olšany. (4) Rationierungsscheine. (5) Das Gebäude des Internationalen Roten Kreuzes. (6) Eine Anzeige für Prager Kohlenhändler. (7) Das Lied »Mein Kamerad«, geschrieben von Karel Hašler (1879–1941), einem der berühmtesten zeitgenössischen Komponisten, zeigt einen tschechischen Soldaten, der von Prag träumt. (8) Eine Weihnachtskarte aus dem Jahr 1916 von der Front. (9) Ein kleines Büchlein mit einer Sammlung von Feldpostbriefen, die Soldaten während des Krieges an ihre Familien und Freunde schrieben.

## Prague en guerre

Bien que loin du théâtre de la guerre, la ville vit ses conditions d'existence se détériorer peu à peu. (1) Elle souffrit de rationnement de nourriture et de multiples difficultés. (3) Bientôt la capitale se transforma en un gigantesque hôpital accueillant des milliers de blessés. Pendant la guerre, des trams-ambulances transportèrent 700 000 soldats blessés vers les hôpitaux. Un wagon fut spécialement aménagé pour les morts (2). La partie inférieure était conçue pour recevoir de deux à quatre cercueils. De 1917 à 1919, 1042 soldats furent ainsi transportés des hopitaux de Vinohrady au cimetière d'Olšany. (4) Coupons de rationnement. (5) Immeuble de la Croix-Rouge internationale. (6) Publicité pour des charbonniers. (7) La chanson « Mon camarade », de Karel Hašler (1879–1941) l'un des plus célèbres compositeurs de chansons populaires de l'époque. Elle décrit un soldat tchèque rêvant de Prague. (8) Carte de vœux de Noël 1916 envoyée par le front. (9) Livret contenant une sélection de lettres de soldats expédiées pendant la guerre à leurs familles et leurs amis.

7

8

9

# The Reign of the Czech Lion
# Unter der Regentschaft des tschechischen Löwen
# Le règne du lion tchèque

The sculpted Czech lion, with a Slovak coat of arms on its chest, on the terrace of the Vítkov Monument. Above it a Czechoslovak airforce squadron displays its strength in celebration of the birth of the new Republic of Czechoslovakia.

Der gemeißelte tschechische Löwe mit dem slowakischen Wappen auf der Brust auf der Basis des Vítkov-Monuments. Über ihm zeigt eine tschechoslowakische Luftwaffeneinheit an einem der Feiertage zur Errichtung der neuen Republik ihre Stärke.

Portant les armes slovaques sur son poitrail, le lion tchèque sculpté de la terrasse du monument Vítkov. Dans le ciel, passe une escadrille de l'armée de l'air tchécoslovaque à l'occasion de l'anniversaire de la naissance de la nouvelle République tchécoslovaque.

### The Birth of the Republic

On 28 October 1918 festive crowds gathered in Wenceslas Square to celebrate the first day of the free Republic. On 18 October, Tomáš Garrigue Masaryk proclaimed in the Washington Declaration that Czechoslovakia had been born as a new independent democratic country. Everybody in the country waited impatiently for the official ending of Austro-Hungarian rule as negotiations were in progress in Geneva. At 10 a.m. news was telegraphed to Prague that Austria-Hungary accepted new conditions proposed by the USA's President Woodrow Wilson. In Prague a spontaneous demonstration erupted: the Czechs started tearing down the two-headed eagle emblems from buildings and putting up red-and-white flags instead. The Austrian military authorities relinquished control in Prague on 30 October, and the war ended with the capitulation of Austria-Hungary on 3 November and of Germany on 11 November.

### Die Geburt der Republik

Am 28. Oktober 1918 versammelte sich eine festlich gestimm-te Menschenmenge auf dem Wenzelsplatz, um den ersten Tag der freien Republik zu feiern. Am 18. Oktober hatte Tomáš Garrigue Masaryk in der Erklärung von Washington die Geburt des neuen unabhängigen demokratischen Landes Tschechoslo-wakei ausgerufen. Jeder im Lande wartete ungeduldig auf das offizielle Ende der österreichisch-ungarischen Herrschaft, über das in Genf verhandelt wurde. Um 10 Uhr morgens telegra-phierte man die Nachricht nach Prag, daß Österreich-Ungarn die neuen, von dem amerikanischen Präsidenten Woodrow Wilson vorgeschlagenen Bedingungen akzeptierte. In Prag brach eine spontane Demonstration aus: Die Tschechen rissen das Emblem mit dem Doppeladler von den Häusern und ersetzten es durch rot-weiße Flaggen. Die österreichischen Militärs über-gaben am 30. Oktober die Kontrolle der Stadt den Tschechen, und der Krieg endete mit der Kapitulation Österreich-Ungarns am 3. und Deutschlands am 11. November.

### Naissance d'une république

Le 28 octobre 1918, une foule en liesse se massa place Venceslas pour célébrer la naissance de la république et le retour à la liberté. Dix jours plus tôt, Tomáš Garrigue Masaryk avait proclamé dans sa déclaration de Washington la naissance de la Tchécoslovaquie, nouvel État indépendant et démocratique. Tout le pays attendait avec impatience la fin officielle de la domination austro-hongroise tandis que les négociations se déroulaient à Genève. À 10 h, Prague reçut un télégramme annonçant que l'Autriche-Hongrie avait accepté les conditions du président américain Woodrow Wilson. Des manifestations spontanées éclatèrent dans la capitale : les Tchèques arrachèrent les emblèmes bicéphales des façades des immeubles et les remplacèrent par des drapeaux rouge et blanc. Les autorités militaires autrichiennes abandonnèrent le contrôle de la ville le 30 octobre, et la guerre s'acheva avec la capitulation de l'Autriche-Hongrie, le 3 novembre, et celle de l'Allemagne, le 11 novembre.

Číslo 243.    V Praze, v pondělí dne 28. října 1918.    Ročník VII. (XXVII.)    Číslo 8 hal.

# VEČERNÍK
## PRÁVA LIDU

## Bezpodmínečná kapitulace Rakousko-Uherska.

## Rakousko-Uhersko žádá své nepřátele o separátní mír a okamžité příměří.

Úplně se podrobuje Wilsonovi.
Uznává práva Čechoslováků a Jihoslovanů.
Konec války. - Konec říše Rakousko-Uherské.

Ministr zahraničních věcí hr. Andrássy uložil včera rakousko-uherskému vyslanci ve Stokholmě, aby požádal královskou švédskou vládu, by doručila vládě Spojených Států amerických tuto odpověď na její notu z 18. t. m.:

### 28 October 1918

(1, 3) Rejoicing crowds celebrating the first day of independence. (2) A newspaper from 28 October 1918 with the headline "Unconditional surrender of Austria-Hungary." Artists expressed their patriotic feelings visually. Since the newly born country did not yet have its symbols worked out, painters often drew a lion, which always represented Bohemia, with some additional images which were later discarded. (4) Here, a lion carrying the tricolor flag (based on the French standard) towards Freedom and Peace. As always in Czech paintings, a beautiful, buxom, bewinged woman makes the best allegory of the new-found democracy. (5) Another symbolic image from the period: the Czech lion chewing the Austro-Hungarian flag with its black double-headed eagle. In the background, the outline of *letohrádek Hvězda* (the Star Summerhouse) on the *Bílá hora* (White Mountain, now a suburb 10km from the center of Prague) where in 1621 Bohemian armies lost their independence to Austria for almost 300 years.

### 28. Oktober 1918

(1, 3) Begeisterte Menschenmassen feiern den ersten Tag der Unabhängigkeit. (2) Eine Zeitung vom 28. Oktober 1918 mit der Schlagzeile »Bedingungslose Kapitulation von Österreich-Ungarn.« Künstler brachten ihre patriotischen Gefühle sichtbar zum Ausdruck. Weil das neu entstandene Land noch keine nationalen Symbole besaß, zeichneten die Maler oft einen Löwen als Sinnbild für Böhmen. Andere Symbole, die ihn umgaben, fielen später weg. (4) Hier trägt der Löwe eine Trikolore (nach dem Vorbild der französischen Fahne) in Richtung Freiheit und Frieden. Wie immer auf tschechischen Gemälden diente eine schöne, geflügelte, vollbusige Frau als Allegorie der neugegründeten Demokratie. (5) Ein anderes Sinnbild aus dieser Zeit: Der tschechische Löwe zerreißt eine österreichisch-ungarische Fahne mit dem schwarzen Doppeladler. Im Hintergrund erkennt man die Silhouette von *letohrádek Hvězda* (Lustschloß Stern) auf dem *Bílá hora* (Weißer Berg, heute ein Vorort zehn Kilometer außerhalb des Prager Stadtzentrums), auf dem die Böhmen 1621 für fast 300 Jahre ihre Unabhängigkeit an Österreich verloren.

### 28 octobre 1918

(1, 3) Une foule joyeuse célébra le premier jour de l'indépendance. (2) Journal du 28 octobre 1918 annonçant la « Reddition sans condition de l'Autriche-Hongrie ». Des artistes exprimèrent dans leurs dessins les sentiments patriotiques. La jeune nation n'avait pas eu le temps de réfléchir à ses symboles, et les peintres la représentaient souvent sous les traits d'un lion, l'ancien symbole de la Bohême, enrichi de quelques emblèmes vite abandonnés. (4) Un lion apportant dans sa gueule le drapeau tricolore à la Paix et à la Liberté. Comme souvent dans les allégories tchèques, c'est une jeune femme ailée et bien en chair qui représente la nouvelle démocratie. (5) Autre image symbolique de la période : le lion tchèque déchirant le drapeau austro-hongrois à l'aigle bicéphale. Dans le fond, figure la silhouette de *letohrádek Hvězda* (Maison d'été de l'étoile) sur la *Bílá hora* (La Montagne blanche, aujourd'hui une banlieue à 10 km du centre de la capitale) où, en 1621, la Bohême avait perdu pour trois siècles son indépendance au profit de l'Autriche.

## The Founding Fathers

(1, 2) On 21 December 1918 Tomáš Garrigue Masaryk arrived in Prague and was welcomed by enthusiastic crowds. The President-Liberator, as he was called, was driven in a car festooned with flowers and the tricolor banner, surrounded by soldiers from the Foreign Legion, *Sokol* members, and men and women in national costume. It was a day of glory for the aged Professor, who, through his negotiating talents, performed the most magnificent diplomatic coup, convincing the Americans, English and French that his Czecho-Slovak model would be of benefit to the Allies and that Austria, which planned to integrate with Germany, should be completely dismantled. The three founders of Czechoslovakia: (3) Tomáš Garrigue Masaryk (1850–1937). (4) Milan Rastislav Štefánik (1880–1919), a Slovak and a legendary hero who organized the Foreign Legions (formed of Czechs and Slovaks, which fought in the war against Austria-Hungary) in France and who, with his connections in French diplomatic circles, helped decisively in the creation of independent Czechoslovakia; he died tragically in an airplane accident on his return. (5) Edvard Beneš (1884–1948).

## Die Gründerväter

(1, 2) Am 21. Dezember 1918 kam Tomáš Garrigue Masaryk nach Prag, wo ihn eine begeisterte Menge empfing. Der Befreiungspräsident, wie man ihn nannte, wurde in einem mit Blumen und der Trikolore geschmückten Wagen gefahren, den Soldaten der Fremdenlegion, *Sokol*-Mitglieder und Männer und Frauen in nationaler Tracht begleiteten. Es war ein Tag des Triumphes für den ältlichen Professor, dem durch sein Verhandlungsgeschick ein großartiger diplomatischer Schachzug gelungen war: Er hatte die Amerikaner, Engländer und Franzosen davon überzeugen können, daß das tschechisch-slowakische Modell für die Alliierten von Vorteil sein würde und ein mit Deutschland verbundenes Österreich komplett aufgesplittert werden sollte. Die drei Gründer der Tschechoslowakei: (3) Tomáš Garrigue Masaryk (1850–1937). (4) Milan Rastislav Štefánik (1880–1919), ein Slowake und legendärer Held, der in Frankreich die Fremdenlegion (aus Tschechen und Slowaken, die im Krieg gegen Österreich-Ungarn gekämpft hatten) organisierte und mit Hilfe seiner Verbindungen zu französischen diplomatischen Kreisen entscheidend zur Gründung der unabhängigen Tschechoslowakei beitrug. Er starb tragischerweise bei einem Flugzeugabsturz auf dem Weg in die Heimat. (5) Eduard Beneš (1884–1948).

## Les pères fondateurs

(1, 2) Le 21 décembre 1918, Tomáš Garrigue Masaryk fit son entrée à Prague où une foule enthousiaste l'acclama. Le président-libérateur – comme on l'appelait alors – fut transporté dans une automobile décorée de fleurs et du drapeau tricolore, entouré de soldats des Légions étrangères, de membres de *Sokol* et d'hommes et de femmes en costumes traditionnels. C'était le triomphe de ce professeur déjà âgé. Par ses talents de négociateur, il avait réussi une brillante manœuvre diplomatique en convainquant les Américains, les Britanniques et les Français que son modèle tchéco-slovaque bénéficierait aux Alliés, puisque l'Autriche, qui projetait de s'intégrer à l'Allemagne serait démantelée. Les trois fondateurs de la Tchécoslovaquie : (3) Tomáš Garrigue Masaryk (1850–1937); (4) Milan Rastislav Štefánik (1880–1919), slovaque et héros légendaire, organisateur des Légions étrangères (formées de Tchèques et de Slovaques qui combattirent contre l'Autriche-Hongrie) en France, et qui, grâce à ses relations dans les cercles diplomatiques français, contribua de façon décisive à la création d'une Tchécoslovaquie indépendante. Il mourut tragiquement à son retour dans un accident d'avion. (5) Edvard Beneš (1884–1948).

VLAJKA STÁTNÍ (NÁRODNÍ)
REPUBLIKY ČESKOSLOVENSKÉ.

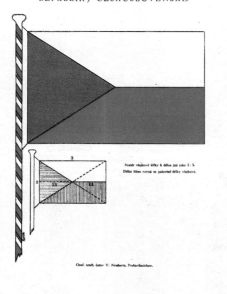

Poměr vlajkové šířky k délce její jako 2 : 3.
Délka klínu rovná se polovině délky vlajkové.

Graf. umělí ústav V. Neuberta, Praha-Smíchov.

MALÝ ZNAK
REPUBLIKY ČESKOSLOVENSKÉ.

STANDARTA PRESIDENTA.

Graf. umělí ústav V. Neuberta, Praha-Smíchov.

3

4

5

## The Castle and the New President

(1) President Masaryk in his study in Hradčany. He was elected by the National Committee on 14 November 1918, the day on which the Habsburgs were officially deposed. Masaryk became the most popular President in Czech history: he was re-elected in 1920, 1927 and 1934. In the first years many ministries, offices and embassies had to be created, new insignia, symbols and money had to be invented (famous artists contributed their designs). Problems with Germans, Hungarians and some Slovak Communists had to be solved. Czechoslovak soldiers from the Foreign Legions had to sort out the territorial claims in the troubled regions. Masaryk stripped the aristocracy of their titles as well as their land. In 1921 the Czechoslovak Parliament reflected the new democratic system: the Social Democrats had 74 seats, the National Socialists 24, the Socialists 3, the Agrarian Party 28, Slovaks 12, Germans 72, Hungarians 10; altogether there were 281 Members of Parliament representing a wide spectrum. (2) A bird's-eye view of the Hradčany compound. The presidential offices are housed in the buildings to the right of St Vitus Cathedral (with its Gothic and neo-Gothic towers). The bodies of Bohemian kings, as well as the remains of the first martyr, St Wenceslas, are interred inside the cathedral. The Czech crown jewels are kept in a treasure chamber just above the St Wenceslas Chapel. In this spot the first Catholic place of worship was erected after the pagan Bohemian tribes accepted Christianity in the 10th century. The hill was settled by Prince Bořivoj in 870–90 and through the centuries Hradčany remained the seat of power from which the princes, from behind their fortifications, ruled the land below the hill. (3) The newly designed Czechoslovak tricolor, with a blue wedge, which won the competition against other designs and was officially approved by Parliament in 1920. (4) The Bohemian lion, with the Slovak cross incorporated on its chest. (5) The presidential flag – two golden lions incorporating the five coats of arms of (clockwise) Slovakia, Transcarpathian Ukraine, Silesia, Moravia and Bohemia in the center. Underneath is embroidered "The truth shall prevail."

## Die Burg und der neue Präsident

(1) Präsident Masaryk in seinem Arbeitszimmer im Hradschin. Am 14. November 1918, dem Tag, an dem die Habsburger offiziell entmachtet wurden, wählte ihn die Nationalversammlung. Masaryk war der populärste Präsident der tschechischen Geschichte: Er wurde 1920, 1927 und 1934 wiedergewählt. In den ersten Jahren mußten viele Ministerien, Büros und Botschaften eingerichtet, neue Insignien, Symbole und Geldscheine (an deren Entwurf berühmte Künstler mitarbeiteten) geschaffen werden. Darüber hinaus galt es, Probleme mit Deutschen, Ungarn und einigen slowakischen Kommunisten zu bewältigen. Tschechoslowakische Soldaten aus der Fremdenlegion kümmerten sich um die territorialen Ansprüche in den Krisengebieten. Masaryk nahm dem Adel Titel und Land. Das neue demokratische System spiegelte sich 1921 in der Zusammensetzung des tschechoslowakischen Parlaments, das ein weites politisches Spektrum abdeckte: von insgesamt 281 Parlamentssitzen gewannen die Sozialdemokraten 74 , die Nationalsozialisten 24, die Sozialisten 3, der Bund der Landwirte 28, die Slowaken 12, die Deutschen 72 und die Ungarn 10 . (2) Der Komplex des Hradschin aus der Vogelperspektive. Die Büros des Präsidenten befinden sich in den Gebäuden rechts des Veitsdomes (mit seinen gotischen und neugotischen Türmen). Die Leichname der böhmischen Könige und die Überreste des ersten Märtyrers, des Heiligen Wenzels, liegen in diesem Dom begraben. Die Kronjuwelen werden in einer Schatzkammer unmittelbar über der Wenzelskapelle aufbewahrt. Nachdem die heidnischen böhmischen Stämme im 10. Jahrhundert das Christentum angenommen hatten, wurde an dieser Stelle das erste katholische Gotteshaus errichtet. Prinz Bořivoj ließ sich zwischen 870 und 890 auf dem Hügel nieder, und über die Jahrhunderte blieb der Hradschin das Machtzentrum, hinter dessen Befestigungen die Prinzen das Land unterhalb des Berges regierten. (3) Die neu entworfene dreifarbige tschechische Flagge mit einem blauen Keil gewann gegen andere Konkurrenten die Ausschreibung und wurde 1920 vom Parlament offiziell angenommen. (4) Der böhmische Löwe mit dem slowakischen Kreuz. (5) Die Präsidentenflagge – zwei goldene Löwen umfassen die fünf im Uhrzeigersinn dargestellten Wappen der Slowakei, der transkarpathischen Ukraine, Schlesiens, Mährens und Böhmens in ihrer Mitte. Darunter ist das Motto »Die Wahrheit wird sich durchsetzen« eingestickt.

## Le château et le nouveau président

(1) Le président Masaryk dans son bureau au château du Hradčany. Il fut élu par le Comité national le 14 novembre 1918, jour de la déposition officielle des Habsbourg. Président le plus populaire de l'histoire tchèque, il sera réélu en 1920, 1927 et 1934. Très vite, il fallut mettre en place des ministères, des administrations, des ambassades, définir les insignes et symboles officiels, créer une monnaie. Les problèmes avec les Allemands, les Hongrois et quelques communistes slovaques pressaient. Les soldats tchécoslovaques des Légions étrangères durent régler les revendications territoriales dans les régions troublées. Masaryk dépouilla l'aristocratie de ses titres et de ses terres. En 1921, le parlement de 281 membres reflétait un large éventail politique et démocratique : les sociaux-démocrates avaient enlevé 74 sièges, les socialistes nationaux 24, les socialistes 3, le parti agrarien 28, les slovaques 12, les Allemands 72, les Hongrois 10. (2) Vue d'avion de l'ensemble du Hradčany. Les bureaux de la présidence se trouvent dans les bâtiments à droite de la cathédrale Saint-Guy, aux flèches gothiques et néogothiques, où sont conservés les corps des rois de Bohême et les restes de saint Venceslas, martyr. Le trésor royal est protégé dans une chambre du trésor juste au-dessus de la chapelle de saint Venceslas. Un premier lieu de culte catholique avait été érigé en cet endroit au Xe siècle, après la conversion des tribus païennes de Bohême au catholicisme. La colline fut occupée par le prince Bořivoj en 870–89, et au cours des siècles, le Hradčany fortifié devait demeurer le siège du pouvoir. (3) Le nouveau drapeau tricolore tchécoslovaque, qui remporta le concours de dessin organisé et fut approuvé par le parlement en 1920. (4) Le lion de Bohême orné de la croix slovaque. (5) Le fanion présidentiel – deux lions d'or tenant les armes de la Slovaquie, de l'Ukraine transcarpatique, de Silésie, de Moravie et de Bohême au centre. La devise brodée dit : « La vérité prévaudra. »

## Prague Incorporates New Townships

(1) Na Příkopě. (2) Wenceslas Square, looking down from above the National Museum. (3) Prague's coat of arms. Initially, Prague (the Old Town) had three houses, a wall and a gate as its symbol. Later it was combined with Přemyslid's dynasty lion. The banners represented the city's 12 army units. The Bohemian lion – the only lion in European heraldry – has two tails (the Bohemian Prince Přemysl Otakar I was granted the second tail by Emperor Otto IV in the 13th century for help against the Saxons). The military banners were replaced with the flags of different communities (on the right 22 and on the left 23). On the ribbon is a golden sign: "Prague the Mother of Cities."
(4) A map of Prague showing the 37 communities (towns and villages) which were incorporated into the capital on 31 December 1921. With the new additions, the capital spread over 17,164 hectares and its population was 676,657. In 1930 the number of inhabitants reached 962,200.

## Die Eingemeindung neuer Stadtteile

(1) Na Příkopě. (2) Der Wenzelsplatz aus der Sicht oberhalb des Nationalmuseums. (3) Das Prager Wappen. Ursprünglich waren die Symbole Prags (die Altstadt) drei Häuser, eine Mauer und ein Tor. Später wurden diese mit dem Löwen der Přemysliden-Dynastie verbunden. Die Banner zeigen die 12 Armee-Einheiten der Stadt. Der böhmische Löwe hat – als einziger in der europäischen Heraldik – zwei Schwänze (im 13. Jahrhundert erlaubte Kaiser Otto IV. dem böhmischen Prinzen Přemysl Otakar I. für seine Hilfe gegen die Sachsen seinem Wappentier das Tragen eines zweiten Schwanzes). Die militärischen Banner wurden durch die Flaggen der einzelnen Gemeinden (22 auf der linken und 23 auf der rechten Seite) ersetzt. Auf dem Band steht mit goldener Schrift: »Prag ist die Mutter der Städte.«
(4) Eine Karte von Prag zeigt die 37 Gemeinden (Städte und Dörfer), die am 31. Dezember 1921 eingemeindet wurden. Mit den Neuerwerbungen dehnte sich die Stadt auf 17.164 Hektar aus und erreichte eine Einwohnerzahl von 676.657 Menschen. 1930 war die Einwohnerzahl auf 962.200 gestiegen.

## Prague s'agrandit

(1) Na Příkopě. (2) La place Venceslas, vue du Musée national. (3) Les armes de la ville de Prague. Initialement, elles ne comportaient que trois maisons, un mur et une porte. Plus tard elles se virent adjoindre le lion dynastique de Přemyslid. Les bannières représentent les 12 quartiers en armes de la ville. Le lion de Bohême possède deux queues (le prince de Bohême Přemysl Otakar I se vit reconnaître le droit à une seconde par l'empereur Otto IV au XIIIe siècle pour l'avoir aidé contre les Saxons). Les bannières militaires furent remplacées par les drapeaux des diverses communautés (22 à droite, 23 à gauche). Sur le ruban figure l'inscription « Prague, mère des villes ».
(4) Plan de Prague détaillant les 37 communautés (villes et villages) incorporées à la capitale le 31 décembre 1921. Avec ces additions, la capitale couvrait maintenant 17 164 hectares pour une population de 676 657 habitants. En 1930, ce chiffre s'élevait déjà à 962 200.

3

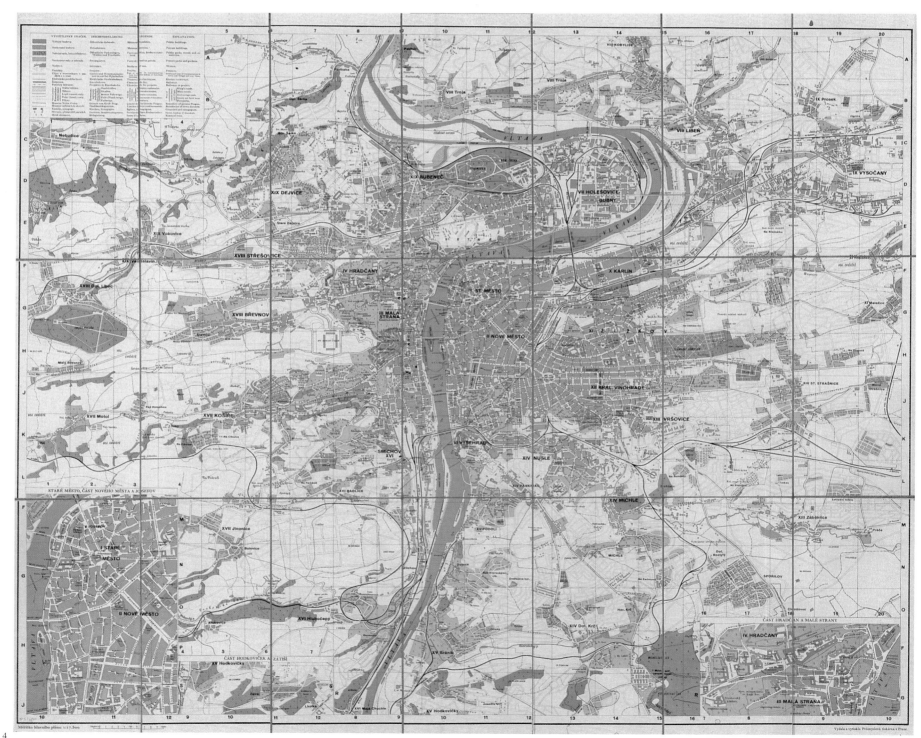

4

### The Old Streets of the New Capital

(1) The Powder Gate, with the Municipial House on the right.
(2) Old Town Square. (3) Hybernská. (4) Rytiřská. (5) Na
Příkopě. (6) The Estates Theater. (7) Celetná.

### Die Altstadt der neuen Hauptstadt

(1) Der Pulverturm, rechts daneben das Repräsentationshaus.
(2) Der Altstädter Ring. (3) Die Hybernská. (4) Die Rytiřská.
(5) Na Příkopě (6) Das Ständetheater. (7) Die Celetná.

### Les rues anciennes de la nouvelle capitale

(1) La Tour des poudres, avec la Maison municipale à sa droite.
(2) La place de la Vieille ville. (3) Hybernská. (4) Rytiřská.
(5) Na Příkopě. (6) le théâtre Stavovské. (7) Celetná.

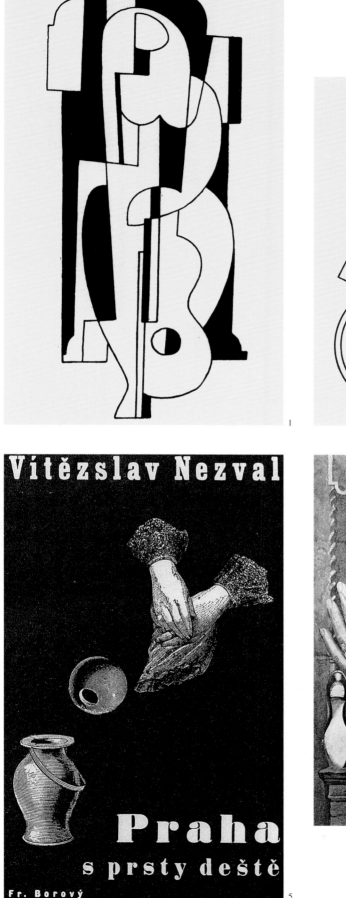

Kavárna „LOUVRE"

KONCERT

Daň 10 h

3

KAVÁRNA UNION

4

Vítězslav Nezval

Praha

s prsty deště

Fr. Borový

5

6

SEIFERT

DISK

PRAHA

DEVĚTSIL

1923

SAMÁ LÁSKA

NAKLADATELSTVÍ VEČERNICE

7

## Café Society

Prague coffeehouses exuded the aroma of fresh coffee, were enveloped in clouds of thick tobacco smoke and were filled with quiet whispers (8–10). Writer Yvan Goll called the cafés of the 1920s "spiritual centers of the world" (*Geistzentrale der Welt*). The history of the Czech avant-garde is closely linked with the Slavia, Union (4, 9), Národní and Demínka coffeehouses. In 1920, young avant-garde poets, painters, architects, theater artists and journalists founded a group named Devětsil, declaring themselves proponents of Marxism and revolution. (1, 2) Drawings by Jindřich Štyrský from a Devětsil book of poems from 1924. (3) A ticket to a concert in Café Louvre. (5) Vítězslav Nezval's (1900–58) collection of poems, *Praha s prsty deště* (Prague with Fingers of Rain). (6) A collage from this book. (7) The cover of Jaroslav Seifert's *Samá láska* (Nothing but Love),1923. It depicts Wenceslas Square in a futuristic fantasy by Otakar Mrkvička at a time when Devětsil was still very enthusiastic and lyrical about the beauty of the future of civilization.

## Cafégesellschaft

Prags Kaffeehäuser verströmten das Aroma von frischem Kaffee, waren eingehüllt in dicke Tabakwolken und angefüllt von leisem Gemurmel. (8–10) Der Schriftsteller Yvan Goll bezeichnete die Cafés der 20er Jahre als »Geistzentrale der Welt«. So ist denn auch die Geschichte der tschechischen Avantgarde eng mit dem Slavia, Union (4, 9), Národní und Demínka verknüpft. 1920 gründeten junge avantgardistische Dichter, Maler, Architekten, Theaterkünstler und Journalisten eine Gruppe namens Devětsil und erklärten sich zu den Vorreitern des Marxismus und der Revolution. (1, 2) Zeichnungen von Jindřich Štyrský aus einem Devětsil-Buch mit Gedichten von 1924. (3) Eine Eintrittskarte für ein Konzert im Café Louvre. (5) Vítězslav Nezvals (1900–58) Gedichtsammlung *Praha s prsty deště* (Prag mit Regenfingern). (6) Eine Kollage aus diesem Buch. (7) Das Umschlagbild zu Jaroslav Seiferts *Samá láska* (Nichts als Liebe) aus dem Jahr 1923. Es zeigt den Wenzelsplatz in einer futuristischen Phantasie von Otakar Mrkvička und entstand zu einer Zeit, als die Devětsil noch sehr enthusiastisch und poetisch über die Zukunft der Zivilisation dachte.

## Les cafés et l'avant-garde

(8–10) Bourdonnement des conversations, odeurs de café frais, fumées de cigares et de cigarettes créaient l'atmosphère des cafés de Prague. L'écrivain Yvan Gol en parlait dans les années 20 comme des «centres spirituels du monde». L'histoire de l'avant-garde tchèque est étroitement liée aux cafés Slavia, Union (4, 9), Národní et Demínka. En 1920, de jeunes poètes, peintres, architectes, acteurs et journalistes fondèrent un groupe nommé Devětsil et se déclarèrent partisans du marxisme et de la révolution. (1, 2) Dessins de Jindřich Štyrský tirés d'un recueil de poèmes Devětsil de 1924. (3) Billet pour un concert au Café Louvre. (5) Recueil de poésie de Vítězslav Nezval, *Praha s prsty deště* (Prague aux doigts de pluie). (6) Un collage de ce livre. (7) Couverture de *Samá láska* de Jaroslav Seifert (Rien que l'amour), 1923, représentant la place Venceslas dans une illustration futuriste d'Otakar Mrkvička, à une époque où Devětsil éprouvait encore de l'enthousiasme pour l'avenir de la civilisation.

8

9

10

### Jaroslav Hašek

(1) Jaroslav Hašek (1883–1923), author of the most famous anti-war novel, *The Good Soldier Švejk*, a vicious satire on the army, a chronicle of the adventures of a "little Czech man," an anarchist and storyteller who wears the mask of simpleton and yet is much smarter than his superiors. Hašek's book inspired several screen adaptations (5–7), including a puppet film by Jiří Trnka (8), theatrical adaptations (2), and many editions (4), including one (3) featuring a collage by John Heartfield with a drawing by Josef Lada.

### Jaroslav Hašek

(1) Jaroslav Hašek (1883–1923), Verfasser des Antikriegsromans *Die Abenteuer des braven Soldaten Schwejk*, eine Satire auf die Armee, eine Chronik der Abenteuer eines »kleinen Tschechen«, eines Anarchisten und Geschichtenerzählers hinter der Maske des Dummkopfs, der am Ende schlauer als seine Vorgesetzten ist. Hašeks Buch ist in vielen Filmen bearbeitet worden (5–7), darunter ein Puppenfilm von Jiří Trnka (8), in Theaterstücken (2) und vielen Buchausgaben (4), u.a. (3) mit einer Kollage von John Heartfield und einer Zeichnung von Josef Lada.

### Jaroslav Hašek

(1) Jaroslav Hašek (1883–1923), auteur du plus célèbre roman antimilitariste, *Le Brave Soldat Švejk*. Satire féroce contre l'armée, l'ouvrage est une chronique des aventures d'un «petit Tchèque», anarchiste mythomane, qui, malgré son air stupide, se révèle plus intelligent que ses supérieurs. Le livre de Hašek inspira plusieurs adaptations au cinéma (5–7), dont une version pour marionnettes de Jiří Trnka (8), adaptions théâtrales (2) et nombreuses éditons (4), l'une d'entre elles (3) avec un collage de John Heartfield et un dessin de Josef Lada.

□PF český film

# DOBRÝ VOJÁK ŠVEJK

režie: Karel Steklý

5

6

7

8

1

4

Anny Ondráková.

2

5

3

6

## The Silver Screen

In the 1920s approximately 20 feature films were made each year. It was a lucrative business, and the concept of "art" was not in the early filmmakers' minds. The silent era, which lasted approximately 30 years, began with the production of simple shorts, which later developed into narrative films in which the psyche and social themes were probed through drama and melodrama. (5) Anny Ondráková (1902–87), with her pencil-thin eyebrows, cupid-bow lips, bleached curls and long legs became the sweetheart of the Czech public. Alfred Hitchcock gave her the leading part in his first sound feature film, *Blackmail*. She became internationally known as Anny Ondra. Silent films were shot predominantly in studios (3, 4, 6) and only occasionally on location (1, 2). (8) A sign for the Lucerna Cinema and (7) a cinema ticket. (9) The Lucerna Cinema, a lavishly decorated movie palace with marbled floors and walls, which was built as part of a complex of buildings (1907–20) just off Wenceslas Square by Vácslav Havel (1861–1921), grandfather of the popular President. His bust decorates the far end of the staircase.

## Das Kino in den 20er Jahren

In den 20er Jahren entstanden durchschnittlich 20 Spielfilme pro Jahr. Das Filmgeschäft war eine lukrative Angelegenheit, der Begriff »Kunst« interessierte die frühen Filmemacher nicht. Die Stummfilm-Ära, die etwa 30 Jahre dauerte, begann mit der Produktion einfacher Kurzfilme, die sich später zu Handlungsfilmen verdichteten, in denen die Psyche und soziale Themen zu Dramen und Melodramen verarbeitet wurden. (5) Anny Ondráková (1902–87) mit ihren bleistiftdünnen Augenbrauen, sinnlich geschwungenen Lippen, gebleichten Locken und langen Beinen wurde der Liebling des tschechischen Publikums. Alfred Hitchcock gab ihr die Hauptrolle in seinem ersten Tonfilm *Erpressung*. Sie wurde international unter dem Namen Anny Ondra bekannt. Stummfilme wurden hauptsächlich in Studios (3, 4, 6) und nur gelegentlich außerhalb (1, 2) gedreht. (8) Ein Schild des Lucerna-Kinos und (7) eine Kinokarte. (9) Das Lucerna-Kino, ein überreich dekorierter Filmpalast mit marmornen Böden und Wänden, das als Teil eines Gebäudekomplexes von Vácslav Havel (1861–1921), dem Großvater des beliebten Präsidenten, direkt am Wenzelsplatz erbaut worden war (1907–20). Havels Büste ziert das äußerste Ende der Treppe.

## Le cinéma des années 20

20 films environ furent produits annuellement au cours des années 20 en Tchécoslovaquie. C'était une activité d'autant plus rentable que les préoccupations artistiques des premiers réalisateurs n'étaient guère ambitieuses. L'ère du film muet, qui dura à peu près 30 ans, commença par la production de courts métrages qui se transformèrent peu à peu en films narratifs abordant des thèmes psychologiques et sociaux à travers des situations dramatiques ou mélodramatiques. (5) Anny Ondráková (1902–1987) – sourcils épilés, lèvres boudeuses, boucles décolorées et longues jambes – était très aimée du public tchèque. Alfred Hitchcock lui confia le rôle principal de son premier film sonore, *Blackmail* (Chantage). Elle se fit connaître dans le monde entier sous le nom d'Anny Ondra. Les films muets étaient essentiellement tournés en studio (3, 4, 6) et rarement en décors naturels (1, 2). (8) Enseigne du cinéma Lucerna et billet de cinéma (7). (9) Le cinéma Lucerna, salle luxueusement décorée, non loin de la place Venceslas, aux sols et murs de marbre, aménagée dans un ensemble immobilier (1907–20) construit par Vácslav Havel (1861–1921), grand-père du président actuel. Son buste figure au sommet de l'escalier.

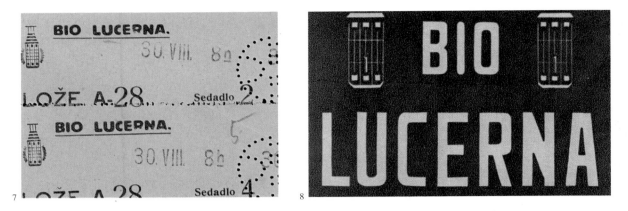

7

8

9

1          2          3

4

## Theater and the Čapek Brothers

In the year of economic crisis, 1933, Prague had 30 permanent theaters and 38 "nomadic" ones (as they were called in Czech). In 1937, 5 million people across Czechoslovakia attended theatrical plays. (1) Leading Czech actor Zdeněk Štěpánek (1896–1968) in the role of Raskolnikov in *Crime and Punishment* (staged in 1926 and again in 1933). (2) Anna Sedláčková (1887–1969) acted in many films as well as theaters: at the Vinohrady and for 30 years at the National Theater. (3) Poster for Oscar Wilde's *The Importance of Being Earnest*, performed in Czech at the Vinohrady Theater on 8 February 1920. (4) The Vinohrady Theater became the city theater in 1907. (5) Poster for *The Insect's Play*, by the Čapek brothers, performed in the National Theater. (6) The Čapek brothers: Karel (1890–1938) was a playwright and journalist; Josef (1887–1945; wearing glasses) was a poet, fairytale-writer and Cubist painter. (7) Josef Čapek's costume design for *The Insect's Play*. (8) Stage design by Bedřich Feuerstein for Karel Čapek's play *RUR* (*Rossum's Universal Robots*;1921). (9) A performance of *RUR* in 1921.

## Das Theater und die Brüder Čapek

1933, im Jahr der Wirtschaftskrise, gab es 30 ständige Theater und 38 Wanderbühnen, die im Tschechischen »Nomaden« genannt wurden. 1937 besuchten 5 Millionen Menschen aus der ganzen Tschechoslowakei Theateraufführungen. (1) Der führende tschechische Star Zdeněk Štěpánek (1896–1968) in der Rolle des Raskolnikov in *Schuld und Sühne* (aufgeführt 1926 und 1933). (2) Anna Sedláčková (1887–1969) spielte in vielen Filmen und Theateraufführungen im Vinohrady und über 30 Jahre im Nationaltheater. (3) Plakate für Oscar Wildes *The Importance of Being Earnest*, das am 8. Februar 1920 in tschechischer Sprache im Vinohrady-Theater Premiere hatte. (4) Das Vinohrady-Theater fungierte ab 1907 als Stadttheater. (5) Plakate zu Karel Čapeks Werk *Aus dem Leben der Insekten*, das im Nationaltheater dargeboten wurde. (6) Die Brüder Čapek: Karel (1890–1938) arbeitete als Dramatiker und Journalist; Josef (1887–1945; mit Brille) war ein Dichter, Märchenerzähler und kubistischer Maler. (7) Josef Čapeks Kostümentwurf für *Aus dem Leben der Insekten*. (8) Bühnendekoration von Bedřich Feuerstein für Karel Čapeks Stück *RUR* (*Rossums universelle Roboter*, 1921). (9) Eine Aufführung von *RUR* 1921.

## Le théâtre et les frères Čapek

L'année de la crise économique – 1933 – Prague comptait 30 théâtres permanents et 30 « nomades » comme on les appelait alors. En 1937, 5 millions de Tchécoslovaques se rendirent dans une salle de théâtre. (1) Le grand acteur tchèque Zdeněk Štěpánek (1896–1968), dans le rôle de Raskolnikov de *Crime et châtiment*, monté en 1926 et repris en 1933. (2) Anna Sedláčková (1887–1969) joua dans de nombreux films et pièces de théâtre au Vinohrady, et, pendant 30 ans, au Théâtre national. (3) Affiche pour la pièce d'Oscar Wilde *De l'importance d'être constant*, interprété en tchèque au Théâtre Vinohrady le 8 février 1920. (4) Le Théâtre Vinohrady devint le Théâtre de la ville en 1907. (5) Affiche pour l'œuvre des frères Čapek, *La pièce de l'insecte*, donnée au Théâtre national. (6) Les frères Čapek. Karel (1890–1938) était auteur dramatique et journaliste ; Josef (1887–1945, avec lunettes) était poète, auteur de contes de fées et peintre cubiste. (7) Dessin de costume de Josef Čapek pour *La pièce de l'insecte*. (8) Décors de Bedřich Feuerstein pour la pièce de Karel Čapek, *RUR* (*Les robots universels de Rossum*), 1921. (9) Une représentation de *RUR* en 1921.

## Fairs, Fun and Radio Days

(1–6) Fairs were very popular in Prague and on St Anna's Day (26 July) people went out to be merry and have a pint of beer. In medieval times fairs always took place in the vicinity of a church and were closely related to various saints' days. Many fairs were gradually forgotten and replaced by new types of entertainment, but the *Matějská* Fair, which usually took place in Dejvice, remained in fashion between the wars. The embankment and the Exhibition Grounds often hosted funfairs (Eden, in Vršovice, was the most famous), which the inhabitants of Prague visited at weekends. (7, 9, 10) Covers of songs written by Karel Hašler: "Prague – the Heart of Europe," "Here Goes Loulila"and "I've Got a Gramophone at Home." Young people danced to gramophone records and to music on the radio. *Radiojournal* was the name given to the first radio station, which started broadcasting on 18 May 1923. (Czechoslovakia was second after the UK to have a radio station.) "Prague is broadcasting" is the proud heading on this poster (8), which shows the Gothic Gate and the Charles Bridge.

## Vergnügungsparks und die Tage des Radios

(1–6) Vergnügungsparks waren in Prag sehr beliebt, und am St. Anna-Tag (26. Juli) gingen die Leute aus, um sich zu amüsieren und ein Glas Bier zu trinken. Im Mittelalter wurden die Jahrmärkte immer in der Nähe einer Kirche abgehalten und waren eng mit den jeweiligen Tagesheiligen verbunden. Viele gerieten jedoch allmählich in Vergessenheit und wurden durch neue Unterhaltungsangebote ersetzt. Die *Matějská*-Kirmes aber, die normalerweise in Dejvice stattfand, erfreute sich auch zwischen den Weltkriegen großer Beliebtheit. Am Flußufer und auf dem Ausstellungsgelände gab es oft Kirmesveranstaltungen (die bekannteste war die Eden-Kirmes), die die Prager Bürger am Wochenende besuchten. (7, 9, 10) Titelblätter zu den Liedern von Karel Hašler: »Prag – das Herz Europas«, »Hier kommt Loulila« und »Ich hab' zu Haus ein Grammophon«. Junge Leute tanzten zu Grammophonplatten und Musik aus dem Radio. Die erste Radiostation, die am 18. Mai 1923 auf Sendung ging, war das *Radiojournal*. (Nach Großbritannien hatte die Tschechoslowakei den ersten Radiosender.) »Prag ist auf Sendung« lautet die stolze Überschrift dieses Plakats (8), auf dem das Gotische Tor und die Karlsbrücke abgebildet sind.

## Fêtes foraines, loisirs et temps de la radio

(1– 6) Les fêtes foraines étaient très populaires à Prague. Le jour de la sainte Anne, le 26 juillet, une foule dense s'y pressait pour s'amuser et boire de la bière. À l'époque médiévale, ces fêtes se tenaient dans le voisinage des églises et étaient liées aux célébrations religieuses. Beaucoup tombèrent peu à peu dans l'oubli, mais la *Matějská*, qui se déroulait généralement à Dejvice, continua à connaître un grand succès entre les deux guerres. Les quais et le Parc des Expositions accueillaient souvent ce genre de fêtes (l'Eden était la plus fameuse) où les Pragois se rendaient en week-end. (7, 9, 10) Couvertures de partitions de chansons composées par Karel Hašler: «Prague – le cœur de l'Europe», «Voilà Loulila», et «J'ai chez moi un gramophone». La jeunesse dansait au son des disques de gramophone ou de la musique diffusée par la radio. *Radiojournal* fut la première station de radio. Elle commença à diffuser le 18 mai 1923 (la Tchécoslovaquie était le second pays après la Grande-Bretagne à posséder une station de radio). «Prague radiodiffuse» est le titre de cette affiche (8) qui montre le pont Charles.

7

8

9

10

### Down by the River

(1) A tramp takes it easy on logs on the banks of the Vltava. (2) A song sheet about a raftsman from Podskalí (an area beneath the Vyšehrad Hill, populated by raftsmen, fishermen, oarsmen and laborers, who were called *Podskaláci*) with the silhouette of Hradčany in the background. Podskalí village was demolished in 1924 and the only building left is a small customs house near the Vyšehrad railway bridge. But not only Podskalí disappeared: gradually salmon, carp, perch, pike, barbel and eel vanished as well. (3) Raftsmen on the Vltava. Different rafts were destined for different purposes: wood for heating houses was different from wood used by bakeries or breweries. The heaviest oak wood was for mills. Other rafts were constructed of deal, which was used for making shingles. On the top of each raft, faggots were carried for the poor to use as firewood. Transporting timber by river continued until 1948. (4) Women did most of their washing in the river, which had accessible sandy banks and a shallow bottom. They used sand for heavily soiled garments and dried the washing on the spot. Often the women scrubbed their children at the same time.

### Unten am Fluß

(1) Ein Landstreicher macht ein Nickerchen auf einem Holzstoß am Ufer der Moldau. (2) Ein Liederbogen über die Flößer von Podskalí (einer Region unter dem Vyšehrad, in der Flößer, Fischer, Ruderer und Arbeiter lebten, die man *Podskaláci* nannte), mit der Silhouette des Hradschin im Hintergrund. Das Dörfchen Podskalí wurde 1924 abgerissen; das einzige Haus, das übrigblieb, war das kleine Zollhaus in der Nähe der Vyšehrader Eisenbahnbrücke. Aber nicht nur Podskalí verschwand: Allmählich starben auch die Lachse, Karpfen, Flußbarsche, Hechte, Barben und Aale aus. (3) Flößer auf der Moldau. Es gab verschiedene Flöße für verschiedene Zwecke: Feuerholz unterschied sich von dem Holz, das man in Bäckereien und Brauereien verwendete. Das schwerste Eichenholz war für die Mühlen. Andere Flöße bestanden aus Fichtenholz, das für den Bau von Schindeln gebraucht wurde. Auf jedem Floß führte man Reisigbündel mit, die die Armen als Feuerholz benutzten. Der Holztransport über den Fluß hielt bis ins Jahr 1948 an. (4) Frauen wuschen den Großteil ihrer Wäsche im Fluß, der über gut erreichbare Sandbänke und flache Stellen verfügte. Zur Reinigung stark verschmutzter Kleidungsstücke verwendeten sie Sand und trockneten die Textilien an Ort und Stelle. Oft wurden gleichzeitig die Kinder abgeschrubbt.

### En descendant la rivière

(1) Un clochard se repose sur des billots de bois le long d'un quai de la Moldau. (2) Partition de chanson sur un flotteur de bois de Podskalí (un bourg au pied de la colline de Vyšehrad, peuplé de flotteurs de bois, de pêcheurs, passeurs et paysans appelés les *Podskaláci*) avec, en fond, la silhouette du Hradčany. Le village fut détruit en 1924, à l'exception d'un petit poste de douane près du pont de chemin de fer de Vyšehrad. Il ne fut pas le seul à disparaître. Peu à peu, saumons, carpes, perches, brochets, barbeaux et anguilles ne furent plus qu'un souvenir. (3) Train de flottage de bois sur la Moldau. Différents bois étaient transportés : celui réservé au chauffage des maisons n'était pas le même que celui des boulangeries ou des brasseries. Le chêne le plus dur était acheté par les scieries. D'autres trains flottaient du bouleau qui servait à faire des tuiles. Des fagots pour les pauvres étaient également transportés au-dessus des billes de bois. Cette méthode de transport dura jusqu'en 1948. (4) Les femmes faisaient l'essentiel de leur lessive au bord de la rivière aux rives sableuses et peu profondes. Elles se servaient de sable pour les taches les plus rebelles et séchaient le linge sur place. Souvent les enfants faisaient leur toilette en même temps.

4

## Rondocubism – the National Style

From 1920–25 the angular prismatic shapes, straight lines and sharp corners of Prague's early buildings were replaced by softer, more cylindrical forms. This was part of the movement known as Rondocubism. Architects searched for national motifs in Czech folklore (including the use of red, blue and white on façades). Curves and circles reminded people of painted Easter eggs, Moravian lace and cottages, and Slovak portals. Roundness came to symbolize the new "National style," as it was called by some. (1) The Adria Palace (1923–25), designed by Pavel Janák and Josef Zasche, had its façade decorated by the sculptors Otto Gutfreund, Karel Dvořák, Bohumil Kafka and Jan Štursa. The sculpted figures break up the rows of plaster ornaments, some of which look like folk embroidery stitches. (2) The Bank of the Czechoslovak Legions, erected in 1921–23, is a good example of Rondocubism. Its red, blue and white façade with semicircular arches recalls robust Russian architecture. The exterior is decorated with sculptures by Jan Štursa and a frieze with figures showing the *Legionnaires' Homecoming* by Otto Gutfreund. Inside (3), the heavy circular granite forms are rich with round and military motifs, which cover the walls, screens and grilles.

## Rondokubismus – der nationale Stil

Zwischen 1920 und 1925 wurden die eckigen, prismatischen Formen, die geraden Linien und scharfen Kanten der frühen Gebäude Prags durch weichere, zylindrischere Gestaltungen ersetzt. Sie waren Teil einer Bewegung, die als Rondokubismus bezeichnet wird. Architekten suchten in der tschechischen Folklore nach nationalen Motiven (einschließlich der Verwendung von Rot, Blau und Weiß an den Fassaden). Kurven und Kreise erinnerten die Menschen an bemalte Ostereier, an mährische Spitzen und Häuschen sowie an slowakische Portale. Die Rundung wurde zum Symbol des »Nationalen Stils«, wie ihn manche nannten. (1) Der Adria-Palast (1923–25), nach Entwürfen von Pavel Janák und Josef Zasche, dessen Fassade die Bildhauer Otto Gutfreund, Karel Dvořák, Bohumil Kafka und Jan Štursa gestalteten. Die Skulpturen unterbrechen die Reihen Stuckornamente, die teilweise an folkloristische Stickereien erinnern. (2) Die zwischen 1921 und 1923 erbaute Tschechoslowakische Legiobank bietet ein gutes Beispiel für den Rondokubismus. Ihre in den Farben Rot, Weiß und Blau gehaltene Fassade mit den halbrunden Fensterbögen erinnert an robuste russische Architektur. Die Außenmauern schmücken Skulpturen von Jan Štursa und ein Fries von Otto Gutfreund mit dem Titel *Die Legionäre kehren heim.* (3) Im Inneren wurden die schweren runden Granitformen reich mit runden und militärischen Motiven verziert, die auch die Wände, Zwischenwände und Fenstergitter bedecken.

## Le rondocubisme, un style national

De 1920 à 1925, les formes anguleuses et raides des premiers grands immeubles pragois furent remplacées par un style plus doux, « le rondocubisme ». Les architectes recherchaient dans le folklore tchèque des motifs spécifiquement nationaux (y compris l'utilisation du rouge et du bleu sur les façades). Les courbes et les cercles rappelaient les œufs de Pâques peints, la dentelle, les maisons moraves et les portails slovaques. Ces rondeurs finirent par représenter ce que certains baptisèrent le « style national ». (1) Le palais Adria (1923–25), dessiné par Pavel Janák et Josef Zasche, eut ses façades décorées par les sculpteurs Otto Gutfreund, Karel Dvořák, Bohumil Kafka et Jan Štursa. Des figures sculptées rompaient les alignements d'ornements en plâtre de style populaire, dont certains évoquaient des points de broderie. (2) La banque des Légions tchécoslovaques, érigée en 1921–1923, est un bon exemple de rondocubisme. Sa façade rouge, bleue et blanche à arches en demi-cercles rappelle la robuste architecture russe. L'extérieur est décoré de sculptures de Jan Štursa et d'une frise de figures d'Otto Gutfreund illustrant *Le retour des Légionnaires*. À l'intérieur, (3) le lourd décor en granit foisonne de motifs militaires et de formes arrondies qui recouvrent les murs, les grilles et les cloisons.

## Lines and Curves

(1, 2) Passageways in multi-purpose buildings. These were the first shopping malls, combining recreational facilities with cafés, restaurants, cinemas, dancehalls, offices, clubrooms and, upstairs, private apartments. (3) ARA (the former textile and fashion department store), on the corner of Perlová, is an elegant white Functionalist building with a slender façade, curved corner and tower with a square clock. (4) The House of the Czechoslovak Firemen's Association represents Constructivism (the form of a building was determined by its structure, which often meant reinforced concrete), which became the prevailing style in the center of Prague. In the late 1920s its name was

## Linien und Bögen

(1, 2) Durchgänge in Mehrzweckbauten: Dies waren die ersten Einkaufszentren, die Erholungsmöglichkeiten mit Cafés, Restaurants, Kinos, Tanzsälen, Büros, Klubräumen und Privatwohnungen in den oberen Geschossen unter einem Dach vereinten. (3) ARA (das ehemalige Textil- und Modekaufhaus) an der Ecke der Perlová ist ein elegantes, weißes funktionalistisches Gebäude mit einer schmalen Fassade, abgerundeten Ecken und einem Turm, den eine eckige Uhr schmückt. (4) Das Haus des Tschechischen Feuerwehrverbands im Stil des Konstruktivismus (die Form des Gebäudes wird von seiner Konstruktion bestimmt, die oft aus Stahlbeton bestand), der im Zentrum von Prag besonders

## Lignes et courbes

(1, 2) Passages dans des immeubles à fonctions multiples. Ce nouveau type d'immeuble regroupait des centres commerciaux, des cafés, des restaurants, des cinémas, des dancings, des bureaux, des clubs privés, et, en étage, des appartements. (3) Le Perla (anciennement grands magasins de tissus et de mode ARA), au coin de la Perlová, élégant immeuble fonctionnaliste aux façades élancées, avec une tour d'angle décorée d'une horloge carrée. (4) Le siège de l'Association des pompiers tchécoslovaques est un bon exemple de ce constructivisme (la forme de l'immeuble est déterminée par sa structure, souvent en béton armé) qui allait s'imposer au centre de la capitale. À la

4

5

6

changed from Constructivism to Functionalism (the emphasis was on the building's purpose and function). (5) A good example of straight clean lines is seen in the Functionalist school in Žižkov. (6) The Prague Insurance Company gave the city a library, which was built in 1926–30. It was designed by František Roith (experienced in ministerial buildings) and its massive walls try to fit in with the 17th-century palaces. Czech architects call the style Traditionalism.

häufig zu finden ist. Am Ende der 20er Jahre wurde der Stil in Funktionalismus umbenannt (um die Zweckbestimmung der Gebäude stärker hervorzuheben). (5) Ein gutes Beispiel für die geraden, klaren Linien dieser Stilrichtung bietet die Schule von Žižkov. (6) Die Prager Versicherungsgesellschaft stiftete der Stadt eine Bücherei, die zwischen 1926 und 1930 nach dem Entwurf von František Roith erbaut wurde. Roith, der bereits mehrere Regierungsgebäude geschaffen hatte, war bestrebt, mit massiven Mauern die Bücherei den Palästen aus dem 17. Jahrhundert anzupassen. Die tschechischen Architekten bezeichneten diesen Stil als Traditionalismus.

fin des années 20 le terme de constructivisme fut abandonné pour celui de fonctionnalisme qui mettait davantage l'accent sur les fonctions de l'immeuble. (5) L'école fonctionnaliste de Žižkov est un bon exemple de ces lignes pures et nettes. (6) La Compagnie d'assurances de Prague offrit à la ville une bibliothèque, édifiée en 1926–30. Œuvre de František Roith, spécialiste des bâtiments officiels, ses murs massifs tentaient de s'harmoniser aux palais baroques du XVIIe siècle. Les architectes tchèques qualifient ce style de traditionalisme.

## The Modernism of the 1930s

(1) The austere Vítkov Monument on the Žižkov Hill was built in 1927–32, to a design by Jan Zázvorka. In the tall, granite-faced cube of the main hall, the remains of an Unknown Soldier are preserved. (2) The Czech National Bank on a crossroads near the Powder Gate, designed by František Roith and clad in granite (1936–38). (3) The Church of the Sacred Heart in Jiří z Poděbrad Square, designed by Jože Plečnik in 1922–33, and considered his masterpiece, was inspired by Classical architecture, especially the Parthenon in Athens. (4) The Mánes Building (1927–30). Behind the old water tower with its Baroque onion dome, a white Functionalist building designed by Otakar Novotný, housing a restaurant, clubroom, and gallery for the artistic group Mánes. (5) Masaryk's Housing Estate. The most famous social project for the old, the disabled and the terminally ill, designed by architect Bohumír Kozák. Part of the estate was opened in 1928 and in it 2000 old people and 300 sick children were given proper medical care. (6) The colony of luxury villas in Baba, designed for clients who were members of the Czechoslovak Decorative Arts Federation and leading personalities of Czech cultural life. It was created as a permanent exhibition of the work of leading architects who designed in the "truly modern style" of the 1930s.

## Die Moderne der 30er Jahre

(1) Das schmucklose Vítkov-Monument auf dem Žižkov-Hügel wurde nach Plänen von Jan Zázvorka zwischen 1927 und 1932 erbaut. In dem hohen, mit Granit verkleideten Quader ruhen die Überreste eines Unbekannten Soldaten. (2) Die Tschechische Nationalbank, ein mächtiger mit Granit verkleideter Palast, an der Straßenkreuzung beim Pulverturm ist ein Werk von František Roith (1936–38). (3) Die Herz-Jesu-Kirche auf dem Jiří-z-Poděbrad-Platz wird als Meisterwerk Jože Plečniks angesehen (1922–1933). Der Entwurf spiegelt den Einfluß klassischer Architektur wider, besonders des Athener Parthenons. (4) Das Mánes-Haus (1927–30). Hinter dem alten Wasserspeicher mit seinem barocken Zwiebelturm wurde ein weißes funktionalistisches Gebäude mit einem Restaurant, einem Klubraum und einer Galerie für die Künstlergruppe Mánes errichtet, das Otakar Novotný entworfen hat. (5) Masaryks Sozialwohnungen. Der berühmteste Sozialbau für Alte, Behinderte und Sterbenskranke stammt von dem Architekten Bohumír Kozák. Ein Teil der Anlage wurde 1928 eröffnet und ermöglichte eine angemessene medizinische Versorgung für 2.000 alte Menschen und 300 kranke Kinder. (6) Die luxuriöse Villenkolonie in Baba entstand für die Mitglieder des Tschechoslowakischen Verbands für Angewandte Kunst und für führende Persönlichkeiten des tschechischen Kulturlebens. Sie war als Dauerausstellung der Arbeiten führender Architekten gedacht, die in den 30er Jahren im »wahrhaft modernen Stil« bauten.

## Monumentalisme et néoclassicisme

(1) L'austère monument Vítkov sur la colline de Žižkov fut élevé en 1927–32 sur les plans de Jan Zázvorka. Dans le hall, un grand cube recouvert de granit abrite les restes d'un soldat inconnu. (2) La Banque nationale tchèque (1936–38), tout en granit, s'élève à un carrefour près de la porte des Poudres. Elle est l'œuvre de František Roith. (3) L'église du Sacré-Cœur (1922–33), place Jiří Poděbrad est due à Jože Plečnik, grand architecte d'inspiration néoclassique. (4) L'immeuble Mánes (1927–30). Derrière l'ancien château d'eau au toit bulbeux baroque, ce bâtiment fonctionnaliste tout blanc dessiné par Otakar Novotný abrite le restaurant, le club et la galerie du mouvement artistique Mánes. (5) Le grand ensemble Masaryk, le plus fameux projet d'habitat social pour personnes âgées, handicapés et grands malades, conçu par l'architecte Bohumir Kozák. Une section pour 2 000 personnes âgées et 300 enfants malades s'ouvrit en 1928. (6) Un groupe de villas de luxe à Baba, destinées à des membres de la Fédération tchécoslovaque des arts décoratifs et des représentants éminents de la vie culturelle tchèque. L'ensemble se voulait une exposition permanente de travaux de grands architectes à l'origine du «style authentiquement moderne» des années 30.

4

5

6

### The Liberated Theater

(1) Jaroslav Ježek (1906–42), a composer of modern classical and popular music, and pioneer of jazz. He became famous for the hits he composed for the Liberated Theater and for films with Jiří Voskovec and Jan Werich. (2, 3, 6) In the 1930s Jiří Voskovec (1905–81) and Jan Werich (1905–80; the round figure in the pictures), known for short as V+W, were the most celebrated and successful stage and screen artists in Czechoslovakia. In their theatrical and film work they produced, wrote, performed and directed shows which revelled in Dada and Surrealism, "intoxicating people with the hashish of improvised comedy," vigorously attacked Fascism and ridiculed dictators. The *Osvobozené divadlo* (Liberated Theater) provided highly intelligent comedy while maintaining popular appeal. (4) The cover of a song, "The Ghost Haunts the House," performed in the Liberated Theater. (5) Promotional leaflet from a V+W film, *The World Belongs to Us* (1937). This aggressive social and anti-Fascist comedy was V+W's most serious and politically committed work. (7) Actors on the stage of the Liberated Theater, which was forced to close down in the autumn of 1938.

### Das Befreite Theater

(1) Jaroslav Ježek (1906–42) war ein Komponist klassischer und populärer Musik und ein Pionier des Jazz. Er wurde durch die Hits berühmt, die er für das Befreite Theater und für Filme mit Jiří Voskovec und Jan Werich komponierte. (2, 3, 6) In den 30er Jahren waren Jiří Voskovec (1905–81) und Jan Werich (1905–80, die rundliche Person auf den Bildern), bekannt durch ihr Kürzel V+W, die gefeiertesten und erfolgreichsten Bühnen- und Leinwandkünstler in der Tschechoslowakei. In ihren Theater- und Filmarbeiten produzierten, schrieben, spielten und organisierten sie Aufführungen, die im Dadaismus und Surrealismus schwelgten, um »die Menschen mit dem Rauschgift der improvisierten Komödie zu infizieren.« Sie griffen vehement den Faschismus an und verspotteten Diktatoren. Das *Osvobozené divadlo* (Befreites Theater) bot höchst scharfsinnige Komödien, die ihre Anziehungskraft auf das Volk nie verloren. (4) Titelbild zu dem Lied »Gespensterspuk im Haus«, das im Befreiten Theater aufgeführt wurde. (5) Flugblatt des V+W-Films *Die Welt gehört uns* (1937). Diese aggressive, soziale und antifaschistische Komödie war V+Ws ernsthafteste und politischste Arbeit. (7) Schauspieler auf der Bühne des Befreiten Theaters, das im Herbst 1938 geschlossen werden mußte.

### Le Théâtre Libéré

(1) Jaroslav Ježek (1906–1942), compositeur de musique classique et populaire et pionnier du jazz. Il composa des succès pour le Théâtre Libéré et des films avec Jiří Voskovec et Jan Werich. (2, 3, 6) Dans les années 30, Jiří Voskovec (1905–1981) et Jan Werich (1905–1980, le personnage au visage tout rond) baptisés V+W furent les deux plus célèbres artistes de la scène et de l'écran en Tchécoslovaquie. Ils écrivaient, produisaient, mettaient en scène et jouaient des pièces et des films d'inspiration dada et surréaliste, « intoxiquant les gens au haschich de la comédie improvisée », attaquaient vigoureusement le fascisme et ridiculisaient les dictateurs. Au *Osvobozené divadlo* (Théâtre Libéré) ils produisaient des comédies intelligentes qui savaient plaire au grand public. (4) Couverture d'une chanson « Le fantôme hante la maison », interprétée au Théâtre Libéré. (5) Brochure promotionnelle d'un film de V+W : *Le monde nous appartient* (1937). (7) Acteurs sur la scène du Théâtre Libéré qui fut obligé de fermer ses portes en 1938 sur ordre du préfet de police.

### Winter

Winter in Prague always reached its climax just before Christmas, when men selling live carp from large barrels appeared, a tradition going back to the Middle Ages. Men swept snow-covered streets, bought Chistmas trees and presents, while women cleaned, scraped and fried the carp, which were served with potato salad. (2) *Eva* was a fashion magazine for women and many well-known artists worked on its graphic design. Milena Jesenská (1896–1944) was one of its journalists. Fashion designers tried to create a "Prague fashion," but on the whole they borrowed ideas from the Parisian catwalks. Sketching at Parisian fashion shows was strictly forbidden, so only people with good photographic memories were sent to attend them. In Prague, fashion shows were introduced in the mid-1920s. The Koruna building and Lucerna Palace (with 300 seats) hosted many. Czech fashion was very practical, relying heavily on accessories. Hat and glove-makers, umbrella and bag producers, manufacturers of buttons, clasps, costume jewelry and beads, embroiderers, furriers, Baťa and his shoes – these were the main pillars of the fashion industry. In 1924 there were 3640 tailors and 210 clothing manufacturers. By 1935, 75 per cent of the population were buying ready-made clothes (compared with 10 per cent in 1919).

### Winter

Der Winter in Prag erreichte kurz vor Weihnachten einen Höhepunkt, wenn lebende Karpfen nach einer mittelalterlichen Tradition aus dem Faß verkauft wurden. Männer räumten schneebedeckte Straßen, kauften Weihnachtsbäume und Geschenke, während Frauen den Karpfen säuberten, schuppten und brieten, der mit Kartoffelsalat gereicht wurde. (2) *Eva* war ein Modemagazin für Frauen, an dessen grafischer Gestaltung viele bekannte Künstler beteiligt waren. Eine der Journalistinnen war Milena Jesenská (1896–1944). Modedesigner versuchten, einen »Prager Stil« zu kreieren, der jedoch im Großen und Ganzen den Einfluß der Pariser Modewelt widerspiegelte. Das Zeichnen bei den Pariser Modenschauen war strengstens verboten, weshalb nur Leute mit gutem fotografischen Gedächtnis zu den Veranstaltungen geschickt wurden. Seit Mitte der 20er Jahre fanden auch in Prag Modenschauen – die meisten im Koruna-Palais und im Lucerna-Palais (mit 300 Sitzen) – statt. Die tschechische Mode war äußerst praktisch und beruhte weitestgehend auf Accessoires. Hut- und Handschuhmacher, Schirm- und Taschenmacher, Hersteller von Knöpfen, Schnallen, Modeschmuck und Ketten, Stickereien, Kürschner, Baťa und seine Schuhe – das waren die Hauptsäulen der Modeindustrie. 1924 gab es 3.640 Schneider und 210 Kleidungshersteller. 1935 kauften bereits 75 Prozent der Bevölkerung fertige Kleidungsstücke (im Vergleich dazu waren es 1919 nur 10 Prozent).

### L'hiver

L'hiver pragois était le plus rigoureux juste avant Noël, lorsque apparaissaient les pêcheurs qui vendaient des carpes vivantes dans de grands barils, vieille tradition du Moyen Âge. (5) Les hommes dégageaient les rues couvertes de neige, achetaient des arbres de Noël et des cadeaux, tandis que les femmes nettoyaient, grattaient et faisaient frire les carpes, servies avec une salade de pommes de terre. (2) *Eva* était un magazine de mode féminine auquel collaborèrent de nombreux artistes connus. Milena Jesenská (1896–1944) y travailla comme journaliste. Les créateurs de mode essayèrent de lancer une « mode de Prague » mais s'inspiraient en fait beaucoup des modèles parisiens. Prendre des croquis pendant les défilés de mode à Paris était strictement interdit, et seuls les professionnels doués d'une bonne mémoire visuelle s'y rendaient. À Prague, les premiers défilés de mode furent introduits au milieu des années 20. Ils se tinrent souvent dans l'immeuble Koruna ou au Lucerna Palace (300 places). La mode tchèque était d'esprit pratique et s'intéressait beaucoup aux accessoires. Chapeliers, gantiers, maroquiniers, fabricants de parapluies et de boutons, de fermoirs, de bijoux, de perles, brodeurs, fourreurs et le chausseur Baťa étaient les piliers de l'industrie de la mode. En 1924, on comptait 3 640 tailleurs et 210 fabricants de vêtements. En 1935, 75 pour cent de la population achetait des vêtements de confection (10 pour cent en 1919).

2

3

4

5

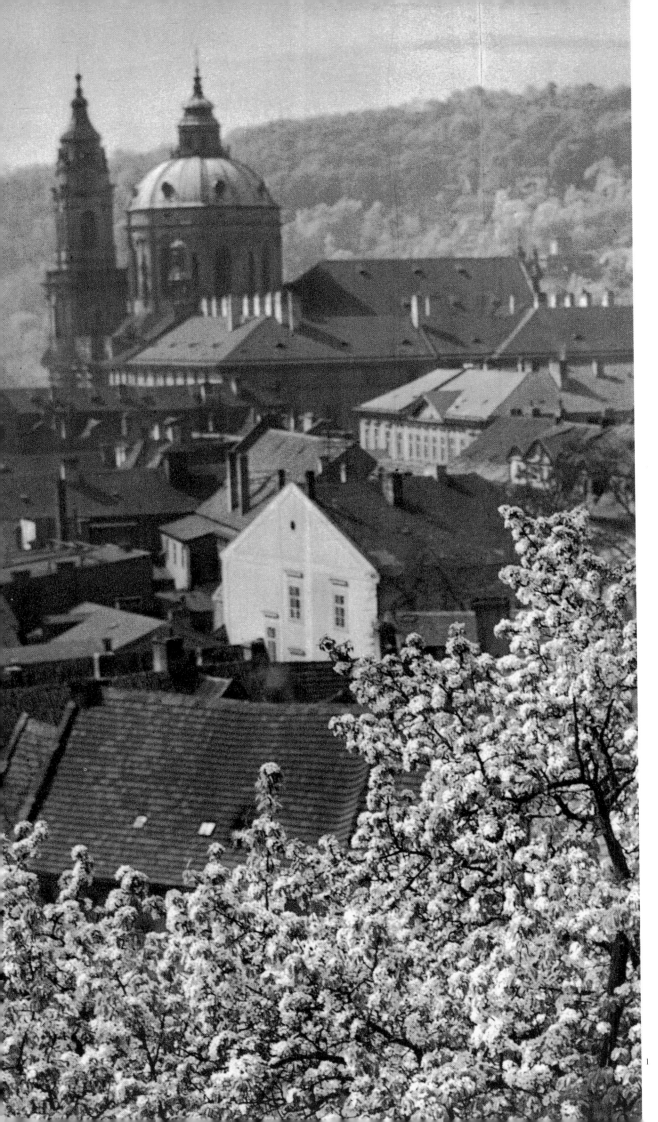

## Spring

Prague came alive in the spring, when the blossoming parks and gardens opened their gates again to the public. The sunshine erased the dark mood of the city's light-starved inhabitants, who, living in the dank Vltava basin and using lignite for heating, spent their winters in a thick cloud of smog. Easter was observed as a religious holiday, although the festivities had their roots in a pagan mating ritual. Men whipped attractive girls with willow sticks and the girls defended themselves by pouring buckets of water on their suitors. Peace was restored when the girl offered a painted egg, a symbol of fertility. The art of drawing intricate designs on eggs with wax, and then dyeing them in a hot dye which melts the wax but leaves the imprint of the pattern (3), is an Eastern European equivalent of the ancient art of batik (or "drawing with wax"). In spring many concert venues opened, people visited galleries and funfairs and ventured outside the city on boats, trains and buses to watch the rebirth of Nature.

## Frühling

Im Frühling, wenn die blühenden Parks und Gärten ihre Tore für das Publikum öffneten, erwachte Prag zu neuem Leben. Die Sonne erhellte die düstere Stimmung der lichthungrigen Städter, die wegen des feuchten Klimas im Moldaubeckens und des Heizens mit Braunkohle den Winter unter einer dicken Smogwolke verbracht hatten. Ostern war ein kirchlicher Feiertag, wenn auch das Fest seine Wurzeln in heidnischen Paarungsbräuchen hatte. Die Männer schlugen die attraktiven Mädchen mit Weidenruten, und die jungen Frauen wehrten sich, indem sie Wassereimer über ihren Verehrern ausschütteten. Der Friede war wieder hergestellt, wenn das Mädchen dem Mann ein bemaltes Ei, das Symbol der Fruchtbarkeit, anbot. Die Kunst, mit Wachs feine Muster auf ein Ei zu malen und sie dann in heißer Farbe zu färben – wobei das Wachs schmolz, aber das Muster auf dem Ei zurückblieb (3) – ist das osteuropäische Äquivalent zur alten Kunst des Batikens (oder »Zeichnen mit Wachs«). Im Frühling öffneten viele Konzerthallen, die Leute besuchten Galerien, gingen auf die Kirmes und unternahmen mit Booten, Zügen und Bussen Ausflüge in die Umgebung, um das Erwachen der Natur zu betrachten.

## Le printemps

Prague s'animait à la belle saison, lorsque les parcs et les jardins en fleurs (1) ouvraient de nouveau leurs portes au public. Le soleil faisait oublier aux habitants la tristesse de l'absence de lumière. Dans le sombre bassin de la Moldau, on se servait de charbon de mauvaise qualité pour se chauffer et les Pragois passaient l'hiver dans *le smog*. Pâques était une fête religieuse, même si les festivités plongeaient leurs racines dans des rituels païens. Les hommes fouettaient les filles les plus belles avec des joncs de roseau, et les jeunes filles se défendaient en versant des baquets d'eau sur leurs soupirants. L'offre d'un œuf peint, symbole de fertilité, ramenait la paix. L'art du décor à la cire sur les œufs teints dans un bain de teinture chaude qui faisait fondre la cire en respectant les motifs dessinés (3) est un art d'Europe de l'Est très ancien, proche du batik (batik signifie d'ailleurs « dessiner avec de la cire »). Le printemps était la saison de nombreux concerts, et les Pragois se rendaient dans les musées et les parcs d'attraction ou s'aventuraient dans les environs en bateau, en train ou en bus pour observer la renaissance de la nature.

### Summer

Summer meant long-deserved holidays, for children and grown-ups alike. Swimming in the Vltava, which had many enclosed swimming facilities, was the main attraction. Some of the swimming areas were for women only. Sunbathing was advised by doctors as healthy, and everybody tried to look a shade darker. The citizens of Prague often went on hiking or boat trips, trying to escape the city heat.

### Sommer

Der Sommer versprach die wohlverdienten Ferien für Kinder und Erwachsene. Das Schwimmen in der Moldau, in der viele abgeschlossene Schwimmbäder eingerichtet waren, gehörte zu den beliebtesten Attraktionen. Einige Schwimmbäder waren nur für Frauen geöffnet. Das Sonnenbad wurde von den Ärzten empfohlen, und jeder versuchte, sich ein bißchen zu bräunen. Die Prager Bürger unternahmen oft Wander- und Radtouren, um der Hitze der Stadt zu entkommen.

### L'été

L'été annonçait les vacances tant attendues, aussi bien par les enfants que les adultes. La principale distraction était de se baigner dans la Moldau dont les rives étaient aménagées pour la natation. Certains endroits étaient réservés aux femmes. Le soleil était recommandé par les médecins et chacun essayait de se faire bronzer. Les Pragois partaient souvent en croisière sur la rivière pour échapper aux chaleurs de la ville.

2

ČÍSLO 18.
ROČNÍK V.

eva

CENA 3 Kč
S POJIŠTĚNÍM 3·50 Kč

3

4

5

## Autumn

In autumn the city changed its colors to melancholy golds and reds, and mushroom-picking enthusiasts scoured the woodlands on the capital's periphery in search of chanterelles, ceps, morels, milk-caps and agarics. These gatherings ended with a picnic and a glass of beer in a nearby tavern. The city markets were stacked with a great variety of fruit and vegetables, the riches of the soil. The adults returned to work, the schools re-opened, the theaters held their premières, and life returned to its accustomed pace.

## Herbst

Im Herbst veränderte die Stadt ihre Farben zu einem melancholischen Gold und Rot. Auf der Suche nach Pfifferlingen, Steinpilzen, Morcheln, Edelreizkern und Blätterpilzen schwärmten die Pilzsammler in die Wälder am Stadtrand aus. Meist endeten diese Unternehmen mit einem Picknick und einem Glas Bier in einer nahegelegenen Taverne. Die Märkte der Stadt waren voll mit allen Sorten von Obst und Gemüse, den Schätzen der Erde. Die Erwachsenen gingen zurück an die Arbeit, die Schulen wurden geöffnet, in den Theatern fanden die Premieren statt, und das Leben nahm wieder seinen gewohnten Gang.

## L'automne

En automne, la ville changeait de couleurs et se couvrait d'ors et de rouges mélancoliques. Les amateurs de champignons parcouraient les bois autour de la capitale à la recherche de chanterelles, de cèpes, de morilles, de bolets et d'oronges. Ces expéditions se terminaient par des pique-niques et un verre de bière dans une taverne. Les marchés foisonnaient de fruits, de légumes et de toutes les richesses de la campagne. Les adultes se remettaient au travail, les écoles rouvraient, les théâtres donnaient des premières et la vie reprenait son cours habituel.

# SLOVENSKA STRELA
## ČSD

### Z BRATISLAVY
### DO PRAHY
### Za 4 hod 51 min

| Odchod Bratislava | 5·30 | Odchod Praha, Wils. nádr. | 18·35 |
| príchod Brno | 7·31 | príchod Brno | 21·43 |
| odchod Brno | 7·34 | odchod Brno | 21·46 |
| príchod Praha, Wils. nádr. | 10·42 | príchod Bratislava | 23·26 |

Len 2. trieda. Zaistite si zavčas miestenky.

1

# PRAHA

If you travel to Europe, why stop, like most tourists from a-broad, in the capitals of Western Europe only, instead of push-ing forward to the very centre of Europe, to Bohemia • Here, at a distance of five hours by aeroplane from London or Paris, two hours from Berlin and one hour from Vienna, you will find

2

3

Kom. 261a. (E. B. 31.)

HOTEL
ESPLANADE
PRAG

DAS HUNDERTTÜRMIGE PRAG · STOVĚŽATÁ PRAHA

5

6

## Tourism in the 1930s

(1) An express train called the Slovak Missile covered the 397km between Prague and Bratislava in 4 hours 51 minutes. The service started in 1936. The locomotive had an M290.0 diesel engine, which cut the previous journey time by one hour. The train made one stop in Brno. (2) A tourist guide book from the inter-war period. (3) A Czechoslovak Railways train ticket. (4) The Hotel Esplanade, which was popular with the more wealthy tourists. During the Second World War top Nazis stayed there. (5, 6) Pictures from tourist brochures showing the sights and also Czechoslovak tourists, who often arrived in the capital wearing their national costumes, which in that period were chic and expressed patriotic feelings. Czechoslovak tourists numbered half a million a year. In 1929, 114,000 foreign tourists visited the city. After that, interest in Prague dwindled. It picked up again in 1937, when the number of tourists reached 100,000. In October 1929 Adolf Hitler planned a motor trip to Czechoslovakia, but he was rejected at the border as an undesirable alien.

## Tourismus in den 30er Jahren

(1) Ein Schnellzug mit dem Namen »Slowakische Rakete« legte in 4 Stunden und 51 Minuten die 397 km zwischen Prag und Bratislava zurück. Die Strecke wurde 1936 in Betrieb genommen. Die Lokomotive besaß einen Dieselmotor der Marke M290.0, der die frühere Reisezeit um eine Stunde verkürzte. Der Zug machte nur einen Halt, in Brno. (2) Ein Reiseführer aus der Zeit zwischen den beiden Weltkriegen. (3) Eine Fahrkarte der Tschechoslowakischen Eisenbahn. (4) Das Hotel Esplanade, das bei den wohlhabenderen Reisenden sehr beliebt war. Während des Zweiten Weltkriegs stiegen hier führende Nazis ab. (5, 6) Bilder aus den Touristeninformationen zeigen sowohl Sehenswürdigkeiten wie auch tschechoslowakische Touristen, die oft in ihrer nationalen Tracht in der Hauptstadt eintrafen, was in der damaligen Zeit als schick und patriotisch galt. Eine halbe Million tschechoslowakischer Besucher reiste pro Jahr nach Prag. 1929 besuchten 114.000 ausländische Touristen die Stadt. Danach ließ das Interesse nach. 1937 zog die Stadt wieder mehr Touristen an: in diesem Jahr kamen 100.000 Menschen. Im Oktober 1929 plante Adolf Hitler eine Autoreise in die Tschechoslowakei, wurde aber an der Grenze als unerwünschter Fremder abgewiesen.

## Le tourisme dans les années 30

(1) Lancé en 1936, un train express appelé le «Missile slovaque» couvrait les 397 km entre Prague et Bratislava en 4 heures 51 minutes. La locomotive était équipée d'un moteur diesel M290.0 qui permettait de raccourcir le voyage d'une heure. Le train ne s'arrêtait qu'à Brno. (2) Un guide touristique de l'entre-deux-guerres. (3) Billet de train des Chemins de fer tchécoslovaques. (4) L'Hôtel Esplanade accueillait les riches touristes. Pendant la Seconde Guerre mondiale il reçut également les dignitaires nazis. (5, 6) Images extraites de brochures touristiques montrant différentes vues de la cité et des Tchèques venus de la campagne dans leurs costumes traditionnels, qui étaient alors considérés comme élégants et exprimaient des sentiments patriotiques. Les touristes tchécoslovaques étaient plus de 500 000 chaque année à visiter la capitale. En 1929, 114 000 étrangers se joignirent à eux. Après cette date la fréquentation des visiteurs faiblit pour remonter à 100 000 en 1937. En octobre 1929, Adolf Hitler qui voulait visiter la Tchécoslovaquie fut refoulé à la frontière comme étranger indésirable.

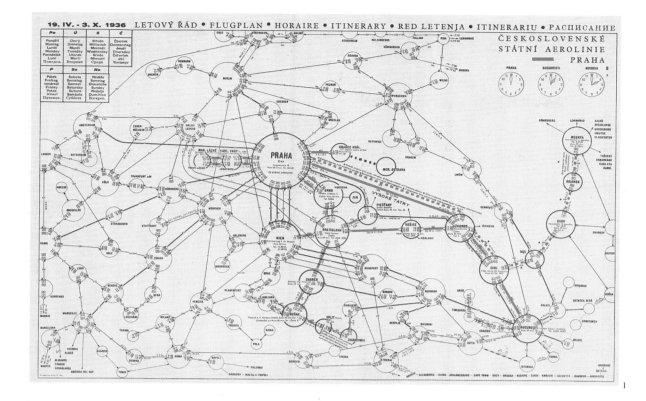

## Air Travel

(1) The Czechoslovak State Airlines air-routes map showing Prague's links with other European cities, giving departure and arrival times as well as distances. (2) A Czechoslovak airline company advertisement assuring "comfort, speed and safety." (3) An advertisement in German for Czechoslovak-manufactured three-engine airplanes. (6) The new modern airport at Ruzyně (1932–36) took over most of the traffic from Kbely (1920–29), which was originally a military airport. In 1937, 22,000 people flew into and 17,000 through Prague. (4, 5) Promotional photographs advertising air travel. In the late 1930s planes from 11 countries were landing at Ruzyně.

## Luftverkehr

(1) Die Flugkarte der Staatlichen Tschechoslowakischen Luftfahrtgesellschaft mit den Verbindungen Prags zu anderen europäischen Städten, einschließlich der Abflugs- und Ankunftszeiten sowie der Entfernungen. (2) Eine Anzeige der Tschechoslowakischen Fluggesellschaft garantiert »Komfort, Schnelligkeit und Sicherheit«. (3) Eine Anzeige auf Deutsch für dreimotorige Flugzeuge aus tschechoslowakischen Fabriken. (4, 5) Werbefotografien für den Luftverkehr. In den späten 30er Jahren landeten Flugzeuge aus 11 Ländern in Ruzyně. (6) Der neue moderne Flughafen von Ruzyně (1932–63) übernahm den größten Teil des Luftverkehrs von Kbely (1920–29), der ursprünglich als Militärflughafen geplant gewesen war. 1937 flogen 22.000 Menschen nach und 17.000 über Prag.

## Les voyages en avion

(1) Carte des lignes aériennes de la Compagnie nationale tchécoslovaque, montrant les liaisons entre Prague et les autres villes européennes, avec indication des horaires et des distances. (2) Publicité d'une compagnie aérienne tchécoslovaque assurant « confort, rapidité et sécurité ». (3) Annonce publicitaire en allemand pour des avions trimoteurs tchécoslovaques. (4, 5) Photographies promotionnelles vantant les voyages en avion. À la fin des années 30, des avions de 11 pays différents atterrissaient déjà à Ruzyně. (6) Le nouvel aéroport moderne de Ruzyně (1932–36) reprit l'essentiel du trafic de Kbely (1920–29) qui était à l'origine une base militaire. En 1937, 22 000 personnes arrivèrent à Prague en avion, 17 000 y firent escale.

4

5

6

### The Busy Metropolis

(1) Heavy traffic in Na Příkopě. Public transport improved and new models of trams were introduced. In 1928 the modernized network of electric rails exceeded 100km. In 1925 buses were successfully reintroduced and in 1936 trolley-buses were added to cope with the demand. (2) Cars neatly parked in Wenceslas Square. The speed limit in the city was 6–8km per hour and the honking of horns was not allowed. When entering Prague one had to pay a "pavement tax" of 1 crown. American cars were much cheaper than domestic ones, so soon a high customs duty was introduced to remedy the situation. By 1925, cars had electric horns, side and headlights, and gears. Leather coats (which protected the early drivers from dust), goggles and gauntlets became museumpieces when cars with roofs came in. A good Škoda *Popular* car just before the Second World War cost 18,000 crowns. The maximum speed was 70km per hour. On average, people drove at 30–40km per hour, and on the left-hand side of the road. In 1938 there were 10,000 petrol pumps in Czechoslovakia.

### Die geschäftige Hauptstadt

(1) Dichter Verkehr in Na Příkopě. Der öffentliche Personen-verkehr wurde verbessert und neue Straßenbahnen eingeführt. 1928 umfaßte das modernisierte Streckennetz der elektrischen Schienen mehr als 100 km. 1925 wurden – mit Erfolg – erneut Busse eingesetzt, und ab 1936 verkehrten aufgrund der gewach-senen Nachfrage zusätzliche Oberleitungsbusse. (2) Ordentlich geparkte Autos am Wenzelsplatz. Die Geschwindigkeitsbe-grenzung in der Stadt lag bei 6–8 km/h, und das Benutzen der Hupe war verboten. Bei der Einfahrt in die Stadt mußte man eine »Pflastersteuer« von einer Krone bezahlen. Weil amerikanische Importe bedeutend billiger als einheimische Autos waren, wurden erstere schon bald mit hohen Zöllen belegt. 1925 besaßen die Autos elektrische Hupen, Stand- und Fahrlicht und Gänge. Als Autos mit Dächern aufkamen, wurden Ledermäntel (die früher die Fahrer vor dem Staub schützen sollten), Schutz-brillen und lange Handschuhe zu Museumsstücken. Ein guter Škoda-*Popular* kostete unmittelbar vor dem Zweiten Welt-krieg 18.000 Kronen. Die Höchstgeschwindigkeit lag bei 70 km/h. Durchschnittlich fuhr man im Linksverkehr 30 bis 40 km/h. 1938 gab es 10.000 Tankstellen in der Tschecho-slowakei.

### Une métropole active

(1) La circulation à Na Příkopě. Les transports publics s'améliorèrent et de nouveaux modèles de trams entrèrent en service. En 1928, le réseau de trams électriques dépassait 100 km. En 1925, des bus furent introduits avec succès ainsi que des trolleybus – en 1936 – pour répondre à une demande grandissante. (2) Voitures sagement alignées place Venceslas. La vitesse autorisée en ville n'était que de 6–8 km/h et le klaxon interdit. En entrant à Prague, il fallait acquitter une « taxe de pavé » d'une couronne. Les voitures américaines étaient moins chères que celles produites dans le pays, ce qui entraîna rapidement l'établissement de droits de douane pour remédier à cette situation. En 1925 furent introduits les klaxons électriques, les feux de stationnement et les phares. Les manteaux de cuir (qui protégeaient les chauffeurs de la poussière), les lunettes et les gants longs devinrent des pièces de musée dès l'apparition des voitures fermées. Juste avant la guerre, une bonne Škoda *Popular* coûtait 18 000 couronnes. La vitesse maximum autorisée sur les routes était de 70 km/h, mais généralement les automobilistes roulaient, à gauche, à 30–40 km/h. En 1938, la Tchécoslovaquie comptait 10 000 pompes à essence.

1

## Street Life

(1) A fancy dress parade advertising Prague restaurants and bars.
(2) The start of a cross-country rally outside the Czechoslovak Automobile Club.

## Straßenleben

(1) Eine Kostümparade, die für Prager Restaurants und Bars wirbt. (2) Start einer Straßen-Ralley vor dem Tschechoslowakischen Automobilclub.

## La vie des rues

(1) Défilé costumé publicitaire pour des restaurants et bars pragois. (2) Départ d'un rallye de cross-country devant l'Automobile-Club Tchécoslovaquie.

2

## Religion

According to the 1921 census, the population of Czechoslovakia belonged to the following churches: Roman Catholic 10,385,000; Evangelical 1,503,000; Lutheran 536,000; Hussite 535,000; and others. The most significant religious celebrations took place in 1929 to commemorate the 1000th anniversary of St Wenceslas's death and in 1935 the First National Congress of Czechoslovak Catholics was held. For the first time in 500 years the Pope's representative visited Jan Hus's Bohemia. (1) People from all over Czechoslovakia attended the Catholic Congress celebrations in Wenceslas Square. (2) *Jezulátko* (the Infant Jesus of Prague) is a 45cm statuette of a toddler, made of colored wax, which was brought to Bohemia in 1587 and stands in the church of Virgin Mary the Victorious. The statue is said to perform miracles and cure the sick. (3) Prague's Archbishop Karel Kašpar (1870–1941) kissing *Jezulátko*'s intricately embroidered dress. (4) The patron saint of the Czechs, St Wenceslas. (5) Archbishop Kašpar blessing the bells at Loreto Church.

## Religion

Nach der Volkszählung von 1921 gehörte die Bevölkerung der Tschechoslowakei folgenden Religionsgemeinschaften an: 10.385.000 waren römisch-katholisch, 1.503.000 evangelisch, 536.000 lutherisch und 535.000 hussitisch; daneben gab es noch weitere Religionsgemeinschaften. Das bedeutendste religiöse Fest fand 1929 zur Erinnerung an den 1.000. Todestag des Heiligen Wenzel statt. 1935 wurde der erste Nationalkongreß der tschechoslowakischen Katholiken abgehalten. Zum ersten Mal seit 500 Jahren besuchten Vertreter des Papstes das Böhmen des Jan Hus. (1) Menschen aus der ganzen Tschechoslowakei kamen zu den Feiern des Katholischen Kongresses auf den Wenzelsplatz. (2) *Jezulátko* (das Jesuskind von Prag) ist die 45 cm große Statuette eines Kleinkindes aus farbigem Wachs, die 1587 nach Böhmen gebracht und in der Kirche der Maria Victoria aufgestellt wurde. Sie soll Wunder vollbringen und Kranke heilen können. (3) Der Prager Erzbischof Karel Kašpar (1870–1941) küßt *Jezulátkos* aufwendig besticktes Kleid. (4) Der Heilige Wenzel, der Schutzheilige der Tschechen. (5) Erzbischof Kašpar weiht die Glocken im Loreto.

## La religion

D'après le recensement de 1921, la population de la Tchécoslovaquie se répartissait entre les confessions suivantes : catholique romaine, 10 385 000 ; évangélique, 1 503 000 ; luthérienne, 536 000 ; hussite, 535 000, et autres. En 1929, de très importantes célébrations commémorèrent le 1 000e anniversaire de la mort de saint Venceslas. En 1935, se tint le premier Congrès national des catholiques, avec la participation de nombreux évêques étrangers. Pour la première fois en 500 ans, des représentants du pape se rendirent dans la Bohême de Jan Huss. (1) Des fidèles venus de toute la Tchécoslovaquie assistèrent aux célébrations du Congrès catholique sur la place Venceslas. (2) Le *Jezulátko* (l'Enfant Jésus de Prague) est une statuette de 45 cm de haut d'un nouveau-né en cire, apporté en Bohême en 1587 et qui se trouve dans l'église Notre-Dame de la Victoire. La statue est censée accomplir des miracles et guérir les malades. (3) L'archevêque de Prague, Karel Kašpar (1870–1941) baisant la robe aux lourdes broderies du *Jezulátko*. (4) Le saint patron des Tchèques : saint Venceslas. (5) L'archevêque Kašpar bénissant les cloches de l'église Loreto.

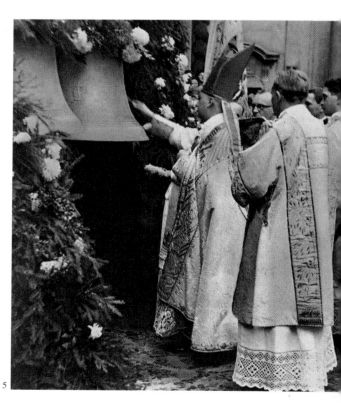

**LETEM SVĚTEM**

*domov a svět*

Obrázkový týdeník, vydávaný za spolupráce Klubu čs. turistů.    Cena 1·50 Kč. — Ročník VIII. — 31. X. 1933. — Číslo **3**.

*Amat. foto V. Jirů.*

**NEJVYŠŠÍ VELITEL PŘIJÍŽDÍ.**
PRESIDENT REPUBLIKY DR. T. G. MASARYK PŘI PŘÍJEZDU K PŘEHLÍDCE VOJSKA NA VÁCLAVSKÉ NÁMĚSTÍ.

## Masaryk's Final Years

(1) T. G. Masaryk on horseback, reviewing troops in Wenceslas Square. (2–5) The funeral of T. G. Masaryk. After his election in 1934, Masaryk suffered a number of strokes. He could no longer sign with his right hand and had difficulties with his speech: sometimes he managed a few sentences in English, but his Czech was even worse. He wanted to stand down but the agrarian parties were trying to gain time, so Masaryk had to persevere. He finally resigned on 14 December 1935 and died on 14 September 1937. His funeral was attended by thousands, who had a dark foreboding that, with the death of the President-Liberator, the country's liberty could be in danger.

## Masaryks letzte Jahre

(1) T. G. Masaryk inspiziert zu Pferd die Truppen auf dem Wenzelsplatz. (2–5) Die Beerdigung von T. G. Masaryk: Nach seiner Wahl 1934 erlitt Masaryk mehrere Schlaganfälle. Er konnte nicht länger mit seiner rechten Hand unterzeichnen und hatte Schwierigkeiten mit dem Sprechen. Manchmal schaffte er es, ein paar Sätze auf Englisch herauszubringen; sein Tschechisch war noch schlimmer. Er wollte sein Amt zur Verfügung stellen, aber da der Bund der Landwirte versuchte, Zeit zu gewinnen, mußte Masaryk durchhalten. Schließlich legte er am 14. Dezember 1935 sein Amt nieder und starb am 14. September 1937. Tausende nahmen mit der dunklen Vorahnung an seiner Beerdigung teil, daß mit dem Tod des Befreiungspräsidenten auch die Freiheit des Landes gefährdet war.

## Les dernières années de Masaryk

(1) T. G. Masaryk à cheval passant les troupes en revue, place Venceslas. (2–5) Les funérailles de Masaryk. Après sa réélection en 1934, Masaryk fut victime de plusieurs attaques. Il ne pouvait plus signer de sa main droite et avait des difficultés à parler. Il pouvait prononcer quelques phrases en anglais, mais son tchèque était devenu incompréhensible. Il voulait démissionner, mais les partis agrariens souhaitaient gagner du temps et le poussèrent à rester au pouvoir. Il quitta finalement ses fonctions le 14 décembre 1935 et mourut le 14 septembre 1937. Ses funérailles furent suivies par des milliers de personnes, avec le sombre pressentiment que la mort du président-libérateur annonçait sans doute une période troublée pour la liberté de la nation.

2

V PRAZE DNE 25. ZÁŘÍ 1937 ★★★ PESTRY ★★★ ROČ. XII · ČÍS. 39 · CENA 3 KČ

Aktuality světa - Sport - Móda    P. Eisner: Požehnaný - J. Mašek:
Romány - Umění - Dětský koutek  Pohřeb T.G.M. - Snímky z pohřbu
Pêle-mêle - Letectví - Motorismus  Poslední chvíle na lánském hřbi-
Českosl. turistika - Divadlo - Film  tově - Pouť lidu na pražský Hrad

# TYDEN

3

4

5

### Edvard Beneš Takes Over

On 14 December 1935 Edvard Beneš was appointed President. He had earlier been recommended by Masaryk as his successor. Beneš, unlike Masaryk, did not have any illusions about Hitler's plans vis-à-vis Czechoslovakia, and for that reason he signed an alliance with the Soviet Union in 1935. Beneš continued Masaryk's policies without any major changes. He had been close to Masaryk and with his wife Hana had often dined with the President in Hradčany or at the presidential summer residence in Lány. (1, 2) Edvard Beneš and his wife Hana. (3) Beneš attending Masaryk's funeral. (4) Beneš working in his office at Hradčany.

### Eduard Beneš übernimmt die Macht

Am 14. Dezember 1935 wurde Eduard Beneš zum Präsidenten gewählt. Masaryk hatte ihn zuvor als seinen Nachfolger vorgeschlagen. Anders als dieser machte sich Beneš keine Illusion über Hitlers Pläne bezüglich der Tschechoslowakei und unterzeichnete deshalb 1935 einen Beistandspakt mit der Sowjetunion. Beneš führte Masaryks Politik ohne große Veränderungen weiter. Er hatte Masaryk sehr nahe gestanden; oft hatten er und seine Frau Hana mit dem Präsidenten auf dem Hradschin oder in seiner Sommerresidenz in Lány zu Abend gegessen. (1, 2) Eduard Beneš mit seiner Frau Hana. (3) Beneš während der Teilnahme an Masaryks Begräbnis. (4) Beneš bei der Arbeit in seinem Büro in Hradschin.

### L'arrivée au pouvoir d'Edvard Beneš

Appuyé par Masaryk, Edvard Beneš fut élu président de la république le 14 décembre 1935. À la différence de son prédécesseur, Beneš ne se faisait guère d'illusions sur les plans de Hitler pour la Tchécoslovaquie, et c'est pour cette raison qu'il signa une alliance avec l'Union soviétique en 1935. Il poursuivit la politique de Masaryk sans changement majeur. Proches de l'ancien président, sa femme et lui dînaient souvent en sa compagnie au Hradčany ou à la résidence présidentielle d'été de Lány. (1, 2) Edvard Beneš et son épouse, Hana. (3) Beneš aux funérailles de Masaryk. (4) Beneš travaillant dans son bureau à Hradčany.

č. 38. 1937.

Ozvěny DOMOVA I SVĚTA

4

## Cinema in the 1930s

In 1924 Prague had 24 cinemas; four years later the number had risen to 115. The film industry was expanding rapidly to accommodate the growing interest in this popular entertainment. (1) A rare picture of actors and crew posing together during the shooting of *Panenka* (The Maiden) at the Barrandov Film Studios. (2) A still from a sound remake of the 1927 silent classic *The Battalion*. (3) The Barrandov Film Studios were built in 1932–33 to the design of Max Urban, who emphasized the functional requirements for making and producing films. (4) A poster for the film *Ekstase* (Ecstasy), directed by Gustav Machatý. It was made in 1933 and was admired by connoisseurs of erotic art. It launched Hedy Lamarr's (Hedwig Kiesler) Hollywood career. (5) A magazine cover featuring the "King of Comedians," Vlasta Burian (1891–1962), a man of mercurial energy, with an exceptional talent for mimicry. He lived for acting, delivering wisecracks and jokes with perfect timing. (6) A poster advertising the 1931 Czech sound film *The Affair of Colonel Redl*, the man who betrayed Austrian military secrets and was a harbinger of the demise of the Empire. The first journalist to find out about Redl's betrayal, and his transvestism, was E. E. Kisch, who co-wrote the film script.

## Das Kino in den 30er Jahren

1924 gab es in Prag 24 Kinos, vier Jahre später war ihre Zahl schon auf 115 angestiegen. Die Filmindustrie expandierte gewaltig, um dem wachsenden Interesse gerecht zu werden. (1) Eine seltene Aufnahme von den Schauspielern und der Filmcrew, die sich während der Aufnahmen für *Panenka* (Das Mädchen) in den Barrandov-Studios vor der Kamera in Pose setzen. (2) Ein Szenenfoto der Tonfilmfassung des Stummfilmklassikers *Das Bataillon* von 1927. (3) Nach den Plänen von Max Urban, der viel Wert auf die funktionalen Anforderungen bei der Herstellung und Produktion von Filmen legte, wurden zwischen 1932 und 1933 die Barrandov Filmstudios erbaut. (4) Ein Filmplakat für *Ekstase* unter der Regie von Gustav Machatý. Der Film entstand 1933 und wurde von Kennern der erotischen Kunst bewundert. Hedy Lamarr (Hedwig Kiesler) begann damit ihre Hollywood-Karriere. (5) Das Titelbild einer Zeitschrift mit dem »König der Komödianten«, Vlasta Burian (1891–1962), einem Mann voller lebendiger Energie und einem außergewöhnlichen Talent für Imitationen. Er widmete sein Leben der Schauspielerei und der Perfektionierung seiner Witze und Sprüche. (6) Ein Plakat wirbt für den 1931 gedrehten tschechischen Tonfilm *Die Affäre des Oberst Redl* – der Mann, der österreichische Militärgeheimnisse verraten hatte und ein Vorbote des Untergangs des Kaiserreiches war. Der erste Journalist, der Oberst Redls Verrat und Transvestitentum entdeckt hatte, war E. E. Kisch, der auch an dem Drehbuch mitarbeitete.

## Le cinéma des années 30

En 1924, Prague comptait 24 cinémas, et 115 quatre ans plus tard. L'industrie cinématographique connaissait une croissance rapide pour répondre à l'intérêt de plus en plus grand pour cette forme de divertissement. (1) Rare portrait de groupe d'acteurs et de techniciens pris pendant le tournage de *Panenka* (La jeune fille) aux studios de Barrandov. (2) Image tirée d'une nouvelle version sonore d'un grand classique du muet *Le Bataillon* de 1927. (3) Les studios de Barrandov furent édifiés en 1932–33 d'après les plans de Max Urban qui avait étudié en détail les contraintes de la production et du tournage de films. (4) Affiche du films *Ekstase* (Extase), réalisé par Gustav Machatý en 1933 et apprécié par les amateurs d'érotisme. Il lança la carrière hollywoodienne d'Hedy Lamarr (Hedwig Kiesler). (5) Couverture de magazine consacrée au « Roi des comédiens » de Vlasta Burian (1891–1962), homme d'une énergie considérable, doué pour le mime, il vivait pour son travail d'acteur, ne cessant de lancer des réparties et des plaisanteries. (6) Affiche du film sonore tchèque de 1931 *L'affaire du Colonel Redl*, l'homme qui trahit les secrets militaires autrichiens et accéléra la fin de l'empire. Le premier journaliste à découvrir la trahison de Redl et son goût pour le travestissement, avait été E. E. Kisch, co-auteur du scénario de ce film.

62/3, J

2

A-B AKCIOVÉ
FILMOVÉ TOVÁRNY

dají k disposici svoje dnes již
světoznámé moderně vybavené

ATELIERY NA
BARRANDOVĚ SE
ŠTÁBEM SVÝCH
TECHNICKÝCH OD-
BORNÍKŮ, JUGO-
SLÁVSKÝ PARTNER
PAKSVŮJ NEJLEPŠÍ

HERECKÝ SOUBOR A
NÁDHERNÉ EXTERIERY.

Produkce A-B, Praha - Barrandov

3

Ekstase

4

5   VLASTA BURIAN PODÁVÁ UKÁZKU SVÉ MISTROVSKÉ KOMIKY VE FILMU „TŘI VEJCE DO SKLA". UVÁDÍ UFAFILM V KINU „ALFA·

6

## Nightlife

(1, 3, 4) Prague's nightlife was concentrated in and around Wenceslas Square, where most of the cinemas, variety theaters, dance halls, cabarets and other entertainment venues were based. Cabarets in Lucerna and Rokoko were famous for their good programs and always attracted great crowds. Television was still a thing of the future, although in 1934 at the Prague Trade Fairs a television set from the Telefunken company was on display. (2) Cover of *Eva* featuring an elegant evening gown. (5) A poster advertising "Evenings of modern dance" in the Lucerna Palace dance hall. The Lucerna hosted many famous balls, which enjoyed a great tradition for matchmaking (one Prague inhabitant called them "a cattle market"). The Lucerna was owned by the Havel family, but from time to time different guests used its large premises – the Communists occasionally rented it for Party gatherings. (6) A poster advertising Vlasta Burian's theater. (7) A romantic scene from the film *Kristián* (1939) starring Adina Mandlová and Raoul Schránil.

## Nachtleben

(1, 3, 4) Prags Nachtleben konzentrierte sich auf und um den Wenzelsplatz, wo die meisten Kinos, Varietétheater, Tanzsäle, Kabaretts und andere Vergnügungsstätten waren. Die Kabaretts im Lucerna-Palais und im Rokoko waren für ihre guten Programme berühmt und zogen immer viele Menschen an. Obwohl auf der Prager Messe 1934 ein Fernsehgerät von Telefunken ausgestellt wurde, lag das Fernsehen noch in weiter Ferne. (2) Titelblatt einer Ausgabe der *Eva*, das ein elegantes Abendkleid zeigt. (5) Ein Plakat wirbt für »Abende mit modernem Tanz« im Lucerna-Palais. In diesem Tanzsaal fanden viele berühmte Bälle statt, die traditionell zur Partnersuche genutzt wurden. (Ein Prager Bürger bezeichnete sie als »einen Viehmarkt«). Das Lucerna gehörte der Familie Havel, aber gelegentlich nutzten auch andere seine großen Räumlichkeiten – beispielsweise die Kommunisten für ihre Parteiversammlungen. (6) Ein Plakat, das für Vlasta Burians Theater wirbt. (7) Eine romantische Szene aus dem Film *Kristián* (1939) mit Adina Mandlová und Raoul Schránil.

## La vie nocturne

(1, 3, 4) La nuit, la vie se concentrait autour de la place Venceslas, où se trouvait la plupart des cinémas, théâtres de variété, dancings, cabarets et autres lieux de distraction. Les cabarets Lucerna et Rokoko étaient réputés pour la qualité de leur programme et attiraient beaucoup de monde. La télévision fit une timide apparition en 1934 lors de la Foire commerciale de Prague à l'occasion d'une démonstration de la marque allemande Telefunken. (2) Couverture de *Eva* montrant une élégante robe du soir. (5) Affiche annonçant des «Soirées de danse moderne» du Lucerna Palace, propriété de la famille Havel. Le lieu était célèbre pour ses bals, qui étaient l'occasion de rapprocher les couples (un Pragois parlait de « marché aux bestiaux »). Les communistes le louèrent parfois pour des réunions. (6) Affiche du théâtre de Vlasta Burian. (7) Scène de séduction tirée du film *Kristián* (1939), entre Adina Mandlová et Raoul Schránil.

5

6

7

# Baťa

Tomaš Baťa began his career before the First World War as a small manufacturer, mainly producing cloth slippers. During the war he became one of the principal suppliers of boots to the Imperial army. He combined cheap labor with mechanization and advanced management methods to cut prices, and sold the shoes in his own chain of shops (the first chain in the country). He aimed at customers who had previously walked barefoot. Zlín, a town in Moravia, where Baťa's factories were based, used to be called the "Detroit of Czechoslovakia". The workers were encouraged to develop loyalty, quality and good service (the company's slogans were: "Our customer is our master," "Professional foot care," "The House of Service") and they were treated well. Baťa developed flexible production methods that enabled him to churn out cheap, stylish shoes for the mass market. By 1938 his company had become one of the first multinationals, but in 1948 it was nationalized by the Communists. (1) The window of a Baťa shop. (2) The Functionalist Baťa department store (built 1927–29) in Wenceslas Square glows with light at night. It was designed for the sole purpose of selling Baťa's footwear. By the early 1930s, Baťa owned 45 buildings and had 16,000 employees producing 150,000 pairs of shoes a day. (3) Advertisements for stockings in the Baťa catalogue. (4, 5) Two advertisements for Baťa's shoes. In the second, the film star Lída Baarová promotes Baťa's sandals.

# Baťa

Tomaš Baťa begann seine Karriere vor dem Ersten Weltkrieg als kleiner Schuhfabrikant und stellte hauptsächlich Stoffschuhe her. Während des Krieges stieg er zu einem der wichtigsten Schuhlieferanten für die kaiserliche Armee auf. Um die Preise niedrig zu halten, verband er niedrige Löhne mit Mechanisierung und modernen Managementmethoden und verkaufte seine Schuhe in einer eigenen Ladenkette (die erste des Landes). Er sprach einen Kundenkreis an, der vorher barfuß gegangen war. Zlín, eine Stadt in Mähren, in der Baťa's Fabriken standen, erhielt den Beinamen »Detroit der Tschechoslowakei«. Die Arbeiter wurden zu Loyalität, Qualitätsarbeit und gutem Service angehalten (die Wahlsprüche des Unternehmens waren »Unsere Kunden sind unsere Herren«, »Professionelle Fußpflege«, »Das Haus des Service«) und fair behandelt. Baťa entwickelte flexible Produktionsmethoden, wodurch er billige, modische Schuhe für die breite Masse auf den Markt bringen konnte. 1938 war seine Firma eines der ersten multinationalen Unternehmen, wurde aber 1948 von den Kommunisten verstaatlicht. (1) Das Fenster eines Baťa-Ladens. (2) Das funktionalistische Baťa-Kaufhaus am Wenzelsplatz (1927–29 erbaut) war in der Nacht hell erleuchtet. Er diente einzig dem Verkauf von Baťa-Schuhen. In den frühen 30er Jahren besaß Baťa 45 Häuser mit 16.000 Angestellten, die 150.000 Paar Schuhe am Tag herstellten. (3) Anzeige für Strümpfe im Baťa-Katalog. (4, 5) Zwei Anzeigen für Baťa-Schuhe. In der zweiten wirbt der Filmstar Lída Baarová für Baťa-Sandalen.

# Baťa

Tomaš Baťa avait entamé sa carrière avant la Première Guerre mondiale comme petit fabricant spécialisé dans les pantoufles en tissu. Pendant la guerre, il devint l'un des principaux fournisseurs de bottes des armées impériales. Grâce à la mécanisation, à une main-d'œuvre bon marché et des méthodes de gestion modernes, il réussit à baisser ses coûts. Il vendait ses chaussures dans sa propre chaîne de magasins (la première chaîne de succursales créée dans le pays) et visait une clientèle qui, il y a peu encore, marchait pieds nus. Zlín, la ville de Moravie où se trouvaient ses usines, était appelée le «Detroit de Tchécoslovaquie». Bien traités, les ouvriers étaient encouragés à développer la loyauté, la qualité et le sens du service (les slogans de la société étaient «Le client est roi», «Le professionnalisme dans la chaussure» et «La maison du service»). Baťa développa des méthodes de production souples qui lui permettaient de produire des chaussures bon marché mais de bonne allure pour un marché de masse. En 1938, sa société devint l'une des premières multinationales tchèques, mais elle fut nationalisée en 1948 par les communistes. (1) Vitrine d'une boutique Baťa. (2) Le grand magasin Baťa de style fonctionnaliste construit en 1927–29 sur la place Venceslas était illuminé la nuit. Il ne vendait que les chaussures de la marque. Dès le début des années 30, Baťa possédait 45 immeubles, employait 16 000 personnes et produisait 150 000 paires de chaussures par jour. (3) Annonce pour des bas dans le catalogue Baťa. (4, 5) Deux annonces publicitaires pour les chaussures Baťa. Dans la seconde, la vedette de cinéma Lída Baarová est mise à contribution.

## Healthy Body, Healthy Spirit

(1) A poster advertising "World and European Championship in Ice Hockey" in 1938. (2) A poster announcing "High School Championship in Ball Games in Prague" in 1932. (3) A 1927 poster advertising the Czechoslovak Workers' Olympics and the program (4) of a sports festival organized by the Workers' Physical Training Units taking place in Prague in 1930. (7, 9–10, 12) Athletic clubs such as Slavia, Sparta and Praha organized championships in football, running, cycling, swimming, rowing and many other disciplines. (5) František Plánička was the country's most famous goalkeeper. (11) For the women, Eliška Junková, driving her Bugatti car, won the Targa Florio race in 1928 and became a famous star. (8) Ms. Haufová, one of the best women motorcyclists, taking part in a race in Prague. Just before the war a tennis talent appeared on the scene: Jaroslav Drobný (in 1954 he won Wimbledon as an Egyptian citizen). The Czech ice-hockey team in that period won the bronze medal in the World Championships three times (6). In five Olympics Czechoslovak sportsmen won 30 medals, mostly in "traditional" disciplines (athletics and gymnastics).

## Ein gesunder Geist in einem gesunden Körper

(1) Ein Plakat kündigt die »Eishockey-Welt- und Europameisterschaften« im Jahr 1938 an. (2) Ein Plakat wirbt für die »Meisterschaft in Ballspielen der Höheren Schulen in Prag« im Jahr 1932. (3) Ein Plakat von 1927 mit der Ankündigung der Tschechoslowakischen Arbeiterolympiade, und das Programm (4) eines von der Arbeitersportvereinigung 1930 in Prag organisierten Sportfestes. (7, 9–10, 12) Sportklubs wie Slavia, Sparta und Praha organisierten Wettbewerbe im Fußball, Wettrennen, Radfahren, Schwimmen, Rudern und vielen anderen Disziplinen. František Plánička war der berühmteste Torwart des Landes (5). Von den Frauen wurde Eliška Junková (11) mit ihrem Bugatti weltberühmt, mit dem sie 1928 die Targa Florio gewann. (8) Frau Haufová, eine der besten Motorradfahrerinnen, bei einem Rennen in Prag. Kurz vor dem Krieg tauchte ein großartiges Tennistalent auf: Jaroslav Drobný (1954 gewann er als ägyptischer Staatsbürger das Turnier von Wimbledon). Das tschechische Eishockeyteam gewann zu dieser Zeit dreimal die Bronzemedaille bei Weltmeisterschaften (6). In fünf Olympischen Spielen errangen tschechoslowakische Sportler 30 Medaillen, die meisten davon in »traditionellen« Disziplinen (Schwerathletik und Turnen).

## Un esprit sain dans un corps sain

(1) Affiche pour le Championnat d'Europe et du monde de hockey sur glace de 1938. (2) Affiche du championnat des sports de ballon à Prague, 1932. (3) Affiche de 1927 des Jeux olympiques des travailleurs tchécoslovaques, et programme (4) d'un festival sportif organisé par les Unions ouvrières d'éducation physique de Prague en 1930. (7, 9–10, 12) Les clubs d'athlétisme comme le Slavia, le Sparta et le Praga organisaient des championnats de football, de natation, de course à pied, de cyclisme, d'aviron et de nombreuses autres disciplines. František Plánička était le plus célèbre gardien de but du pays (5). Eliška Junková (11) remporta au volant de sa Bugatti la course de la Targa Florio en 1928 et devint une véritable vedette. (8) Mademoiselle Haufová, l'une des meilleures pilotes de moto féminines, praticipant à une course à Prague. Juste avant la guerre, un remarquable tennisman fit son apparition : Jaroslav Drobný. Il remporta en 1954 le tournoi de Wimbledon pour l'équipe égyptienne. L'équipe tchèque de hockey sur glace de cette période gagna trois fois la médaille de bronze du Championnat du monde (6). En cinq Jeux olympiques, les sportifs tchécoslovaques s'attribuèrent 30 médailles, principalement dans des disciplines «traditionnelles» comme l'athlétisme et la gymnastique.

5

6

7

8

9

10

11

12

## Prague Trade Fairs

In 1921 Prague Trade Fairs were established in order to give a boost to Czechoslovak industry and commerce. They took place in March and September. The Exhibition Grounds and the Trade Fair Palace were the two main centers in which industrial achievements were displayed. Czechoslovakia was the 10th richest country in the world. In 1929 one Czech crown had a value of 44.58mg in gold. Foreign investment (especially English and French) was high, one third of the country's capital. Czechoslovakia's metallurgy and engineering industries, and textile manufacture (linen, cotton, jute and hemp) were its trademarks. The country also had natural resources such as coal and iron ore. It exported hosiery, leather accessories, boots, shoes, gloves, hats, toys, glass and porcelain, as well as costume jewelry (Hollywood bought large amounts of beads and rhinestones for decorating film stars' costumes). (1–6) Posters advertising Prague Trade Fairs. (7) The interior of the Trade Fair Palace. (8) Bělského třida (now called Dukelských hrdinu) with the Grand Exhibition Hall in the background.

## Prager Messen

1921 wurden die Prager Messen zur Förderung der tschechischen Industrie und des Handels gegründet. Sie fanden regelmäßig im März und im September statt. Das Ausstellungsgelände und der Messepalast waren die beiden Hauptzentren, in denen industrielle Errungenschaften vorgeführt wurden. Unter den reichsten Ländern der Welt nahm die Tschechoslowakei Platz 10 ein. 1929 hatte eine tschechische Krone einen Goldwert von 44,58 mg. Der Anteil ausländischen Investitionen (vor allem aus England und aus Frankreich) lag mit einem Drittel des Landeskapitals sehr hoch. Die tschechischen Metall- und Maschinenindustrien sowie die Textilherstellung (Leinen, Baumwolle, Jute und Hanf) waren die wichtigsten Industriezweige. Auch verfügte das Land über Bodenschätze wie Kohle und Eisenerz. Man exportierte Feintextilien, Lederaccessoires, Stiefel, Schuhe, Handschuhe, Hüte, Spielzeug, Glas, Porzellan sowie Modeschmuck (Hollywood kaufte große Mengen an Perlen und Bernstein für die Kostüme seiner Filmstars). (1–6) Plakate werben für die Prager Messen. (7) Der Innenraum der Messepalastes. (8) Bělského třida (jetzt Dukelských hrdinu) mit der großen Ausstellungshalle im Hintergrund.

## Les foires commerciales de Prague

Fondées en 1921, les foires commerciales de Prague avaient pour objectif de promouvoir l'industrie et le commerce tchécoslovaques. Elles se déroulaient en mars et en septembre. Le Parc des expositions et le Palais de la Foire accueillaient les exposants. La Tchécoslovaquie était le dixième pays le plus riche du monde en 1929, date à laquelle la couronne valait 44,58 mg d'or. Les investissements étrangers (en particulier britanniques et français) étaient abondants et représentaient un tiers de la richesse capitalistique du pays. La métallurgie, les usines de mécanique et les usines textiles (lin, coton, jute et chanvre) étaient florissantes. Le pays possédait également des ressources naturelles comme le charbon et le minerai de fer. Il exportait de la lingerie, de la maroquinerie, des bottes, des chaussures, des gants, des chapeaux, des jouets, du verre et de la porcelaine, des bijoux fantaisie (dont Hollywood était un grand client pour les costumes de ses stars). (1–6) Affiches des foires de Prague. (7) Intérieur du Palais de la foire. (8) Bělského třida (aujourd'hui Dukelských hrdinu) avec le Palais de la Foire dans la perspective.

7

8

Tatra razí cestu vozům zítřka!

Již před mnoha lety přišla TATRA mezi prvními — a často byla vůbec první v tom, co je dnes znakem moderního automobilu. Co mnohde je poslední novinkou, je u TATRY dlouho samozřejmou věcí. Každý nový vůz TATRA zajišťuje přednosti, jež zevšeobecní v automobilismu až za několik let. Váš příští vůz by měla býti proto TATRA.

ZÁVODY RINGHOFFER-TATRA A. S.

## Advertising

Advertising from the period 1927–29 depicted the achievements and economic prosperity of the First Republic in its carefree days with humor and imagination. In 1928–29 the average monthly pay of a farmer was 550 crowns; a worker 850 crowns; a chemist 1300 crowns; an engineer 1750 crowns; and a minister 9000 crowns. A large beer cost 1.30 crowns; bread 2 crowns; 1kg of meat 15 crowns; a pair of shoes 19 crowns; a shirt 24 crowns; a vacuum cleaner 1500 crowns; and a car 18,000 crowns. (1–7) Posters advertising Praga and Tatra cars, Prague ham, vinegar, cigarettes and Radion washing powder.

## Werbung

Die Werbung aus der Zeit zwischen 1927 und 1929 zeigt die Errungenschaften und die wirtschaftliche Prosperität der Ersten Republik in ihren sorgenfreien Tagen voller Humor und Phantasie. 1928–29 lag das durchschnittliche Monatseinkommen eines Bauern bei 550 Kronen; ein Arbeiter verdiente 850 Kronen, ein Chemiker 1.300 Kronen, ein Ingenieur 1.750 Kronen und ein Minister 9.000 Kronen. Ein großes Bier kostete 1,30 Kronen, Brot 2 Kronen, 1 kg Fleisch 15 Kronen, ein Paar Schuhe 19 Kronen, ein Hemd 24 Kronen, ein Staubsauger 1.500 Kronen und ein Auto 18.000 Kronen. (1–7) Plakate werben für den Praga und den Tatra, für Prager Schinken, Essig, Zigaretten und Radion-Waschpulver.

## Publicité

La publicité de la période 1927–29 décrit avec humour et imagination les réussites et la prospérité économique de la première république, encore insouciante. En 1928–29, le revenu moyen d'un fermier était de 550 couronnes, celui d'un ouvrier 850, d'un chimiste 1300, d'un ingénieur 1750, et d'un ministre 9000. Une pinte de bière coûtait 1,3 couronne, le pain 2 couronnes, 1 kg de viande 15 couronnes, une paire de chaussures 19 couronnes, une chemise 24 couronnes, un aspirateur 1500 couronnes et une automobile 18 000 couronnes. (1–7) Affiches pour les automobiles Praga et Tatra, les jambons de Prague, du vinaigre, des cigarettes et la poudre à laver Radion.

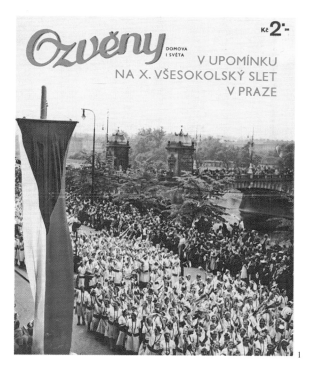

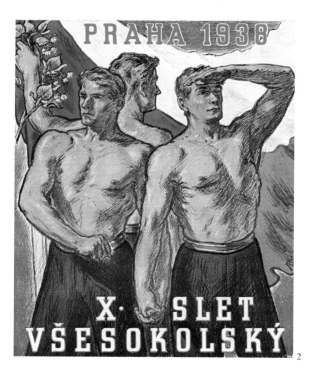

### Sokol 1938 (I)

The last *Sokol* rally before the war. On the eve of the German invasion of Czechoslovakia more than 2 million people turned out at Prague's Strahov stadium over four days to witness 350,000 men, women and children display the strength of the Czech nation, many of them dressed in military uniform. The festival reached its climax during the men's exercises, as planes flew overhead and 28,000 men finished their routine with a mass oath declaring their readiness to defend the Republic. On 12 June President Beneš attended the rally to watch the patriotic display. (4) The *Sokols* marching across the Legionnaires Bridge.

### Sokol 1938 (I)

Die letzte *Sokol*-Treffen vor dem Krieg. Am Vorabend der deutschen Invasion in die Tschechoslowakei erschienen mehr als 2 Millionen Menschen im Prager Strahov-Stadion, um sich vier Tage lang die 350.000 Männer, Frauen und Kinder – viele von ihnen in Uniform – anzusehen, die dort die Stärke der tschechischen Nation zur Schau stellten. Während der Veranstaltungen der Männer erreichte das Fest seinen Höhepunkt, als Flugzeuge über die 28.000 Sportler flogen, die am Ende ihrer Übungen gemeinsam den Eid ablegten, zur Verteidigung der Republik bereitzustehen. Am 12. Juni besuchte Präsident Beneš das Treffen und sah den patriotischen Bezeugungen zu. (4) *Sokol*-Mitglieder marschieren über die Brücke der Legionen.

### Sokol 1938 (I)

Le dernier grand rassemblement *Sokol* avant la guerre. À la veille de l'invasion allemande, plus de 2 millions de personnes se rendirent en quatre jours dans le stade Strahov de Prague pour applaudir 350 000 hommes, femmes et enfants, et témoigner de la vitalité de la nation tchèque. Beaucoup d'entre eux étaient vêtus d'uniformes militaires. La fête atteignit son sommet lors des exercices physiques masculins, tandis que des avions passaient dans le ciel et que 28 000 hommes prêtaient serment de défendre la république. Le 12 juin, le président Beneš assista à ce rassemblement patriotique. (4) Les *Sokol* défilant sur le pont des Légionnaires.

### Sokol 1938 (II)

(Overleaf) *Sokol* members performing at Strahov sports stadium.

### Sokol 1938 (II)

(Folgende Seiten) *Sokol*-Mitglieder treten im Strahov-Stadion auf.

### Sokol 1938 (II)

(Pages suivantes) Membres de *Sokol* à l'exercice dans le stade de Strahov.

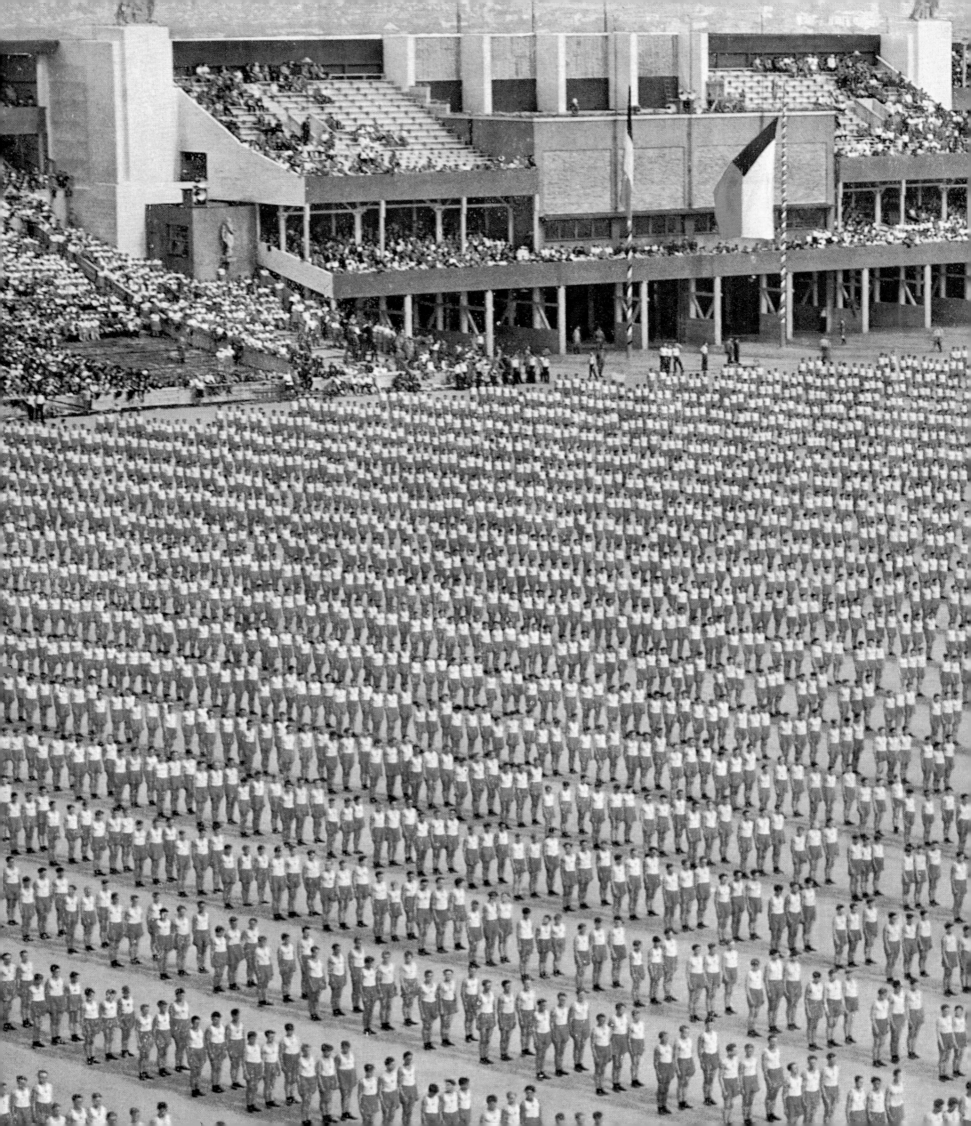

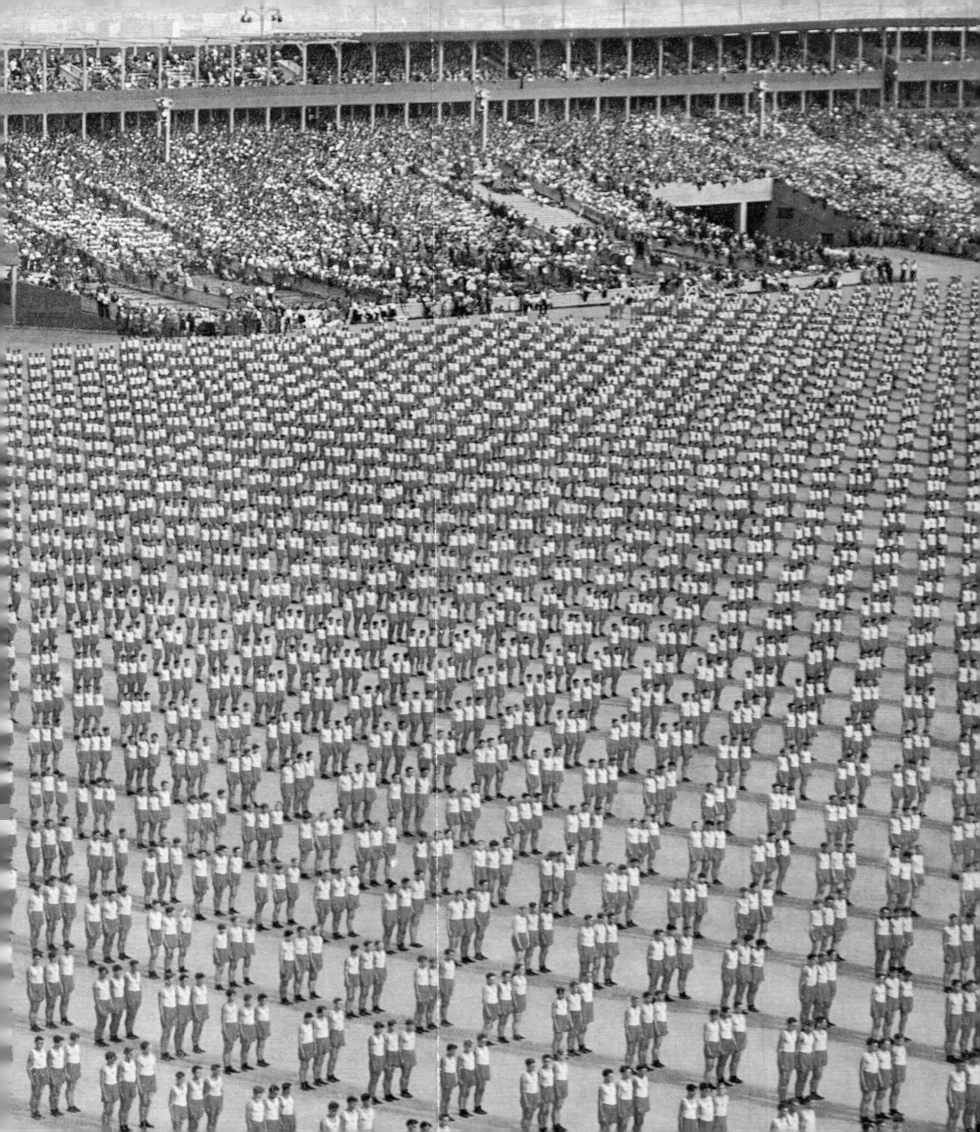

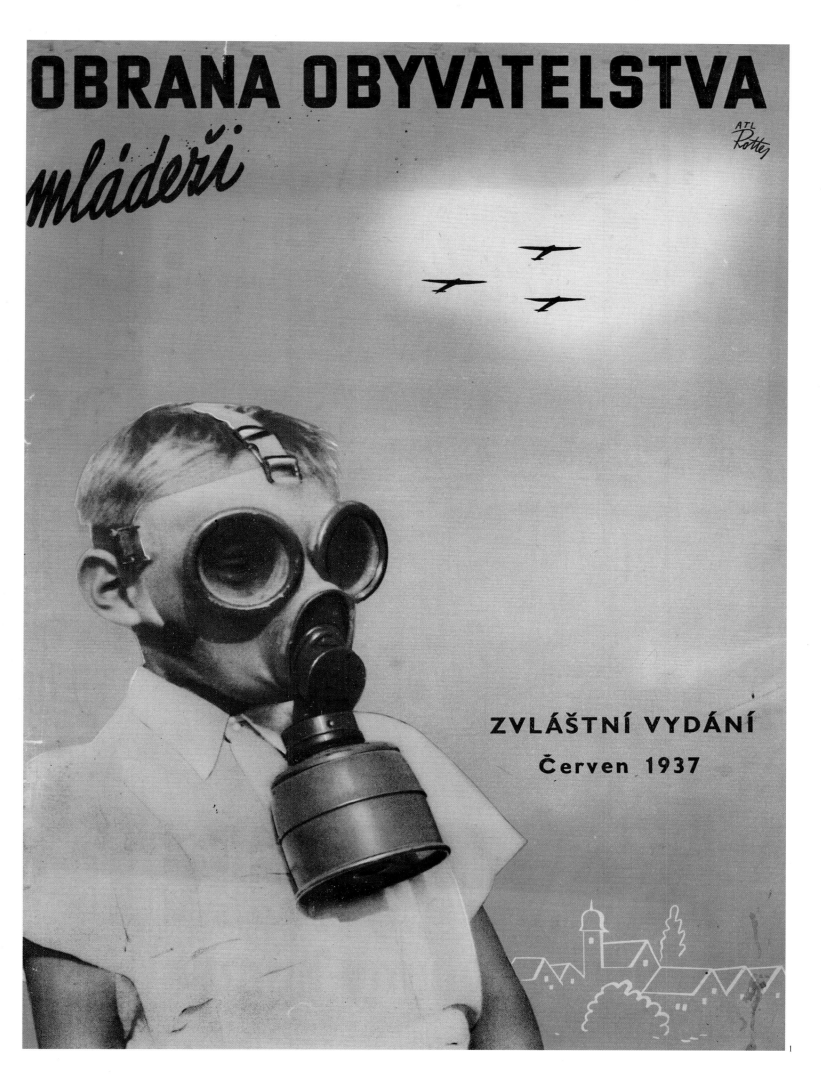

OBRANA OBYVATELSTVA

*mládeži*

ATL
Rotter

ZVLÁŠTNÍ VYDÁNÍ

Červen 1937

## The Gathering Storm

The Nazis financed a Sudeten German Party from 1935, which agitated for cession from Czechoslovakia, providing popular support for Hitler's claim to the region. The Sudeten Germans demanded a separate state with its own government, and freedom to propagate Nazi ideology. In a directive of 30 May 1938 Hitler said: "It is my unalterable decision to smash Czechoslovakia by military action within the foreseeable future." He gave 1 October as the deadline. Beneš was ready to accept a peaceful solution, but on 13 September the Sudeten Germans tried to take over power in 60 places (the Sudetendeutsches Freikorps killed 37 Czech border guards and wounded 132). The Czechoslovak government declared martial law in the Sudetenland. (1) A 1937 special edition of a civil-defense manual for teaching Czech youth. (2) A 1936 Czech edition of *Mein Kampf* (My Struggle). (3) A satirical cartoon of Hitler by the famous cartoonist Josef Bidlo. It is captioned: "Be ready, that's all." (4) A Czech magazine cover showing the Czechoslovak army ready to defend its borders. On 20 May 1938 the Czechs called for mobilization.

## Der aufziehende Sturm

Seit 1935 wurde die Sudetendeutsche Partei von den Nazis finanziell unterstützt: Mit ihrer Autonomieforderung bot sie Hitler öffentlichen Beistand für seine Ansprüche in der Region. Die Sudetendeutschen verlangten einen separaten Staat mit einer eigenen Regierung und die Freiheit, die Naziideologie zu propagieren. In einer Direktive vom 30. Mai 1938 sagte Hitler: »Es ist meine unabänderliche Entscheidung, die Tschechoslowakei in einer militärischen Aktion in nächster Zukunft zu zerschlagen.« Als Ultimatum setzte er den 1. Oktober. Beneš war zu einer friedlichen Lösung bereit, aber am 13. September versuchten die Sudetendeutschen an 60 Orten, die Macht zu übernehmen (dabei töteten sudetendeutsche Freikorps 37 und verwundeten 132 tschechische Grenzbeamte). Daraufhin rief die tschechoslowakische Regierung im Sudetenland das Kriegsrecht aus. (1) Sonderausgabe eines Zivilschutzhandbuchs zur Unterweisung der tschechischen Jugend von 1937. (2) Eine tschechische Ausgabe von *Mein Kampf*. (3) Ein satirischer Cartoon über Hitler von dem bekannten tschechischen Cartoonisten Josef Bidlo mit der Überschrift: »Seid bereit. Das ist alles.« (4) Eine tschechische Zeitschrift zeigt auf ihrem Titelblatt die tschechoslowakische Armee in Bereitschaft, ihre Grenzen zu verteidigen. Am 20. Mai 1938 machte die Tschechoslowakei mobil.

## Les nuages s'accumulent...

Les nazis finançaient depuis 1935 le parti des Allemands des Sudètes qui revendiquait leur sécession de la Tchécoslovaquie, et préparaient le terrain aux revendications territoriales de Hitler. Ils réclamaient un État séparé avec leur propre gouvernement et la liberté de propager l'idéologie nazie. Dans une directive du 30 mai 1938, Hitler déclara : « J'ai pris la décision irrévocable d'écraser la Tchécoslovaquie par la force militaire dans un futur prévisible. » Il fixa le 1er octobre comme limite. Beneš était prêt à accepter une solution pacifique, mais, le 13 septembre, les Allemands des Sudètes essayèrent de prendre le pouvoir dans 60 localités (le *Freikorps* tua 37 gardes-frontière tchèques et en blessa 132). Le gouvernement déclara la loi martiale dans les Sudètes. (1) Édition d'un manuel de défense civile pour les jeunes Tchèques (1937). (2) Édition tchèque de *Mein Kampf* (1936), sous-titrée « Hitler parle de lui et de ses objectifs ». (3) Dessin satirique de Hitler par le célèbre caricaturiste Josef Bidlo. La légende dit : « Soyez prêts, c'est tout. » (4) Couverture de magazine tchèque montrant l'armée tchécoslovaque prête à défendre les frontières. Le 20 mai 1938, la mobilisation générale fut proclamée.

80 hal. PRAŽSKÝ ILUSTROVANÝ ZPRAVODAJ

SPOLEČENSKÝ NEPOLITICKÝ TÝDENÍK
VYCHÁZÍ VE ČTVRTEK ČÍSLO 40 (922) ROČ. 1938

5

## The Sudetenland

In the autumn of 1938 Hitler demanded the "return" of the German-speaking Sudetenland. Eventually, the Führer accepted a "compromise" at the Munich Conference on 28 September 1938: annexation of the Sudetenland in stages. In Munich an agreement was reached between Britain, Germany, France and Italy to partition Czechoslovakia by forcing the cession of the Sudetenland to Germany, as Hitler had demanded. The agreement was the culmination of British Prime Minister Neville Chamberlain's appeasement policy. The Czechs were not invited to the negotiations ("*o nás, bez nás*" – about us, without us). Hitler made it clear that he would not deal with the Czechoslovak state as long as Beneš remained President. Hitler hated him, identifying him with the spirit of Czech nationalism. (1) Beneš visiting the grave of Tomáš Masaryk on the anniversary of his death. (2) The cover of a magazine picturing "the men who decided the fate of Europe." (3) Men marching off at the time of mobilization. (4) A cover story on mobilization. (5) A map of Czechoslovakia showing the Sudetenland border regions which were lost to Germany after the Munich Treaty.

## Das Sudetenland

Im Herbst 1938 verlangte Hitler die »Rückführung« des deutschsprachigen Sudetenlandes. Schließlich akzeptierte er auf der Münchener Konferenz vom 28. September 1938 einen »Kompromiß«: die schrittweise Annexion des Sudetenlandes. In München kamen Großbritannien, Deutschland, Frankreich und Italien überein, die Forderungen Hitlers zu erfüllen und das Sudetenland den Deutschen zu übergeben. Dieses Abkommen bildete den Höhepunkt der Appeasement-Politik des britischen Premierministers Neville Chamberlain. Die Tschechen waren nicht zu den Verhandlungen eingeladen worden (»*o nás, bez nás*« – über uns, ohne uns). Hitler machte deutlich, daß er nicht mit der Tschechoslowakei verhandeln würde, solange Beneš Präsident war. Hitler haßte ihn, weil er in ihm den Geist des tschechischen Nationalismus verkörpert sah. (1) Zu seinem Todestag besuchte Beneš das Grab von Tomáš Masaryk. (2) Das Titelblatt einer Zeitung zeigt »die Männer, die über das Schicksal Europas entschieden haben«. (3) Marschierende Männer während der Mobilmachung. (4) Die Titelgeschichte über die Mobilmachung. (5) Eine Karte der Tschechoslowakei mit dem Grenzgebiet des Sudetenlandes, das nach dem Münchener Abkommen an Deutschland verloren ging.

## Les Sudètes

À l'automne 1938, Hitler demanda le « retour » des Sudètes germanophones à l'Allemagne. Il accepta le «compromis» d'une annexion par étapes lors de la conférence de Munich le 28 septembre 1938. Des accords furent signés entre l'Allemagne, la Grande-Bretagne, la France et l'Italie pour la partition de la Tchécoslovaquie en l'obligeant à céder les Sudètes, comme Hitler le voulait. Ces accords étaient le fruit de la politique d'apaisement du Premier ministre britannique, Neville Chamberlain. Les Tchèques ne furent pas invités aux négociations («*o nás, bez nás*» – sur nous, sans nous). Hitler fit comprendre qu'il ne traiterait pas avec l'État tchécoslovaque tant que Beneš en serait le président. Il le haïssait et l'identifiait au nationalisme tchèque. (1) Beneš devant la tombe de Tomáš Masaryk pour l'anniversaire de sa mort. (2) Couverture d'un magazine montrant « les hommes qui ont décidé du sort de l'Europe ». (3) Hommes défilant lors de la mobilisation. (4) La mobilisation en première page des journaux. (5) Carte de la Tchécoslovaquie avec les régions frontalières des Sudètes abandonnées à l'Allemagne par les Accords de Munich.

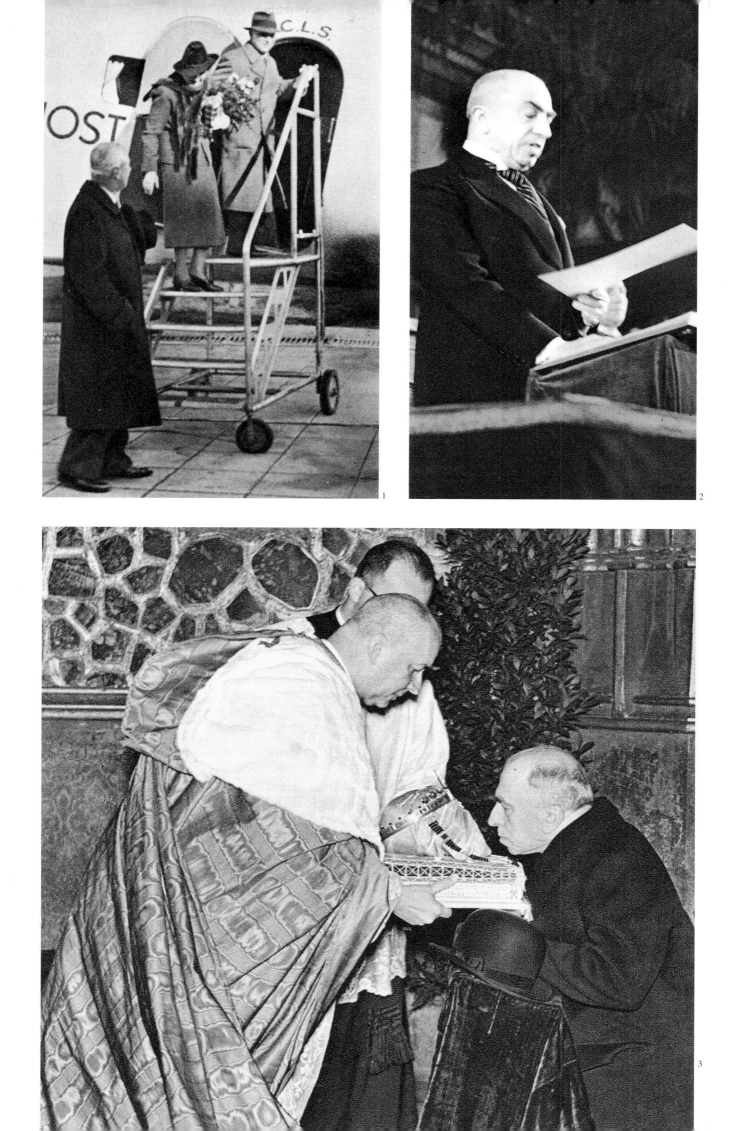

## The Dismemberment of Czechoslovakia

Under pressure from politicians who thought that the President's resignation and emigration would save the country and stop Hitler in his expansionist schemes, Edvard Beneš resigned on 5 October 1938 and left for England (1) with his wife, Hana, on 22 October. (2) Emil Hácha (1872–1945) was politically conservative, an expert on English law and President of the Supreme Court. He was elected President on 30 November 1938 (out of 312 votes, 272 were for Hácha). He took an oath: "I swear on my honor and in accordance with my conscience that I shall take care of the well-being of the Republic and people and safeguard the constitutional laws...". (3) A mass celebrating the occasion was held in St Vitus Cathedral, at which Archbishop Karel Kašpar held the crowned skull of St Wenceslas for Hácha to kiss (an old remedy practised in times of trouble). The ceremony took place in the splendor of the St Wenceslas Chapel, studded with precious stones set in gold mortar. (4) Hitler's armies invaded the Sudetenland on 1 October 1938 and Germans tore down the Czechoslovak border posts. (5) Hitler visited the Sudetenland in the first days of October in his familiar three-axle Mercedes G4, surrounded by his henchmen, who often had to walk or trot alongside the car. He inspected Czech fortifications, which he found quite impressive. He was welcomed by Konrad Henlein's pro-Nazi Party (Sudetendeutsche Partei) supporters and enthusiastic crowds flooded the streets, threw flowers, offered baskets of fruit and waved little flags with swastikas.

## Die Zerstückelung der Tschechoslowakei

Unter dem Druck der Politiker, die hofften, daß der Rücktritt des Präsidenten und seine Emigration das Land retten und Hitler von seinen expansionistischen Absichten abbringen würde, trat Eduard Beneš am 5. Oktober 1938 zurück und (1) reiste zusammen mit seiner Frau Hana am 22. Oktober nach England. (2) Emil Hácha (1872–1945), ein Konservativer und Experte für englisches Recht, Präsident des Obersten Gerichtes, wurde am 30. November 1938 zum Präsidenten gewählt (mit 272 von 312 Stimmen). Er legte folgenden Eid ab: »Ich schwöre bei meiner Ehre und meinem Gewissen, daß ich für das Wohl der Republik und ihrer Bürger sorgen und die Verfassung schützen werde ...«. (3) Aus diesem Anlaß wurde im Veitsdom eine Messe gelesen, bei der Erzbischof Karel Kašpar den gekrönten Schädel des Heiligen Wenzel Hácha zum Kuß hinhielt (ein altes Ritual aus Krisenzeiten). Die Zeremonie fand in der prächtigen Wenzelskapelle statt, die mit Halbedelsteinen auf goldenem Mörtel geschmückt ist. (4) Am 1. Oktober 1938 marschierten Hitlers Armeen im Sudetenland ein und Deutsche rissen die tschechoslowakischen Grenzpfähle nieder. (5) Hitler besuchte das Sudetenland in den ersten Oktobertagen in seinem dreiachsigen Mercedes G4, umgeben von Gefolgsleuten, die oft neben dem Wagen herlaufen mußten. Er inspizierte tschechische Befestigungsanlagen, die ihn sehr beeindruckten. Anhänger von Konrad Henleins nationalsozialistischer Sudetendeutschen Partei begrüßten ihn, und begeisterte Menschenmengen säumten die Straßen, warfen Blumen, boten ihm Obstkörbe an und schwenkten kleine Hakenkreuzflaggen.

## Le démembrement de la Tchécoslovaquie

Sous la pression de politiciens qui pensaient que sa démission et son départ sauveraient le pays et mettraient fin aux visées expansionnistes de Hitler, Edvard Beneš démissionna le 5 octobre 1938, et parti le 22 octobre pour la Grande-Bretagne, accompagné de sa femme, Hana. (2) Emil Hácha (1872–1945) était un conservateur, expert en droit anglais et président de la Cour suprême. Élu président le 30 novembre 1938 (par 272 voix sur 312), il prêta le serment suivant : « Je jure sur mon honneur et selon ma conscience de prendre en charge le devenir de la République et de son peuple et la sauvegarde de la constitution... ». (3) Une messe se tint dans la cathédrale Saint-Guy, l'archevêque Karel Kašpar présenta la couronne de saint Venceslas à Hachá qui l'embrassa (ancien rite en temps de crises). La cérémonie se déroula dans la splendide chapelle de saint Venceslas, décorée de pierres semi-précieuses serties dans un mortier à l'or. Les armées de Hitler envahirent les Sudètes le 1er octobre 1938. (4) Allemands arrachant les poteaux de la douane tchécoslovaque. (5) Hitler se rendit dans les Sudètes dès les premiers jours d'octobre dans sa Mercedes G4 à triple essieu, entouré de ses sbires, qui marchaient souvent à côté de la voiture. Il inspecta les fortifications tchèques qu'il jugea impressionnantes. Il fut accueilli par les membres enthousiastes du parti pronazi de Konrad Henlein (Sudetendeutsche Partei) et des foules qui envahirent les rues, jetant des fleurs, offrant des paniers de fruits et agitant de petits drapeaux ornés de la croix gammée.

# Aufruf an die Bevölkerung!

Auf Befehl des Führers und Obersten Befehlshabers der Deutschen Wehrmacht habe ich im Lande Böhmen mit dem heutigen Tage die vollziehende Gewalt übernommen.

Hauptquartier Prag, den 15. März 1939.

Der Oberbefehlshaber der Heeresgruppe 3

## Blaskowitz
General der Infanterie.

---

# Výzva obyvatelstvu!

Na rozkaz Vůdce a vrchního velitele Německé armády převzal jsem v zemi české dnešním dnem vykonávací moc.

Hlavní stan v Praze, dne 15. března 1939.

Vrchní velitel armádní skupiny 3

## Blaskowitz
generál pěchoty.

# Under the Swastika
# Unter dem Hakenkreuz
# Dans l'ombre de la croix gammée

An announcement by the commander of the German occupation forces, General Blaskowitz, stating that on the orders of the Führer he has assumed total power. On 15 March 1939 Czechoslovakia ceased to exist and the "Protectorate of Bohemia and Moravia" was established.

Eine Bekanntmachung des Kommandanten der deutschen Besatzungmacht, General Blaskowitz, mit der Erklärung der völligen Machtübernahme durch den Führer. Am 15. März 1939 verlor die Tschechoslowakei ihre Souveränität, das Land hieß jetzt »Protektorat Böhmen und Mähren«.

Déclaration du commandant des forces d'occupation allemandes, le général Blaskowitz, annonçant que, sur les ordres du *Führer*, il assume la totalité des pouvoirs. Le 15 mars 1939, la Tchécoslovaquie cesse d'exister pour être remplacée par un « Protectorat de Bohême et de Moravie ».

PRAŽSKÝ ILUSTROVANÝ

**80** hal

SPOLEČENSKÝ
NEPOLITICKÝ TÝDENÍK
VYCHÁZÍ VE ČTVRTEK
ČÍSLO 12 (955)
ROČNÍK 1939

# ZPRAVODAJ

*V těsném semknutí nás všech a v řádném plnění národních povinností bude nejlepší záruka naší zdárné budoucnosti.*

(Z rozhlasového projevu
dr. Háchy 16. března.)

## PRESIDENT Dr. EMIL HÁCHA V BERLÍNĚ

14. března po 22. hodině byl uvítán na Anhaltském nádraží v Berlíně státním ministrem dr. Meissnerem (vpravo) a berlínským velitelem generálem-poručíkem Seifertem (vlevo). V pozadí vidíme našeho ministra zahraničí dr. Chvalkovského.

Nakladatel: Melantrich, Praha.                          Snímek: Keystone, Berlín.

## 14 March 1939 and the German Invasion

A convenient excuse for the German invasion of Czechoslovakia was provided by German riots in Prague and other cities. President Emil Hácha arrived in Berlin in order to solve the crisis. Adolf Hitler gave him an ultimatum: a peaceful occupation, or the total destruction of Czechoslovakia. Hácha fainted and when he came round he signed a paper presented to him, requesting Hitler to take the Czech people under the protection of the Reich. It was 3.55 a.m., 15 March 1939. The radio announcement before dawn came as a shock to the people of Czechoslovakia. The previous day, the Slovak government had declared an independent Fascist state, leaving the Czechs to their fate. (1) Magazine title page covering Emil Hácha's visit to Berlin on 14 March 1939. (2) The presidential flag of Bohemia and Moravia. (3) The Reichsprotektor's standard on the roof of Hradčany. (4) Hácha and Hitler at Hradčany on 16 March 1939. (5) A small force of 7000 lightly armed men as a ceremonial guard was all that the Czech State President Hácha was allowed to retain.

## Der 14. März 1939 und die deutsche Invasion

Die deutschen Aufstände in Prag und in anderen Städten lieferten den willkommenen Anlaß für den Einmarsch der Deutschen in die Tschechoslowakei. Präsident Emil Hácha war nach Berlin gekommen, um die Krise beizulegen. Adolf Hitler aber stellte ihm ein Ultimatum: entweder eine friedliche Besetzung oder die völlige Zerstörung der Tschechoslowakei. Hácha verlor das Bewußtsein – als er wieder zu sich kam, unterzeichnete er das ihm vorgelegte Papier. Darin wurde Hitler aufgefordert, das tschechische Volk unter den Schutz des Reiches zu stellen. Es war 3.55 Uhr am Morgen des 15. März 1939. Die Nachricht wurde im Morgengrauen im Radio verbreitet und kam für die Menschen in der Tschechoslowakei wie ein Schock. Am vorangegangenen Tag hatte die slowakische Regierung ihr Land zu einem unabhängigen faschistischen Staat erklärt und die Tschechen ihrem Schicksal überlassen. (1) Titelblatt einer Zeitschrift anläßlich Emil Háchas Besuch in Berlin am 14. März 1939. (2) Die Präsidentenflagge von Böhmen und Mähren. (3) Die Standarte des Reichsprotektors auf dem Dach des Hradschin. (4) Hácha und Hitler am 16. März 1939 auf dem Hradschin. (5) Eine kleine Truppe von 7.000 leicht bewaffneten Männern als symbolische Wache war alles, was dem tschechischen Staatspräsidenten Hácha blieb.

## Le 14 mars 1939 et l'invasion allemande

Des émeutes allemandes à Prague et dans d'autres villes fournirent un prétexte à l'invasion allemande de la Tchécoslovaquie. Le président Emil Hácha se rend à Berlin pour tenter de résoudre la crise. Adolf Hitler lui lança un ultimatum : une occupation pacifique ou la destruction totale du pays. Hácha s'évanouit puis signa, à 3 h 55 du matin le 15 mars 1939, le document qu'on lui présenta demandant à Hitler de prendre le peuple tchèque sous la protection du Reich. La nouvelle fut annoncée à l'aube à la radio provoquant une énorme émotion parmi les Tchécoslovaques. La veille, le gouvernement fasciste slovaque avait proclamé l'indépendance de la Slovaquie, abandonnant les Tchèques à leur destin. (1) Couverture de magazine : Emil Hácha à Berlin le 14 mars 1939. (2) Le drapeau présidentiel de Bohême et Moravie. (3) Le drapeau du Protecteur du Reich flottant sur les toits du Hradčany. (4) Hácha et Hitler au Hradčany le 16 mars 1939. (5) Seule une petite formation de 7 000 hommes équipés d'armes légères et de fonction purement honorifique fut laissée au président tchèque.

2

3

4

5

## 15 March 1939: The Wehrmacht Takes Over

The advance German troops, from Army Group Three under General Blaskowitz, reached Prague at 9 a.m. on 15 March 1939. They were cheered by the local Germans, who gave the Hitler salute and waved swastika flags. The Czechs were grief-stricken, some cried, others sang the National Anthem. The main German objectives were the airfields at Ruzyně and Kbely, the War Ministry buildings in Dejvice and Hradčany, the residence of the Czech President. A curfew was proclaimed (only railwaymen and doctors were excepted). Popular gatherings and acts hostile

## 15. März 1939: Die Wehrmacht übernimmt das Kommando

Die einmarschierenden deutschen Truppen von der Dritten Armee unter General Blaskowitz erreichten Prag am 15. März 1939 um 9 Uhr morgens. Sie wurden von den einheimischen Deutschen mit dem Hitlergruß und Hakenkreuzfähnchen jubelnd empfangen. Die Tschechen waren verzweifelt; einige weinten, andere sangen die Nationalhymne. Die Deutschen wollten vor allem die Flugplätze von Ruzyně und Kbely, das Kriegsministerium in Dejvice und die Residenz des Präsidenten auf dem Hradschin in ihre Hand bekommen. Sie verhängten eine Ausgangssperre (von der nur tschechische Eisenbahner und Ärzte ausgenommen waren). Öffentliche Versammlungen und anti-

## 15 mars 1939: la Wehrmacht prend le contrôle du pays

Les troupes de l'avant-garde allemande du troisième corps d'armée sous le commandement du général Blaskowitz atteignirent Prague à 9 h du matin le 15 mars 1939. Elles furent ovationnées par les Allemands de Prague, qui les saluèrent le bras tendu en agitant des drapeaux à croix gammée. Les Tchèques étaient atterrés, certains pleuraient, d'autres chantaient l'hymne national. Les principaux objectifs allemands étaient: l'aéroport de Ruzyně et de Kbely, les bâtiments du ministère de la Guerre à Dejvice et le Hradčany, résidence du président. Un couvre-feu fut proclamé (dont seuls les médecins et les employés des chemins de fer étaient dispensés). Tout rassemblement et

to Germans were forbidden. Apart from a few scattered incidents of minor sabotage, in which the tyres of German lorries were slashed, there was no resistance. The police co-operated with the invaders, giving directions to troops lost in the medieval streets. (1) German troops march into the First Courtyard of Hradčany. (2) German motorcycle troops at Hradčany. (3) A German sentry keeps watch over the conquered city, with the snow-covered Hradčany in the background. (4) A German soldier on a streetcorner near the Charles Bridge.

deutsche Aktivitäten wurden verboten. Abgesehen von ein paar verstreuten Sabotageakten, bei denen die Reifen deutscher Lastwagen zerstochen wurden, gab es keinen Widerstand. Die Polizei kooperierte mit den Invasoren und half den Truppen, sich in den mittelalterlichen Straßen zurecht zu finden. (1) Deutsche Truppen marschieren in den ersten Innenhof des Hradschins. (2) Eine deutsche Motorradstaffel auf dem Hradschin. (3) Ein deutscher Wachposten in der besetzten Stadt, im Hintergrund der schneebedeckte Hradschin. (4) Ein deutscher Soldat an einer Straßenecke in der Nähe der Karlsbrücke.

actes hostiles aux Allemands étaient interdits. En dehors de quelques incidents de sabotage mineurs, comme la crevaison des pneus de camions militaires, il n'y eut pas de résistance. La police coopéra avec les envahisseurs, guidant les troupes égarées dans le dédale des ruelles médiévales. (1) Les troupes allemandes pénètrent dans l'avant-cour du Hradčany. (2) Troupes allemandes motorisées devant le Hradčany. (3) Une sentinelle allemande observe la ville conquise, sur fond de Hradčany enneigé. (4) Officier allemand à un angle de rue, près du pont Charles.

3

4

### Hitler in Prague

On 15 March 1939 Hitler took a train to Česká Lípa in the Sudetenland and from there traveled by car to Prague. (1) An enthusiastic German crowd salutes Hitler as he appears in the upper window of the Castle. (2) Adolf Hitler (1889–1945) in the First Courtyard at Hradčany, accompanied by the SS Reichsführer, Heinrich Himmler (on the left) and his deputy, Reinhard Heydrich, head of the Nazi security police (on the right). (3) The newspaper *Národní Politika* (National Politics) announces that Hitler "entered Prague by the shortest possible route from Česká Lípa at 5 p.m." (4) Hitler surveying his new conquest from a window of the Castle. Exhilarated by the ease with which the task had been completed, and dazzled by the Castle's splendors, he tasted Prague ham and drank a small glass of Pilsner beer. (5) Hitler stroking the head of a girl who hands him flowers. (6) A Protectorate stamp based on the famous photograph of Hitler. (7) Hitler departs from the Castle, as German soldiers and Prague Germans line the cobbled street. On the morning of 16 March a decree signed by Hitler proclaimed the "Protectorate of Bohemia and Moravia."

### Hitler in Prag

Am 15. März 1939 reiste Hitler mit dem Zug nach Česká Lípa im Sudetenland und fuhr von dort aus mit dem Auto nach Prag weiter. (1) Eine begeisterte deutsche Menge begrüßt Hitler, als er sich am oberen Fenster der Burg zeigt. (2) Adolf Hitler (1889–1945) mit dem SS Reichsführer Heinrich Himmler (links) und dessen Stellvertreter Reinhard Heydrich, dem Chef des Reichssicherheitshauptamtes (rechts), im ersten Burghof des Hradschin. (3) Die Zeitung *Národní Politika* (Nationale Politik) berichtet, Hitler habe »Prag auf dem schnellsten Weg von Česká Lípa um 5 Uhr morgens erreicht.« (4) Vom Fenster der Burg aus inspiziert Hitler seinen neuen Besitz. Begeistert von der Mühelosigkeit, mit der er sein Ziel erreichte, und verblüfft von der Schönheit der Burg probierte er Prager Schinken und trank ein kleines Glas Pilsener Bier. (5) Hitler streicht einem kleinen Mädchen übers Haar, das ihm Blumen schenkt. (6) Eine Briefmarke des Protektorats mit einem berühmten Hitlerbild. (7) Deutsche Soldaten und Prager Deutsche säumen die kopfsteingepflasterten Straßen, als Hitler die Burg verläßt. Am Morgen des 16. März hatte Hitler einen Erlaß unterschrieben, durch den das »Protektorat Böhmen und Mähren« geschaffen wurde.

### Hitler à Prague

Le 15 mars 1939, Hitler prit un train pour Česká Lípa dans les Sudètes, et se rendit à Prague en voiture. (1) Une foule allemande enthousiaste salue Hitler qui apparaît à l'une des fenêtres du château. (2) Adolf Hitler (1889–1945) dans l'avant-cour du château, accompagné du *SS Reichsführer* Heinrich Himmler (à gauche) et de son représentant, Reinhard Heydrich, responsable des services de sécurité nazis (à droite). (3) Le quotidien *Národní Politika* (Affaires politiques nationales) annonce que Hitler «est arrivé à Prague venant de Česká Lípa à 17 h». (4) Hitler observe sa nouvelle conquête d'une fenêtre du château. Mis de bonne humeur par la facilité de la tâche et émerveillé par les splendeurs du château, il goûta au jambon de Prague et but un petit verre de bière de Pilsen. (5) Hitler remerciant une petite fille qui lui tend des fleurs. (6) Timbre du Protectorat réalisé à partir de la célèbre photographie de Hitler au Hradčany. (7) Hitler quitte le château entre des haies de soldats allemands et d'Allemands de Prague. Au matin du 16 mars, un décret signé de sa main avait proclamé le «Protectorat de Bohême et Moravie».

Dnes v listě:

Politik odbírá se blanenka a Foltouraské Rock

Chvistací mrsobá.

Objasněný obraz národnických politik.

Ěko so vál nejlídilejšíba selstve na sobě.

# NÁRODNÍ POLITIKA

V Praze ve čtvrtek 16. března 1939.

50 hal.

O politických jars a málib.

Veborová vlisch nemocze.

Zúcbovací potvorémí nebezpečen.

Přiravry na olymnitáde ber 1949 zdal ozdravel.

Ročník LVII. Číslo 75.D

Telefony ★ 293-51.

## Říšský kancléř Adolf Hitler v Praze

V jeho průvodu ministr zahraničí šl. Ribbentrop, vůdce ochranných oddílů Himmler, vrchní velitel německé branné moci Keitel a tiskový náčelník dr. Dietrich.

3

6

7

### The Arrival of the Reichsprotektor

The Reichsprotektor, with his seat in Prague, became Hitler's representative, guaranteeing that the Czech government acted in conformity with German interests. He could veto Czech legislation and dismiss Czech ministers. On 5 April 1939, at the main station in Prague, bands played "Deutschland Über Alles" and the "Horst Wessel Song," the anthem of the Nazi Party, to welcome the new Reichsprotektor Konstantin von Neurath (1873–1956). The crowds were sparse, with only Germans and a few Czech Fascists showing any enthusiasm as von Neurath's car passed. Accompanied by a motorized guard of honor, von Neurath was driven to watch a military parade in Wenceslas Square. It was a show of military force, with tanks and heavy guns grinding through the streets while bombers droned through the sky above the National Museum. (1) Neurath welcomed by Hácha. (2, 3) The German military parade in Wenceslas Square to mark von Neurath's arrival in the city.

### Die Ankunft des Reichsprotektors

Der Reichsprotektor mit Sitz in Prag war als Hitlers Stellvertreter dafür verantwortlich, daß die tschechische Regierung in Übereinstimmung mit den deutschen Interessen handelte. Er besaß Vetorecht in Fragen der tschechischen Gesetzgebung und konnte tschechische Minister entlassen. Zur Begrüßung des neuen Reichsprotektors Konstantin von Neurath (1873–1956) spielten am 5. April 1939 auf dem Prager Hauptbahnhof Blaskapellen das Deutschland- und das Horst-Wessel-Lied, die Hymne der NSDAP. Nur wenige Menschen – hauptsächlich Deutsche und ein paar tschechische Faschisten – waren gekommen, um von Neuraths vorbeifahrendem Wagen zuzujubeln. In Begleitung einer Ehrengarde fuhr von Neurath auf den Wenzelsplatz, wo er eine Militärparade abnahm. Es war eine Demonstration militärischer Stärke, bei der Panzer und schwere Waffen durch die Straßen zogen und Bomber am Himmel über dem Nationalmuseum dröhnten. (1) Begrüßung Neuraths durch Hácha. (2, 3) Eine deutsche Militärparade spielt auf dem Wenzelsplatz zu Ehren der Ankunft von Neuraths in der Stadt.

### L'arrivée du Protecteur du Reich

Le *Reichsprotektor*, siégeant à Prague, était le représentant de Hitler et garantissait que le gouvernement tchèque agisse en conformité avec les intérêts allemands. Il pouvait opposer son veto aux lois tchèques et démettre des ministres. Le 5 avril 1939, devant la gare principale de Prague, des orchestres militaires interprétèrent « Deutschland über alles » et le « Horst Wessel Lied », hymne du parti nazi, pour accueillir le nouveau Reichsprotektor, Konstantin von Neurath (1873–1956). La foule était peu nombreuse, uniquement composée d'Allemands et de quelques fascistes tchèques qui saluèrent la voiture de Neurath. Accompagné d'une garde d'honneur motorisée, celui-ci passa les troupes en revue sur la place Vencelas. C'était une démonstration de force militaire, avec déploiement de chars et d'armes lourdes et survol de la ville par des bombardiers. (1) Hácha salue Neurath. (2, 3) Parade militaire allemande place Vencelas à l'occasion de l'arrivée du *Reichsprotektor*.

3

## Prague Becomes German

(1) All car registration plates bore the stamp of the Protectorate. (2) A billboard announcing that from 26 March 1939 traffic will change to right-hand drive. (3) This magazine cover graphically reminds drivers of the new regulations by placing arrows for car- and tram-drivers on the right side of the road. (4) In front of the Powder Gate a Czech policeman supervises the new traffic system. The poster reads: "Prague is now driving on the right." It took only 11 days to implement the change. On 11 July Karl Hermann Frank issued a decree ordering the use of German and Czech on all official correspondence. The German language was to appear first and was to take legal precedence in the event of a disputed translation. Certain words, including "Führer" and "Reichsprotektor" could appear only in German form. (5, 7) Bilingual roadsigns, railway-station names and street-signs. (6) A restaurant on Strossmayer Square advertising in German and Czech a "one dish" menu. (8) A sign on Národní třída advertising the "White Horse" – a German beer cellar offering music, dancing and "good cheer."

## Prag wird deutsch

(1) Alle Nummernschilder wurden mit einer Plakette des Protektorats gestempelt. (2) Ein Schild weist darauf hin, daß ab dem 26. März 1939 der Rechtsverkehr gilt. (3) Das Titelblatt einer Zeitschrift erinnerte die Verkehrsteilnehmer mit Pfeilen an die neuen Bestimmungen des Rechtsverkehrs. (4) Vor dem Pulverturm regelt ein tschechischer Polizist den Verkehr nach den neuen Bestimmungen. Auf dem Plakat ist zu lesen: »In Prag wird rechts gefahren.« – Die Umstellung wurde nach nur 11 Tagen eingeführt. Am 11. Juli veröffentlichte Karl Hermann Frank einen Erlaß, der den Gebrauch der deutschen und der tschechischen Sprache im offiziellen Schriftverkehr regelte. Die deutsche Sprache sollte als erste verwendet werden und hatte in Rechtsfällen bei unterschiedlichen Übersetzungen Priorität. Einige Worte wie »Führer« und »Reichsprotektor« gab es nur auf deutsch. (5, 7) Zweisprachige Verkehrszeichen, Bahnhofsnamen und Straßenschilder. (6) Ein Restaurant auf dem Strossmayer-Platz wirbt in deutscher und in tschechischer Sprache für ein Eintopfgericht. (8) Ein Werbeschild auf der Národní třída lädt in das »Weiße Rössel« ein, einen deutschen Bierkeller mit Musik, Tanz und Stimmung.

## La germanisation de Prague

(1) Toutes les plaques minéralogiques des voitures durent porter le timbre du Protectorat. (2) Affiche annonçant qu'à partir du 26 mars 1939, le sens de la circulation passera de gauche à droite. (3) La couverture de magazine rappelle aux conducteurs la nouvelle réglementation au moyen de flèches peintes sur la chaussée. (4) Devant la Porte des poudres, un policier tchèque supervise la nouvelle circulation. L'affiche annonce : « Prague roule maintenant à droite. » Il ne fallut que 11 jours aux Allemands pour la mettre en œuvre. Le 11 juillet, Karl Hermann Frank signa un décret ordonnant l'usage de l'allemand et du tchèque dans toutes les correspondances officielles. La langue allemande devait occuper la première place, et faisait seule foi en cas de contestation de la traduction. Certains termes, comme *Führer* ou *Reichsprotektor* ne devaient apparaître que sous leur forme allemande. (5, 7) Panneaux signalétiques en deux langues. (6) Un restaurant de la place Strossmayer annonce en allemand et en tchèque son menu « plat unique ». (8) *Národní třída*, panneau publicitaire pour le « Cheval blanc », une brasserie allemande qui proposait de la musique, de la danse et « une joyeuse atmosphère ».

5

6

7

8

# Bekanntmachung!

Trotz wiederholter ernster Warnungen versucht seit einiger Zeit eine Gruppe tschechischer Intellektueller in Zusammenarbeit mit Emigranten= kreisen im Ausland durch kleine oder größere Widerstandsakte die Ruhe und Ordnung im Protektorat Böhmen und Mähren zu stören. Es konnte dabei festgestellt werden, daß sich Rädelsführer dieser Widerstandsakte besonders auch in den tschechischen Hochschulen befinden.

Da sich am 28. Oktober und am 15. November diese Elemente hin= reißen ließen, gegen einzelne Deutsche tätlich vorzugehen, wurden

die tschechischen Hochschulen

auf die Dauer von drei Jahren geschlossen,

neun Täter erschossen

und

eine größere Anzahl Beteiligter in Haft genommen.

Prag, den 17. November 1939.

Der Reichsprotektor in Böhmen und Mähren
gez. Freiherr von Neurath.

Ačkoliv byl
doby skupir
skými kruhy
rušiti klid
Při tom byl
zvláště také
Ježto tyto
strhnouti k

byly

devě

a vět

# yhláška!

ně vážně varováno, pokouší se od nějaké

h intelektuálů ve spolupráci s emigrant-

, menšími nebo většími akcemi odporu

k v Protektorátu Böhmen und Mähren.

o, že původci těchto aktů odporu jsou

ých vysokých školách.

se ve dnech 28. října a 15. listopadu

činům proti jednotlivým Němcům,

soké školy na dobu tři roků uzavřeny,

elů bylo zastřeleno

účastníků vzat do vazby.

**V Praze, dne 17. listopadu 1939.**

### Crushing the Czech Intelligentsia

(1) A poster dated 17 November 1939 announcing the closing of Czech universities and draconian anti-student measures. A peaceful demonstration by Czech students on 28 October ended in the death of Jan Opletal. Frank ordered heavy reprisals – nine student leaders were shot and 1200 sent to Oranienburg concentration camp. (2) Karl Hermann Frank (1898–1946) was promoted to the rank of SS Gruppenführer on 30 October.

### Unterdrückung der tschechischen Intelligenzia

(1) Auf einem Plakat vom 17. November 1939 werden die Schließung der tschechischen Universitäten und drakonische Maßnahmen gegen Studenten verkündet. Eine friedliche Demonstration tschechischer Studenten am 28. Oktober endete mit dem Tod von Jan Opletal. Frank ordnete schwere Vergeltungsmaßnahmen an – 9 Studentenführer wurden erschossen, 1.200 Studenten in das Konzentrationslager Oranienburg geschickt. (2) Am 30. Oktober wurde Karl Hermann Frank (1898–1946) in den Stand eines SS Gruppenführers befördert.

### La répression de l'intelligentsia tchèque

(1) Affiche datée du 17 novembre 1939, annonçant la fermeture des universités tchèques et la prise de mesures draconiennes contre les étudiants. Une manifestation pacifique de ceux-ci, le 28 octobre, s'acheva par la mort de Jan Opletal. Frank ordonna des représailles sanglantes : 9 responsables étudiants furent fusillés et 1 200 envoyés au camp de concentration d'Oranienburg. (2) Karl Hermann Frank (1898–1946) fut promu au rang de *SS Gruppenführer* (lieutenant-général) le 30 octobre.

## Hitler's Birthday

Czechs stayed away from Hitler's birthday parade on 20 April 1940. Two years later, when the Nazi grip on the country had tightened, the Hácha government tried to appease Hitler by giving him a hospital train to carry wounded soldiers as a birthday present. (1) The Černín Palace, offices of the Reichsprotektor's administration. (2) A commemorative sheet featuring Hradčany with a swastika flag and the flag of the Protectorate. (3) A Nazi parade in Wenceslas Square. (4) The heading "Towards sincere co-operation" on another commemorative sheet, issued on Hitler's 50th birthday. (5) The Municipal House was often used for exhibitions, like this one of Nazi architecture advertised above the main entrance. (6) Celetná festooned with swastikas. (7) The "Deutsches Haus" – the Nazi social and cultural center on Na Příkopě. Next door, swastikas hang over the Prague branch of the Thomas Cook travel agency, which was condemned by the Germans as a front for Anglo-French subversion. (8) Hitler's birthday celebrations in the Old Town Square in front of the Týn Church.

## Hitlers Geburtstag

Die Tschechen boykottierten die Paraden zu Hitlers Geburtstag am 20. April 1940. Zwei Jahre später, als der Druck der Nazis auf die Stadt gewachsen war, versuchte die Regierung Hácha, Hitler gnädig zu stimmen und schenkte ihm zum Geburtstag einen Hospitalzug für den Transport verwundeter Soldaten. (1) Der Czernin-Palast, Sitz des Reichsprotektors. (2) Ein Ersttagsbrief mit dem Hradschin, an dessen Spitze die Hakenkreuzflagge und die Flagge des Protektorats flattert. (3) Eine Naziparade auf dem Wenzelsplatz. (4) Die Überschrift »In aufrichtiger Mitarbeit« auf einem Ersttagsbrief, der anläßlich Hitlers 50. Geburtstag herausgegeben wurde. (5) Im Repräsentationshaus fanden oft Kulturveranstaltungen statt; das Plakat über dem Haupteingang wirbt für eine Ausstellung der Nazi-Architektur. (6) Die mit Hakenkreuzen geschmückte Celetná. (7) Das soziale und kulturelle Zentrum der Deutschen befand sich im »Deutschen Haus« auf der Straße Na Příkopě. Nebenan flatterten Hakenkreuzflaggen über der Reiseagentur Thomas Cook, die von den Nazis als Zentrum anglo-französischer subversiver Aktivitäten verdammt wurde. (8) Feiern zu Hitlers Geburtstag auf dem Altstädter Ring vor der Teynkirche.

## L'anniversaire de Hitler

Les Tchèques restèrent à l'écart de la parade donnée à l'occasion de l'anniversaire du dictateur le 20 avril 1940. Deux ans plus tard, lorsque la mainmise nazie se fut renforcée, le gouvernement Hácha essaya de s'attirer les bonnes grâces de Hitler en lui offrant pour son anniversaire un train de transport de blessés. (1) Le palais Černín, bureaux du *Reichsprotektor*. (2) Feuille commémorative du Hradčany surmonté du drapeau à la croix gammée. (3) Parade nazie place Venceslas. (4) Sous l'intitulé « Vers une coopération sincère », une autre feuille commémorative, éditée à l'occasion du cinquantième anniversaire de Hitler. (5) La Maison municipale servait souvent à des expositions, comme celle-ci consacrée à l'architecture nazie et annoncée au-dessus de l'entrée du bâtiment. (6) La Celetná décorée de croix gammées. (7) « La Maison allemande », centre culturel national-socialiste, rue Na Příkopě. L'agence des Wagons-Lits Cook avait été fermée par les Allemands qui l'accusaient d'être un nid d'espions franco-anglais. (8) Célébration de l'anniversaire d'Hitler sur la place de la Vieille ville, devant l'église Notre-Dame de Týn.

5

6

7

8

## Propaganda Minister Joseph Goebbels Visits Prague

Joseph Goebbels (1) visited Prague in 1940 and was dazzled by it. "I have fallen totally in love with this city. It exudes the German spirit and must become German again one day," he wrote in his diary. His visit to the Barrandov Film Studios combined business with pleasure. (2) Czech star Lída Baarová had a notorious pre-war affair with Goebbels. The dangerous liaison was brought to an end by Hitler himself (after Magda, Goebbels' wife, had complained bitterly to him): Hitler decided that his minister was a family man and should remain so. Goebbels, "the family man," killed his six children and committed suicide with his wife on 30 April 1945. (3) Goebbels inspecting plans for the expansion of the Barrandov studios. He enlarged the studio complex, building the largest sound stage in Europe.

## Propagandaminister Joseph Goebbels besucht Prag

Joseph Goebbels (1) besuchte Prag 1940 und war von der Stadt bezaubert. »Ich habe mich total in diese Stadt verliebt. Sie atmet den deutschen Geist und muß eines Tages wieder deutsch werden«, schrieb er in sein Tagebuch. Bei seinem Besuch der Barrandov-Filmstudios verband er das Angenehme mit dem Nützlichen. (2) Der tschechische Filmstar Lída Baarová hatte vor dem Krieg eine allgemein bekannte Affäre mit Goebbels. Hitler selbst beendete diese gefährliche Liebschaft (nachdem Goebbels Frau Magda sich bitter bei ihm beschwert hatte) und entschied, daß sein Minister ein Familienvater war und es auch bleiben sollte. Goebbels, der »Familienvater«, tötete am 30. April 1945 seine sechs Kinder und nahm sich zusammen mit seiner Frau das Leben. (3) Goebbels begutachtet Pläne zum Ausbau der Barrandov-Studios. Er erweiterte den Studiokomplex und ließ die größte Tonfilmbühne Europas bauen.

## Goebbels, ministre de la propagande, visite Prague

Joseph Goebbels (1) se rendit à Prague en 1940 et en fut ébloui. «Je suis tombé totalement amoureux de cette ville. Elle exsude l'esprit allemand et doit redevenir allemande un jour», écrivit-il dans son journal. Sa visite au Théâtre national associait le travail au plaisir. (2) La liaison de Goebbels et de la star tchèque Lída Baarová était bien connue avant-guerre. Hitler y avait mis fin lui-même après que Magda, l'épouse de Goebbels, s'en fut amèrement plainte auprès de lui. Le dictateur décida que son ministre était un père de famille respectable et devait le rester. Goebbels «le bon père de famille» tua ses six enfants et se suicida avec sa femme le 30 avril 1945. (3) Goebbels supervisant les plans pour l'agrandissement des studios de Barrandov que les nazis contrôlaient aux deux tiers. Il fit construire le plus grand studio pour films sonores d'Europe.

2

3

### The SS City

The leading role of the SS in the Nazi "New Order" was constantly promoted through parades, propaganda campaigns and acts of terror against the population. The SS, with Heinrich Himmler and Reinhard Heydrich at the top and Frank as their tool, were constantly plotting to take over the wealthy Bohemia–Moravia and turn it into a model SS state, the springboard to total power in the Nazi's growing empire. Prague was to become the model SS city. (1) An SS guard battalion marching across the Charles Bridge. (2) Frank (second from right) attending a parade of SS recruits. (3) Newly-weds posing against a background of SS signs. (4, 5) Recruits of the *SS Totenkopf* (Death's-head) Infantry Regiment take an oath of allegiance to Hitler in the Old Town Square. (6) Frank takes the salute at a parade near the Old Town Square.

### Die Stadt der SS

Die führende Rolle der SS innerhalb der »neuen Ordnung« der Nazis wurde ununterbrochen durch Paraden, Propagandakampagnen und Terrorakte gegen die Bevölkerung unter Beweis gestellt. Die SS, mit Heinrich Himmler und Reinhard Heydrich an der Spitze und Frank als ihrem Vollstrecker, arbeitete beständig an Plänen, das reiche Böhmen und Mähren zu übernehmen und in einen SS-Modellstaat zu verwandeln, der zum Sprungbrett für das wachsende Imperium der Nazis werden sollte. Prag war darin als modellhafte SS-Stadt vorgesehen. (1) Ein Wachbatallion der SS marschiert über die Karlsbrücke. (2) Frank (der zweite von rechts) besucht eine Parade der SS-Rekruten. (3) Frischvermählte stellen sich für ein Foto in Pose. Im Hintergrund erkennt man SS-Zeichen. (4, 5). Rekruten der SS-Totenkopf-Infanteriebataillone schwören auf dem Altstädter Ring den Treueeid auf Hitler. (6) Frank nimmt in der Nähe des Altstädter Rings eine Parade ab.

### La ville SS

Le rôle pilote des SS dans le nouvel ordre nazi était sans cesse mis en avant dans des parades, des campagnes de propagande et des opérations visant à terroriser la population. Avec Heinrich Himmler et Reinhard Heydrich à leur tête et Frank comme marionnette, ils voulaient faire de la Bohême-Moravie un État-modèle SS, base de la conquête totale du pouvoir dans l'empire nazi en cours de constitution. Prague devait devenir la cité-modèle SS. (1) Un bataillon de gardes SS sur le pont Charles. (2) Frank (second à partir de la droite) assistant à une parade. (3) Nouveaux mariés et panneaux signalétiques SS. (4, 5) Les recrues du régiment d'infanterie *SS Totenkopf* (tête de mort) prêtent serment d'allégeance à Hitler sur la place de la Vieille ville. (6) Frank saluant lors du défilé près de la place de la Vieille ville.

3

4

5

6

## The New Ruler Arrives

On 27 September 1941 a more lethal ruler, SS Obergruppenführer and General of Police Reinhard Heydrich (1902–42), arrived in Prague. Within a month nearly 5000 suspects were arrested and over 400 death sentences passed. (1) Official portrait of the new Acting Reichsprotektor. (2) On 19 November President Hácha, in a symbolic gesture of subservience to Nazi Germany, presented Heydrich with seven keys to the city's treasure chamber, which contained the most precious possession of the Czech nation: the crown of St Wenceslas. Heydrich and Hácha looking at the Bohemian

## Die Ankunft des neuen Führers

Am 27. September 1941 kam ein neuer, todbringender Führer, der SS Obergruppenführer und Chef der Sicherheitspolizei Reinhard Heydrich (1902–1942) nach Prag. Innerhalb eines Monats wurden beinahe 5.000 Verdächtige verhaftet und über 400 Menschen hingerichtet. (1) Offizielles Porträt des neuen Stellvertretenden Reichsprotektors. (2) Am 19. November übergab Hácha in einer symbolischen Geste der Unterwerfung Heydrich die sieben Schlüssel zur Schatzkammer der Stadt, in der kostbarste Besitz des tschechischen Volkes aufbewahrt wurde: die Krone des Heiligen Wenzel. Heydrich und Hácha

## Le nouveau souverain

Le 27 septembre 1941, un chef plus redoutable encore prit ses fonctions à Prague : le *SS Obergruppenführer* et général de la police Reinhard Heydrich (1902–1942). En l'espace d'un mois, 5000 suspects furent arrêtés et 400 personnes exécutées. (1) Portrait officiel du nouveau *Reichsprotektor*, plusieurs fois médaillé. (2) Le 19 novembre, Emil Hácha, dans un geste symbolique de soumission à l'Allemagne nazie, remit à Heydrich les sept clés de la chambre du trésor de la ville qui contenait le bien le plus précieux de la nation tchèque : la couronne de saint Venceslas. Heydrich et Hácha regardant les joyaux de

crown jewels. (3) SS Reichsführer Heinrich Himmler arriving at Hradčany on 29 October 1941. He and his protégé Heydrich were plotting to divert Czech arms production, which amounted to one third of the total arms production of occupied Europe, to serve the needs of the Waffen SS. (4) Himmler in the courtyard of Hradčany shaking hands with one of the officers. Heydrich stands behind him. (5) Heydrich attending a performance in the German Opera House. (6) Frank (left) and Heydrich (right) giving the Nazi salute in the Hradčany courtyard.

betrachten die Kronjuwelen. (3) SS Reichsführer Heinrich Himmler besuchte am 29. Oktober 1941 den Hradschin. Um dem Bedarf der Waffen-SS zu entsprechen, planten er und sein Protegé Heydrich eine Ausweitung der tschechischen Rüstungsindustrie, die schon ein Drittel der gesamten Waffen im besetzten Europa produzierte. (4) Himmler bei der Begrüßung einiger Offiziere im Hradschin. Heydrich steht hinter ihm. (5) Heydrich besucht eine Aufführung in der Deutschen Oper. (6) Frank (links) und Heydrich (rechts) heben auf dem Hradschin die Hand zum Nazigruß.

la couronne de Bohême. (3) Le *SS Reichsführer* Heinrich Himmler arrive au Hradčany le 29 octobre 1941. Lui et son protégé Heydrich complotaient de détourner la production tchèque d'armement, qui représentait un tiers du total de la production de l'Europe occupée, au bénéfice du *Waffen SS*. (4) Himmler dans la cour du château, serrant la main d'un officier. Derrière lui, Heydrich. (5) Heydrich assistant à une représentation à l'Opéra allemand. (6) Frank (à gauche) et Heydrich (à droite) faisant le salut nazi dans la cour du Hradčany.

5

6

## Propaganda Campaigns

The Czechs participated in the "V" campaign mounted by the BBC in January 1941, which called for the peoples of the occupied countries to paint the "V" for victory sign on walls and buildings under cover of the blackout. The campaign was so successful throughout Europe that the Germans cunningly adopted it as their own. In the summer of 1941 Prague was suddenly decorated with huge "V" signs and banners proclaiming faith in German victory. (1) A propaganda poster, "Germany will liberate Europe from Jewish–Bolshevik terror." (2) Prague trams were decorated with the "V" sign. (3) Under the "V" sign, suspended from a balcony of the Municipal House, Prague citizens queuing for their cigarette rations. (4) A huge "V" in the Old Town Square. (5) "The Soviet Paradise" anti-Soviet propaganda exhibition staged in the winter of 1941. (6) The *Winterhilfe* (Winter Help) campaign rally in the Old Town Square to appeal for warm clothing for German soldiers fighting in the East. Germany attacked the Soviet Union in June 1941.

## Propagandakampagnen

Die Tschechen beteiligten sich an dem von der BBC im Januar 1941 initiierten Unternehmen »V«, das die Bevölkerung der besetzten Länder aufforderte, im Schutz der Verdunkelungen das Siegeszeichen V auf alle Häuser und Mauern zu malen. Die Kampagne war überall in Europa so erfolgreich, daß die Nazis sie schließlich geschickt für ihre eigene Sache nutzten. Im Sommer 1941 war Prag plötzlich mit großen »V«-Zeichen und Standarten geschmückt, die das Vertrauen in den deutschen Sieg symbolisieren sollten. (1) Ein Propagandaplakat »Deutschland befreit Europa vom jüdisch-bolschewistischen Terror«. (2) Prags Straßenbahnen wurden mit dem »V«-Zeichen geschmückt. (3) Unter dem »V«-Zeichen, das von dem Balkon des Repräsentationshauses entrollt worden ist, stehen Prager Bürger für Zigaretten an. (4) Ein großes »V« auf dem Altstädter Ring. (5) »Das Sowjet-Paradies« – eine antisowjetische Propaganda-ausstellung im Winter 1941. (6) Auf dem Altstädter Ring bittet die Aktion »Winterhilfe« um Kleiderspenden für deutsche Soldaten an der Ostfront. Im Juni 1941 marschierten die Deutschen in der Sowjetunion ein.

## Les campagnes de propagande

Les Tchèques participèrent à la campagne du « V » organisée par la BBC en janvier 1941, qui demandait aux peuples des pays occupés de peindre le signe du V de la victoire sur les immeubles pendant le black-out. La campagne connut un tel succès en Europe que les Allemands la détournèrent. Pendant l'été 1941, Prague fut brusquement décorée d'immenses « V » proclamant la foi dans la victoire allemande. Effacer, modifier ou ridiculiser ce signe était un délit. Le cas échéant, tout le voisinage était puni d'une amende collective et de la confiscation des postes de radio. (1) Affiche de propagande : « L'Allemagne libérera l'Europe de la terreur judéo-bolchevique. » (2) Les trams de Prague décorés du « V » de la victoire allemande. (3) Sous le symbole du « V » dominant un balcon de la Maison municipale, les citoyens de Prague font la queue pour leur ration de cigarettes. (4) Un énorme « V » peint sur la place de la Vieille ville. (5) « Le paradis soviétique », exposition de propagande anti-soviétique organisée en hiver 1941. (6) Rassemblement pour la campagne de la *Winterhilfe* (Secours d'hiver) place de la Vieille ville, afin de réunir des vêtements chauds pour les soldats allemands combattant sur le front de l'Est. L'Allemagne attaqua l'Union soviétique en juin 1941.

5

6

## The Terror

(1) The Petschek Palace, headquarters of the Prague Gestapo, on Bredauer Gasse (today Political Prisoners' Street), where people were tortured, often to death. (2) SS Standartenführer Dr Hans Ulrich Geschke, head of the Prague Gestapo in the first half of the war. (3) Frank and his henchmen walking through the streets of Prague. (4) Frank and Heydrich (right) planning their reign of terror. (5) The execution chamber at the Pankrác prison and the guillotine used by the Nazis. People were hanged or beheaded. The relatives of the condemned had to pay for the execution and for the cost of public posters announcing the sentence. They were allowed to pay in instalments. In 1943– 45, 920 men and 155 women were executed at Pankrác. (6) A victim of the Prague Gestapo. Over 2000 men were executed by firing squad at Kobylisy in the evenings between 6.30 and 9.00. They were brought from the Pankrác prison and shot in groups of ten. (7) Horst Böhme and Frank (center) inspecting a clandestine printing press uncovered by the Prague Gestapo.

## Der Terror

(1) Das Petschek-Haus, Hauptquartier der Prager Gestapo, auf der Bredauer Gasse (heute Straße der Politischen Gefangenen), wo Menschen – oft zu Tode – gequält wurden. (2) SS Standartenführer Dr. Hans Ulrich Geschke, der in der ersten Hälfte des Krieges Kommandant der Prager Gestapo war. (3) Frank und seine Gefolgsleute auf den Straßen von Prag. (4) Frank und Heydrich (rechts) planen ihr Terrorregime. (5) Der Hinrichtungsraum im Pankratius-Gefängnis mit der Guillotine der Nazis. Die Opfer wurden gehängt oder enthauptet. Die Angehörigen der Verurteilten mußten für die Hinrichtung und deren öffentliche Bekanntmachung bezahlen; Ratenzahlung war möglich. Zwischen 1943 und 1945 wurden 920 Männer und 155 Frauen im Pankratius-Gefängnis hingerichtet. (6) Ein Opfer der Prager Gestapo. Über 2.000 Männer wurden insgesamt von Erschießungskommandos in Kobylisy abends, zwischen 18.30 und 21.00 Uhr, getötet. Sie wurden vom Pankratius-Gefängnis hierher gebracht und in Gruppen zu zehn Mann erschossen. (7) Horst Böhme und Frank (Mitte) inspizieren eine verbotene Druckerpresse, die von der Gestapo entdeckt worden war.

## La terreur

(1) Le palais Petschek, siège de la Gestapo à Prague, rue Bredauer (aujourd'hui, rue des Prisonniers politiques), où les gens étaient torturés, souvent à mort. (2) Le *SS Standartenführer* (colonel) Doktor Hans Ulrich Geschke, responsable de la Gestapo pragoise pendant la première moitié de la guerre. (3) Frank et ses sbires se promenant dans les rues de Prague. (4) Frank et Heydrich (à droite) travaillant à l'organisation de la terreur. (5) La salle des exécutions à la prison de Pankrác et la guillotine alors utilisée. La lame de l'engin pesait 65 kg. Les condamnés étaient pendus ou décapités. De 1943 à 1945, 920 hommes et 155 femmes furent exécutés à Pankrác. Leurs parents devaient payer pour leur exécution et le coût des affiches annonçant la sentence. La dette pouvait se régler en plusieurs fois. (6) Une victime de la Gestapo. Plus de 2 000 hommes furent fusillés à Kobylisy, le soir de 18 h 30 à 21 h. Ils étaient amenés de la prison de Pankrác et exécutés par groupes de dix. (7) Horst Böhme et Frank (au centre) inspectant une imprimerie clandestine découverte par la Gestapo.

5

6

7

231

## Anti-Jewish Legislation

Before the war almost 50 per cent of Czech Jews lived in Prague. The new government was under great pressure from Germany to introduce anti-Jewish legislation on the pattern of the Nazi Nuremberg Laws. At first the Nazis attempted to stir up popular anti-Semitism with exhibitions, books and other campaigns. Then the Jews were robbed of their assets and excluded from the economic life of the country. Many were forced out of the best apartments and from 1 September 1940 they were ordered to wear a Yellow Star of David. They were not allowed to leave their local area. (1) As the sign in the window of this tram shows, Jews were not allowed to use trams or other public transport. (2) A sign in a library: "Jews excluded from the library." (3) A book cover: *About the Jews.* (4) An anti-Semitic publication, *Golem, the Scourge of the Czechs.* (5) A poster for the anti-Semitic film *Jud Süss*, shot partially in the Barrandov Film Studios. (6) An anti-Semitic newspaper, *The Aryan War*, which reports the story of a love-affair with a Jewish woman and mentions that from 13 March 1942 intimate relationships between Jews and non-Jews were forbidden by law. (7) A sign proclaims: "No entry for Jews."

## Antijüdische Gesetze

Vor dem Krieg lebten fast 50 Prozent aller tschechischen Juden in Prag. Die neue Regierung stand unter starkem Druck aus Deutschland, das die Einführung antijüdischer Verordnungen im Geist der Nürnberger Rassengesetze forderte. Anfänglich versuchten die Nazis durch Ausstellungen, Bücher und andere Kampagnen, eine antijüdische Stimmung zu schüren. Dann beraubte man die Juden ihres Vermögens und schloß sie vom wirtschaftlichen Leben im Lande aus. Die besseren Wohnungen mußten sie räumen, und seit dem 1. September 1940 war das Tragen des gelben Davidsterns Pflicht. Auch durften sie ihre unmittelbare Umgebung nicht verlassen. (1) Eine Hinweistafel im Fenster einer Straßenbahn, die besagt, daß Juden von der Benutzung der öffentlichen Transportmittel ausgeschlossen waren. (2) Eine Tafel in einer öffentlichen Bücherei mit der Aufschrift: »Juden sind aus dieser Bücherei ausgeschlossen«. (3) Ein Buch mit dem Titel: *Über die Juden.* (4) Die antisemitische Publikation: *Golem, die Geißel der Tschechen.* (5) Ein Plakat für den antisemitischen Film *Jud Süss*, der teilweise in den Barrandov-Studios gedreht wurde. (6) Eine antisemitische Zeitung, *Der arische Krieg*, die über eine Liebesaffäre mit einer jüdischen Frau berichtet und bekannt gibt, daß ab dem 13. März 1942 intime Beziehungen zwischen Juden und Nicht-Juden gesetzlich verboten waren. (7) Ein Schild mit der Aufschrift »Juden nicht zugänglich«.

## La législation antisémite

Avant la guerre, presque 50 pour cent des Juifs tchèques vivaient à Prague. Le nouveau gouvernement était sous forte pression allemande pour introduire une nouvelle législation antisémite sur le modèle des lois nazies de Nuremberg. Au début, les nazis tentèrent de nourrir un antisémitisme populaire par des expositions, des livres et diverses campagnes. Puis les Juifs furent dépouillés de leurs biens et exclus de la vie économique du pays. Beaucoup furent expulsés de leurs appartements et, à partir du 1er septembre 1940, tous durent porter l'étoile jaune. Il leur était interdit de quitter leur quartier. (1) Comme le montre le placard sur la fenêtre du tram, les Juifs n'avaient pas le droit d'utiliser les transports publics. (2) Panneau dans une bibliothèque « Interdit aux Juifs. » (3) Couverture de livre : *Les Juifs.* (4) Publication antisémite : *Le Golem, le fléau des Tchèques.* (5) Affiche du film antisémite *Le Juif Süss*, tourné en partie aux studios de Barrandov. (6) Journal antisémite, *La Guerre aryenne*, qui raconte une relation amoureuse avec une femme juive et rappelle qu'à partir du 13 mars 1942 toutes relations entre Juifs en non-Juifs sont interdites par la loi. (7) « Entrée interdite aux Juifs. »

3

4

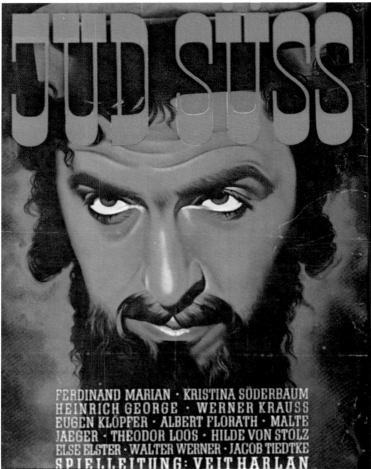

5

6

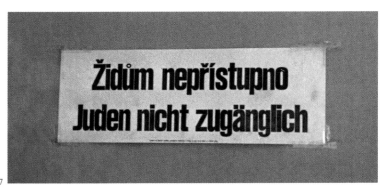

7

## Confiscation of Property and Deportation

In November 1941, in the fortress town of Terezín (64km north of Prague), Heydrich set up a transit camp for all Czech Jews. From here Jewish men, women and children were sent to death camps in occupied Poland. Their property, left behind, was redistributed to Germans. (1–6) Forty-five warehouses in the city were stacked with confiscated goods. Religious objects were to form the basis of a museum of the extinct Jewish race after the Final Solution had been concluded. (7) The decree of 1 September 1941 required Jews to wear a Yellow Star of David sewn on their clothes. (8) Jews were forced to register for deportation to the new ghetto established by the Nazis at Terezín. (9) Bubny, from where Prague Jews were deported to the Terezín ghetto. Before being put on the trains they were assembled in a fenced-off area with a few shabby huts at the Trade Fair Grounds near Stromovka Park. Then the groups were marched to nearby Bubny station. Of 39,395 Jews deported from Prague to Terezín, 31,709 were murdered in extermination camps. Of the 92,199 Jews who had lived in Bohemia and Moravia in 1941, only 14,045 survived the war.

## Konfiszierung des Eigentums und Deportation

Im November 1941 richtete Heydrich in dem Garnisonsort Theresienstadt (64 km nördlich von Prag) ein Durchgangslager für alle tschechischen Juden ein. Von hier aus wurden jüdische Männer, Frauen und Kinder in die Todeslager im besetzten Polen deportiert. Das Eigentum der Juden, das sie zurücklassen muß-ten, wurde unter den Deutschen verteilt. (1– 6) In 45 Waren-häusern der Stadt waren konfiszierte Güter aufgestapelt. Nach der »Endlösung« sollten religiöse Objekte den Grundstock für ein Museum über die ausgerottete jüdische Rasse bilden. (7) Ein Dekret vom 1. September 1941 forderte die Juden auf, den gel-ben Davidstern an ihre Kleidung nähen. (8) Die Juden wurden gezwungen, sich für die Deportation in das neue Ghetto, das die Nazis in Theresienstadt eingerichtet hatten, registrieren zu las-sen. (9) Von Bubny wurden die Juden in das Ghetto Theresien-stadt abtransportiert. In ein paar schäbigen Hütten innerhalb eines abgezäunten Gebiets auf dem Messegelände nahe des Stromovka-Parkes mußten sie auf die Ankunft der Züge warten. Dann wurde die Gruppe zur benachbarten Bubny-Station geführt. Von 39.395 Juden, die von Prag nach Theresienstadt deportiert wurden, kamen 31.709 in den Konzentrationslagern ums Leben. Nur 14.045 der 92.199 Juden, die 1941 in Böhmen und Mähren gewohnt hatten, überlebten den Krieg.

## Les biens confisqués et la déportation

En novembre 1941, Reinhard Heydrich créa un camp de transit pour les Juifs tchèques dans la ville fortifiée de Terezín (à 64 km au nord de Prague). De là, ils étaient envoyés dans les camps de la mort installés en Pologne occupée. (1– 6) Quarante-cinq entrepôts furent bourrés des biens confisqués. Objets de culte devaient former le noyau d'un musée de la race juive, une fois celle-ci annihilée par la politique de la solution finale. (7) Décret du 7 septembre 1941 obligeant les Juifs à porter une étoile jaune cousue sur leurs vêtements. (8) Les Juifs étaient obligés de faire enregistrer leur déportation au nouveau ghetto de Terezín, aménagé par les nazis. (9) Prague-Bubny, d'où les Juifs tchèques étaient envoyés au ghetto de Terezin. Avant d'être expédiés en train, ils étaient rassemblés sur un terrain entouré de barrières sur le champ de foire du parc de Stromova. Puis les groupes se rendaient à pied à la gare de Bubny. Sur les 39 395 Juifs déportés de Prague à Terezin, 31 709 furent assassinés dans les camps d'extermination. Seuls 14 045 Juifs – sur les 92 199 vivant en Bohême et Moravie en 1940 – survécurent à la guerre.

7

8

9

235

## The Assassination of Heydrich

On the evening of 26 May 1942 Reinhard Heydrich inaugurated the Prague Music Weeks with a concert of his father Bruno Heydrich's chamber works. (1) Heydrich and his wife, Lina, entering the concert hall in the Wallenstein Palace. The next day, on his way to the Castle, Heydrich was attacked by two parachute agents sent by the Czech government-in-exile in London, Jan Kubiš and Jozef Gabčík. Gabčík's sten-gun failed, but Kubiš's impact bomb, designed by the English SOE (Special Operations Executive), fatally wounded the Acting Reichsprotektor. He died on 4 June from infected wounds. (2) A special edition of a Czech newspaper reports the attack on Heydrich, the proclamation of martial law and a reward of 10 million crowns for information leading to the capture of the assassins. (3) A Gestapo photograph of the bomb damage to Heydrich's car. (4) Heydrich's open Mercedes on the sharp corner in V Holešovičkách (in the suburbs of Libeň), where his driver had to slow down dramatically, offering a good target for the Czechoslovak soldiers.

## Die Ermordung Heydrichs

Am Abend des 26. Mai 1942 eröffnete Heydrich die Prager Musikwochen mit einem Konzert der Kammermusik seines Vaters Bruno Heydrich. (1) Heydrich und seine Frau Lina betreten die Konzerthalle im Wallenstein-Palais. Am nächsten Tag wurde Heydrich auf dem Weg zur Burg von Jan Kubiš und Jozef Gabčík, zwei Mitgliedern einer Fallschirmspringereinheit, die im Auftrag der Exilregierung in London handelten, überfallen. Gabčíks Maschinengewehr versagte, aber Kubiš' Handgranate aus der Werkstatt des englischen SOE (Special Operation Executive) verwundete den amtierenden Reichsprotektor schwer. Er starb am 4. Juni an einer Wundinfektion. (2) Eine Sonderausgabe einer tschechischen Zeitung berichtet über den Angriff auf Heydrich, die Verhängung des Kriegsrechts und eine Belohnung von 10 Millionen Kronen für Hinweise zur Ergreifung der Täter. (3) Ein von der Gestapo aufgenommenes Foto der Bombenschäden an Heydrichs Wagen. (4) Heydrichs offener Mercedes in der scharfen Kurve (in V Holešovičkách im Vorort Libeň), in der sein Fahrer die Geschwindigkeit erheblich reduzieren mußte und damit den tschechoslowakischen Soldaten ein gutes Ziel bot.

## L'assassinat d'Heydrich

Au soir du 26 mai 1942, Reinhard Heydrich assista au concert d'ouverture des Semaines musicales de Prague, composé d'œuvres de musique de chambre de son père, Bruno Heydrich. (1) Heydrich et son épouse Lina entrant dans la salle des concerts du Palais Wallenstein. Le lendemain, en se rendant à son château, Heydrich fut attaqué par deux parachutistes envoyés par le gouvernement tchèque en exil, Jan Kubiš et Jozef Gabčík. La mitraillette de Gabčík s'enraya, mais la bombe à impact de Kubiš conçue par les services secrets britanniques (SOE) blessa à mort le *Reichsprotektor* qui mourut le 4 juin de l'infection de ses blessures. (2) Édition spéciale d'un journal tchèque annonçant l'attentat contre Heydrich, la proclamation de la loi martiale et une récompense de 10 millions de couronnes pour toute information permettant la capture des assassins. (3) Photographie prise par la Gestapo de la voiture après l'attentat. (4) La Mercedes décapotable de Heydrich dans un virage de V Holešovičkách (banlieue de Libeň) qui avait obligé le chauffeur à ralentir fortement, facilitant du même coup l'attaque des agents tchécoslovaques.

2

3

4

## POPIS PACHATELŮ ATENTÁTU NA ZASTUPUJÍCÍHO ŘÍŠSKÉHO PROTEKTORA

## Manhunt and Terror

Late in the afternoon of 27 May Frank proclaimed a state of emergency and a curfew. Anyone who helped the attackers was to be executed along with his entire family. A massive search operation began: 21,000 men were involved in checking 36,000 houses. By 4 June, 157 people had been executed as a result of the reprisals, but the assassins had not been found and no information was forthcoming. (1) Gestapo-circulated photographs of objects left at the scene of the attack. The bicycle, coat and briefcases which Gabčík and Kubiš abandoned in a hurry when making their getaway were displayed in the windows of the Baťa store at the bottom of Wenceslas Square. (2) A further 10 million crowns were offered by Emil Hácha, who described Beneš as the number-one enemy of the Czech nation. (3) A poster announcing executions (the name, date of birth and death were given). (4) Registration document. (5) Kurt Daluege (1897–1946), head of the Ordnungspolizei (the Nazi uniformed police) and Heydrich's successor. (6) Following the assassination, everyone had to register their place of residence. People queuing outside a police station to register.

## Menschenjagd und Terror

Am späten Nachmittag des 27. Mai rief Frank den Notstand aus und verhängte eine Ausgangssperre. Jeder, der den Attentätern half, sollte mit seiner gesamten Familie exekutiert werden. Eine großangelegte Suchaktion begann: 21.000 Männer durchkämmten 36.000 Häuser. Bis zum 4. Juni waren in einer Vergeltungsaktion 157 Menschen hingerichtet worden, aber von den Attentätern fehlte jede Spur. (1) Die Gestapo veröffentlichte Gegenstände, die am Tatort gefunden worden waren. Das Fahrrad, der Mantel und die Aktenkoffer, die Gabčík und Kubiš auf der Flucht zurückgelassen hatten, wurden in den Fenstern des Baťa-Kaufhauses am unteren Ende des Wenzelsplatzes ausgestellt. (2) Emil Hácha, der Beneš als den größten Feind der tschechischen Nation bezeichnete, setzte weitere 10 Millionen Kronen aus. (3) Ein Plakat gibt Exekutionen bekannt (mit Angabe des Namens, des Geburts- und Todestages des Opfers). (4) Registrierungsdokument. (5) Kurt Daluege (1897–1946), Chef der Ordnungspolizei (der uniformierten Nazi-Polizei) und Heydrichs Nachfolger. (6) Nach dem Attentat mußte jeder Einwohner seinen Wohnsitz registrieren lassen. Hier stehen Menschen außerhalb einer Polizeistation zur Registrierung an.

## Chasse à l'homme et terreur

À la fin de l'après-midi du 27 mai, Frank proclama l'état d'urgence et un couvre-feu. Tous ceux qui aideraient les «terroristes» seraient exécutés avec toute leur famille. Une impressionnante chasse à l'homme commença: 21 000 hommes contrôlèrent 36 000 maisons. Le 4 juin, 157 personnes avaient déjà été exécutées en représailles, mais les assassins restaient introuvables. (1) La Gestapo fit diffuser des photographies d'objets abandonnés après l'attaque. La bicyclette, un manteau et des serviettes laissés, dans leur fuite par Gabčík et Kubiš, furent exposés dans les vitrines du magasin Baťa en bas de la place Venceslas. (2) 10 millions de couronnes supplémentaires furent offerts par Emil Hácha, qui qualifia Beneš d'ennemi public n°1 de la nation tchèque. (3) Affiche annonçant des exécutions, avec mention du nom, de la date de naissance et celle du décès. (4) Un document d'enregistrement. (5) Kurt Daluege (1897–1946) chef de l'*Ordnungspolizei* (la police nazie en uniforme) et successeur de Heydrich. (6) Après l'assassinat, tous les Pragois durent déclarer leur lieu de résidence. Queue devant un commissariat de police pour faire cette déclaration.

5

6

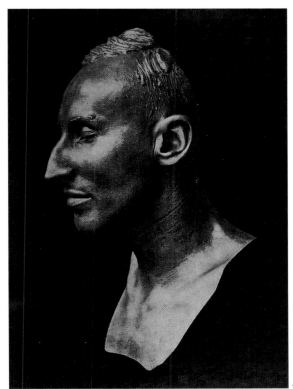

### Heydrich's Funeral and the Destruction of Lidice

Heydrich was the only leading Nazi to be assassinated by the resistance during the Second World War. On 7 June his coffin was paraded on a gun carriage across the Charles Bridge (1) and through the Old Town to the main station, where a special funeral train was waiting to take him on his last journey to Berlin. (3) The funeral cortège in Wenceslas Square on the way to the main railway station. (2) Heydrich was treated as a Nazi martyr. His death mask was unveiled at the corner of V Holešovičkách where the attack took place and was given a perpetual guard of honor. It was torn to pieces by the Czechs in 1945. On the evening of 9 June, shortly after Heydrich's funeral, Hitler ordered the total destruction of Lidice village near Prague, which the Gestapo had mistakenly implicated in the case. The SS shot 173 men on the spot; another 11 men who were not in the village that day were arrested and murdered soon afterwards, as were eight men and seven women already under arrest because they had relations serving with the army in exile in Britain; 203 women were deported to concentration camps; 105 children were separated from their parents: a few considered racially suitable for germanization were handed over to SS families and the rest were sent to camps. Only 153 women and 17 children returned after the war. The buildings were destroyed and the village levelled to the ground. (4) The bodies of the men of Lidice who were shot against a wall lined with mattresses to prevent ricochets.

### Heydrichs Begräbnis und die Zerstörung von Lidice

Heydrich war der einzige hochrangige Nazi, der von Widerstandskämpfern während des Zweiten Weltkriegs ermordet worden ist. Am 7. Juni wurde sein Sarg auf einem Waffentransporter über die Karlsbrücke (1) durch die Altstadt zum Hauptbahnhof gebracht, von wo er mit einem Sonderzug seine letzte Reise nach Berlin antrat. (3) Der Leichenzug vom Wenzelsplatz in Richtung Hauptbahnhof. (2) Heydrich wurde zum Märtyrer der Nazis stilisiert. Man stellte seine Totenmaske am Tatort an der Ecke von V Holešovičkách auf und postierte dort eine Ehrenwache. Die Maske wurde 1945 von den Tschechen zerschlagen. Am Abend des 9. Juni ordnete Hitler kurz nach der Beerdigung Heydrichs die völlige Zerstörung des Dörfchens Lidice in der Nähe von Prag an, das die Gestapo fälschlicherweise mit dem Fall in Verbindung gebracht hatte. Die SS erschoß 173 Männer direkt vor Ort; weitere 11 männliche Einwohner, die an diesem Tag nicht im Dorf waren, wurden später ermordet. Dasselbe Schicksal erlitten die acht Männer und sieben Frauen, die bereits im Gefängnis saßen, weil sie Verwandte in der Exilarmee in Großbritannien hatten. 203 Frauen wurden in Konzentrationslager deportiert und 105 Kinder von ihren Eltern getrennt; einige von ihnen, die als »rassisch geeignet« galten, kamen zur Arisierung in SS-Familien, der Rest kam in die Lager. Nur 153 Frauen und 17 Kinder kehrten nach dem Krieg zurück. Das Dorf wurde dem Erdboden gleichgemacht. (4) Die Leichen der Männer von Lidice, die man an einer mit Matrazen ausgepolsterten Mauer erschossen hatte, um Querschläger zu vermeiden.

### Les funérailles de Heydrich et la destruction de Lidice

Heydrich a été le seul haut responsable nazi assassiné pendant la Seconde Guerre mondiale. Le 7 juin, son cercueil fut transporté sur un affût de canon par le Pont Charles (1) et à travers la Vieille ville jusqu'à la gare principale où un train funéraire spécial l'attendait pour l'emporter à Berlin. (2) Heydrich fut érigé en martyr par les nazis. Son masque mortuaire fut posé à l'angle de V Holešovičkách où l'attentat avait eu lieu, gardé en permanence par une garde d'honneur. Il fut mis en pièces par les Tchèques en 1945. Le 9 juin au soir, peu après les funérailles de Heydrich, Hitler ordonna la destruction totale du village de Lidice, près de Prague, dont la Gestapo pensait, à tort, qu'il était impliqué dans l'attentat. Les SS abattirent 173 hommes, et 11 autres qui ne se trouvaient pas au village ce jour-là furent arrêtés et exécutés, ainsi que huit hommes et sept femmes déjà emprisonnés pour avoir des parents exilés en Grande-Bretagne. 203 femmes furent déportées en camp de concentration. Des 105 enfants séparés de leurs parents, quelques-uns furent jugés racialement aptes à la germanisation, et remis à des familles SS, et les autres envoyés dans des camps. Seuls 153 femmes et 17 enfants revinrent après la guerre. Les maisons furent détruites et le village rasé. (3) Le cortège funéraire sur la place Venceslas, en route vers la gare. (4) Corps des hommes de Lidice fusillés contre un mur garni de matelas pour éviter les ricochets.

4

242

### The Siege of Resslova and Demonstration of Loyalty

(2, 4) Jan Kubiš and Jozef Gabčík, a Czech and a Slovak, were the brave soldiers who assassinated Heydrich. On 18 June, betrayed by Karel Čurda, a fellow soldier whom they knew from England, Gabčík and Kubiš, along with five other Czech parachutists (who had been on sabotage missions), were attacked by the Waffen SS in the church of St Cyril and St Methodius in Resslova (1) where they were hiding. After a gun battle, they committed suicide with their last bullets rather than surrender. (3) Frank standing astride the bodies of Heydrich's assassins and their colleagues, which were identified for the Gestapo by the traitor Čurda. They were laid outside the church on the pavement, except for Kubiš, who was badly wounded when he fell into the hands of the Germans. He died on the way to hospital. (5) A Czech magazine cover showing the demonstration of loyalty to the Reich in Wenceslas Square on 3 July 1942 with Hácha's puppet government standing under the Wenceslas statue. 250,000 Czechs sang the National Anthem whilst giving the Nazi salute and pledging allegiance to the Third Reich.

### Die Belagerung in der Resslova und die Loyalitätskundgebungen

(2, 4) Der Tscheche Jan Kubiš und der Slowake Jozef Gabčík waren die tapferen Soldaten, die Heydrich ermordeten. Am 18. Juni wurden sie von ihrem Kameraden Karel Čurda, den sie aus England kannten, mit fünf weiteren Fallschirmspringern (die einen Sabotageauftrag erfüllt hatten) verraten. Die Waffen-SS stellte sie in der Kirche St. Kyrill und St. Method (1) in der Resslova, wo sie sich versteckt hielten. Nach einem Feuergefecht begingen sie Selbstmord mit den letzten Kugeln, um der Kapitulation zu entgehen. (3) Frank steht breitbeinig vor den Leichen der Heydrich-Attentäter und ihrer Kameraden, die von dem Verräter Čurda für die Gestapo identifiziert wurden. Mit Ausnahme von Kubiš, der den Nazis schwer verwundet in die Hände fiel, legte man ihre Leichen außerhalb der Kirche auf den Bürgersteig. Kubiš starb noch auf dem Weg ins Krankenhaus. (5) Das Titelbild einer tschechischen Zeitschrift zeigt die Loyalitätsbekundungen für das Reich auf dem Wenzelsplatz am 3. Juli 1942, anläßlich denen sich Háchas Marionettenregierung an der Wenzelsstatue aufgestellt hatte. 250.000 Tschechen sangen die Nationalhymne, hoben die Hand zum Nazigruß und gelobten ihre Treue zum Dritten Reich.

### Le siège de la rue Resslova et la manifestation de loyauté

(2, 4) Jan Kubiš et Josef Gabčik, un Tchèque et un Slovaque, furent aidés par les membres d'une résistance en perte de vitesse (composée entre autres de membres de Sokol). Parachutés en Tchécoslovaquie en décembre 1941, ils avaient passé cinq mois à suivre Heydrich et à préparer l'attentat. Le 18 juin, trahis par Karel Čurda, un soldat qu'ils connaissaient de Grande-Bretagne, Gabčik, Kubiš et cinq autres parachutistes tchèques en mission de sabotage furent attaqués par les Waffen SS dans l'église de St. Cyrille et St. Méthode rue Resslova, où ils se cachaient. Après une bataille au fusil, ils se suicidèrent avec leurs dernières munitions plutôt que de se rendre. (3) Les corps des meurtriers de Heydrich et de leurs compagnons furent identifiés par la Gestapo par le traître Čurda qui avait auparavant essayé de les convaincre de se rendre. Ils furent exposés sur les pavés devant l'église, sauf Kubiš grièvement blessé qui était tombé aux mains des Allemands mais mourut pendant son transport à l'hôpital. (5) Couverture de magazine tchèque montrant la manifestation de loyauté envers le IIIe Reich tenue sur la place Venceslas le 3 juillet 1942. Le gouvernement fantoche de Hachá se tient au pied de la statue de Venceslas. 250 000 Tchèques chantèrent l'hymne national et jurèrent allégeance au IIIe Reich.

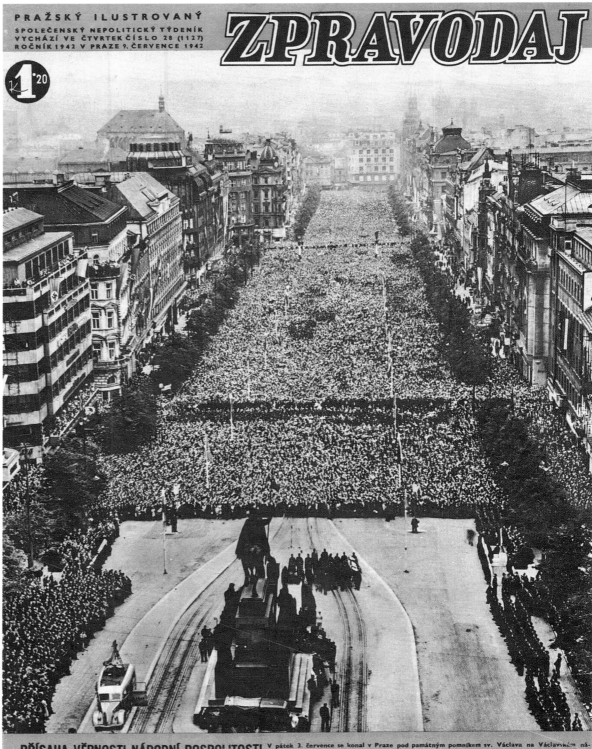

5

## Work and Entertainment

(1–3) German-language manuals for workers were printed during the occupation in order to germanize the population. The Nazis cultivated the working class, whose contribution was vital for the efficient operation of war industry, favoring the heavy industrial, chemical and electrical sectors. (4, 5) Wartime advertisements for industrial plants (the Škoda works was the most important armament factory in the whole of Bohemia). (6) Adina Mandlová (1910–91), one of the biggest Czech stars, was rumored to have had a relationship with Karl Hermann Frank. (7) Frank with Nazi cultural officials on a tour of inspection at the Barrandov Film Studios. (8) Matinee idol Oldřich Nový (1899–1983) in the film *Men Don't Grow Old*. (9) R. A. Dvorský (1899–1966), composer and singer of many hits and of dance music influenced by jazz. Jazz was popular amongst younger Czechs, but the Nazis frowned on jazz as racially degenerate, the product of Blacks and Jews and a symbol of all that was wrong with America (especially after December 1941, when the USA became involved in the war on the side of the Allies). (10) *The Night Butterfly* featured another well-known female star, Hana Vítová (1914–85).

## Arbeit und Unterhaltung

(1–3) Während der Besatzung wurden in großer Zahl deutschsprachige Arbeitsanweisungen gedruckt, um die Bevölkerung zu »germanisieren«. Die Nazis bemühten sich um die Arbeiterklasse, deren Mitwirkung für eine effiziente Rüstungsindustrie unersetzlich war. Sie förderten vor allem die Schwerindustrie sowie den Chemie- und Elektrobereich. (4, 5) Kriegspropaganda für Industriewerke (die Škoda-Fabriken waren die wichtigsten Waffenproduzenten in ganz Böhmen). (6) Adina Mandlová (1910–91), einem der größten tschechischen Filmstars, wurde eine Affäre mit Karl Hermann Frank nachgesagt. (7) Frank inspiziert mit Mitarbeitern der Kulturabteilung die Barrandov-Studios. (8) Filmidol Oldřich Nový (1899–1983) in dem Film *Männer werden nicht alt*. (9) R. A. Dvorský (1899–1966), Komponist und Sänger vieler populärer Schlager und vom Jazz beeinflußter Tanzmusik. Der Jazz war unter den jüngeren Tschechen sehr beliebt, bei den Nazis aber als rassisch entartet verpönt. Er galt als Produkt Schwarzer und Juden und war (besonders nach dem Kriegseintritt der USA auf der Seite der Alliierten im Dezember 1941) ein Symbol für alles Schlechte in Amerika. (10) *Der Nachtfalter* mit der bekannten Schauspielerin Hana Vítová (1914–1985).

## Travail et loisirs

(1–3) Des manuels en allemand pour les ouvriers furent imprimés sous l'occupation pour germaniser la population. Les nazis prenaient soin de la classe ouvrière dont la collaboration était vitale pour l'industrie de guerre, et en particulier l'industrie lourde, la chimie et l'électricité. (4, 5) Publicité du temps de guerre pour les implantations industrielles. Les usines Škoda étaient le plus important producteur d'armes de toute la Bohême. (6) Adina Mandlová (1910–1991), l'une des plus grandes vedettes tchèques, aurait eu une liaison avec Karl Hermann Frank. (7) Frank avec des responsables culturels nazis en inspection aux studios de Barrandov. (8) Vedette populaire Oldřich Nový (1899–1983) dans le film *Les hommes ne vieillissent pas*. (9) R. A. Dvorský (1899–1966), compositeur et interprète de nombreux succès et de musique de danse influencée par le jazz. Le jazz était apprécié de la jeunesse tchèque, mais les nazis trouvaient qu'il s'agissait là d'une musique dégénérée, production de Juifs et de Noirs et symbole de l'Amérique, surtout après 1941, lorsque les États-Unis entrèrent en guerre. (10) *Papillon de nuit*, avec une autre grande star de l'époque, Hana Vitová (1914–1985).

6

7

8

9

10

## Hard Times

People had to work long hours, food shortages became acute, and infectious diseases were common. (1, 4) The population was urged to heat economically and save electricity, gas and water. (2) This shop was closed for the duration of the war. (3) A sign chalked on a Prague wall proclaims in German: "We want Peace." (5) An empty shop window displaying a sign: "Closed for the victory of the Reich," because the staff were working elsewhere. (6) A poster urging women "all to work side by side with your men." (7, 8) Rationing coupons. In the last two years of the Protectorate rations were restricted. In the autumn of 1944 the average weekly allowance was one egg, 0.25kg meat (usually horse), 1.5kg bread and 3.5kg potatoes. There was also a monthly allowance of 140g butter, 60g fat, 160g artificial fat, 1.2kg sugar and 16 bread rolls. The cigarette ration was reduced from 35 to 25 a week. (9) The cover of a handbook on the use of gas fuel. Efforts were made to increase food production. Throughout the city, parks and open spaces were ploughed up to grow potatoes and other vegetables. (10) A magazine cover showing men ploughing the fields on the Letná Plain.

## Schwere Zeiten

Die Menschen mußten länger arbeiten, Lebensmittel wurden knapp und Infektionskrankheiten traten gehäuft auf. (1, 4) Schilder, die die Bevölkerung zum sparsamen Umgang mit Elektrizität, Gas und Wasser auffordert. (2) Dieses Geschäft war für die Dauer des Krieges geschlossen. (3) Die Aufforderung auf Deutsch »Wir wollen Frieden«, mit Kreide an die Wand gemalt. (5) Ein leeres Schaufenster mit dem Hinweisschild »Für den Sieg des Reiches geschlossen«, weil die Belegschaft an anderer Stelle arbeitet. (6) Ein Plakat, das alle Frauen auffordert: »Arbeite an der Seite deines Mannes.« (7, 8) Rationierungsmarken. In den letzten zwei Jahren des Protektorats waren die Lebensmittelrationen streng eingeteilt. Im Herbst 1944 bestand die durchschnittliche wöchentliche Zuteilung aus einem Ei, 0,25 kg Fleisch (in der Regel vom Pferd), 1,5 kg Brot und 3,5 kg Kartoffeln. Darüber hinaus gab es pro Monat 140 Gramm Butter, 60 Gramm Fett, 160 Gramm künstliches Fett, 1,2 kg Zucker und 16 Brötchen. Die wöchentliche Ration Zigaretten wurde von 35 auf 25 Stück reduziert. (9) Titelblatt einer Gebrauchsanweisung für Autogas. Man bemühte sich, die Lebensmittelproduktion zu erhöhen. Überall in der Stadt wurden Parks und andere freie Flächen umgepflügt und mit Kartoffeln und anderen Gemüsen bepflanzt. (10) Das Titelblatt einer Zeitschrift zeigt einen Mann beim Pflügen der Felder auf dem Letná-Plateau.

## Les temps difficiles

Les Tchèques travaillaient de longues heures, les pénuries devenaient de plus en plus fréquentes, les maladies infectieuses se répandirent. (1, 4) Affiches incitant la population à économiser l'électricité, le gaz et l'eau. (2) Ce magasin était fermé pour la durée de la guerre. (3) Marque à la craie sur un mur : « Nous voulons la paix. » (5) Vitrine de magasin vide, avec inscription : « Fermé pour la victoire du Reich », parce que le personnel travaillait ailleurs. (6) Affiche pressant les femmes «de travailler aux côtés de leurs maris». (7, 8) Coupons de rationnement. Au cours des deux dernières années, les rations furent encore réduites. En automne 1944, l'allocation hebdomadaire moyenne était de 1 œuf, 250 g de viande (généralement du cheval), 1,5 kg de pain et 3,5 kg de pommes de terre. À cela s'ajoutaient chaque mois 140 g de beurre, 60 g de matières grasses, 160 g de matières grasses synthétiques, 1,2 kg de sucre et 16 petits pains. La ration de cigarettes passa au cours de la guerre de 35 à 25 par semaine. (9) Couverture d'un manuel sur l'utilisation du gaz comme carburant. Des efforts furent déployés pour augmenter la production de produits alimentaires. Dans toute la ville, les parcs et les espaces verts furent labourés pour faire pousser des pommes de terre et divers légumes. (10) Couverture de magazine montrant les labours sur la plaine de Letná.

Všechny
do práce
po boku
mužů!

Mladým
ženám
v Protektorátě.

POSTKARTE
DOPISNICE

6

7

8

TŮMA — FRČEK

# PLYNNÁ PALIVA
## PRO POHON AUTOMOBILŮ
### (svítiplyn, methan, acetylen, tekutý plyn)

VYDALA MOTOR REVUE PRAHA

9

PESTRÝ TÝDEN

ROČ. XIX     V Praze dne 28. října 1944     ČÍS. 43 - K 3

Podzimní sklizeň ve velkoměstě, kde
všechny volné plochy byly letos jako
loni zemědělsky využity.
FOTO: PESTRÝ TÝDEN.

10

## Bombing Raids

(1) A Prague policeman directs traffic during a wartime blackout. Prague was spared the destructive bombing suffered by other major cities during the war. The first raid did not take place until 15 November 1944, when five stray bombs hit a suburban electricity station, killing four and injuring 30. Then on 14 February 1945 American bombers attacked the city and Mozart Bridge (today Palacký Bridge) and many neighboring buildings were hit, including several hospitals. The American pilots had mistaken Prague for Dresden. The raid killed 413 and wounded 1455. But on 25 March 1945 industrial targets, including the Böhmen and Mähren Engine Works, which was producing self-propelled guns for the Germans, were deliberately attacked. The death toll was over 500. (2) An American air raid on the ČKD factory in Vysočany on 25 March 1945. (3) A house on the corner of Heydrich Ufer (Rašín Embankment) and Resselgasse (Resslova).

## Bombenangriffe

(1) Ein Prager Polizist lenkt den Verkehr durch die verdunkelte Stadt. Anders als andere Großstädte blieb Prag von den verheerenden Bombenangriffen während des Krieges verschont. Erst am 15. November 1944 erfolgte der erste Luftangriff, bei dem fünf verirrte Bomben ein Elektrizitätswerk trafen, vier Menschen töteten und 30 verletzten. Am 14. Februar 1945 griffen amerikanische Bomber die Stadt an und trafen die Mozart-Brücke (heute Palacký-Brücke) und verschiedene angrenzende Gebäude einschließlich mehrerer Krankenhäuser. Die amerikanischen Piloten hatten Prag mit Dresden verwechselt. Bei dem Angriff kamen 413 Menschen ums Leben, 1.455 wurden verletzt. Am 25. März wurden Luftangriffe auf industrielle Ziele geflogen. Dazu gehörten auch die Böhmischen und Mährischen Motorenwerke, in denen Kanonen mit Selbstfahrlafetten für die Deutschen hergestellt wurden. Der Angriff kostete mehr als 500 Menschen das Leben. (2) Ein amerikanischer Luftangriff auf die ČKD-Werke in Vysočany am 25. März 1945. (3) Ein Eckhaus zwischen Heydrich-Ufer (Rašín-Kai) und Resselgasse (Resslova).

## Les bombardements aériens

(1) Un policier pragois dirige la circulation pendant le blackout. Prague fut pratiquement épargnée par les bombardements aériens, à la différence de nombreuses autres grandes villes européennes. Le premier raid n'eut lieu que le 15 novembre 1944, lorsque cinq bombes perdues touchèrent un poste d'électricité en banlieue, faisant 4 morts et 30 blessés. Puis, le 14 février 1945, les bombardiers américains attaquèrent la ville, touchant le pont Mozart (aujourd'hui pont Palacký) et de nombreux immeubles avoisinants, dont plusieurs hôpitaux. Les pilotes américains avaient pris Prague pour Dresde. Ce raid fit 413 morts et 1 455 blessés. Le 25 mars 1945, en revanche, se déroula une attaque délibérée sur des cibles industrielles dont les usines de mécanique Böhmen und Mähren qui fabriquaient des canons automoteurs pour les Allemands. Il y eut plus de 500 morts. (2) Raid américain sur l'usine ČKD de Vysočany le 25 mars 1945. (3) Immeuble bombardé à l'angle du Heydrich Ufer (quai Rašín) et de la Resselgasse (Resslova).

2

3

## The Uprising

On 5 May 1945 the uprising erupted spontaneously. The Czech National Committee (ČNR), representing Communists and non-Communists, took over the leadership. By the end of the day, most of Prague east of the river was in Czech hands with the exception of Gestapo headquarters at the Petschek Palace and three other centers. The Czechs thought that the Americans, who were near Plzeň, were going to help. (1–6) The inhabitants of Prague tore down German signs and flags, burnt Nazi books and fought street battles. (5) A German policeman lays down his machine gun, but the German soldiers were reluctant to do the same, fearing lynching. (7) A Prague Radio announcer (wearing a helmet) started the uprising when he announced the time in Czech and broadcast only in Czech therafter. (8) People gathered outside the radio station. (9) Prague policemen decided to join the uprising. (10) A street scene from the uprising.

## Der Aufstand

Am 5. Mai 1945 brach plötzlich der Aufstand aus. Der Tschechische Nationalrat (ČNR), in dem Kommunisten und Nichtkommunisten vertreten waren, übernahm die Führung. Am Ende des Tages war der größte Teil der Stadt östlich des Flusses, mit Ausnahme des Gestapo-Hauptquartiers im Petschek-Haus und drei weiterer Zentren, in tschechischer Hand. Die Tschechen hofften auf Hilfe der Amerikaner, die bei Pilsen standen. (1–6) Prager Bürger rissen deutsche Schilder und Flaggen herunter, verbrannten Nazi-Bücher und nahmen an Straßenkämpfen teil. (5) Ein deutscher Polizist legt sein Maschinengewehr ab, aber die deutschen Soldaten zögerten aus Angst vor Lynchjustiz, dasselbe zu tun. (7) Ein Prager Radiosprecher (mit Stahlhelm) begann den Aufstand, als er die Zeit auf Tschechisch ansagte und alles weitere nur noch auf Tschechisch vermeldete. (8) Vor der Radiostation versammelten sich Menschen. (9) Prager Polizisten schlugen sich auf die Seite des Aufstandes. (10) Eine Straßenszene während des Aufstandes.

## Le soulèvement

Le 5 mai 1945, le soulèvement éclata spontanément. Le Comité national tchèque (ČNR) composé de communistes et de non-communistes en prit la tête. À la fin de cette journée, la plus grande partie de la ville à l'est de la rivière se trouvait en ses mains, à l'exception du siège de la Gestapo, du palais Petschek et des trois autres lieux. Les Tchèques pensaient que les Américains qui se trouvaient non loin de Plzeň allaient les aider. (1–6) Les Pragois détruisirent les signes et les drapeaux allemands, brûlèrent les livres nazis et participèrent aux combats de rue. (5) Un policier allemand déposant sa mitraillette, mais les soldats allemands hésitèrent de faire de même car ils craignaient d'être lynchés. (7) Un présentateur de Radio Prague (portant un casque) donna le signal du soulèvement en annonçant l'heure en tchèque et en ne parlant plus qu'en tchèque à partir de ce moment. (8) Des Pragois réunis près de la gare. (9) Les policiers pragois décidèrent de rejoindre le soulèvement. (10) Scène de rue pendant le soulèvement.

7

8

9

10

## Fighting

The Germans were no longer fighting to reconquer the city, but to negotiate an agreement which would allow them to disengage and withdraw. Heavy shelling form German artillery destroyed the Gothic Old Town Hall and many houses in the Old Town Square. The SS units in Krč and Pankrác were burning buildings, looting shops and killing men, women and children indiscriminately. At Hiberner Bahnhof (now Masaryk railway station) and in Jelení příkop (Deer Moat in Hradčany) Czechs were massacred.

## Die Kämpfe

Die Deutschen kämpften nicht länger um die Rückeroberung der Stadt, sondern handelten in einem Abkommen den freien Abzug aus. Heftiger Beschuß der deutschen Artillerie zerstörte das gotische Altstädter Rathaus und viele Gebäude am Altstädter Ring. Die SS-Einheiten in Krč und Pankratz brannten Häuser nieder, plünderten Geschäfte und töteten wahllos Männer, Frauen und Kinder. Am Hiberner Bahnhof (heute Masaryk-Bahnhof) und in Jelení příkop (Hirschgraben auf dem Hradschin) wurden unbewaffnete Zivilisten niedergemetzelt.

## Les combats

Les Allemands ne se battaient plus pour reconquérir la ville, mais pour négocier un accord leur permettant de se retirer. Des bombardements allemands nourris détruisirent l'ancien hôtel de ville gothique et de nombreuses maisons de la place de la Vieille ville. Les unités SS de Krč et Pankrác incendièrent des maisons, pillèrent les magasins et tuèrent hommes, femmes et enfants sans discrimination. À la gare de Hiberner (aujourd'hui gare de Masaryk) et à Jelení příkop (des douves du Hradčany), de nombreux Tchèques furent massacrés.

### Capitulation

At 2.41 a.m. on 7 May, a German delegation signed an act of unconditional surrender at Rheims. In the early morning of 8 May, the Vlasov Army hurried towards the American lines near Plzeň, fleeing the approaching Red Army. The German reinforcements started heavy fighting, with the SS committing the worst atrocities, but the German leadership, fearing the Red Army, asked the Czechs to be allowed to pull out of Prague unhindered and requested a guarantee of safety for German civilians. Isolated and short of weapons, the Czechs agreed to the German "offer" (otherwise the Germans were prepared to destroy Prague). The ceasefire was agreed, the Czechs opened their barricades and the troops started leaving the city at 6 p.m. (1) German emissaries. (2) Negotiations for ceasefire. (3) Germans were forced to clear the streets. (4) Some were lynched. (5) High-ranking Germans (one already dressed in civilian clothes) leaving the Alcron Hotel. (6) The German army withdraws from Prague.

### Die Kapitulation

Um 2:41 Uhr am Morgen des 7. Mai unterzeichnete eine deutsche Delegation in Reims die bedingungslose Kapitulation. In den frühen Morgenstunden des 8. Mai marschierte Wlassows Armee auf der Flucht vor der Roten Armee in aller Eile in Richtung der amerikanischen Linien bei Pilsen. Die deutschen Verstärkungstruppen begannen heftige Gefechte, bei denen die SS die schlimmsten Greueltaten verübte, aber die deutschen Generäle, die die Rote Armee fürchteten, baten die Tschechen um einen ungehinderten Abzug aus Prag und um eine Sicherheitsgarantie für die deutschen Zivilisten. Isoliert und schlecht bewaffnet stimmten die Tschechen dem deutschen Ultimatum zu (andernfalls hatten die Deutschen mit der völligen Zerstörung Prags gedroht). Man vereinbarte einen Waffenstillstand, die Tschechen öffneten ihre Barrikaden und die Deutschen begannen um 6 Uhr abends mit dem Abzug aus der Stadt. (1) Deutsche Unterhändler. (2) Waffenstillstandsverhandlungen. (3) Deutsche wurden gezwungen, die Trümmer wegzuschaffen. (4) Einige wurden gelyncht. (5) Hochrangige deutsche Offiziere (darunter bereits einer in Zivilkleidung) verlassen das Hotel Alcron. (6) Die deutsche Armee zieht sich aus Prag zurück.

### La capitulation

Le 7 mai à 2h 41, une délégation allemande signa une reddition inconditionnelle à Reims. Au petit matin du 8 mai, l'armée de Vlasov se précipita vers les lignes américaines près de Plzeň, pour fuir l'armée soviétique qui approchait. Les renforts allemands se livrèrent à de nouveaux combats, accompagnés d'atrocités SS, mais l'état-major allemand plus conscient des risques demanda aux Tchèques l'autorisation de se retirer de Prague en sûreté et avec des garanties de sécurité pour les civils allemands. Isolés et à court de munitions, les Tchèques accédèrent à cette proposition (en cas de refus, les nazis étaient prêts à détruire la capitale). Le cessez-le-feu fut déclaré, les Tchèques ouvrirent leurs barricades, et les troupes d'occupation commencèrent à évacuer la ville vers 18 h. (1) Émissaires allemands. (2) Négociations de cessez-le-feu. (3) Les Allemands furent obligés de dégager les rues. (4) Certains furent lynchés. (5) Des Allemands de haut rang (l'un déjà en costume civil) quittent l'hôtel Alcron. (6) L'armée allemande quitte Prague.

# PRÁCE

LIST REVOLUČNÍHO ODBOROVÉHO HNUTÍ

PRAHA, VE STŘEDU 9. KVĚTNA 1945
Cena 70 haléřů

### České povstání skončilo vítězstvím

# Slavná Rudá armáda vstoupila do Prahy

*Bouřlivé a srdečné uvítání pražským obyvatelstvem · Poslední odpor nacistických banditů likvidován.*

Praha, 9. května. Devátý květen je historickým dnem v našich dějinách. Čtyřdenní povstání pražského lidu se skončilo vítězstvím. Slavná Rudá armáda vstoupila do Prahy, provázena bouřlivým jásotem českého obyvatelstva. Německá vojska se vzdávají do moci naší a Rudé armády a v proudech putují do zajateckých táborů. Jen v několika místech v Praze se ještě ozývají třesky strojních pušek. Poslední odpor nacistických banditů je drcen a bude nemilosrdně zlikvidován. Veškeré důležité vojenské opěrné body byly dobyty a zajištěny.

## Rudé tanky v Praze

Praha, 9. května. — Dnes krátce před 5. hod. ranní dojel na Prahou. Obyvatelstvo se připravila k jejich přivítání a připra-
Bořislavku v Dejvicích předvoj vítězné Rudé armády v počtu asi vila průchody v barikádách. Předem však se nutno přesvědčit.

## The Red Army Arrives

On 9 May, in the early hours of the morning, the first Soviet tanks entered the northern suburbs of Prague. The ceasefire collapsed and the German rearguard was attacked. Roving bands of SS looted the shops and fired at passersby. Czech resistance fighters hunted down German stragglers, who were hanged from lamp posts and set on fire. Shortly after midday, Marshal Ivan S. Koniev's troops (which came from Berlin) were joined by an element of the 2nd Ukrainian Front from the east and the last pockets of Nazi resistance were overcome. The people rejoiced, greeting their Soviet liberators and garlanding their tanks with flowers. The uprising was finally over, at the cost of 1694 Czech lives. The Reds hunted down the Vlasov soldiers and often shot them without trial. (1) A newspaper headline announces: "Czech Uprising finished with a victory: the famous Red Army entered Prague... Only in a couple of places can one still hear gunfire..." (2–5) The Red Army on the streets of Prague, jubilant crowds welcoming the soldiers with lilacs.

## Die Ankunft der Roten Armee

In den frühen Morgenstunden des 9. Mai fuhren die ersten sowjetischen Panzer durch die nördlichen Vororte Prags. Der Waffenstillstand brach zusammen, als die deutsche Nachhut angegriffen wurde. Marodierende Banden der SS plünderten Geschäfte und schossen auf Passanten. Tschechische Widerstandskämpfer jagten versprengte Deutsche, hängten sie an Laternenpfählen auf und zündeten sie an. Kurz nach Mittag erhielten General Iwan S. Koniews Truppen (die aus Berlin angerückt waren) Verstärkung durch Einheiten der Zweiten Ukrainischen Front aus dem Osten und vernichteten die letzten Widerstandsnester der Nazis. Die Bevölkerung jubelte, begrüßte die Sowjets als Befreier und schmückte die russischen Panzer mit Blumengirlanden. Der Aufstand, der 1.694 Tschechen das Leben gekostet hatte, war zu Ende. Die Rote Armee verfolgte Wlassows Soldaten, die oft ohne Prozeß erschossen wurden. (1) Eine Zeitungsüberschrift mit den Worten: »Der tschechische Aufstand endete mit einem Sieg: Die berühmte Rote Armee marschierte in Prag ein ... Nur an wenigen Plätzen kann man noch Gewehrfeuer vernehmen ... « (2–5) Die Rote Armee auf den Straßen von Prag, wo die Soldaten von der begeisterten Menge mit Fliedersträußen begrüßt werden.

## L'arrivée de l'Armée rouge

Le 9 mai, à l'aube, les premiers tanks soviétiques pénétrèrent dans la banlieue nord de Prague. Le cessez-le-feu fut interrompu et l'arrière-garde allemande attaquée. Des bandes de SS pillaient les magasins et tiraient sur les passants. La résistance tchèque fit la chasse aux retardataires allemands, qui furent pendus à des lampadaires et brûlés vifs. Peu après midi, les troupes du maréchal Ivan S. Koniev (arrivé de Berlin) furent rejointes par d'autres venues du second front d'Ukraine et les dernières poches de la résistance nazie furent anéanties. Le peuple accueillit ses libérateurs soviétiques, ornant leurs chars de fleurs. Le soulèvement était terminé. 1 694 Tchèques y avaient perdu la vie. Les Rouges pourchassèrent les soldats de Vlasov et les abattirent souvent sans procès. (1) Titre de journal : « Le soulèvement tchèque se termine par la victoire : la grande Armée rouge entre à Prague… on entend encore quelques échanges de tirs… » (2–5) L'Armée rouge dans les rues de Prague, accueillie par une foule en liesse qui couvre les soldats de fleurs.

3

4

5

## The Aftermath

(1) A smashed bust of Hitler on a Prague street. (2–9) The destruction around the Old Town Square, Wenceslas Square and in the vicinity of the National Museum, where the heaviest fighting took place. The rest of the city was relatively unscathed, thanks to the Vlasov soldiers and their participation in the uprising. Those who were not shot by Red Army soldiers reached American lines and were handed over to the Soviet authorities. A labor camp and death awaited them in the Soviet Union. A year later President Beneš claimed credit for Prague's lack of injuries: "The only undamaged city in Central Europe and all my doing."

## Nachspiel

(1) Eine zertrümmerte Hitlerbüste auf einer Prager Straße. (2–9) Die Zerstörungen um den Altstädter Ring, am Wenzelsplatz und in der Nähe des Nationalmuseums, wo die heftigsten Gefechte stattfanden. Das übrige Stadtgebiet blieb weitgehend verschont, dank der Wlassow Soldaten und ihrer Beteiligung am Aufstand. Diejenigen, die nicht von Soldaten der Roten Armee erschossen wurden, erreichten die amerikanischen Reihen und wurden den sowjetischen Behörden übergeben. In der Sowjetunion erwartete sie ein Arbeitslager und der Tod. Ein Jahr später schrieb sich Präsident Beneš das Verdienst für die relative Unversehrtheit von Prag zu: »Die einzige unbeschädigte Stadt in Mitteleuropa und alles mein Werk.«

## Les lendemains

(1) Buste de Hitler fracassé sur le sol dans une rue de Prague. (2–9) Les destructions autour de la place de la Vieille ville, de la place Venceslas et du Musée national, lieux des combats les plus durs. Le reste de la ville fut relativement épargné grâce à la participation des soldats de Vlasov au soulèvement. Ceux qui ne furent pas abattus par l'Armée Rouge se réfugièrent derrière les lignes américaines, mais furent remis aux autorités soviétiques. Les camps de travail forcé et la mort les attendaient. Un an plus tard, le président Beneš s'attribua le crédit de la préservation de la capitale : « La seule citée intacte de l'Europe centrale, et cela grâce à moi. »

4

5

6

7

8

9

3

## Edvard Beneš Returns

In the spring of 1945 Edvard Beneš went to Moscow, taking with him only men who would be acceptable to Stalin. After talking to the Soviets, who were obviously taking the fullest advantage of their military successes and of the powerful group of Czech Communists led by Klement Gottwald, a new Czech government was set up in Košice (Slovak soil liberated by the Soviets). In this new government, Communists held all the most important posts – an inevitable prelude to a Communist takeover. They had been imposed on Beneš by Stalin, and they were the first to be returned to Prague, in a Soviet transport plane, one week before the President. Beneš was kept captive under the pretext of security and illness; he had no freedom of movement or communication. (1) Edvard Beneš and his wife finally returning to Prague on 16 May 1945. (2) Beneš arrives in the First Courtyard of Hradčany. (3) Jubilant crowds in the Old Town Square, gathered around the Jan Hus monument.

## Die Rückkehr von Eduard Beneš

Im Frühling 1945 reiste Eduard Beneš in Begleitung von Politikern, die für Stalin akzeptabel sein würden, nach Moskau. Nach Gesprächen mit den Sowjets, die offensichtlich ihre militärischen Erfolge und den großen Einfluß der tschechischen Kommunisten unter Klement Gottwald ausnutzten, wurde in Košice (auf slowakischem Boden, den die Sowjets befreit hatten) eine neue Regierung gebildet. In dieser Regierung besetzten die Kommunisten die wichtigsten Ministerien – ein unvermeidliches Vorspiel zur kommunistischen Machtübernahme. Sie waren Beneš von Stalin aufgezwungen worden und kehrten in einer sowjetischen Transportmaschine als erste nach Prag zurück – eine Woche vor dem Präsidenten. Unter dem Vorwand seiner Sicherheit und seiner Gesundheit wurde Beneš gefangengehalten – er durfte sich weder frei bewegen noch mit der Außenwelt Kontakt aufnehmen. (1) Eduard Beneš und seine Frau kehrten schließlich am 16. Mai 1945 nach Prag zurück. (2) Beneš fährt durch den ersten Burghof des Hradschin. (3) Jubelnde Menschen auf dem Altstädter Rathaus, die sich um das Jan-Hus-Monument versammelt haben.

## Le retour d'Edvard Beneš

Au printemps 1945, Edvard Beneš se rendit à Moscou, accompagné de ses seuls collaborateurs qui pouvaient être acceptés par Staline. Après ses discussions avec les Soviétiques, qui tiraient déjà le maximum d'avantages de leurs succès militaires et de la présence d'un puissant groupe de communistes dirigés par Klement Gottwald, un nouveau gouvernement tchèque fut établi à Košice (en Slovaquie libérée par les Russes). Les communistes y détenaient tous les postes les plus importants, prélude au coup d'État qui se préparait. Imposés par Staline, ils furent les premiers à revenir à Prague dans un avion de transport soviétique, une semaine avant le président. Beneš fut retenu sous prétexte de sécurité et de santé. Il n'avait plus aucune liberté de mouvement ou de communication. (1) Edvard Beneš et son épouse reviennent enfin à Prague le 16 mai 1945. (2) Arrivée de Beneš dans l'avant-cour du Hradčany. (3) Une foule radieuse place de la Vieille ville, autour du monument à Jan Hus.

# In the Shadow of the Red Star
# Im Schatten des Roten Stern
# Dans l'ombre de l'étoile rouge

In the foreground, a Socialist Realist sculpture from the 1950s and in the background, a 216m-high television transmitter built towards the end of the Communist period. They encompass over 40 years of Communist regime in Czechoslovakia.

Die Skulptur im Stil des Sozialistischen Realismus aus den 50er Jahren im Vordergrund und der 216 Meter hohe Fernsehturm, der gegen Ende der kommunistischen Ära gebaut wurde, bezeichnen Anfang und Ende des mehr als 40 Jahre währenden kommunistischen Regimes in der Tschechoslowakei.

Au premier plan, une sculpture de style réaliste socialiste des années 50 et, dans le fond, la tour de télévision de 216 m de haut élevée à la fin de la période communiste : quarante années de régime communiste en Tchécoslovaquie les séparent.

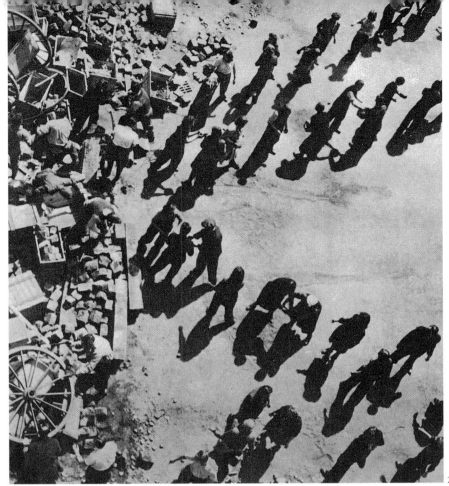

## Cleaning Up

Cleaning up got under way as soon as the war ended. Although Prague survived the war relatively unscathed, unlike other European cities, the Old Town Square witnessed some heavy fighting during the uprising. (1) The historic Old Town Hall (left) was damaged by German shells on 8 May 1945. (Týn Church can be seen in the center.) (2) Clearing the barricades. (3) The neo-Gothic east wing of the Old Town Hall (looking from Celetná) was partially burnt (together with many precious manuscripts, maps and engravings, since here was the main archive of Prague). (4) Rationing coupon. (5) Five-crown banknote from the period. (6) A banknote bearing the portrait of T. G. Masaryk, which was printed in London in 1943 and used just after the war. (7) The Old Town Hall without its neo-Gothic addition, which was removed and the space left empty as a visible scar.

## Aufräumarbeiten

Sofort nach Kriegsende begannen die Aufräumarbeiten. Prag hat – im Gegensatz zu anderen europäischen Großstädten – den Krieg relativ unbeschadet überstanden; lediglich der Altstädter Ring war während des Aufstandes Schauplatz heftiger Gefechte. (1) Das historische Altstädter Rathaus (links) wurde am 8. Mai 1945 von deutschen Bomben beschädigt. (In der Bildmitte erkennt man die Teynkirche.) (2) Beseitigung der Barrikaden. (3) Der neugotische Ostflügel des Altstädter Rathauses (von der Celetná aus gesehen) brannte teilweise ab. Der Brand vernichtete auch das Stadtarchiv mit vielen wertvollen Manuskripten, Karten und Stichen. (4) Rationierungskarten. (5) Eine Fünf-Kronen-Banknote der damaligen Zeit. (6) Eine Banknote mit den Porträt T.G. Masaryks, die 1943 in London gedruckt worden war und unmittelbar nach dem Krieg in Umlauf kam. (7) Das Altstädter Rathaus ohne seine neugotischen Anbauten, die nicht wieder instandgesetzt, sondern als sichtbare Narben belassen wurden.

## La reconstruction

La reconstruction démarra dès la fin de la guerre. Bien que Prague ait été relativement épargnée par le conflit – à la différence d'autres cités européennes – la place de la Vieille ville fut témoin de quelques combats acharnés pendant le soulèvement. (1) L'Ancien hôtel de ville (à gauche) endommagé par des bombes allemandes le 8 mai 1945 (au centre, l'église Notre-Dame-de-Týn). (2) La démolition des barricades. (3) L'aile Est néogothique de l'ancien hôtel de ville (vue de Celetná) fut en partie incendié, et de nombreux manuscrits, cartes et gravures des archives municipales disparurent. (4) Carte de rationnement. (5) Billet de 5 couronnes de l'époque. (6) Billet de banque à l'effigie de T. G. Masaryk, imprimé à Londres en 1943 et utilisé après guerre. (7) L'ancien hôtel de ville sans son extension néogothique qui fut détruite et non reconstruite, laissée telle une cicatrice bien visible.

7

### The Trial of Karl Hermann Frank and the Post-war Years

Karl Hermann Frank was caught in Rokycany and handed over by the Americans to the Czechoslovak authorities. He was tried for war crimes in May 1946. (1) Frank facing the death penalty (listening to a German translation on earphones). (2) A ticket to Frank's execution. (3) The hanging at Pankrác prison on 22 May 1946. (4) Edvard Beneš was re-elected President on 19 June 1946. (5) Prague Germans were forced to leave the city as part of the nationwide expulsion of the German population (estimated at 2.5 million). The expulsions were initiated by President Beneš, who considered them necessary retaliation for the Munich treaty and a guarantee against any possible future threat from the German minorities. Immediately after the war the Czechoslovak government embarked on a large-scale nationalization program in the key industries. On 24 October 1945 the President issued a decree nationalizing mines, banks, the food industry and insurance companies (altogether 3000 enterprises). The next day the legislation was announced at a mass rally in Wenceslas Square (6).

### Der Prozeß gegen Karl Hermann Frank und die Nachkriegsjahre

Karl Hermann Frank wurde in Rokycany von den Amerikanern gefangengenommen und an die tschechoslowakischen Behörden ausgeliefert. Im Mai 1946 klagte man ihn der Kriegsverbrechen an. (1) Frank in dem Augenblick, in dem man die Todesstrafe verkündet (die deutsche Übersetzung per Kopfhörer). (2) Eine Eintrittskarte zur Exekution Franks. (3) Die Hinrichtung im Pankratius-Gefängnis am 22. Mai 1946. (4) Am 19. Juni 1946 wurde Eduard Beneš erneut zum Staatspräsidenten gewählt. (5) Im Zusammenhang mit der landesweiten Vertreibung von etwa 2,5 Millionen Deutschen wurden auch die Prager Deutschen gezwungen, die Stadt zu verlassen. Die Ausweisung war von Beneš initiiert worden, der darin eine notwendige Vergeltung für das Münchener Abkommen und eine Garantie gegen jegliche zukünftige Bedrohung durch deutsche Minderheiten sah. Unmittelbar nach dem Krieg startete die tschechoslowakische Regierung ein großangelegtes Programm zur Verstaatlichung der Schlüsselindustrien. Am 24. Oktober 1945 unterzeichnete der Präsident ein Dekret zur Verstaatlichung der Bergwerke, Banken, der Lebensmittelindustrie und der Versicherungsgesellschaften (insgesamt 3000 Unternehmen). Am nächsten Tag wurden die neuen Gesetze während einer Massenkundgebung auf dem Wenzelsplatz veröffentlicht (6).

### Le procès de Karl Hermann Frank et les années d'après-guerre

Karl Hermann Frank fut capturé à Rokycany et remis par les Américains aux autorités tchécoslovaques. En mai 1946, il fut accusé de crimes de guerre. (1) Frank au moment de sa condamnation à mort qu'il écoute dans une traduction en allemand. (2) Billet d'entrée pour assister à l'exécution de Frank. (3) La pendaison à la prison de Pankrác le 22 mai 1946. (4) Edvard Beneš, réélu président le 19 juin 1946. (5) Les Allemands de Prague furent contraints de quitter la ville dans le cadre de l'expulsion générale de toute la population allemande (estimée à 2,5 millions de personnes) de Tchécoslovaquie. Les expulsions furent décidées par le président Beneš, qui y voyait une vengeance nécessaire pour faire oublier le traité de Munich et une garantie contre toute future menace des minorités allemandes. Immédiatement après la guerre, le gouvernement tchécoslovaque lança un programme de nationalisation à grande échelle dans le secteur des industries clés. Le 24 octobre 1945, le président signa un décret nationalisant les mines, les banques, l'industrie alimentaire et les compagnies d'assurance (300 sociétés en tout). La nouvelle législation fut annoncée le lendemain, lors d'un énorme rassemblement place Venceslas (6).

4

5

6

271

VIII. sjezd
KOMUNISTICKÉ STRANY
ČESKOSLOVENSKA
sněm budovatelů silné a šťastné republiky
Praha 28.-31. III. 1946

PŘÍKAZ NAŠÍ SVOBODY, NAŠÍ VLÁDY I NÁRODA
ROZTOČTE KOLA!

VOLÍME
1
KOMUNISTY

RUDÉ PRÁVO
ÚSTŘEDNÍ ORGÁN KOMUNISTICKÉ STRANY ČESKOSLOVENSKA

KSČ daleko největší stranou v českých zemích

Komunisté vedoucí silou
národa

KSČ nejsilnější stranou v hlavním
městě republiky

Předběžné výsledky hlavního města Prahy

## Gottwald's Road to Power

In the free election of 1946 – the country's last for many years – the Czechoslovak population demonstrated their confidence by awarding the Communists almost 38 per cent of the vote. (1, 2) Klement Gottwald (1896–1953) was appointed Prime Minister of the coalition government. He imitated Stalin's warm, modest image, including his pipe-smoking. (3) Poster announcing the VIII Congress of the Communist Party of Czechoslovakia. (4) Gottwald attended rallies organized by the dynamic Communist Party, which rolled out various infectiously optimistic and catchy slogans. This one exclaims "Our freedom, government and nation commands: get the wheels moving!" (5) Pre-election campaign leaflet, "Vote Communist the No.1 Party." (On the election card they were allocated first place on the list, which proved to be very convenient.) (6) *Rudé Právo*, the Communist newspaper, reports on the election victory in the capital. (7) The master and his pupil: Josef Stalin and Klement Gottwald. (8) The uneasy partnership between Prime Minister, Gottwald, and President, Beneš. (9) People cheering Gottwald after the elections.

## Gottwalds Weg zur Macht

In den freien Wahlen von 1946, die für lange Zeit die letzten im Lande sein sollten, sprach die tschechoslowakische Bevölkerung den Kommunisten mit einem Stimmenanteil von fast 38 Prozent ihr Vertrauen aus. (1, 2) Klement Gottwald (1896–1953) wurde zum Ministerpräsidenten der Koalitionsregierung ernannt. Er imitierte Stalins freundliches, bescheidenes Image – bis hin zum Pfeiferauchen. (3) Auf einem Plakat wird der VIII. Kongreß der Kommunistischen Partei der Tschechoslowakei angekündigt. (4) Gottwald besucht die von der tatkräftigen Kommunistischen Partei organisierten Demonstrationen, bei denen verschiedene Plakate mit ansteckend optimistischen und eingängigen Slogans entrollt wurden. Dieses hier verkündet: »Unsere Freiheit, unsere Regierung und unser Volk fordern: Bringt die Räder zum Rollen!« (5) Wahlkampfbroschüren: »Wählt die Kommunisten – Partei Nummer 1.« (Auf der Wahlliste standen sie auf Platz 1, was sich als sehr vorteilhaft erwies.) (6) *Rudé Právo*, die kommunistische Zeitung, berichtet über den Wahlsieg in der Hauptstadt. (7) Der Meister und sein Schüler: Josef Stalin und Klement Gottwald. (8) Die prekäre Partnerschaft zwischen Ministerpräsident Gottwald und Präsident Beneš. (9) Jubelnde Anhänger Gottwalds nach der Wahl.

## L'ascension de Gottwald

Aux élections libres de 1946 – les dernières qu'allait connaître le pays pour une longue période – la population tchécoslovaque fit preuve de confiance en accordant aux communistes près de 38 pour cent des voix. (1, 2) Klement Gottwald (1896–1953) fut désigné Premier ministre de la coalition gouvernementale. Il s'inspirait de l'image chaleureuse et pleine de modestie de Staline, pipe comprise. (3) Affiche annonçant le VIIIe Congrès du Parti communiste de Tchécoslovaquie. (4) Gottwald assistait aux rassemblements organisés par son parti qui affichait des slogans accrocheurs d'un optimisme contagieux. Cette banderole proclame : « Notre liberté, notre gouvernement et notre nation l'exigent : il faut faire bouger les choses! » (5) Brochure de campagne pré-électorale : « Votez communiste, le Parti n°1. » (Sur le bulletin de vote, les communistes occupaient la première place, ce qui était très pratique.) (6) *Rudé Právo*, le quotidien communiste, traitant de la victoire électorale dans la capitale. (7) Le maître et son élève : Joseph Staline et Klement Gottwald. (8) Le partenariat difficile entre le premier ministre, Gottwald, et le président Beneš. (9) La foule acclamant Gottwald après les élections.

7

8

9

### The Communist Coup: February 1948

A number of actions undertaken by the Communists led to a crisis in the government. Twelve non-Communist ministers resigned in protest at the Communist infiltration of the police, the security services and the army. Klement Gottwald speaking in the Old Town Square on 21 February (2). At 4 p.m. on 25 February 1948, he announced to crowds assembled in Wenceslas Square (1) that Beneš had accepted the ministerial resignations and that a new Communist government had been created. The whole Communist campaign was orchestrated under the explicit threat of armed People's Militias which forced Beneš to yield to Gottwald's demands. The day when the transfer of power to the "working class" was achieved became officially known as the "Victorious February."

### Der kommunistische Staatsstreich: Februar 1948

Verschiedene Aktionen der Kommunisten lösten eine Regierungskrise aus. Zwölf nicht-kommunistische Minister legten aus Protest gegen die kommunistische Unterwanderung der Polizei, der Sicherheitskräfte und der Armee ihr Amt nieder. Klement Gottwald hält am 21. Februar eine Rede auf dem Altstädter Ring (2). Um 16 Uhr am 25. Februar 1948 verkündete er den auf dem Wenzelsplatz versammelten Massen (1), daß Beneš das Rücktrittsgesuch der Minister angenommen habe und eine neue kommunistische Regierung gebildet worden sei. Die gesamte Kampagne der Kommunisten war von Einschüchterungen durch bewaffnete Volksmilizen begleitet, die Beneš dazu zwangen, sich Gottwalds Forderungen zu beugen. Der Tag der Machtübernahme durch die »Arbeiterklasse« wurde allgemein als der »Siegreiche Februar« bekannt.

### Le coup d'État communiste de février 1948

Un certain nombre de manœuvres communistes entraînèrent une crise gouvernementale. Douze ministres non-communistes démissionnèrent pour protester contre l'infiltration communiste de la police, des services de sécurité et de l'armée. Klement Gottwald fait un discours sur la Place de la Vieille ville le 21 février (2). Dans l'après-midi du 25 février 1948, il annonça à une foule rassemblée place Venceslas que Beneš avait accepté les démissions des ministres et la création d'un nouveau gouvernement communiste. L'ensemble de la campagne communiste se développa sous la menace explicite de milices populaires armées qui obligèrent le Président à céder aux demandes de son Premier ministre. Le jour du transfert du pouvoir à la « classe ouvrière » fut baptisé « La victoire de février ».

## The People's Militia

The Communists, fearing the army which was strongly influenced by Western democratic ideals, created a paramilitary group called the People's Militia. They equipped factory workers with new rifles, gave them a limited number of bullets and told them to be vigilant against "reactionaries." The militias came under the direct command of the KSČ (Czechoslovak Communist Party) and the Party's First Secretary, Rudolf Slánský, and were there to fulfil one function: to intimidate the "counterrevolutionaries" in the government and democratically oriented groups within the population. (1) Members of the People's Militia posing for a photograph. (2) On 28 February 1948 Gottwald publicly thanked the People's Militia unit and the National Security Guards for their participation in the February coup. (3, 5) LM (*Lidová milice*: People's Militia) armband. (4) Militia unit marching across the Charles Bridge. (6) A pleased Klement Gottwald inspecting the SNB and LM units in the Old Town Square on 28 February 1948. (7) Armed militia unit.

## Die Volksmiliz

Aus Angst vor der Armee, die stark von demokratischen Idealen des Westens beeinflußt war, riefen die Kommunisten unter dem Namen »Volksmiliz« eine paramilitärische Organisation ins Leben. Sie bewaffneten Fabrikarbeiter mit neuen Gewehren und einer begrenzten Anzahl Patronen und forderten sie zur Wachsamkeit gegen »Reaktionäre« auf. Die Miliz wurde dem direkten Befehl der KSČ (Tschechoslowakische Kommunistische Partei) und ihrem Generalsekretär Rudolf Slánský unterstellt. Sie hatte nur eine Aufgabe: Die Einschüchterung der »Konterrevolutionären« in der Regierung und demokratisch gesinnter Gruppen in der Bevölkerung. (1) Mitglieder der Volksmiliz stellen sich für die Kamera in Pose. (2) Am 28. Februar bedankte sich Gottwald öffentlich bei der Volksmiliz und den Nationalen Sicherheitstruppen für ihre Mithilfe beim Februarcoup. (3, 5) Armbinde der LM (*Lidová milice*: Volksmiliz). (4) Eine Milizeinheit marschiert über die Karlsbrücke. (6) Am 28. Februar 1948 inspiziert ein zufriedener Klement Gottwald die SNB- und LM-Einheiten auf dem Altstädter Ring. (7) Eine bewaffnete Milizeinheit.

## Les milices populaires

Les communistes, craignant une armée fortement imprégnée d'idées occidentales, créèrent des groupes paramilitaires, les milices populaires. Ils équipèrent des ouvriers d'usine de fusils du dernier modèle (mais avec un nombre de munitions limité) et leurs demandèrent d'être vigilants envers les «réactionnaires». Les milices étaient sous le commandement direct du Parti et du Premier secrétaire de celui-ci, Rudolf Slánský. Leur unique fonction était d'intimider les «contre-révolutionnaires» du gouvernement et les organisations démocrates au sein de la population. (1) Membre des milices populaires posant devant l'objectif. (2) Le 28 février 1948, Gottwald remercie publiquement les milices et les gardes de la Sécurité nationale pour leur participation au coup de février. (3, 5) Le bandeau de la milice populaire LM (*Lidová milice*). (4) Unité de la Milice traversant le pont Charles. (6) Un Gottwald très satisfait inspecte des unités de la LM et de la SNB sur la place de la Vieille ville le 28 février 1948. (7) Unité armée de la milice.

6

7

## The End of Democracy

On 10 March 1948 Jan Masaryk (1), Foreign Minister and son of the founder of the Czechoslovak Republic, Tomáš Masaryk, was found dead in the courtyard of the Černín Palace. According to František August, a senior officer in the Czechoslovak State Security Organization (StB), Masaryk was murdered on the orders of the NKVD because he planned to leave Czechoslovakia and the Communist Party was afraid of the enormous damage he could inflict by revealing the truth about dirty Communist tactics. The man who organized the killing (with the help of four others) was Major Augustin Schramm, an NKVD officer. (2) The shocked nation turned up in thousands to mourn the last great democrat, who once said, "Very few people know what a beautiful gift one's life is. A big gift from an anonymous donor. And this donor would have liked that people should 'wear' their lives lightly, like a carnation in a buttonhole." (3) Beneš and his wife posing outside their country house in Sezimovo Ústí in the south of Bohemia. He resigned on 7 June and (4) died on 3 September 1948. (5) Pass for inclusion in his funeral cortège. (6) Gottwald greeting crowds on the day of his inauguration as President, 14 June 1948.

## Das Ende der Demokratie

Am 10. März 1948 wurde Jan Masaryk, Außenminister und Sohn des Gründers der tschechoslowakischen Republik, Tomáš Masaryk, tot im Innenhof des Czernin-Palastes aufgefunden. Nach den Aussagen von František August, einem höheren Offizier des Tschechoslowakischen Staatssicherheitsdienstes (StB), war Masaryk auf Anordnung des NKWD ermordet worden, weil er die Tschechoslowakei verlassen wollte und die Kommunistische Partei den enormen Gesichtsverlust fürchtete, den sie erleiden würde, wenn ihre schmutzigen Tricks an die Öffentlichkeit gelangten. Der Mann, der die Ermordung (mit der Hilfe von vier anderen) organisiert hatte, war der NKWD-Offizier Major August Schramm. (2) Zu Tausenden erschien die erschütterte Nation, um den letzten großen Demokraten zu betrauern, der einmal gesagt hatte: »Nur wenige Menschen wissen, was für ein wunderbares Geschenk das eigene Leben ist. Ein großes Geschenk von einem unbekannten Gönner. Und dieser Gönner hätte es gern gesehen, wenn die Menschen ihr Leben leicht genommen hätten, wie eine Nelke im Knopfloch.« (3) Beneš und seine Frau stehen vor ihrem Landsitz in Sezimovo Ústí im südlichen Böhmen vor der Kamera. Er trat am 7. Juni zurück und (4) starb am 3. September 1948. (5) Ausweis zur Teilnahme an seinem Leichenzug. (6) Gottwald winkt der Menschenmenge am Tage seiner Amtseinführung als Staatspräsident, dem 14. Juni 1948, zu.

## La fin de la démocratie

Le 10 mars 1948, le corps de Jan Masaryk (1), ministre des Affaires étrangères et fils du fondateur de la République tchécoslovaque, Tomáš Masaryk, fut découvert dans la cour du palais Černin. Selon František August, haut responsable du Service de la Sécurité d'État (StB), Masaryk fut assassiné sur les ordres du NKVD parce qu'il projetait de quitter le pays et que le parti communiste avait peur de l'effet de ses révélations sur sa tactique. L'homme qui organisa ce meurtre (avec l'aide de quatre comparses) était le major Augustin Schramm, officier du NKVD. (2) Devant le palais Černin: des milliers de Tchèques bouleversés vinrent rendre un dernier hommage au grand démocrate qui avait déclaré un jour: «Très peu de gens savent à quel point la vie est un merveilleux cadeau. Le grand cadeau d'un donateur anonyme. Et ce donateur aurait aimé que les gens vivent leur existence avec légèreté comme un œillet dans une boutonnière.» (3) Beneš et son épouse devant leur résidence de campagne de Sezimovo Ústí dans le sud de la Bohême. Il abdiqua le 7 juin et (4) mourut le 3 septembre 1948. (5) Laissez-passer pour son cortège funéraire. (6) Gottwald saluant la foule, le jour de sa nomination, le 14 juin 1948.

3

4

5

6

# směna

KULTURNÍ ČTRNÁCTIDENÍK MLÁDEŽE   9. V. 1951 • CENA 5 Kčs • ČÍSLO **9**

LETNÍ
MAGAZIN

ČASOPISU
*Žena*
A MÓDA
ČERVEN 1949

40 Kčs

FOTO V. JÍRŮ

2

ŽENA
MÓDA

Ročník VII
číslo 5
Květen 1955
Cena Kčs 4
PNS 489

3

JARNÍ
MAGAZIN VLASTY

4

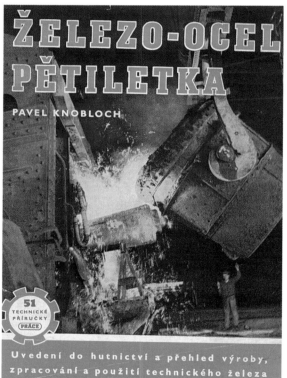

ŽELEZO-OCEL
PĚTILETKA

PAVEL KNOBLOCH

51
TECHNICKÉ
PŘÍRUČKY
PRÁCE

Uvedení do hutnictví a přehled výroby,
zpracování a použití technického železa

5

ČSR
5
1951

6

Pojď s námi!
Budujeme
NOVOU PRAHU

7

## Communist Propaganda

(1) Cover of the Czechoslovak Communist Youth magazine *Směna* (meaning "The Shift"), depicting an enthusiastic member of the organization marching in a May Day parade. (2–7) Communist propaganda posters promoting the new Socialist woman and working women's fashion; encouraging iron and steel production and the five-year plan in factories (modeled on the Soviet economy, with the emphasis on heavy industry); and building a new Prague.

## Kommunistische Propaganda

(1) Die Titelseite des tschechischen kommunistischen Jugend-magazins *Směna* (Der Wandel) zeigt ein begeistertes Mitglied der Organisation beim Marsch während einer Parade zum Ersten Mai. (2–7) Kommunistische Propagandaplakate werben für die neue sozialistische Frau und die Mode der Arbeiterin, für die Unterstützung der Eisen- und Stahlindustrie, den Fünfjahres-plan in den Fabriken (der nach dem sowjetischen Modell beson-ders auf die Schwerindustrie angelegt war) und den Bau eines neuen Prags.

## La propagande communiste

(1) Couverture du magazine de la jeunesse communiste tchécoslovaque *Směna* (le changement) montrant l'enthousiasme de jeunes défilant pour le 1er Mai. (2–7) Affiches de propagande communiste mettant en valeur la nouvelle femme socialiste et les femmes au travail ; encourageant la production de fer et d'acier et le plan quinquennal dans les usines (calqué sur l'organisation soviétique) ; édifiant la Prague nouvelle.

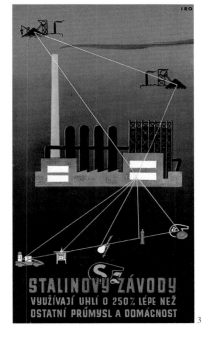

STALINOVY ZÁVODY
VYUŽÍVAJÍ UHLÍ O 250% LÉPE NEŽ
OSTATNÍ PRŮMYSL A DOMÁCNOST

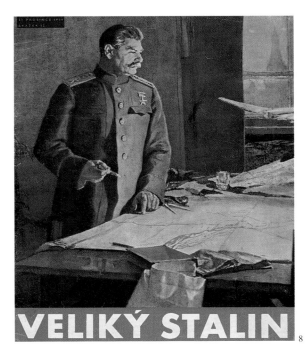

## The Cult of Personality

(1) A monument to Czechoslovak–Soviet friendship: a Czech soldier embraces a Soviet soldier (holding lilacs) in gratitude for the liberation of his country. (2, 3, 7–9) Stalin's face, name and "works" appeared everywhere. (4) A poster "With the Soviet Union for Permanent Peace in the World." (5) A poster proclaiming "With the Soviet Union For Ever." (6) A Czechoslovak–Soviet Friendship Union membership card. (10) Workers writing letters to Stalin. (11) Gottwald and Marshal Ivan Koniev watching the 9th of May parade. (12) Sportswomen carrying portraits of Gottwald and Stalin in Wenceslas Square.

## Der Personenkult

(1) Ein Denkmal der tschechoslowakisch-sowjetischen Freundschaft: Ein tschechischer Soldat umarmt einen sowjetischen Kameraden (mit Flieder in der Hand) aus Dankbarkeit für die Befreiung seines Landes. (2, 3, 7–9) Stalins Gesicht, sein Name und seine »Werke« erscheinen überall. (4) Ein Plakat mit dem Titel »Mit der Sowjetunion für einen dauerhaften Frieden in der Welt.« (5) Ein anderes Plakat fordert: »Für immer mit der Sowjetunion.« (6) Eine Mitgliedskarte der tschechoslowakisch-sowjetischen Freundschaftsunion. (10) Arbeiter schreiben Briefe an Stalin. (11) Gottwald und Marschall Iwan Koniew nehmen die Parade zum 9. Mai ab. (12) Sportlerinnen tragen Porträts von Gottwald und Stalin auf dem Wenzelsplatz.

## La culte de la personnalité

(1) Monument à l'amitié tchécoslovaco-soviétique : un soldat tchèque embrasse un soldat soviétique (des lilas à la main) pour le remercier d'avoir libéré son pays. (2, 3, 7–9) Le visage, le nom et les «travaux» de Staline apparaissent partout. (4) Affiche : « Avec l'Union Soviétique pour la paix permanente dans le monde. » (5) Affiche proclamant : « Avec l'Union Soviétique pour toujours. » (6) Carte de membre de l'Union de l'amitié tchécoslovaco-soviétique. (10) Lettres de travailleurs à Staline. (11) Gottwald et le maréchal Ivan Koniev assistant au défilé du 9 mai. (12) Sportives arborant des portraits de Staline et de Gottwald sur la place Venceslas.

10

11

## Russian-style Military Parades

(Previous pages) The 9th of May, Liberation Day, was celebrated as a national holiday. (1) Army units marching along the Avenue of the Defenders of Peace (today Milady Horákové). (2) May Day crowds in Wenceslas Square; attendance was compulsory.

## Militärparaden im russischen Stil

(Vorherige Seiten) Der 9. Mai, der Tag der Befreiung, war ein Nationaler Feiertag. (1) Armee-Einheiten marschieren auf der Straße der Verteidiger des Friedens (heute Milady Horákové). (2) Menschenmassen bei den Mai-Versammlungen auf dem Wenzelsplatz, deren Teilnahme Pflicht war.

## Les parades militaires à la russes

(Pages précédentes) Le 9 mai, anniversaire de la Libération, était jour férié. (1) Des unités de l'armée défilent avenue des Défenseurs de la paix (aujourd'hui, avenue Milady Horákové). (2) Place Venceslas, la foule se presse ; la présence aux manifestations était obligatoire.

12

## Socialist Realism I

The concept of Socialist Realism was credited to Stalin himself and was defined as true and historically concrete depiction of reality in its revolutionary development. (1–6) Details on the door to the Hall of the Soviet Army (an addition to the Vítkov Monument built for the 10th anniversary of the "liberation") celebrating Soviet soldiers, workers and the revolution. The hammer and sickle – the symbol of the new order – suggested that workers and peasants were the new rulers. Inside, the Soviet Army Hall is decorated with a bust of the Soviet Marshal P. S. Rybalko and the walls are covered with mosaics (1953–54) of Soviets soldiers by Vladimir Sychra accompanied by Vítězslav Nezval's verses. A sarcophagus contains the remains of an Unknown Soviet Soldier. (7) Smíchov railway station (1953–54), built in Socialist Realist style by J. David. (8) Czech artists imitated their Soviet colleagues, who specialized in the "genre

## Sozialistischer Realismus I

Das Konzept des Sozialistischen Realismus geht auf Stalin selbst zurück und bezeichnet eine getreue und historisch korrekte Abbildung der Wirklichkeit in ihrem revolutionären Fortschritt. (1–6) Details auf der Tür zur Halle der Sowjetischen Armee (eine Erweiterung des Vítkov-Monuments, das anläßlich des 10. Jahrestages der »Befreiung« zum Ruhm der sowjetischen Soldaten und Arbeiter und der Revolution erbaut wurde). Hammer und Sichel, die Symbole der neuen Ordnung, sollen zeigen, daß Arbeiter und Bauern die neuen Herrscher sind. Den Innenraum des Saals der Sowjetischen Armee dekoriert eine Büste des sowjetischen Marschalls P. S. Rybalko, die Wände sind mit Mosaiken russischer Sodaten von Vladimir Sychra (1953–54) geschmückt, neben denen Verse von Vítězslav Nezval stehen. In einem Sarkophag ruhen die Gebeine eines unbekannten russischen Soldaten. (7) Der Smíchov-Bahnhof wurde im Stil des sozialistischen Realismus von J. David (1953–54) erbaut. (8) Tschechische Künstler imitieren ihre sowjetischen Kolle-

## Le réalisme socialiste I

Le concept du réalisme socialiste est dû à Staline en personne. Son objectif était de donner une représentation authentique et historique de la réalité dans ses développements révolutionnaires. (1–6) Sculptures du portail d'acier du Hall de l'Armée soviétique, une extension du Monument Vitkov construit pour le dixième anniversaire de la «libération» et célébrant les soldats, les travailleurs et la révolution soviétiques. Le marteau et la faucille – symboles de l'ordre nouveau – suggéraient que les ouvriers et les paysans étaient dorénavant au pouvoir. L'intérieur du hall, dont les murs sont recouverts de mosaïques (1953–54) de Vladimir Sychra, accompagnées de vers de Vítězslav Nezval, représentent des soldats soviétiques. Il est également décoré d'un buste du maréchal soviétique P. S. Rybalko et abrite un sarcophage contenant les restes d'un soldat soviétique inconnu. (7) La gare de Smíchov, édifiée en style réaliste socialiste par J. David. (8) Des artistes tchèques imitèrent leurs confrères

of a leader." A painting of Klement Gottwald looking into the bright Socialist future surrounded by grateful workers. (9) Prague art students discussing the statue of a miner. (10) A model worker's family (detail) depicted on a mural inside Smíchov station. Richard Wiesner was the author of the unsmiling row of workers and peasants who perform their tasks while, at the far left, a guard with a dog watches Czechoslovakia's borders, which were closed in 1948. He protects them and guards them at the same time. (11) Oil painting of a miliatiaman. The keepers of the Socialist order (militiamen, border guards, and their dogs) became the new heroes of the art of that period. (In 1975, the Museum of Security Forces was created. Its most famous exhibit was a stuffed dog, Brek, which in its short life caught 60 men who were trying to quit the "Socialist paradise").

gen, die sich auf das »Genre eines Führers« spezialisiert haben. Ein Bild von Klement Gottwald, der, umgeben von dankbaren Arbeitern, in eine helle sozialistische Zukunft blickt. (9) Prager Kunststudenten diskutieren über die Statue eines Bergarbeiters. (10) Wandgemälde im Innern des Smíchov-Bahnhofs, das eine Musterfamilie der Arbeiterklasse darstellt (Ausschnitt). Richard Wiesner war der Maler dieser ernst blickenden Arbeiter und Bauern bei der Arbeit. Ganz links beobachtet ein Wachposten mit Hund die tschechoslowakische Grenze, die 1948 geschlossen wurde; er beschützt und bewacht sie zugleich. (11) Ölgemälde eines Milizionärs. Die Hüter der sozialistischen Ordnung (Milizionäre, Grenzposten und ihre Hunde) avancierten zu den neuen Helden dieser Kunstperiode. (1975 wurde das Museum der Sicherheitskräfte eröffnet. Sein bekanntestes Ausstellungsobjekt war ein ausgestopfter Hund namens Brek, der in seinem kurzen Leben 60 Menschen angefallen hatte, die dem »Sozialistischen Paradies« zu entfliehen versuchten.

soviétiques qui se spécialisaient dans le « genre d'un leader ». Peinture de Klement Gottwald tourné vers le lumineux avenir socialiste et entouré de travailleurs reconnaissants. (9) Des étudiants praguois discutent de la représentation d'un mineur. (10) Une famille ouvrière exemplaire (détail) sur une fresque de la gare de Smíchov, Richard Wiesner est l'artiste auteur de ces rangées d'ouvriers et de paysans qui accomplissent leur tâche sans un sourire. A l'extrême-gauche, un garde accompagné d'un chien surveille la frontière tchécoslovaque, fermée en 1948. Il protège et surveille en même temps. (11) Peinture à l'huile représentant un milicien, Les défenseurs de l'ordre socialiste (miliciens, gardes-frontière, et leurs chiens) devinrent les sujets préférés de l'art de cette période ( En 1975, fut crée le Musée des forces armées, dont la pièce la plus fameuse était un chien empaillé, Brek, qui avait attrapé 60 hommes coupables d'essayer de fuir le « paradies socialiste ».

7

8

9

10

11

## Socialist Realism II

(1) The cover of a songbook, *We Are Singing [while fulfilling] the Five Year Plan*. Audio-indoctrination was adopted from the Soviet Union and many poets in the 1950s wrote verses about beautiful tractors, the wisdom of Stalin and peace. (2, 3) Two covers of the *Kino* (Cinema) magazine, featuring optimistic young workers, the builders of the new system (who chanted at mass rallies: "We are the new generation, we are Gottwald's generation"). (4) A factory set built inside the Barrandov Film Studios used for propaganda movies (7). Barrandov Studios were nationalized after the war and run by workers who were devout Communists (one of the first managing directors of the film studios was called "our Barrandov Lenin" by the film technicians). (5) A choir under a large portrait of young Communist Julius Fučík, who was made into a martyr by the Communist department of propaganda. While in the hands of the Gestapo, Fučík not only refused to reveal the names of his

## Sozialistischer Realismus II

(1) Umschlag eines Liederbuches mit dem Titel »*Wir singen, [während wir] den Fünfjahresplan [erfüllen]*«. Die Indoktrination über den Weg der Sprache und der Lieder wurde von der Sowjetunion übernommen. Viele Dichter der 50er Jahre schrieben Gedichte über die Schönheit von Traktoren, die Weisheit Stalins und über den Frieden. (2, 3) Zwei Titelbilder des Kinomagazins *Kino* mit der Darstellung optimistischer junger Arbeiter, den Baumeistern des neuen Systems, die auf den Massenkundgebungen sangen: »Wir sind die neue Generation, wir sind Gottwalds Generation«. (4) Eine Fabrikkulisse in den Barrandov-Filmstudios, die für Propagandafilme genutzt wurde (7). Die Barrandov-Studios wurden nach dem Kriegsende verstaatlicht und von Arbeitern betrieben, die treue Kommunisten waren (einen der ersten Studioleiter nannten die Filmtechniker »unser Lenin von Barrandov«). (5) Ein Chor unter dem großen Porträt des jungen Kommunisten Julius Fučik, der von der Propagandaabteilung der Kommunistischen Partei zum Märtyrer stilisiert wurde. In der Gewalt der Gestapo hatte Fučik sich nicht nur geweigert, die Namen seiner Kameraden zu verraten, son-

## Le réalisme socialiste II

(1) Couverture d'un recueil de chansons *Nous chantons le plan quinquennal*! L'endoctrinement sonore fut développé par l'Union soviétique, et de nombreux poètes des années 50 composèrent des vers aussi bien sur des tracteurs que sur Staline et la paix. (2, 3) Deux couvertures du magazine *Kino* (cinéma) montrant de jeunes ouvriers optimistes, constructeurs du nouveau système, qui criaient dans les manifestations de masse : « Nous sommes la nouvelle génération, nous sommes la génération Gottwald. » (4) Décor d'usine construit dans les studios de Barrandov et utilisé pour les films de propagande (7). Les studios de Barrandov furent nationalisés après la guerre et gérés par des ouvriers communistes convaincus (l'un des premiers directeurs des studios était surnommé « notre Lénine de Barrandov » par les techniciens de cinéma). (5) Chœur sous un grand portrait du jeune communiste Julius Fučík, intronisé martyr par les services de la propagande communiste. Tombé aux mains de la Gestapo, non seulement il refusa de livrer les noms de ses camarades, mais

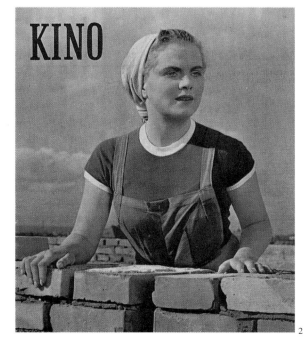

comrades but also managed to write a book, *The Report from the Gallows.* One Czech historian called the phenomenon "a miracle in Pankrác." Filmgoers were numbed with stories of happy workers building the Socialist paradise and grossly exaggerated tales of Communist resistance during the war. They were fed a diet of anti-American propaganda films, such as *The Hijacking* (6), made in 1952 by Ján Kádar and Elmar Klos. *The Silent Barricade* (8), directed by Otakar Vávra in 1949, presented a distorted history of the Prague uprising. The director finished the film with shots of Soviet tanks rushing to liberate Prague and big close-ups of the Soviet soldiers' medals, in order to improve its ideological content. When showing his film in Poland, Vávra shouted enthusiastically, "Long live Comrade Stalin." He survived successive regimes in his country and made more films than anybody else.

dern auch ein Buch mit dem Titel *Reportage unter dem Strang* verfaßt. Ein tschechischer Historiker nannte sein Verhalten »ein Wunder in Pankratius«. Die Kinogäger stumpften gegenüber den Geschichten glücklicher Arbeiter, die das sozialistische Paradies aufbauen, und den stark übertriebenen Erzählungen des kommunistischen Widerstandes währen des Krieges ab. Ihnen wurden zahlreiche antiamerikanische Propagandafilme wie *Entführung* (6), 1952 unter der Regie von Jan Kádar und Elmar Klos entstanden, vorgeführt. *Die schweigende Barrikade* (8), ein Werk des Regissiurs Otokar Vávra aus dem Jahre 1949, erzählte eine verzerrte Geschichte des Prager Aufstandes. Der Regisseur ließ den Film mit den Schüssen sowjetischer Panzer, die Prag im Sturm befreiten, und mit Großaufnahmen von den Verdienstorden russischer Soldaten enden, um den ideologischen Inhalt zu unterstreichen. Als der Film in Polen gezeigt wurde, schrie Vávra begeistert: »Lang lebe der Genosse Stalin«. Er überlebte die aufeinanderfolgenden Regimes in seinem Lande und produzierte mehr Filme als jeder andere.

il réussit à rédiger le livre *Rapport des geôles.* Un historien tchèque qualifia le phénomène de « miracle à Pankrác ». Les spectateurs se virent submergés d'histoires de travailleurs heureux de participer à la construction du « paradis socialiste » et de récits grossièrement exagérés sur la résistance communiste pendant la guerre. Ils durent subir un régime de films de propagande anti-américaine, comme *L'Enlèvement* (6), réalisé en 1952 par Ján Kádar et Elmar Klos. *La Barricade silencieuse* (8), de Otakar Vávra en 1949, présentait une version inexacte du soulèvement de Prague. Pour renforcer le contenu idéologique, le réalisateur acheva son film par des plans de tanks soviétiques roulant à grande vitesse pour aller libérer la capitale, et des gros plans de médailles de soldats soviétiques. En présentant son œuvre en Pologne, Vávra cria avec enthousiasme « Vive le camarade Staline! ». Survivant à tous les régimes, il fut le plus prolifique des réalisateurs tchécoslovaques.

4

5

6

7

8

### Emil Zátopek

(1) Dana Zátopková (b. 1922) and Emil Zátopek (b.1922; holder of nine world records). Husband and wife were both Olympic gold medal winners and became the embodiment of Communist success in international sport. In 1952 at the Helsinki Olympics, Zátopek became the only man in history to win the 5km, 10km and marathon run. Dana Zátopková won a gold medal in the javelin. (2) Zátopek was welcomed enthusiastically by crowds in Wenceslas Square after the London Olympics in 1949. (3) Medal for a race named in honor of Zátopek. He was often seen in his army uniform (he graduated from a military school) and the Communist government gave him the title of Honored Master of Sport for his various achievements (some of them not connected with sport). (4) Zátopek was the best runner in Czechoslovakia's history.

### Emil Zátopek

(1) Dana Zátopková (geboren 1922) und Emil Zátopek (geboren 1922, Inhaber von neun Weltrekorden). Beide Ehepartner gewannen olympische Goldmedaillen und verkörperten die kommunistischen Erfolge im internationalen Sport. Bei den Olympischen Spielen in Helsinki 1952 wurde Zátopek als einziger Mann in der olympischen Geschichte Sieger in den Rennen über 5 und 10 Kilometer und im Marathonlauf. Dana Zátopková gewann eine Goldmedaille im Speerwerfen. (2) Zátopek wurde nach den Olympischen Spielen in London 1949 von einer begeisterten Menschenmenge auf dem Wenzelsplatz begrüßt. (3) Medaille für ein Rennen, das zu Ehren Zátopeks nach ihm benannt ist. Er zeigte sich oft in Militäruniform (er hatte eine Militärschule besucht), und die kommunistische Regierung verlieh ihm für seine vielen Erfolge (darunter einige, die mit dem Sport nichts zu tun hatten) den Titel »Ehrenmeister des Sports«. (4) Zátopek war der beste Läufer in der Geschichte der Tschechoslowakei.

### Emil Zátopek

(1) Dana Zátopková (née en 1922) et Emil Zátopek (né en 1922, détenteur de neuf records du monde). Tous deux remportèrent des médailles d'or olympiques et incarnèrent la percée communiste dans le sport international. En 1952, aux Jeux olympiques d'Helsinki, Zátopek fut le seul athlète de l'histoire à remporter les 5 km, 10 km et le marathon. Dana Zátopková s'attribua la médaille d'or du lancer de javelot. (2) Zátopková fut accueilli par une foule en délire sur la place Venceslas après les Jeux olympiques de Londres en 1949. (3) Médailles pour une course nommée en l'honneur de Zátopek. Il arborait souvent son uniforme de l'armée et était diplômé d'une académie militaire. Le gouvernement communiste lui accorda le titre de «Maître honoré du Sport» pour ses nombreux succès (certains sans rapport avec le sport). (4) Zátopek est le meilleur coureur de l'histoire de la Tchécoslovaquie.

3

4

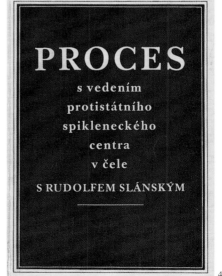

PROCES

s vedením
protistátního
spikleneckého
centra
v čele

S RUDOLFEM SLÁNSKÝM

5

6

## "Final Solution" Soviet-style

Rudolf Slánský (1901–52) was, after Gottwald, the most important man in the Czechoslovak Communist Party. In 1945 he became First Secretary and in the next three years he played an active part in the political purges. In 1952 he himself became the victim of those purges and, together with 13 other Communists, he was arrested as the leader of "the Zionist international conspiracy" and as "an imperialist spy." The 14 accused, of whom 11 were Jewish, were without exception former high Party and government officials. The Stalin-orchestrated purges within the Communist parties of the Soviet satellite countries were directed against Jewish Communists, who were "too Jewish" for his liking. The interrogations of the victims were prepared by agents sent from Moscow, from the special VI Department of the NKVD, known colloquially as the "Jew section." The confessions in court, so carefully rehearsed by the interrogators, were obtained by extreme physical and psychological torture, including beating, sleep deprivation, administration of drugs and intense questioning over long periods. On 27 November 1952, 11 of the defendants, including Slánský, were sentenced to death; the other three were given life imprisonment. Gottwald stayed silent, and in so doing he became a passive accomplice in the murder of his comrades. The sentences were carried out on 3 December 1952 and the ashes of the dead men were scattered on an icy road outside Prague. (1) Rudolf Slánský (left) and Klement Gottwald (center). (2) Slánský and Gottwald before the laughter died out. (3) Pankrác court and prison, where the trials took place. (4) A book published from the trials: *The Trial Against the Leading Anti-State Spy Center with Rudolf Slánský as its Leader*. (6) A retouched photograph of Klement Gottwald. After the executions, the men who always stood behind Gottwald (5) had to be erased from many photographs. The men were legally rehabilitated in 1963 and by the Party in 1968.

## Die »Endlösung« im sowjetischen Stil

Rudolf Slánský (1901–52) war nach Gottwald der wichtigste Mann in der KSČ. 1945 wurde er Generalsekretär und spielte während der folgenden drei Jahre eine aktive Rolle bei den politischen Säuberungen. 1952 fiel er selbst diesen Säuberungen zum Opfer und wurde zusammen mit 13 anderen Kommunisten als Führer »der zionistischen internationalen Verschwörung« und als »imperialistischer Spion« verhaftet. Die 14 Angeklagten, von denen 11 Juden waren, stammten ohne Ausnahme aus den höheren Partei- und Regierungsorganen. Die von Stalin angeordneten Säuberungen in den kommunistischen Parteien der sowjetischen Satellitenstaaten richteten sich gegen die jüdischen Kommunisten, die ihm »zu jüdisch« waren. Die Verhöre hatten Moskauer Agenten der Sondereinheit VI des NKWD, die allgemein unter dem Spitznamen »Judensektion« bekannt war, vorbereitet. Die Geständnisse vor Gericht waren im Verhör sorgfältig einstudiert und unter extremer physischer und psychischer Gewaltanwendung, einschließlich Schlägen, Schlafentzug, Drogeneinsatz und Dauerverhören, erpreßt worden. Am 27. November 1952 verurteilte das Gericht 11 der Angeklagten, darunter Slánský, zum Tode; die übrigen erhielten lebenslange Haftstrafen. Gottwald verhielt sich ruhig und machte sich so zum passiven Komplizen der Mörder seiner Kameraden. Am 3. Dezember 1952 wurde das Urteil vollstreckt. Die Asche der toten Männer verstreute man auf einer vereisten Straße außerhalb Prags. (1) Rudolf Slánský (links) und Klement Gottwald (Mitte). (2) Slánský und Gottwald – bevor ihnen das Lachen verging. (3) Der Pankratius-Gerichtshof und das Gefängnis, in dem die Prozesse stattfanden. (4) Zu den Prozessen erschien ein Buch mit dem Titel *Die Prozesse gegen das wichtigste antistaatliche Spionagezentrum unter der Führung von Rudolf Slánský*. (6) Eine retuschierte Fotografie von Klement Gottwald. Nach der Hinrichtung mußten die Männer, die immer hinter Gottwald gestanden hatten (5), von vielen Fotografien verschwinden. Die Männer wurden 1963 durch den Obersten Gerichtshof und 1968 auch durch die Partei posthum rehabilitiert.

## La « solution finale », style soviétique

Après Gottwald, Rudolf Slánský (1901–1952) était le plus important responsable du Parti communiste. En 1945, il fut nommé Premier secrétaire et joua un rôle actif dans les purges politiques des trois années qui suivirent. En 1952, il en fut à son tour victime et arrêté, avec 13 autres membres du Parti, comme chef de « la conspiration sioniste internationale » et « espion impérialiste ». Les 14 accusés, dont 11 étaient juifs, étaient sans exception de hauts responsables du Parti et du gouvernement. Orchestrées par Staline, les purges des divers partis communistes des satellites soviétiques furent dirigées contre les communistes juifs, « trop juifs » à son goût. Les interrogatoires étaient préparés par des agents envoyés par Moscou (Département spécial VI du NKVD, appelé couramment « section juive »). Les confessions publiques devant le tribunal, répétées avec soin, étaient obtenues au moyen de tortures physiques et psychologiques extrêmes, dont la violence, la privation de sommeil, l'administration de drogues et d'interminables séances de questions. Le 27 novembre 1952, 11 des accusés, y compris Slánský, furent condamnés à mort, les autres à la prison à vie. Gottwald se tut, complice du même coup de la mort de ses camarades. Les sentences furent exécutées le 3 décembre 1952 et les cendres des suppliciés dispersées sur une route gelée des environs de Prague. (1) Rudolf Slánský (à gauche) et Klement Gottwald (au centre). (2) Slanský et Gottwald quelque temps avant les procès. (3) Le tribunal et la prison de Pankrác où se déroulèrent les procès. (4) Livre publié sur les procès: *Procès contre la principale centrale d'espionnage antiétatique, dirigée par Rudolf Slánský*. (6) Photo retouchée de Klement Gottwald. Après les exécutions, les hommes qui se tenaient souvent près de Gottwald (5) furent supprimés de nombreuses photographies. Les condamnés furent réhabilités en 1963 et par le Parti en 1968.

### The Deaths of Stalin and Gottwald; Antonín Zápotocký – the New President

(1) Gottwald, greeted by saluting soldiers, as he arrives at Ruzyně airport after attending Stalin's funeral in Moscow. (2) Gottwald looking at a smiling Antonín Zápotocký (1884–1957), the man who was soon to become the next President. (3) *The World of Soviets* announces Stalin's death on 5 March 1953. (4) *New Prague* reports Gottwald's death on 14 March 1953. Gottwald died of syphilis, which he caught before penicillin became widely available and which was never properly cured. His body was embalmed and displayed in a sarcophagus in the Vítkov Monument. It was kept on display by an army of doctors and make-up artists from the Barrandov Film Studios but by 1963 it had disintegrated so badly that it had to be cremated. (5) Thousands lined the streets for Gottwald's funeral.

### Der Tod von Stalin und Gottwald; Antonín Zápotocký – der neue Präsident

(1) Gottwald wird nach seiner Rückkehr von Stalins Beerdigung in Moskau bei seiner Ankunft auf dem Flughafen Ruzyně von salutierenden Soldaten begrüßt. (2) Gottwald schaut auf einen strahlenden Antonín Zápotocký (1884–1957), der bald darauf der nächste Präsident werden sollte. (3) *Die Welt der Sowjets* gab am 5. März 1953 Stalins Tod bekannt. (4) *Das Neue Prag* berichtet über Gottwalds Tod am 14. März 1953. Gottwald starb an der Syphillis, an der er vor der Zeit, als Penicillin überall erhältlich war, erkrankt war und die er nie richtig auskuriert hatte. Sein Leichnam wurde einbalsamiert und im Vítkov-Monument in einem Sarkophag ausgestellt. Er wurde von einer ganzen Armee von Doktoren und Maskenbildnern aus den Barrandov-Studios konserviert; 1963 war der Leichnam aber bereits soweit verfallen, daß er verbrannt werden mußte. (5) Tausende säumen die Straßen anläßlich Gottwalds Beerdigung.

### Morts de Staline et de Gottwald; Antonín Zápotocký nouveau président

(1) Gottwald salué par les troupes arrive à l'aéroport de Ruzyně de retour des funérailles de Staline à Moscou. (2) Gottwald souriant à Antonín Zápotocký (1884–1957), son futur successeur. (3) *Le Monde des Soviets* annonce la mort de Staline le 5 mars 1953. (4) *Le Nouveau Prague* annonce la mort de Gottwald le 14 mars 1953. Gottwald mourut de syphilis attrapée avant que la pénicilline ne soit disponible et jamais bien soignée. Son corps fut embaumé et exposé dans un sarcophage du monument de Vítkov. Entouré des soins d'une armée de médecins et de maquilleurs des studios de cinéma de Barrandov, il était en si piètre état en 1963 qu'on dut l'incinérer. (5) Des milliers de personnes suivent les funérailles de Gottwald.

## SVĚT SOVĚTŮ 11

Nesmrtelné Stalinovo jméno bude navždy žít
v srdcích všeho pokrokového lidstva

3

## NOVÁ PRAHA

ČASOPIS PRAŽSKÉ LIDOVÉ SPRÁVY

Věčně bude žít v československém lidu jméno soudruha Klementa Gottwalda

56. ROČNÍK ● ČÍSLO 6
V PRAZE 25. BŘEZNA 1953
Cena jednotlivého čísla Kčs 3.50

4

5

5

### The Stalin Monument

(1) A rare picture of film technicians and workers from the Barrandov Film Studios, dressed by the costume department, posing for the sculptor Otakar Švec (2), who (together with two architects, Jiří and Vlasta Štursovi) designed the largest monument to Stalin ever built. The film electrician, who after his "modeling job" was nicknamed "Stalin", became an alcoholic and died a few years later. The statue was built in Letná and unveiled on 1 May 1955. It weighed 14,000 tons and was 30m high; 7000m³ of granite were used; 600 workers struggled with the job for 500 days. The workers were paid handsomely and received medals. Several of them died in accidents while erecting the monument and Otakar Švec committed suicide just before the unveiling. Seen from the Čech Bridge, the statue of Stalin seemed larger than the figures standing behind him. Looking from the east, three Soviet men and a woman were queuing behind the Generalissimo; looking from the west (5), a Czech worker, a woman-farmer with a sickle, a "working intellectual" and a soldier completed the symmetry. The monument symbolized both nations marching towards Communism, led by the Man of Steel (Stalin). But the inhabitants of Prague ignored the ideological content and many jokes circulated: "Why is Stalin reaching for his inside pocket? He is trying to get his wallet to pay for the sculpture."

### Das Stalin-Monument

(1) Eine seltene Aufnahme von Technikern und Arbeitern der Barrandov-Filmstudios, die, von der Kostümabteilung ausgestattet, für den Bildhauer Otakar Švec (2) Modell stehen. Švec entwarf (zusammen mit den beiden Architekten Jiří und Vlasta Štursovi) das größte Stalin-Monument, das je errichtet wurde. Der Filmtechniker, dem man wegen seiner Arbeit als Modell den Spitznamen Stalin gab, wurde alkoholkrank und starb ein paar Jahre später. Am 1. Mai 1955 wurde die in Letná gebaute Statue enthüllt. Für das 14.000 Tonnen schwere und 30 Meter hohe Monument wurden 7.000 m³ Granit benötigt, 600 Arbeiter waren über 500 Tage mit dem Auftrag beschäftigt. Die Arbeiter erhielten ansehnliche Löhne und Ehrenmedaillen. Einige von ihnen kamen dabei ums Leben, und Otakar Švec verübte kurz vor der Enthüllung Selbstmord. Von der Čech-Brücke aus erscheint Stalin größer als die Figuren hinter ihm. Blickt man von Osten auf das Monument, stehen drei sowjetische Männer und eine Frau hinter dem Generalissimus; vom Westen aus (5) sind es ein tschechischer Arbeiter, eine Bäuerin mit einer Sichel, ein »arbeitender Intellektueller« und ein Soldat. Das Monument symbolisiert beide Völker auf ihrem Weg zum Kommunismus unter der Führung des Mannes aus Stahl (Stalin). Aber die Prager Bürger ignorierten die ideologische Botschaft und erzählten sich Witze wie diesen: »Warum greift Stalin in seine Innentasche? Er sucht seine Geldbörse, um für das Monument zu bezahlen.«

### Le Monument à Staline

(1) Rare image de techniciens et d'ouvriers des studios de Barrandov habillés par le département des costumes et posant pour le sculpteur Otakar Švec (2) qui, avec les architectes Jiří et Vlasta Štursovi, éleva le plus grand monument jamais dédié à Staline. L'électricien de cinéma surnommé « Staline » qui servit de modèle sombra dans l'alcoolisme et mourut quelques années plus tard. La statue fut édifiée à Letná et inaugurée le 1er mai 1955. Elle pesait 14 000 tonnes et mesurait 30 m de haut. 7000 m³ de granit furent utilisés et 600 ouvriers participèrent à sa construction qui dura 500 jours. Ils étaient bien payés et furent récompensés par des médailles. Plusieurs moururent accidentellement pendant les travaux, et Otakar Švec se suicida peu avant l'inauguration. Vue du Pont Čech, la statue de Staline paraissait plus grande que celles des personnages qui l'accompagnaient. Côté est, trois Soviétiques et une femme se tiennent derrière le maréchal. Côté ouest (5), un ouvrier tchèque, une fermière avec faucille, un « travailleur intellectuel » et un soldat assurent la symétrie. Le monument symbolisait les deux nations marchant vers le Communisme sous la conduite de l'homme d'acier (Staline), mais les Pragois ignorèrent ce contenu idéologique et de nombreuses plaisanteries circulèrent : « Pourquoi Staline a-t-il la main dans son manteau ? Pour prendre son portefeuille et payer la sculpture ? »

## Now You See It, Now You Don't

Soon after the XX Congress of the Soviet Communist Party in October 1956, at which Stalin's personality cult was publicly criticized, his corpse was removed from Lenin's Mausoleum. Nikita Khrushchev made his famous speech denouncing Stalin's crimes and charging him with the murder of 20–40 million Russians. The speech shook the Communist world. Finally, in 1962, the Czech Communists received explicit orders from Moscow to get rid of the embarrassing Stalin monument and 800kg of explosives and 1650 detonators were used to blow it up over a period of several weeks (1). It was a top-secret operation, which in true Švejk fashion was watched with delight by all the inhabitants of Prague, including schoolchildren who were brought by their teachers to experience a lesson in history. The remains were later driven in an open truck through the medieval streets of Prague, adding a surreal touch to this political happening. The only thing left was the medal given to the builders (2). The space was left empty (3) until the 1990s, when the Metronome sculpture was put up (4), and on one occasion in 1996 a statue of Michael Jackson appeared as he tried to re-launch his career. Nowadays Prague's teenagers use the granite pedestal to perform acrobatics on their skateboards.

## Sinnestäuschungen

Kurz nach dem XX. Kongreß der KPdSU im Oktober 1956, auf dem der Personenkult um Stalin öffentlich kritisiert wurde, entfernte man seinen Leichnam aus dem Lenin-Mausoleum. Nikita Chruschtschow hielt seine berühmte Rede über die Verbrechen Stalins und warf ihm den Mord an 20 bis 40 Millionen Russen vor. Diese Rede erschütterte die kommunistische Welt. 1962 schließlich erhielten die tschechischen Kommunisten aus Moskau den direkten Befehl, das peinliche Stalin-Monument zu entfernen. 800 kg Sprengstoff und 1.650 Detonatoren waren notwendig, um das Werk in die Luft zu sprengen. Diese Aktion dauerte mehrere Wochen. (1) Sie sollte unter größter Geheimhaltung stattfinden; aber in echter Schwejk-Manier sahen alle Einwohner Prags mit Begeisterung zu. Lehrer brachten ihre Schulkinder mit, um ihnen eine Lektion in Geschichte zu erteilen. Später fuhr man die Überreste auf offenen Lastwagen durch die mittelalterlichen Straßen von Prag, was diesem politischen Ereignis einen surrealen Unterton verlieh. Das einzige, was übrig blieb, waren die Medaillen für die Erbauer (2). Der Platz blieb leer (3), bis man in den 90er Jahren die Metronom-Skulptur dorthin stellte (4). 1996 baute man eine Figur von Michael Jackson auf, der hier seine festgefahrene Karriere wieder in Gang bringen wollte. Heute nutzen Prager Teenager die Granitplattform, um ihre akrobatischen Kunststücke auf dem Skateboard vorzuführen.

## Une brève existence

Peu après le XXe Congrès du Parti communiste soviétique d'octobre 1956 au cours duquel le culte de la personnalité stalinien fut publiquement dénoncé, le cadavre du dictateur fut enlevé du Mausolée Lénine. Nikita Kroutchev prononça son fameux discours dénonçant les crimes de Staline et l'accusa d'avoir fait assassiner de 20 à 40 millions de Russes. Cette intervention bouleversa le monde communiste. Finalement, en 1962, les communistes tchèques reçurent des ordres explicites de Moscou d'avoir à faire disparaître le monument à Staline. En quelques semaines 800 kg d'explosifs et 1 650 détonateurs le firent partir en fumée (1). C'était une opération secrète, mais dans un style très Švejk, et tout Prague en fit des gorges chaudes. Les professeurs profitèrent de l'occasion pour donner une leçon d'histoire à leurs élèves. Les restes furent ultérieurement transportés en camion découvert dans les rues médiévales de la capitale, ajoutant une touche surréaliste à ce happening politique. (2) Le seul souvenir qui subsiste de ce monument est la médaille offerte aux ouvriers. L'emplacement fut abandonné (3) jusque dans les années 1990, date de la mise en place de la sculpture du métronome (4) et, en 1996, une effigie de Michael Jackson fut dressée au même endroit. Aujourd'hui, les adolescents pragois s'exercent à la planche à roulettes acrobatique sur son socle de granit.

2

3

4

### Spartakiáda

The last *Sokol* rally took place on 28 March 1948 (one month after the Communist coup) and turned into a gigantic act of defiance towards the Communist regime. During the opening and closing parades, thousands shouted their support for President Beneš and when Gottwald took the stage many in the crowd openly jeered. Soon after, *Sokol* was denounced as a "bourgeois" organization and its leaders were arrested. The festivals were replaced with *spartakiáda* – a similarly monolithic event, but stripped of Czech patriotism. The first National *Spartakiáda* in 1955 celebrated the 10th anniversary of "the liberation of Czechoslovakia by the Soviet Army." Fireworks and festivities concluded the festival, with a re-enactment of the Czechs' joy at being "liberated" by the Soviet army. (1–5) Pictures from the 1955 *spartakiáda*.

### Die Spartakiade

Am 28. März 1948 (einen Monat nach dem kommunistischen Staatsstreich) fand die letzte *Sokol*-Veranstaltung statt, das sich zu einer riesigen Demonstration gegen das kommunistische Regime entwickelte. Während der Eröffnungs- und der Abschlußparaden forderten Tausende die Rückkehr von Präsident Beneš, und als Gottwald auf der Tribüne erschien, wurde er von vielen öffentlich ausgebuht. Kurz darauf wurde die *Sokol* als »bürgerliche« Organisation denunziert, ihre Anführer kamen ins Gefängnis. Die Spartakiaden traten an die Stelle ihrer Festivals – ähnlich monolithische Veranstaltungen, aber ohne den tschechischen Patriotismus. Die erste nationale Spartakiade fand 1955 anläßlich des 10. Jahrestages der »Befreiung der Tschechoslowakei durch die sowjetische Armee« statt. Das Festival endete mit einem Feuerwerk und anderen Festlichkeiten, die die tschechische Freude über die »Befreiung« durch die sowjetische Armee widerspiegeln sollte. (1–5) Bilder von der Spartakiade 1955.

### Les Spartakiades

Le dernier *Sokol* rassemblement se déroula le 28 mars 1948 (un mois après le coup d'État communiste) et se transforma en une gigantesque manifestation de défiance envers le régime communiste. Au cours du défilé d'ouverture et de clôture, des milliers de participants demandèrent le retour du président Beneš et lorsque Gottwald parut, de nombreuses huées s'élevèrent dans la foule. Peu après, *Sokol* fut dénoncé comme une organisation « bourgeoise » et ses responsables arrêtés. Les rassemblements furent remplacés par des Spartakiades, manifestations similaires, mais débarrassées de tout patriotisme. Annoncée comme le plus grand événement sportif jamais organisé, la première Spartakiade nationale de 1955 célébrait le dixième anniversaire de « la libération de la Tchécoslovaquie par l'Armée soviétique ». Des feux d'artifice et des festivités conclurent le festival mettant en scène la joie des Tchèques d'avoir été « libérés » par l'Armée rouge. (1–5) Images des Spartakiades de 1955.

### Optimistic Predictions

A map of blossoming Socialist industries in the Czechoslovak Republic, showing the smoking chimneys of factories which in 30–40 years would completely destroy some of the areas ecologically (especially the northern parts), leaving dead forests and poisonous, unbreathable air.

### Optimistische Prognosen

Eine Karte der blühenden sozialistischen Industrien in der tschechoslowakischen Republik zeigt die rauchenden Schornsteine der Fabriken, die in 30 bis 40 Jahren einige Regionen (besonders den Norden) ökologisch total zerstörten und nur abgestorbene Wälder und vergiftete Luft zurückließen.

### Une carte optimiste

Cette carte des industries socialistes en plein essor montre également les cheminées fumantes des usines qui, en 30 ou 40 ans, allaient totalement détruire l'écologie de certaines régions (en particulier dans le Nord), détruisant les forêts et empoisonnant l'air.

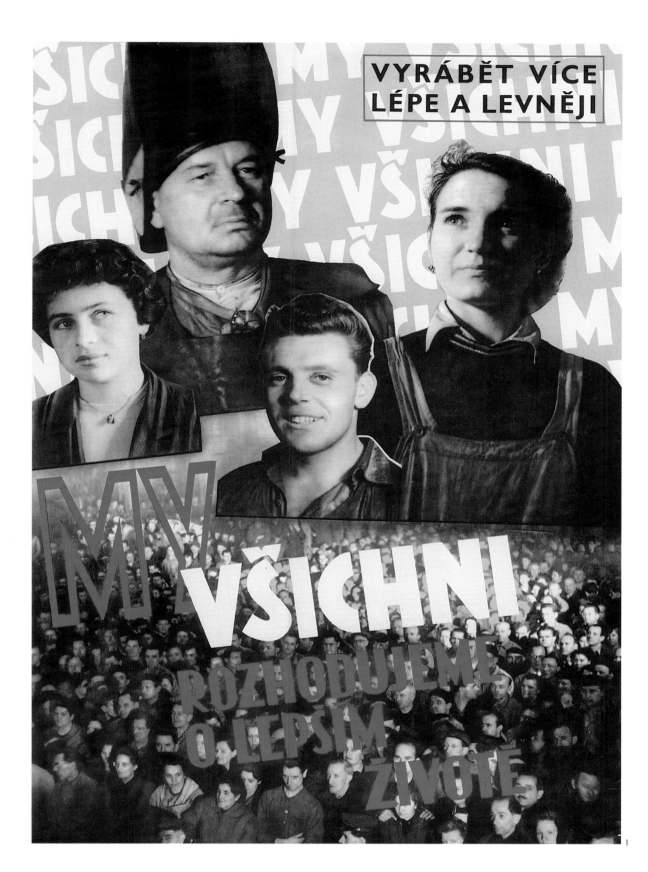

VYRÁBĚT VÍCE
LÉPE A LEVNĚJI

MY VŠICHNI
ROZHODUJEME
O LEPŠÍM
ŽIVOTĚ

### A Dose of Austerity

(Pages 304–309) The dream and reality of 1950s Socialism were very different and slogans about "everybody producing more, better and cheaper" were hollow (1). The system was unprofitable and, although people were provided with basic economic security, including guaranteed full employment, the goods they produced were inferior in quality. Inefficiency was covered up with false statistics. People struggled to make ends meet. Many democrats were imprisoned (some were executed – the most famous case was that of Milada Horáková, a hero of the wartime resistance). Thousands of shopkeepers and tradesmen were dragged to prison. 1950 alone saw 14 executions and 52 life sentences; 50,000 were arrested; 2500 monks and Catholic priests were jailed. The monasteries and churches were closed down. Fear and paranoia prevailed. But the Czech sense of humor thrived. A Czech joke: "Why are capitalists teetering on the edge of an abyss? So they can have a better look at us."

### Die Härte des Alltags

(304–309) Im Gegensatz zur sozialistischen Utopie sah die Realität der 50er Jahre ganz anders aus, und Schlagworte wie »alle produzieren mehr, besser und billiger« waren leeres Gerede (1). Das System arbeitete nicht profitabel; obwohl die wirtschaftliche Grundversorgung der Menschen sichergestellt und Vollbeschäftigung garantiert war, waren die produzierten Güter von minderwertiger Qualität. Ineffizienz wurde durch falsche Statistiken geschönt. Die Menschen mußten hart arbeiten, um über die Runden zu kommen. Viele Demokraten saßen in Strafanstalten (einige wurden hingerichtet – der bekannteste Fall war der von Milada Horáková, einer Widerstandsheldin des Krieges). Tausende von Ladenbesitzern und Kaufleuten wanderten ins Gefängnis. Allein im Jahr 1950 gab es 14 Hinrichtungen und 52 Verurteilungen zu lebenslangen Haftstrafen. 50.000 Menschen wurden verhaftet, 2.500 Mönche und katholische Priester inhaftiert und Klöster und Kirchen geschlossen. Angst und Verfolgungswahn gingen um. Aber der tschechische Sinn für Humor blühte auf. Ein typischer tschechischer Witz lautete: »Warum schwanken die Kapitalisten am Rande des Abgrunds? Damit sie uns besser sehen können.«

### Une vie difficile

(Pages 304–309) La réalité de l'utopie socialiste des années 50 était très différente des creux slogans obligatoires comme : « Tout le monde produit plus, mieux et moins cher. » (1) Le système n'était pas rentable et si tout le monde bénéficiait d'une sécurité de base, dont le plein-emploi, les biens produits restaient de qualité insuffisante. L'inefficacité était masquée par des statistiques mensongères. Il fallait se battre pour arriver à vivre correctement. De nombreux démocrates furent jetés en prison (certains exécutés, dont en particulier Milada Horáková, héros de la Résistance). Des milliers de commerçants et de vendeurs furent traînés en prison. Rien qu'en 1950, 14 condamnations à mort et 52 à l'emprisonnement à perpétuité furent prononcées. 50 000 personnes furent arrêtées et 2 500 moines et prêtres catholiques jetés en prison. Les monastères et les églises furent fermés. La peur et la paranoïa s'installèrent, même si le sens de l'humour tchèque persista : « Pourquoi les capitalistes sont-ils au bord du gouffre ? Pour avoir un meilleur point de vue sur nous. »

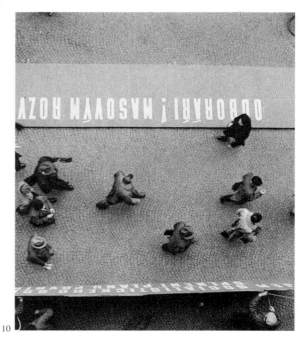

## Antonín Novotný

After Zápotocký's death in 1957, Antonín Novotný (1904–75) became Czechoslovakia's third working-class President. At the end of the 1950s he decided that Socialism had been achieved in Czechoslovakia and he added one important word to its official name: in 1960 the country became the Czechoslovak Socialist Republic. During the Novotný era (1957–68) people were demoralized because the judicial system became a blatant tool of the top Communists and StB. A new phrase, *vnitřní emigrace* (inner emigration), was coined. In the early 1960s, however, Novotný did recognize the country's economic problems and some reforms were undertaken. (1) Novotný delivering a speech. He was known for not being able to pronounce multisyllable words of foreign origin, such as *imperialismus*, *supervelmoc* (imperialism, superpower), so his relationship with the Czechoslovak intelligentsia was always strained. (2) Soviet leader Nikita Khrushchev with Novotný, surveying Prague from the top of the Old Town Hall tower.

## Antonín Novotný

Nach dem Tod Zápotockýs 1957 wurde Antonín Novotný (1904–75) der dritte Präsident der Tschechoslowakei, der aus der Arbeiterklasse kam. Ende der 50er Jahre entschied er, daß der Sozialismus in der Tschechoslowakei vollendet sei und ergänzte den offiziellen Staatsnamen durch ein wichtiges Wort: 1960 wurde das Land in Tschechoslowakische Sozialistische Republik umbenannt. In der Ära Novotný (1957–68) sank die Stimmung der Bevölkerung auf einen Tiefpunkt, weil die Justiz zu einem willigen Werkzeug der obersten Kommunisten und des StB wurde. Ein neues Schlagwort, *vnitřní emigrace* (innere Emigration) machte die Runde. In den früher 60er Jahren erkannte allerdings auch Novotný die wirtschaftlichen Probleme des Landes und leitete verschiedene Reformen ein. (1) Novotný hält eine Rede. Er war dafür bekannt, daß er mehrsilbige Worte fremdsprachlicher Herkunft – wie *imperialismus* und *supervelmoc* (Supermacht) nicht aussprechen konnte. Seine Beziehungen zur tschechoslowakischen Intelligenz waren immer gespannt. (2) Der sowjetische Führer Nikita Chruschtschow mit Novotný bei einem Blick über Prag von der Spitze des Altstädter Rathausturms.

## Antonín Novotný

Après la mort de Zápotocký en 1957, Antonín Novotný (1904–1975) fut désigné président tchécoslovaque. Il était le troisième président issu de la classe ouvrière. En 1960, il décida que le pays avait accédé au socialisme et ajouta un qualificatif à sa dénomination officielle qui devint: République socialiste tchécoslovaque. Pendant l'ère Novotný (1957–68), le peuple perdit tout courage tant le système juridique était ouvertement aux mains des responsables communistes et du StB. Une nouvelle expression fit son apparition: la *vnitřní emigrace* (l'émigration intérieure). Au début des années 60 cependant, Novotný reconnut l'existence des problèmes économiques et quelques réformes furent entreprises. (1) Discours de Novotný. Il était réputé pour être incapable de prononcer des mots d'origine étrangère de plus d'une syllabe comme *imperialismus* ou *supervelmoc* (impérialisme et superpuissance) et ses relations avec l'intelligentsia restèrent toujours tendues. (2) Le leader soviétique Nikita Kroutchev et Novotný observant Prague du haut du beffroi de l'ancien hôtel de ville.

2

## 1960s Optimism

The thaw in the 1960s brought slow but significant changes in people's lives. A relatively free decentralized market economy brought a certain prosperity and increased spending. The number of cars in the country increased from 69,591 to 235,000 between 1966 and 1978. *Škoda Spartak* cars and motorcycles (1, 4, 5) became an accessible dream that allowed people to visit their weekend log cabins (*chatas*). (3) Butchers, bakers and patisseries sold a wider variety of products. (6) Interesting shows and plays were staged in the capital's theaters. (7) Large department stores, such as *Bílá Labuť* (White Swan), were frequented by people who, through their moonlighting jobs, had some extra cash to spend. (2) A new banknote issued in 1962.

## Der Optimismus der 60er Jahre

Das Tauwetter der 60er Jahre brachte langsame, aber bedeutende Veränderungen in das Leben der Menschen. Eine relativ freie, dezentralisierte Marktwirtschaft führte zu einem gewissen Wohlstand und größerer Kaufkraft. Im ganzen Land stieg die Zahl der Autos Marke *Škoda Spartak* zwischen 1966 und 1978 von 69.591 auf 235.000, und der Traum von einem Motorrad (1, 4, 5), mit dem man in die Wochenendhäuschen (*chatas*) fahren konnte, ging nun für manche in Erfüllung. (3) Metzger, Bäcker und Konditoren boten eine größere Auswahl an Waren an. (6) Interessante Shows und Theaterstücke wurden in den Schauspielhäusern der Hauptstadt gezeigt. (7) Große Kaufhäuser, wie das *Bílá Labuť* (Weißer Schwan), zogen Leute an, die durch Schwarzarbeit ein wenig Geld gespart hatten. (2) 1962 kam ein neuer Geldschein in Umlauf.

## L'optimisme des années 60

Le dégel des années 60 apporta quelques changements – lents mais significatifs – dans la vie des gens. Une économie de marché relativement libre facilita une certaine prospérité et favorisa la consommation. Dans tout le pays, le nombre de voitures passa de 69 591 à 235 000 de 1966 à 1978. Les voitures et motos *Škoda Spartak* devenaient un rêve accessible (1, 4, 5) et permettaient aux Pragois de se rendre dans leurs cabanes de week-end (*chatas*). (3) Boucheries, boulangeries et pâtisseries proposaient désormais davantage de produits. (6) Des pièces et des spectacles intéressants étaient enfin montés dans les théâtres de la capitale. (7) De nouveaux grands magasins, comme *Bílá Labuť* (Cygne blanc), séduisaient une clientèle à laquelle le travail au noir donnait davantage de moyens financiers. (2) Nouveau billet de banque, diffusé en 1962.

6

7

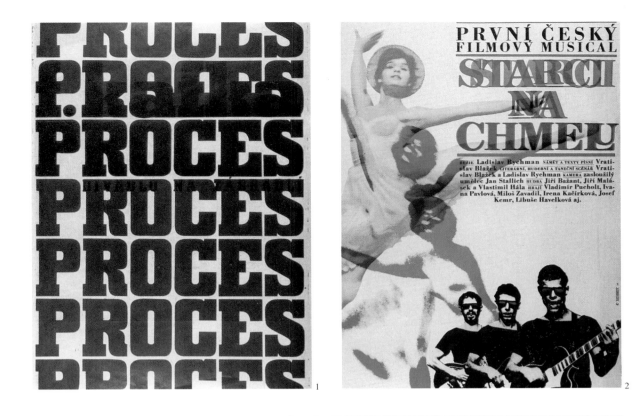

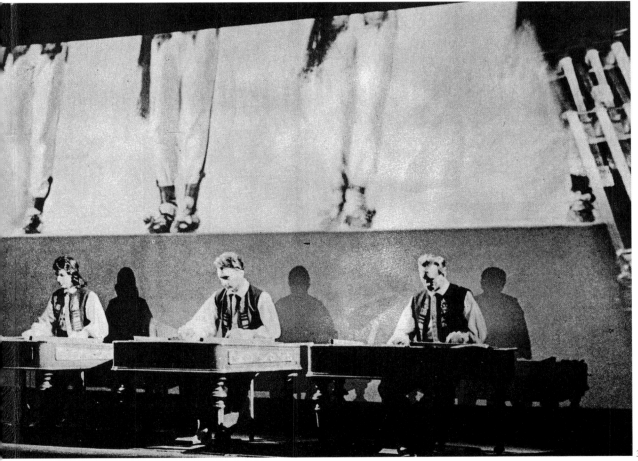

### The Cultural Thaw

(1) A poster for a dramatization of Franz Kafka's *The Trial*, staged by Jan Grossman (1925–93) at the Theater on the Balustrade, which became one of the most exciting stages in the capital. (2) The first Czech musical, *The Hop-Pickers*, produced in 1964. (3) Alfréd Radok (1914–76) and his Magic Lantern Show became famous for combining live performance with film projection and audio-visual effects. (4) Karel Gott (b. 1939), a popular singer often called the "Golden Nightingale" (from the name of the popular Czechoslovak award which he won many times). (5) The Semaphore Theater specialized in musicals, comedy, recitation, dance, art, film and songs. In the 1960s it became famous for its originality, wit and many hits under the direction of two talented artists, Jiří Suchý (b. 1931; playwright, prolific lyricist and performer) and Jiří Šlitr (1924–69; composer of over 300 songs, jazz musician and graphic artist). (6) Women's fashion reflected the changes taking place in the late 1960s. (7) Ladislav Fialka (1931–91), mime artist, director and choreographer, creator of the *Pantomime On the Balustrade*. (8) Jiří Trnka (1906–69), Czech painter and animator famous for his puppet films.

### Tauwetter im kulturellen Bereich

(1) Ein Plakat für eine Bühnenfassung von Franz Kafkas *Der Prozeß*, die Jan Grossman (1925–93) im Theater am Geländer inszenierte, welches zu den interessantesten Bühnen der Stadt wurde. (2) 1964 entstand das erste tschechische Musical, *Die Hopfenpflücker*. (3) Alfréd Radok (1914–76) und seine *Laterna Magica* wurden durch die Kombination der Schauspielervorführungen mit Filmprojektionen und audiovisuellen Effekten bekannt. (4) Karel Gott (geboren 1939), ein beliebter Sänger mit dem Spitzname »die Goldene Nachtigall« (nach dem Titel einer begehrten tschechoslowakischen Auszeichnung, die er mehrfach gewann). (5) Die Semafor-Kleinbühne war auf Musicals, Komödien, Lesungen, Tanz-, Kunst-, Film- und Gesangsveranstaltungen spezialisiert. In den 60er Jahren wurde sie für ihre Originalität, ihren Witz und die vielen Schlagererfolge ihrer beiden Direktoren berühmt, den Künstlern Jiří Suchý (ein 1931 geborener Dramatiker, ausgezeichneter Lyriker und Schauspieler) und Jiří Šlitr (1924–69, Verfasser von über 300 Liedern, Jazzmusiker und Grafikkünstler). (6) Die Damenmode spiegelte die Veränderungen der 60er Jahre wider. (7) Ladislav Fialka (1931–91), Pantomine, Schauspieldirektor und Choreograph, Gründer der *Pantomime am Geländer*. (8) Jiří Trnka (1906–1969), tschechischer Maler und Animateur, berühmt für seine Puppenfilme.

### La culture tchèque

(1) Affiche pour un montage théâtral d'après *Le Procès* de Kafka, mis en scène par Jan Grossman (1925–1993) au Théâtre sur la balustrade qui devint l'une des meilleures scènes de la capitale. (2) La première comédie musicale tchèque *Les Cueilleurs de houblon* produite en 1964. (3) Alfréd Radok (1914–1976) et son spectacle de lanterne magique devinrent célèbres en combinant le jeu d'acteurs à des projections de film et des effets audiovisuels. (4) Karel Gott (né en 1939), chanteur populaire, souvent appelé « la voix d'or », d'après le nom d'un prix tchécoslovaque qu'il remporta plusieurs fois. (5) Le Théâtre du Sémaphore était spécialisé dans les comédies musicales, les comédies, les récitals de poésie, la danse, l'art, le cinéma et la chanson. Dans les années 60, il se fit remarquer par son originalité et ses nombreux succès sous la direction de deux artistes de talent Jiří Suchý (auteur dramatique né en 1931, parolier prolifique et acteur) et Jiří Šlitr (1924–1969), compositeur de plus de 300 chansons, musicien de jazz et graphiste. (6) La mode féminine reflétait les changements politiques. (7) Ladislav Fialka (1931–1991), mime, metteur en scène et chorégraphe est le célèbre créateur du théâtre *Pantomime sur la balustrade*. (8) Jiří Trnka (1906–1969), peintre tchèque et animateur célèbre pour ses films de marionnettes.

5

6

7

8

## The Czech New Wave

In the late 1950s and 1960s Czechoslovak films turned away from Socialist Realism and embraced national traditions, Surrealism and lyricism, as well as a large dose of irony, wit and a keen sense of the absurd. Highly acclaimed by critics, the films won numerous awards, including two Oscars, and throughout the world were labeled the Czechoslovak New Wave. (1) Miloš Forman (b. 1932), one of the most famous Czechoslovak New Wave film directors, who in his films presented raw life with a large dose of ironic humor. (2) A poster for one of Forman's films, *Blonde in Love*, a painful comedy about a petty middle-class world within the Socialist economy. Stills from *Blonde in Love* (8) and *Peter and Paula* (4). Scene from *Intimate Lighting* (5) by Ivan Passer. Forman's film *The Firemen's Ball* (3), a satire on Socialist bureaucracy, did not go down too well with the authorities, who banned it "for all time" (it was briefly released in 1968 and banned again until 1989). (6) Jan Němec's unconventional film *Diamonds of the Night* has almost no dialogue and fantasy sequences which break up any psychological motivation. It tries to convey a state of mind, the fear of two men on the run. (7) A poster for František Vláčil's film *Markéta Lazarová* (9), a tale of barbarity set in 13th-century Bohemia.

## Die tschechische »Neue Welle«

In den späten 50er und 60er Jahren kehrten die tschechoslowakischen Filmer dem Sozialistischen Realismus den Rücken und machten sich ihre nationalen Traditionen, den Surrealismus, den lyrischen Stil sowie eine große Portion Ironie, Witz und Sinn für das Absurde zu eigen. Von den Kritikern hochgelobte Filme gewannen zahllose Auszeichungen, einschließlich zweier Oscars, und wurden als »tschechoslowakische Neue Welle« bezeichnet. (1) Miloš Forman (geboren 1932) ist einer der bekanntesten tschechoslowakischen Filmemacher der Neuen Welle, der in seinen Filmen das Leben mit viel Ironie darstellte. (2) Ein Plakat zu Formans Film *Die Lieben einer Blondine*, eine schmerzhaftwitzige Komödie über die kleinbürgerliche Welt in der sozialistischen Wirtschaft. Szenen aus *Die Lieben einer Blondine* (8) und *Peter und Paula* (4). Szene aus *Intime Beleuchtung* (5) von Ivan Passer. Formans Film *Feuerwehrball* (3), eine Satire auf die sozialistische Bürokratie, erzürnte die Behörden, die ihn »auf ewig« verboten (er wurde 1968 für eine kurze Zeit freigegeben, dann aber wieder bis 1989 unter Verschluß gehalten). (6) Jan Němecs unkonventioneller Film *Diamanten der Nacht* enthält fast keine Dialoge, dafür phantastische Sequenzen, die jede psychologische Deutung sprengen. Der Autor versucht, einen Gemütszustand darzustellen: die Angst der beiden Männer auf der Flucht. (7) Ein Plakat von František Vláčils Film *Markéta Lazarová* (9), eine Geschichte über die Grausamkeit im Böhmen des 13. Jahrhunderts.

## La nouvelle vague tchèque

À la fin des années 50 et dans les années 60, le cinéma tchécoslovaque se détourna du réalisme socialiste pour se rapprocher de traditions nationales, du surréalisme et d'un certain lyrisme. Il faisait preuve de beaucoup d'ironie, d'esprit et d'un sens très développé de l'absurde. Très applaudis par la critique, ces films remportèrent de nombreux prix dont deux Oscars, et l'on vit apparaître une sorte de label « nouvelle vague tchèque ». (1) Miloš Forman (né en 1932), l'un des plus célèbres metteurs en scène de la nouvelle vague, qui montrait la vraie vie avec beaucoup d'ironie et d'humour. (2) Affiche pour l'un des films de Forman *Les Amours d'une blonde*, comédie douce-amère sur la petite-bourgeoisie socialiste. Images des *Amours d'une blonde* (8) et de *Peter et Paula* (4). Scène d'*Éclairage intime* (5), d'Ivan Passer. Le film de Forman *Au feu les pompiers* (3), satire de la bureaucratie socialiste, ne plut guère aux autorités qui l'interdirent « à perpétuité » (il fut brièvement projeté en 1968, puis interdit de nouveau jusqu'en 1989). (6) Le film peu conventionnel de Jan Němec, *Les Diamants de la nuit*, était presque sans dialogues et comportait des séquences oniriques qui rompaient le développement psychologique. Il essayait de traduire l'état d'esprit, la peur de deux hommes en fuite. (7) Affiche du film de František Vláčil *Markéta Lazarová* (9), récit barbare situé dans la Bohême du XIIIe siècle.

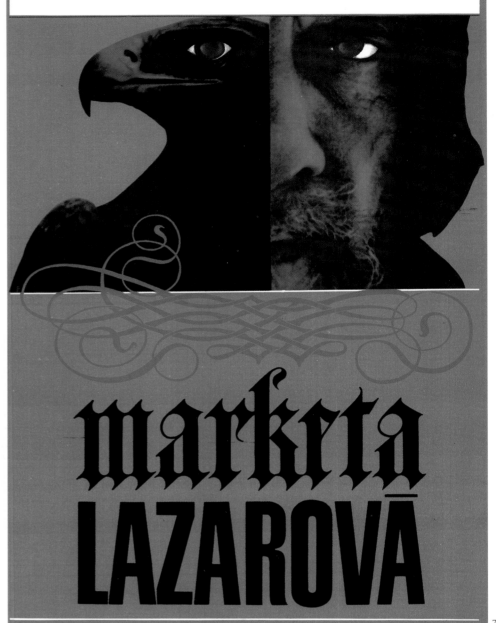

FILMOVÝ EPOS PODLE LITERÁRNÍ PŘEDLOHY VLADISLAVA VANČURY
Scénář: FRANTIŠEK PAVLÍČEK, FRANTIŠEK VLÁČIL ⁓ Režie: FRANTIŠEK VLÁČIL ⁓ Kamera: BEDŘICH BAŤKA
Hudba: ZDENĚK LIŠKA ⁓ ČESKÝ FILM ⁓ Hrají: MAGDA VÁŠÁRYOVÁ, MICHAL KOŽUCH, JOSEF KEMR,
PAVLA POLÁŠKOVÁ, FRANTIŠEK VELECKÝ, VLASTIMIL HARAPES, IVO PALUCH aj.

marketa
LAZAROVA

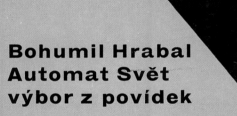

## Bohumil Hrabal

(1) A poster from the film *Closely Observed Trains*, which in 1967 won an Academy Award for director (6) Jiří Menzel (b. 1928). The film is based on a slim novel by Bohumil Hrabal (1914–97). (4, 7) Stills from the film, which is a sophisticated, small-town tale full of quirky moments of passion and humor (one scene shows an assistant stationmaster rubber-stamping a girl telegrapher's buttocks). The film subverts stereotypes, showing everyone as human, war as absurd and heroism as accidental. Its poetic charge is indebted to Surrealism. (2) Bohumil Hrabal drinking beer at U Tygra pub. Despite his fame, he was an accessible man, although he did not suffer fools and servile admirers gladly. Hrabal is the most imaginative Czech

## Bohumil Hrabal

(1) Ein Filmplakat zu *Reise nach Sondervorschrift*, *Zuglauf überwacht*, dessen Regisseur (6) Jiří Menzel (geboren 1928) 1967 den Academy Award erhielt. Der Film basiert auf einer kleinen Novelle von Bohumil Hrabal (1914–97). (4, 7) Szenen aus dem Film, der mit viel Witz und Leidenschaft eine intelligente Geschichte aus der Kleinstadt erzählt (in einer Szene stempelt der Stationsvorsteher die Pobacken der jungen Telegraphistin). Der Film macht sich über Stereotypen lustig und zeichnet alle Beteiligten von ihrer menschlichen Seite, erklärt den Krieg für absurd und Heldentum für ein Zufallsprodukt. Seine poetische Linie ist dem Surrealismus angelehnt. (2) Bohumil Hrabal bei einem Bier in der Kneipe U Tygra. Trotz seiner Berühmtheit

## Bohumil Hrabal

(1) Affiche du film *Trains étroitement surveillés* qui rapporta un Academy Award en 1967 à son metteur en scène (6) Jiří Menzel (né en 1928). Le film s'inspire d'un petit roman de Bohumil Hrabal (1914–1997). (4, 7) Images du film, portrait sophistiqué d'une petite ville, riche en expressions maladroites de passion et d'humour (une scène montre un aide-chef de gare tamponnant les fesses d'une télégraphiste). Le film détourne les stéréotypes du moment. Il montre l'humanité présente en chaque protagoniste, que la guerre est absurde et que l'héroïsme est un accident. Ses qualités poétiques doivent beaucoup au surréalisme. (2) Bohumil Hrabal buvant une bière dans la brasserie U Tygra. Malgré sa réputation, il était resté accessible,

4

5

6

7

writer of the 20th century. His name became well known in the West not only for *Closely Observed Trains* but also for *Too Loud a Solitude* and *I Served the King of England*. His tales are populated with outcasts, pub braggarts and down-and-outs. (3) The cover of Hrabal's book *A Bistro Called the World*, a selection of short stories which contain uniquely perceptive visions of a world full of the grotesque, where beauty is hidden under triviality. (5) It was filmed in 1965 by Věra Chytilová.

blieb er ein Mann, mit dem man reden konnte; Dummköpfe und Schmeichler duldete er allerdings nicht in seiner Nähe.Im Westen fand er nicht nur mit *Reise nach Sondervorschrift, Zuglauf überwacht*, sondern auch mit *Eine zu laute Einsamkeit* und *Ich habe den englischen König bedient* eine breite Leserschaft. Seine Geschichten sind bevölkert von Außenseitern, Kneipengängern und Aussteigern. (3) Das Titelbild von Hrabals Buch *Ein Bistro namens Welt*, einer Sammlung von Kurzgeschichten mit einem ungewöhnlich scharfsichtigen Blick auf die Welt und ihre Grotesken, in der die Schönheit des Lebens und die Trivialität des Alltags verborgen liegt. (5) Dieses Werk wurde 1965 von Věra Chytilová verfilmt.

même s'il n'appréciait pas les excès et la servilité de certains de ses admirateurs. Hrabal est le plus imaginatif des écrivains tchèques du XXe siècle. Son nom devint célèbre à l'Ouest à travers le succès de *Trains étroitement surveillés*, mais également *Une Trop bruyante solitude*, et *Moi qui ai servi le roi d'Angleterre*. Ses récits sont remplis de ratés, de piliers de brasseries et de clochards. (3) Couverture du livre d'Hrabal *Un Bistro appelé Monde*, sélection de nouvelles faites de visions pleines de sensibilité d'un monde grotesque où la beauté se cache sous la vulgarité. (5) Filmé en 1965 par Věra Chytilová.

## The Prague Spring Festival

The international music festival called the Prague Spring has been held in the city every year since 1946. The government of President Beneš decided that an international music festival would be the perfect tribute to mark the 50th anniversary of the Czechoslovak Philharmonic. The victorious Allies each sent a representative and the festival took off in spectacular style. Although conceived as a one-off celebration, after its initial success it became an annual event. The festival takes place during the three weeks following 12 May, the anniversary of Bedřich Smetana's death in 1884. The opening concert takes place in the Smetana Hall in the Municipal House. The national anthem, "Kde domov můj?" (Where Is My Home?) opens the festival, followed by Smetana's *Má vlast* (My Country), a cycle of six symphonic poems. "Vltava" is the most famous (often referred to by its German name, "Moldau"). The other five are: "From Bohemian Woods and Fields", "Tábor," "Blaník," "Vyšehrad" and "Šárka". Smetana once proclaimed: "Music is the life of the Czechs." His rise to fame in Communist Czechoslovakia was partially due to the fact that Zdeněk Nejedlý (Czech Minister of Culture under Gottwald) promoted him as a more patriotic composer than Dvořák (although Smetana could neither speak nor write proper Czech, unlike Dvořák). (1) Posters advertising concerts during the festival. (2) A poster from the 1947 Prague Spring festival. (3, 4, 6) Prague Spring concerts take place in different venues all over the city – in parks, gardens, churches, as well as in concert halls. (5) Herbert von Karajan (1908–89) conducting the Czechoslovak Philharmonic Orchestra.

## Das Prager Frühlingsfestival

Seit 1946 findet alljährlich in der Stadt ein internationales Musikfest mit dem Namen »Prager Frühling« statt. Die Regierung Beneš hatte beschlossen, anläßlich des 50. Geburtstages der Tschechischen Philharmoniker ein internationales Musikfest zu veranstalten. Das Festival, zu dem jeder der siegreichen Alliierten einen Vertreter schickte, wurde in großem Stil begangen. Ursprünglich als einmalige Veranstaltung geplant, wurde es wegen seines großen Erfolges von nun an jährlich wiederholt. Das Festival findet in den drei Wochen nach dem 12. Mai, dem Todestag von Bedřich Smetana im Jahre 1884 statt. Das Eröffnungskonzert wird in der Smetana-Halle im Repräsentationshaus der Stadt gegeben. Es beginnt mit der Nationalhymne, »Kde domov můj?« (Wo ist meine Heimat?), darauf folgen Smetanas *Má vlast* (Mein Heimatland) und ein Zyklus aus sechs symphonischen Gedichten. Das bekannteste ist »Vltava« (das oft unter seinem deutschen Namen »Die Moldau« zitiert wird). Die anderen sind »Aus böhmischen Wäldern und Feldern«, »Tábor«, »Blaník«, »Vyšehrad« und »Šárka«. Smetana hatte einst gesagt: »Musik ist das Leben der Tschechen.« Sein Aufstieg zum Ruhm in der kommunistischen Tschechoslowakei lag unter anderem daran, daß ihn Zdeněk Nejedlý (der tschechische Kulturminister unter Gottwald) als einen Komponisten förderte, der stärker als Dvořák die patriotische Gesinnung verkörperte (obwohl Smetana im Gegensatz zu Dvořák tschechisch weder richtig lesen noch schreiben konnte). (1) Plakate werben für die Konzerte während des Festivals. (2) Ein Plakat zum Prager Frühlingsfestival 1947. (3, 4, 6) Das Prager Frühlingsfestival findet an verschiedenen Orten überall in der Stadt statt – in Parks, Gärten, Kirchen und Konzertsälen. (5) Herbert von Karajan (1908–1989) dirigiert das Tschechoslowakische Philharmonieorchester.

## Le Festival du Printemps de Prague

Un festival international de musique, le «Printemps de Prague» fut organisé en 1946. Le gouvernement du président Beneš pensait qu'une manifestation internationale de ce type conviendrait au cinquantième anniversaire de la Philharmonie tchécoslovaque. Les Alliés victorieux envoyèrent chacun un représentant et le festival connut un lancement spectaculaire. Devant son succès, il fut décidé d'en faire un événement annuel. Il se déroula tout au long de trois semaines après le 12 mai, anniversaire de la mort de Bedřich Smetana en 1884. Le concert d'ouverture fut donné dans la Salle Smetana de la Maison municipale. L'hymne national, «Kde domov můj?» (Où est mon foyer?) ouvrit le festival, suivi par *Má vlast* (Ma patrie), cycle de six poèmes symphoniques. «Vltava» («La Moldau») est le plus connu. Les cinq autres sont: «Par les prés et les bois de Bohème», «Tábor», «Blaník», «Vyšehrad» et «Šárka». Smetana avait dit un jour: «La musique est la vie des Tchèques.» Son accession à la gloire dans la Tchécoslovaquie communiste est due en partie à ce que Zdeněk Nejedlý (Ministre tchèque de la culture sous Gottwald) le jugeait plus patriote que Dvořák (bien que Smetana ait pu à peine parler ou écrire le tchèque à la différence de Dvořák). (1) Affiches annonçant les concerts. (2) Affiche du Festival de 1947. (3, 4, 6) Les concerts du Printemps de Prague se déroulent en divers lieux : parcs, jardins, églises, et salles de concert. (5) Herbert von Karajan (1908–1989) dirigeant l'orchestre philharmonique tchécoslovaque.

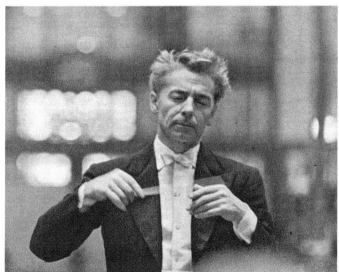

3

4

5

6

PRVNÍ TAJEMNÍK ÚV KSČ ALEXANDER DUBČEK

Jsme s vámi          buďte s námi!

### Alexander Dubček

Alexander Dubček (1921–92), a Slovak Communist, was liked and admired not only for his desire to reform the country but also for his decency. He often drove his Simca, avoiding the chauffeured limousine that went with his office, and in a 1968 television broadcast he addressed the people as "Dear friends, dear citizens," which everybody found very refreshing. He came to embody "Socialism with a human face" (the period also became known as the Prague Spring, the name taken from the music festival). Dubček became Party leader in January 1968 and a pent-up demand for reforms gathered momentum. The lifting of censorship, demand for respect for civil rights, protection for minorities, the settling of the Slovak problem, a comprehensive reform of the economy and criticism of "the leading role of the Party" put Moscow on the alert. (1) Photograph of Alexander Dubček: "We are with you, be with us." (3, 4) Dubček was everywhere greeted with spontaneous applause. (2) Dubček and General Ludvík Svoboda (1895–1979), who during the Prague Spring in March 1968 became President.

### Alexander Dubček

Alexander Dubček (1921–92), ein slowakischer Kommunist, wurde nicht nur wegen seines Reformeifers, sondern auch wegen seiner Aufrichtigkeit geliebt und bewundert. Er fuhr oft mit seinem Simca anstatt in seiner Limousine mit Chauffeur, die seinem Amt zugestanden hätte. In einer Fernsehsendung von 1968 begrüßte er die Zuschauer mit den Worten: »Liebe Freunde, liebe Bürger«, was als sehr erfrischend empfunden wurde. Er verkörperte den »Sozialismus mit menschlichem Antlitz« (in der Periode, die nach dem Prager Musikfestival als »Prager Frühling« bezeichnet wird). Im Januar 1968 wurde Dubček Parteivorsitzender, was dem lange schwelenden Wunsch nach Reformen neuen Aufschwung gab. Die Aufhebung der Zensur, die Forderung nach Bürgerrechten, Minderheitenschutz, die Lösung der slowakischen Frage, eine umfassende Wirtschaftsreform und die Kritik an der »Führungsrolle der Partei« alarmierten Moskau. (1) Ein Foto von Alexander Dubček: »Wir sind bei dir, sei du bei uns.« (3, 4) Überall empfing man Dubček mit spontanem Applaus. (2) Dubček und General Ludvík Svoboda (1895–1979), der während des Prager Frühlings im März 1968 Präsident wurde.

### Aleksander Dubček

Aleksander Dubček (1921–1992), communiste slovaque, fut aimé et admiré non seulement pour son désir de réformer le système mais aussi pour sa modestie. Il conduisait lui-même sa Simca, évitant la limousine avec chauffeur à laquelle il avait droit, et dans une émission télévisée de 1968, s'adressa aux téléspectateurs en leur disant: «Chers amis, chers concitoyens», ce que tout le monde trouva rafraîchissant dans le contexte de la rhétorique communiste en vigueur. Il en vint à incarner le «socialisme à visage humain» et la période appelée Printemps de Prague, comme le Festival. Dubček devint leader du Parti en janvier 1968 et la pression pour les réformes atteignit alors son apogée : fin de la censure, respect des droits civils, textes sur la protection des minorités, résolution du problème slovaque, réforme globale de l'économie et critique du «rôle moteur du Parti». Cette agitation alerta Moscou. (1) Photographie d'Aleksander Dubček: «Nous sommes avec vous, soyez avec nous!» (3, 4) Dubček était partout salué par des applaudissements spontanés. (2) Dubček et le général Ludvík Svoboda (1895–1979) qui devint président pendant le Printemps de Prague en mars 1968.

1

# DUBČEK

PŘIPRAVILI: PŘEMYSL VEVERKA A KAREL HVIŽĎALA

FOTOGRAFIE: MIROSLAVA ZAJÍCE, PETRA HODANA, ANTONA ŠMOTLÁKA A ČTK

Dubček je pojem. Chtějí si ho dát do londýnského muzea voskových figur, dávají ho k dispozici panu Nobelovi, dávají ho do každých zpráv a do každé výkladní skříně.

Je to bezesporu překrásné, mají-li o něj zájem i strážci muzeí. Ale ti ho neuhlídají. Šaňo, jak mu říkají v Bratislavě, je pro ně příliš živý. Nenajdete-li ho nahoře na ÚV, je na horách. On je Jánošík.

2

den před ÚV KSČ

3

na 1. máje 1968

4

21. 8. 1968

Tak už jste tady... vitejte!
Vitejte, letní hosté
z hlubin mrazu,
vitejte nám
po starém obyčeji
s pancířem chleba,
s tímto krystalem
        slzotvorné soli
jež rozežírá,
vše, co padlo s nebe.
Vitejte v láskyplném objetí,
v němž prašti kosti,
sákne krev
z plodů
na sklonku výsluní.
A znovu
hluchoněmí
        s hluchoněmými.
A znovu osiky,
osiky, které se otřásaji
při pouhém pomyšlení
        na Jidáše
Na úsvitě zařičel kohout.

Zapírám,
že jsem vás kdy znal.
Zapírám podruhé,
potřetí

24. 8. 1968

Záběr situace před pražským rozhlasem 21. srpna 1968 v 10,35 min. Z budovy se ještě vysílalo.

# PROČ? ПОЧЕМУ?

**SVĚT** V OBRAZECH

21. srpna 1968

Ve chvílích, kdy Prahu okupovaly sovětské tanky, kdy sovětská armáda internovala
presidenta republiky, řádně volené ústavní činitele, členy vlády, čelné funkcionáře
předsednictva ÚV KSČ i Národní fronty, kdy vojska pěti armád začala obracet vniveč
československo-sovětské přátelství, kdy byla věrolomně porušena Varšavská smlouva,
kdy jednostranně byly porušeny výsledky porad v Čierne a ujednání v Bratislavě
připravujeme tento dokument doby. Desítky našich bezbranných lidí byly už zabity
a postřeleny, začalo zatýkání čestných osob, ničí se majetek českého a slovenského
národa. Náš odpor proti násilí však nikdy neustane! Chceme, aby to byl odpor klidu,
rozvahy a duševní vyspělosti, který je našim národům vlastní a s nimž má své histo-
rické zkušenosti.

# SVĚT V OBRAZECH
24. srpna 1968
JSME S VÁMI - BUĎTE S NÁMI !

## BYLI JSME
## A BUDEM!

Okupantské tanky obsadily stát, neotřás-
ly však našimi národy. Avšak uvažujme:
Existuje ještě pro nás nějaký důvod se-
trvávat ve svazku Varšavské smlouvy,
když jsme poznali tuto otřesnou zkuše-
nost? Není pro naši budoucnost neutra-
lita spolehlivější zárukou?

## The Invasion: 21 August 1968

On 20 August 1968, shortly after 11 p.m., Soviet commandos landed at Ruzyně airport. Tanks disembarked from the heavy Antonov planes. By dawn the massive airlift had deposited an entire airborne division, which was led by KGB and StB agents to various ministries. Concurrently, Soviet, Polish, Hungarian and Bulgarian troops crossed Czechoslovakia's borders. These were the first units of the half million Warsaw Pact troops and 5000 tanks that were to occupy Czechoslovakia in the next few days. Dubček and his group of reformers were kidnapped and flown to Moscow, where they were intimidated and bullied by the Soviet Communists. In the end they (except for František Kriegel) signed the Moscow agreement which rolled back the reforms of the Prague Spring, brought back censorship and legalized the invasion. They returned to Prague, beaten men, on 28 August. In Prague, tanks were positioned at all strategic places, the bridges were guarded and streets leading towards the presidential quarter in Hradčany were closed. A typical Soviet tank was a rough-hewn affair with two spare barrel-shaped diesel-oil canisters attached to a wooden plank at the back. They fired at the National Museum, mistaking it for the building of the Central Committee of the KSČ. The situation around Prague Radio looked more dramatic when about five juggernauts caught fire from the leaking fuel. Demonstrations took place in all towns and the Czechoslovak flag became a symbol of opposition. Shocked and angry, the capital's citizens expressed their hostility with anti-Soviet posters and graffiti, mass demonstrations and acts of sabotage.They tried unceasingly to convince the foreign soldiers that the invasion was wrong, that no one had asked them to come and that they had no right to be in Czechoslovakia. In 1996 Boris Yeltsin sent Václav Havel a letter written in 1968 by five Czechoslovak hardliners inviting the Soviets to come and save endangered Socialism. The letter was written in Russian and opened "Dear Leonid Iljich..." This was the official Soviet excuse. The population was defiant in support of their reformers. Although newspaper offices, radio and television were occupied by the Soviet forces, the underground free transmitters continued to keep the population abreast of the current news, and underground presses printed posters and handbills informing people about the resistance. The unprecedented unity of the Czechoslovak people achieved two objectives: it prevented the establishment of a quisling government and forced Brezhnev to return the Czechoslovak leaders unharmed. Meanwhile, food supplies were shrinking (one of the favorite tricks of the Soviet Communists was to starve people out in order to bring them to their senses). After long days and sleepless nights, the opposition diminished. In Prague 25 people died in skirmishes with the armed invaders, who used live ammunition. In the whole of the country, 72 Czechs and Slovaks were shot or killed by armoured vehicles, 267 suffered serious injuries and 422 were wounded slightly; 172 were kidnapped by the invading forces, though all but eight were later released. (1–4) Covers of magazines from August 1968. The cover of *The World* (3) asks: "Why?" in Czech and Russian. (2) The St Wenceslas statue covered with defiant slogans. Often signs in Russian urged the Soviet soldiers to return home. In order to prevent morale sinking among the Russians, who were slowly becoming aware of their role, they were quickly replaced with new units from Central Asia and Siberia. (4) Soviet tanks with a chalked-on swastika at the Powder Gate.

## Die Invasion: 21. August 1968

Am 20. August 1968, kurz nach 23.00 Uhr, landeten sowjetische Kommandos auf dem Flughafen Ruzyně. Aus den schweren Antonow-Flugzeugen wurden Panzer entladen. Bis zum Morgengrauen hatte man eine komplette Luftlandedivision abgesetzt, die von KGB- und StB-Agenten zu verschiedenen Ministerien geführt wurden. Gleichzeitig überquerten sowjetische, polnische, ungarische und bulgarische Truppen die Grenzen. Es waren die ersten Einheiten von einer halben Million Soldaten und 5.000 Panzern aus dem Warschauer Pakt, die in den nächsten Tagen die Tschechoslowakei besetzen sollten. Dubček und seine Reformer wurden entführt und nach Moskau geflogen, wo sie Schikanen und Einschüchterungsversuchen der sowjetischen Kommunisten ausgesetzt waren. Schließlich unterzeichneten sie (mit der Ausnahme von František Kriegel) das Moskauer Abkommen, durch das die Reformen des Prager Frühlings zurückgenommen, die Zensur wieder eingeführt und die Invasion legalisiert wurde. Als geschlagene Männer kehrten sie am 28. August nach Prag zurück. In der Stadt wurden an allen strategisch wichtigen Stellen Panzer postiert, die Brücken bewacht und die Straßen zum Regierungsviertel auf dem Hradschin gesperrt. Ein typischer sowjetischer Panzer war ein grobschlächtiges Gefährt mit zwei zusätzlichen Kanisterfäßchen für Diesel, die auf man Holzplanken an der Rückseite angebracht hatte. Die Russen griffen das Nationalmuseum an, das sie irrtümlich für die Zentrale der KSČ hielten. Die Situation um die Prager Radiostation nahm dramatische Züge an, als fünf Lastwagen aufgrund eines lecken Dieselkanisters in Flammen aufgingen. In allen Städten fanden Demonstrationen statt, bei denen die tschechoslowakische Flagge zum Symbol des Widerstands wurde. Schockiert und wütend brachten die Bürger der Hauptstadt ihren Widerstand mit anti-sowjetischen Plakaten und Wandmalereien, Massendemonstrationen und Sabotageakten zum Ausdruck. Sie versuchten unermüdlich, die Soldaten davon zu überzeugen, daß die Invasion unrecht sei, daß niemand sie eingeladen habe und sie kein Recht hätten, in der Tschechoslowakei zu sein. 1996 sandte Boris Jelzin Václav Havel einen Brief aus dem Jahr 1968, in dem fünf tschechoslowakische Hardliner die Sowjets aufforderten, den gefährdeten Sozialismus zu retten. Der Brief war auf russisch verfaßt und begann mit den Worten »Lieber Leonid Iljitsch...«. Das war der offizielle Vorwand der Sowjets. Die Bevölkerung widersetzte sich und unterstützte ihre Reformer. Obwohl die Zeitungen, Radiostationen und Fernsehsender von den sowjetischen Kräften besetzt waren, hielt man die Leute mit freien, illegalen Radioübertragungen auf dem laufenden und druckte heimlich Plakate und Handzettel mit Nachrichten über den Widerstand. Die unvorhergesehene Einigkeit des tschechoslowakischen Volkes erreichte zwei Ziele: Sie verhinderte die Einsetzung einer Marionettenregierung und zwang Breschnew, die tschechoslowakischen Führer unverletzt zurückzuschicken. In der Zwischenzeit waren die Lebensmittelvorräte zusammengeschrumpft (zu den beliebtesten Methoden der sowjetischen Kommunisten gehörte es, die Menschen auszuhungern, bis sie wieder linientreu waren). Nach vielen Tagen und schlaflosen Nächten zerfiel auch die Opposition. In Prag starben 25 Menschen bei den Auseinandersetzungen mit den bewaffneten Invasoren, die mit scharfer Munition schossen. Im ganzen Land kamen 72 Tschechen und Slowaken durch Geschütze oder Unfälle mit Panzerfahrzeugen ums Leben, 267 erlitten schwere, 422 leichte Verletzungen. 172 Menschen wurden von den Invasoren entführt, mit Ausnahme von acht Personen später allerdings wieder freigelassen. (1–4) Titelblätter von Zeitschriften im August 1968. Das Titelbild von *Die Welt* (3) fragte in russischer und in tschechischer Sprache »Warum?«. (2) Die Wenzelsstatue, bedeckt mit Parolen des Widerstands. Häufig forderten Plakate die sowjetischen Soldaten in russischer Sprache zur Rückkehr nach Hause auf. Als sie merkten, welche Rolle sie hier spielten und ihre Moral allmählich nachließ, wurden sie durch neue Einheiten aus Zentralasien und Sibirien ersetzt. (4) Sowjetische Panzer, auf denen mit Kreide Hakenkreuze gemalt sind, auf der Pulverbrücke.

## L'invasion : 21 août 1968

Le 20 août 1968, peu après 11 h du soir, des commandos soviétiques atterrirent à l'aéroport de Ruzyně. Des tanks débarquèrent des lourds transporteurs Antonov. À l'aube, l'opération avait déposé toute une division aéroportée, orientée par des agents du KGB et de la StB vers les divers ministères. Dans le même temps, des troupes soviétiques, polonaises, hongroises et bulgares franchissaient la frontière, avant-garde d'un demi-million de soldats du Pacte de Varsovie et de 5 000 tanks qui allaient occuper la Tchécoslovaquie au cours des journées suivantes. Dubček et son groupe de réformateurs furent enlevés et envoyés à Moscou, où ils furent soumis à des manœuvres d'intimidation et des pressions des Soviétiques. Finalement (à l'exception de František Kriegel), ils signèrent l'Accord de Moscou qui annulait les réformes, rétablissait la censure et légalisait l'invasion. Ils rentrèrent à Prague, humiliés, le 28 août. Dans la capitale, les tanks étaient positionnés à tous les carrefours stratégiques, les ponts étaient gardés et les rues vers le Hradčany fermées. Beaucoup de ces chars étaient rouillés, avec deux malheureux bidons de carburant de secours attachés sur des planches à l'arrière. Ils tirèrent sur le Musée national, le prenant pour le Comité central du Parti. La situation autour de Radio Prague était plus dramatique : cinq mastodontes prirent feu à la suite de fuites d'essence. Des manifestations se déroulèrent dans toutes les villes et le drapeau national devint le symbole de l'opposition. Choqués et en colère, les Pragois montrèrent leur hostilité par des affiches et des graffitis anti-soviétiques, des manifestations de masse et des actes de sabotage. La population essaya de convaincre les soldats étrangers que l'invasion était une grave erreur, que personne ne leur avait demandé de venir et qu'ils n'avaient pas le droit d'être là. En 1996, Boris Eltsine envoya à Václav Havel une lettre écrite en 1968 par cinq communistes tchécoslovaques de la ligne dure demandant aux Soviétiques d'intervenir pour sauver le socialisme. La lettre était rédigée en russe et commençait par « Cher Leonid Illitch ». C'était la grande excuse officielle soviétique. La population était sans le moindre doute derrière les réformateurs. Bien que les journaux, les radios et la télévision aient été occupés par les forces soviétiques, des émetteurs clandestins libres continuèrent à informer la population abasourdie des développements tandis que des imprimeries clandestines imprimaient des affiches et des tracts appelant le peuple à la résistance. L'unité sans précédent du peuple tchécoslovaque atteignit deux objectifs : elle empêcha la création d'un gouvernement type Quisling et força Brejnev à laisser rentrer les leaders réformateurs. Dans le même temps l'approvisionnement de la capitale se réduisait de jour en jour, c'était l'une des techniques favorites des communistes : affamer les peuples pour les forcer à adopter leurs idées. Après de longues journées et des nuits sans sommeil, l'opposition commença à faiblir. 25 personnes perdirent la vie dans des accrochages avec les troupes soviétiques, qui se servirent de leurs armes. Dans le pays, 72 Tchèques et Slovaques furent tués par des véhicules blindés, 267 furent blessés grièvement et 422 légèrement. 172 furent enlevés par les forces d'invasion, 164 relâchés. (1– 4) Couvertures de magazine d'août 1968. Celle *du Monde* (3) demande « Pourquoi ? » en tchèque et en russe. (2) Des pancartes en russe pressaient les soldats soviétiques de retourner chez eux. Afin de prévenir des problèmes de moral dans l'Armée rouge, les troupes furent rapidement remplacées par des unités envoyées d'Asie centrale et de Sibérie. (4) Des chars soviétiques marqués d'une croix gammée à la craie devant la Porte des poudres.

## Invasion II

(1) Czech men on a truck wave Czechoslovak flags, trying to invigorate the spirit of resistance. (2) People marched through the streets carrying blood-stained flags, protesting against the invasion. (4) Places where someone had been killed were marked with flowers. Some Russians were puzzled and many soldiers from the invading forces were starving because they were ordered not to loot (although some could not resist when they saw goods unavailable in their country). There were cases of soldiers who were reduced to begging for food and water. Food and sanitary supplies were not taken sufficiently into account by the Soviet generals. (3) Russian soldier with *Pravda* (Truth), the Soviet Communist newspaper which to most people in Socialist countries meant the opposite. In their debates with the Czechs, soldiers often repeated stock phrases about counterrevolution and Fascism taken from *Pravda*. One Soviet soldier committed suicide in front of the Central Committee of the KSČ building.

## Invasion II

(1) Tschechische Männer auf einem Lastwagen schwingen die tschechoslowakische Flagge, um zum Widerstand aufzurufen. (2) Aus Protest gegen die Invasion marschierten die Menschen mit blutverschmierten Fahnen durch die Straßen. (4) Orte, an denen jemand ermordet worden war, wurden mit Blumen geschmückt. Einige Russen waren erstaunt, und viele Soldaten der Invasionsarmee litten Hunger, da man ihnen Plünderungen verboten hatte (denen manche allerdings nicht widerstehen konnten, als sie all die Waren sahen, die sie in ihrem eigenen Land nicht bekommen konnten). In einigen Fällen mußten die Soldaten sogar um Lebensmittel und Wasser bitten. Die sowjetischen Generäle hatten die Versorgung mit Lebensmitteln und sanitären Gütern nicht ausreichend eingeplant. (3) Ein russischer Soldat mit der *Pravda* (Wahrheit), die Zeitung der sowjetischen Kommunisten, die für die meisten Bürger der sozialistischen Länder eher das Gegenteil von dem verbreitete, was der Titel versprach. In ihren Diskussionen mit den Tschechen zitierten die Soldaten oftmals Standardsätze aus der *Pravda* über die Konterrevolution und den Faschismus. Ein sowjetischer Soldat nahm sich vor der Zentrale der KSČ das Leben.

## Invasion II

(1) Des Tchèques sur un camion, brandissant des drapeaux tchécoslovaques, essayent de soulever une résistance. (2) Des gens défilent dans les rues montrant des drapeaux tachés de sang, en signe de protestation contre l'invasion. (4) Les endroits où des personnes avaient été tuées furent recouverts de fleurs. Certains Russes étaient surpris par ces réactions. De nombreux soldats mourraient de faim parce qu'il leur était interdit de se livrer au pillage (même si certains ne purent résister devant des produits introuvables chez eux). Ils furent contraints de mendier de la nourriture et de l'eau, car la logistique avait été mal préparée par les généraux soviétiques. (3) Un soldat russe, la *Pravda* (vérité) en main, le grand quotidien soviétique qui pour la plupart des habitants des pays socialistes signifiait mensonge. Dans leurs discussions avec les Tchèques, les soldats répétaient des phrases sur la contre-révolution et le fascisme lues dans la *Pravda*. Un soldat soviétique se suicida devant le Comité central du KSČ.

## Invasion III and Jan Palach

(Page 328) Street scenes from the invasion. (Page 329) Five months later, Prague inhabitants grieved the death of a young student who had sacrificed himself.

## Invasion III und Jan Palach

(Seite 328) Straßenszenen von der Invasion. (Seite 329) Fünf Monate später trauerten die Prager Bürger um einen jungen Studenten, der sein Leben geopfert hatte.

## Invasion III et Jan Palach

(Page 328) Scènes de rues de l'invasion. (Page 329) Cinq mois plus tard, les Pragois allaient pleurer la mort d'un jeune étudiant qui s'était immolé.

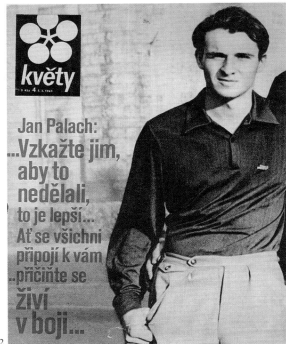

### Jan Palach

Cover of *Květy* (2) showing Jan Palach, student of history and political science at the Charles University, aged twenty. On 16 January 1969 he poured petrol over himself and set himself alight in Wenceslas Square in protest against the Soviet occupation. He died three days later. On 25 January his funeral was attended by half a million people and became a solemn, silent demonstration of grief. The procession left the University and proceeded to the Old Town Square where it stopped at the Jan Hus monument (1). Palach was buried in Olšany cemetery and for the next four years the StB harassed people who came to pay their respects. In September 1973 Palach's mother buried the ashes of her son at her local cemetery in Všetaty.

### Jan Palach

Ein Bild des 20jährigen Geschichts- und Politikstudenten Jan Palach von der Karlsuniversität auf dem Titelblatt der Zeitschrift *Květy* (2). Am 16. Januar 1969 übergoß er sich auf dem Wenzelsplatz aus Protest gegen die sowjetische Besetzung mit Benzin und zündete sich an. Er starb drei Tage später. An seiner Beerdigung am 25. Januar, die zu einer feierlichen, stillen Demonstration wurde, nahm eine halbe Million Menschen teil. Die Prozession verlief von der Universität zum Altstädter Ring, wo sie am Denkmal für Jan Hus eine Pause einlegte (1). Palach wurde auf dem Olšany-Friedhof beerdigt; und für die nächsten vier Jahre vertrieben StB-Agenten Menschen, die seinem Grab einen Besuch abstatten wollten. Im September 1973 überführte Palachs Mutter die Asche ihres Sohnes auf ihren Heimatfriedhof in Všetaty.

### Jan Palach

Couverture de *Květy* (2) montrant Jan Palach, âgé de vingt ans, étudiant en histoire et en sciences politiques á l'université Charles. Le 16 janvier 1969, il versa du pétrole sur ses vêtements et se laissa brûler vif sur la place Venceslas en signe de protestation contre l'occupation soviétique. Il mourut trois jours plus tard. Le 25 janvier, ses funérailles se déroulèrent devant 500 000 personnes, démonstration silencieuse de la douleur d'un peuple. La procession quitta l'Université et s'avança vers la place de la Vieille ville où elle s'arrêta devant le monument à Jan Hus (1). Palach furent enterré au cimetière d'Olšany, et pendant quatre ans, la StB harcela ceux qui venaient lui rendre hommage. En 1973, ses cendres furent remises à la mère du jeune homme, et elle eut enfin l'autorisation de l'enterrer dans le petit cimetière local de Všetaty.

### After the Ice-Hockey Match

In March 1969 the Czechoslovak ice-hockey team defeated the Soviet Union 3–2 in Stockholm. A large crowd gathered in Wenceslas Square to celebrate the event. The KGB and StB used the occasion to stage a provocation. Intelligence agents stoned the offices of the Soviet airline Aeroflot, but in the Communist press the inhabitants of Prague were blamed for the disorder.

### Nach dem Eishockeyspiel

Im März 1969 schlug das tschechoslowakische Eishockeyteam die Mannschaft der Sowjetunion in Stockholm mit 3:2. Auf dem Wenzelsplatz versammelten sich viele Menschen, um den Sieg zu feiern. KGB und StB nutzten die Gelegenheit, um eine Provokation zu inszenieren. Geheimagenten warfen Steine auf die Büros der sowjetischen Fluggesellschaft Aeroflot, und die kom-

### Après le match de hockey sur glace

En mars 1969, l'équipe de hockey sur glace tchécoslovaque battit celle de l'Union soviétique par 3 à 2 à Stockholm. Une immense foule se rassembla place Venceslas pour célébrer l'événement. Le KGB et la StB profitèrent de l'occasion pour monter une provocation. Des agents secrets jetèrent des pierres sur les bureaux de la ligne aérienne soviétique Aéroflot, rejetant via

Dubček was held responsible for being unable to maintain order: on 17 April 1969 he was forced to resign and was pushed from political life.

munistische Presse machte die Prager Bürger für die Unruhen verantwortlich. Dubček warf man vor, er sei unfähig, die Ordnung aufrecht zu erhalten. Am 17. April 1969 wurde er zum Rücktritt gezwungen und vom politischen Leben ausgeschlossen.

la presse la responsabilité de cet acte sur les Pragois. Dubček fut accusé de ne pas savoir maintenir l'ordre et tenu responsable : le 17 avril, il était forcé de démissionner et exclu de la vie politique.

### "Normalization" and Gustáv Husák

Gustáv Husák's offer to the Czechoslovak people was: forget the past and your rights in return for food and a quiet life. The Husák period was called "normalization." (1) Gustáv Husák (1913–91), a Slovak hardliner. His career took off after the invasion of 1968, which catapulted him to the post of Czechoslovak Governor on behalf of the Soviet Union, and in 1975 he was made President. On the advice of Leonid Brezhnev, he expelled half a million Party members for supporting the reforms, 1 million were fired or demoted and many were imprisoned. The children of these people were banned from entering higher education. University professors had to clean windows; artists worked in boiler rooms; poets measured water-levels in reservoirs; political prisoners made crystal chandeliers (the most famous chandelier-maker was Václav Havel). (2) Leonid Brezhnev and Gustáv Husák. (3) Poster honoring the Russian Revolution of October 1917. (4, 5) Strengthening ties with Russia: attending parades and rallies.

### Die »Normalisierung« unter Gustáv Husák

Gustáv Husák machte dem tschechischen Volk folgendes Ange-bot: Vergeßt die Vergangenheit und eure Rechte, dafür erhaltet ihr Lebensmittel und ein ruhiges Dasein. Die Ära Husák wurde als Zeit der »Normalisierung« bezeichnet. (1) Gustáv Husák (1913–91), ein slowakischer Hardliner. Seine Karriere begann nach der Invasion von 1968, die ihn auf einen Posten in der Regierung von Moskaus Gnaden katapultierte; 1975 wurde er zum Präsidenten gemacht. Auf Weisung Leonid Breschnews schloß er eine halbe Million Menschen wegen Unterstützung der Reformen aus der Partei aus; eine Million Menschen ver-loren ihren Arbeitsplatz, wurden strafversetzt oder wanderten ins Gefängnis. Ihre Kinder durften keine höheren Schulen besu-chen. Universitätsprofessoren mußten Fenster putzen, Künstler arbeiteten als Kesselreiniger, Dichter maßen den Wasserstand der Stauseen, politische Gefangene fertigten Kristalleuchter (der berühmteste Lampenhersteller war Václav Havel). (2) Leonid Breschnew und Gustáv Husák. (3) Plakate zur Erinnerung an die Oktoberrevolution. (4, 5) Die Bindungen zu Rußland wur-den gefestigt: Besuch der Paraden und Demonstrationen.

### La «normalisation» et Gustáv Husák

L'offre de Gustáv Husák au peuple tchécoslovaque était la suivante : oubliez le passé et vos droits et vous aurez de quoi manger et mener une vie tranquille. Cette période fut baptisée «normalisation». (1) Gustáv Husák (1913–1991), slovaque et membre «dur» du Parti. Sa carrière démarra après l'invasion de 1968 qui le catapulta au poste de Gouverneur avant d'être fait Président en 1975. Suivant les conseils de Leonid Brejnev, il expulsa 500 000 membres du Parti pour avoir soutenu les réformes ; 1 million de personnes furent licenciées ou rétrogradées et beaucoup emprisonnées. Leurs enfants ne purent suivre d'études supérieures. Les professeurs de l'université se firent laveurs de carreaux, des artistes travaillèrent dans des chaufferies, des poètes mesurèrent la hauteur de l'eau dans les réservoirs, des prisonniers politiques fabriquèrent des lustres en cristal (dont Václav Havel). (2) Leonid Brejnev et Gustáv Husák. (3) Affiche en l'honneur de la révolution d'Octobre. (4, 5) Renforcement des liens avec la Russie : la présence aux défilés était obligatoire.

3

4

5

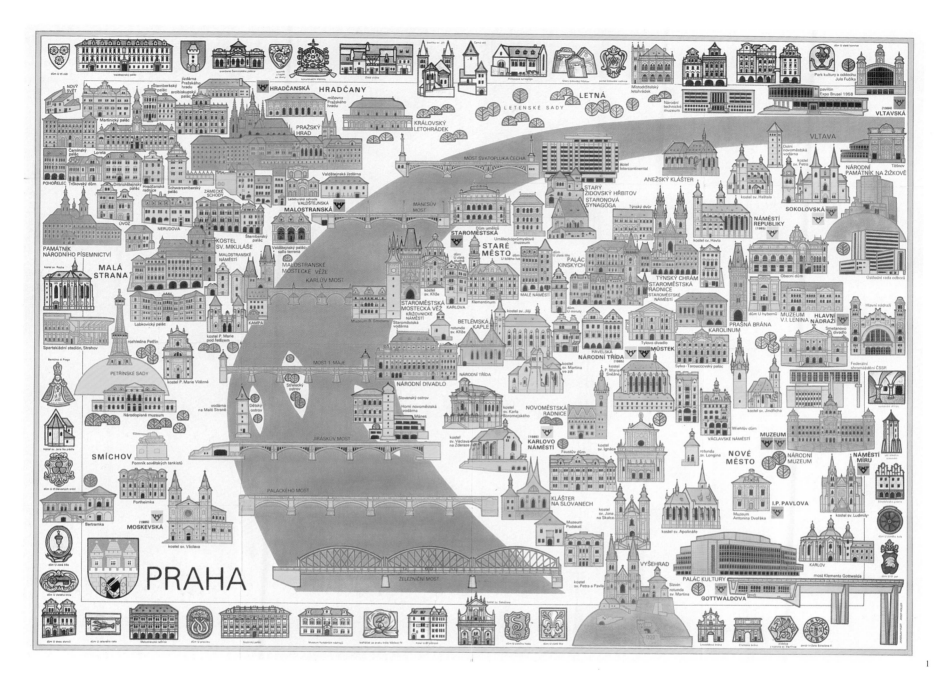

## Underground

Prague's medieval streets and many steep slopes created a problem for municipal transport. After two aborted attempts (one before the Second World War), the construction of the city's underground network began in 1967. Soviet architects contributed their expertise to the grand project. The C Line became operational in 1974, Line A in 1978 and Line B in 1985. The stations were designed by 39 architects and were embellished with metallic-colored plates, ceramic tiles, marble wall-facing and granite flooring. It is one of the most efficient public transport systems in Europe. (1) Map of the underground with its Communist names: the Moskevská station (now called Anděl), Sokolovská (Florenc), Gottwald Bridge (Nusle Bridge), and the Soviet Tank (in the 1990s removed to a museum). (4) Building the underground. (5) An underground station. (2) Since the former Stock Exchange was no longer necessary under the new Communist system, the building was redeveloped by the architect Karel Prager, who added a square two-storey structure and a façade with massive granite pillars, creating the gloomy Federal Assembly (Parliament) building. (3) Prager was also responsible for the heavy glass cube, the New Stage, next to the neo-Renaissance National Theater. Architects call the style Brutalism.

## Die U-Bahn

Prags mittelalterliche Straßen und die steilen Böschungen waren für das öffentliche Transportwesen problematisch. Nach zwei vergeblichen Versuchen (einer vor dem Zweiten Weltkrieg) begann man 1967 mit dem Bau einer U-Bahn. Sowjetische Architekten stellten ihre Erfahrungen dem großen Unternehmen zur Verfügung. Linie C wurde 1974 eröffnet, Linie A nahm 1978 ihren Dienst auf, Linie B 1985. Am Bau der Stationen, die mit metallfarbenen Tafeln, Kacheln, Marmorplatten und Granitböden ausgestattet wurden, waren 39 Architekten beteiligt. Die U-Bahn gehört zu den effizientesten öffentlichen Nahverkehrssystemen in Europa. (1) Plan der U-Bahn-Stationen mit ihren kommunistischen Namen: die Moskevská-Station (jetzt Anděl), Sokolovská (Florenc), Gottwald-Brücke (Nusle-Brücke), und der Sowjetische Panzer (der in den 90er Jahren in ein Museum gebracht wurde). (4) Bau der U-Bahn. (5) Eine U-Bahn-Station. (2) Nachdem man unter dem kommunistischen System die Börse nicht mehr benötigte, wurde das Gebäude nach Plänen des Architekten Karel Prager umgebaut. Er fügte eine zweigeschossige quadratische Konstruktion und eine Fassade mit massiven Granitsäulen hinzu, die zusammen das düstere Tagungsgebäude der Bundesversammlung (das Parlament) ergeben. (3) Prager war auch für die schweren Glaskuben der »Neuen Szene« neben dem im Neorenaissance-Stil erbauten Nationaltheater verantwortlich. Architekten nannten diesen Stil »Brutalismus«.

## Le métro

Les rues médiévales de la capitale et leurs nombreux escaliers ne facilitaient pas les transports publics. Après deux tentatives avortées (dont une avant la Seconde Guerre mondiale), la construction d'un réseau de métro commença en 1967. Des architectes soviétiques apportèrent leur expertise à ce grand projet. La ligne C fut opérationnelle en 1974, la ligne A en 1978 et la ligne B en 1985. Conçues par 39 architectes, les stations sont décorées de panneaux métalliques, de carrelages, de marbre sur les murs et de granit au sol. Le métro pragois est l'un des plus efficaces d'Europe. (1) Plan du métro avec encore les noms communistes : la station Moskěvská (aujourd'hui Anděl), Sokolovská (Florenc), Pont Gottwald (Pont Nusle), et le Char soviétique (garé dans un musée dans les année 90). (4) La construction du métro. (5) Une station de métro. (2) Comme l'ancienne Bourse n'avait plus d'utilité sous un régime communiste, le bâtiment fut transformé par l'architecte Karel Prager qui lui ajouta deux étages et une façade à piliers massifs en granit pour abriter le sinistre siège de l'Assemblée fédérale. (3) Prager est également l'auteur du gros parallélogramme de verre de la Nouvelle Scène, près du Théâtre national néo-Renaissance. Les architectes appellent ce style : le brutalisme.

2

3

4

5

2

## Ecological Devastation

(Previous pages, 1) The polluted river looks more like tar than
water, one of the legacies of disastrously short-sighted ecological
policies. (2) Industrial suburbs of Prague, polluted by smoking
factory chimneys.

## Ökologische Verwüstung

(Vorherige Seiten, 1) Der verunreinigte Fluß scheint eher Teer
als Wasser zu führen – eine der Hypotheken der katastrophalen,
kurzsichtigen Umweltpolitik. (2) Industrievororte Prags, ver-
schmutzt durch die rauchenden Fabrikschornsteine.

## La pollution dévastatrice

(Pages précédentes, 1) La rivière polluée évoque plus le goudron
que l'eau: c'est l'un des héritages d'une politique écologique
à courte vue. (2) Les banlieues industrielles de Prague sont
polluées par les émissions des usines.

2

## Socialist Holidays

(1) The citizens of Prague attending yet another Socialist rally.
(2) People returning home after fulfilling their Socialist duty of cheering and marching.

## Sozialistische Ferien

(1) Prager Bürger besuchen wieder einmal eine sozialistische Massenveranstaltung. (2) Menschen auf dem Weg nach Hause, nachdem sie ihre sozialistische Pflicht der Jubelns und Marschierens erfüllt haben.

## Vacances socialistes

(1) Les Pragois participent à un nouveau défilé. (2) Retour à la maison après avoir accompli son devoir civique de défilé et d'applaudissements.

1

## Dissidents

(Page 342) Pavel Landovský (left), the actor, and Václav Havel, the playwright and future President, in the carefree days when harassment by the StB was still hardly known to them. In 1977 a group of civil rights campaigners – among them Jan Patočka, Jiří Hájek and Václav Havel – formed the Charter 77 group, demanding basic human rights. The authorities retaliated by arresting the signatories, but by 1980 Charter 77 had over 1000 signatures. Among them was a core of about 100 dissidents. Václav Havel (who was imprisoned in 1977 and 1979) said of the Czechoslovak Communist system, one of the most repressive in the Socialist bloc: "This developed totalitarian system is more cunning. It actually seeps through the whole of society, each person carries with them a bit of the system. They are their creator and their victim." Havel's talent for making brilliant political speeches was spotted by one Communist, who after listening to the tumultuous applause Havel received at the Writer's Union, spoke the immortal words, "This guy is going to be dangerous to us."

## The Velvet Revolution

(Overleaf) On 17 November 1989, to mark the 50th anniversary of the death of Czech students murdered by the Nazis, inhabitants of Prague (most of them students) marched from the cemetery to Wenceslas Square via the National Avenue. They were met by armed riot police (4) and "red beret" special squads. Large groups were surrounded and cut off. They chanted "Freedom!" and tried to hand flowers to the police. They placed lighted candles on the ground and raised their arms, chanting, "We have bare hands" (3). The police and the special units attacked them with truncheons, wounding many. Students, supported by actors who turned the city's theaters into political forums, decided to call a general strike. Three days later, the Civic Forum was organized and assumed leadership of the revolution, calling for the resignation of Communist leaders, demanding that those who had beaten up the students be called to account and asking for the immediate release of prisoners of conscience. The Magic Lantern Theater (2) became the headquarters of Civic Forum and Václav Havel's charisma glued the varied assortment of banned writers, journalists, actors, workers, students and economists (Václav Klaus) together. In the next few days, strike committees were set up in factories, hospitals, offices and schools. Demonstrations took place after working hours, supporting the slogan "Objectivity, truth, productivity, freedom." The Wenceslas statue was covered with posters, photographs, graffiti and candles. People chanted, "Resign," "Now's the time." Foreign journalists arrived with their cameras, changing the events into telerevolution and thus providing the world's protection. The Soviet Embassy courteously welcomed the Civic Forum members, which meant that Mikhail Gorbachev had given a green light to the changes. On 24 November Alexander Dubček (5), Cardinal František Tomášek and Václav Havel appeared on the balcony of *Svobodné slovo* (offices of the Socialist Party newspaper, The Free Word) in Wenceslas Square and made speeches about freedom to the sound of 300,000 keyrings being waved in jubilation. Towards the end of the day the whole politburo and Central Committee secretariat resigned and jubilant crowds celebrated their first glimpse of a free Czechoslovakia, parliamentary democracy, the rule of law and market economy.

## Dissidenten

(Seite 342) Der Schauspieler Pavel Landovský (links) und der Dramatiker und spätere Präsident Václav Havel während der sorglosen Tage, in denen sie noch nicht vom StB belästigt wurden. 1977 gründeten Menschenrechtsaktivisten – unter ihnen Jan Patočka, Jiří Hájek und Václav Havel – die Charta 77, die die Einhaltung der Menschenrechte forderte. Die Behörden reagierten mit der Verhaftung der Unterzeichner, aber 1980 trug die Charta 77 bereits mehr als 1.000 Unterschriften. Unter ihnen gab es einen harten Kern von etwa 100 Dissidenten. Václav Havel (der 1977 und 1979 im Gefängis saß) nannte das kommunistische System der Tschechoslowakei eines der härtesten innerhalb des sozialistischen Blocks. »Dieses ausgefeilte totalitäre Regime ist gerissener. Es durchdringt die ganze Gesellschaft, und jedes Mitglied trägt es ein kleines bißchen mit. Jeder einzelne ist Baumeister und Opfer zugleich.« Havels Talent für brillante politische Reden wurde von einem Kommunisten erkannt, der, nachdem er Zeuge des tosenden Applauses gewesen war, den Havel nach einer Rede vor der Schriftsteller gewerkschaft bekommen hatte, die unvergeßlichen Worte aussprach: »Dieser Typ wird uns gefährlich werden.«

## Die Samtene Revolution

(Folgende Seiten) Am 17. November 1989 marschierten Prager Bürger (die meisten von ihnen waren Studenten) aus Anlaß des 50. Todestages der tschechischen Studenten, der von den Nazis ermordet worden war, von seinem Grab über die Nationalstraße auf den Wenzelsplatz. Bewaffnete Überfallkommandos der Polizei (4) und Eliteeinheiten der Armee stellten sich ihnen in den Weg. Große Gruppen wurden eingekreist und isoliert. Sie sangen: »Freiheit!« und versuchten, den Polizisten Blumen zu übergeben. Sie stellten brennende Kerzen auf den Boden, hoben die Hände und sangen: *Unsere Hände sind leer.*« (3). Die Polizei und die Spezialeinheiten attackierten die Demonstranten mit Schlagstöcken, wobei viele verletzt wurden. Mit Unterstützung der Schauspieler, die die Theater zu politischen Foren umfunktionierten, riefen die Studenten einen Generalstreik aus. Drei Tage später wurde das Bürgerforum gegründet und übernahm die Führung der Revolution. Man forderte den Rücktritt der kommunistischen Führer, eine Untersuchung gegen diejenigen, die die Studenten zusammengeschlagen hatten und die sofortige Freilassung der politischen Gefangenen. Das Laterna-Magica-Theater (2) wurde zum Hauptquartier des Bürgerforums, und Václav Havel gelang es mit seinem Charisma, so unterschiedliche Gruppen wie verbotene Schriftsteller, Journalisten, Schauspieler, Arbeiter, Studenten und Wirtschaftswissenschaftler (Václav Klaus) zu vereinen. In den nächsten Tagen entstanden in Fabriken, Krankenhäusern, Behörden und Schulen Streikkomitees. Nach Arbeitsende fanden Demonstrationen unter dem Slogan »Objektivität, Wahrheit, Produktivität, Freiheit« statt. Die Wenzelsstatue wurde mit Plakaten, Fotografien, Graffiti und Kerzen bedeckt. Die Menschen riefen: »Rücktritt« und »Es ist Zeit!« Ausländische Journalisten reisten mit ihren Kameras an und verwandelten die Ereignisse in eine »Telerevolution«, um den Aktivisten durch die Weltöffentlichkeit Schutz zu gewähren. Mitglieder des Bürgerforums wurden in der sowjetischen Botschaft höflich empfangen, was bedeutete, daß Michail Gorbatschow grünes Licht für Veränderungen gegeben hatte. Am 24. November erschienen Alexander Dubček (5), Kardinal František Tomášek und Václav Havel auf dem Balkon von *Svobodné slovo* (dem Büro der Zeitung der sozialistischen Partei, Die Freie Welt) auf dem Wenzelsplatz und hielten unter den Klängen von 300.000 Schlüsselringen, die als Zeichen der Freude geschüttelt wurden, Reden über die Freiheit. Am Ende des Tages trat das gesamte Politbüro und das Sekretariat des Zentralkomitees zurück, und eine jubelnde Menschenmenge feierte die ersten Anzeichen einer freien Tschechoslowakei: parlamentarische Demokratie, Rechtsstaatlichkeit und Marktwirtschaft.

## Les dissidents

(Page 342) Pavel Landovský (à gauche), acteur, et Václav Havel, auteur et futur président avant qu'ils ne soient harcelés par les hommes du StB. En 1977, un groupe de défenseurs des droits civils – dont Jan Patočka, Jiří Kájek et Václav Havel – constituèrent la Charte 77 réclamant l'application des droits fondamentaux. Les autorités répliquèrent en faisant arrêter les signataires, mais en 1980, la Charte comptait déjà plus de 1 000 signatures. Parmi elles se trouvait un noyau d'environ 1 000 dissidents. Václav Havel (emprisonné en 1977 et 1979) disait du système communiste tchécoslovaque, l'un des plus répressifs du bloc socialiste : «Ce système totalitaire développé est plus rusé. Il se diffuse en fait à travers l'ensemble du corps social, chacun en transportant un peu avec soi. Ils sont leur créateur et leur victime.» Le talent d'orateur de Havel avait été remarqué par un communiste qui, après avoir entendu les applaudissements passionnés remportés par l'auteur dramatique à l'Union des écrivains, eut ces paroles immortelles : «Ce type représente un danger pour nous.»

## La Révolution de velours

(Pages suivantes) Le 17 novembre 1989, cinquantième anniversaire d'étudiants assassinés par les nazis, les Pragois (des étudiants pour la plupart) marchèrent du cimetière à la place Venceslas par l'Avenue nationale. Ils furent arrêtés par la police anti-émeute (4) armée et les escadrons spéciaux des «bérets rouges» qui les divisèrent en petits groupes. Ils criaient «Liberté,» tendaient des fleurs à la police, déposaient de petites bougies sur le sol, levaient la main vers le ciel, criaient «Nos mains sont nues.» (3) La police et les unités spéciales les attaquèrent avec violence, faisant de nombreux blessés. Les étudiants soutenus par les comédiens qui transformèrent les théâtres en forums politiques, décidèrent d'en appeler à une grève générale. Trois jours plus tard, le Forum civique était sur pied et prenait la tête de la révolution, réclamant la démission des leaders communistes, le jugement de ceux qui avaient fait battre les étudiants, et la libération immédiate des prisonniers de conscience. Le Théâtre de la Lanterne magique (2) devint le siège du Forum et le charisme de Václav Havel attira écrivains bannis, journalistes, acteurs, ouvriers, étudiants et économistes (Václav Klaus). Dans les jours qui suivirent, des comités de grève furent constitués dans les usines, les hôpitaux, les bureaux et les écoles. Des manifestations se déroulèrent après les heures de travail sur le slogan «Objectivité, vérité, productivité, liberté». La statue de Venceslas fut recouverte d'affiches, de photographies, de graffiti et de bougies. Les gens criaient «Démission!»,«Le moment est venu!» Les journalistes étrangers affluèrent avec leurs caméras transformant les événements en télé-révolution et apportant du même coup la protection de l'opinion internationale. L'ambassade soviétique accueillit avec courtoisie les membres du Forum civique, ce qui signifiait que Gorbatchev avait donné son feu vert au changement. Le 24 novembre, Aleksander Dubček (5), František Cardinal Tomášek et Václav Havel apparurent au balcon de *Svobodné slovo* (le journal du parti socialiste, Le monde libre) sur la place Venceslas et firent des discours sur la liberté au son de 300 000 trousseaux de clés agités en signe de jubilation. Vers la fin de la journée, la totalité du Politburo et du Comité central démissionnait et des foules en liesse célébraient les premiers pas d'une Tchécoslovaquie libre, de la démocratie parlementaire, de l'état de droit et de l'économie de marché.

### Scenes from the revolution

(1) Wencelas Square, 23 November 1989. (2) Václav Havel and Civic Forum in The Magic Lantern Theater. (3) The crowd raising their arms and chanting "We have bare hands". (5) They are met by armed riot police and "red beret" special squads. (4) On 24 November, Alexander Dubček and VáclavHavel appear on the balcony of *Svobodné slovo* in Wencelas Square.

### Bilder von der Revolution

(1) Der Wenzelsplatz am 23. Nobember 1989. (2) Václav Havel und das Bürgerforum im Laterna-Magica-Theater. (3) Die Menge hebt die Arme und singt »Unsere Hände sind leer«. (5) Bewaffnete Überfallkommandos der Polizei und Eliteeinheiten der Armee stellen sich ihnen in den Weg. (4) Am 24. November erscheinen Alexander Dubček und Václav Havel auf dem Balkon von *Svobodné slove* auf dem Wenzelplatz.

### Scènes de la Révolution

(1) Place Venceslas, le 23 novembre 1989. (2) Václav Havel et le Forum Civique au Théâtre de la Lanterne magique. (3) La foule levant les bras en chantant « Nos mains sont nues ». (5) La police anti-émeutes et les pelotons spéciaux de «bérets rouges» intervinrent. (4) Le 24 novembre, Alexander Dubček et Václav Havel apparurent au balcon de *Svobodné slovo*, place Venceslas.

4

5

1

### Václav Havel Elected President

(1) A poster from the period: *Havel na Hrad* (Havel to the Castle). (2) Havel reviewing troops in the courtyard of Hradčany. (3) Havel was elected President on 29 December 1989 at a festive ceremony in the Coronation Hall of Hradčany. A mass in the Cathedral, conducted by Cardinal Tomášek, followed and in the evening people danced in the streets, celebrating the second President-Liberator. In his 1990 New Year's presidential address, Havel said that the worst thing in Czechoslovakia was "the devastated moral environment. We are all morally sick, because we all got used to saying one thing and thinking another."

### Der gewählte Präsident Václav Havel

(1) Plakat mit dem Slogan *Havel na Hrad* (Havel auf den Hradschin). (2) Havel inspiziert Truppen im Innenhof des Hradschins. (3) Am 29. Dezember 1989 wurde Havel in einer feierlichen Zeremonie in der Krönungshalle des Hradschins zum Präsidenten gewählt. Im Anschluß zelebrierte Kardinal Tomášek eine Messe im Dom, und am Abend feierten die Menschen in den Straßen den zweiten Befreier-Präsidenten. In seiner Neu-jahrsansprache 1990 bezeichnete Havel als das Schlimmste in der Tschechoslowakei »... die ruinierte Moral. Wir sind alle moralisch krank, weil wir alle daran gewöhnt sind, das eine zu tun und das andere zu denken.«

### Václav Havel élu président

(1) Poster *Havel na Hrad* (Havel au château). (2) Havel passant les troupes en revue dans la cour du château. (3) Havel fut élu président le 29 décembre 1989 à l'occasion d'une joyeuse cérémonie dans la Salle du couronnement du Hradčany. Après une messe dans la cathédrale célébrée par le cardinal Tomášek, les Pragois dansèrent dans les rues, célébrant leur second président-libérateur. Dans son discours du Nouvel An, Havel déclara que le pire qui était arrivé à la Tchécoslovaquie était « notre environnement moral dévasté. Nous sommes tous moralement malades, parce que nous avons tous pris l'habitude de dire une chose et d'en penser une autre. »

### Hradčany – Prague Castle

(Overleaf) The city on the Vltava is dominated by Hradčany (the Castle), the seat of power of princes, kings, emperors, Nazis, Communists and democratic presidents. It is a place where charlatans conversed with spirits seen in a magic mirror; where a hypochondriac sovereign collected thousands of art objects, hoping to discover the elixir of life and gold; where some mediocre people, elevated to their grand posts by a stroke of Fate, held sway; and from where some outright gangsters, who seized the place by force, spread terror on the people below the hill. But this hill has always been surrounded by a sea of hope, an infinite proud patience, and an awareness of the vanity of all things and of the frailty of the world.

### Der Hradschin – die Prager Burg

(Folgende Seiten) Die Stadt an der Moldau wird vom Hradschin (der Prager Burg) beherrscht, dem Machtzentrum der Prinzen, Könige, Kaiser, der Nazis, Kommunisten und der demokratischen Präsidenten. Hier diskutierten Scharlatane mit Geistern, die ihnen im Spiegel begegneten; hier sammelten hypochondrische Herrscher Tausende von Kunstobjekten in der Hoffnung, eines Tages das Lebenselixir oder Gold herstellen zu können; hier residierten durchschnittliche Menschen, die nur durch einen Streich des Schicksals auf große Posten gehoben worden waren. Von hier aus richteten Gangster, die die Burg mit Gewalt eingenommen hatten, ihre terroristischen Aktionen gegen die Menschen unterhalb des Hügels. Trotzdem war dieser Berg immer von einem Meer der Hoffnung umgeben, mit einer unendlichen, stolzen Geduld und dem Bewußtsein für die Eitelkeit aller Dinge und die Vergänglichkeit der Welt.

### Hradčany – le château de Prague

(Pages suivantes) La ville sur le Moldau est dominée par le Hradčany (le château), siège des princes, des rois, des empereurs, des nazis, des communistes et des présidents démocratiquement élus. C'est un lieu étrange où des charlatans conversèrent avec des esprits aperçus dans un miroir magique, où un souverain hypocondriaque réunit des milliers d'objets d'art en espérant découvrir un élixir de longue vie, où quelques personnages médiocres élevés à leur poste par un coup du destin confisquèrent le pouvoir, et où d'authentiques gangsters imposés par la force répandirent la terreur sur le peuple qui vivait au pied de la colline. Mais cette colline a toujours été entourée d'un océan d'espoir, d'une infinie patience, et de la conscience de la vanité de toute chose et de la fragilité du monde.

# CHRONOLOGICAL TABLE

**1900**    *Klub za starou Prahu* (Club for the Preservation of Old Prague) founded.
Realistic Party founded by followers of T. G. Masaryk.
City's population reaches 514,345.

**1901**    Première of Dvořák's opera *Rusalka* (The Water Nymph) at the National Theater.
Emperor Franz Bridge opened in the presence of the Emperor.
Barnum and Bailey Circus visits Prague.

**1902**    Auguste Rodin attends opening of an exhibition of his work in Prague.
Guillaume Apollinaire visits Prague; the visit inspires several verses in his famous poem *Zone*.

**1903**    Laying of foundation stone for Jan Hus statue by Ladislav Šaloun in Old Town Square.

**1904**    First Motorcycle Exhibition held at Žofín Island.
National Museum of Technology founded.
Antonín Dvořák dies.

**1905**    Edvard Munch Exhibition held in Mánes Pavilion, making great impact on young Czech artists.
Sparta soccer stadium (largest in Bohemia) opens.
On 12 May, Prague sees last horse-drawn tram in streets, making a final journey across Charles Bridge.
300,000 people attend mass demonstrations in support of election reforms.

**1906**    Velká Chuchle racecourse opens.
Czech male population over age of 24 granted voting rights.

**1907**    Emperor Franz Josef I visits Prague.
Austrian Speed-Skating Championship takes place at Střelecký Island.
First permanent cinema in Bohemia opens in Karlova.
Praga Automobile Works founded.
First taxis appear in streets of Prague.
Vinohrady City Theater begins first season.

**1908**    Jubilee Exhibition held in Exhibition Grounds to mark 60th anniversary of Emperor's coronation.
Svatopluk Čech Bridge opens.
Czech Ice-Hockey Association founded.
First motor-car race (from Zbraslav to Jíloviště).

**1909**    National Museum of Technology opens.
Czech Rowing Club organizes Prague's first Mayor's Boat Race on the Vltava (Moldau).
Prague's Franz Josef railway station completed.

**1910**    Prague's population reaches 616,631.
After many years abroad, painter Alfons Mucha returns to Prague.
Prague's first air show takes place at Letná Plain.
Lucerna Cabaret in Vodičkova opens.

**1911**    Building of Municipal House completed.
Jan Kašpar flies from Pardubice to Prague (194km) in 92 minutes.
František Bílek villa built.
Albert Einstein becomes Professor of Theoretical Physics at Prague German University.

**1912**    Josef Hlávka Bridge opened.
V. I. Lenin attends Russian Social Democratic Party conference held in Hybernská Street.
St Wenceslas statue by J. V. Myslbek unveiled.

**1913**    Building of Koruna Palace completed.

---

# ZEITTAFEL

**1900**    Gründung des *Klub za starou Prahu* (Club zur Erhaltung des alten Prag).
Gründung der Realistischen Partei durch Anhänger T. G. Masaryks.
Anstieg der Stadtbevölkerung auf 514.345 Einwohner.

**1901**    Premiere von Dvořáks Oper *Rusalka* (Die Wassernixe) im Nationaltheater.
Eröffnung der Franz-Brücke im Beisein des Kaisers.
Der Zirkus Barnum and Bailey gastiert in der Stadt.

**1902**    Auguste Rodin nimmt an der Eröffnung einer Ausstellung seiner Werke in Prag teil.
Guillaume Apollinaire besucht Prag; der Aufenthalt inspiriert ihn zu einigen Versen seines berühmten Gedichtes *Zone*.

**1903**    Grundsteinlegung für die Jan-Hus-Statue durch Ladislav Šaloun auf dem Altstädter Ring.

**1904**    Erste Motorradausstellung auf der Sophieninsel.
Grundsteinlegung für das Technische Nationalmuseum.
Tod des tschechischen Komponisten Antonín Dvořáks.

**1905**    Die Edvard-Munch-Ausstellung im Mánes-Pavillon beeinflußt viele junge tschechische Künstler.
Das Sparta-Fußballstadion (das größte seiner Art in Böhmen) öffnet seine Tore.
Am 12. Mai sehen die Prager Bürger zum letzten Mal eine Pferdebahn auf ihren Straßen. Ihre letzte Fahrt führt über die Karlsbrücke.
300.000 Menschen nehmen an einer Massendemonstration für Wahlrechtsreformen teil.

**1906**    Eröffnung der Velká-Chuchle-Rennbahn.
Wahlrecht für tschechische Männer über 24 Jahre.

**1907**    Kaiser Franz-Josef I. besucht Prag.
Die österreichischen Meisterschaften im Eisschnellaufen finden auf der Insel Střelecký statt.
Auf der Karlova eröffnet das erste ständige Lichtspielhaus Böhmens.
Gründung der Praga-Automobilwerke.
Das erste Taxi fährt durch die Straßen von Prag.
Das Stadttheater in Vinohrady beginnt seine erste Spielsaison.

**1908**    Aus Anlaß des 60. Thronjubiläums des Kaisers wird eine Jubiläumsausstellung abgehalten.
Eröffnung der Svatopluk-Čech-Brücke.
Gründung des tschechischen Eishockeyverbandes.
Das erste Autorennen findet statt (von Zbraslav nach Jíloviště).

**1909**    Eröffnung des Technischen Nationalmuseums.
Der tschechische Ruderclub veranstaltet Prags erstes sogenanntes Bürgermeister-Bootsrennen auf der Moldau.
Fertigstellung des Prager Franz-Josefs-Bahnhofs.

**1910**    Prags Bevölkerung steigt auf 616.631 Menschen.
Nach vielen Jahren im Ausland kehrt der Maler Alfons Mucha nach Prag zurück.
Prags erste Flugschau findet auf dem Letná-Plateau statt.
In der Vodičkova eröffnet das Kabarett Lucerna.

**1911**    Fertigstellung des Rathauses.
In 92 Minuten fliegt Jan Kašpar von Pardubice nach Prag (194 km).
Bau der Villa František Bílek.
Albert Einstein wird Professor für Theoretische Physik an der Deutschen Universität in Prag.

**1912**    Eröffnung der Josef-Hlávka-Brücke.
V. I. Lenin nimmt an der Konferenz der Russischen Sozialdemokratischen Partei in der Hybernská teil.
Enthüllung der Statue des Heiligen Wenzel von J.V. Myslbek.

**1913**    Fertigstellung des Koruna-Palastes.

---

# CHRONOLOGIE

**1900**    Fondation du *Klub za starou Prahu* (Club pour la préservation du Vieux Prague).
Création du Parti réaliste par les partisans de T. G. Masaryk.
Prague compte 514 345 habitants.

**1901**    Première de l'opéra de Dvořák *Rusalka* (La nymphe des eaux) au Théâtre national.
Le pont François est inauguré en présence de l'Empereur.
Les cirques Barnum et Bailey en tournée à Prague.

**1902**    Auguste Rodin assiste à l'inauguration d'une exposition de son œuvre à Prague.
Guillaume Apollinaire visite la ville qui lui inspire plusieurs vers de son célèbre poème *Zone*.

**1903**    Pose de la première pierre de la statue de Jan Hus, du sculpteur Ladislav Šaloun.

**1904**    Premier salon de l'automobile sur l'île de Žofín.
Fondation du Musée national de la technologie.
Mort d'Antonín Dvořák.

**1905**    L'exposition d'Edvard Munch au Pavillon Mánes exerce un fort impact sur les jeunes artistes tchèques.
Ouverture du stade de football Sparta (le plus vaste de Bohême).
12 mai : dernier voyage du dernier tram tiré par un cheval.
300 000 personnes participent à des manifestations pour la réforme électorale.

**1906**    Ouverture du champ de course de Velká Chuchle.
Le droit de vote est accordé à tous les hommes tchèques de plus de 24 ans.

**1907**    Visite de l'empereur François-Joseph à Prague.
Championnat de patinage de vitesse sur glace autrichien sur l'île de Střelecký.
Le premier cinéma permanent de Bohême ouvre ses portes rue Karlova.
Création d'une usine d'automobiles Praga.
Première apparition d'un taxi automobile dans les rues de la capitale.
Première saison du théâtre de Vinohrady.

**1908**    Exposition du Jubilé au palais de la foire pour marquer le 60e anniversaire du couronnement de l'Empereur.
Ouverture du pont Svatopluk Čech.
Fondation de l'Association tchèque de hockey sur glace.
Première course automobile (de Zbraslav à Jíloviště).

**1909**    Ouverture du Musée national de la technologie.
Le Club d'aviron tchèque organise la première course du Maire sur la Moldau.
Achèvement de la gare François-Joseph.

**1910**    La population atteint le chiffre de 616 631 habitants.
Le peintre Alfons Mucha rentre à Prague après de nombreuses années passées à l'étranger.
Première exposition aéronautique de Prague sur la plaine de Letná.
Ouverture du cabaret Lucerna, rue Vodičkova.

**1911**    Achèvement de la construction de la Maison municipale.
Le pilote Jan Kašpar accomplit le vol Pardubice-Prague (194 km) en 92 minutes.
Construction de la villa de František Bílek.
Albert Einstein devient professeur de physique théorique à l'Université allemande de Prague.

**1912**    Ouverture du pont Josef Hlávka.
Lénine assiste à une conférence du parti social-démocrate russe, rue Hybernská.
Inauguration de la statue de saint Venceslas de J. V. Myslbek.

**1913**    Achèvement de la construction du palais Koruna.

| | | | | | |
|---|---|---|---|---|---|
| | First Czech Care Center for disabled youth founded at Vyšehrad. Cubist houses designed by J. Chochol built under Vyšehrad Hill. Cabaret Montmartre opens in Řetězová. | | In Vyšehrad wird das erste tschechische Heim für behinderte Jugendliche eröffnet. Auf dem Vyšehrad entstehen kubistische Häuser nach den Plänen J. Chochols. An der Řetězová eröffnet das Kabarett Montmartre. | | Fondation du premier centre de soins tchèque pour jeunes handicapés à Vyšehrad. Construction de maisons cubistes par J. Chochol au pied de la colline de Vyšehrad. Ouverture du cabaret Montmartre, rue Řetězová. |
| **1914** | On 28 June, assassination in Sarajevo of Archduke Franz Ferdinand d'Este (owner of Konopiště Estate south of Prague) provides direct impetus for outbreak of First World War. | **1914** | Die Ermordung von Erzherzog Franz Ferdinand (dem Besitzer von Anwesen in Konopiště, südlich von Prag) am 28. Juni ist der Auslöser für den Ausbruch des Ersten Weltkriegs. | **1914** | Assassinat de l'archiduc François-Ferdinand à Sarajevo (propriétaire du domaine de Konopiště au sud de Prague) le 28 juin, qui déclenche la Première Guerre mondiale. |
| **1915** | Jan Hus statue unveiled in Old Town Square. Clandestine "Maffia" organization founded by followers of T. G. Masaryk. | **1915** | Auf dem Altstädter Ring wird die Jan-Hus-Statue enthüllt. Anhänger T. G. Masaryks gründen die Geheimorganisation »Maffia«. | **1915** | Inauguration de la statue de Jan Hus sur la place de la Vieille ville. Création d'une organisation clandestine par les partisans de T. G. Masaryk, la «Maffia». |
| **1916** | Trial of leading members of "Maffia." Emperor Franz Josef dies and is succeeded by Archduke Karl. | **1916** | Führende Mitglieder der »Maffia« werden vor Gericht gestellt. Tod des Kaisers Franz-Josef. Sein Nachfolger wird Erzherzog Karl. | **1916** | Procès des principaux membres de «Maffia»; Mort de l'empereur François-Joseph, auquel succède l'archiduc Charles. |
| **1917** | Public gatherings officially banned. | **1917** | Verbot öffentlicher Versammlungen. | **1917** | Interdiction de toute manifestation publique. |
| **1918** | General strike by Czech workers. War brings collapse of Austro-Hungarian Empire. On 28 October, Czechoslovak independence officially proclaimed in Wenceslas Square. T. G. Masaryk elected first President of Czechoslovakia. On 18 December, first Czechoslovak postage stamp issued, featuring Hradčany. On 21 December, T. G. Masaryk returns to Prague. | **1918** | Generalstreik der tschechischen Arbeiter. Zusammenbruch des österreichisch-ungarischen Reiches durch den Krieg. Am 28. Oktober wird auf dem Wenzelsplatz offiziell die tschechische Unabhängigkeit proklamiert. T. G. Masaryk ist der erste gewählte Präsident der Tschechoslowakei. Am 18. Dezember erscheint die erste tschechische Briefmarke mit dem Bild des Hradschin. Am 21. Dezember kehrt T. G. Masaryk nach Prag zurück. | **1918** | Grève générale des ouvriers tchèques. Effondrement de l'empire austro-hongrois. Le 28 octobre, proclamation de l'indépendance tchèque place Venceslas. T. G. Masaryk est élu premier président de Tchécoslovaquie. Le 18 décembre, édition du premier timbre-poste tchèque, reproduisant le château du Hradčany. T. G. Masaryk rentre à Prague le 21 décembre. |
| **1919** | Following temporary closure during war, Prague Stock Exchange re-opens. Three airplane factories (Walter, Avia and Military Aircraft Factory in Kbely) begin production in Prague. | **1919** | Nach vorübergehender, kriegsbedingter Schließung wird die Prager Börse wiedereröffnet. Drei Flugzeugfabriken (Walter, Avia und die Militärflugzeugfabrik in Kbely) beginnen in Prag mit der Produktion. | **1919** | Réouverture de la Bourse de Prague close pendant la guerre. Trois usines aéronautiques sont créées : Walter, Avia et une militaire à Kbely. |
| **1920** | On 29 February, Czechoslovak legal and governmental system finalized and constitution formally approved. Prague proclaimed capital of Czechoslovak Republic. Parliamentary elections take place in April. Czech avant-garde art group Devětsil founded. Czechoslovak Travel Bureau (Čedok) founded. | **1920** | Am 29. Februar ist das tschechoslowakische Rechtsund Regierungssystem komplettiert und die Verfassung offiziell angenommen. Prag wird zur Hauptstadt der tschechoslowakischen Republik ausgerufen. Im April finden Parlamentswahlen statt. Gründung der tschechischen Avantgarde-Künstlergruppe Devětsil. Eröffnung der Tschechoslowakischen Reiseagentur (Čedok). | **1920** | Approbation de la constitution le 29 février. Prague est proclamée capitale de la République tchécoslovaque. Élections au parlement en avril. Création du groupe artistique d'avant-garde Devětsil. Création de l'agence de voyage tchécoslovaque Čedok. |
| **1921** | Population of Prague reaches 676,657. Czechoslovak Communist Party (KSČ) founded. Exhibition of modern Italian art held in Rudolfinum. Karel Čapek's play *R.U.R.* produced by National Theater. | **1921** | Die Bevölkerung Prags wächst auf 676.657 Menschen. Gründung der Kommunistischen Partei der Tschechoslowakei (KSČ). Im Rudolfinum wird eine Ausstellung moderner italienischer Kunst eröffnet. Das Nationaltheater führt Karel Čapeks Drama *R.U.R.* auf. | **1921** | Prague compte 676 657 habitants. Fondation du Parti communiste tchécoslovaque (KSČ). Exposition d'art moderne italien au Rudolfinum. La pièce de Karel Čapek, *R.U.R.*, est donnée au Théâtre national. |
| **1922** | Greater Prague formed by incorporating more than 35 outlying districts and villages. Initial instalments of Jaroslav Hašek's novel *The Good Soldier Švejk* published. Piccasso Exhibition held in Prague. | **1922** | Über 35 Vororte und Dörfer werden in das Stadtgebiet Prags eingemeindet. Jaroslav Hašeks *Der brave Soldat Schwejk* erscheint als Fortsetzungsroman. Eröffnung einer Ausstellung mit Werken von Picasso in Prag. | **1922** | Formation du grand Prague par l'intégration de 35 communes avoisinantes. Début de la publication du *Brave Soldat Švejk* de Jaroslav Hašek. Exposition de Picasso à Prague. |
| **1923** | Finance Minister Alois Rašín assassinated. Czechoslovak Radio *(Radiojournal)* begins broadcasting from a tent in Kbely. Major exhibition of modern French art held in Municipal House. Poet Marina Tsvetaeva, one of many Russians fleeing Soviet regime, settles in Prague. Jaroslav Hašek dies. Regular scheduled flights between Prague and Bratislava introduced. Bazaar of Modern Art, organized by Devětsil, held at Artists' Emporium. | **1923** | Ermordung von Finanzminister Alois Rašín. Von einem Zelt in Kbely beginnt das Tschechoslowakische Radio *(Radiojournal)* seine Übertragungen. Im Rathaus wird eine bedeutende Ausstellung moderner französischer Kunst eröffnet. Auf der Flucht vor dem sowjetischen Regime läßt sich die russische Dichterin Marina Zwetajeva in Prag nieder. Tod des Schriftstellers Jaroslav Hašeks. Beginn des regulären Flugverkehrs zwischen Prag und Breslau. Die Künstlergruppe Devětsil eröffnet im Künstler-Emporium einen Basar der modernen Kunst. | **1923** | Assassinat du ministre des finances, Alois Rašín. Première émission de la radio tchécoslovaque *(Radiojournal)* depuis une tente à Kbely. Grande exposition d'art moderne français à l'hôtel de ville. La poétesse Marina Tsvetaeva, fuyant le régime soviétique, s'installe à Prague. Mort de Jaroslav Hašek. Ouverture de vols réguliers entre Prague et Bratislava. Devětsil organise le «Bazar de l'art moderne» dans l'Emporium des artistes. |

**1924** Czechoslovak Airlines founded.
Architects Club in Prague organizes series of lectures by leading architects, including Le Corbusier, Loos and Gropius.
Franz Kafka dies.

**1925** Europe's first radio broadcast of an entire opera (Bedřich Smetana's *The Two Widows*, staged at National Theater).
Anniversary of Jan Hus's death celebrated for first time as national holiday.

**1926** Avant-garde Liberated Theater (*Osvobozené divadlo*) begins performances.
First Czech live radio broadcast of soccer match.
Douglas Fairbanks and Mary Pickford visit Prague.

**1927** *The Vest Pocket Revue* by Jiří Voskovec and Jan Werich premières at Liberated Theater.
Dada Theater founded.

**1928** City Public Library building opens.
Mánes House of Artists built.
Construction of Barrandov Villa development completed.

**1929** Liberated Theater moves to U Nováků premises.
Klement Gottwald, representative of radical young Stalinists, assumes leadership of Communist Party.
Prague's first "talking picture" (*Showboat*) shown at Lucerna Cinema.
St Vitus Cathedral reconsecrated as part of large-scale celebrations to mark 1000th anniversary of death of St Wenceslas.

**1930** City's population reaches 848,823.
Czechoslovak Airlines launch their first international air route (Prague to Zagreb).
Villa by architect Adolf Loos built in Střešovice.
First entirely Czech, full-length sound film (*Fidlovačka*) produced.

**1931** Alois Jirásek Bridge built.
First artificial ice-skating rink built on Štvanice Island.
Prague Zoo opens to public.

**1932** National Liberation Monument (designed by J. Zázvorka) completed on Žižkov Hill.
US General McArthur visits Prague.

**1933** Construction of Barrandov Film Studios completed.
Number of unemployed in Prague reaches 28,461.
Over next few years, Prague becomes destination of many German refugees fleeing Hitler's regime, among them authors Thomas Mann, Stefan Zweig and Bertold Brecht.

**1934** President Masaryk re-elected.
The Surrealist Group of Prague (Teige, Nezval, Toyen, Štyrský and others) founded.

**1935** First Surrealist Group exhibition opens at Mánes House.
French Surrealists André Breton and Paul Éluard visit Prague.
President Masaryk retires.
On 18 December, Dr Edvard Beneš elected President of Czechoslovakia.

**1936** Trolley buses introduced as part of public-transport system.
New international airport in Ruzyně opened.

**1937** City's population reaches estimated 945,000.
Hollywood mogul Luis B. Mayer visits Prague.
On 14 September, Tomáš Masaryk dies in his residence in Lány.

---

**1924** Gründung der tschechoslowakischen Luftfahrtgesellschaft.
Der Club der Architekten in Prag organisiert eine Vorlesungsreihe mit führenden Architekten, darunter Le Corbusier, Loos und Gropius.
Tod Franz Kafkas.

**1925** Erstmals wird in Europa eine ganze Oper im Radio übertragen (Bedřich Smetanas am Nationaltheater aufgeführtes Werk *Die zwei Witwen*).
Zum ersten Mal wird der Todestag von Jan Hus als nationaler Feiertag begangen.

**1926** Das avantgardistische Befreite Theater (*Osvobozené divadlo*) beginnt mit seinem Programm.
Erste tschechische Live-Übertragung eines Fußballspiels im Radio.
Douglas Fairbanks und Mary Pickford besuchen Prag.

**1927** *Die Westentaschenrevue* von Jiří Voskovec und Jan Werich wird zum ersten Mal im Befreiten Theater aufgeführt.
Gründung des Dada-Theaters.

**1928** Eröffnung der Stadtbibliothek.
Bau des Mánes-Hauses der Künstler.
Fertigstellung der Barrandov-Villen.

**1929** Das Befreite Theater zieht in das Spielhaus U Nováků.
Klement Gottwald, der Vertreter der radikalen jungen Stalinisten, übernimmt den Vorsitz der Kommunistischen Partei.
Im Kino Lucerna wird erstmals in Prag ein Film mit »sprechenden Bildern« (*Showboat*) gezeigt.
Zu den umfangreichen Feierlichkeiten zum 1000. Todestag des Heiligen Wenzel wird der Veitsdom neu geweiht.

**1930** Die Bevölkerung der Stadt steigt auf 848.823 Einwohner.
Die tschechoslowakische Luftfahrtgesellschaft bietet ihre erste internationale Reise (von Prag nach Zagreb) an.
In Střešovice baut der Architekt Adolf Loos eine Villa.
Produktion des ersten tschechischen Films in Spielfilmlänge (*Fidlovačka*).

**1931** Bau der Alois-Jirásek-Brücke.
Auf der Insel Štvanice wird die erste künstliche Eisbahn eingerichtet.
Eröffnung des Prager Zoos.

**1932** Auf dem Žižkov-Hügel wird das (von J. Zázvorka entworfene) Nationaldenkmal fertiggestellt.
Der amerikanische General McArthur besucht Prag.

**1933** Fertigstellung der Barrandov-Filmstudios.
In Prag beträgt die Zahl der Arbeitslosen 28.461 Personen.
Auf der Flucht vor Hitlers Regime wird Prag in den folgenden Jahren zum Ziel vieler deutscher Auswanderer, darunter Thomas Mann, Stefan Zweig und Bertold Brecht.

**1934** Wiederwahl von Präsident Masaryk.
Gründung der Surrealistischen Gruppe von Prag (Teige, Nezval, Toyen, Štyrský u.a.).

**1935** Die erste Ausstellung der Surrealisten wird im Mánes-Haus eröffnet.
Die französischen Surrealisten André Breton und Paul Éluard besuchen Prag.
Präsident Masaryk tritt zurück.
Am 18. Dezember wird Dr. Eduard Beneš zum Präsidenten der Tschechoslowakei gewählt.

**1936** Im öffentlichen Transportwesen werden Oberleitungsbusse eingeführt.
Eröffnung des neuen internationalen Flughafens in Ruzyně.

**1937** Die Bevölkerungszahl steigt auf schätzungsweise 945.000 Personen an.
Der Hollywood-Mogul Luis B. Mayer besucht Prag.
Am 14. September stirbt Tomáš Masaryk auf seinem Alterssitz in Lány.

---

**1924** Création de la compagnie aérienne tchécoslovaque.
Le Cercle des architectes de Prague organise une série de conférences données par de grands architectes comme Le Corbusier, Loos et Gropius.
Mort de Franz Kafka.

**1925** Première retransmission radiophonique d'un opéra entier en Europe (*Les Deux Veuves*, de Bedřich Smetana, depuis le Théâtre national).
L'anniversaire de la mort de Jan Hus devient jour férié.

**1926** Début des représentations du groupe d'avant-garde du Théâtre Libéré (*Osvobozené divadlo*).
Première retransmission radiophonique tchèque d'un match de football.
Douglas Fairbanks et Mary Pickford en visite à Prague.

**1927** Première de *la Revue du gousset*, de Jiří Voskovec et Jan Werich, au Théâtre Libéré.
Fondation du Théâtre Dada.

**1928** Inauguration de la Bibliothèque municipale.
Construction de la Maison des artistes de Mánes.
Achèvement de la construction de lotissement de villas de Barrandov.

**1929** Le Théâtre Libéré s'installe à U Nováků.
Klement Gottwald, représentant les jeunes stalinistes radicaux, devient chef du Parti communiste.
Première projection d'un film parlant (*Showboat*) au Cinéma «Lucerna».
La cathédrale Saint-Guy est reconsacrée à l'occasion d'importantes célébrations pour le 1 000e anniversaire de la mort de saint Venceslas.

**1930** La population de Prague atteint 848 823 habitants.
La Compagnie aérienne tchécoslovaque lance sa première liaison internationale: Prague-Zagreb.
Adolf Loos construit une villa à Střešovice.
Production du premier grand film tchèque parlant (*Fidlovačka*).

**1931** Construction du pont Alois Jirásek.
Construction de la première patinoire artificielle sur l'île de Štvanice.
Ouverture au public du zoo de Prague.

**1932** Monument de la Libération nationale (dessiné par J. Zázvorka) sur la colline de Žižkov.
Le général américain McArthur en visite à Prague.

**1933** Achèvement de la construction des studios de cinéma de Barrandov.
Le nombre de chômeurs praguois s'élève à 28 461.
De nombreux réfugiés allemands fuyant le régime hitlérien commencent à se réfugier à Prague.
Parmi eux, des écrivains comme Thomas Mann, Stefan Zweig et Bertold Brecht.

**1934** Réélection du président Masaryk.
Création du groupe surréaliste praguois: Teige, Nezval, Toyen, Štyrský…

**1935** Première exposition du groupe des surréalistes à la maison Mánes.
André Breton et Paul Éluard visitent Prague.
Masaryk se retire de la vie politique.
Le Docteur Edvard Beneš est élu président de la République le 18 décembre.

**1936** Introduction de trolleys dans les transports publics.
Ouverture du nouvel aéroport international de Ruzyně.

**1937** La population de la capitale atteint 945 000 habitants.
Luis B. Mayer, le producteur d'Hollywood, visite Prague.
Mort de Tomáš Masaryk dans sa résidence de Lány, le 14 septembre.

| | | |
|---|---|---|
| **1938** | Population reaches 962,200.<br>Prague hosts European Ice-Hockey Championship.<br>Sudeten German Party, under Konrad Henlein, demands autonomy for Sudetenland.<br>On 20–22 May, partial mobilization declared.<br>10th *Sokol* (Falcon) gymnastic rally takes place in July.<br>US aviator Charles Lindbergh visits Prague.<br>On 7 September, President Beneš offers to meet Sudeten German demands.<br>On 23 September, overall mobilization declared.<br>On 29 September, at Munich Conference, Hitler, Mussolini, Chamberlain and Daladier agree to cede Sudetenland to Germany.<br>On 1 October, German troops begin to occupy Sudetenland.<br>On 5 October, President Beneš resigns.<br>On 22 October, Beneš flees to England.<br>On 11 November, Dr Emil Hácha elected President of the Republic.<br>Writer Karel Čapek dies. |
| **1939** | On 15 March, German troops occupy Prague; Hitler arrives and spends one night at Hradčany.<br>On 16 March, Hitler proclaims Protectorate of Bohemia and Moravia.<br>K. H. Frank becomes State Secretary of Protectorate.<br>Hitler appoints Konstantin von Neurath as Reichsprotektor.<br>So-called "Nuremberg Laws" implemented, excluding Czech Jews from economic life of Protectorate.<br>On 28 October, a peaceful demonstration to commemorate National Day ends in violence provoked by Nazis.<br>On 17 November, all Czech universities and technical colleges closed down; 9 student leaders executed, 1200 students deported to concentration camps. |
| **1940** | Nazi Propaganda Minister Dr Josef Goebbels visits Prague.<br>Czechoslovak pilots take part in Battle of Britain. |
| **1941** | Czechoslovak government-in-exile recognized by the governments of Britain and the Soviet Union.<br>Czech Jews ordered to wear yellow star.<br>On 27 September, Reinhard Heydrich, appointed Acting Reichsprotektor of Bohemia and Moravia, arrives in Prague.<br>Martial law declared; Nazis resort to mass arrests and executions to crush resistance and wipe out intelligentsia.<br>Terezín transit ghetto set up.<br>*Sokol* organization banned by Nazis. |
| **1942** | On 27 May, Czechoslovak parachutists sent from London attempt to assassinate Heydrich.<br>Martial law imposed.<br>Hitler appoints Kurt Daluege as Acting Reichsprotektor.<br>On 4 June, Heydrich dies.<br>On 10 June, village of Lidice destroyed, its men shot, its women sent to concentration camps. On 18 June, Heydrich's assassins and five colleagues die in siege of St Cyril and St Methodius Church in Resslova.<br>On 3 July, 250,000 people take part in oath of allegiance to Third Reich at mass rally in Wenceslas Square. |

---

| | | |
|---|---|---|
| **1938** | Die Bevölkerung wächst auf 962.200 Menschen.<br>In Prag finden die Eishockey-Europameisterschaften statt.<br>Unter der Führung Konrad Henleins fordert die Sudetendeutsche Partei die Selbständigkeit des Sudetenlandes.<br>Am 20.–22. Mai wird die Teilmobilmachung erklärt.<br>Im Juli finden die 10. Turnertage der *Sokol* (Falken) statt.<br>Der amerikanische Flieger Charles Lindbergh besucht Prag.<br>Am 7. September erklärt sich Präsident Beneš bereit, den Forderungen der Sudetendeutschen entgegenzukommen.<br>Am 23. September wird die totale Mobilmachung erklärt.<br>Auf der Münchener Konferenz am 29. September einigen sich Hitler, Mussolini, Chamberlain und Daladier auf die deutsche Übernahme des Sudetenlandes.<br>Am 1. Oktober beginnt die deutsche Besetzung des Sudetenlandes.<br>Am 5. Oktober tritt Präsident Beneš zurück.<br>Am 22. Oktober flieht Beneš nach England.<br>Am 11. November wird Dr. Emil Hácha zum Präsidenten der Republik gewählt.<br>Tod des Schriftstellers Karel Čapek. |
| **1939** | Am 15. März besetzen deutsche Truppen Prag. Hitler besucht die Stadt und verbringt eine Nacht im Hradschin.<br>Am 16. März richtet er das Protektorat Böhmen und Mähren ein.<br>K. H. Frank wird Staatssekretär des Protektorats.<br>Hitler ernennt Konstantin von Neurath zum Reichsprotektor.<br>In Prag werden die sogenannten »Nürnberger Gesetze« eingeführt. Dadurch schließt man die tschechischen Juden vom wirtschaftlichen Leben des Protektorats aus.<br>Eine friedliche Demonstration zum Nationalfeiertag am 28. Oktober endet mit von den Nazis provozierten Gewaltanwendungen.<br>Am 17. November werden alle tschechischen Universitäten und technischen Hochschulen geschlossen. Die Nazis richten neun Studentenführer hin und deportieren 1.200 Kommilitonen in Konzentrationslager. |
| **1940** | Josef Goebbels, der Propagandaminister der Nazis, besucht Prag.<br>Tschechische Piloten nehmen an der Luftschlacht um England teil. |
| **1941** | Die tschechoslowakische Exil-Regierung wird von England und der Sowjetunion anerkannt.<br>Die tschechischen Juden müssen den gelben Stern tragen.<br>Am 27. September trifft der neue stellvertretende Reichsprotektor von Böhmen und Mähren, Reinhard Heydrich, in Prag ein.<br>Ausrufung des Kriegsrechts: Die Nazis führen Massenverhaftungen und Exekutionen durch, um den Widerstand zu brechen und die Intellektuellen zu vernichten.<br>Das Ghetto Theresienstadt wird eingerichtet.<br>Die Organisation *Sokol* wird von den Nazis verboten. |
| **1942** | Am 27. Mai werden aus London tschechoslowakische Fallschirmspringer zur Ermordung Heydrichs geschickt.<br>Das Kriegsrecht wird verschärft.<br>Hitler ernennt Kurt Daluege zum Reichsprotektor.<br>Am 4. Juni stirbt Reinhard Heydrich.<br>Am 10. Juni zerstören die Nazis das Dorf Lidice; die Männer werden erschossen, die Frauen in Konzentrationslager deportiert. Am 18. Juni sterben Heydrichs Mörder und fünf Kameraden während der Belagerung der Kirche St. Kyrill und Method auf der Resslova.<br>Am 3. Juli nehmen 250.000 Menschen an einer Massendemonstration für die Nazis auf dem Wenzelsplatz teil und schwören den Treueeid auf das Dritte Reich. |

---

| | | |
|---|---|---|
| **1938** | La population atteint 962 200 habitants. Prague accueille le Championnat d'Europe de hockey sur glace.<br>Le parti allemand des Sudètes, dirigé par Konrad Henlein, réclame l'autonomie des Sudètes.<br>20–22 mai: mobilisation partielle.<br>Le 10e Festival de gymnastique de l'Association *Sokol* se déroule en juillet.<br>L'aviateur américain Charles Lindbergh visite Prague.<br>Le 7 septembre, le président Beneš accepte les revendications des Allemands des Sudètes.<br>Le 23 septembre, mobilisation générale.<br>Le 29 septembre, à la conférence de Munich, Hitler, Mussolini, Chamberlain et Daladier décident de la cession de la région des Sudètes à l'Allemagne.<br>Le 1er octobre, les troupes allemandes commencent à occuper les Sudètes.<br>Le 5 octobre, le président Beneš démissionne.<br>Le 22 octobre, Beneš fuit en Grande-Bretagne.<br>Le 11 novembre, le Dr. Emil Hácha est élu président de la République.<br>Mort de l'écrivain Karel Čapek. |
| **1939** | Le 15 mars, les troupes allemandes occupent Prague. Hitler passe une nuit au château de Hradčany.<br>Le 16 mars, Hitler proclame son protectorat sur la Bohême et la Moravie.<br>K. H. Frank devient secrétaire d'État du Protectorat.<br>Hitler nomme Konstantin von Neurath, *Reichsprotektor*.<br>Les «Lois de Nuremberg» entrent en vigueur, excluant les Juifs tchèques de la vie économique du Protectorat.<br>Le 28 octobre, une manifestation paisible à l'occasion de la fête nationale dégénère en violences provoquées par les nazis.<br>Le 17 novembre, toutes les universités et les collèges techniques tchèques sont fermés. 9 leaders étudiants sont exécutés, 1 200 étudiants déportés dans les camps de concentration. |
| **1940** | Goebbels, ministre de la propagande nazie, visite Prague.<br>Des pilotes tchécoslovaques participent à la Bataille d'Angleterre. |
| **1941** | Le gouvernement tchécoslovaque en exil est reconnu par la Grande-Bretagne et l'Union soviétique.<br>Les Juifs tchèques sont contraints de porter l'étoile jaune.<br>27 septembre: Reinhard Heydrich est nommé *Reichsprotektor* de Bohême et de Moravie.<br>Déclaration de la loi martiale. Arrestations en masse et exécutions pour briser la résistance et anéantir l'intelligentsia.<br>Création du ghetto de Terezin.<br>L'Association *Sokol* interdite par les nazis. |
| **1942** | 27 mai: des parachutistes tchécoslovaques envoyés de Londres tentent d'assassiner Heydrich.<br>Loi martiale.<br>Hitler nomme Kurt Daluege au poste de *Reichsprotektor*.<br>4 juin: mort de Heydrich.<br>10 juin: le village de Lidice est rasé, ses hommes fusillés, ses femmes envoyées en camp de concentration. Le 18 juin, les assassins d'Heydrich et cinq hommes sont tués au cours du siège de l'église Saint-Cyrille et Saint-Méthode, rue Resslova.<br>3 juillet: 250 000 personnes participent à une manifestation d'allégeance au Troisième Reich, place Venceslas. |

| 1943 | First Prague Youth Week takes place. Hitler appoints Wilhelm Frick as new Reichs-protektor. |
|------|------|

**1943**
First Prague Youth Week takes place.
Hitler appoints Wilhelm Frick as new Reichs-protektor.

**1944**
Frank establishes League Against Bolshevism.
First air raid on Prague.

**1945**
On 14 February, Prague bombed during Anglo-American air raid.
On 25 March, last bombing raid on Prague.
On 5 May, Prague Uprising starts; over 1600 barricades built across city.
On 6 May, well-armed Vlasov Army (anti-Communist Russians who fought with Germans) reaches Prague and decides to switch sides in order to help inhabitants of Prague and save own skins.
On 7 May, Vlasov Army continues to fight Germans and later withdraws towards Plzeň, seeking protection from Soviet army.
On 8 May, ceasefire concluded; German troops begin to withdraw from Prague.
On 9 May, Red Army arrives in Prague.
On 16 May, President Beneš returns to Prague.
In August, Czechoslovaks, with Allied approval, begin expulsion of 2.5 million Germans to Germany.
In October, key industries nationalized.
Transcarpathian Ruthenia, part of pre-war Czechoslovak state, annexed by Soviet Union.

**1946**
In first post-war elections, Communists win almost 38 per cent of vote.
Annual "Prague Spring" music festival established.
Nazi Secretary of State K. H. Frank tried and executed in Pankrác prison.
New Czechoslovak government elected; Klement Gottwald appointed Prime Minister.
State Jewish Museum founded.

**1947**
Prague hosts First World Festival of Youth and Students.
World Ice-Hockey Championship takes place in Prague.
Exhibition of International Surrealist art held in Prague.
Soviets veto Czechoslovak participation in Marshall Plan.

**1948**
On 20 February, 12 ministers from non-Communist parties resign in protest against Communist advance.
On 25 February, Communists seize power as President Beneš, under threat of armed militia units, is forced to accept resignation of democratic ministers.
On 10 March, Jan Masaryk found dead in grounds of Černín Palace.
On 7 June, Beneš resigns.
Gottwald elected President.
On 3 September, Edvard Beneš dies.
Purge trials begin to eliminate "enemies of the state."

**1949**
On 25 February, Communist Party celebrates first anniversary of "Victorious February" coup.

**1950**
Show trial of democratic Member of Parliament Milada Horáková on trumped-up charges of treason.
14 executions and 52 life-sentences carried out in this one year.
First Czechoslovak Communist Youth rally.

**1951**
Jan Šverma Bridge opens.

**1952**
Czechoslovak Academy of Sciences founded.
Series of "conspiracy" trials, modeled on Soviet purge trials of 1930s, leads to execution of 11 top Communists (including Rudolf Slánský).
Puppet Theater Academy (first of its kind in world) founded in Prague.

---

**1943**
Eröffnung der ersten Prager Jugendwoche.
Hitler ernennt Wilhelm Frick zum neuen Reichspro-tektor.

**1944**
Frank gründet die Liga gegen den Bolschewismus.
Erste Luftangriffe auf Prag.

**1945**
Während eines anglo-amerikanischen Luftangriffs am 14. Februar fallen Bomben auf Prag.
Letzter Luftangriff auf Prag am 25. März.
Am 5. Mai beginnt der Prager Aufstand: 1.600 Barrikaden werden in der Stadt errichtet.
Die gut ausgerüstete Wlassow-Armee (antikommunistische Russen in der deutschen Armee) erreicht am 6. Mai Prag und kämpft gegen die SS-Truppen.
Am 7. Mai zieht sich die Wlassow-Armee unter weiteren Gefechten gegen die SS nach Pilsen zurück, um dort Schutz gegen die sowjetische Armee zu suchen.
Am 8. Mai wird ein Waffenstillstand vereinbart; die deutschen Truppen beginnen mit dem Abzug aus Prag.
Am 9. Mai trifft die Rote Armee in Prag ein.
Am 16. Mai kehrt Präsident Beneš zurück.
Im August beginnen die Tschechen unter Zustimmung der Alliierten mit der Vertreibung von 2,5 Millionen Deutschen nach Westen.
Im Oktober werden Schlüsselindustrien verstaatlicht.
Das transkarpartische Ruthenien, ehemals Teil der Tschechoslowakei, wird von der Sowjetunion annektiert.

**1946**
In den ersten Nachkriegswahlen erhalten die Kommunisten fast 38 Prozent der Stimmen.
Der »Prager Frühling« (ein jährlich stattfindendes Musikfest) findet zum ersten Mal statt.
Der NS-Staatssekretär K. H. Frank wird vor Gericht gestellt und im Pankratius-Gefängnis hingerichtet.
Wahl einer neuen tschechoslowakischen Regierung; Klement Gottwald wird zum Premierminister ernannt.
Gründung des Jüdischen Museums.

**1947**
In Prag findet das erste Weltfestival der Jugend und der Studenten statt.
Die Weltmeisterschaften im Eishockey werden in der Stadt ausgetragen.
Eröffnung einer Ausstellung mit Werken internationaler Surrealisten.
Die Sowjets verbieten die tschechoslowakische Beteiligung am Marshallplan.

**1948**
Aus Protest gegen die kommunistischen Vorstöße treten am 20. Februar 12 Minister nicht-kommunistischer Parteien zurück.
Nachdem Präsident Beneš unter dem Druck bewaffneter Milizen gezwungen wird, den Rücktritt demokratischer Minister anzuerkennen, übernehmen die Kommunisten am 25. Februar die Macht.
Am 10. März wird Jan Masaryk tot im Czernin-Palast gefunden.
Am 7. Juni tritt Beneš zurück.
Gottwald wird zum neuen Präsidenten gewählt.
Am 3. September stirbt Eduard Beneš.
Säuberungsprozesse zur Vernichtung der »Staatsfeinde« beginnen.

**1949**
Am 25. Februar feiert die Kommunistische Partei den ersten Jahrestag des »Siegreichen Februars«.

**1950**
Gegen die demokratische Parlamentsabgeordnete Milada Horáková wird mit gefälschten Verratsanklagen ein Schauprozeß veranstaltet.
In diesem Jahr werden 14 Hinrichtungen und 52 lebenslange Haftstrafen verhängt.
Erste Großveranstaltung der tschechoslowakischen kommunistischen Jugend.

**1951**
Eröffnung der Jan-Šverma-Brücke.

**1952**
Gründung der Tschechoslowakischen Akademie der Wissenschaften.
Eine Reihe von »Verschwörungs«-Prozessen in Stil der sowjetischen Schauprozesse der 30er Jahre führt zur Hinrichtung von elf hochrangigen Kommunisten (einschließlich Rudolf Slánský).
Die Akademie für Puppentheater (die weltweit erste dieser Art) wird in Prag gegründet.

---

**1943**
Ouverture de la première semaine de la jeunesse de Prague.
Hitler nomme Wilhelm Frick *Reichsprotektor*.

**1944**
Frank fonde la Ligue contre le bolchevisme.
Premier raid aérien sur Prague.

**1945**
14 février : Prague bombardée lors d'un raid anglo-américain.
25 mars : dernier raid aérien sur Prague.
5 mai : soulèvement de la capitale. 1600 barricades sont élevées.
6 mai : l'armée de Vlasov, bien équipée (Russes anti-communistes qui avaient combattu contre les Soviétiques) atteint Prague et se bat contre les troupes SS.
7 mai : l'armée de Vlasov se bat, puis se retire vers Plzeň, cherchant à se protéger de l'armée soviétique.
8 mai : cessez-le-feu. Les troupes allemandes commencent à se retirer de Prague.
9 mai : l'Armée rouge atteint Prague.
16 mai : le président Beneš rentre dans la capitale.
En août, les Tchécoslovaques, avec l'accord des Alliés, commencent l'expulsion de 2,5 millions d'Allemands des Sudètes vers l'Allemagne.
Octobr : nationalisation des industries-clés.
La Ruthénie transcarpatienne, qui appartenait avant-guerre à la Tchécoslovaquie, est annexée par l'Union soviétique.

**1946**
Les communistes remportent près de 38 pour cent des voix aux premières élections d'après-guerre.
Création du festival de musique « le Printemps de Prague ».
Procès du secrétaire d'État nazi K. H. Frank qui est exécuté dans la prison de Pankrác.
Nouveau gouvernement tchécoslovaque. Klement Gottwald est nommé Premier ministre.
Fondation du Musée juif d'État.

**1947**
Prague accueille le premier festival mondial de la jeunesse et des étudiants.
Championnats du monde de hockey sur glace à Prague.
Exposition d'art surréaliste à Prague.
Les Soviétiques interdisent à la Tchécoslovaquie de bénéficier du plan Marshall.

**1948**
20 février : 12 ministres de partis non-communistes démissionnent pour protester contre la pression communiste.
25 février : les communistes prennent le pouvoir lorsque le président Beneš est forcé d'accepter la démission des ministres démocrates sous la menace de milices armées.
10 mars : Jan Masaryk est découvert mort sous les fenêtres du palais Černín.
7 juin : démission de Beneš.
Gottwald élu président.
3 septembre : mort d'Edvard Beneš.
Débuts de procès d'élimination des «ennemis de l'État».

**1949**
25 février : le Parti communiste célèbre le premier anniversaire du coup d'état victorieux de février.

**1950**
Procès-spectacle du député démocrate Milada Horáková sous prétexte de trahison.
14 exécutions et 52 condamnations à la prison à vie sont prononcées au cours de l'année.
Premier rassemblement de la jeunesse communiste tchécoslovaque.

**1951**
Inauguration du pont Jan Šverma.

**1952**
Fondation de l'Académie tchécoslovaque des Sciences.
Séries de procès de «conspiration» à l'instar des purges soviétiques des années 30. Exécution de 11 responsables communistes de haut niveau, dont Rudolf Slánský.
Fondation de l'Académie du théâtre de marionnettes (première au monde).

| | | |
|---|---|---|
| **1953** On 14 March, Gottwald dies (just over a week after attending Stalin's funeral in Moscow). Antonín Zápotocký elected President. On 1 May, Czechoslovak Television begins regular broadcasting. Museum of National Literature opens in Strahov. On 1 June, currency reform takes place. Letná Tunnel opens. | **1953** Am 14. März stirbt Gottwald (eine Woche, nachdem er an der Beerdigung Stalins in Moskau teilgenommen hatte). Antonín Zápotocký wird zum Präsidenten gewählt. Das tschechoslowakische Fernsehen beginnt am 1. Mai mit regelmäßigen Übertragungen. In Strahov eröffnet das Museum für Nationale Literatur. Am 1. Juni führt man eine Währungsreform durch. Eröffnung des Letná-Tunnels. | **1953** 14 mars : mort de Gottwald une semaine après son retour des funérailles de Staline. Antonín Zápotocký est élu président. 1er mai : premières émissions régulières de la télévision tchécoslovaque. Inauguration du Musée national de la littérature à Strahov. 1er juin : réforme monétaire. Ouverture du tunnel de Letná. |
| **1954** Prague's second crematorium opens in Motol. Klement Gottwald Museum opens. | **1954** Prags zweites Krematorium nimmt in Motol seine Arbeit auf. Eröffnung des Klement-Gottwald-Museums. | **1954** Ouverture d'un second crématorium à Motol. Ouverture du Musée Klement Gottwald. |
| **1955** Stalin Monument (by sculptor Otakar Švec) unveiled. First *spartakiáda* held at Strahov Stadium. | **1955** Enthüllung des Stalin-Monuments (vom Bildhauer Otakar Švec). Im Strahov-Stadion findet die erste Spartakiade statt. | **1955** Inauguration d'un monument à Staline, œuvre du sculpteur Otakar Švec. Première Spartakiade au stade Strahov. |
| **1956** "House of Fashion" opens in Wenceslas Square. | **1956** Eröffnung des »Hauses der Mode« auf dem Wenzelsplatz. | **1956** Ouverture d'une « Maison de la mode » place Venceslas. |
| **1957** Soviet leader Nikita Khruschev visits Prague. On 11 November, President Zápotocký dies. Antonín Novotný elected President. Czechoslovak Airlines introduce first jetliner on Prague–Moscow route. | **1957** Der sowjetische Parteichef Nikita Chruschtschow besucht Prag. Am 11. November stirbt Präsident Zápotocký. Antonín Novotný wird zu seinem Nachfolger gewählt. Die tschechoslowakische Luftfahrtgesellschaft stellt ihren ersten Düsenflieger auf der Route Prag-Moskau vor. | **1957** Nikita Kroutchev en visite à Prague. 11 novembre : mort du président Zápotocký. Antonín Novotný est élu président. La Compagnie aérienne tchécoslovaque ouvre une ligne Prague-Moscou par avion à réaction. |
| **1958** Jalta Hotel opens in Wenceslas Square. Theater on the Balustrade opens. | **1958** Eröffnung des Hotels Jalta auf dem Wenzelsplatz. Das Theater am Geländer öffnet seine Pforten. | **1958** Ouverture de l'hôtel Jalta, place Venceslas. Ouverture du Théâtre sur la Balustrade. |
| **1959** Magic Lantern multimedia show opens in Adria Palace. Semaphore Theater founded. Jaroslav Heyrovský receives Nobel Prize for Chemistry. | **1959** Im Adria-Palast wird eine Laterna-magica-Show gezeigt. Gründung des Theaters Semafor. Jaroslav Heyrovský erhält den Nobelpreis für Chemie. | **1959** Show multimédia « Lanterne magique » au palais Adria. Fondation du théâtre du Sémaphore. Jaroslav Heyrovský reçoit le prix Nobel de chimie. |
| **1960** Second *spartakiáda* takes place. World Postage Stamp Exhibition held in Prague. On 11 July, National Assembly approves new constitution and new official name of state: the Czechoslovak Socialist Republic. | **1960** In Prag findet die zweite Spartakiade statt. Die Briefmarken-Weltausstellung wird in Prag gezeigt. Am 11. Juli verabschiedet die Nationalversammlung eine neue Verfassung. Der neue offizielle Name des Staates lautet: Tschechoslowakische Sozialistische Republik. | **1960** Seconde Spartakiade. Exposition mondiale de philatélie à Prague. 11 juillet : l'Assemblée nationale approuve la nouvelle constitution et la nouvelle dénomination officielle de l'État : République socialiste tchécoslovaque. |
| **1961** Department of "Supreme Architect of the City of Prague" founded, to supervise all building projects in the city. Soviet astronaut Yuri Gagarin visits Prague. | **1961** Die Abteilung »Oberster Architekt der Stadt Prag« wird zur Überwachung aller Bauprojekte der Stadt eingerichtet. Der sowjetische Astronaut Juri Gagarin besucht Prag. | **1961** Création du poste d'« architecte suprême de la ville de Prague », doté d'importants pouvoirs. Le cosmonaute Youri Gagarine en visite à Prague. |
| **1962** Stalin statue demolished. New Sports Hall opens. | **1962** Sprengung des Stalin-Monuments. Eröffnung der neuen Sportstätten. | **1962** La statue de Staline est abattue. Ouverture de la nouvelle salle des sports. |
| **1963** Gallery of the City of Prague founded. | **1963** Gründung der »Galerie der Stadt Prag«. | **1963** Création de la Galerie municipale de Prague. |
| **1964** Gallery of Vincenc Kramář opens in Dejvice. | **1964** In Dejvice eröffnet die Galerie Vincenc Kramář. | **1964** Ouverture de la galerie de Vincenc Kramář à Dejvice. |
| **1965** Third *spartakiáda* takes place. Theater Behind the Gate founded. Major restoration of Charles Bridge begins. | **1965** Austragung der dritten Spartakiade. Das Theater hinter dem Tor wird eröffnet. Beginn umfangreicher Restaurierungen der Karlsbrücke. | **1965** Troisième Spartakiade. Fondation du Théâtre derrière la porte. Début d'importants travaux de restauration du pont Charles. |
| **1966** Preparatory work on construction of Prague Metro. | **1966** Erste Arbeiten an der Prager U-Bahn. | **1966** Travaux préparatoires pour le métro de Prague. |
| **1967** Czech film *Closely Observed Trains* wins Academy Award for Best Foreign Film. Fourth Congress of Czechoslovak writers. Strahov student protests. | **1967** Der tschechische Film *Reise nach Sondervorschrift, Zuglauf überwacht* gewinnt den Academy Award als bester ausländischer Film. Vierter Kongreß der tschechoslowakischen Schriftsteller. Studentenproteste in Strahov. | **1967** Le film tchèque *Trains étroitement surveillés* remporte un *Academy Award* du meilleur film étranger. Quatrième congrès des écrivains tchécoslovaques. Manifestation des étudiants de Strahov. |
| **1968** Alexander Dubček elected First Secretary of Central Committee of Czechoslovak Communist Party. On 22 March, Antonín Novotný resigns presidency. On 30 March, General Ludvík Svoboda elected President of the Republic. New air terminal building opens at the Ruzyně airport. At its April session, Central Committee accepts reformers' Action Program. By end of May, Central Committee agrees introduction of new model for national economy. New organizations, such as K 231 (former political prisoners) and KAN (Club of Engaged Non-Party Members), founded. On 20 June, National Assembly approves new law abolishing censorship. On 21 August, Soviet-led invasion of Czechoslovakia by Warsaw Pact member states begins; Dubček and colleagues kidnapped and flown to Moscow, where | **1968** Alexander Dubček wird zum Ersten Sekretär des Zentralkomitees der Tschechoslowakischen Kommunistischen Partei gewählt. Am 22. März tritt Präsident Antonín Novotný zurück. General Ludvík Svoboda wird am 30. März zum neuen Präsidenten der Republik gewählt. Auf dem Flughafen Ruzyně wird ein neuer Terminal eröffnet. Auf ihrer Aprilsitzung nimmt das Zentralkomitee das Aktionsprogramm der Reformer an. Bis Ende Mai einigt sich das Zentralkomitee auf ein neues Modell für die nationale Wirtschaft. Neue Organisationen, wie beispielsweise K 231 (für ehemalige politische Gefangene) und KAN (Der Club Engagierter Parteiloser), werden gegründet. Am 20. Juni verabschiedet die Nationalversammlung ein neues Gesetz zur Aufhebung der Zensur. Am 21. August beginnt die von der Sowjetunion geführte Invasion der Tschechoslowakei durch Mit- | **1968** Alexander Dubček est élu premier secrétaire du Comité central du parti communiste. 22 mars : démission de la présidence d'Antonín Novotný. 30 mars : le général Ludvík Svoboda est élu président de la République. Construction d'un nouveau terminal à l'aéroport de Ruzyně. Lors de sa session d'avril, le Comité central accepte le programme des réformateurs. Fin mai, le Comité central donne son accord à l'introduction d'un nouveau modèle économique. Création de nouveaux mouvements comme le K 231 (anciens prisonniers politiques) et le KAN (cercle des membres engagés non-membres du Parti) 20 juin : l'Assemblée nationale approuve l'abrogation de la censure. 21 août : invasion de la Tchécoslovaquie par les troupes du Pacte de Varsovie à l'instigation de l'URSS. Dubček et ses collègues sont emmenés à |

under duress they sign Moscow Agreement; the Prague Spring is over.

**1969** Self-immolations of students Jan Palach and Jan Zajíc, protesting against Soviet occupation.
At World Ice-Hockey Championship in Sweden, Czechoslovakia beats Soviet Union 3:2; crowds in Wenceslas Square celebrate while StB *agents provocateurs* smash Aeroflot office.
On 17 April, Dubček replaced as First Secretary of Czechoslovak Communist Party by Gustáv Husák. "Normalization" process begins.
On 21 August, first anniversary of Soviet invasion, Prague citizens stage demonstration which is brutally dispersed by joint police and army forces.

**1970** Czechoslovak Television launches second channel.

**1971** House of Soviet Science and Culture opens.

**1972** Building of concrete panel-house "Southern City" estate begins.

**1973** Klement Gottwald Bridge opens.

**1974** Prague Metro's "C" line (6.7km) opens.
Palace of Trade Fair in Holešovice burns down.

**1975** Kotva and Máj department stores open.
On 25 May, Gustáv Husák elected President of Czechoslovak Socialist Republic.
Fourth *spartakiáda*.

**1976** Members of underground rock band Plastic People of the Universe imprisoned.

**1977** Dissident group demands basic human rights in manifesto Charter 77, signed by 1000 Czechoslovaks; Husák regime retaliates with harassment and arrests.

**1978** Prague Metro's "A" line opens.

**1979** Playwright Václav Havel and several other signatories of Charter 77 imprisoned.

**1980** City's population reaches 1,182,294.
Exhibition of 19th-century art opens in newly restored former St Agnes convent.
Fifth *spartakiáda*.

**1981** Palace of Culture opens.

**1982** Prague's former abattoir converted into large outdoor market.

**1983** National Theater's "New Stage" opens.

**1984** Czech poet Jaroslav Seifert awarded Nobel Prize for Literature.

**1985** Population of Prague reaches 1.2 million.
Sixth *spartakiáda*.
Construction of 216m-high TV tower begins.

**1986** New tennis stadium complex opens on Štvanice Island.

**1987** Soviet leader Mikhail Gorbachev visits Prague.

**1988** Mass rally to commemorate 20th anniversary of Soviet invasion disrupted by police.

**1989** On 17 November, security police forces brutally intervene against student demonstration on 50th anniversary of execution of Czech student leaders by Nazis.
Large-scale strikes by university students and actors.
Civic Forum co-ordination center founded.
Mass demonstrations take place in Wenceslas Square and Letná Plain.
On 24 November, Communists capitulate, handing power to opposition.

gliedstaaten des Warschauer Paktes; Dubček und seine Mitarbeiter werden entführt und nach Moskau geflogen, wo sie unter Druck das Moskauer Abkommen unterzeichnen. Der Prager Frühling ist vorbei.

**1969** Selbstverbrennungen der Studenten Jan Palach und Jan Zajíc aus Protest gegen die sowjetische Besetzung.
Bei der Eishockeyweltmeisterschaft in Schweden schlägt die Tschechoslowakei die Sowjetunion mit 3:2; auf dem Wenzelsplatz feiern die Menschenmassen, während StB-Agenten das Aeroflot-Büro beschädigen.
Am 17. April wird Dubček von Gustav Husák als Erster Sekretär der Tschechoslowakischen Kommunistischen Partei abgelöst.
Der sogenannte Prozeß der »Normalisierung« beginnt.
Zum ersten Jahrestag der sowjetischen Invasion findet am 21. August in Prag eine Demonstation statt, die von Polizei- und Armee-Einheiten brutal aufgelöst wird.

**1970** Das tschechoslowakische Fernsehen führt einen zweiten Kanal ein.

**1971** Das »Haus der sowjetischen Wissenschaft und Kultur« wird eröffnet.

**1972** Baubeginn der Plattenbausiedlung »Südstadt«.

**1973** Eröffnung der Klement-Gottwald-Brücke.

**1974** U-Bahn-Linie C (6,7 km) nimmt ihren Betrieb auf.
Der Handelspalast in Holešovice brennt ab.

**1975** Das Kaufhaus Kotva und Máj öffnet seine Pforten.
Am 25. Mai wird Gustáv Husák zum Präsidenten der Tschechoslowakischen Sozialistischen Republik gewählt.
Vierte Spartakiade.

**1976** Mitglieder der Untergrund-Rockgruppe Plastic People of the Universe werden verhaftet.

**1977** In ihrem Manifest Charta 77, das von 1000 Bürgern unterschrieben wurde, fordert eine Dissidentengruppe die Anerkennung und Einhaltung der Menschenrechte; Husáks Regime reagiert mit Verfolgungen und Verhaftungen.

**1978** Die Prager U-Bahn-Linie A nimmt ihren Betrieb auf.

**1979** Der Dramatiker Václav Havel und verschiedene andere Unterzeichner der Charta 77 werden verhaftet.

**1980** Die Bevölkerung der Stadt wächst auf 1.182.294 Menschen.
Eine Ausstellung zur Kunst des 19. Jahrhunderts wird im restaurierten ehemaligen St. Agnes-Konvent gezeigt.
Fünfte Spartakiade.

**1981** Eröffnung des Kulturpalastes.

**1982** Das ehemalige Schlachthaus von Prag wird als großer offener Markt wiedereröffnet.

**1983** Das Nationaltheater »Neue Bühne« öffnet seine Pforten.

**1984** Der tschechische Lyriker Jaroslav Seifert erhält den Nobelpreis für Literatur.

**1985** Die Bevölkerung Prags wächst auf 1,2 Millionen Menschen.
Sechste Spartakiade.
Baubeginn für den 216 Meter hohen Fernsehturm.

**1986** Auf der Insel Štvanice wird ein neues Tennisstadion gebaut.

**1987** Der sowjetische Führer Michail Gorbatschow besucht Prag.

**1988** Eine Massendemonstration zum 20. Jahrestag der sowjetischen Invasion wird von der Polizei zerschlagen.

**1989** Polizeikräfte gehen am 17. November brutal gegen eine Studentendemonstration zur Erinnerung an den 50. Jahrestag der Ermordung eines Kommilitonen durch die Nazis vor.
Massive Streiks von Studenten und Schauspielern.
Einrichtung des Koordinationszentrums des »Bürgerforums«.
Auf dem Wenzelsplatz und auf dem Letná-Plateau finden die Massendemonstrationen statt.

Moscou, où ils sont contraints de signer l'Accord de Moscou. Le «Printemps de Prague» est terminé.

**1969** Les étudiants Jan Palach et Jan Zajíc s'immolent par le feu, pour protester contre l'occupation soviétique.
Au Championnat du monde de hockey, en Suède, la Tchécoslovaquie bat les Soviétiques, 3 à 2. Allégresse de la foule sur la place Venceslas tandis que des agents provocateurs du Stb brisent les vitrines de l'Aéroflot.
17 avril: Dubček est remplacé au poste de premier secrétaire par Gustav Husák.
Le processus de «normalisation» débute.
21 août: premier anniversaire de l'invasion soviétique.
Manifestation des Praguois, brutalement dispersée par la police et l'armée.

**1970** Lancement de la seconde chaîne de télévision.

**1971** Ouverture de la Maison de la science et de la culture soviétiques.

**1972** Construction du grand ensemble en béton «Cité du Sud».

**1973** Inauguration du pont Klement Gottwald.

**1974** Ouverture de la ligne C du métro (6,7 km).
Incendie du palais de la foire d'Holešovice.

**1975** Ouverture des grands magasins Kotva et Máj.
25 mai: Gustáv Husák est élu président de la République.
Quatrième Spartakiade.

**1976** Les membres du groupe rock clandestin «Plastic People of the Universe» sont jetés en prison.

**1977** Un groupe de dissidents demande le respect des droits de l'homme dans la Charte 77, signée par 1000 Tchécoslovaques. Le régime d'Husák réplique par des manœuvres de harcèlement et des arrestations.

**1978** Ouverture de la ligne de métro A.

**1979** L'auteur dramatique Václav Havel et plusieurs autres signataires de la Charte 77 sont emprisonnés.

**1980** La population de Prague atteint 1 182 294 habitants.
Inauguration d'une Exposition d'art du XIXe siècle dans l'ancien couvent Sainte-Agnès restauré.
Cinquième Spartakiade.

**1981** Inauguration du Palais de la Culture.

**1982** L'ancien abattoir de Prague est converti en marché.

**1983** Inauguration de la «Nouvelle scène» du Théâtre national.

**1984** Le poète tchèque Jaroslav Seifert reçoit le prix Nobel de littérature.

**1985** Prague compte 1,2 millions d'habitants. Sixième Spartakiade.
Début de la construction d'une tour de télévision de 216 m de haut.

**1986** Ouverture d'un nouveau stade de tennis sur l'île de Štvanice.

**1987** Mikhaïl Gorbatchev en visite à Prague.

**1988** Manifestation de masse à l'occasion du 20e anniversaire de l'invasion soviétique, dispersée par la police.

**1989** 17 novembre: les forces de sécurité interviennent avec brutalité contre une manifestation d'étudiants pour le 50e anniversaire de l'exécution de leaders étudiants tchèques par les nazis.
Importantes grèves d'étudiants et d'acteurs.
Fondation d'un centre de coordination, le Forum civique.
Manifestations de masse place Venceslas et sur la plaine de Letná.

On 10 December, President Husák resigns.
Alexander Dubček elected Chairman of Federal Assembly (parliament).
On 29 December, Václav Havel elected President of the Republic.

1990    On 8–9 June, free parliamentary elections (won in Czech Lands by Civic Forum).
Official name of state changed to the Czech and Slovak Federal Republic.
On 5 June, Václav Havel re-elected President of the Republic.
Pope John Paul II visits Prague.

1991    Federal Assembly accepts Charter of Fundamental Human Rights and Liberties.
Civic Forum splits into Civic Movement Party (OH) led by Jiří Dienstbier, Civic Democratic Party (ODS) led by Václav Klaus, Civic Democratic Alliance (ODA) led by Jan Kalvoda, and Christian Party (KDU-ČSL) led by Josef Lux.
First wave of coupon privatization begins.
Restitution of private property begins.
Rolling Stones perform at Strahov stadium.

1992    June parliamentary elections won in Czech lands by ODS (Civic Democratic Party) and in Slovakia by left-oriented HZDS (Movement for a Democratic Slovakia).
Representatives of ODS and HZDS agree to dismantle Czechoslovak federation.
On 25 November, Federal Assembly declares termination of Czechoslovakia at midnight on 31 December.

1993    On 26 January, Václav Havel elected President of Czech Republic.
Young artist David Černý shocks Soviets and amuses many Prague citizens with his Pink Tank *akce* (happening).
Prince and Princess of Wales visit Prague.

1994    US President Bill Clinton visits Prague.

1995    Second Rolling Stones concert in Prague.
National Gallery opens permanent exhibition of Czech modern art 1900–60 in Palace of Trade Fair.

1996    Queen Elizabeth II visits Prague.
Singer Michael Jackson begins the "HIStory" world tour in Prague.
Magnificent retrospective exhibition of Surrealist movement (first since 1946) opens in Gallery of the City of Prague.
First elections to Upper House of Czech Parliament.

1997    During German Chancellor's visit to Prague, Helmut Kohl and Czech government sign Czech–German declaration.
Bohumil Hrabal dies.
One year after Olga Havel's death, Václav Havel marries Dagmar Veškrnová.
Czech film *Kolya* by Jan Svěrák wins Academy Award for Best Foreign Film.

Am 24. November kapitulieren die Kommunisten und übergeben die Macht der Opposition.
Am 10. Dezember tritt Präsident Husák zurück.
Alexander Dubček wird zum Vorsitzenden der Bundesversammlung (dem Parlament) gewählt.
Am 29. November wird Václav Havel Präsident der Republik.

1990    Vom 8. bis 9. Juni finden freie Parlamentswahlen statt (die in den tschechischen Landesteilen vom Bürgerforum gewonnen werden).
Der offizielle Name des Staates lautet nun Tschechische und Slowakische Bundesrepublik.
Am 5. Juni wird Václav Havel als Präsident bestätigt.
Papst Johannes Paul II besucht Prag.

1991    Die Bundesversammlung nimmt eine Charta der Menschen- und Freiheitsrechte an.
Das Bürgerforum spaltet sich in die Partei der Bürgerbewegung unter der Führung von Jiří Dienstbier (OH), die Demokratische Bürgerpartei (ODS) unter dem Vorsitz von Václav Klaus, die Bürgerlich-Demokratische Allianz (ODA) unter Jan Kalvoda und die Christliche und Demokratische Union (KDU-ČSL) unter Josef Lux.
Erste Privatisierungswellen.
Beginn der Rückführung von Privateigentum.
Die Rolling Stones treten im Strahov-Stadion auf.

1992    Bei den Parlamentswahlen in den tschechischen Ländern gewinnt im Juni die ODS (Demokratische Bürgerpartei) und in der Slowakei die linksgerichtete HZDS (Bewegung für eine Demokratische Slowakei).
Vertreter der ODS und der HZDS einigen sich auf die Auflösung der tschechoslowakischen Föderation.
Am 25. November erklärt die Bundesversammlung für Mitternacht des 31. Dezember das Ende der Tschechoslowakei.

1993    Am 26. Januar wird Václav Havel zum Präsidenten der Tschechischen Republik gewählt.
Der junge Künstler David Černý schockiert die Russen und erheitert viele Prager Bürger mit seinem Rosa-Panzer-Happening.
Der Prinz und die Prinzessin von Wales besuchen Prag.

1994    Der amerikanische Präsident Bill Clinton besucht Prag.

1995    Die Rolling Stones treten erneut in Prag auf.
Im Handelspalast eröffnet die Nationalgalerie eine Dauerausstellung tschechischer moderner Kunst von 1900 bis 1960.

1996    Königin Elisabeth II. besucht Prag.
Der Sänger Michael Jackson beginnt seine »HIStory«-Welttournee in Prag.
In der »Galerie der Stadt Prag« wird eine großartige Ausstellung der Surrealisten (die erste seit 1946) eröffnet.
Erste Wahlen zum Oberhaus des tschechischen Parlaments.

1997    Während des Besuchs des deutschen Bundeskanzlers in Prag unterzeichen Helmut Kohl und die tschechische Regierung die deutsch-tschechische Erklärung.
Bohumil Hrabal stirbt.
Ein Jahr nach dem Tod von Olga Havel heiratet Vaclav Havel die Schauspielerin Dagmar Veškrnová.
Der tschechische Film *Kolya* von Jan Šverák gewinnt den Academy Award als bester ausländischer Film.

24 novembre : les communistes capitulent et remettent le pouvoir à l'opposition.
10 décembre : démission du président Husák.
Alexander Dubček est élu président de l'Assemblée fédérale (le parlement).
29 décembre : élection de Václav Havel à la présidence de la République.

1990    8–9 juin : élections libres au parlement, remportées dans les régions tchèques par le Forum civique.
La dénomination officielle de l'État devient : République fédérale tchèque et slovaque.
5 juin : Václav Havel réélu président de la République.
Le pape Jean-Paul II en visite à Prague.

1991    L'Assemblée fédérale accepte la Charte des Droits de l'homme et des libertés fondamentales.
Le Forum civique éclate en un Mouvement civique, animé par Jiří Dienstbier (OH), le Parti civique démocratique (ODS) dirigé par Václav Klaus, l'Alliance civique démocratique (ODA) mené par Jan Kalvoda et l'Union démocratique chrétienne (KDU-ČSL) ayant à sa tête Josef Lux.
Première vague de privatisations.
Débuts de la restitution des biens nationalisés.
Concert des Rolling Stones au stade de Strahov.

1992    Les élections au parlement sont remportées dans les régions tchèques par l'ODS, et en Slovaquie par le parti de gauche HZDS (Mouvement pour une Slovaquie démocratique).
Les représentants de l'ODS et l'HZDS s'accordent pour démanteler la fédération tchécoslovaque.
25 novembre : l'Assemblée fédérale déclare la fin de la Tchécoslovaquie le 31 décembre à minuit.

1993    26 janvier : Václav Havel est élu président de la République tchèque.
Le jeune artiste David Černý choque les Soviétiques et amuse de nombreux Pragois avec son happening de tank peint en rose.
Le prince et la princesse de Galles visitent Prague.

1994    Le président américain Bill Clinton en visite à Prague.

1995    Second concert des Rolling Stones à Prague.
La Galerie nationale ouvre une exposition permanente d'art tchèque moderne (1900–1960) au Palais de la foire.

1996    La Reine Elizabeth II en visite à Prague.
Le chanteur Michael Jackson commence son « HIStory » tour à Prague.
Superbe rétrospective du mouvement surréaliste (la première depuis 1946) au Musée municipal.
Premières élections à la chambre haute du parlement tchèque.

1997    Le chancelier allemand visite Prague, Helmut Kohl et le gouvernement tchèque signent une déclaration tchéco-allemande.
Mort de Bohumil Hrabal.
Václav Havel épouse Dagmar Veškrnová, un an après le décès de sa première femme Olga.
Academy Award du meilleur film étranger pour *Kolya* de Jan Svěrák.

# INDEX

## SELECTED BIBLIOGRAPHY
## AUSWAHLBIBLIOGRAPHIE
## BIBLIOGRAPHIE SÉLECTIONNÉE

Ash, Timothy Garton: *The Magic Lantern*, New York 1990
August, František & Rees, David: *Red Star Over Prague*, London 1984
Bartoš, J. & Kovářová, S. & Trapl, M.: *Osobnosti českých dějin*, Olomouc 1995
Bittman, Ladislav: *The Deception Game*, New York 1972
Churan, Milan, a kol.: *Kdo byl kdo v našich dějinách ve 20. století*, Praha 1994
Cibula, Václav: *Objevujeme Prahu*, Praha 1988
Czech Modernism 1900–1945, Houston 1989
Doležal, Jiří: *Česká kultura za protektorátu*, Praha 1996
Fischl, Victor: *Hovory s Janem Masarykem*, Praha 1996
Forman, Miloš & Novák, Jan: *Turnaround*, London 1993
Frolík, Josef: *Interview with a Senior Czechoslovak Secret Agent Josef Frolík, Communist Bloc Intelligence Activities in the United States: Hearing before the Subcommittee to Investigate the Administration of the Internal Security Act and Other Internal Security Laws of the Committee on the Judiciary United States Senate, Ninety-Fourth Congress*, Washington 1975
Fučík, Julius: *Report from the Gallows*, London 1951
Hames, Petr: *The Czechoslovak New Wave*, Los Angeles 1985
Hermann, A.H.: *A History of the Czechs*, London 1975
Hojda, Zdeněk & Pokorny, Jiří: *Pomníký a zapomníky*, Paseka Praha-Litomyšl 1996
Kovály, Heda, Kohák, Erazim: *The Victors and the Vanquished*, New York 1973
Kriseová, Edá: *Václav Havel*, New York 1993
Kusin, Vladimír V.: *From Dubček to Charter 77*, Edinburgh 1978
Kuraš, Benjamin: *Czechs and Balances – a Nation's Survival Kit*, Praha 1996
Levy, Alan: *So Many Heroes*, New York 1980
MacDonald, Callum & Kaplan, Jan: *Prague in the Shadow of the Swastika*, Praha 1995
MacDonald, Callum: *The Assassination of SS Obergruppenführer Reinhard Heydrich*, London 1989
Moorhouse, Geoffrey: *Prague*, Amsterdam 1980
Navrátilová, Martina: *Being Myself*, London 1985
Ripellino, Angelo Maria: *Magic Prague*, Los Angeles 1994
Seifert, Jaroslav: *The Selected Poetry of Jaroslav Seifert*, London 1986
Šejna, Jan: *We Will Bury You*, London 1982
Staňková, Jaroslava & Štursa, Jiří & Voděra, Svatopluk: *Prague Eleven Centuries of Architecture: Historical Guide*, Praha 1992
Sterling, Clare: *The Masaryk Case – The Murder of Democracy in Czechoslovakia*, Boston 1982
Tigrid, Pavel: *Kapesní průvodce inteligentní ženy po vlastním osudu*, Praha 1988
Weisskopf, Kurt: *The Agony of Czechoslovakia '38/'68*, London 1968

## ACKNOWLEDGEMENTS

We should like to thank the following individuals and institutions, who placed photographs and documentary material from their collections at our disposal:

PhDr Michal Ajvaz, Ing. Miroslav Burdatš, Claudia Carrington, Jaromír Červenka, Miroslav Chloupek, The Czechoslovak National House (London), PhDr. Gustav Erhart, Fotogalerie-Dobra, Anita Franková (Jewish Museum, Prague), Ing. Bohumil Hajný, Jan Hajný, Antoní Herudek, Jindřiška Hlonžková, Marta Horniková, Pavlína Horská, Pavel Hořejši, Dr Jan Hozák (National Technical Museum, Prague), Josef Hrubeš, Petr Hruška, Pavel Hudec Ahasver, Ing. Michal Hulla, Josef Janda, Jiří Jiras (the Barrandov Film Studios Archive), Jitka Karasová, Jiří Karhan, Tolja Kohut, Simona Koulová, Václav Kratěk, Adam Krejčík, Milan Kocourek (Sokol London), Vladimir Korouš, PhDr Martin Krajíček, PhDr Aleš Kýr, Alan Levy (*The Prague Post*), Josef Macela, Ladislav Moučka, PhDr Jakub Outrata, Pavel Pekník, Josef Peitz, Slávek Pilman, Petr Popelka, Regula Pragensis Foundation, Reproslužby s.r.o., Bohumil Sladký, Dr Dagmar Šmatláková, Jan Švankmajer, Vetešnictvi ve Vítězně, Jaroslava Zbíralová & Allan Teller (the Collected Image, Chicago).

## DANKSAGUNG

Wir möchten den folgenden Personen und Institutionen danken, die uns Fotografien und dokumentarisches Material aus ihren Sammlungen zur Verfügung gestellt haben:

PhDr Michal Ajvaz, Ing. Miroslav Burdatš, Claudia Carrington, Jaromír Červenka, Miroslav Chloupek, The Czechoslovak National House (London), PhDr. Gustav Erhart, Fotogalerie-Dobra, Anita Franková (Jüdisches Museum, Prag), Ing. Bohumil Hajný, Jan Hajný, Antoní Herudek, Jindřiška Hlonžková, Marta Horniková, Pavlína Horská, Pavel Hořejši, Dr Jan Hozák (National Technical Museum, Prague), Josef Hrubeš, Petr Hruška, Pavel Hudec Ahasver, Ing. Michal Hulla, Josef Janda, Jiří Jiras (Archiv der Barrandov-Filmstudios), Jitka Karasová, Jiří Karhan, Tolja Kohut, Simona Koulová, Václav Kratěk, Adam Krejčík, Milan Kocourek (Sokol London), Vladimir Korouš, PhDr Martin Krajíček, PhDr Aleš Kýr, Alan Levy (*The Prague Post*), Josef Macela, Ladislav Moučka, PhDr Jakub Outrata, Pavel Pekník, Josef Peitz, Slávek Pilman, Petr Popelka, Regula Pragensis Foundation, Reproslužby s.r.o., Bohumil Sladký, Dr Dagmar Šmatláková, Jan Švankmajer, Vetešnictvi ve Vítězně, Jaroslava Zbíralová & Allan Teller (the Collected Image, Chicago).

## REMERCIEMENTS

Nous souhaitons remercier les personnes et institutions citées ci-dessous, qui ont mis leurs photographies et les documents de leurs collections à notre disposition:

PhDr Michal Ajvaz, Ing. Miroslav Burdatš, Claudia Carrington, Jaromír Červenka, Miroslav Chloupek, The Czechoslovak National House (Londre), PhDr. Gustav Erhart, Fotogalerie-Dobra, Anita Franková (Musée juif, Prague), Ing. Bohumil Hajný, Jan Hajný, Antoní Herudek, Jindřiška Hlonžková, Marta Horniková, Pavlína Horská, Pavel Hořejši, Dr Jan Hozák (National Technical Museum, Prague), Josef Hrubeš, Petr Hruška, Pavel Hudec Ahasver, Ing. Michal Hulla, Josef Janda, Jiří Jiras (Les Archives des Barrandov Film Studios), Jitka Karasová, Jiří Karhan, Tolja Kohut, Simona Koulová, Václav Kratěk, Adam Krejčík, Milan Kocourek (Sokol Londres), Vladimir Korouš, PhDr Martin Krajíček, PhDr Aleš Kýr, Alan Levy (*The Prague Post*), Josef Macela, Ladislav Moučka, PhDr Jakub Outrata, Pavel Pekník, Josef Peitz, Slávek Pilman, Petr Popelka, Regula Pragensis Foundation, Reproslužby s.r.o., Bohumil Sladký, Dr Dagmar Šmatláková, Jan Švankmajer, Vetešnictvi ve Vítězně, Jaroslava Zbíralová & Allan Teller (the Collected Image, Chicago).


With love to Henryka
In memory of Marian and Callum

I have tried my best to produce something which should be more than just "putting lips in motion." However, if I have failed then surely Jan Kaplan's visual tale, full of surprises (rare photographs) and unexpected twists, will do justice to this extraordinary city, which always gave her artists the sense of being saved from the dullness of existence.

Krystyna Nosarzewska


In Liebe für Henryka,
In Erinnerung an Marian und Callum

Ich habe mein Möglichstes versucht, um etwas zu schaffen, das mehr sein soll als nur »Lippen sprechen zu lassen«; sollte mir das jedoch nicht gelungen sein, wird sicherlich Jan Kaplans Bildergeschichte, die so voller Überraschungen (seltenen Fotografien) und unerwarteter Wendungen steckt, dieser außergewöhnlichen Stadt gerecht werden, die ihren Künstlern immer das Gefühl gegeben hat, vor der Stumpfsinnigkeit der Existenz sicher zu sein.

Krystyna Nosarzewska


À Henryka, avec amour
En souvenir de Marian et Callum

J'ai essayé de mon mieux de parler de Prague d'une façon qui soit un peu plus que « d'actionner les lèvres. » Si je n'y ai pas réussi, je suis certaine que l'iconographie de Jan Kaplan, riche en surprises, images rares et rapprochement inattendus, rendra justice à cette ville extraordinaire qui a toujours aidé ses artistes à se sauver de la banalité de l'existence.

Krystyna Nosarzewska


Pages 2/3: Na Slupi, street in Prague at the turn of the century.
Seiten 2/3: Na Slupi, Prager Straße während der Jahrhundertwende.
Pages 2/3: Na Supi, rue à Prague au tournant du siècle.

Art direction and design: Peter Feierabend
Project manager: Sally Bald
Editing: Brenda Updegraff
Translation into German: Raingard Esser
Translation into French: Jacques Bosser
Layout and typesetting: Claudia Faber
Production manager: Detlev Schaper
Reproductions: Omniascanners
Printing and binding: Partenaires Livres
Printed in France
on SCA Paper

ISBN 3-89508-528-6

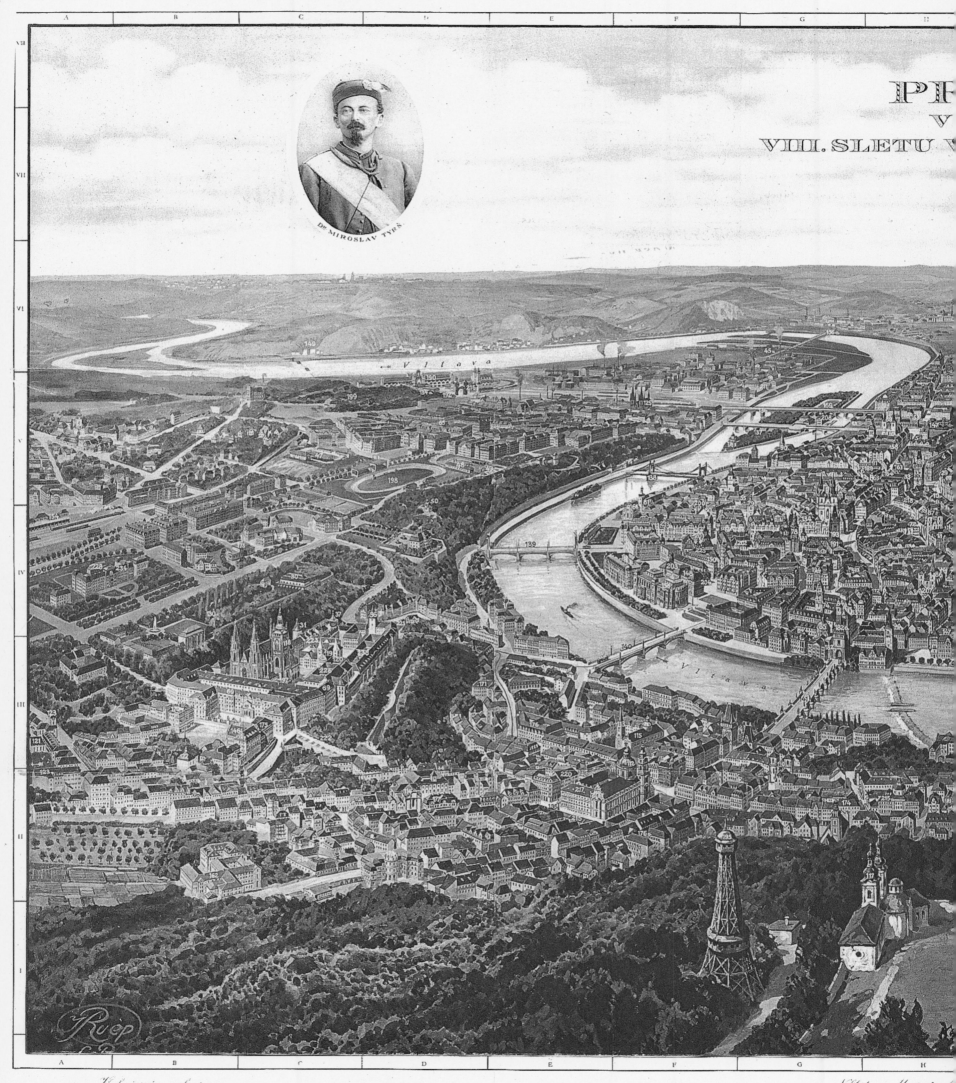

Dr MIROSLAV TYRŠ

Nákladem Mentor nakl
spol s r o